The Supreme Court and Capital Punishment

The Supreme Court's Power in American Politics Series

Melvin I. Urofsky, *Series Editor*

The Supreme Court and Capital Punishment: Judging Death

Michael E. Parrish

CQ PRESS
A Division of SAGE
Washington, D.C.

CQ Press
2300 N Street, NW, Suite 800
Washington, DC 20037

Phone: 202-729-1900; toll-free, 1-866-4CQ-PRESS (1-866-427-7737)

Web: www.cqpress.com

Cover design: Matthew Simmons
Composition: C&M Digitals (P) Ltd.
Photo credits:
AP Images: cover, 65, 71, 129, 194, 208, 338, 349
The Granger Collection, New York: 20, 60
The Library of Congress: 22, 25

Text credits:
Page 87: © 1931 American Civil Liberties
   Union, and used with permission
Page 103: © 2001 Jenner & Block, LLP, and
   used with permission
Page 157: © 1972 H. L. Richardson and used
   with the author's permission
Page 158: © 1972 Anthony Amsterdam and
   used with the author's permission
Page 219: ©1997 Norman Mailer. Courtesy of
   Polaris Communications, Inc.
Page 270: © 1992 *San Francisco Chronicle* and
   used with permission

♾ The paper used in this publication exceeds the requirements of the American National Standard for Information Sciences—Permanence of Paper for Printed Library Materials, ANSI Z39.48-1992.

Printed and bound in the United States of America

13 12 11 10 09   1 2 3 4 5

Library of Congress Cataloging-in-Publication Data
The Supreme Court and Capital Punishment: Judging Death / Michael Parrish.
   p. cm. — (The Supreme Court's power in American politics series)
   Includes bibliographical references and index.

   ISBN 978-0-87289-773-1 (alk. paper)
   1. Capital punishment—United States—History I. Title . II. Series.

KF9227.C2P37 2009
345.73'0773—dc22   2009020104

For Peggy, Without Whom, Not.

Summary Contents

Contents

Foreword

Scholars of the Supreme Court have long known that while a particular opinion may have powerful and even eloquent language in it, the words themselves mean nothing until translated into action. Chief Justice Earl Warren declared in *Brown v. Board of Education* (1954) that "in the field of public education the doctrine of 'separate but equal' has no place. Separate educational facilities are inherently unequal," but it took more than two decades of congressional and executive action before legalized segregation disappeared from the states. In *Gideon v. Wainwright* (1963) the Court expanded the right of counsel, but it meant nothing until the states actually implemented the ruling.

Most studies of the Court are doctrinal, in that they view the decisions of the Court in a particular area to see how they have developed, what rules have been created, what arguments and precedents are established. This is all legitimate and is primarily what we do in law schools. Historians and political scientists also tend to look at the impact that Court decisions have had on different groups and agencies. They want to know how the Court's decisions affected the actions of the states, the president, Congress, and other parts of society—how words translated into action.

The books in this series, while not ignoring doctrinal issues, focus more on how Court decisions are translated into practice. What does it mean, for example, in actual police work when a court says that officers must follow certain rules in gathering evidence or making arrests? What does it mean to a state legislature when the high court holds current schemes of apportionment to be unconstitutional? How does an administrative agency respond when courts have held that it has overstepped its authority?

In some areas, the responses have been simple if not always straightforward. For all of the furor raised by critics of the ruling in *Miranda v. Arizona* (1966), within a relatively short time police departments made the *Miranda* warning part of the routine for an arrest. On the other hand, decisions regarding school prayer and abortion have met with opposition, and the responses of state and local governments have been anything but simple or straightforward.

Judges, as well as senators and members of Congress, like the president take an oath of office to preserve, protect, and defend the Constitution. While the Constitution is quite explicit in some areas (such as the length of a term of office), the Framers deliberately wrote other provisions in broad strokes, so that the document could grow and adapt to the needs of future ages. What specific meanings should be attached to various constitutional clauses is a task that lies not only with the courts, but on the other branches of the government as well. The meaning of the Constitution in our times is the result of the interaction of the three branches of our government.

In this volume, *The Supreme Court and Capital Punishment* by Michael E. Parrish, we see how the Court has dealt with one of the most troubling aspects of the criminal justice system—the death penalty. The only thing that had differentiated the American colonies from the mother country prior to 1776 is that the colonies had a far more restrictive list of crimes for which a criminal could be put to death. But there is no question that at the time of the drafting of the Constitution and the Bill of Rights in the late eighteenth century, capital punishment was accepted in each of the states. Well into the nineteenth century, in both England and the United States, public hangings were part of normal life, a public ceremony to warn those of less than pure heart that should they stray off the path, a grisly ending awaited them.

In the past 150 years a great deal has happened, both in the United States and around the world, and at the beginning of the twenty-first century there are only a dozen or so nations that still employ capital punishment. Although there has been a serious debate about the efficacy of the death penalty as well as the fairness in its application to minorities and the poor, a majority of the Supreme Court as well as three-fourths of the American states still favor death as the appropriate sentence for heinous crimes.

The Supreme Court has been a central participant in this debate for the past four decades, and the question that has come before the bench is not whether imposition of death violates due process but whether the death penalty runs counter to the Eighth Amendment ban on cruel or unusual punishment. This debate has at least twice put a hold on executions all across the country, as the states waited to hear whether they could put condemned prisoners to death or how they might do it.

The constitutional dialogue involves many questions, as Professor Parrish shows, and while the answers are far from clear, they do bring into sharp relief some key issues. Jurists who advocate "original intent" argue that since capital punishment was accepted at the time of the ratification of the Eighth Amendment, it did not violate then or now the ban against cruel and unusual punishment. Opposed are those who believe in a "living Constitution" and those who claim that changing moral beliefs make the death penalty unacceptable in our time. While the latter group has managed to carve out certain categories, such as the mentally incompetent and children, from application, the originalists still prevail in their claim that there is nothing inherently unconstitutional about capital punishment.

In his discussion, Professor Parrish portrays the intensity of the issue through the eyes of the Court, the individual justices, the states, and, of course, the men and women who have been put to death after conviction for crimes, some of which can only be described as heinous. But over the past forty years the imposition of the death penalty has changed, and the Court has slowly erected a series of obstacles to guarantee procedural fairness and to avoid the arbitrariness that often characterized how judges and juries imposed this punishment before 1970.

The debate, of course, is far from over, but as Parrish indicates, the basic issues have now been aired, and the questions that will confront the Court and the states in the years ahead is whether the answers will reflect what conservatives call original intent or what liberals describe as modern sensibilities.

Melvin I. Urofsky
May 2009

Introduction

On June 29, 1972, in the case of *Furman v. Georgia* and its companions, a majority of the justices of the Supreme Court of the United States ruled that the existing death penalty laws in America constituted "cruel and unusual punishment" under the Eighth Amendment and were therefore unconstitutional.[1] The decision struck down the capital punishment regimes in thirty-nine states and the District of Columbia and spared the lives of over six hundred death row inmates. Each member of the majority (Justices William O. Douglas, Potter Stewart, Byron White, William Brennan, and Thurgood Marshall) wrote a separate opinion, and although they could not agree upon a single rationale for their collective conclusion, each found the existing state statutes to be defective because they vested too much discretion in juries and judges to determine who among those convicted of a capital crime would live or die.

Four members of the majority hoped that the *Furman* decision would lead either to the complete abolition of the death penalty in the United States (Douglas, Brennan, and Marshall) or generate revised statutes that so restricted discretion that only "the worst of the worst" offenders would suffer the supreme criminal punishment (Stewart). Justice White, on the other hand, believed that fine-tuning those eligible for the death penalty and narrowing discretion would restore public confidence in capital punishment and result in more executions, which had declined precipitously since 1966.

Four members of the Court, all appointed by President Richard Nixon and led by the new chief justice, Warren Burger, dissented. Each dissenter wrote an opinion as well. Among them was Justice Harry Blackmun, a close friend of the chief justice, a one-time general counsel to the Mayo Clinic, and a former federal appeals judge. Blackmun and Burger, who both hailed from the land of ten thousand lakes, had earned the sobriquet "the Minnesota Twins." Just a week before the *Furman* decision, Blackmun had authored an opinion reaffirming baseball's exemption from the federal antitrust laws in rhapsodic words, even reciting the classic poem "Casey at the Bat."[2] A year later, Blackmun would write the majority opinion in *Roe v. Wade* (1973), which struck down state criminal abortion laws and upheld a married woman's right to terminate a pregnancy during her first trimester.[3]

In his separate *Furman* dissent, Blackmun expressed deep personal opposition to capital punishment and recounted how such cases on the Eighth Circuit Court of Appeals had generated for him "an excruciating agony of the spirit." Were he a member of the legislature, he would do "all I could to sponsor and to vote for . . .

abolishing the death penalty." As a governor he would be "tempted to exercise executive clemency." But this was not his function as a judge. Expressing what had become with few exceptions the orthodoxy of post–New Deal judicial philosophy, Blackmun opined that "our task here . . . is to pass upon the constitutionality of legislation that has been enacted and challenged. This is the sole task for judges. We should not allow our personal preferences as to the wisdom of legislative and congressional actions, or our distaste for such actions, to guide our judicial decisions in cases such as these. The temptations to cross that policy line are very great. In fact, as today's decision reveals, they are almost irresistible."[4]

Four years later, when the Court sustained revised death penalty laws from Georgia, Florida, and Texas in *Gregg v. Georgia* (1976), Blackmun briefly concurred in the lead opinion written jointly by Justices Stewart, Lewis Powell, and John Paul Stevens, citing only his dissent in *Furman*.[5] That same day in *Woodson v. North Carolina* and *Roberts v. Louisiana*, a different coalition struck down mandatory death penalty laws from North Carolina and Louisiana. Justice Blackmun was again among the dissenters, again citing only his views in *Furman*.[6]

The quartet of cases from *Furman* to *Gregg-Woodson-Roberts* in the early 1970s closed one chapter in the Court's confrontation with capital punishment in America and opened a new one that remains unfinished today. Although in the early days of the republic both the individual states and the national government carried out executions, usually by firing squad or hanging, capital punishment received negligible attention from the Court until the third decade of the twentieth century when the justices turned their attention more broadly to issues of civil liberties and civil rights.

Apart from a few notorious cases, such as the execution of the conspirators charged with President Abraham Lincoln's assassination, the Native American victims of the Dakota War, and military courts-martial, the states, not the federal government, dominated the business of capital punishment from 1789 into the 1920s, and did so with minimal constitutional interference from the Court. Although the Fourteenth Amendment, added to the Constitution in 1868, prohibited the states from depriving persons of "life, liberty or property without due process of law," it played an insignificant role in the development of capital punishment jurisprudence until after World War I. Prior to this the justices held steadfast to a traditional commitment and deference to the federal structure. The nation's long-standing plague of racial discrimination, and the impact of such discrimination on the criminal justice system, began to fundamentally rearrange the landscape of the law in the 1920s and 1930s.

In the years since *Furman*, the Eighth Amendment, which prohibits "cruel and unusual punishment," has emerged as the core of the Court's constitutional universe with respect to capital punishment. But this provision, like the Fourteenth Amendment, remained largely dormant as well until the twentieth century. Beginning in 1833 the Court ruled that the original Bill of Rights, including the Eighth Amendment, restricted only the federal government, not the law-making authority of the individual states. Not until the twentieth century did the Court rule that specific provisions of the Bill of Rights also applied to the states by virtue of the liberty provision of the Fourteenth Amendment. Thus the Eighth Amendment, as well as the First and Fifth, did not impose any restraints upon the states' death penalty regimes until made part of the Court's Fourteenth Amendment's due process revolution in the 1930s and 1940s.

The justices, for example, rejected a claim that the firing squad constituted cruel and unusual punishment in 1878 in a federal case from the Utah territory and deferred to state courts on the question of electrocution as well. Its most important Eighth Amendment decisions prior to *Furman* arose in non-capital cases in which the justices ruled that "evolving standards of decency" would always inform the constitutional standard of what constituted cruel and unusual punishment.

In *Furman* only two justices, Brennan and Marshall, adopted the position that capital punishment could never survive constitutional scrutiny under the Eighth Amendment however legislatures might strive to narrow the category of those eligible for death or cabin the choices made by prosecutors, juries, and judges. In their view, the procedures for determining who would live and who would die could never be so refined as to eliminate human error and discretion and the penalty could not be justified in the closing decades of the twentieth century on grounds of either deterring crime or retribution. They were alone in these views on the Court until Blackmun changed his mind in 1994. By then, Brennan had retired and Marshall had died.

On February 22, 1994, the Court, now led by Chief Justice William Rehnquist, refused to review the pending execution of Bruce Edwin Callins, who had been convicted of robbery and murder and sentenced to death by lethal injection in Texas (see **Document 5.3**). Blackmun dissented from this denial of certiorari (the Court's discretionary writ) and took the occasion to announce that "from this day forward, I no longer shall tinker with the machinery of death." He and other members of the Court had struggled for over twenty years, Blackmun continued, to develop procedures and rules that would lend the "mere appearance of fairness to the death penalty endeavor." But rather than "coddle the Court's delusion that the desired level of fairness has been achieved," he now felt morally and intellectually obligated to concede that "the death penalty experiment has failed."[7]

Blackmun confessed that he had dissented in *Furman* on the grounds that the Court majority in 1972 had too suddenly reversed its position on the constitutionality of capital punishment, but that he had come to accept its essential ruling—later articulated in *Gregg v. Georgia*: "where discretion is afforded a sentencing body on . . . whether a human life should be taken or spared, that discretion must be suitably directed and limited so as to minimize the risk of wholly arbitrary and capricious action."[8] He had also endorsed and continued to support later Court rulings such as *Lockett v. Ohio* (1978) that required individualized sentencing in all capital cases as a matter of constitutional law because "American standards of decency could no longer tolerate a . . . sentencing process that failed to afford a defendant individualized consideration in the determination whether he or she should live or die."[9]

Furman mandated strict restraints on sentencing discretion to achieve consistency and prevent arbitrariness in the administration of the death penalty, but *Lockett* required that sentencers retain unbridled discretion to afford mercy. Blackmun believed these two constitutional principles to be both necessary and correct, but he had also come to see that they were irreconcilable. He would not sacrifice either. In addition, he concluded, the death penalty could never be constitutionally administered fairly and without discrimination because of recent decisions that ignored the continuing plague of racism in the prosecution of capital offenses, decisions that failed to monitor the rulings of state appellate courts, and decisions that sharply restricted appeals from state prisoners under sentence of death. The death penalty could not be reconciled with the Eighth Amendment.[10]

Blackmun's *cri de coeur* provoked a response from Justice Antonin Scalia. Long Blackmun's antagonist on the Court, Scalia seldom voted to overturn a death sentence and prided himself on his fidelity to the words of the Constitution and what he usually referred to as the original understanding of those who framed it and the Bill of Rights. Blackmun had voiced personal, moral, and intellectual objections to the death penalty, Scalia argued, but seldom mentioned "the text or tradition of the Constitution." The Fifth Amendment, he pointed out, sanctioned capital punishment when it declared that "[n]o person shall be held to answer for a capital . . . crime, unless on a presentment or indictment of a Grand Jury . . . nor be deprived of life . . . without due process of law."[11]

Beginning with *Furman* and continuing through its progeny, Scalia pointed out, the Court itself had created the warring principles that Blackmun now believed made it impossible to administer the death penalty in accord with the Constitution. Unlike Blackmun, Scalia suggested that at least one of these "judicially announced irreconcilable commands which cause the Constitution to prohibit what its text implicitly permits must be wrong." Scalia concluded by noting that the dissent had chosen in Callins' case "one of the less brutal of the murders that regularly come before us." Callins' victim had been "ripped by a bullet suddenly and unexpectedly . . . and left to bleed to death on the floor of a tavern. The death-by-lethal-injection that Justice Blackmun describes looks pretty desirable next to that."[12] Texas executed Bruce Callins on May 21, 1997.

As the 1994 debate between Blackmun and Scalia demonstrates, legal and personal perceptions about the constitutionality and morality of capital punishment remain potent sources of conflict on the Court and among the American people as well. Prepared, despite his own objections, to sanction the death penalty in the early 1970s, Justice Blackmun had come by 1994 to believe it could not be reconciled with the commands of the Constitution, including the Eighth Amendment and the due process and equal protection clauses of the Fourteenth. As the dissents of Brennan and Marshall always suggested, he was not alone in this judgment. Scalia, echoing the views of Rehnquist, White, and a majority of the justices who sat on the Court between the 1950s and the year 2000, believed with equal passion that the Constitution sanctioned the death penalty and that the Court, beginning in the 1970s, had often erected unnecessary barriers to its enforcement and thwarted the will of those states that had decided to maintain it.

The following chapters trace both the history that brought the justices to the debate in *Callins v. Collins* and what has ensued in the years since 1994. Two major themes are clear in a review of the history of the Supreme Court and capital punishment. First, prior to the third decade of the twentieth century, the constitutional issue played a miniscule role on the justices' agenda, apart from a few landmark cases that injected meaning into the Eighth Amendment's ban on cruel and unusual punishment. Second, beginning in the wake of World War I, it was the nation's long-festering ordeal with racial discrimination that finally brought the issue to center stage, reaching its climax in *Furman v. Georgia*.

In the nearly four decades since *Furman*, despite Blackmun's harsh indictment, the Court has significantly narrowed the categories of those eligible for the death penalty and surrounded its procedures with new constitutional protections that irritated not only Scalia but many other proponents of capital punishment as well. The ironic effect of those decisions, also examined in the pages that follow, has been the realization generally of the goals of the late Justice White, who had endorsed *Furman*'s conclusions with the objective of making capital punishment once again tolerable to the American people. When the Court under the present chief justice, John Roberts, rejected claims that lethal injection constituted cruel and unusual punishment in *Baze v. Rees* (2008), it very likely barred the door to significant constitutional challenges to capital punishment in the near future. Only Justice Stevens, now the senior associate justice, may still choose the path trod by Brennan, Marshall, and Blackmun. The prospects of another *Furman* decision seem remote in 2009, which leaves the future of the death penalty where in 1972 Justice Blackmun said it should belong: to state legislatures and governors. After all, it was in states such as Wisconsin, Minnesota, and Michigan that the movement to abolish the death penalty first gained momentum in the nineteenth century, and it is in states such as New Jersey and New Mexico that that momentum continues today.

Notes

1. *Furman v. Georgia*, 408 U.S. 238 (1972), decided together with *Jackson v. Georgia* and *Branch v. Texas.*
2. *Flood v. Kuhn*, 407 U.S. 258 (1972).
3. *Roe v. Wade*, 410 U.S. 113 (1973).
4. *Furman v. Georgia*, at 407–409.
5. *Gregg v. Georgia*, 428 U.S. 153 (1976), at 422.
6. *Woodson v. North Carolina*, 428 U.S. 280 (1976); and *Roberts v. Louisiana*, 428 U.S. 153 (1976).
7. *Callins v. Collins*, 510 U.S. 1141 (1994), at 1145.
8. *Gregg v. Georgia*, at 189.
9. *Lockett v. Ohio*, 438 U.S. 586 (1978).
10. *Callins v. Collins*, at 1155–1158.
11. Ibid., at 1141.
12. Ibid.

CHAPTER 1

Before *Moore v. Dempsey*
Judging Death, 1789–1923

Phillips County, Arkansas, lies along the Mississippi River on the state's eastern border. There, in the 1820s, Sylvanus Phillips and other white settlers arrived in the 1820s to cultivate cotton in the river's soil-rich delta. They brought with them African American slaves. One hundred years later, by the end of World War I, the county's black population, mostly sharecroppers, outnumbered the whites who owned the land and the local businesses by a ratio of 2 or 3 to 1. On the morning of October 1, 1919, one hundred sharecroppers gathered at the Hoop Spur Church in Elaine, the second largest town in the county, to discuss how to confront the landowners of Phillips over the unfair prices offered for their cotton. Some urged members of the gathering to join the Progressive Farmers and Household Union of America, an African American tenant farmers union that had been organized in Arkansas by tenant farmer Robert Hill. Others hoped to pursue a lawsuit against the landowners for breach of contract.

A number of those at the church that morning brought with them rifles and shotguns in fear that white officials and landowners would attempt to disrupt the meeting. A deputy sheriff and a railroad detective soon arrived. A fight broke out, and in the ensuing exchange of gunfire the detective was killed and the deputy wounded. Frank Kitchens, the sheriff of Phillips County, quickly organized a posse to track down the blacks who had fled the church on the correct assumption that they would be held responsible for the violence. In the summer and fall of 1919, with the country rocked by urban race riots, industrial strikes, and fears of the burgeoning Bolshevik Revolution, rumors soon spread throughout neighboring counties that the Hoop Church gathering had been only a prelude to a murderous insurrection aimed at all whites in Phillips County.

In this fraught climate Kitchens' posse soon numbered close to one thousand armed men. During a two-day rampage, members of the posse shot and killed over 150 blacks. The bloodshed only ended when Gov. Charles Hillman Brough sought the help of federal troops to quell the disorder. Within the month, an all-white Arkansas grand jury had indicted 122 of the blacks; 73 of those soon faced charges of murder, conspiracy, and insurrection. In a series of trials that lasted less than one hour each, with no witnesses called by the defense, twelve defendants were convicted of murder and sentenced to death in the state's electric chair. In each case the all-white juries had deliberated for less than ten minutes. The Arkansas supreme court reversed the sentences of six defendants on grounds that the trial judge had improperly instructed the jury of the difference between first- and second-degree murder. When the case of the remaining six Elaine defendants reached the Supreme Court in 1923, it changed the course of constitutional history with respect to the Court's role in American life, criminal justice, and capital punishment.[1]

American Federalism and the Limits of Judicial Intervention

In the 136 years of its existence prior to 1923, capital punishment did not loom large on the Court's docket. In large part this was due to a federal structure that left the definition and punishment of ordinary crimes, including murder, to the discretion of state and local authorities. At the national level, Congress prior to the twentieth century had declared few crimes against the United States punishable by death. A strict regard for the federal system narrowed the Court's jurisdiction over state criminal trials, even after the Fourteenth Amendment in 1868 imposed new constitutional limits on state legislatures and courts. The first federal criminal code, for example, made treason against the United States punishable by death, but under defined constitutional limitations that required two witnesses to overt acts of levying war against the government or aiding enemies in time of war. The first federal treason convictions saw the leaders of the Whiskey Rebellion and John Fries' Rebellion sentenced to death by three-judge federal courts of appeal. Presidents George Washington and John Adams pardoned the defendants, and none of the cases came before the justices.[2]

In addition to treason, Congress provided the death penalty for homicides committed on federal property or in a federal institution, such as a prison, and invoked its admiralty jurisdiction to make piracy and murder on the high seas punishable by death as well. The first criminal code for the District of Columbia, also subject to exclusive federal jurisdiction, authorized the death penalty for offenses ranging from homicide to inciting a slave rebellion. Territorial legislatures, subject to congressional oversight, mandated death for crimes such as intentional murder. Finally, by means of courts-martial and military commissions, the U.S. Army and Navy tried, convicted, and executed Native Americans defeated in war and military servicemen guilty of desertion and capital felonies while on duty. These proceedings, including the most notorious, remained immune to inquiry by the federal courts on the grounds that such military tribunals did not derive their authority from Article III of the Constitution, which fixed the jurisdiction of the civil courts.[3]

Taken together, these federal statutory provisions and the cases they generated constituted only a small volume of capital offenses in the United States. Most such cases were prosecuted and carried through to execution under state law by state courts. In 1833, in the case of *Barron v. Baltimore,* the Court drew a sharp line between federal and state authority when it ruled that the Bill of Rights in the

Constitution of the United States did not impose any restrictions upon the procedural or substantive laws of the individual states.[4] As we shall see, not even the adoption of the Fourteenth Amendment in 1868, which required the states to respect the privileges and immunities of citizens of the United States and guarantee all persons due process of law and equal protection of the laws, significantly moved that rigid and imposing federal-state boundary until after World War I. And even at the federal level, the Court moved cautiously with respect to capital punishment, usually shaping its rulings along narrow procedural lines. Shortly after the Civil War, for example, the justices overturned a death sentence imposed by a military commission on a Confederate sympathizer and curbed the president's suspension of the writ of habeas corpus. The ruling applied narrowly, only affecting suspensions carried out by the president acting without congressional approval and forbidding the use of military tribunals to try civilians in areas remote from combat where the civil courts remained open.[5]

In its first decision involving capital punishment, the Court under Chief Justice John Marshall displayed procedural scruples that would subsequently mark its death penalty decisions. Congress intended robbery and murder to constitute piracy, punishable by death, when accomplished on the high seas by U.S. citizens against a U.S. vessel, the Court noted, but it threw out an indictment against defendants who had accomplished their crime against foreign nationals aboard a Spanish ship.[6] The Court did not again address capital punishment until shortly before the Civil War, when it ruled that a congressional expansion of the federal circuit courts in the Arkansas Territory did not deprive the original eastern circuit of jurisdiction to try one James L. Dawson for murder, although his crime had been committed in what now constituted the newly formed western federal circuit.[7]

The First Eighth Amendment Case

The Mormon-dominated Utah territory provided the justices with their initial opportunity to overturn a capital conviction, and two years later for the first time to interpret the constitutional ban on cruel and unusual punishments. In *Wiggins v. People* (1876) the Court set aside the death sentence of, and ordered a new trial for, the owner of a Salt Lake City saloon who had been convicted of shooting to death a patron he had earlier disarmed and ejected from his establishment. The defendant claimed self-defense, and various witnesses remained uncertain who had fired first. Over defense objections, however, the trial judge had excluded the testimony of another witness who claimed the victim had brazenly displayed a pistol to him before returning to the saloon where the fatal gun battle erupted. Justice Samuel Miller and the majority ruled that this excluded testimony constituted a serious procedural error that called for reversal of the conviction, even though the defendant had not known of the incident, because it tended to indicate the mind of the deceased.[8]

Two years later, in *Wilkerson v. Utah* (1878), a convicted Utah murderer was not so lucky. The justices affirmed his death sentence by firing squad and first opined on the meaning of the Eighth Amendment's ban on cruel and unusual punishments. If Wallace Wilkerson had been tried, convicted, and sentenced to death before a revision of the territorial laws in 1876, he would have been given the option under a territorial 1862 statute of "being shot, hanged, or beheaded." But the legislature had eliminated that option in 1876 and delegated the method of execution to the trial court in situations where juries did not recommend life imprisonment. The only questions on appeal before the justices were therefore narrow ones: had the Utah courts correctly construed the revised territorial statute to give the trial judge discretion and did a congressional statute mandating death by hanging as the mode of execution when imposed by federal circuit courts trump the territorial law? Justice Nathan Clifford answered "yes" for the Court to the first question and "no" to the second, which sealed Wilkerson's fate.

In his opinion, although it was not absolutely necessary to the result, Clifford noted that had the Utah statute fixed the method of execution the trial court would have been obliged to follow it, "unless the punishment to be inflicted was cruel and unusual within the meaning of the Eighth Amendment to the Constitution, *which is not pretended by the counsel of the prisoner.*"[9] Although Wilkerson's lawyer had not challenged the use of the firing squad, Clifford proceeded to find it constitutional, along with hanging, the two methods customarily used by the military (**Document 1.1**). "Difficulty would attend the effort to define with exactness the extent of the constitutional provision . . . that cruel and unusual punishments shall not be inflicted," Clifford wrote. Drawing upon William Blackstone, an authoritative source on the common law of England, he catalogued a few punishments that likely fell within the prohibition: emboweling alive, beheading, quartering, public dissection, and burning alive in cases of treason "committed by a female." Fortunately, Clifford concluded with Blackstone, "the humanity of the nation" had mitigated such parts of those punishments "as savored of torture or cruelty" or what he later described as "unnecessary cruelty."[10]

When Wilkerson faced a Utah firing squad a year later, the execution did not go well, which led one newspaper to remind the territory that "the French guillotine never fails." The condemned man, obviously intoxicated, refused to be tied to a chair and declined a blindfold, telling the sheriff he intended to look his executioners in the eye and "die like a man." After putting a white patch over Wilkerson's heart, the sheriff stepped away and ordered the shooters, twenty feet away, to fire. As the guns commenced Wilkerson drew up his shoulders, and four rounds ripped his body. None hit his heart. "Oh, my God! My God! They have missed," he screamed. Wilkerson writhed on the ground in agony before the spectators, his chest bleeding from three wounds. The fourth shot had only shattered his left arm. It took Wilkerson twenty-seven minutes to die (**Document 1.2**). One journalist later described the event as "the most bizarre, grotesque and horribly botched Utah execution on record."[11]

Weems and the Future of the Eighth Amendment

In *Weems v. United States* (1910), a disbursing officer for the U.S. Coast Guard stationed in the Philippines offered the justices the opportunity to expound at much greater length on the meaning of cruel and unusual punishment in a non-capital case when he appealed his conviction and sentence for falsifying public payroll records in the amount of 616 pesos.[12] The Philippine court sentenced Paul Weems to fifteen years at hard labor under a statute that permitted imprisonment from twelve to twenty years and included provisions for "the carrying of a chain at the ankle, hanging from the wrists," and no communication or assistance from anyone outside the prison. In addition, the court imposed a fine of 4,000 pesos and certain "accessory penalties"—loss of parental authority, loss of guardianship rights over persons or property, loss of marital authority, and loss of the right to dispose of his property.[13]

At trial Weems' lawyer had raised various procedural objections, including a claim of improper arraignment and notice of a defective description of his client's office in the indictment. Nowhere, however, had he lodged a claim of cruel and unusual punishment, a provision against which could be found in the Philippine bill of rights that mirrored the Eighth Amendment. Three years earlier, in *Paraiso v. United States* (1907), a similar case of falsifying records in the Philippines where constitutional claims had not been raised at trial, the Court summarily refused to consider such errors on appeal and dismissed the writ.[14]

The *Paraiso* decision, however, presented no obstacle to Justice Joseph McKenna, a former attorney general of the United States, who noted that the Court's own Rule 35 allowed the justices themselves to consider what he called "a plain error not assigned" at trial, regardless of "what may have been done at other times," and especially "when rights are asserted which are of such high character as to find expression and sanction in the Constitution or Bill of Rights . . . [as] asserted in this case."[15] An Eighth Amendment claim, McKenna ruled, constituted just such a fundamental right, one that trumped any technical procedural barrier.

McKenna, a former U.S. representative from California, apparently thought so little of his legal experience that he took several law courses at Columbia University before taking his seat on the Court. Now, in *Weems*, he proceeded to write one of the landmark opinions of constitutional law with respect to the meaning of cruel and unusual punishments. McKenna reversed the disbursing officer's conviction and held the Philippine statute unconstitutional on the grounds that it violated both the island's bill of rights and the Eighth Amendment, which "must have the same meaning" (**Document 1.3**).

The penalties imposed on Weems, McKenna began, could only "amaze those . . . who believe that it is a precept of justice that punishment for crime should be graduated and proportioned to offense," a not entirely original statement on the need for the punishment to fit the crime, but one that would echo down future years when the Court considered other Eighth Amendment claims.[16] McKenna noted that Justice Joseph Story, in his *Commentaries on the Constitution of the United States* (1833), traced the words of the Eighth Amendment back to the English bill of rights of 1688. The language of the amendment served to warn all departments of the government of the United States against "such violent proceedings as had taken place in England in the arbitrary reigns of some of the Stuarts." But words etched by history did not finally control, the justice added, because "general language should not . . . be necessarily confined to the form that evil had theretofore taken. Time works changes, brings into existence new conditions and purposes."[17]

McKenna drove his point home with language that evoked Marshall's admonition in *McCulloch v. Maryland* (1819): the Constitution provided a framework of government intended to endure for ages to come.[18] McKenna also anticipated what later justices would call evolving standards of decency, or a living Constitution. A constitutional principle such as the Eighth Amendment, he wrote, "must be capable of wider application than the mischief which gave it birth." When interpreting a constitutional provision the Court should consider not only the past, but how the principle applies to new, unforeseen circumstances. A provision of the Constitution, McKenna concluded, "may acquire meaning as public opinion becomes enlightened by a humane justice."[19]

Chief Justice Edward White, joined by Justice Oliver Wendell Holmes, believed the *Paraiso* decision required the dismissal of the writ of error. In addition, White denounced McKenna's ruling in *Weems* because it "rests upon an interpretation of the cruel and unusual punishment clause of the Eighth Amendment, never before announced, which is repugnant to the natural import of the language employed in the clause, and which interpretation curtails the legislative power of Congress to define and punish crime by asserting a right of judicial supervision over the exertion of that power."[20]

Weems, with its emphasis upon a constitution whose meaning could evolve over time, spoke to a distant future of Eighth Amendment and capital punishment jurisprudence. It had little immediate impact upon death penalty cases, especially at the federal level. In *Johnson v. United States,* decided in 1912 two years after *Weems,* the Court affirmed a death sentence from the District of Columbia by dismissing a challenge to the competency of jurors as raised too late in the proceedings and rejecting the claim that the district's criminal code had to conform to the U.S. code, which afforded juries the opportunity of recommending life imprisonment following a conviction for murder. Justice McKenna wrote the unanimous opinion.[21] In

Stroud v. United States (1919), the Court rejected a double jeopardy claim by a federal prisoner. Robert Stroud's first murder conviction for stabbing to death a guard at Leavenworth Federal Penitentiary came without a jury recommendation of death. That conviction had been overturned on appeal. A jury then convicted Stroud again at his second trial, but this time without a recommendation for mercy.[22]

From the 1890s until the end of World War I, the justices overturned only two capital convictions secured under federal law. In 1895 they reversed the conviction and sentence of a seaman charged with murder on the high seas when the trial judge allowed into the record a confession by a co-conspirator.[23] And in 1899 they ordered a new trial for a defendant based on improper jury instructions in the District of Columbia.[24] But they affirmed a death sentence from the Alaska Territory in *Hardy v. United States* (1902) when they rejected claims that the trial judge abused his discretion in failing to grant the defendant a continuance and also allowed voluntary statements made by the defendant during a preliminary examination to be introduced as evidence by the prosecution.[25]

In *Hotema v. United States* (1902), one of the more bizarre cases decided in the new century, the Court affirmed the death penalty for a member of the Choctaw tribe whose apparent belief in witches and witchcraft led him on a murderous rampage that resulted in the deaths of three people on a single day. One jury found him not guilty by reason of insanity for two of the killings. A second panel could not reach a verdict regarding the third homicide. Finally, a third jury rejected the same insanity plea and sentenced him to death. The justices rejected his plea of double jeopardy.[26]

The Bill of Rights, Federalism, and the States

In their review of capital sentences secured under state law prior to 1923, the justices exhibited a firm adherence to conceptions of federalism shaped by the Marshall and Taney Courts in the pre–Civil War era. Those concepts attempted to maintain clear boundaries between state and national authority with respect to both legislative and judicial power. With the exception of certain specific powers allocated to the national government (such as declaring war or entering into treaties) or denied to the states (such as coining money or impairing the obligations of contracts), traditional federalism left the states with broad discretion to manage their own affairs—including the punishment of crimes—free from supervision by Congress, the president, and the federal courts. In the landmark expression of this traditional federalism, 1833's *Barron,* the Marshall Court ruled that the just compensation clause of the Fifth Amendment, and by implication the other first eight amendments to the Constitution, did not apply as limitations upon the individual states or their subdivisions. A subsequent ruling reaffirmed this view with respect to other provisions of the original Bill of Rights.[27]

The Fourteenth Amendment, ratified in 1868 as part of congressional Reconstruction following the Civil War, imposed new and, many believed, radical limitations upon the states. Section 1 of the amendment prohibited any state from "abridging the privileges or immunities of citizens of the United States" (**Document 1.4**). Echoing the original Fifth Amendment, the section also affirmed that "no state shall deprive a person of life, liberty or property without due process of law," and, finally, that no state "shall deny to any person within its jurisdiction the equal protection of the laws." What were the "privileges and immunities of citizens of the United States" if not the words of the Constitution itself and its amendments, including the Bill of Rights?

But in the same year in which the Fourteenth Amendment was ratified, the Court again rejected a claim that specific provisions of the Bill of Rights applied to the states. In *Twitchell v. Commonwealth* (1868), the justices turned away an appeal from an inmate under sentence of death in Pennsylvania whose attorney argued that he had been denied rights secured through the Fifth and Sixth Amendments by a state law that did not require an indictment for murder to "set forth the manner in which, or the means by which[,] the death of the deceased was caused." A federal criminal indictment required that a defendant "be informed of the nature and cause of the accusation," but the Sixth Amendment did not constrain the states. Again citing *Barron,* the Court refused to hear the case for want of federal jurisdiction.[28]

Many of the leading members of Congress who framed the Fourteenth Amendment, notably Ohio representative John Bingham and Sen. Jacob Howard of Michigan, asserted that the privileges and immunities clause extended the protections of the Bill of Rights, especially the First Amendment, to the states, thus overruling *Barron* and its progeny.[29]

The Court Limits the Scope of the Fourteenth Amendment

When the Court first addressed the scope of the Fourteenth Amendment in the *Slaughterhouse Cases* (1872), the majority opinion by Justice Samuel Miller rejected a sweeping view of incorporating the Bill of Rights into the privileges and immunities clause.[30] A group of discontented butchers in New Orleans challenged a state law that required them to practice their trade only within a single slaughterhouse to which they would pay a use fee. The butchers argued that the law abridged their privilege of pursuing their occupation, deprived them of property without due process, and violated equal protection. Five justices rejected their arguments, but Miller's discussion of the privileges and immunities clause did include a significant reference to at least one piece of the First Amendment: the right to peaceably assemble and petition for redress of grievances (**Document 1.5**).[31] Among the dissenters, Justice Joseph Bradley did not hesitate to declare that "among the privileges and immunities of citizens of the United States" were the free exercise of religion, freedom from unreasonable searches, freedom of speech and press "and still others . . . specified in the original Constitution, or in the early amendments of it."[32]

Justice Noah Swayne may have been too harsh when he declared that Justice Miller's conception of the privileges and immunities clause turned "what was meant for bread into a stone."[33] Later justices and attorneys did not take Miller's hint. Instead they adopted the understanding that *Slaughterhouse* had completely rejected the idea of applying the Bill of Rights against the states via the privileges and immunities clause of the Fourteenth Amendment. The constitutional door it was assumed had been partially closed against state criminal defendants who sought relief in the federal courts from violations of the Bill of Rights by invoking the Fourteenth Amendment. Even state prisoners under sentence of death would be limited to state constitutional remedies, not federal ones.

Two years after *Slaughterhouse* the justices further narrowed the path of plaintiffs seeking relief in the federal courts from state laws when it interpreted the Judiciary Act of 1867, which delineated the Court's jurisdiction over cases decided by the highest courts of the individual states. Writing for the Court in *Murdock v. Memphis* (1875), Justice Miller held that when exercising such review the justices were limited to the "federal" questions presented in the case and excluded from considering "questions of common law, of State statutes, of controverted facts, and conflicting evidence."[34] The state courts were the appropriate tribunals for deciding all questions arising under local law, statutory or otherwise. The Court's jurisdiction over appeals from state court judgments would be limited therefore to "the correction of errors relating solely to Federal law."[35]

The Limits of Ex Post Facto Claims

In the face of *Murdock*'s limitations and the accepted understanding of *Slaughterhouse*, state prisoners under sentence of death did not fare well after 1875 when they sought relief from the Court. James J. Medley, on death row in the Colorado state penitentiary, was the exception who proved the rule. Medley, who killed his wife on May 13, 1889, had been convicted of that crime and sentenced to death by hanging on November 29, 1889. On July 19, 1889, soon after his indictment by a grand jury, however, the Colorado legislature rewrote its capital punishment statute, including the procedures for carrying out the death penalty, which mandated some twenty changes between the new statute and the old one in existence at the time Medley killed his wife.

Medley would still suffer death by hanging under the new procedures, but his date with the hangman would take place within 28 days of sentencing in contrast to the 25 days fixed in the past. Instead of confinement in the county jail prior to execution he would be confined in the penitentiary and the warden, not the county sheriff, would serve as his executioner. Finally, under the old law Medley would have been kept in solitary confinement prior to his execution with only his attorney allowed to visit. The new statute gave greater access to more persons prior to the execution, but only at the discretion of prison officials.

In re Medley (1890) raised a challenge to Medley's conviction and sentence before a federal appeals court on grounds that Colorado's revisions constituted an ex post facto law prohibited by Article I, Section 10, of the Constitution, the only section in the original Constitution that imposed substantive limitations on state power.[36] The appeals court rejected this argument, but in a habeas corpus proceeding the Court, speaking through Justice Miller, agreed that the statute under which Medley had been condemned was an ex post facto law and ordered him released from the penitentiary, with the proviso that the state's attorney general be notified by the warden ten days before the release (**Document 1.6**).

Miller and the majority realized that their strict interpretation of the ex post facto clause had left the state in an untenable position with regard to a future prosecution of someone guilty of first-degree murder because the statute under which Medley had been held repealed the statute under which he might have been legally punished. A murderer would be set free. Such rigor was too much for Justices David Brewer and Bradley, who joined in an angry dissent. "Was there ever a case in which the maxim '*de minimis non curat lex*' [about minimal things], had more just and wholesome application?" Brewer asked. "Yet on account of these differences, a convicted murderer is to escape the death he deserves, and be turned loose on society."[37]

Medley appears to have been lucky. Five months after announcing the Court's opinion Justice Miller died, and two months after that the justices turned away a similar ex post facto claim in *Holden v. Minnesota* (1890). Between the time Clifton Holden committed first-degree murder and his sentencing, the Minnesota legislature revised its procedures to provide that a prisoner under sentence of death would be kept in solitary confinement until the time of execution with access limited to a defined list of visitors and witnesses. In addition, the date and time of the execution were to be fixed by the governor instead of the trial court. Distinguishing these facts from those presented in *Medley,* and concluding that the Minnesota revisions were only minimal, the Court, with Justice John Marshall Harlan now speaking for a new majority that included Justices Brewer and Bradley, affirmed Holden's conviction and sentence.[38]

The death of Justice Miller soon after the *Medley* decision, and the passing of three other justices by 1900, brought to the Court new members with a less scrupulous perspective on what constituted state violations of the ex post facto clause in capital cases. *Medley* was not even cited when the justices upheld the death sentences of John Rooney in North Dakota and Joe Malloy in South Carolina. Rooney had committed murder in August 1902, when North Dakota's death penalty statute required execution six months after sentencing and gave the task of hanging the condemned to the county sheriff inside a county jail.

North Dakota, like Minnesota and other states at the time, centralized its procedures shortly before a court sentenced Rooney in 1903 by moving all executions to the state penitentiary out of public view, limiting the number of witnesses and affording the condemned an additional three months before walking to the gallows. Without dissent, Justice Harlan, in *Rooney v. North Dakota* (1905), disposed of Rooney's claim in several short paragraphs by citing his own opinion in *Holden* and noting as well that at least one of the statutory revisions worked to his benefit.[39] In *Holden* and *Rooney,* the Court heralded a less rigorous standard when it came to the ex post facto clause. At the same time the justices ratified the growing tide of legislative sentiment that sought to remove executions as far as possible from the community and dilute their significance as public spectacles and rituals. The privatizing of executions, sanctioned by the Court, had less to do with preserving the dignity of the condemned than with preventing outbreaks of disorder and violence that often accompanied public executions.[40]

At the time he committed his crime, convicted murderer Malloy also faced death by hanging in a county jail. But in 1912 the state of South Carolina introduced the electric chair and mandated its use only in the penitentiary. In *Malloy v. South Carolina* (1915), the Court rejected Malloy's claim that this revision constituted an ex post facto law that worked to his prejudice and injury. Justice James McReynolds observed that the clause had been intended "to secure substantial rights against arbitrary and oppressive legislative action, and not to obstruct mere alterations in conditions deemed necessary for the orderly infliction of humane punishment."[41]

State prisoners under sentence of death who raised constitutional claims other than the ex post facto clause fared no better than Holden, Rooney, and Malloy. Invoking *Murdock,* the justices usually dismissed most appeals for lack of a "federal question" in situations where the claim had not been raised at trial, where the claim challenged an interpretation of state law as determined by the state's highest court, or where a state court's interpretation of a federal constitutional right agreed with prior Court rulings. As Chief Justice Melville Fuller wrote in *Leeper v. State of Texas* (1891): "Whether the statutes of a legislature of a state have been duly enacted in accordance with the requirements of the constitution of such state is not a federal question, and the decision of state courts as to what are the laws of the state is binding upon the courts of the United States. . . . The sufficiency of the indictment, the degree of the offense charged, the admissibility of the testimony objected to, and the alleged disqualification of the juror because he was not a freeholder, were all matters with the disposition of which . . . we have nothing to do."[42]

Reaffirming the Limits of the Fourteenth Amendment

Those in the shadow of the gallows or facing the electric chair who invoked either the due process clause or privileges and immunities clause of the Fourteenth Amendment were no more successful than the New Orleans butchers in *Slaughterhouse*. A majority of the justices construed the amendment as simply reaffirming a traditional federal system, not enlarging federal judicial authority over state law, as evidenced in an 1884 case, *Hurtado v. California*.[43] Joseph Hurtado, sentenced to death in California for shooting to death his wife's lover, attempted to escape the hangman's noose by claiming that the state's failure to indict him by a grand jury violated due process of law as it had been known to the common law and as required by the Fourteenth Amendment.

In a 7–1 decision the Court disposed of this argument on both historical and logical grounds (**Document 1.7**). Justice Stanley Matthews argued persuasively for the majority that indictment by grand jury had not been considered an indispensable requirement of due process at common law in either England or America and that had the framers of the Fourteenth Amendment intended to include it within the concept of due process they would have explicitly provided for it in the text of the amendment, making it identical with the guarantee contained in the Fifth Amendment.[44] Harlan's dissent challenged Matthews' account of the common law's history and protested that, however logical, Matthews' argument would leave other guarantees of the Bill of Rights unprotected through the Fourteenth Amendment's due process clause, a prediction that proved prescient for many years.[45]

Three years after *Hurtado*, the justices for the first time turned away a challenge to a death sentence rooted in the privileges and immunities clause, a claim thoughtfully raised by J. Randolph Tucker. Tucker represented August Spies, editor of the anarchist newspaper *Arbeiter Zeitung*, who had been convicted in Chicago along with other radicals for plotting the bombing that killed policemen during the Haymarket Riot.[46] The judge who presided at Spies' trial had permitted two members of the jury to serve who admitted under examination that they had already formed an opinion about the case, including the guilt or innocence of the defendants.[47] Illinois law, however, permitted the seating of such a juror "if he shall upon oath state that he believes he can fairly and impartially render a verdict therein in accordance with the law and the evidence and the court shall be satisfied of the truth of such statement."[48]

Testifying in his own defense, Spies had been interrogated at length by the prosecution about his anarchist beliefs. Tucker alleged that such questioning strayed so far from the issue in the case that it forced the defendant to become a witness against himself. Additionally, Tucker asserted that evidence had been introduced at the trial that had been seized from Spies' office without a proper warrant. Tucker argued that the statute and the judge's decision to seat the jurors violated Spies' right to "an impartial jury," language derived from the Sixth Amendment, while the other violations were condemned in the Fifth and Fourteenth Amendments. Making a clever distinction, Tucker did not claim that those amendments by their own force applied to Illinois, a losing argument in 1887 given the Court's devotion to *Barron* and its progeny. Instead, Tucker asserted that the rights claimed had been rooted in the common law and given fundamental protection against the national government in the Bill of Rights. As such they could be considered among the privileges and immunities of a U.S. citizen now protected by the Fourteenth Amendment.

Chief Justice Morrison Waite, writing for a unanimous court, brushed aside Tucker's Fourteenth Amendment arguments with the observation that "the federal questions presented by counsel . . . are not involved in the determination of the case as it appears on the face of the record." On the impartial jury issue, Waite declared that the case must be one where the law left "nothing to the 'conscience or discretion' of the [trial] court," and where "the error complained of is so gross as to amount in law to a denial by the state of a trial by an impartial jury." The self-incrimination claim "is certainly a question of state law, as administered in the courts of the state, and not of federal law," while the unlawful seizure objection had not been raised at trial and could not be examined on appeal.[49] Spies and three other Haymarket defendants went to their deaths nine days later.

Cruel and Unusual Punishment

William Kemmler's attempt to avoid electrocution in New York by invoking both the privileges and immunities clause and the due process clause proved equally unavailing. Three New York courts had rejected his claim that this new method of execution violated the state's constitutional ban on cruel and unusual punishment by deferring to the legislature's determination that it "constituted a more humane method [that] . . . must result in instantaneous, and consequently in painless, death."[50] As for the similar language in the Constitution of the United States, the state courts noted only "we have no present concern, as the prohibition therein . . . is addressed solely to the national government."[51]

Chief Justice Fuller's opinion for the Court in *In re Kemmler* (1890) simply affirmed the correctness of the New York courts on both the state and federal issues (**Document 1.8**). "It is not contended, as it could not be," he wrote, "that the Eighth Amendment was intended to apply to the States," and he went on to dismiss Kemmler's Fourteenth Amendment claims as well. In case anyone missed the point, Fuller concluded, "the Fourteenth Amendment did not radically change the whole theory of the relations of the state and the federal government to each other."[52]

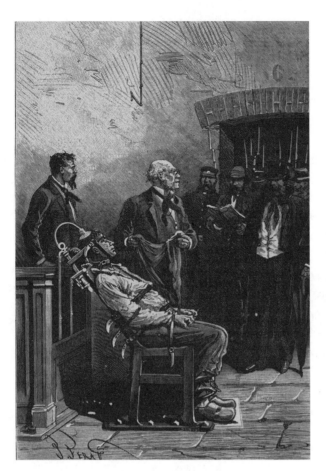

By rejecting the claim that the Eighth Amendment applied to the states, the Court permitted the electrocution of William Kemmler in August 1890. In his opinion, Chief Justice Melvin Fuller also clarified that in order for a punishment to be considered cruel and unusual it must "involve torture or a lingering death." The gruesome scene that unfolded at Kemmler's execution, seen above in a contemporary engraving, left some disgusted witnesses questioning the efficacy and humaneness of this new technology.

Although it was not necessary to the decision, Fuller added several observations about what forms of punishment fell within the constitutional ban, including "burning at the stake, crucifixion, breaking on the wheel, or the like. . . . Punishments are cruel when they involve torture or a lingering death. . . . It implies there is something inhuman and barbarous—something more than the mere extinguishment of life."[53] In fact, Kemmler's execution three months after the Court's decision proved to be neither "instantaneous" nor "painless" (**Document 1.9**). The electricity had to be turned on twice to end the condemned man's life. Witnesses described for reporters a scene "so terrible that the word fails to convey the idea," as Kemmler's blood vessels began to burst, the hair and skin under the electrodes burned, "the stench was unbearable," and people collapsed.[54] Even so, electrocution endured with the public's support as a form of "humane" execution (**Document 1.10**).

By the spring of 1915, a year before the United States entered World War I, the Court had all but sealed the door on efforts by state prisoners, including those under death sentence, to challenge their convictions by claiming a violation of rights protected by the Fourteenth Amendment. In *Maxwell v. Dow* (1900), with Justice Harlan the lone dissenter, the Court ruled that a jury of eight persons in a state criminal proceeding did not offend the privileges and immunities clause when it convicted the defendant of robbery.[55] "The privileges and immunities of citizens of the United States do not necessarily include all the rights protected by the first eight amendments to the Federal Constitution against the powers of the Federal Government," Justice Rufus Peckham reaffirmed.[56]

Eight years later, in *Twining v. New Jersey* (1908), Justice William Moody conceded that "some of the personal rights safeguarded by the first eight Amendments against national action may also be safeguarded against state action, because a denial of them would be a denial of due process of law."[57] But the Fifth Amendment's prohibition on compulsory self-incrimination was not among them, he concluded, because it was not "an immutable principle of justice which is the inalienable possession of every citizen of a free government" (**Document 1.11**). Nor was the prohibition on compulsory self-incrimination among the privileges and immunities of a citizen protected by the Fourteenth Amendment.[58] The Fifth Amendment right claimed in *Twining*, Moody noted, "cannot be ranked with the right to hearing before condemnation, the immunity from arbitrary power . . . *and the inviolability of private property.*"[59]

Moody's reference to "the inviolability of private property" recognized that eleven years prior to *Twining* the justices had suddenly begun to apply at least one explicit provision of the Bill of Rights—the just compensation clause of the Fifth Amendment—against the states in the landmark decision *Chicago, Burlington & Quincy Railroad Company v. Chicago* (1897). There the justices overturned an Illinois supreme court ruling that upheld a jury award of one dollar when a street was opened across the railroad's tracks.[60] The justices found both the Illinois condemnation procedures as well as the substance of the jury's award "inadequate" under the due process clause of the Fourteenth Amendment, the first example of incorporating a substantive portion of the Bill of Rights into that clause.[61]

Without overruling *Barron* the Court had effectively rendered it superfluous by means of the Fourteenth Amendment. And that the first incorporation decision through the due process clause protected property rather than other constitutional liberties was not lost on some members of the Court. When the justices upheld the conviction of Joseph Gilbert for seditious speech under a Minnesota law during the war, Justice Louis Brandeis dissented with the observation, "I cannot believe that the liberty guaranteed by the Fourteenth Amendment includes only the liberty to acquire and enjoy property."[62]

Brandeis' complaint anticipated the birth of a new constitutional regime with respect to the Fourteenth Amendment, liberty, and capital punishment. The prosecution of Leo Frank for murder in 1913 and his petition to the Supreme Court for a writ of habeas corpus two years later opened a new chapter in the

Court's role in state capital cases under the Fourteenth Amendment and set the stage for the even more dramatic events generated by the Elaine massacre and the trial of the six African American defendants sentenced to death in Arkansas.

The Ordeal of Leo Frank

Leo Frank, a twenty-nine-year-old engineering graduate of Cornell, managed the National Pencil Factory in Atlanta, where he and his wife had become pillars of the local Jewish community. In the spring of 1913 the factory's night watchman discovered the body of thirteen-year-old Mary Phagan, who had been strangled and raped. Suspicion fell initially on the night watchman and an African American janitor, John Conley, after the discovery of what appeared to be Conley's blood-soaked shirt and two notes, allegedly written by Phagan as she lay dying, that accused a "Negro" of attacking her. Conley soon shifted the blame to Frank, claiming that Frank had forced him to write the Phagan notes and that he had received $200 from Frank for helping him move the body, although he could not produce the so-called hush money.

Indicted on May 24, 1913, Frank's murder trial began two months later amidst a blitz of sensational local newspaper coverage in a courthouse surrounded by a mob that cheered the chief prosecutor each day as he entered and left the building

Leo Frank, manager of the National Pencil Factory in Atlanta, was convicted and sentenced to electrocution for the 1913 rape and death of a thirteen-year-old girl. The sensationalism that accompanied his trial stirred ethnic hatred. Frank appealed his conviction, arguing that his right to due process had been violated by the intimidation and potential threat posed by the mobs that congregated during his trial. The Supreme Court sided with the lower courts and rejected the claims that events surrounding the trial had stripped Frank of his Fourteenth Amendment right to due process.

(**Document 1.12**). Georgia's aging populist leader, Tom Watson, regularly stirred the pot of ethnic and religious hatred throughout the proceedings to the point where the trial judge became so fearful for the safety of Frank and his lawyers in the event of an acquittal that they were asked to waive Frank's right to be present when the verdict was read. Frank was convicted and sentenced to death in the electric chair. His two motions for a new trial rejected, and his appeals turned down on three occasions by the Georgia supreme court, Frank's lawyers sought a writ of habeas corpus from the federal district court on the grounds that Frank had been denied due process of law in violation of the Fourteenth Amendment. When the district court, without holding a hearing to examine the conflicting evidence, refused the writ, Frank appealed to the Supreme Court, which heard the case over two days at the end of February 1915.[63]

Frank's lawyers raised two interwoven claims. First, they argued that Frank had been denied due process guaranteed by the Fourteenth Amendment. They maintained that the presence of the mob outside the courtroom had been so intimidating that it overwhelmed the proceedings and essentially stripped the court of jurisdiction so that its proceedings became *coram non judice* (literally, "not in the presence of a judge"). In addition, they claimed that Frank's absence from the court at the time of the verdict, secured under threat of violence voiced by the trial judge, conclusively demonstrated mob domination. Seven members of the Court, led by Justice Mahlon Pitney, found no merit to these claims and refused the writ, thereby closing the door on a further inquiry by the district court.

Pitney's opinion in *Frank v. Mangum* (1915) showed extraordinary deference to the conclusions of the Georgia courts on all matters of fact and law. Claims of disorder during a trial "calculated to influence court or jury, are matters [not] to be lightly treated," Pitney affirmed, but Georgia's decisions demonstrated that such disorders had been repressed in the past by sturdy judges and by means of various other methods, including postponing the trial, changing the venue, and granting a new trial. Frank's due process claims would require the states to take even greater protective measures any time a trial became threatened by outside interference. The state might be forced to abandon jurisdiction over the trial altogether and refrain from further inquiry into the question of guilt. Such a radical result, Pitney said, "would . . . impair the power of the States to repress and punish crime; for it would render their courts powerless to act in opposition to lawless public sentiment. The argument is not only unsound in principle, but is in conflict with the practice that prevails in all of the States, so far as we are aware."[64]

The Georgia courts refused a new trial, Pitney wrote, "only because they found his charges untrue save in a few minor particulars not amounting to more than irregularities, and not prejudicial to the accused. There was here no denial of due process of law."[65] As for Frank's absence during the reading of the verdict, it was only "an incident of the right of trial by jury," according to Pitney, and a state, without infringing the Fourteenth Amendment, "may limit the effect to be given to an error respecting one of the incidents of such trial."[66]

Justice Holmes, seldom one to wring his hands over the fate of criminal defendants,[67] penned a devastating dissent, joined by Charles Evans Hughes, soon to become the Republican candidate for president and a future chief justice (**Document 1.13**). Holmes reminded the Court that the issue before them was the simple question of whether the district court should have tried the facts before refusing the writ. He then proceeded to catalogue the parade of horrors that infected Leo Frank's right to due process of law:

> The hostility surrounding the trial was sufficient on one day to lead the judge to confer in the presence of the jury with the chief of police for Atlanta and the colonel of the Fifth Georgia Regiment.
>
> Before charging the jury, the judge expressed the view to one of Frank's lawyers that there existed "danger of violence" if the jury acquitted his client or could not reach a verdict.
>
> Before the jury could be polled there was such a roar of applause that the polling could not go on and the judge could not hear the answers.[68]

Habeas corpus, Holmes wrote in memorable words, "cuts through all forms and goes to the very tissue of the structure. It comes from outside, not in subordination to the proceedings, and although the forms may have been preserved opens the inquiry whether they have been more than an empty shell."[69] Reasonable judges might debate the meaning of due process of law, he continued, but there could be no doubt that at a minimum it embraced the fundamental conception of a fair trial. Frank had not been given one. "Mob law does not become due process of law by securing the assent of a terrorized jury."[70]

No decision by a higher court in Georgia, Holmes concluded, could overcome the loss of jurisdiction by the trial court manifested in the record. The duty of the Court should be "to declare lynch law as little valid when practiced by a regularly drawn jury as when administered by one elected by a mob intent on death."[71] Pitney and his six colleagues had apparently cleared the way for Frank's date with Georgia's electric chair.

Georgia's lame duck governor, John M. Slaton, who read the same trial record as Pitney, reached a different conclusion (**Document 1.14**). Shortly after the Court handed down its decision denying the writ, he commuted Frank's sentence to life in prison, an action that prompted threats on Slaton's life and necessitated the posting of a national guard detail around the governor's mansion.

On August 17 a mob intent on death styled itself "the Knights of Mary Phagan," broke into the penitentiary, kidnapped Frank, drove him to Marietta, and there lynched him. The Knights, led by former governor Joseph Mackey Brown and aided by a local sheriff, included the former mayor of Marietta and the son of a former U.S. senator. Crowds swarmed to the sight of the hanging, photographed Frank's body, and took pieces of the tree and rope that had served

Justice Oliver Wendell Holmes's sharp dissent in Frank v. Mangum *outlined the litany of due process barriers facing Leo Frank during his trial. Justice Holmes would be vindicated eight years later when the Court overruled the* Frank *decision in* Moore v. Dempsey.

as the instruments of his death. Seventy-one years after this grizzly event, Frank received a pardon from the Georgia board of pardons and parole.

Saving the Elaine Six

The violent martyrdom of Leo Frank, a Jew, probably saved the lives of the African Americans under sentence of death for the Elaine riot and massacre eight years later. So, too, did other developments in American life. Between 1915 and 1923 the nation experienced wartime induced social disorders, including labor strikes, race riots, and vigilante activities, that shocked government leaders who demanded a restoration of law and order.[72] The Court that had decided *Frank v. Mangum* also underwent profound changes. Justice Hughes, who had joined Holmes' dissent, was gone, but so, too, was Justice Pitney, the author of the majority opinion, who retired in 1922. A new chief justice, William Howard Taft, now presided over the Court. He was joined by two other Republican appointees, George Sutherland and Pierce Butler. Both men had been appointed by the new Republican president, Warren G. Harding, who, in contrast to departed president Woodrow Wilson, had spoken out against racial discrimination. The defendants in Elaine now called upon the Court to step forward and uphold the rule of law.

Represented in their appeals by a legendary African American lawyer from Little Rock, Scipio Africanus Jones, and by Col. George M. Murphy, a Confederate veteran and former attorney general of Arkansas, the Elaine Six had no success with the state's supreme court, which ruled against their claims that African Americans had been excluded from the jury and that the trial had been dominated by a mob (**Document 1.15**). Their initial efforts to secure review from the Supreme Court also failed when the justices refused to hear the case on direct appeal. Fortunately, a state chancery judge postponed their execution long enough to permit the filing of a writ of habeas corpus with the federal district court. The district court also denied the writ on the authority of the *Frank* decision, but the judge certified probable cause for allowing an appeal of his habeas ruling to the Supreme Court. That was sufficient for Holmes, who secured five votes—including Taft, Butler, and Sutherland—to reverse the district court, ordering that court to hold a hearing on the defendants' claims and thereby overruling *Frank v. Mangum sub silentio* (**Document 1.16**).[73]

He began his opinion in *Moore v. Dempsey* with a chilling account of the course of justice before and during the Elaine trial:

> How mobs marched on the jail after the arrest of the defendants to lynch them, but were prevented by the presence of federal troops and promises by local leading officials that if they refrained from violence the African Americans would be executed according to the form of law.
>
> How African American witnesses were "whipped and tortured until they would say what was wanted . . . to prove the petitioners' guilt."
>
> How African Americans were systematically excluded from the grand and petit juries.
>
> How the trial court and neighborhood "were thronged with an adverse crowd that threatened the most dangerous consequences to anyone interfering with the desired result."
>
> How counsel for the accused had no opportunity to consult with them, did not request a change of venue or separate trials, and called no witnesses for the defense.

Holmes next paid brief deference to Justice Pitney, who had retired the year before, by noting that *Frank v. Mangum* recognized that if a trial is dominated by a mob to the extent that it prevents the course of justice and if the state's corrective processes do not afford a remedy such circumstances deprives the accused of due process of law. If the corrective processes of the state are adequate, federal courts must stay their hand with respect to habeas corpus.

He then added the devastating exception taking the present case outside that rule: "But if the case is that the whole proceeding is a mask—that counsel, jury and judge were swept away to the fatal end by an irresistible wave of public passion, and that the State Courts failed to correct the wrong, neither perfection in the machinery for correction nor the possibility that the trial court and counsel saw no other way of avoiding an immediate outbreak of the mob can prevent this Court from securing to the petitioners their constitutional rights." The district court was ordered to examine the facts presented and "if true as alleged they make the trial absolutely void."[74]

Given a new trial as a result of the Court's decision, the six Elaine defendants received twelve-year sentences, but left the state safely after Arkansas governor Thomas McRae granted them indefinite furloughs. For the first time since the adoption of the Fourteenth Amendment, the justices had effectively overturned a state criminal conviction on grounds of due process and expanded the possibilities of reviewing state criminal trials by means of habeas corpus. *Moore v. Dempsey* had initiated the redesign of the jurisprudence of death in America.

Document 1.1
Justice Nathan Clifford Examines the Meaning of the Eighth Amendment's Prohibition on Cruel and Unusual Punishment in *Wilkerson v. Utah*, March 17, 1879

Wallace Wilkerson, convicted of murder in the Utah Territory and sentenced to death by firing squad, appealed his sentence to the Supreme Court on various statutory grounds. In the course of rejecting his appeal, the Court, speaking through Justice Nathan Clifford in Wilkerson v. Utah, *examined the Eighth Amendment's prohibition on cruel and unusual punishments.*

MR. JUSTICE CLIFFORD delivered the opinion of the Court.

. . . Cruel and unusual punishments are forbidden by the Constitution, but the authorities referred to are quite sufficient to show that the punishment of shooting as a mode of executing the death penalty for the crime of murder in the first degree is not included in that category within the meaning of the Eighth Amendment. . . . Cases mentioned by the author are where the prisoner was drawn or dragged to the place of execution, in treason; or where he was emboweled alive, beheaded, and quartered, in high treason. Mention is also made of public dissection in murder, and burning alive in treason committed by a female. . . . Difficulty would attend the effort to define with exactness the extent of the constitutional provision . . . but it is safe to affirm that punishments of torture, such as those mentioned . . . and all others in the same line of unnecessary cruelty, are forbidden by that amendment to the Constitution. . . .

Source: Wilkerson v. Utah, 99 U.S. 130 (1878), at 135–137.

Document 1.2
An Account of the Execution of Wallace Wilkerson, May 23, 1879

Wallace Wilkerson's execution by firing squad in 1879 was anything but quick and painless, as described in this contemporary newspaper account.

Mormon Execution—Shot to Death.

Wallace Wilkerson, who murdered William Baxter at Homansville, Utah, in June 1877, was executed at Provo on the 16th. The doomed man had expressed a desire to be shot to death, which was granted. At twelve o'clock P.M. he was lead [sic] out into the courthouse yard and was seated on a chair. Railroad ties were piled at his back, and upon his heart a white mark was placed, as a target for the four marksmen, who were in concealment, about fifteen paces off. The prisoner, neatly dressed, sat stolidly indifferent, and after he had made a brief speech and said farewell to the Sheriffs and others near by, the word was given, and four rifles cracked simultaneously. Springing into the air, Wilkerson, mortally wounded, shouted out: "O, God! O, God! They have missed!" He then fell forward and died in about 27 minutes. About 225 people witnessed the execution from inside and around the stockade. The remains were turned over to his wife and friends, who conveyed them to Payson, Utah, for burial. He was a Mormon, and was the second person ever executed by shooting in the territory, John D. Lee, the Mountain Meadows murderer, being the first.

Source: The Weekly Arizona Miner, May 23, 1879, Issue 22, column D.

Document 1.3
The Supreme Court Reverses the Philippine Court, Ruling That Penalties Imposed Violate Eighth Amendment, May 2, 1910

In reversing the conviction and sentence imposed by a Philippine court on Paul Weems, Justice Joseph McKenna, in Weems v. United States, *offered an expansive reading of the Eighth Amendment's ban on cruel and unusual punishment.*

MR. JUSTICE MCKENNA delivered the opinion of the Court.
   . . . He [Weems] must bear a chain night and day. He is condemned to painful as well as hard labor. . . . Such penalties for such offenses amaze those who have formed their conception of the relation of a state to even its offending citizens from the practice of the American commonwealths, and believe that it is a precept of justice that punishment for crime should be graduated and proportioned to offense.

Is this also a precept of the fundamental law? We say fundamental law, for the provision of the Philippine Bill of Rights, prohibiting the infliction of cruel and unusual punishment, was taken from the Constitution of the United States, and must have the same meaning. . . .

Legislation, both statutory and constitutional, is enacted, it is true, from an experience of evils but its general language should not, therefore, be necessarily confined to the form that evil had theretofore taken. Time works changes, brings into existence new conditions and purposes. Therefore a principle, to be vital, must be capable of wider application than the mischief which gave it birth. This is peculiarly true of constitutions. They are not ephemeral enactments, designed to meet passing occasions. . . . In the application of a constitution, therefore, our contemplation cannot be only of what has been, but of what may be. Under any other rule, a constitution would indeed be as easy of application as it would be deficient in efficacy and power. Its general principles would have little value, and be converted by precedent into impotent and lifeless formulas. Rights declared in words might be lost in reality. . . .

The clause of the Constitution . . . may be therefore progressive, and is not fastened to the obsolete, but may acquire meaning as public opinion becomes enlightened by a humane justice. . . .

Source: Weems v. United States, 217 U.S. 349 (1910), at 368–378.

Document 1.4
Ratification of the Privileges or Immunities Clause of the Fourteenth Amendment, July 9, 1868

In 1868 Congress adopted, and the states ratified, the Fourteenth Amendment to the Constitution of the United States. The amendment's first section provided national citizenship for all persons born or naturalized in the United States, effectively nullifying the Supreme Court's 1857 Dred Scott decision that had excluded African Americans from citizenship. In addition, it prohibited the states from abridging the privileges and immunities of citizens or denying persons due process of law and the equal protection of the laws.

Section 1: All persons born or naturalized in the United States, and subject to the jurisdiction thereof, are citizens of the United States and of the State wherein they reside. No State shall make or enforce any law which shall abridge the privileges or immunities of citizens of the United States; nor shall any State deprive any person of life, liberty, or property, without due process of law; nor deny to any person within its jurisdiction the equal protection of the laws.

Source: U.S. Constitution, Amendment XIV, Section 1.

Document 1.5
Justice Samuel Miller on the Application of the Fourteenth Amendment in the *Slaughterhouse Cases*, April 14, 1873

In the 1873 Slaughterhouse Cases, *the Supreme Court for the first time was called upon to interpret the Fourteenth Amendment. In his decision for the Court, Justice Samuel Miller explicitly noted "the right to peaceably assemble and petition for redress of grievances," a right derived from the First Amendment.*

MR. JUSTICE MILLER delivered the opinion of the Court.

. . . Of the privileges and immunities of the citizen of the United States, and of the privileges and immunities of the citizen of the State, and what they respectively are, we will presently consider; but we wish to state here that it is only the former which are placed by this clause under the protection of the Federal Constitution, and that the latter, whatever they may be, are not intended to have any additional protection by this paragraph of the amendment. . . .

. . . [W]e venture to suggest some which own their existence to the Federal government, its National character, its Constitution, or its laws . . . the right of the citizen of this great country, protected by implied guarantees of its Constitution, to come to the seat of government to assert any claim he may have upon that government, to transact any business he may have with it, to seek its protection, to share its offices, to engage in administering its functions. He has the right of free access to its seaports . . . to the subtreasuries, land offices, and courts of justice in the several States. . . .

Another privilege of a citizen of the United States is to demand the care and protection of the Federal government over his life, liberty, and property when on the high seas or within the jurisdiction of a foreign government. . . . The right to peaceably assemble and petition for redress of grievances, the privilege of the writ of habeas corpus, are rights of the citizen guaranteed by the Federal Constitution. . . .

To these may be added the rights secured by the thirteenth and fifteenth articles of amendment, and by the other clause of the fourteenth. . . .

Source: The *Slaughterhouse Cases,* 83 U.S. 36 (1872), at 77–80.

Document 1.6
The Court Orders James J. Medley Freed after Ruling Colorado Statute Unconstitutional in *In Re Medley*, March 3, 1890

Finding some twenty variances between the Colorado statute in force when James J. Medley committed murder and the new statute under which he was sentenced to death, the Supreme Court ordered his release on grounds that the state had violated the constitutional ban on ex post facto laws.

MR. JUSTICE MILLER delivered the opinion of the Court.

. . . But under the writ of habeas corpus we cannot do anything else than discharge the prisoner from the wrongful confinement in the penitentiary under the statute of Colorado invalid as to this case. . . .

We do not think that we are authorized to remand the prisoner to the custody of the sheriff of the proper county to be proceeded against, in the court of Colorado which condemned him, in such a manner as they may think proper; because it is apparent that, while the statute under which he is now held in custody is an ex post facto law in regard to the offense, it repeals the former law, under which he might otherwise have been punished, and we are not advised whether that court possesses any power to deal further with the prisoner or not. Such a question is not before us, because it has not been acted upon by the court below, and it is neither our inclination nor our duty to decide what the court may or what it may not do in regard to the case as it stands. Upon the whole, after due deliberation, we have come to the conclusion that the attorney general of the state of Colorado shall be notified by the warden of the penitentiary of the precise time when he will release the prisoner from his custody under the present sentence and warrant, at least 10 days beforehand, and after doing this, and at that time, he shall discharge the prisoner from his custody; and such will be the order of this court. . . .

BREWER, J. (dissenting.)

. . . The differences between the two [statutes], as to the manner in which this sentence of death shall be carried into execution, are trifling. What are they? By the old law, execution must be within 25 days from the day of sentence; by the new, within 28 days. By the old, confinement prior to execution was in the county jail; by the new, in the penitentiary. By the old, the sheriff was the hangman; by the new, the warden. . . . Under the old, his confinement might be absolutely solitary, at the discretion of the sheriff, but with a single interruption; under the new, access is given to him, as a matter of right, to all who ought to be permitted to see him. . . .

Was there ever a case in which the maxim, *'de minimis non curat lex,'* had more just and wholesome application? Yet, on account of these differences, a convicted murderer is to escape the death he deserves, and be turned loose on society. I am authorized to say that Mr. Justice BRADLEY concurs in this dissent.

Source: In Re Medley, 134 U.S. 160 (1890), at 174–176.

Document 1.7
The Court Rules That Grand Juries Are Not a Constitutional Right in Capital Cases, March 3, 1884

In the case of Hurtado v. California (1884), the Supreme Court majority rejected the argument that the due process clause of the Fourteenth Amendment required the states to indict by grand jury in all capital cases. Justice Stanley Matthews explained why due process remained a separate requirement from the grand jury provision in both the Fifth and Fourteenth Amendments.

MR. JUSTICE MATTHEWS delivered the opinion of the Court.

. . . According to a recognized canon of interpretation . . . we are forbidden to assume, without clear reason to the contrary, that any part of this most important amendment is superfluous. The natural and obvious inference is that, in the sense of the Constitution, 'due process of law' was not meant or intended to include . . . the institution and procedure of a grand jury in any case. The conclusion is equally irresistible that, when the same phrase was employed in the fourteenth amendment to restrain the action of the states, it was used in the same sense and with no greater extent; and that if in the adoption of that amendment it had been part of its purpose to perpetuate the institution of the grand jury in all the states, it would have embodied, as did the fifth amendment, express declarations to that effect. . . .

Source: Hurtado v. California, 110 U.S. 516 (1884), at 534–535.

Document 1.8
The Supreme Court Upholds the Constitutionality of Electrocution, May 23, 1890

In 1890 the Supreme Court upheld the first execution by electrocution when it rejected claims by lawyers representing William Kemmler that New York's use of the electric chair violated the state's constitutional ban on cruel and unusual punishment, language identical to that found in the Eighth Amendment, as well as the Fourteenth Amendment's guarantees of privileges and immunities and due process.

CHIEF JUSTICE FULLER delivered the opinion of the Court.

. . . It is not contended, as it could not be, that the Eighth Amendment was intended to apply to the States, but it is urged that the provision of the Fourteenth Amendment, which forbids a State to make or enforce any law which shall abridge the privileges or immunities of citizens of the United States, is a prohibition on the State from the imposition of cruel and unusual punishments, and that such punishments are also prohibited by inclusion in the term 'due process of law.' . . . So that, if the punishment prescribed for an offense against the laws of the State were manifestly cruel and unusual as burning at the stake, crucifixion, breaking on the wheel, or the like, it would be the duty of the courts to adjudge such penalties to be within the constitutional prohibition. And we think this equally true of the eighth amendment, in its application to Congress. . . . Punishments are cruel when they involve torture or a lingering death, but the punishment of death is not cruel within the meaning of that word as used in the Constitution. It implies something inhuman and barbarous—something more than the extinguishment of life. . . . The decision of the state courts sustaining the validity of the act under the state Constitution is not reexaminable here, nor was that decision against any title, right, privilege, or immunity specially set up or claimed by the petitioners under the Constitution of the United States. . . .

The Fourteenth Amendment did not radically change the whole theory of the relations of the state and federal governments to each other, and of both governments to the people. . . . Undoubtedly the Amendment forbids any arbitrary deprivation of life, liberty, or property. . . . But it was not designed to interfere with the power of the State to protect the lives, liberties, and property of its citizens. . . . The enactment of this statute was, in itself, within the legitimate sphere of the legislative power of the State. . . . We cannot perceive that the State has thereby abridged the privileges or immunities of the petitioner, or deprived him of due process of law.

In order to reverse the judgment of the highest court of the state of New York, we should be compelled to hold that it had committed an error so gross as to amount in law to a denial by the state of due process of law to one accused of crime, or of some right secured to him by the constitution of the United States. We have no hesitation in saying that this we cannot do upon the record before us. The application for a writ of error is denied.

Source: In re Kemmler, 136 U.S. 436 (1890), at 446–448.

Document 1.9
"Far Worse Than Hanging": The Execution of William Kemmler, August 6, 1890

William Kemmler, a convicted murderer, became the first person executed in the electric chair. The execution took place at the Auburn prison in New York state. As the following account by a reporter for the New York Times *suggests, Kemmler's death was not instantaneous.*

AUBURN, N.Y., Aug. 6—A sacrifice to the whims and theories of the coterie of cranks and politicians who induced the Legislature of this State to pass a law supplanting hanging by electrical execution was offered to-day in the person of William Kemmler, the Buffalo murderer. He died this morning under the most revolting circumstances, and with his death there was placed to the discredit of the State of New-York an execution that was a disgrace to civilization.

Probably no convicted murder[er] of modern times has been made to suffer as Kemmler has suffered. Unfortunate enough to be the first man convicted after the passage of the new execution law, his life has been used as the bone of contention between the alleged humanitarians who supported the law on the one side, and the electric-light interests, who hated to see the commodity in which they deal reduced to such a use as that. . . .

The uncertainty in which he has so long lived would have driven any ordinary man insane. That suffering has culminated in a death so fearful that people throughout the country will read of it with horror and disgust.

The execution can not merely be characterized as unsuccessful. It was so terrible that the word fails to convey the idea. . . .

Fortunately there was no difficulty in getting the full details of the affair, despite the fact that the advocates of the law attempted to do their work concealed from the eyes of the public. . . .

Words will not keep pace with what followed. Simultaneously with the click of the lever the body of the man in the chair straightened. Every muscle of it seemed to be drawn to its highest tension. It seemed as though it might have been thrown across the chamber were it not for the straps that held it. There was no movement of the eyes. The body was as rigid as though cast in bronze, save for the index finger of the right hand, which closed up so tightly that the nail penetrated the flesh on the first joint and blood trickled out the arm of the chair. Drs. Spitzka and Macdonald stood in front of the chair, closely watching the dead or dying man. . . .

Dr. Spitzka, shaking his head, said: "He is dead." Warden Durston pressed the signal button, and at once the dynamo was stopped. . . . Then the eyes that had been momentarily turned from Kemmler's body returned to it and gazed with horror on what they saw. The men rose from their chairs impulsively and groaned at the agony they felt. "Great God! he is alive!" someone said; "Turn on the current," said another; "See, he breathes," said a third; "For God's sake kill him and have it over," said a representative of one of the press associations, and then, unable to bear the strain, he fell on the floor in a dead faint. . . .

Kemmler's body had become limp and settled down in the chair. His chest was raising and falling and there was a heavy breathing that was perceptible to all. Kemmler was, of course, entirely unconscious. Drs. Spitzka and Macdonald kept their wits about them. Hastily they examined the man, not touching him, however.

Turning to Warden Durston, who had just finished getting the head electrode back in place, Dr. Spitzka said: "Have the current turned on again, quick—no delay." . . .

Again came that click as before and again the body of the unconscious wretch in the chair became as rigid as one of bronze. It was awful, and the witnesses were so horrified by the ghastly sight that they could not take their eyes off it. The dynamo did not seem to run smoothly. . . . Blood began to appear on the face of the wretch in the chair. It stood on the face like sweat.

The capillary or small blood vessels under the skin were being ruptured. But there was worse than that. An awful odor began to permeate the death chamber, and then, as though to cap the climax of this fearful sight, it was seen that the hair under and around the electrode on the head and the flesh under and around the electrode at the base of the spine was singeing. The stench was unbearable.

How long this second execution lasted—for it was a second execution, if there was any real life in the body when the current was turned on for the second time—is not really known by anybody. Those who held watches were too much horrified to follow them. . . . They all seemed to act as though they felt that they had taken part in a scene that would be told to the world as a public shame, as a legal crime. . . .

"First, the guillotine; second, the gallows, and last of all, electrical execution." That is the way that Dr. Spitzka expressed his preference for methods of capital punishment just after witnessing the execution to-day. . . . "What I have seen has impressed me deeply, not exactly with what you would call horror, but rather with wonder and doubt. I have seen hangings that were immeasurably more brutal than this execution, but I have never seen anything so awful. . . ."

There can be no doubt that the result was unsatisfactory to Deputy Coroner Jenkins of New York. He was one of the first to leave the prison . . . and when The Times's correspondent talked to him he was visibly unnerved by his recent experience. . . . "I would rather see ten hangings than one such execution as this. In fact I never care to witness such a scene again. It was fearful. No humane man could witness it without the keenest agony. . . ."

Source: "Far Worse than Hanging," *New York Times,* August 7, 1890, 1.

Document 1.10
A Response to the Botched Execution of William Kemmler,
September 5, 1890

In response to the problematic electrocution of William Kemmler in August 1890, Kate Fields reminded readers that despite the deficiencies associated with the new technology the hangman's noose was not always the most expedient and efficient manner of death. She cautioned against hasty abandonment of electrocution;

instead, she encouraged further use so as to advance the technology and avoid the mistakes that occurred in Kemmler's execution. In the article the author mentions inventor Thomas Edison, who had earlier testified in an investigation into the effectiveness of electrocution as a manner of execution.

IS IT A SUCCESS?

Kate Fields Thinks "Electrocution" Not Altogether a Failure.

Kate Field [sic] Washington: The problem which was to be solved by Kemmler's death is as far from solution as ever. We are no nearer having an ideal plan for putting a human being out of the world by jueicial [sic] process than we were two years ago, when the friends of the electrical execution project were in the midst of their campaign for its incorporation in the statutes of New York. Even the physicians who formed the expert jury in Kemmler's case are of two opinions as to the precise moment of his death, though generally agreed as to the time at which he became unconscious; and the newspaper accounts of the affair differ so as to justify a suspicion that they have, as a rule, sacrificed accuracy of detail to the desire for a "good story." Hence we have neither scientific data nor an exact statement of unrelated facts to draw upon in forming an estimate of the value of electricity as an agent for the vindication of outraged justice.

Down at the bottom of the whole failure lies the nervousness of Warden Durston and his assistants in making a first experimental test of a natural force which they only meagerly understood. I cannot blame them for their feeling of uncertainty and dread. My only regret is that the public, who, as the ultimate court of appeal, must pass judgment on the result, do not seem to take this phase of the case enough into consideration. Electrocution may not be a perfect method for disposing of murderers, but that is not the question. The one thing to be decided is whether it compares well or ill with hanging. The day has not yet arrived when legislatures generally will consent to abolish capital punishment; hence the repeal of the law under which Kemmler was killed will mean simply a return to the old and familiar machinery of the gallows. I am sure, no one could have the hardihood to claim perfection for that. Almost every hanging which has occured [sic] in a civilized community for the last dozen years has called forth a chorus of horrified protests from the press on account of its incidental brutalities. In nearly every case where a new hangman has officiated mistakes have been made which involved positive torture to the poor wretch on the scaffold, and this, at least, cannot be charged against the electrical apparatus in Kemmler's case. However long it may have taken him to die, there is every evidence that he knew nothing of his surroundings from the instant the first current passed through his frame. One serious error probably was that, in the general anxiety to avoid a scene of horror, the arrangements were too complex. Mr. Edison expressed this very well when he said that the criminal ought to be made simply to lay hold of a surcharged wire with both hands, as the victims of the electric light apparatus do now and then by accident. The skull cap and the spinal attachment, and all the rest of the involved mechanism, represent a great waste of inventive energy.

If the courts will but do their duty, we shall soon learn more about the effectiveness of "electrocution" than we know now. There are several criminals a waiting death in New York state; and in each successive case, if the law is permitted to take its course, we ought to get better results, through increasing familiarity with the conditions. The danger is, however, that judges whose interference is besought will be tempted to listen to the clamor of a few noisy conservatives and decide against putting any more men to death by the application of electricity. There are people who oppose everything that savors of progress. They hold fast to the beam and rope because those implements had the sanction of use by two English-speaking nations for several generations, just as they fight against cremation because Abraham buried his wife, and against public baths because the lusty Spartans never washed themselves. The Kemmler episode, as I said some time ago, has solved no problem, but that is because it was a first experiment and unquestionably faulty in several particulars. There was certainly nothing about it that need frighten us off from further trials in the same direction. Perhaps the next one will bear better fruit.

Source: "Is It a Success?" *Omaha Daily Bee,* September 5, 1890, 6.

Document 1.11
Justice William Moody Explores the Applicability of Constitutional Protections to the States in *Twining v. New Jersey,* November 9, 1908

In Maxwell v. Dow *(1900) and* Twining v. New Jersey *(1908), the Supreme Court once again turned away claims that the Fourteenth Amendment's privileges and immunities clause or due process clause "incorporated" specific provisions of the Bill of Rights and made them applicable to the states. In the course of his opinion for the majority in* Twining, *however, Justice William Moody opened the door to future consideration of the relationship between the due process clause and the Bill of Rights.*

MR. JUSTICE MOODY delivered the opinion of the Court.

Indeed, since, by the unvarying decisions of this court, the first ten Amendments of the Federal Constitution are restrictive only of national action, there was nowhere else to look up to the time of the adoption of the 14th Amendment, and the state, at least until then, might give, modify, or withhold the privilege at its will. . . .

We conclude, therefore, that exemption from compulsory self-incrimination is not a privilege or immunity of national citizenship guaranteed by this clause of the 14th Amendment against abridgment by the states.

The defendants, however, do not stop here. They appeal to another clause of the 14th Amendment, and insist that the self-incrimination which they allege the instruction to the jury compelled was a denial of due process of law. This contention requires separate consideration, for it is possible that some of the personal rights safeguarded by the first eight Amendments against national action may also be safeguarded against state action, because a denial of them would be a denial of due process of law. . . .

Even if the historical meaning of due process of law and the decisions of this court did not exclude the privilege [against compulsory self-incrimination] from it, it would be going far to rate it as an immutable principle of justice which is the inalienable possession of every citizen of a free government. Salutary as the principle may seem to the great majority, it cannot be ranked with the right to hearing before condemnation, the immunity from arbitrary power not acting by general laws, and the inviolability of private property. . . .

We do not pass upon the conflict, because, for the reasons given, we think that the exemption from compulsory self-incrimination in the courts of the states is not secured by any part of the Federal Constitution.

Judgment affirmed.

Source: Twining v. New Jersey, 211 U.S. 78 (1908), at 97–101.

Document 1.12
The *Kansas City Star* Investigates the Leo Frank Trial, January 17, 1915

A reporter for the Kansas City Star *who went to Atlanta to investigate the* Frank *case filed a detailed report that documented all aspects of the murder of Mary Phagan, the trial of Leo Frank, and the extent of anti-Semitism in Atlanta. In these excerpts, the author details the mobs that assembled at the courthouse and the threats and overt anti-Semitism that swirled around the trial.*

Has Georgia Condemned an Innocent Man to Die?

Is Leo Frank Guilty of Murder or Has Race Prejudice Blinded Justice?

Foreword

Leo M. Frank, a Jew, graduate of Cornell University, president of the B'Nai Brith of Atlanta, Ga., is under sentence of death in that city for the murder of a 14-year-old girl who worked in a pencil factory of which he was superintendent.

Frank is 30 years old. His wife is a member of one of the best Jewish families in Atlanta.

It is the contention of Frank and his friends that he is innocent; that there was and is not any evidence that points to his guilt, or that even points the finger of suspicion to him; that the real murderer is a negro who gave the testimony that convicted Frank; that the trial of Frank established beyond doubt the guilt of the negro; that the police and the newspapers of Atlanta well know this to be true; but that the authorities and the newspapers of Atlanta were goaded on by public sentiment and a mob spirit to the sacrifice of Frank largely because he was a Jew accused of murdering a Gentile girl.

Frank and his friends contend that this racial prejudice and passion for his sacrifice dominated the court that condemned him, and that his trial was unfair; that the jury knew it would be lynched had it acquitted him; that this same inflamed prejudice spread throughout the state of Georgia and influenced the supreme court that denied him a new trial.

Frank's case is in the supreme court of the United States. If it refuses to interfere he will surely be hanged.

The Frank case is attracting wide attention throughout the Northern states. Jewish men of greatest prominence have interested themselves in his behalf, solely because they believe he is innocent and was convicted largely because of racial prejudice. The case will go down in history as one of the most remarkable in American jurisprudence.

The *Star* sent a reporter to Atlanta to investigate the Frank case, to learn if his trial measured up to the American standard of fair play to which every man accused of crime is entitled, no matter what his race, creed or condition in life.

This reporter, in his investigation, paid no heed to gossip or rumor. He went for his facts to the court records and to newspaper files.

By A.B. MacDonald

[Chapters I–V have been omitted. They detail the murder of Mary Phagan and the investigation into her death.]

Chapter VI

The Trial.

Frank's trial lasted thirty days. It was held in August, in a small courtroom, the windows of which on one side opened upon a street, and on the other opened on an alley. The mob dominated the trial. There can be no doubt about that.

The motion for a new trial certified to by the trial judge as correct in its statements, cites many instances of loud and continuous applause by the spectators when any ruling adverse to Frank was made, or when a point was made against him. There were sneers and hisses, the demonstrations always being against Frank. The judge refused at any time to clear the courtroom, although requested many times by Frank's attorneys to do so.

The alley and street outside was always filled with a mob through which the jury was led daily, and through which Frank was taken daily by an armed guard, with revolvers drawn.

It was a noisy mob. Some reviewers of the trial have said there were cries to the jury of "Hang the Jew or we will hang you."

There is no proof that this occurred, but it is true that the spirit of the mob breathed upon the jury and the court, and that the jurors knew their lives would be in danger if they acquitted Frank. The judge knew it and said so. . . .

Such a mob surrounded the courtroom on Saturday while Dorsey was speaking that the editors of the three newspapers of Atlanta, supposing that the case would [go] to the jury that day, joined in a written request to Judge Roan to not permit a verdict to be returned that day, as they feared mob violence in any event.

But Dorsey carried his speech over into Monday, and when he finished it the crowd sent up a cheer and lifted Dorsey upon shoulders and carried him in triumph in the streets.

Amid such a scene the jury retired to consider a verdict.

Judge Roan called Frank's lawyers to him. He told them it would be unsafe for Frank or either of them to be in the courtroom when the verdict was returned. He told them he feared the mob would kill them, and he advised them to stay away. Frank's lawyers agreed, if Judge Roan would poll the jury. The judge promised he would do so.

The judge also sent for E.E. Pomeroy, colonel of the local militia, and warned him to have the militia ready to put down a riot.

That much is all in the court record, certified as correct by the judge himself, Frank's lawyers say, but it is not in the record that Judge Roan asked of them at that time:

"What do you think the verdict will be?"

"Guilty, of course," replied Mr. Rosser.

"Yes," said Judge Roan. "If Christ and his angels came down here and showed this jury that Frank was innocent, it would bring him in guilty."

The jury did find him guilty, and the crowd of thousands set up such a cheering that Judge Roan, as he certified, could not hear the responses of the jurors as an effort was made to poll them.

Frank was in his cell a half mile away, and not a lawyer representing him was in court when the verdict was returned.

[Chapters VII and VIII have been omitted. They provide additional details, evidence, and testimony on the murder and the trial.]

Chapter IX

The Poison of Unspeakable Things.

The people of Georgia honestly believe that Frank is guilty and that the rich Jews of the North have raised a fund of millions of dollars to save his life. It is not fair to criticize them for that. They have been deceived and "fooled" by the clique of political office holders who have worked the ruin of Frank.

A newspaper man of Atlanta, who reported the Frank case from its inception, told me that Frank was innocent. I repeated that to an official who had helped convict Frank, and he put the hollow of his hand to his mouth and whispered in all earnestness:

"He has been bought with Jew money. But don't say I told you."

I assured him that the reporter of another Atlanta paper, who had attended each session of the trial, had also told me that Frank was innocent.

"He got some of the Jew money, too. They've scattered it all around," he answered.

Anyone who raises his voice in favor of Frank is accused of being bought by "Jew money."

A young woman of unusual intelligence, connected with a photograph gallery in Atlanta, said to me that she would like to see Frank hanged by the tongue at the "Five Points," the center of Atlanta.

"But I believe he is innocent," I said.

"Oh, you have gotten some of the Jew money," she retorted.

The managing editor, associate editor, city editor, assistant city editor and court reporter of an Atlanta newspaper said to me they knew Frank was entitled to a new trial; his trial was not fair.

"Then why don't you say so?" I asked. "We dare not; we would be accused of being bought by Jew money," they answered.

Judge Roan, who tried Frank, said publicly from the bench when denying a motion for a new trial:

"I have given this question long consideration. It has given me more concern than any other case I was ever in, and I want to say right here that, although I heard the evidence and arguments during those thirty days, I do not know this morning whether Leo Frank is innocent or guilty. But I was not the one to be convinced. The jury was convinced, and I feel it my duty to overrule the motion."

The next day the *Atlanta Georgian,* in a double-leaded editorial on the first page said:

"When Judge Roan, the trial judge, is in doubt, and boldly says so, is it [not?] time to pause before legal murder is added to the long list of other crimes [in?] our state?"

But the public raised such a storm [word unclear] this that the *Georgian,* from that day to this, has not dared to say a word in Frank's favor.

March 1[0?], 191[4?], the *Atlanta Journal,* conscience stricken and determined to try and undo some of the wrong done to Frank, printed an editorial in large type, filling four full columns, headed,

"Frank Should Have a New Trial"

Here are a few paragraphs from that editorial:

"Leo Frank has not had a fair trial. He has not been fairly convicted and his death without a fair trial and legal conviction will amount to judicial murder.

"It was not within the power of human judges, human lawyers and human jurymen to decide impartially and without fear the guilt or innocence of an accused man under the circumstances that surrounded the trail [sic]. The very atmosphere of the courtroom was charged with an electric current of indignation which flashed and scintillated before the eyes of the jury. The courtroom and streets were filled with an angry, determined crowd, ready to seize the defendant if the jury had found him not guilty.

"A verdict of acquittal would have caused a riot such as would shock the country and cause Atlanta's streets to run with innocent blood.

"Unless the courts interfere we are going to murder an innocent man by refusing to give him an impartial trial."

For this the *Journal* was accused of being bought with Jew money and was so threatened with ruin that it dared not continue the policy it set out on, and it has never said a word since then about unfairness to Frank nor a new trial. . . .

The wife and daughter of [L?]. Z. Rosser, who defended Frank, have been called on the telephone many times and told that he was going to be killed unless he ceased his efforts to save Frank.

W. J. Burns, the famous detective, who went to Atlanta and investigated the Frank case and declared he was innocent and that Conley was the murderer, had to leave the city hurriedly to escape threatened indictment, and his agents were not permitted to operate in Atlanta, and he was forced to close his office there. . . .

The evidence in the Frank case has never been reviewed by an appellate court, although it is generally supposed that it has been. Under the Georgia laws the supreme court cannot review the evidence. It can only pass upon the rulings of the trial court; it can only consider errors of law and not errors of testimony. The Supreme Court of Georgia, in a recent decision, said it was not satisfied that the evidence was sufficient to convict, but with that it could not interfere; the jury was the sole judge of it, and the supreme court affirmed the conviction.

Frank has been thrice sentenced to die and three times has come very near to the gallows. The battle to get him a new trial has made his case one of the most noted in criminal annals. His first appeal was denied by the supreme court. His lawyers then filed an "extraordinary motion" for a new trial, raising the point that he was not in court when the verdict was returned and citing newly discovered evidence of his innocence, and further evidence of perjury at his trial, and affidavits showing that several of the twelve jurors had asserted before the trial their belief in his guilt, one, in particular, having declared that he hoped he could get on the jury so he could "crack his damned neck."

This motion was denied by the supreme court.

Then Frank was examined by a commission of experts who declared he was sane and normal in every way and not a pervert.

Another motion to annul the verdict was made and denied by the supreme court.

December [2?]1, last, a motion for a certificate of "probabl[e] cause" for appeal was denied by Judge Newman of the United States District Court in Atlanta. This decision was overruled by Associate Justice Lamar of the United States Supreme Court and thus Frank's case went at least to the highest tribunal in the land. This acts as a stay of execution of the death sentence, which was to have been carried out January 23.

The point to be passed upon by the United States Supreme Court is whether at the supreme moment of his trial, when the verdict was returned, Frank was denied his constitutional right of being present and looking his condemners in the face. The supreme court of this country has never decided this question before.

If the supreme court decides in his favor it will discharge him, a free man, he cannot be tried again. . . .

Source: Kansas City Star (Mo.), January 17, 1915.

Document 1.13
Justice Oliver Wendell Holmes Sharply Criticizes the Court's Ruling and the Due Process Violations during the Trial of Leo Frank, April 19, 1915

The Supreme Court, in the 1915 case of Frank v. Mangum, *refused to grant relief through habeas corpus to Leo Frank, under death sentence in Georgia, following a trial dominated by threats of mob violence. The Court majority, speaking through Justice Mahlon Pitney, found no violation of due process, but the decision provoked a sharp dissent from Oliver Wendell Holmes, joined by Charles Evans Hughes. Georgia's governor commuted Frank's death sentence, but a mob kidnapped him from a prison hospital and lynched him.*

MR. JUSTICE HOLMES dissenting, joined by MR. JUSTICE HUGHES.

Mr. Justice Hughes and I are of opinion that the judgment should be reversed. The only question before us is whether the petition shows on its face that the writ of habeas corpus should be denied, or whether the District Court should have proceeded to try the facts. The allegations that appear to us material are these: the trial began on July 28, 1913, in Atlanta, and was carried on in a court packed with spectators and surrounded by a crowd outside, all strongly hostile to the petitioner. On Saturday, August 23, this hostility was sufficient to lead the judge to confer in the presence of the jury with the Chief of Police of Atlanta and the Colonel of the Fifth Georgia Regiment stationed in that city, both of whom were known to the jury. On the same day, the evidence seemingly having been closed, the public press, apprehending danger, united in a request to the Court that the proceedings should not continue on that evening. Thereupon, the Court adjourned until Monday morning. On that morning, when the Solicitor General entered the court, he was greeted with applause, stamping of feet and clapping of hands, and the judge, before beginning his charge, had a private conversation with the petitioner's counsel in which he expressed the opinion that there would be "probable danger of violence" if there should be an acquittal or a disagreement, and that it would be safer for not only the petitioner but his counsel to be absent from Court when the verdict was brought in. At the judge's request they agreed that the petitioner and they should be absent, and they kept their word. When the verdict was rendered, and before more than one of the jurymen had been polled there was such a roar of applause that the polling could not go on until order was restored. The noise outside was such that it was difficult for the judge to hear the answers of the jurors although he was only ten feet from them. With these specifications of fact, the petitioner alleges that the trial was dominated by a hostile mob and was nothing but an empty form. . . .

Whatever disagreement there may be as to the scope of the phrase "due process of law," there can be no doubt that it embraces the fundamental conception of a fair trial, with opportunity to be heard. Mob law does not become due process of law by securing the assent of a terrorized jury. We are not speaking of more disorder, or more irregularities in procedure, but of a case where the processes of justice are actually subverted. In such a case, the Federal court has jurisdiction to issue the writ. The fact that the state court still has its general jurisdiction and is otherwise a competent court does not make it impossible to find that a jury has been subjected to intimidation in a particular case. The loss of jurisdiction is not general but particular, and proceeds from the control of a hostile influence. . . .

The single question in our minds is whether a petition alleging that the trial took place in the midst of a mob savagely and manifestly intent on a single result, is shown on its face unwarranted, by the specifications, which may be presumed to set forth the strongest indications of the facts at the petitioner's command. This is not a matter for polite presumptions; we must look facts in the face. Any judge who has sat with juries knows that, in spite of forms, they are extremely likely to be impregnated by the environing atmosphere. And when we find the judgment of the expert on the spot,— of the judge whose business it was to preserve not only form, but substance—to have been that if one juryman yielded to the reasonable doubt that he himself later expressed in court as the result of most anxious deliberation, neither prisoner nor counsel would be safe from the rage of the crowd, we think the presumption overwhelming that the jury responded to the passions of the mob. Of course we are speaking only of the case made by the petition, and whether it ought to be heard. Upon allegations of this gravity in our opinion it ought to be heard, whatever the decision of the state court may have been, and it did not need to set forth contradictory evidence, or matter of rebuttal, or to explain why the motions for a new trial and to set aside the verdict were overruled by the state court. There is no reason to fear an impairment of the authority of the state to punish the guilty. We do not think it impracticable in any part of this country to have trials free from outside control. But to maintain this immunity it may be necessary that the supremacy of the law and of the Federal Constitution should be vindicated in a case like this. It may be that on a hearing a different complexion would be given to the judge's alleged request and expression of fear. But supposing the alleged facts to be true, we are of opinion that if they were before the Supreme Court, it sanctioned a situation upon which the courts of the United States should act; and if, for any reason, they were not before the Supreme Court, it is our duty to act upon them now, and to declare lynch law as little valid when practiced by a regularly drawn jury as when administered by one elected by a mob intent on death.

Source: Frank v. Mangum, 237 U.S. 309 (1915), at 346–349.

Document 1.14
Georgia Governor John M. Slaton Commutes Leo Frank's Death Sentence, June 21, 1915

On June 21, 1915, Gov. John M. Slaton commuted the death sentence of Leo Frank after reviewing the evidence in the case and concluding with the trial judge that too much doubt remained concerning Frank's guilt. What follows is a portion of the draft of the governor's clemency decision.

In Re Leo M. Frank, Fulton Superior Court, Sentenced to be executed, June 22nd, 1915.

Saturday, April 26th, 1913, was Memorial Day in Georgia and a general holiday. At that time Mary Phagan, a white girl, of about 14 years of age was in the employ of the National Pencil Company located near the corner of Forsyth & Hunter Sts. in the City of Atlanta. She came to the Pencil Factory a little after noon to obtain the money due her for her work the preceding Monday, and Leo M. Frank, the defendant, paid her $1.20, the amount due her and this was the last time she was seen alive.

Frank was tried for the offense and found guilty the succeeding August. Application is now made to me for clemency.

This case has been the subject of extensive comments through the newspapers of the United States and has occasioned the transmission of over 100,000 letters from various States requesting clemency. Many communications have been received from citizens of this State advocating or opposing interference with the sentence of the court. . . .

Many newspapers and multitudes of people have attacked the State of Georgia, because of the conviction of Leo M. Frank and have declared the conviction to have been through the domination of a mob with no evidence to support the verdict. This opinion has been formed to a great extent by those who have not read the evidence and who are unacquainted with the judicial procedure in our State.

I have been unable to even open a large proportion of the letters sent me, because of their number and because I could not through them gain any assistance in determining my duty.

The murder committed was a most heinous one. A young girl was strangled to death by a cord tied around her throat and the offender deserves the punishment of death. The only question is as to the identity of the criminal.

The responsibility is upon the people of Georgia to protect the lives of her citizens and to maintain the dignity of her laws, and if the choice must be made between the approbation of citizens of other States and the enforcement of our laws against offenders whether powerful or weak, we must choose the latter alternative.

Mobs.

It is charged that the court and jury were terrorized by a Mob and the jury were coerced into their verdict. . . .

If the audience in the court room manifested their deep resentment toward Frank, it was largely by this evidence of feeling beyond the power of a court to correct. It would be difficult anywhere for an appellate court, or even a trial court, to grant a new trial in a case which occupied thirty days, because the audience in the court room upon a few occasions indicated their sympathies. However, the deep feeling against Frank which developed in the progress of the evidence was in the atmosphere and regardless of the commission of those acts of which the court would take cognizance, the feeling of the public was strong.

Since Gov. Brown has related secret history [sic] in his public argument before me, I may state that Friday night before the verdict was expected Saturday, I had the Sheriff to call at the Mansion and inquired whether he anticipated trouble. This was after many people had told me of possible danger and an editor of a leading newspaper indicated his anticipation of trouble. The Sheriff stated he thought his deputies could avert any difficulty. Judge Roan telephoned me that he had arranged for the defendant [sic] to be absent when the verdict was rendered. Like Gov. Brown, I entered into communication with the Colonel of the Fifth Regiment, who stated he would be ready if there were necessity. . . .

Judge Roan, in the exercise of precaution, requested that both counsel and defendant be absent when the verdict was rendered, in order to avoid any possible demonstration in the event of acquittal.

The jury found the defendant guilty and with the exception of demonstration outside the court room, there was no disorder. . . .

Racial Prejudice.

The charge against the State of Georgia of racial prejudice is unfair. A conspicuous Jewish family in Georgia is descended from one of the original colonial families of the State. Jews have been presidents of our Boards of Education, principals of our schools, Mayors of our cities, and conspicuous in all our commercial enterprises. . . .

Defense.

. . . One fact in the case, and that of most important force in arriving at the truth, contradicts Conley's testimony. It is disagreeable to refer to it, but delicacy must yield to necessity when human life is at stake.

The mystery in the case is the question as to how Mary Phagan's body got into the basement. It was found 136 feet away from the elevator and the face gave evidence of being dragged through the dirt and cinders. She had dirt in her eyes and mouth. Conley testified that he and Frank took the body down to the basement in the elevator on the afternoon of April 26th, 1913, and leaves for inference that Frank removed the body 136 feet toward the end of the building, where the body was found at a spot near the back door which led out towards the street in the rear. Conley swears he did not return to the basement, but went back up in the elevator, while Frank went back on the ladder, constituting the only two methods of ingress and egress to the basement, excepting through the back door. This was between one and two o'clock on the afternoon of April 26th. . . .

Frank is delicate in physique, while Conley is strong and powerful. Conley's place for watching, as described by himself, was in the gloom a few feet from the hatchway, leading by way of ladder to the basement. Also he was in a few feet of the elevator shaft on the first floor. Conley's action in the elevator shaft was in accordance with his testimony that he made water twice against the door of the elevator shaft on the morning of the 26th, instead of doing so in the gloom of his corner behind the boxes where he kept watch.

Mary Phagan in coming down stairs was compelled to pass within a few feet of Conley, who was invisible to her and in a few feet of the hatchway.

Frank could not have carried her down the hatchway. Conley might have done so with difficulty. If the Elevator Shaft was not used by Conley and Frank in taking the body to the basement, then the explanation of Conley, who admittedly wrote the notes found by the body, cannot be accepted. . . .

Conley's Affidavits.

The defense procured under notice one statement and three affidavits taken by the Detectives from Conley and introduced in evidence. . . .

On May 24, 1913, he made for the Detectives an affidavit in which he says that on Friday before the Saturday on which the murder was committed, Frank asked him if he could write. This would appear strange, because Frank knew well he could write and had so known for months, but according to Conley's affidavit Frank dictated to him practically the contents of one of the notes found by the body of Mary Phagan. Frank, then, according to Conley's statement, took a brown scratch pad and wrote on that himself, and then gave him a box of cigarettes in which was some money and Frank said to him that he had some wealthy relatives in Brooklyn, and said "why should I hang."

This would have made Frank guilty of the contemplated murder on Friday which was consummated Saturday and which was so unreasonable, it could not be accepted. . . .

On the 29th of May, 1913, Conley made another affidavit, in which he said that Frank told him that he had picked up a girl and let her fall and Conley hollered to him that the girl was dead, and told him to go to the cotton bag and get apiece [sic] of cloth, and he got a big wide piece of cloth and took her on his right shoulder, when she got too heavy for him and she slipped off when he got to the Dressing Room. He called Frank to help and Frank got a key to the elevator and the two carried the body down stairs and Frank told him to take the body back to the saw dust pile and Conley says, he picked up the girl and put her on his shoulder, while Frank went back up the ladder.

It will be observed that the testimony and the appearance of the girl indicated that she was dragged through the cinders and debris on the floor of the basement, yet Conley says he took her on his shoulder. . . .

Detective Scott, who was introduced by the State, testified regarding Conley's statement and affidavits as follows:

> "We tried to impress him with the fact that Frank would not have written those notes on Friday, that that was not a reasonable story. That it showed premeditation and that would not do. We pointed out to him why the first statement would not fit. We told him we wanted another statement. He declined to make another statement. He said he had told the truth." . . .

Conley in explaining why his affidavits varied said: "The reason why I told that story was I do not want them to know that these other people passed by me for they might accuse me. I do not want people to think that I was the one that done the murder." . . .

Jury's Verdict.

The jury which heard the evidence and saw the witnesses found the defendant, Leo M. Frank, guilty of murder. They are the ones, under our laws, who are chosen to weigh evidence and to determine its probative value. They may consider the demeanor of the witnesses upon the stand and in the exercise of common sense will arrive with wonderful accuracy at the truth of the contest. . . .

Judiciary.

. . . But under our judicial system, the trial judge is called upon to exercise his wise discretion, and he cannot permit a verdict to stand which he believes to be unjust. A suggestion in the order over-ruling a motion for a new trial, that the judge was not satisfied with the verdict, would demand a reversal by the Supreme Court.

In this connection Judge Roan declared orally from the bench that he was not certain of the defendant's guilt—that with all the thought he had put on this case, he was not thoroughly convinced whether Frank was guilty, or innocent—but that he did not have to be convinced—that the jury was convinced and that there was no room to doubt that—that he felt it was his duty to order that the motion for a new trial be over-ruled. . . .

Judge Roan, however, misconstrued his power, as evidence by the following charge to the jury in the case of the State against Frank:

"If you believe beyond a reasonable doubt from the evidence in this case that this defendant is guilty of murder, then, you would be authorized in that event to say, "We, the jury, find the defendant guilty." Should you go further, gentlemen, and say nothing else in your verdict, the court would have to sentence the defendant to the extreme penalty of murder, to-wit: "To be hanged by the neck until he is dead."

Surely, if Judge Roan entertained the extreme doubt indicated by his statement and had remembered the power granted him by the Code, he would have sentenced the defendant to life imprisonment.

In a letter written to counsel he says, "I shall ask the Prison Commission to recommend to the Governor to commute Frank's sentence to life imprisonment. It is possible that I showed undue deference to the jury in this case, when I allowed the verdict to stand. They said by their verdict that they had found the truth. I was in a state of uncertainty, and so expressed myself. After many months of continued deliberation, I am still uncertain of Frank's guilt. The state of uncertainty is largely due by the character of the Conley testimony, by which the verdict was largely reached." . . .

In any event, the performance of my duty under the Constitution is a matter of my conscience. The responsibility rests where the power is reposed. Judge Roan, with that awful sense of responsibility, which probably came over him as he thought of that Judge before whom he would shortly appear, calls to me from another world to request that I do that which he should have done. I can endure misconstruction, abuse and condemnation, but I cannot stand the constant companionship of an accusing conscience, which would remind me in every thought that I, as a Governor of Georgia, failed to do what I thought to be right. There is a territory "beyond a REASONABLE DOUBT and absolute certainty," for which the law provides in allowing life imprisonment instead of execution. This case has been marked by doubt. The trial judge doubted. Two Judges of the Supreme Court of Georgia doubted. Two Judges of the Supreme Court of the United States doubted. One of the three Prison Commissioners doubted.

In my judgement, by granting a commutation in this case, I am sustaining the jury, the judge, and the appellate tribunals, and at the same time am discharging that duty which is placed on me by the Constitution of the State.

Acting, therefore, in accordance with what I believe to be my duty under the circumstances of this case, it is

ORDERED: That the sentence in the case of Leo M. Frank is commuted from the death penalty to imprisonment for life.

This 21st day of June, 1915.

John M. Slaton

GOVERNOR

Source: "Decision by Governor John Slaton to Grant Executive Clemency to Leo Frank, June 21, 1915." Georgia Archives. http://sos.georgia.gov/archives/what_do_we_have/online_records/leo_frank/ (accessed February 20, 2009).

Document 1.15
Circuit Court Denies New Trial for Phillips County "Rioters," December 27, 1919

The Chicago Defender, *a leading African American newspaper, published the following account of the appeal by twelve African American men charged with murder and sentenced to death for their alleged participation in the Phillips County "riots" in October 1919. Their failed appeals for new trials cited a lack of access to proper counsel, the threat of mob violence, and prejudiced juries. Despite this setback to the accused, the article expresses optimism, saying that "the fight has just begun." The Supreme Court heard the case, and in its landmark 1923 ruling* Moore v. Dempsey *reversed the convictions and ordered new trials.*

Arkansas "Rioters" Refused New Trial

Court Turns Down Appeal of Helena Farmers Who Face Electric Chair
(By Century News Service)

Helena, Ark., Dec. 26.—Motion for a new trial in the cases of twelve men sentenced to the electric chair for murder alleged to have been committed in connection with the Phillips county riots on Oct. 1, was denied by Judge J.M. Jackson of the Phillips County Circuit court here last Saturday. The twelve condemned men are: Edward Ware, Albert Giles, Joseph Fox, John Martin, Alf Banks Jr., William Wordlow, Frank Moore, Edward Hicks, J.E. Knox, Edward Coleman, Paul Hall and Frank Hicks. Col. George W. Murphy (white) of Little Rock, former attorney general of Arkansas, and Sciopo [sic] A. Jones, prominent lawyer of Little Rock, are representing the prisoners.

Appeal Stays Execution

Six of the twelve men were sentenced to die on Friday, Dec. 26, and the remainder on Friday, Jan. 2. When the appeal was denied the lawyers were given sixty days to file exceptions preparatory to an appeal to the Supreme court. This actions [sic] automatically stayed the executions.

All Petitions Alike

The motion for the new trial in each of the twelve cases was couched in practically identical language. The petition in the case of Frank Hicks is typical and reads as follows:

"That Clinton Lee was killed on the first day of October by parties unknown to him in a deadly conflict following a disturbance between the white and black races of Phillips county on the night previous, for which he is no wise responsible; that the feeling of the white people was intense against the black, and against the defendant it was bitter, active and persistent; that in the course of the conflict five whites were killed and between [text illegible] opportunity to converse with friends after being incarcerated in the county jail and could not seek assistance for his defense or relief that while he was confined in the county jail several hundred white men assembled at the jail for the purpose of mobbing him, and only through the efforts of the United States soldiers were they dispersed; that the feeling was so intense among the whites that an unprejudiced jury could not be obtained; that the verdict of the jury was contrary to law and evidence in the case."

Supporters Gain Hope

The refusal to grant a new trial was expected by persons here who have followed the case throughout. In fact, it is said that the action on the part of the court in denying a rehearing gives renewed hope to the supporters of the convicted farmers, rather than discouragement. It is declared that the fight has just begun, and that should the State Supreme court affirm the decision of the lower court, the case will be carried to the United States Supreme court for final adjustment.

Evidence Collected

At the next trial it is the purpose of the counsel for the prisoners to show that the Progressive Farmers' Household Union was an organization primarily created to further the interest of the farm laborers and protect them from becoming victims of white land owners. It was the existence of this order that caused the white farmers to accuse the laborers of trying to start an insurrection. Investigation has demonstrated that highway robbery methods were practiced by some of the farmers, and records to substantiate this statement are on file at the N.A.A.C.P. headquarters. . . .

Source: The Chicago Defender, December 27, 1919, 1.

Document 1.16
The Supreme Court Overturns a State Capital Case on Due Process Grounds in *Moore v. Dempsey*, February 19, 1923

Eight years after Frank v. Mangum, *the Supreme Court in* Moore v. Dempsey *overturned a state capital conviction and sentence for the first time on grounds the trial violated the due process clause of the Fourteenth Amendment. The case arose out of the Elaine riot and massacre in Arkansas and trial circumstances similar to those in the* Frank *case. Writing now for the majority, Justice Oliver Wendell Holmes invoked the* Frank *decision, but in effect overruled the earlier decision.*

MR. JUSTICE HOLMES delivered the opinion of the Court.

. . . In *Frank v. Mangum*, it was recognized of course that if in fact a trial is dominated by a mob so that there is an actual interference with the course of justice, there is a departure from due process of law; and that, "if the State, supplying no corrective process, carries into execution a judgment of death or imprisonment based upon a verdict thus produced by mob domination, the State deprives the accused of his life or liberty without due process of law." We assume in accordance with that case that the corrective process supplied by the State may be so adequate that interference by habeas corpus ought not to be allowed. It certainly is true that mere mistakes of law in the course of a trial are not to be corrected in that way. But if the case is that the whole proceeding is a mask—that counsel, jury and judge were swept to the fatal end by an irresistible wave of public passion, and that the State Courts failed to correct the wrong, neither perfection in the machinery for correction nor the possibility that the trial court and counsel saw no other way of avoiding an immediate outbreak of the mob can prevent this Court from securing to the petitioners their constitutional rights. . . .

We shall not say more concerning the corrective process afforded to the petitioners than that it does not seem to us sufficient to allow a Judge of the United States to escape the duty of examining the facts for himself when if true as alleged they make the trial absolutely void. We have confided the statement to the facts admitted by the demurrer. We will not say that they cannot be met, but it appears to us unavoidable that the District Judge should find whether the facts alleged are true and whether they can be explained so far as to leave the state proceedings undisturbed.

Order reversed. The case to stand for hearing before the District Court.

Source: Moore v. Dempsey, 261 U.S. 86 (1923), at 90–92.

NOTES

1. A substantial body of literature exists on the Elaine riot and the massacre that followed. See Robert Whitaker, *On the Laps of Gods: The Red Summer of 1919 and the Struggle for Justice That Remade a Nation* (New York: Crown, 2008); Grif Stockley Jr., *Blood in*

Their Eyes: The Elaine Race Massacre of 1919 (Fayetteville: University of Arkansas Press, 2001); and Richard Cortner, *A Mob Intent on Death: The NAACP and the Arkansas Race Cases* (Middletown, Conn.: Wesleyan Publishing House, 1988).

2. *United States v. Mitchell*, 26 F. Cas. 1277 (C.C. Pa. 1795) (No. 15,788); *United States v. Vigol*, 28 F. Cas. 376 (C.C. Pa. 1795) (No. 16,621); and *United States v. Fries*, 3 U.S. (3 Dall.) 515 (1799). See also Thomas P. Slaughter, *The Whiskey Rebellion: Frontier Epilogue to the American Revolution* (New York: Oxford University Press, 1986).

3. In the aftermath of the so-called Dakota War of 1862, waged by the U.S. Army against several bands of eastern Sioux, or Dakota, Indians in southwestern Minnesota, the army interned over a thousand Native Americans and carried out the largest one-day execution in American history when it hanged 38 Dakota men. President Abraham Lincoln had commuted the death sentences of 264 of the Dakota warriors. See Bill Yenne, *Indian Wars: The Campaign for the American West* (Yardley, Pa.: Westholme, 2005); and Hank H. Cox, *Lincoln and the Sioux Uprising of 1862* (Nashville: Cumberland House, 2005). The Houston Riot of 1917, sparked by a clash between African American soldiers and white civilians, led to the courts-martial of 59 soldiers charged with mutiny and murder. Fourteen were executed in the second largest mass execution in U.S. history. See Robert V. Haynes, *A Night of Violence: The Houston Riot of 1917* (Baton Rouge: Louisiana State University Press, 1976); and Frederick Bernays Wiener, "The Seamy Side of the World War I Court Martial Controversy," *Military Law Review* 123 (Winter 1989): 109.

4. *Barron v. Baltimore*, 32 U.S. (7 Pet.) 243 (1833).

5. *Ex parte Milligan*, 71 U.S. (4 Wall.) 2 (1866). Two years earlier the justices avoided a constitutional confrontation with the president when they declined to review the decision of a military commission to banish Confederate sympathizer and former Ohio representative Clement Vallandigham. The Court ruled that military commissions were not tribunals established under Article III of the Constitution and therefore not subject to its jurisdiction. *Ex parte Vallandigham*, 68 U.S. (1 Wall.) 243 (1864).

6. *United States v. Palmer*, 16 U.S. (3 Wheat.) 610 (1818).

7. *United States v. Dawson*, 56 U.S. (15 How.) 467 (1854).

8. *Wiggins v. People*, 93 U.S. (3 Otto) 465 (1876).

9. *Wilkerson v. Utah*, 99 U.S. 130 (1878), at 137 (emphasis added). Later justices have cited *Wilkerson* as the foundational case for the Eighth Amendment and the proposition that death by firing squad does not constitute cruel and unusual punishment, although this was not the central issue in the case and unnecessary for its resolution.

10. Ibid., at 135–137. The Court decided *Wilkerson* in the same term it unanimously affirmed the conviction of Mormon leader George Reynolds for violating the federal anti-polygamy law, rejecting his claim that the statute violated the Constitution's free exercise clause. For his offense, Reynolds was sentenced to two years and hard labor and fined $500. *Reynolds v. United States*, 98 U.S. 145 (1878).

11. Hal Schindler, "Taylor's Death Was Quick . . . But Some Weren't So Lucky: Executioner's Song—A Utah Reprise," *Salt Lake Tribune*, January 28, 1996, A1.

12. *Weems v. United States*, 217 U.S. 349 (1910).

13. Ibid., at 217.

14. *Paraiso v. United States*, 207 U.S. 368 (1907).

15. *Weems v. United States,* at 363.
16. Ibid., at 367
17. Ibid., at 372–373.
18. *McCulloch v. Maryland,* 17 U.S. 316 (1819).
19. Ibid., at 374, 378, 380. At the conclusion of his opinion McKenna noted various crimes that carried lighter punishments than that inflicted on Weems, including several degrees of homicide, misprision of treason, inciting rebellion, forgery of letters patent, robbery, and larceny.
20. Ibid., at 385–386.
21. *Johnson v. United States,* 225 U.S. 405 (1912).
22. *Stroud v. United States,* 251 U.S. 15 (1919).
23. *Sparf and Hansen v. United States,* 156 U.S. 51 (1895). Justices Horace Gray and George Shiras would have reversed both convictions on the grounds that the judge had taken from the jury the power to decide both the law and the facts with respect to whether the defendants had committed murder or manslaughter.
24. *Winston v. United States,* 172 U.S. 303 (1899).
25. *Hardy v. United States,* 186 U.S. 224 (1902).
26. *Hotema v. United States,* 186 U.S. 413 (1902).
27. See *Permoli v. Municipality of the City of New Orleans,* 44 U.S. 589 (1845).
28. *Twitchell v. Commonwealth,* 74 U.S. (7 Wall.) 321 (1868).
29. The scholarly debate over the intention of the framers of the Fourteenth Amendment and the Bill of Rights has raged for decades, with the weight of opinion favoring those who hold to the incorporation theory. For a sample of the arguments, see Charles Fairman, "Does the Fourteenth Amendment Incorporate the Bill of Rights? 2 *Stanford Law Review* 5 (1949); Raoul Berger, "Incorporation of the Bill of Rights in the Fourteenth Amendment: A Nine Lived Cat," 42 *Ohio State Law Journal* 435 (1981); Michael K. Curtis, "The Bill of Rights as a Limitation on State Authority: A Reply to Professor Berger," 16 *Wake Forest Law Review* 45 (1980); and Michael K. Curtis, " Further Adventures of the Nine Lived Cat: A Response to Mr. Berger on Incorporation of the Bill of Rights," 43 *Ohio State Law Journal* 89 (1982).
30. The Slaughterhouse Cases, 83 U.S. 36 (1872).
31. The New Orleans butchers who filed the suit against a state law regulating the business of meatpacking had alleged a constitutional right to pursue their occupation free of the proposed regulations that required them to slaughter animals within a single facility. Miller and the majority rejected the claim that the Constitution secured such economic rights, but affirmed that privileges and immunities included, in addition to the petition clause of the First Amendment, "the rights secured by the thirteenth and fifteenth articles of amendment, and by the [due process and equal protection] clauses of the fourteenth."
32. Ibid., at 119.
33. Ibid., at 130.
34. *Murdock v. Memphis,* 87 U.S. (20 Wall.) 590 (1875).
35. Ibid., at 630.
36. *In re Medley,* 134 U.S. 160 (1890).
37. Ibid., at 176.
38. *Holden v. Minnesota,* 137 U.S. 483 (1890).
39. *Rooney v. North Dakota,* 196 U.S. 319 (1905).
40. See Louis P. Masur, *Rites of Execution: Capital Punishment and the Transformation of American Culture, 1776–1865* (New York: Oxford University Press, 1991); and

Michael Madow, "Forbidden Spectacle: Executions, the Public and the Press in Nineteenth Century New York," 43 *Buffalo Law Review* 461 (1995).

41. *Malloy v. South Carolina*, 237 U.S. 180 (1915), at 184.

42. *Leeper v. State of Texas*, 139 U.S. 462 (1891), at 468. See also *McNulty v. California*, 149 U.S. 645 (1893), in which the Court held that the question of whether an amendment to the California penal code repealed an earlier statute under which the defendant had been convicted and sentenced was solely a matter of state law; and *Nobles v. Georgia*, 168 U.S. 398 (1897), in which the Court held that the state's procedures for determining insanity did not raise a federal question.

43. *Hurtado v. California*, 110 U.S. 516 (1884). California's constitution permitted indictment solely by information "after examination and commitment by a magistrate."

44. Ibid., at 533–537. Matthews' argument in *Hurtado* respecting the inclusion of the grand jury requirement in addition to due process in the Fifth Amendment has always presented a logical difficulty for those who claim that the framers of the Fourteenth Amendment intended to apply the Bill of Rights to the states via the due process clause. The better argument, suggested by Miller in *Slaughterhouse* but subsequently rejected by the Court, rests on the privileges and immunities clause. See Kevin Christopher Newsom, "Setting Incorporation Straight: A Reinterpretation of the Slaughter-House Cases," 109 *Yale Law Journal* 643 (2000).

45. Ibid., at 549–555.

46. James R. Green, Death in the Haymarket: A Story of Chicago, the First Labor Movement and the Bombing That Divided Gilded Age America (New York: Pantheon, 2006).

47. *Spies v. Illinois*, 123 U.S. 131 (1887), at 175–176.

48. Ibid., at 133.

49. Ibid., at 179–181.

50. *In re Kemmler*, 136 U.S. 436 (1890), at 443–444.

51. Ibid., at 442.

52. Ibid., at 448.

53. Ibid., at 446–447.

54. Quoted in Jurgen Martschukat, "'The Art of Killing by Electricity': The Sublime and the Electric Chair," *Journal of American History* 89 (December 2002): 918. See also Michael Madow, "Forbidden Spectacle: Executions, the Public and the Press in Nineteenth Century New York," 43 *Buffalo Law Review* 461 (1995); and Mark Essig, *Edison and the Electric Chair* (New York: Walker, 2003).

55. *Maxwell v. Dow*, 176 U.S. 581 (1900).

56. Ibid., at 598–599.

57. *Twining v. New Jersey*, 211 U.S. 78 (1908). Moody held that the Fifth Amendment's prohibition on self-incrimination was not among the privileges and immunities of U.S. citizenship or included within the due process clause of the Fourteenth Amendment.

58. Ibid., at 85.

59. Ibid. (emphasis added).

60. *Chicago, Burlington & Quincy Railroad Company v. Chicago*, 166 U.S. 226 (1897).

61. The decision had been foreshadowed in *Davidson v. New Orleans*, 96 U.S. 97 (1878). Justice Bradley noted that when judging "what is 'due process of law,' respect must be had to the cause and object of the taking, whether under the taxing power, the power of eminent domain, or the power of assessment for local

improvements . . . [and] if found to be arbitrary, oppressive, and unjust, it may be declared to be not 'due process of law,' " at 108.

62. *Gilbert v. Minnesota*, 254 U.S. 325 (1920), at 343.

63. This account of the Frank case is based on the following: Nancy MacLean, *Behind the Mask of Chivalry* (New York: Oxford University Press, 1994); Leonard Dinnerstein, *The Leo Frank Case* (Athens: University of Georgia Press, 1987); and Albert Lindemann, *The Jew Accused: Three Anti-Semitic Affairs: Dreyfus, Beilis, Frank, 1894–1915* (New York: Cambridge University Press, 1991).

64. *Frank v. Mangum*, 237 U.S. 309 (1915), at 337–338.

65. Ibid., at 338.

66. Ibid., at 343.

67. Four years after *Frank v. Mangum*, Holmes would write for the Court to sustain convictions under the Espionage Act by invoking the "clear and present danger" test. See *Schenck v. United States*, 249 U.S. 47 (1919); *Frohwerk v. United States*, 249 U.S. 204 (1919); and *Debs v. United States*, 249 U.S. 211 (1919).

68. *Frank v. Mangum*, at 346.

69. Ibid.

70. Ibid., at 347.

71. Ibid., at 350.

72. On war-time social disorder and vigilantism, see Christopher Capozzola, *Uncle Sam Wants You: World War I and the Making of the Modern American Citizen* (New York: Oxford University Press, 2008), 55–143.

73. *Moore v. Dempsey*, 261 U.S. 86 (1923), at 88.

74. Ibid., at 91–92.

The Road to *Furman*

The Due Process Revolution, 1923–1971

In 1923 *Moore v. Dempsey* opened a new chapter in the Supreme Court's relationship to capital punishment in America.[1] In 1972 *Furman v. Georgia*, a 5–4 decision that included nine separate opinions covering over 230 pages in the official *United States Reports*, opened the next chapter.[2] *Furman* declared that the existing death penalty statutes of the states and the federal government constituted cruel and unusual punishment prohibited by the Eighth and Fourteenth Amendments to the Constitution. The decision overturned the death sentences of 631 men and 2 women then awaiting execution in states from Florida to California. It elated opponents of capital punishment throughout the country and generated vitriolic attacks upon the justices by those who believed the penalty essential to the nation's war on crime.

Furman struck some observers as a bolt from the blue, a sudden departure from what the Court had done only a year earlier in *McGautha v. California* (1971) when it affirmed capital sentences under laws similar to those invalidated in 1972.[3] But as we shall see the Court had undergone significant personnel changes during that brief period, and public opinion by 1972 appeared to be moving inexorably against the death penalty, as reflected in both polling data and the decline in the number of executions. Only two persons had been executed in 1967, and none in the years from 1968 to 1971. *Furman* in effect ratified an existing national moratorium on the death penalty with the Court asking the political branches whether that moratorium should be made permanent.

This chapter revisits the long jurisprudential road the Court traveled to reach *Furman*, an era during which the justices imposed, often cautiously, new procedural limitations upon how the states wielded capital punishment. In the nearly half century that separated *Moore v. Dempsey* from *Furman*, death penalty cases on the Court's annual docket provided the occasion for many of the justices' most controversial and contested decisions, including:

- *Ex parte Quirin* (1942) and *In re Yamashita* (1946), in which the Court decided whether German enemy saboteurs and a Japanese commanding general, respectively, could be put to death by American military tribunals without affording to the accused the full protections of the Bill of Rights.[4]

57

- *Louisiana ex rel. Francis v. Resweber* (1947), which raised the question of whether the state of Louisiana could carry out a second electrocution of a condemned inmate after the first attempt failed without violating the Fourteenth Amendment's due process clause and, by implication, the Eighth Amendment's ban on cruel and unusual punishment.[5]

- *Palko v. Connecticut* (1937) and *Adamson v. California* (1947), which again presented the issue of whether specific guarantees of the Bill of Rights, such as the double jeopardy clause or the self-incrimination clause, applied to the states by virtue of the Fourteenth Amendment's due process clause. *Adamson* provoked an epic debate between Justices Hugo Black and Felix Frankfurter over the history of the Fourteenth Amendment, the meaning of due process, and the intention of the framers of the Reconstruction amendment.[6]

- *Rosenberg v. United States* (1953), in which a sharply divided Court upheld the death sentences of convicted spies Julius and Ethel Rosenberg, the only American citizens ever executed for conspiracy to commit espionage.[7] The *Rosenberg* case represents the single instance that the Court vacated a stay of execution granted by one of its members. The case provoked Justice Frankfurter to observe that "men's devotion to law is not profoundly rooted"; he described it as "the most disturbing single experience I have had during my term of service on the Court."[8]

- *Brown v. Allen* (1953), in which prisoners under sentence of death in North Carolina challenged their convictions on grounds of racial discrimination through habeas corpus after the Court had declined to review their claims on direct appeal.[9] A majority affirmed the sentences, but the case provoked the most contentious debate among the justices concerning the scope of federal habeas corpus jurisdiction over state criminal trials since *Frank v. Mangum*[10] and *Moore v. Dempsey.*

- *Chessman v. Teets* (1955; 1957), which involved the fate of convicted California rapist Caryl Chessman, the alleged "Red Light Bandit."[11] Chessman avoided eight dates over 12 years with the state's gas chamber, including one successful appeal that led the Court to order the state of California to hold a hearing on the adequacy of the original trial transcript. That review concluded that the transcript was substantially accurate, and Chessman, denied clemency by California's governor, was executed in 1960.[12]

- *Sheppard v. Maxwell* (1966), in which the Court overturned the conviction and death sentence of Ohio physician Samuel H. Sheppard on grounds of prejudicial pre-trial newspaper publicity.[13] Found not guilty in a second trial, Sheppard became the subject of both a fictional television series and a motion picture.[14]

- *Rudolph v. Alabama* (1963), in which three members of the Court, led by Justice Arthur Goldberg, dissented from a denial of certiorari and for the first time urged the justices to consider whether the death penalty for the crime of rape violated the constitutional ban on cruel and unusual punishment.[15]

The Crucible of Race

Four of the famous capital cases noted above—*Louisiana ex rel. Francis v. Resweber, Adamson v. California, Brown v. Allen,* and *Rudolph v. Alabama*—and *Furman* each touched on the one issue that drove the Court's death penalty jurisprudence throughout the half century following *Moore v. Dempsey:* the racially motivated and brutal treatment of African American defendants in the criminal justice regimes of the South. Slavery and its racist legacy infected Southern law long after formal emancipation. Both the slave codes of the Old South and the Black Codes that followed provided that African Americans would be punished more severely than whites for the same offenses. In addition, crimes against whites drew harsher punishments than similar crimes against African Americans.

Between 1930, when official statistics begin, and 1970, nearly half of all persons executed for murder in the United States and 90 percent of those condemned to death for rape were African Americans, although African Americans never constituted more than 11 percent of the population.[16] In 1951, for example, Virginia put to death seven African Americans on a single day for the crime of rape. Mississippi executed Willie McGee a few months later for allegedly raping a white woman, despite claims that their relationship had been consensual until McGee sought to end it. No white man had ever been executed for rape in Mississippi when the state electrocuted McGee.[17]

Sometimes the justices noted the racial component in capital cases, but often they did not. Writing for the majority in the botched execution case of Willie Francis, Justice Stanley Reed described the petitioner as "a colored citizen of Louisiana," while in *Brown* Reed identified all four of the defendants as "Negroes." In *Adamson,* by contrast, despite the rhetorical fireworks over the intention of those who wrote the Fourteenth Amendment, no member of the Court described the defendant, Admiral Dewey Adamson, as an African American. And none of the nine justices who wrote in *Furman* focused on the fact that the three men under death sentence—William Henry Furman, Lucious Jackson, and Elmer Branch—were African Americans. Jackson and Branch had been convicted of raping a white woman, the most frequent offense for which African Americans were executed in the South during the twentieth century.

The Court's squeamishness on the issue of race and the death penalty found echoes in popular culture, notably in motion pictures, where producers seldom confronted directly the racial dimensions of capital punishment in America during the pre-*Furman* era. Until very recently, classic American films that focused on capital punishment sent only white actors to the electric chair or the gas chamber: Clark Gable in *Manhattan Melodrama,* James Cagney in *Angels with Dirty Faces,* and Montgomery Clift in *A Place in the Sun.* When Hollywood brought Sister Helen Prejean's death row memoir *Dead Man Walking* to the silver screen

Cinematic portrayals of capital punishment have historically masked the racial dimension of those put to death. Here, James Cagney walks to his execution in the 1938 film Angels with Dirty Faces.

in 1995 the central condemned inmate became a poor white man played by Sean Penn, not one of the African Americans actually executed in Prejean's book. In 1999 and 2001, *The Green Mile* and *Monster's Ball* broke modestly with this tradition by executing African Americans, but the films focused largely on white guilt, not black agony. The Court's—and Hollywood's—caution aside, the pervasive environment of Southern racism played the silent but transformative role in changing the constitutional boundaries of capital punishment in the United States from *Moore v. Dempsey* to *Furman*.

The case of the Elaine Six did not produce an immediate systemic change in the Court's death penalty jurisprudence. Three years after the Arkansas decision, the justices unanimously dismissed a writ of error in *Gaines v. Washington* by holding that the public trial provision of the Sixth Amendment did not apply to the states via the Fourteenth Amendment and that indictment without a grand jury did not constitute a constitutional violation in a state criminal trial.[18] But the arrival of a new chief justice in 1930, Charles Evans Hughes, the onset of the worst economic calamity in the nation's history, and a trial in a tiny Alabama town suddenly changed the landscape of law, politics, and capital punishment in the South.

Scottsboro

As the youngest associate justice prior to World War I, Hughes had displayed sensitivity to the pathology of racism in American life and the constitutional command of equal protection of the laws. In 1908 he wrote for the Court in *Bailey v. Alabama* to strike down Alabama's debt peonage laws that had ensnared black tenant farmers as a violation of the Thirteenth Amendment,[19] and in 1914 he spoke again for a majority in *McCabe v. Atchison, Topeka and Santa Fe Railroad* to invalidate an Oklahoma statute that permitted railroads to refuse certain services to African American passengers.[20]

One year after his return to the Court as its twelfth chief justice, Hughes commanded majorities that dramatically extended the scope of Fourteenth Amendment guarantees that applied specific provisions of the Bill of Rights to the states. In *Stromberg v. California* (1931), the Hughes majority for the first time overturned a state law on the grounds that the liberty protected by the due process clause included freedom of speech.[21] That same term the Court ruled in *Near v. Minnesota* that the Fourteenth Amendment also prohibited the states from engaging in prior restraint of the press.[22] Hughes and his brethren launched a due process revolution in *Stromberg* and *Near* that soon reached the law of capital punishment as well.

The Great Depression and Franklin Roosevelt's New Deal focused the nation's attention as never before on issues of poverty and economic inequality in America, but this environment also heightened public fears about crime and lawlessness and proved inhospitable to arguments against capital punishment. The states kept their death rows full and their executioners very busy between 1930 and 1940 when they electrocuted, gassed, shot, and hanged 1,791 inmates, an average of 163 per year. The decade of the Great Depression became simultaneously the busiest time for executioners in the history of the United States as well as the years when the Court took major steps towards placing some procedural limits on the nation's capital punishment regime. In Scottsboro, Alabama, racism, poverty, death sentences, due process, and the Hughes Court all came together in 1932 and 1935.

In late March 1931 two groups of people were riding the Southern Railroad's freight train between Chattanooga and Memphis in search of work: nine young African Americans and a number of whites, including two females, Victoria Price and Ruby Bates. When a fight erupted, the African Americans, led by Haywood Patterson, Ozie Powell, and Clarence Norris, forced the whites off the train. The whites then walked to the nearest station where they reported an assault by a gang of blacks. Within hours, a white posse stopped the train in Paint Rock, Alabama, arrested all nine of the African Americans, including twelve-year-old Roy Wright and thirteen-year-old Eugene Williams, loaded them onto a truck, and locked them up in the nearby Scottsboro jail. In the course of the arrests the charges mounted against the nine when either Price or Bates, likely fearing a charge of prostitution, alleged sexual assault. Only a detachment of Alabama National Guardsmen sent by Gov. B. M. Miller prevented a mob from lynching the Scottsboro prisoners that night.

Soon known as the "Scottsboro Boys" to their defenders—but as "Nine Black Fiends" in the local press—the defendants went on trial in groups of two or three twelve days later in a courtroom presided over by Judge A. E. Hawkins. Hawkins initially appointed "all members of the bar" to represent the defendants for the purpose of their arraignment, but on the morning of their trials they remained without specific counsel. Hawkins finally named two lawyers to defend them: Stephen Roddy, an alcoholic real estate attorney from Chattanooga, who claimed to have been sent by friends of the defendants, and Milo Moody, a seventy-year-old local practitioner, who had never tried a capital case. The lawyers first consulted with their clients only on the day of the trials.

In the course of the trials, Roddy and Moody failed to explore the contradictory testimony of Price and Bates or to cross-examine the doctors who had treated Price on March 25. Six of the defendants denied even seeing the two women—one, Olen Montgomery, nearly blind, had been found in a freight car near the end of the train, and another, Willie Roberson, suffered so severely from syphilis he could barely walk at the time of the alleged crime. Two of the defendants confessed, but later testified to being beaten in jail; Norris, attempting to save himself, blamed the others. All-white juries, cheered by crowds outside the courtroom, returned guilty verdicts in the four separate trials and sentenced eight of the nine to death in the electric chair. Judge Hawkins declared a mistrial in the case of Wright when the jury insisted upon a death sentence despite his age and a plea for leniency by the prosecution (**Document 2.1**).[23]

When the National Association for the Advancement of Colored People (NAACP) did not immediately come to their aid, the Scottsboro defendants became the clients of the International Labor Defense, the legal arm of the American Communist Party, headed by Joseph Brodsky. Brodsky represented them on appeal before the Alabama supreme court, which affirmed eight of the nine death sentences in early 1932.[24] When the case reached the Hughes Court in the fall of 1932, the defense team included Walter H. Pollak, who had graduated from the Harvard Law School in 1910. Pollak had worked for the New York law firm of Simpson, Warren and Cardozo, one of whose partners, Benjamin N. Cardozo, now sat on the Supreme Court. Pollak had argued on behalf of Benjamin Gitlow seven years earlier in *Gitlow v. New York* (1925). It was in that case that the Court first extended the protections of the due process clause and the First Amendment to the states, although Gitlow ended up in prison.[25] Pollak fared better with the remaining Scottsboro defendants and left a lasting imprint upon American constitutional law.

In *Powell v. Alabama*, Pollak and his co-counsel argued that the convictions and sentences should be set aside on three grounds: the defendants had not received a fair, impartial trial; the defendants had been denied the right to counsel "with the accustomed incidents of consultation and opportunity of preparation for trial"; and the defendants had been tried by a jury from which qualified members of their own race had been "systematically excluded."[26] The Court chose to reverse the Alabama supreme court only on the right to counsel issue in an opinion by Justice George Sutherland, a former U.S. senator from Utah who remained among the more conservative members of the Court when matters touched property rights and economic regulations. Sutherland crafted an opinion that blazed a new constitutional trail with respect to the rights of defendants in capital cases, but also drew clear boundaries around that right (**Document 2.2**).

In excruciating detail, Justice Sutherland reviewed the feckless process through which Judge Hawkins had appointed "all members of the bar" to represent the defendants for arraignment, but left them only with Roddy and Moody on the morning of the trial. Sutherland labeled this judicial performance as "little more than an expansive gesture, imposing no substantial or definite obligation upon any one," which meant that "from the time of their arraignment until the beginning of their trial, when consultation, thoroughgoing investigation and preparation were vitally important, the defendants did not have the aid of counsel in any real sense, although they were as much entitled to such aid during that period as at the trial itself."[27]

But was the right to counsel, explicitly protected by the Sixth Amendment, also embraced within the Fourteenth Amendment's due process clause? Here Sutherland had to overcome the reasoning embedded in *Hurtado v. California*, where in 1884 Justice Stanley Matthews had argued that specific constitutional guarantees in the Bill of Rights, such as indictment by grand jury, remained wholly separate from the concept of due process.[28] That logic, if extended from the Fifth Amendment to the Sixth, would have doomed the Scottsboro defendants. But Sutherland had at his disposal more recent decisions in which the Court had incorporated portions of the Bill of Rights (*Gitlow*, *Stromberg v. California*, and *Near v. Minnesota*) into the due process clause of the Fourteenth Amendment. And for good measure, he cited Justice William Moody's language in *Twining v. New Jersey*: "it is possible that some of the personal rights safeguarded by the first eight Amendments against national action may also be safeguarded against state action, because a denial of them would be a denial of due process of law." The "right to the aid of counsel," Sutherland concluded, "is of this fundamental character."[29]

The failure of the trial court to give the defendants "reasonable time and opportunity to secure counsel," Sutherland wrote, denied them due process of law considering "the ignorance and illiteracy of the defendants, their youth, the circumstances of public hostility, the imprisonment and the close surveillance . . . by military forces, the fact that their friends and families were all in other states . . . and, above all that they stood in deadly peril of their lives.[30] In addition to the issue of time and opportunity, Sutherland added that "the failure . . . to make *an effective appointment of counsel* was likewise a denial of due process."[31] With this statement the Court opened the door to further constitutional questions concerning the broad right to counsel. Did "effective appointment" include the legal competence and diligence of attorneys so appointed by the court? And how were such judgments to be made?

But having opened one door, Sutherland closed another when he made it clear that this second due process rule applied only in a capital case "where the defendant is unable to employ counsel, and is incapable adequately of making his own defense because of ignorance, feeble mindedness, illiteracy, or the like." With this qualification, Sutherland appeared to exclude from consideration other circumstances he had previously noted, such as the age of the defendant, public hostility, imprisonment and close surveillance by military forces, and isolation from friends and family. The Scottsboro defendants would be given new trials, but the scope of the right to counsel rule announced in *Powell* remained limited and vague. Even so, Sutherland's opinion drew a sharp dissent from Justice Pierce Butler, who accepted the time and opportunity conclusion but blanched at the rule requiring "an effective appointment of counsel." Butler argued that such a requirement "is an extension of federal authority into a field hitherto occupied exclusively by the several States."[32] The future would prove Butler right.[33]

Scottsboro: Round Two

The second round of trials was held in Decatur, Alabama, in the spring of 1933. Haywood Patterson was again found guilty of rape and sentenced to die, despite dazzling defense work by his new attorney, Samuel Leibowitz, and a dramatic reversal in the testimony of Ruby Bates. Bates now claimed that the crime had never occurred and that Victoria Price had invented the story in order to avoid police inquiry into their own behavior. Dr. R. R. Bridges, who had physically examined the two women, confirmed Bates' recantation when he testified that the sperm he identified had been non-motile, which suggested that intercourse had taken place long before the alleged crime on March 25. Two months after the guilty verdict, trial judge James Horton, acting in the belief that neither the evidence nor Price's testimony was convincing, set aside both the jury verdict and sentence and ordered a new trial, an act of judicial courage that brought down on Horton the wrath of his hometown of Athens, Alabama, and subsequently cost him reelection.

Undeterred by that outcome, the state of Alabama put Patterson and Norris on trial for a third time in November 1933, with the other five Scottsboro defendants scheduled to follow. William Callahan, the new trial judge, told the jury that no white woman in Alabama would ever consent to have sex with a black man and initially refused to provide the jury with a form for acquittal. Again, the prosecution won guilty verdicts and death sentences. Two years later, when the Court heard the second Scottsboro appeal in *Norris v. Alabama*, Leibowitz placed squarely before the justices the jury issue first raised by Pollak in the *Powell* case.[34] When asked by the chief justice if he could prove his claim of racial discrimination,

After the Supreme Court ruled in 1932 that the "Scottsboro Boys" had been denied "an effective appointment of counsel," the defendants were given new trials. In this November 1933 photo, the seven defendants leave the Scottsboro jail for a third trial. In 1935 the Court weighed in again on a second appeal. After reviewing proof of the exclusion of blacks from jury pools, the Court threw out the convictions on equal protection grounds.

the attorney presented to the Court the actual jury rolls from Jackson and Morgan counties, which Hughes and the other justices scrutinized from the bench. They found overwhelming written proof that blacks had been excluded from local juries (**Document 2.3**). On April 1, 1935, a unanimous Court threw out Norris' conviction and sentence on equal protection grounds by holding that both the indictment and trial had taken place in counties riddled with "continuous and systematic exclusion of statutorily qualified African Americans from jury panels."[35]

The two Scottsboro cases remain landmarks of both constitutional development and death penalty litigation, but they also reveal the limited reach of Supreme Court rulings in both areas. Eight years after *Powell*, the justices rejected a right-to-counsel claim in another Alabama capital case, where court-appointed lawyers, having had just five days prior to trial to consult with their clients, requested a continuance that the trial judge denied. Justice Black, an Alabama native, wrote the opinion affirming the conviction and death sentence.[36] A decade after *Powell*, in addition, the Court refused to extend its right-to-counsel rule to non-capital, indigent defendants who did not fit the social profile of the Scottsboro nine, a decision that stood until the 1960s.[37]

Racially biased juries remained a pervasive part of Southern justice long after *Norris*, especially with African Americans' continued systematic exclusion from voting rolls into the late 1960s. In *Akins v. Texas*, for example, decided a decade after *Norris*, the Court sustained a death sentence, although only a single African American had been empanelled on either the grand jury or the trial jury. Writing against the three dissenters, Justice Reed declared that fairness in the selection of jurors did not require proportional representation of African Americans from the community, although lawyers for the petitioner had not raised the issue.[38] Not until the 1980s did the Court place significant restrictions upon the use of racially motivated peremptory challenges by prosecutors—an issue that continues to plague the justices, some of whom have argued that racial discrimination can only be expunged from the criminal justice system by a total ban on such preemptory challenges.[39]

The Limits of *Powell* and *Norris*

Powell and *Norris* did not immediately provide justice to the Scottsboro defendants, who continued to face local prosecutors bent upon their punishment for a crime few believed they had committed. Tried for a fourth time, Patterson was again convicted of rape, but this time given a sentence of seventy-five years. Patterson was serving time in Kilby Prison near Birmingham when in 1948 he escaped and fled North. Arrested in Michigan after the publication of his book *Scottsboro Boy,* Patterson remained outside the grip of Alabama law when Michigan governor G. Mennen Williams refused Alabama's extradition request. Powell was not so lucky. Shot in the head during an alleged escape attempt, he suffered brain damage, pled guilty to assault, and remained in prison until 1948. Norris escaped a death sentence after his third trial in 1937, but remained behind bars for over a decade. Alabama finally dropped charges against Roberson, Montgomery, Williams, and Wright, although all of them had been in jail for over six years.

In the same term that it reversed Norris' conviction, the Hughes Court again expanded the meaning of due process of law in the Fourteenth Amendment when it overturned the California conviction of labor organizer Tom Mooney, who had initially been sentenced to death for allegedly detonating a bomb during a pro-war parade in San Francisco in 1917. Following worldwide protests and an investigation by the federal government, California's governor commuted Mooney's sentence to life in prison. Mooney's lawyers continued to seek relief in the federal courts after a key witness admitted that he had lied during the trial with the encouragement of the chief prosecutor. In *Mooney v. Holohan* (1935) the Hughes Court ruled that the knowing use of perjured testimony by prosecutors violated the Fourteenth Amendment.[40]

Due Process and Coerced Confessions

The *Mooney* decision set the stage for an even more critical due process decision by the Court a year later that had long-term consequences for capital cases. In *Brown v. Mississippi,* with Hughes again taking the lead, the justices overturned convictions and death sentences secured by the state on the basis of confessions extorted by what the chief justice called "violence and brutality."[41] Ed Brown and two others, described in the state court as "ignorant Negroes," had been indicted for the murder of Raymond Stewart on April 4, 1934, tried and convicted two days later, and sentenced to death.

Over the objections of court-appointed lawyers, the trial judge admitted into evidence confessions secured by the systematic physical torture of Brown and the other defendants inflicted by a deputy sheriff and white vigilantes. They hung one defendant twice from a tree and whipped him until he agreed to sign a confession; Brown and the others had been stripped and beaten with a leather strap in the local jail. The Mississippi supreme court affirmed the convictions, with two judges dissenting, although no one disputed the facts of the torture, including the deputy sheriff who, when asked during the trial about the severity of the whippings, said: "Not too much for a Negro; not as much as I would have done if it were left to me."[42]

A majority on the Mississippi supreme court, citing *Twining v. New Jersey,* argued that the Fourteenth Amendment did not provide an exemption in a state trial from compulsory self-incrimination, to which Hughes responded tartly that the *Twining* rule referred only to "the processes of justice by which the accused may be called as a witness and required to testify. Compulsion by torture to extort a confession is a different matter." In the case of *Brown v. Mississippi,* Chief Justice Hughes concluded, "it would be difficult to conceive of methods more revolting to the sense of justice than those taken to procure the confessions of these petitioners, and the use of the confessions thus obtained . . . as a clear denial of due process."[43] The defendants were entitled to a new trial with the confessions excluded (**Document 2.4**).

Brown gave birth to a long series of coerced confession cases over the next three decades, many of them involving African Americans sentenced to death by Southern courts. Where, as in *Brown,* the record demonstrated elements of mistreatment, physical abuse, or physical threats prior to a confession, the Court went on to overturn state convictions, particularly where defendants had been subjected to prolonged interrogations and denied access to lawyers, friends, or families.[44] By the late 1940s, long interrogations alone in the absence of counsel became grounds for setting aside murder convictions in non-capital cases,[45] but the justices affirmed death sentences when the record remained conflicted on such issues.[46]

In the face of conflicting precedents that often rested on retrospective, subjective judgments about the voluntariness of a particular confession, the Warren Court in the 1960s shifted the burden of proof to law enforcement officials and prosecutors. The Court required them to demonstrate that a person taken into custody had been informed of his right to counsel and the privilege against self-incrimination and had knowingly waived these rights before a confession could be introduced at trial.[47]

In less than a decade, the Hughes Court had dramatically reshaped constitutional law with respect to the Fourteenth Amendment's due process clause and capital punishment by broadening access to federal review through habeas corpus; requiring the states to provide counsel to impoverished defendants in special circumstances, such as Scottsboro; placing limits on the most blatant forms of racial discrimination in the empanelling of grand and petit juries; and restricting the most brutal methods used to extract confessions from criminal suspects in capital and non-capital cases. But the Hughes Court and its immediate successors also placed some clear limits on the due process revolution and the judicial machinery of death.

Cardozo and the Limits of Due Process

The first indication of those limits came in *Snyder v. Massachusetts,* decided in 1934 by a narrow 5–4 vote, with Justice Cardozo writing for the majority.[48] The state initially charged Herman Snyder and two others with robbery and murder at a Somerville gas station, but one of the suspects confessed and testified for the prosecution that his confederates had been the ones who pulled the trigger, a charge they vehemently disputed. The jury spared the prosecution's witness, but sentenced Snyder and his companion to death, despite conflicting testimony concerning the physical layout of the station and the location of the victim's body. When the prosecution moved that the jury visit the crime scene at the opening of the trial, the judge granted the request, permitted Snyder's attorney to attend the site, but barred the defendant from the view. Snyder's lawyer objected that the exclusion deprived his client of due process guaranteed by the Fourteenth Amendment.

Cardozo began by invoking *Twining v. New Jersey* to make it clear at the outset that Massachusetts remained free to regulate the procedure of its courts "unless, in so doing, it offends some principle of justice so rooted in the traditions and conscience of our people as to be ranked as fundamental." He conceded that the Sixth Amendment guaranteed a defendant the privilege to confront his accusers and cross-examine them face to face "in prosecutions in the federal courts," and that "the privilege is reinforced by the Fourteenth Amendment, though this has not been squarely held." But the Fourteenth Amendment privilege applied only "whenever his presence has a relation, reasonably substantial, to the fullness of his opportunity to defend against the charge," and "nowhere in the decisions of this court is there a dictum, and still less a ruling, that the . . . Amendment assures the privilege of presence when presence would be useless, or the benefit but a shadow."[49] In other words, Cardozo and the majority found Snyder's absence from the crime scene a harmless error that did not reach the threshold of a fundamental constitutional right (**Document 2.5**).

From that opening, Cardozo marched easily to the retrospective conclusion that Snyder's presence at the view would not have altered the outcome of the jury's decision and had not deprived him of "the fundamental justice assured to him by the Constitution of the United States." Snyder had not been denied something "indispensable," such as an opportunity to be heard or defended, but only a privilege "not explicitly conferred" because the "Fourteenth Amendment has not said in so many words that he must be present every second or minute, or even every hour, of the trial. . . . Due process of law requires that the proceedings shall be fair, but fairness is a relative, not an absolute, concept. . . . The due process clause does not impose upon the States a duty to establish ideal systems for the administration of justice, with every modern improvement and with provision against every possible hardship that may befall."[50]

In conclusion, despite a powerful dissent by Justice Owen Roberts, who pointed out that Snyder's presence at the view might have contributed to his lawyer's defense strategy, Cardozo dismissed the claim as trivial and a threat to the integrity of the entire criminal justice system. "But justice, though due to the accused, is due to the accuser also. The concept of fairness must not be trained till it is narrowed to a filament. . . . There is danger that the criminal law will be brought into contempt . . . if gossamer possibilities of prejudice to a defendant are to nullify a sentence pronounced by a court of competent jurisdiction in obedience to local law, and set the guilty free."[51]

The Hughes Court had been engaged in a constitutional struggle against state jurisdictions that operated "in obedience to local law," especially in the South. But Cardozo's opinion in *Snyder* sharply narrowed that commitment. Three years later, Cardozo and the Court took another step back in *Palko v. Connecticut.*[52] In *Palko* the Court reaffirmed once again the core principles of *Hurtado, Twining,* and *Maxwell v. Dow* (1900)[53] with respect to the guarantees of the Bill of Rights and the Fourteenth Amendment.

Frank Palka (the Court reporter got his name wrong) shot and killed two police officers in his attempt to elude arrest for a robbery at a music store. Indicted and tried on a charge of first-degree murder, the jury returned a verdict of murder in the second degree and the judge sentenced him to life in prison. Under an 1886 statute that permitted the state to appeal matters of law, the prosecutors petitioned for a new trial on the grounds that the judge had excluded certain testimony and improperly instructed the jury as to the difference between first- and second-degree murder. The Connecticut supreme court of errors reversed the judgment and ordered a new trial at which Palka was convicted of first-degree murder and sentenced to death. He alleged that the statute placed him in double jeopardy, barred by the privileges and immunities clause and the due process clause of the Fourteenth Amendment.

Echoing his reasoning in *Snyder*, Cardozo conceded that the double jeopardy provision of the Fifth Amendment would have barred a second trial in the federal courts, but Palka's attorneys now argued that "whatever would be a violation of the original bill of rights . . . if done by the federal government is now equally unlawful by force of the Fourteenth if done by a state." To this claim, Cardozo declared, "There is no such general rule." Only certain immunities, he quickly added, all "implicit in the concept of ordered liberty," such as freedom of speech, freedom of the press, the right to benefit of counsel, or the right of peaceable assembly, had become through the Fourteenth Amendment valid against the states. Other specific guarantees in the Bill of Rights, including trial by jury, indictment by grand jury, or immunity from compulsory self-incrimination, were not "of the very essence of a scheme of ordered liberty," because to abolish them "is not to violate a 'principle of justice so rooted in the traditions and conscience of our people as to be ranked as fundamental'" (**Document 2.6**).

The Connecticut statute permitting Palka's second trial on the original indictment fell into the second category because it, too, did not infringe those "fundamental principles of liberty and justice which lie at the basis of all our civil and political institutions." The state, Cardozo concluded, had asked only that the case against Palka "go on until there shall be a trial free from the corrosion of substantial legal error. This is not cruelty at all, nor even vexation in any immoderate degree." Palka could have appealed if the trial had been infected with errors adverse to him. "A reciprocal privilege . . . has now been granted to the state. There is no seismic innovation. The edifice of justice stands, its symmetry, to many, greater than before."[54]

Among those who joined Cardozo's opinion in *Palko* was the newest justice, Hugo Black, the former senator from Alabama and the first of Roosevelt's eight appointments to the Court. Arriving on the bench with limited judicial experience, Black survived a scandal soon after his confirmation when news reports documented his earlier membership in the Ku Klux Klan. Black promptly immersed himself in the history of the Court and the Constitution. After a close study of the debates surrounding the adoption of the Fourteenth Amendment in 1868, he came to the conclusion, earlier held by Justice John Marshall Harlan, that the framers of the Fourteenth Amendment had intended to apply all of the first eight amendments of the original Bill of Rights as limitations upon the states by means of the first section of the Fourteenth Amendment.

Two years after authoring *Palko*, Cardozo was dead from heart failure and stroke, but his doctrinal legacy lived on in the new justice confirmed to replace him, former law professor Felix Frankfurter, a long-time confidante to President Roosevelt and associate of Justices Oliver Wendell Holmes and Louis Brandeis. Frankfurter was unbending in his intellectual commitment to the independent constitutional status of due process in the Fourteenth Amendment. Frankfurter's views resembled those of Justice Matthews in *Hurtado* even more than Cardozo's in *Palko*, although he accepted the selective incorporation precedents that had been fashioned by the Court since the turn of the century. This position put him in opposition to Black and his total incorporation position, which Frankfurter labeled naive positivism that imposed a doctrinal straightjacket that would inhibit progressive constitutional evolution directed by sagacious justices. The Black-Frankfurter debate largely dominated the two most controversial death penalty cases of the late 1940s, those involving Willie Francis and Admiral Dewey Adamson.

The Ordeal of Willie Francis

On one level, the Willie Francis case exposed how little had changed in Southern justice accorded to African Americans as a result of Supreme Court decisions since Scottsboro. Seventeen years old, barely literate, poor, and plagued by a speech impediment, Francis was convicted of the murder of a local druggist in St. Martinville, Louisiana, and sentenced to die in the state's traveling electric chair after a perfunctory trial void of even a stenographic record. His court-appointed lawyers called no witnesses and did not cross-examine the prosecution's witnesses, challenge the voluntariness of Francis' confession, or file an appeal after his conviction and sentence.

The case of *Louisiana ex rel. Francis v. Resweber* probably would not have reached the Court, even given these circumstances, but for the botched execution that followed on May 3, 1946, when Francis was strapped into the chair in the St. Martin parish courthouse. For several minutes, electric current surged into Francis's body, but he did not die due to a malfunction in the generator or the incompetence of the executioner, even after a second charge lasting several additional minutes was applied. Guards removed Francis from the chair and

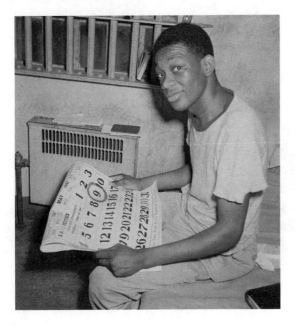

After the electric chair malfunctioned during his execution, Willie Francis appealed his case to the Supreme Court, arguing that a return to the electric chair would violate his due process rights and constitutional protections from double jeopardy and cruel and unusual punishment. The Court rejected these arguments, and Louisiana sent Francis back to the electric chair in 1947.

returned him to his cell where he remained while the state, supported by the Louisiana supreme court, moved to electrocute him a second time and opponents struggled to save him from that fate. The Louisiana court declined to intervene on the grounds that no electricity had actually reached Francis' body, a fact denied by some witnesses and the condemned man's own words in the electric chair. The state court therefore concluded that Francis had not been harmed and that a second execution constituted only an executive decision, one that didn't raise judicial questions.[55]

Represented before the Court by Bertrand DeBlanc, a local Louisiana attorney, and Skelly Wright, a future federal appeals judge, Francis challenged the state's effort to execute him again by arguing that to do so would violate the due process clause of the Fourteenth Amendment, the double jeopardy provision of the Fifth Amendment, and the cruel and unusual punishment provision of the Eighth Amendment. Francis' appeal provoked discord and strategizing as the Court struggled to bring forth its final opinion (**Document 2.7**). When the justices voted after hearing argument, six (the new chief justice, Fred Vinson, Reed, Frankfurter, Black, William O. Douglas, and Robert Jackson) voted to affirm the Louisiana high court; Frank Murphy, Harold Burton, and Wiley Rutledge registered dissents. Reed's initial draft for the majority rejected all three claims, finding explicitly no violation of due process when measured by "national standards of decency," but he avoided discussion of incorporation, selective or total. This draft led Douglas to defect and brought separate concurring opinions from Frankfurter and Jackson.[56]

Burton's dissent, which now commanded four votes, implicitly accepted the argument that the Fourteenth Amendment incorporated the Eighth by noting that when the former had been adopted in 1868 "there long had been embedded deeply in the standards of this nation a revulsion against subjecting guilty persons to torture culminating in death." Subjecting Francis to a second electrocution would sanction such torture, or "death by installments," not the "instantaneous death" required under Louisiana's own execution statute, which provided that the condemned receive "a current of electricity of sufficient intensity to cause death." Burton and the dissenters urged that the case be returned to the Louisiana supreme court pending further review of the evidence concerning Francis' claim that he had endured electricity, which, if confirmed, would render the second attempt unconstitutional because "it exceeds any punishment prescribed by law. There is no precedent for it. What then is it, if it be not cruel, unusual and unlawful."[57]

Reed also faced a revolt by Jackson and Black, both of whom proposed concurring opinions. Jackson expressed disapproval of the death penalty, but rejected Reed's "national standards of decency" test for due process in favor of what he called "Louisiana's own law and sense of decency," criteria that would have abandoned plaintiffs such as Francis to the mercies of white Southern justice. Black urged explicit incorporation of the Fifth and Eighth Amendments into the Fourteenth, but did not believe a second try at electrocution violated either provision. He vehemently condemned what he called "a mystic natural law" interpretation of the due process clause, with its reliance on "standards of decency" or "fundamental principles," words that left judges "free to substitute their ideas of natural justice for the considered policies of state and federal legislatures."[58]

Black's proposed concurrence provoked Frankfurter to write one of his own, which echoed *Hurtado, Twining,* and *Palko* in affirming the independent status of the Fourteenth Amendment's due process clause. The amendment, he said, withdrew from the states "the right to act in ways that are offensive to a decent respect for the dignity of man, and heedless of his freedom." When enforcing due process a judge should not impose his "private view rather than that consensus of society's opinion which, for purposes of due process, is the standard enjoined by the Constitution." In his final conclusion Frankfurter again invoked Cardozo: "I cannot say that it would be 'repugnant to the conscience of mankind,' for Louisiana to exercise the power on which she here stands. I cannot say that the Constitution withholds it."[59] Determined to trump Black on the meaning of due process and display his own fidelity to judicial restraint, Frankfurter refused to join the dissenters and spare Francis, although he made a futile attempt, which he later kept secret from all but Burton, to influence a clemency decision from Louisiana governor Jimmie Davis.[60]

Once he gained a major concession from Reed on the issue of incorporation, Black had no incentive to join the dissenters, although he might have done so. In order to keep Black in the majority, Reed modified his opinion by arguing that "to determine whether or not the execution of the petitioner may fairly take place . . . we shall examine the circumstances under the assumption, *but without so deciding, that violation of the principles of the Fifth and Eighth Amendments . . . would be violative of the due process clause of the Fourteenth Amendment.*"[61] Four months after the Court's plurality decision came down, Louisiana successfully electrocuted Francis, gaining what Frankfurter had called "its pound of flesh."[62]

Debating Incorporation Again

If Justice Black believed that Reed's concession to him on incorporation and the Bill of Rights in his Willie Francis opinion signaled a decisive shift in the Court's approach to due process, he was sorely disappointed six months later when the justices voted again, 5–4, to affirm the conviction and death sentence of Admiral Dewey Adamson. Previously convicted of burglary, larceny, and robbery, Adamson declined to testify at his California murder trial for fear that to do so would permit prosecutors during cross-examination to parade his entire criminal record before the jury deciding his fate. California, however, was among the few states that still permitted its courts and prosecutors to comment upon a defendant's failure "to explain or to deny by his testimony any evidence or facts in the case against him."[63] The court and prosecutors informed the jury of Adamson's past convictions, and the jury convicted him of first-degree murder without a recommendation of mercy.

Reed, writing for the Court, reaffirmed the doctrines of both *Twining* and *Palko* in rejecting Adamson's arguments that Section 1 of the Fourteenth Amendment required the states to observe the privilege against self-incrimination. The amendment's due process clause, he wrote, guaranteed only a fair trial, not the specific protections of the Fifth Amendment. It prohibited the use of confessions secured "by fear of hurt, torture or exhaustion . . . [and] forbids any other type of coercion." But Adamson's refusal to testify in his own defense represented a voluntary choice on his part, and hence the Court saw "no reason why comment should not be made upon his silence."[64]

Black now gave full voice to his views on the amendment and the Bill of Rights by arguing that Section 1 "as a whole" had been intended to apply the first eight amendments to the states without exception, no more and no less. He correctly observed that Justice Samuel Miller's opinion in *Slaughterhouse* had not emphatically closed the door on his interpretation, but he lavished more attention upon the due process clause than upon the privileges and immunities clause in the course of his historical analysis and roundly condemned the *Hurtado-Twining-Palko* line of decisions as a departure from *Slaughterhouse*. Black characterized those decisions as evil expressions of a "natural law" jurisprudence that gave the Court too much power over legislatures. He recited the list of economic statutes, state and federal, struck down by the justices between the 1890s and 1937 under this approach and noted that in the recent past the Court had begun to selectively incorporate bits and pieces of the Bill of Rights. The Court should now, Black argued, complete the process by announcing total incorporation, the intent of the framers.[65]

Frankfurter, rising to Black's challenge, advanced his own historical analysis that reaffirmed the correctness of *Hurtado*, *Twining*, and *Palko*. When a state criminal conviction reached the Court, he said, the question was not whether a specific provision of the first eight amendments has been violated, but whether the proceedings "taken as a whole" violated due process of law, "those canons of decency and fairness which express the notions of justice of English-speaking peoples even toward those charged with the most heinous offenses."[66] Justices Murphy and Rutledge joined Black's dissent, along with Justice Douglas, but added that Section 1 should not be limited exclusively to the first eight amendments, dicta that Black regarded as another invitation to unbounded judicial discretion.[67]

With the exception of the case of Willie Francis, all the capital cases before the Court in this era after *Moore v. Dempsey* raised only procedural due process issues, some of which the justices resolved by forcing modest changes on state officials who arrested, tried, convicted, and sentenced persons to death. The Francis decision briefly forced the justices to confront a substantive question: did a second attempt at execution violate due process and, by implication, constitute cruel and unusual punishment? A bare majority answered that question in the negative. Claims of insanity by death row inmates awaiting execution confronted the justices with another invitation to address a substantive issue. Most chose to avoid it.

Due Process and Insanity Pleas

In 1897 the Court first addressed the question of insanity and the death penalty in the case of *Nobles v. Georgia*. In July 1895 in Twiggs County, Georgia, Elizabeth Nobles was found guilty of murder and sentenced to death. The justices unanimously rejected Nobles' claim that due process of law required a trial by judge and jury to determine her soundness of mind prior to execution following an initial procedure whereby the conclusion of an earlier jury, summoned by the county sheriff, had found her insane and stayed her execution. Georgia's insanity law ultimately vested broad power in the presiding trial judge by providing that "at any time . . . when it shall appear to [him] *either by inquisition or otherwise,* that the said convict is of sound mind, the said [trial] judge shall issue a new warrant, directing the sheriff to do execution."[68] The Court conceded that the common law prohibited punishment of the insane, but the Georgia method for determining that fact without trial by jury did not violate due process. Such an absolute right, wrote Chief Justice Edward White, "would be wholly at the will of a convict . . . [and] would depend solely upon his fecundity in making suggestion after suggestion of insanity, to be followed by trial upon trial."[69]

A year after the Willie Francis case, in *Phyle v. Duffy,* the justices rejected the claim of another death row inmate who had been found mentally competent to be executed by the medical superintendent of the state hospital for the insane. In making his decision, the superintendant had acted without notice or hearing, eighteen days after the inmate's admission to the hospital. The trial jury had previously found the defendant insane, which barred his execution under California law. But the decision to begin a further sanity hearing rested with the warden of the prison alone "if . . . there is good reason to believe that a defendant, under judgment of death, has become insane." But the medical superintendent's final determination was not subject to further judicial inquiry. Phyle's lawyers argued that such discretion deprived their client of due process.[70]

Writing for the majority, Justice Black noted that *Nobles* had not addressed the broad discretion vested by California in a single medical official. The decision had, however, clearly ruled that "a condemned defendant cannot automatically block execution by suggestions of insanity, and that . . . a judge, must be left free to exercise a reasonable discretion in determining whether the facts warrant a full inquiry and hearing upon the sanity of a person sentenced to death."[71] Having said that much, the majority upheld a denial of habeas corpus by the California supreme court on the grounds that the defendant retained a separate state remedy of a mandatory writ to challenge the California procedure.[72]

Black's conclusion drew a sharp concurrence from Frankfurter, who was joined by three of his peers in wanting to make it clearly understood that their support for the decision and opinion rested upon the understanding that the mandatory state remedy proposed by the majority "enables the present petitioner to secure a judicial determination of his present sanity. . . . It presupposes that California affords petitioner the means of challenging in a substantial way the *ex parte* finding of the Superintendent of the State Hospital . . . and enables him to secure judicial determination of the claims he has made. . . ."[73] Frankfurter and the others voiced their concern that the ruling might not give Phyle and his lawyers the opportunity to challenge the conclusions of the warden and the medical superintendent. The California supreme court later denied relief in *Phyle* when it found no evidence showing "a good reason to believe" that the condemned man was insane and that the warden should have initiated another trial of the insanity question.[74]

Frankfurter's concurrence in *Phyle* became a long and impassioned dissent in 1950 when the Court upheld a Georgia procedure that gave to the governor, acting with the advice of three physicians, exclusive authority to determine the sanity of the condemned without a hearing or judicial review of the findings. Black opened his majority opinion in *Solesbee v. Balkcom* by stating that the issue of whether executing an insane person constituted cruel and unusual punishment was not the question before the Court. Georgia law, he noted, banned such a practice and the petitioner was not about to be executed "on such a premise." He then slammed the door more tightly against any judicial inquiry into such claims by holding that judgments about insanity bear "a close affinity not to trial . . . but to reprieves of sentences in general," thus sustaining the governor's discretion because "seldom, if ever, has this power of executive clemency been subjected to review by the courts."[75]

Frankfurter attacked Black's framing of the case, which, as he saw it, clearly raised the question of putting to death an insane person, an outcome long condemned by the common law, by Georgia's own statute, and by the laws of every other state. Georgia's governor, aided by three physicians, had made a factual determination that would send the defendant to the electric chair. Frankfurter contended that it was this precise issue that Black's opinion swept under the rug by focusing upon the procedure, not the outcome. Frankfurter demonstrated that among the states only Georgia and five others provided that such an inquiry "may be [made] entirely behind closed doors without any opportunity for submission of facts on behalf of the person whose sanity is to be determined as a prerequisite to killing him" (**Document 2.8**). Nine states made the inquiry entirely judicial, while fourteen others provided for a judicial inquiry with various alternatives of judge and jury.[76]

By making an inventory of state laws and counting legislative noses with respect to the process of determining sanity, Frankfurter departed from his usual open-ended approach to due process and suggested a new framework for how the Court could determine a standard for due process and cruel and unusual punishment that echoed the views of McKenna in *Weems:* "the clause . . . may acquire meaning as public opinion becomes enlightened by a humane justice."[77] Georgia's process, he concluded, violated due process when it risked "the barbarous execution of an insane man because of a hurried, one-sided, untested determination of the question of insanity."[78] Frankfurter returned to this standard two years later in *Leland v. Oregon,* in which the Court affirmed a conviction and death sentence under a statute that placed upon the defendant the burden of proving his insanity "beyond a reasonable doubt."[79] That Oregon was the only state to impose such a burden upon a defendant did not mean, according to Justice Tom Clark and the majority, that it violated due process by offending what Cardozo had called "some principle of justice so rooted in the traditions and conscience of our people as to be ranked as fundamental."[80] Now joined by Black in dissent, Frankfurter noted that the Oregon statute dated from 1864, and that unlike every other state its insanity test subverted the ancient standard of the criminal law by demanding that "the accused person must satisfy a jury beyond a reasonable doubt that, being incapable of committing murder, he has not committed murder."[81]

The Warren Court Revolution

The arrival of a new chief justice, former California governor Earl Warren, in the summer of 1953 opened an extraordinary new chapter in the history of the Court and the Constitution. Over the next sixteen years, Warren and his brethren completed the revolution begun by the Hughes Court in the 1930s by striking at racial discrimination in public and private life and incorporating more provisions of the Bill of Rights against state action through the Fourteenth Amendment.[82]

Preoccupied with the issues of race, freedom of expression, and basic criminal procedure, the Warren Court did not lavish its full attention upon capital punishment, but several of its rulings, notably on the Eighth Amendment in non-capital cases, had important implications for the future of the death penalty.

For the first time since *Weems,* a plurality of the Court struck down a statute on the grounds that it violated the Eighth Amendment. The petitioner in *Trop v. Dulles* (1958), an army private convicted and sentenced by court-martial to six years in prison for wartime desertion and dishonorably discharged from the military, had been subsequently stripped of his citizenship under a section of the Nationality Act of 1940 that provided denationalization for persons so convicted and discharged.[83] Warren's opinion for the plurality echoed the broad language of Justice Moody in *Weems* by arguing that the amendment mandated basic respect for what he called "the dignity of man" and fixed governmental power "within the limits of civilized standards" that drew their meaning "from the evolving standards of decency that mark the progress of a maturing society."[84] And in an attempt to define those "evolving standards of decency," the chief justice went beyond U.S. case law by invoking for comparison the laws of eighty-four other nations, only two of which—the Philippines and Turkey—"impose denationalization as a penalty for desertion."[85]

Justice William Brennan's separate opinion, anticipating his later views on capital punishment, explored the justifications for the punishment of denationalization authorized by Congress under its war powers and found them lacking either a rational basis or wholly beyond the legislature's constitutional power. Denationalization could hardly be justified on grounds of rehabilitation since the provision amounted to excommunication from society and made the offender an outlaw. A deserter who was not deterred by the punishment of imprisonment or death was not likely to be swayed by the future penalty of expatriation. That left only the justification of retribution, which Brennan described as "naked vengeance," a statutory purpose, he concluded, beyond the war powers of Congress.[86]

Four years after *Trop*, the Court for the first time explicitly held the Eighth Amendment binding upon the states through the Fourteenth Amendment when it overturned the California conviction of Lawrence Robinson, who had been found guilty under a statute and jury instructions that made it criminal "either to use narcotics, or to be addicted to the use of narcotics."[87] California might constitutionally criminalize the purchase, sale, or possession of narcotics or anti-social behavior resulting from their use, Justice Potter Stewart wrote, and it might require compulsory treatment for addicts, but it could not, consistent with the Eighth Amendment, adopt a statutory provision that made the status of narcotic addiction a crime without any proof of use within the state or possession. To do so was the equivalent, Stewart wrote, of making it a criminal offense "for a person to be mentally ill, or a leper, or to be afflicted with a venereal disease."[88]

The *Robinson* case set the stage for Justice Arthur Goldberg's dissent from the Court's denial of certiorari in the 1963 case of Frank Lee Rudolph, an African American convicted and sentenced to death in Alabama for the rape of a white woman. Rudolph's lawyers had attempted without success to have his conviction overturned by the Alabama supreme court on the grounds that his confession had been coerced and that significant racial disparities existed in Alabama between African American and white males convicted of the same crime.[89] Joined by Justices Douglas and Brennan, Goldberg restated a position he had outlined in an earlier memorandum to the other justices asking them to consider the Eighth Amendment implications of the death penalty.[90]

Goldberg's dissent in *Rudolph v. Alabama* focused narrowly, however, on the crime of rape (**Document 2.9**). The Court, Goldberg wrote, should consider whether the Eighth and the Fourteenth Amendments permitted the death penalty for a convicted rapist who had neither taken nor endangered human life. Noting that thirty-three states had abolished the death penalty for the offense, Goldberg wanted the Court to determine whether the punishment for rape violated "evolving standards of decency . . . or standards of decency more or less universally accepted," language that drew upon *Trop* and Frankfurter's concurrence in the Willie Francis case. The Court should also decide, he wrote, whether capital punishment employed to protect "a value other than human life" constituted punishment "greatly disproportioned to the offense charged," and whether death as opposed to lesser punishments for rape constituted "unnecessary cruelty."[91]

By raising the Eighth Amendment question with respect to rape, the trio of Goldberg, Douglas, and Brennan invited anti–death penalty advocates to launch a frontal assault on the death penalty. But the majority of the justices on the Warren Court, often led by Justice Stewart, remained far more cautious and inclined to chip away at the death penalty through procedural rulings that resembled the Court's other criminal justice landmarks. Even on this level of intervention into state criminal procedures, the Court faced determined resistance from Justice Harlan, who carried forward the torch of judicial restraint and rigid federalism articulated by the now-departed Frankfurter. In 1967 *Spencer v. Texas* exposed these divisions when the justices had their first encounter with the issue of a unitary criminal trial where juries determined both guilt and sentencing in a single proceeding, an issue that soon became central to death penalty litigation.[92]

Stewart Spencer had been convicted and sentenced to death under Texas' habitual-criminal statute, which at the time of his trial permitted evidence of prior convictions to be introduced before jury deliberations, albeit with instructions from the court that such matters were not to be taken into account in assessing the defendant's guilt or innocence. Texas, along with several other states, subsequently revised its repeat offender statute to provide for a second-stage jury deliberation where evidence of prior convictions could be considered with respect to the enhancement of punishment. Harlan and the majority sustained the old statute on the grounds that the unitary procedure did not violate the due process clause, although it presented some danger that despite court instructions to the contrary a jury might be swayed to a guilty verdict by the introduction of evidence concerning prior offenses.

The Fourteenth Amendment, Harlan wrote, echoing Cardozo and Frankfurter, guaranteed only "fairness in a criminal trial," but "has never been thought [to] establish this Court as a rule-making organ for the promulgation of state rules of criminal procedure." A two-stage jury trial that separated guilt from the question of enhanced punishment might be more desirable, but to compel this standard as a matter of constitutional law would dictate "substantial changes in trial procedure in countless local courts around the country" and would constitute "a wholly unjustifiable encroachment by this Court upon the constitutional powers of States to promulgate their own rules of evidence to try their own state-created crimes in their own state court."[93]

Warren's dissent, joined by Justices Abe Fortas, Brennan, and Douglas, found a clear violation of due process in the Texas statute that, they argued, inevitably tipped the scales in favor of a defendant's guilt, contrary to the purpose and justification of all recidivist statutes previously sustained by the Court. Brennan and Douglas would have overturned the convictions and sentences and, in addition, made the ruling retroactive.[94] Although *Spencer* technically concerned only a habitual-offender statute, it would soon play a decisive role in broader capital-sentencing cases.

Although he reluctantly joined Harlan's opinion in *Spencer,* Justice Stewart soon broke ranks and advanced the procedural attack on the death penalty in the 1968 case *United States v. Jackson*.[95] By then, five years after *Rudolph*, Goldberg had resigned from the Court to accept appointment as U.S. ambassador to the United Nations, thereby reducing the liberal wing on the Warren Court and making Stewart the important swing vote. The defendants in *Jackson* had been indicted under the Federal Kidnapping Act, which provided the death penalty if the kidnap victim had been injured and the defendant opted for a jury trial and was found guilty without a recommendation of mercy. A defendant who pled guilty avoided a possible death sentence. The federal district court had quashed the indictment and declared the entire statute unconstitutional on the grounds that it coerced defendants to plead guilty and to forgo their Sixth Amendment right to a jury trial.

Like rape, kidnapping that did not result in the taking of life raised the Eighth Amendment question of proportionality and "unnecessary cruelty" that the Goldberg dissent urged the Court to examine. Justice Stewart's opinion for the Court in *Jackson,* however, tacked closely to the district court procedural rationale by finding the death penalty clause unconstitutional on Sixth Amendment grounds, but saving the remainder of the federal kidnapping statute on grounds that other sections did not pose constitutional problems.[96]

The Court's narrow procedural assault on the death penalty continued a few months later in *Witherspoon v. Illinois,* with Justice Stewart again writing for the majority.[97] William Witherspoon had been convicted of the murder of a policeman in the course of a robbery and sentenced to death by a jury under an Illinois statutory provision that permitted the prosecution to exclude from the jury "any juror who . . . has conscientious scruples against capital punishment, or . . . is opposed to the same."[98] Prosecutors eliminated for cause nearly half the pool of prospective jurors who expressed doubts about capital punishment, without any inquiry whether such doubts would automatically dispose them to vote against death. On his fourth appeal following conviction, Witherspoon's lawyers, Thomas Sullivan and Albert Jenner Jr., first challenged the impartiality of the jury, a claim rejected by the Illinois supreme court.

Justice Stewart and a majority of the Court saw the issue differently. Putting aside the question of Witherspoon's guilt, Stewart focused only on the penalty decision by noting that Illinois law gave juries the authority to determine life or death in a capital case, discretion that made them "the conscience of the community," the basic link between "contemporary community values and the penal system," without which punishment could not reflect "the evolving standards of decency that mark the progress of a maturing society."

Stewart then cited recent public opinion polls indicating a narrow plurality opposed to capital punishment and highlighted the fact that only a single execution had taken place in the United States in 1966 to drive home his point: the Illinois statute "culled . . . all who harbor doubts about the wisdom of capital punishment," creating a jury that could "speak only for a distinct and dwindling minority." Stewart and the majority made the ruling on sentencing retroactive over the state's objections and condemned Illinois for sanctioning "a hanging jury" that "stacked the deck" against Witherspoon. The opinion also made it clear, however, that Illinois and other states could exclude jurors who would automatically vote against the death penalty or jurors whose attitude toward it would prevent them from making an impartial decision about a defendant's guilt.[99] These exceptions made it possible for prosecutors to still fill the jury box with members very likely to impose death, what critics called "death qualified" juries.

Douglas, writing separately, questioned the separation of guilt from punishment and argued that the majority had defeated its avowed purpose of guaranteeing a jury that reflected "the conscience of the community" by continuing to sanction the exclusion of those who fundamentally opposed capital punishment. "I see no constitutional basis for excluding those who are so opposed to capital punishment that they would never inflict it on a defendant. Exclusion of them means the selection of jurors who are either protagonists of the death penalty or neutral concerning it. That results in a systematic exclusion of qualified groups, and the deprivation to the accused of a cross-section of the community for decision on both his guilt and his punishment."[100] Despite its procedural limitations, *Witherspoon* had the largest impact on the death penalty prior to *Furman*. As a result of the decision, more than 350 inmates, including Witherspoon, saw their sentences reversed (**Document 2.10**).

The dissenters in *Witherspoon,* led by Black and White, chided the majority for not directly holding capital punishment unconstitutional, but, as Black put it, "making it impossible for States to get juries that will enforce the death penalty." The majority's "fine line" between jurors with "conscientious or religious scruples" against the death penalty and those who would "automatically vote against" created only a "semantic illusion" that would not produce significantly different juries from Witherspoon's and would put the states to a great deal of legislative effort for nothing.[101] Justice White argued that he saw no difference between a state law that mandated death for specific crimes, which he presumed would be constitutional, and the Illinois law that tipped the scales in favor of jurors who would impose death more often than a group chosen differently.[102]

Despite Justice Black's fears, *Witherspoon* demonstrated how a major Court ruling on capital punishment did not become suddenly operational at the level of judicial compliance by lower courts, especially at the state level where most death sentences were imposed. Jurors who expressed conscientious or religious scruples against capital punishment could not be excluded, the justices held, unless they clearly stated that their views would prevent them from imposing the penalty without regard to any evidence in the case before them, or that their views would prevent them from making an impartial decision with respect to the defendant's guilt. Lower federal courts and several state supreme courts, notably California's, complied with the decision fully by requiring an unambiguous declaration by jurors with respect to the two exemptions before allowing prosecutors to exclude them.[103]

Other state courts, however, including the Illinois supreme court, resisted and frustrated compliance with the *Witherspoon* ruling through a variety of devices that allowed death qualified juries to continue to send defendants to their doom. The Illinois supreme court simply ignored the two exceptions outlined by Stewart and the requirement that each juror satisfy the test unambiguously during the questioning of proposed jurors. It instead adopted a "fair atmosphere" standard that deemphasized the relevance of individual questioning.[104] Other states continued to apply state statutory requirements in lieu of *Witherspoon,* adopted "harmless error" rules when only individual jurors were excluded in violation of the Court's standard, or, like the Arkansas supreme court, flatly rejected Stewart and the *Witherspoon* majority (**Document 2.11**).[105]

Witherspoon reverberated beyond the judicial system into the hall of academia. Stewart's opinion focused narrowly on the question of the death penalty and noted that the evidence concerning the impact of death qualified juries on the separate issues of guilt or innocence remained "too tentative and fragmentary" for decision. That part of the decision soon launched a minor academic industry in the social sciences by researchers who took up the Court's challenge and began to investigate the question *Witherspoon* left open: was a death qualified jury more likely to convict? Empirical studies on death qualified juries and deterrence began to play a significant role in shaping legal arguments regarding the efficacy and fairness of the death penalty. Many studies generated by *Witherspoon* indicated that prolonged exposure to discussion of the penalty at the outset of jury qualification inclined jurors to presume the defendant's guilt and increased both the likelihood of conviction and a willingness to vote for the death penalty.[106]

During Chief Justice Warren's last term in 1969, the justices avoided another substantive ruling on the death penalty. Edward Boykin Jr., a twenty-seven-year-old African American, had pleaded guilty to five counts of armed robbery and had been sentenced to death by an Alabama jury. On direct appeal to the Alabama supreme court, Boykin's lawyers argued that the penalty of death for common law robbery constituted cruel and unusual punishment. The state tribunal rejected this claim, although three of the justices argued in dissent that the trial record failed to demonstrate that Boykin had intelligently and knowingly entered his guilty plea. Led by Jack Greenberg and Anthony Amsterdam of the NAACP's Legal Defense Fund, which had filed a broad *amicus curiae* (friend of the court) brief in *Boykin v. Alabama* attacking use of the death penalty on grounds of the Eighth Amendment and racial discrimination (**Document 2.12**), Boykin and his lawyers chose not to highlight the pleas issue except during oral argument.[107] Justice Douglas and the majority nevertheless seized on it to reverse Boykin's conviction and to compel the states to follow the federal rule of criminal procedure, which required judges to fully inform a defendant about the consequences of a guilty plea. This now became for state courts a constitutional requirement of due process.[108]

Several months after agreeing to hear *Boykin*, the justices also granted certiorari in another Arkansas case, *Maxwell v. Bishop*. The case was limited to two specific questions: Did the state's practice of allowing juries absolute discretion to impose the death penalty violate the Fourteenth Amendment? And, did the state's single-verdict procedure, requiring the jury to find both guilt and fix the sentence, violate the Fifth and Fourteenth Amendments by forcing the defendant to choose between presenting mitigating evidence on the punishment issue or maintaining his privilege against self-incrimination on the question of guilt?[109] William Maxwell, an African American, had been convicted of rape without a jury recommendation of life imprisonment and sentenced to death by the trial court. The NAACP's Amsterdam argued *Maxwell* on the same day he argued *Boykin*, supported by amicus briefs from the American Civil Liberties Union, the Synagogue Council of America, the American Friends Service Committee, and a group of distinguished lawyers that included William T. Coleman, Samuel Dash, Burke Marshall, Whitney North Seymour, and Cyrus Vance (**Document 2.13**). All hoped that *Maxwell* would begin to fulfill the promise of Goldberg's dissent in *Rudolph* by becoming a vehicle for an important substantive ruling on the death penalty.

Those hopes were dashed, however, when two members of the Court, Thurgood Marshall and Harry Blackmun, did not participate in the decision. Marshall had long represented the Legal Defense Fund, while Blackmun, the newest justice, had written the opinion at the Eighth Circuit Court of Appeals rejecting Maxwell's habeas corpus claims, the most important of which had focused on racial disparities in sentencing involving black-on-white rape cases.[110] A divided seven-member Court therefore elected to avoid a ruling on the two questions originally presented and to send the case back to the federal district court for consideration of an issue not previously raised: Had jury selection in *Maxwell* offended the *Witherspoon* rule by excluding those who expressed conscientious or religious scruples against the death penalty? Justice Black, still opposed to the result in *Witherspoon,* dissented from the solution offered by the majority in an unsigned opinion. At the same time, however, the justices announced that the two questions not addressed would be considered soon in *McGautha v. California* and *Crampton v. Ohio,* both set for argument in the fall of 1970.

The Court Retreats

When the *McGautha* and *Crampton* cases finally came down in the spring of 1971, they marked an abrupt retreat from the death penalty jurisprudence that had distinguished the Court's progress since Goldberg's dissent in *Rudolph.*[111] Both defendants had been convicted and sentenced to death under statutes in California and Ohio that gave broad discretion to juries to decide guilt and fix the punishment at either death or life imprisonment. The Ohio law empowered the jury to make those decisions in a single verdict. It also barred the defendant, James Edward Crampton, from offering any testimony regarding mitigating circumstances unless he chose to testify in his own defense, which exposed him to cross-examination about past criminal convictions. Dennis McGautha had been sentenced to death by the same California jury in a separate penalty proceeding where mitigating evidence had been permitted.

Two old antagonists, Justices Black and Harlan, each sitting in his final term, led the majority in sustaining both convictions and sentences against claims that the unguided jury discretion in both cases deprived McGautha and Crampton of due process of law. Crampton specifically challenged the Ohio statute on the grounds that it violated his Fifth and Fourteenth Amendment rights against compulsory self-incrimination by denying him the opportunity to offer mitigating testimony during the trial that combined guilt and punishment. Long a biting critic of the due process analysis favored by Frankfurter and Harlan, Black nonetheless concurred in the latter's opinion for the Court, which rang all the traditional due process and federalism bells to conclude that any attempt to require explicit statutory governing standards for juries in capital cases would be a deadly assault on the sovereignty of the states. "Our function," wrote Harlan, "is not to impose on the States, ex cathedra [with full authority], what might seem to us a better system for dealing with capital cases. Rather, it is to decide whether the Federal Constitution proscribes the present procedures of these two States in such cases."[112]

The new chief justice, Warren Burger, who had been nominated by President Richard Nixon and was a vocal critic of many Warren Court decisions, joined the majority, as did his Minnesota colleague, Blackmun, who had not participated in *Maxwell*. Justice White, a dissenter in *Jackson* and *Witherspoon*, predictably sided with Harlan. The surprise vote for the majority came from Justice Stewart, who had authored the majority opinions in both *Jackson* and *Witherspoon*.

Harlan interpreted the discretionary capital sentencing statutes as an example of the progressive and enlightened development of the law from the days when the death penalty had been mandatory in many cases. Stealing a page from Stewart's opinion in *Witherspoon*, where he had dissented, Harlan also claimed that absolute jury discretion guaranteed that punishment would be inflicted consistent with the conscience of the community. Finally, he argued that any attempt to develop governing standards in such cases would be doomed to frustration and failure. "To identify before the facts those characteristics of criminal homicide and their perpetrators which call for the death penalty," Harlan wrote, "and to express these characteristics in language which can be fairly understood and applied by the sentencing authority, appears to be tasks which are beyond present human ability."[113]

Harlan disposed of the Fifth Amendment claim raised in *Crampton* by noting that Crampton retained the customary common law right of allocution to speak to the court prior to sentencing, which guaranteed he would not be tried, convicted, and sentenced to death "in complete silence." Black simply reminded everyone that the due process clause did not empower the justices to reverse criminal convictions because of personal beliefs that certain procedures were "unfair," "arbitrary," or "shocking to the conscience." Moreover, both the due process clause and the Eighth Amendment could not be vehicles for overturning the death penalty on constitutional grounds. The former assumed its existence; the latter had been adopted by the first Congress when the penalty had been in common use and authorized by law.[114]

Justice Douglas focused his dissent on unitary trial procedure in the Ohio statute and its violation of the prohibition against self-incrimination. The trial judge in Crampton's case instructed the jury that they "must not be influenced by any consideration of sympathy or prejudice . . . so that the State of Ohio and the defendant will feel that their case was fairly and impartially tried." That instruction tipped the scales against Crampton because his right of making a statement before sentencing, emphasized by Harlan and the majority, could occur only after the jury's verdict of death had been rendered. "If the right to be heard were to be meaningful," Douglas wrote, "it would have to accrue before sentencing; yet . . . any attempt on the part of the accused during the trial to say why the judgment of death should not be pronounced against him entails a surrender of his right against self-incrimination."[115]

By 1970 Justice Brennan had become the acknowledged leader of the Court's liberal wing. During the Warren years he had written many of the Court's memorable majority opinions on issues ranging from freedom of speech to reapportionment.[116] His dissent in *McGautha* was a masterpiece that attacked both Harlan's opinion on grounds of its departure from established due process requirements and its pessimism concerning the possibility of articulating standards for capital sentencing (**Document 2.14**). By sustaining the unguided discretion of juries, Brennan suggested, the majority had declared that the rule of law and the power of the state to kill remained in irreconcilable conflict. He rejected that conclusion and its corollary, that "the 50 States are so devoid of wisdom and the power of rational thought that they are unable to face the problem of capital punishment directly, and to determine for themselves the criteria under which convicted felons should be chosen to live or die."[117]

Across a wide range of constitutional issues, Brennan pointed out, the Court had historically insisted on clear statutory guidelines as a fundamental component of due process of law. Many state criminal laws had been struck down on grounds of vagueness or overbreadth. Others had fallen because the statutes vested too much discretion in particular officials wielding power. When Congress delegated authority to the president and other executive branch officials on economic matters, the justices had insisted on an explicit statement of legislative objectives and the standards to be applied. The entire body of federal and state administrative law from public utilities to environmental policy did not leave regulators at sea without articulated legislative goals and objectives. Without such statutory standards, Brennan noted, judicial review over the exercises of state power became virtually impossible. Why should the state's power to kill be subject to a lower due process requirement than its power to take property or regulate other aspects of social life? Brennan concluded: "We are not presented with the slightest attempt to bring the power of reason to bear on the considerations relevant to capital sentencing. We are faced with nothing more than stark legislative abdication. Not once in the history of this Court, until today, have we sustained against a due process challenge such an unguided, unbridled, unreviewable exercise of naked power."[118]

McGautha and *Crampton* appeared to bury any hope that the Court would mandate further limits on capital punishment even as public opinion appeared to turn against the practice. No executions had taken place since that of Luis Jose Monge in Colorado in 1967. Brennan's powerful dissent offered a framework with respect to the setting of capital sentencing standards, preparing the ground for another day. Then, barely a month after *McGautha* was handed down, the justices granted certiorari in five capital cases from Georgia, Texas, and California. Three involved homicide and two involved rape.[119] In *Furman v. Georgia, Jackson v. Georgia, Branch v. Texas,* and *Aikens v. California,* the grant of review was limited to the question whether "the imposition and carrying out of the death penalty in [these cases] constitutes cruel and unusual punishment in violation of the Eighth and Fourteenth Amendments."[120]

McGautha, of course, had not addressed the Eighth Amendment question. But at least one member of that majority, either White or Stewart, must have voted with the dissenters to accept review of the five cases. Two months later, in 1971, illness and death itself added another unexpected twist to these developments. Justice Black, felled by a stroke, entered Bethesda Naval Hospital on August 28, announced his retirement two weeks later, and died on September 25. Justice Harlan, author of *McGautha,* nearly blind and suffering from spinal cancer, had stepped down from the Court two days before Black passed away and died on December 29. In consequence, two of the most stalwart defenders of the death penalty in *McGautha* were no longer on the Court by the time the justices heard argument in three of the five cases on January 17, 1972. Although their replacements, Lewis Powell and William Rehnquist, nominated by Nixon and confirmed by the Senate, were not likely to immediately shift the balance of power on the Burger Court, the Court's chemistry had nevertheless significantly changed, and with it the fate of capital punishment. Moreover, at about the same time the respected California supreme court had under consideration the question of whether the state's death penalty statute violated California's constitutional provision prohibiting "cruel or unusual punishment."[121]

Furman, therefore, would be decided in a legal environment that differed starkly from that in existence at the time of the *McGautha* decision. The landmark decision of capital punishment and the Supreme Court that *Furman* became merits separate attention in the next chapter.

Document 2.1
Hollace Ransdell Reports for the ACLU on the Scottsboro, Alabama Case, May 1931

Hollace Ransdell, a young teacher, reporter, and social activist, went to Scottsboro, Alabama, in early May 1931 on behalf of the American Civil Liberties Union to investigate the first trial of the Scottsboro defendants. She spent ten days in the area where the trial took place, interviewing many of the participants in the trial and other residents. She filed this report on the conclusion of the trial.

. . . The first case went to the jury Tuesday afternoon at 3 o'clock, and a verdict calling for the death penalty was returned in less than two hours. The Judge had previously warned the courtroom that no demonstration must be staged when the verdict was announced. In spite of this the room resounded with loud applause, and the mass of people outside, when the news spread to them, cheered wildly.

The next day, Wednesday, April 8, Haywood Patterson . . . 18 years old, was tried alone, as the second case. In three hours the jury returned with the death penalty verdict. It was met with silence in the courtroom.

In the third case, five of the six remaining boys were tried: Olin Montgomery . . . 17 years old, and nearly blind; Andy Wright . . . 18 years old; Eugene Williams . . . 15 years old; Willie Robeson . . . 17 years old; Ozie Powell . . . 16 years old.

It was brought out in this trial that Willie Robeson was suffering from a bad case of venereal disease, which would have made it painful, if not impossible for him to have committed the act of which he was accused. The case went to the jury at 4 p.m. on Wednesday, April 8, and early Thursday morning, the jury again turned in the verdict calling for the death penalty, received without demonstration in court.

Judge Hawkins proceeded at once after the convictions returned against the five Negroes in the third case, to pronounce the death sentence on the eight who had been tried. He set the day of execution for July 10, the earliest date he was permitted to name under the law, which requires that 90 days be allowed for filing an appeal of a case.

In three days' time, eight Negro boys all under 21, four of them under 18 and two of them sixteen or under, were hurried through trials which conformed only in outward appearance to the letter of the law. Given no chance to communicate with their parents and without even as much as the sight of one friendly face, these eight boys, little more than children, surrounded entirely by white hatred and blind, venomous prejudice, were sentenced to be killed in the electric chair at the earliest possible moment permitted by law. It is no exaggeration certainly to call this a legal lynching.

The most shameful of the cases was left to the last. This was the trial of fourteen-year-old Roy Wright, of Chattanooga, a young brother of another of the defendants. Perhaps because of his youthfulness, the white authorities who had him at their mercy, seemed to be even more vicious in their attitude toward him than toward the older defendants. They may unconsciously have been trying to cover up a sense of uneasiness at what they were doing to a child. Several of the authorities at the trial assured me that he was really the worst of the lot and deserved no lenience on account of his youth. But for the sake of outside public opinion, the State decided to ask for life imprisonment instead of the death penalty, in view of the youth of the defendant.

At two o'clock on the afternoon of Thursday, April 9, the jury announced that they were dead-locked and could not agree on a verdict [for Wright]. Eleven of them stood for the death penalty and one for life imprisonment. Judge Hawkins declared a mistrial, and the child was ordered back to jail to await another ordeal at a later date. He is now in the Birmingham jail. The other eight defendants were kept a short time also in Birmingham, and then moved to Kilby prison, about four miles from Montgomery. I visited them there in their cells in the death row on May 12, locked up two together in a cell, frightened children caught in a terrible trap without understanding what it is all about.

Source: Hollace Ransdell, "Report on the Scottsboro, Alabama Case for the American Civil Liberties Union, May 27, 1931," unpublished. Full report available at the Famous Trials Web site created by Prof. Douglas O. Linder at www.law.umkc.edu/faculty/projects/FTrials/scottsboro/Scottsbororeport.pdf.

Document 2.2
Justice George Sutherland Rules on the Denial of the Right of Counsel in *Powell v. Alabama*, November 7, 1932

In the first Scottsboro *case, known as* Powell v. Alabama *(1932), the Supreme Court reversed the convictions and death sentences of young African American defendants who had been charged with rape.*

MR. JUSTICE SUTHERLAND delivered the opinion of the Court.

It thus will be seen that until the very morning of the trial no lawyer had been named or definitely designated to represent the defendants. Prior to that time, the trial judge had "appointed all the members of the bar" for the limited "purpose of arraigning the defendants." Whether they would represent the defendants thereafter if no counsel appeared in their behalf, was a matter of speculation only, or, as the judge indicated, of mere anticipation on the part of the court. Such a designation, even if made for all purposes, would, in our opinion, have fallen far short of meeting, in any proper sense, a requirement for the appointment of counsel. How many lawyers were members of the bar does not appear; but, in the very nature of things, whether many or few, they would not, thus collectively named, have been given that clear appreciation or responsibility or impressed with that individual sense of duty which should and naturally would accompany the appointment of a selected member of the bar, specifically named and assigned.

That this action of the trial judge in respect to appointment of counsel was little more than an expansive gesture, imposing no substantial or definite obligation upon any one. . . . In any event, the circumstance lends emphasis to the conclusion that during perhaps the most critical period of the proceedings against these defendants, that is to say, from the time of their arraignment until the beginning of their trial, when consultation, thoroughgoing investigation and preparation were vitally important, the defendants did not have the aid of counsel in any real sense, although they were as much entitled to such aid during that period as at the trial itself. . . .

With this dubious understanding, the trials immediately proceeded. The defendants, young, ignorant, illiterate, surrounded by hostile sentiment, haled back and forth under guard of soldiers, charged with an atrocious crime regarded with especial horror in the community where they were to be tried, were thus put in peril of their lives within a few moments after counsel for the first time charged with any degree of responsibility began to represent them. . . .

Under the circumstances disclosed, we hold that defendants were not accorded the right of counsel in any substantial sense. To decide otherwise, would simply be to ignore actualities. . . .

The Sixth Amendment, in terms, provides that in all criminal prosecutions the accused shall enjoy the right "to have the assistance of counsel for his defense." In the fact of the reasoning of the *Hurtado* case, if it stood alone, it would be difficult to justify the conclusion that the right to counsel, being thus specifically granted by the Sixth Amendment, was also within the intendment of the due process clause. But the *Hurtado* case does not stand alone. . . . This court has considered that freedom of speech and of the press are rights protected by the due process clause of the Fourteenth Amendment, although in the First Amendment, Congress is prohibited in specific terms from abridging the right.

These later cases establish that notwithstanding the sweeping character of the language in the *Hurtado* case, the rule laid down is not without exception. The rule is an aid to construction, and in some instances may be conclusive; but it must yield to more compelling considerations whenever such considerations exist. The fact that the right involved is of such a character that it cannot be denied without violating those "fundamental principles of liberty and justice which lie at the base of all our civil and political institutions," is obviously one of those compelling considerations which must prevail in determining whether it is embraced within the due process clause of the Fourteenth Amendment, although it be specifically dealt with in another part of the federal Constitution. . . .

In light of the facts outlined—the ignorance and illiteracy of the defendants, their youth, the circumstances of public hostility, the imprisonment and the close surveillance of the defendants by the military forces, the fact that their friends and families were all in other states and communication with them necessarily difficult, and above all that they stood in deadly peril of their lives—we think the failure of the trial court to give them reasonable time and opportunity to secure counsel was clear denial of due process.

But passing that, and assuming their inability, even if opportunity had been given, to employ counsel, as the trial court evidently did assume, we are of the opinion that, under the circumstances just stated . . . the failure of the trial court to make an effective appointment of counsel was likewise a denial of due process within the meaning of the Fourteenth Amendment. Whether this would be so in other criminal prosecutions, or under other circumstances, we need not determine. All that it is necessary now to decide, as we do decide, is that in a capital case, where the defendant is unable to employ counsel, and is incapable adequately of making his own defense because of ignorance, feeble mindedness, illiteracy, or the like, it is the duty of the court, whether requested or not, to assign counsel for him as a necessary requisite of due process of law; and that duty is not discharged by an assignment at such a time or under such circumstances as to preclude the giving of effective aid in the preparation and trial of the case. . . .

Source: *Powell v. Alabama*, 287 U.S. 45 (1932), at 57–59, 66–72.

Document 2.3
Chief Justice Charles Evans Hughes, in *Norris v. Alabama*, Discusses the Exclusion of African Americans from Juries, April 1, 1935

In the second Scottsboro *case,* Norris v. Alabama *(1935), the Supreme Court reversed the defendants' convictions and death sentences on grounds that the systematic exclusion of African Americans from the grand and petit juries had denied them equal protection of the law.*

CHIEF JUSTICE HUGHES delivered the opinion of the Court.

. . . Defendant adduced evidence to support the charge of unconstitutional discrimination in the actual administration of the statute in Jackson County. The testimony, as the state court said, tended to show that "in a long number of years no negro had been called for jury service in that county." It appeared that no Negro had served on any grand or petit jury in that county within the memory of witnesses who had lived there all their lives. . . . Their testimony was uncontradicted. . . . The court reporter, who had not missed a session in that county in twenty-four years, and two jury commissioners testified to the same effect. One of the latter, who was a member of the commission which made up the jury roll for the grand jury which found the indictment, testified that he had "never known a single instance where any negro sat on any grand or petit jury in the entire history of that county." . . .

The population of Morgan County, where the trial was had, was larger than that of Jackson County, and the proportion of Negroes was much greater. . . .

Within the memory of witnesses, long resident there, no Negro had ever served on a jury in that county or had been called for such service. . . . Their testimony was not contradicted. A clerk of the circuit court, who had resided in the county for thirty years, and who had been in office for over four years . . . did not recall "ever seeing any single person of the colored race serve on any jury in Morgan County." . . .

In *Neal v. Delaware,* supra, decided over fifty years ago, this Court observed that it was a "violent presumption," in which the state court had there indulged, that the uniform exclusion of Negroes from juries, during a period of many years, was solely because, in the judgment of officers, charged with the selection of grand and petit jurors, fairly exercised, "the black race in Delaware were utterly disqualified by want of intelligence, experience, or moral integrity to sit on juries." Such a presumption at the present time would be no less violent with respect to the exclusion of the Negroes of Morgan County. And, upon the proof contained in the record now before us, a conclusion that their continuous and total exclusion from juries was because there were none possessing the requisite qualifications, cannot be sustained.

We are concerned only with the federal question which we have discussed, and in view of the denial of the federal right suitably asserted, the judgment must be reversed and the cause remanded for further proceedings not inconsistent with this opinion.

It is so ordered.

Source: Norris v. Alabama, 294 U.S. 587 (1935), at 591–592, 596–597, 599.

Document 2.4
Chief Justice Charles Evans Hughes Rules on the Inadmissibility of Coerced Confessions in State Criminal Trials, February 17, 1936

In Brown v. Mississippi *(1936), the Hughes Court again expanded upon the meaning of due process in the Fourteenth Amendment when it ruled that confessions secured by violence and physical torture were inadmissible in a state criminal trial. The ruling voided the death sentences of three African Americans.*

CHIEF JUSTICE HUGHES delivered the opinion of the Court.

The question in this case is whether convictions, which rest solely upon confessions shown to have been extorted by officers of the State by brutality and violence are consistent with the due process of law required by the Fourteenth Amendment of the Constitution of the United States. . . .

The opinion of the state court did not set forth the evidence as to the circumstances in which the confessions were procured. That the evidence established that they were procured by coercion was not questioned. . . . There is no dispute as to the facts upon this point and as they are clearly and adequately stated in the dissenting opinion of Judge Griffith . . . showing both the extreme brutality of the measures to extort the confessions and the participation of the state authorities, we quote this part of his opinion in full, as follows:

"The crime with which these defendants, all ignorant negroes, are charged, was discovered about 1 o'clock p.m. on Friday, March 30, 1934. On that night one Dial, a deputy sheriff, accompanied by others, came to the home of Ellington, one of the defendants. . . . [T]hey seized him, and with the participation of the deputy they hanged him by a rope to the limb of a tree, and having let him down, they hung him again, and when he was let down the second time, and he still protested his innocence, he was tied to a tree and whipped. . . . A day or two thereafter the said deputy, accompanied by another, returned to the home of the said defendant and arrested him, and departed with the prisoner towards the jail in an adjoining county, but went by a route which led into the State of Alabama; and while on the way, in that state, the deputy stopped again and severely whipped the defendant, declaring that he would continue the whipping until he confessed and the defendant then agreed to confess to such a statement as the deputy would dictate, and he did so, after which he was delivered to jail.

"The two other defendants, Ed Brown and Henry Shields, were also arrested and taken to the same jail. . . . [T]he two last named defendants were made to strip and they were laid over chairs and their backs were cut to pieces with a leather strap with buckles on it . . . and in this manner the defendants confessed the crime, and as the whippings progressed and were repeated, they changed or adjusted their confessions in all particular of details so as to confirm to the demands of their torturers. . . .

"This deputy was put on the stand by the state in rebuttal and admitted the whippings . . . and in response to the inquiry as to how severely he was whipped, the deputy stated, 'Not too much for a negro; not as much as I would have done if it were left to me.'" . . .

It would be difficult to conceive of methods more revolting to the sense of justice than those taken to procure the confessions of these petitioners, and the use of the confessions thus obtained as the basis for conviction and sentence was a clear denial of due process. . . .

Source: Brown v. Mississippi, 297 U.S. 278 (1936), at 281–286.

Document 2.5
The Supreme Court Applies the Sixth Amendment's Confrontation Clause to the States through the Fourteenth Amendment, January 8, 1934

Herman Snyder, sentenced to death in Massachusetts for his role in a gas station robbery and murder, challenged his conviction on the grounds that he had been excluded by the trial judge from the crime scene when the jury, prosecutors, and his defense lawyers visited the site in the course of the trial. A third defendant testified for the state against Snyder and escaped the death penalty. Snyder disputed that testimony and claimed that he had not been the one to fire the fatal shot. His exclusion from the crime view, he argued, denied him the constitutional right to confront his accusers, protected by the Sixth Amendment and incorporated within the Fourteenth Amendment's due process clause. Writing for the five-justice majority in Snyder v. Massachusetts, *Justice Benjamin Cardozo accepted part of this argument, but narrowed its application in Snyder's case to the cross-examination of witnesses, not his presence at every stage of the trial. Justice Owen Roberts dissented for himself and Justices Louis Brandeis, George Sutherland, and Pierce Butler.*

MR. JUSTICE CARDOZO delivered the opinion of the Court.

. . . At the opening of the trial, there was a motion by the Commonwealth that the jury be directed to view the scene of the crime. . . . Counsel for Snyder moved that his client be permitted to view the scene with the jury, invoking the protection of the federal constitution. This motion was denied. The jurors were then placed in charge of bailiffs duly sworn. Accompanied by these bailiffs and also by the judge, the court stenographer, the District Attorney, and the counsel for the defendants, they went forth to make their view. . . .

After the completion of the view, the group returned to the courthouse, and the trial went on. In charging the jury, the judge said, "Now what have you before you on which to form your judgment and to render your finding and your verdict? The view, the testimony given by the witnesses, and the exhibits comprise the evidence that is before you." The question in this court is whether a view in the absence of a defendant who has made a demand that he be present is a denial of due process under the Fourteenth Amendment. . . .

We assume in aid of the petitioner that, in a prosecution for a felony, the defendant has the privilege under the Fourteenth Amendment to be present in his own person whenever his presence has a relation, reasonably substantial, to the fullness of his opportunity to defend against the charge. Thus, the privilege to confront one's accusers and cross-examine them face to face is assured to a defendant by the Sixth Amendment in prosecutions in the federal courts. . . . For present purposes, we assume that the privilege is reinforced by the Fourteenth Amendment, though this has not been squarely held. . . . Nowhere in the decisions of this court is there a dictum, and still less a ruling, that the Fourteenth Amendment assures the privilege of presence when presence would be useless, or the benefit but a shadow. . . . Confusion will result again if the privilege of presence be identified with the privilege of confrontation, which is limited to the stages of the trial when there are witnesses to be questioned. "It [the privilege] was intended to prevent the conviction of the accused upon depositions or ex parte affidavits, and particularly to preserve the right of the accused to test the recollections of the witness in the exercise of the right of cross-examination." . . .

The Fourteenth Amendment does not assure to a defendant the privilege to be present at such a time. There is nothing he could do if he were there, and almost nothing he could gain. The only shred of advantage would be to make certain that the jury had been brought to the right place, and had viewed the right scene. If he had any doubt about this, he could examine the bailiffs at the trial and learn what they had looked at. The risk that they would lie is no greater than the risk that attaches to testimony about anything. . . . There is no immutable principle of justice that secures protection to a defendant against so shadowy a risk. . . .

But here, in the case at hand, the privilege, if it exists, is not explicitly conferred, nor has the defendant been denied an opportunity to answer and defend. The Fourteenth Amendment has not said in so many words that he must be present every second or minute, or even every hour, of the trial. . . . Due process of law requires that the proceedings shall be fair, but fairness is a relative, not an absolute, concept. It is fairness with reference to particular conditions or particular results. . . .

To say that the defendant may be excluded from the scene if the court tells the jury that the view has no other function than to give them understanding of the evidence, but that there is an impairment of the constitutional privileges of a defendant thus excluded if the court tells the jury that the view is part of the evidence—to make the securities of the constitution depend upon such quiddities is to cheapen and degrade them. . . .

But justice, though due to the accused, is due to the accuser also. The concept of fairness must not be strained till it is narrowed to a filament. We are to keep the balance true. . . .

The judgment is

Affirmed.

MR. JUSTICE ROBERTS, dissenting.

. . . The concept of due process is not technical. Form is disregarded if substantial rights are preserved. In whatsoever proceeding, whether it affects property or liberty or life, the Fourteenth Amendment commands the observance of that standard of common fairness, the failure to observe which would offend men's sense of the decencies and proprieties of civilized life. It is fundamental that there can be no due process without reasonable notice and a fair hearing. . . .

Our traditions, the Bill of Rights of our federal and state constitutions, state legislation and the decisions of the courts of the nation and the states, unite in testimony that the privilege of the accused to be present throughout his trial is of the very essence of due process. The trial, as respects the prisoner's right of presence in the constitutional sense, does not include the formal procedure of indictment or preliminary steps antecedent to the hearing on the merits, or stages of the litigation after the rendition of the verdict, but does comprehend the inquiry by the ordained trier of fact from beginning to end. . . .

Accordingly, the courts have uniformly and invariably held that the Sixth Amendment, as respects federal trials, and the analogous declarations of right of the state constitutions touching trials in state courts, secure to the accused the privilege of presence at every state of his trial. This court has so declared. . . .

In light of the universal acceptance of this fundamental rule of fairness that the prisoner may be present throughout his trial, it is not a matter of assumption, but a certainty, that the Fourteenth Amendment guarantees the observance of the rule.

It has been urged that the prisoner's privilege of presence is for no other purpose than to safeguard his opportunity to cross-examine the adverse witnesses. But the privilege goes deeper than the mere opportunity to cross-examine, and secures his right to be present at every state of the trial. . . .

The accused cannot cross-examine his own witnesses. Will it be suggested that, for this reason, he may be excluded from the courtroom while they give their evidence? . . . The opportunity for cross-examination of witnesses is only one of many reasons for the defendant's presence throughout the trial. In no State save in the Commonwealth of Massachusetts, and in no cases save in those there recently decided, has the privilege or the fundamental nature of the right it preserves been questioned or denied. . . .

In this case, the view was a part of the trial. The jury were not sent to the scene in the custody of bailiffs who had no knowledge of the place or the circumstances of the crime. They were not instructed to view the premises so as to better understand the testimony. They went forth with the judge presiding, the stenographer officiating, the District Attorney and the counsel of the defendants. As has been shown, more than a mere view of the premises was had. Matters were called to the jury's attention in detail so that they could form judgments of distance, relative position, the alignment of objects, all having a crucial bearing upon the truthfulness of the testimony subsequently given. . . . Little wonder, in these circumstances, that the court felt it right to appoint the defendants' counsel to accompany the jury on the view. If the prisoners were entitled to this protection, by the same token, they were entitled themselves to be present.

I think that the petitioner was deprived of a constitutional right, and that the judgment should be reversed.

Source: Snyder v. Massachusetts, 291 U.S. 97 (1934), at 103, 105–107, 115–116, 122, 127–131, 137–138.

Document 2.6
Justice Benjamin Cardozo Rejects the Claim That the Double Jeopardy Clause Applies to the States through the Fourteenth Amendment, December 6, 1937

Frank Palka (misspelled in the official Supreme Court report as Palko), convicted of murder and sentenced to life in prison, was subjected to a second trial for the same offense in Connecticut under a state law that permitted the prosecution to appeal errors of law made by the trial judge. Palka was convicted again at his second trial, but then sentenced to death. He appealed, claiming the state law and the second trial violated the double jeopardy clause of the Fifth Amendment made applicable to the states by the Fourteenth Amendment. Over one dissent, Justice Cardozo and the Court rejected these claims in Palko v. Connecticut, *ruling that the Fourteenth Amendment incorporated only those rights "implicit in the concept of ordered liberty," principles of justice "so rooted in the traditions and conscience of our people as to be ranked as fundamental." Double jeopardy was not such a principle, nor, Cardozo added, was the right to trial by jury or indictment by grand jury.*

MR. JUSTICE CARDOZO delivered the opinion of the Court.

. . . The argument for appellant [Palka] is that whatever is forbidden by the Fifth Amendment is forbidden by the Fourteenth also. . . . To retry a defendant, though under one indictment and only one, subjects him, it is said, to double jeopardy in violation of the Fifth Amendment if the prosecution is one on behalf of the United States. From this the consequence is said to follow that there is a denial of life or liberty without due process of law, if the prosecution is one on behalf of the People of a State. . . .

Is double jeopardy in such circumstances, if double jeopardy it must be called, a denial of due process forbidden to the states? The tyranny of labels . . . must not lead us to leap to a conclusion that a word which in one set of facts may stand for oppression or enormity is of like effect in every other.

We have said that, in appellant's view, the Fourteenth Amendment is to be taken as embodying the prohibitions of the Fifth. His thesis is even broader. Whatever would be a violation of the original bill of rights (Amendments I to VIII) if done by the federal government is now equally unlawful by force of the Fourteenth Amendment if done by a state. There is no such general rule. . . .

On the other hand, the due process clause of the Fourteenth Amendment may make it unlawful for a state to abridge by its statutes the freedom of speech which the First Amendment safeguards against encroachment by Congress or the like freedom of the press, or the free exercise of religion, or the right of peaceable assembly, without which speech would be unduly trammeled, or the right of one accused of crime to the benefit of counsel. In these and other situations, immunities that are valid as against the federal government by force of the specific pledges of particular amendments have been found to be implicit in the concept of ordered liberty, and thus, through the Fourteenth Amendment, become valid as against the states. . . .

There emerges the perception of a rationalizing principle which gives to discrete instances a proper order and coherence. The right to trial by jury and the immunity from prosecution except as the result of an indictment may have value and importance. Even so, they are not of the very essence of a scheme of ordered liberty. To abolish them is not to violate a "principle of justice so rooted in the traditions and conscience of our people as to be ranked as fundamental." Few would be so narrow or provincial as to maintain that a fair and enlightened system of justice would be impossible without them. What is true of jury trials and indictments is true also, as the cases show, of the immunity from compulsory self-incrimination. This, too, might be lost, and justice still be done. . . .

Is that kind of double jeopardy to which the statute has subjected him a hardship so acute and shocking that our polity will not endure it? Does it violate those "fundamental principles of liberty and justice which lie at the base of all our civil and political institutions"? The answer surely must be "no." . . . There is here no seismic innovation. The edifice of justice stands, its symmetry, to many, greater than before.

2. The conviction of appellant is not in derogation of any privilege or immunities that belong to him as a citizen of the United States. There is argument in his behalf that the privileges and immunities clause of the Fourteenth Amendment as well as the due process clause has been flouted by the judgment. . . .

The judgment is affirmed.

Source: Palko v. Connecticut, 302 U.S. 319 (1937), at 322–325, 328.

Document 2.7
The Supreme Court on the Constitutionality of Sending Willie Francis Back to the Electric Chair, January 13, 1947

In January 1947, by a vote of 5–4 in the case of Louisiana ex rel. Francis v. Resweber, *the Court allowed the state of Louisiana to attempt a second electrocution of Willie Francis, a seventeen-year-old African American. The justices assumed that the first execution had failed due to a "mechanical failure" in the equipment, but later research determined that the executioner who pulled the switch had been intoxicated. The Court addressed the question of whether the second execution would deprive Francis of due process of law under the Fourteenth Amendment and whether the Fifth Amendment's prohibition on double jeopardy and the Eighth Amendment's ban on cruel and unusual punishment had been incorporated into that clause. The Court decided these questions against Francis, who was executed on the second attempt.*

MR. JUSTICE REED delivered the judgment of the Court in an opinion in which CHIEF JUSTICE VINSON, MR. JUSTICE BLACK and MR. JUSTICE JACKSON joined.

. . . By the applications the petitioner claimed the protection of the due process clause of the Fourteenth Amendment on the ground that an execution under the circumstances detailed would deny due process to him because of the double jeopardy provision of the Fifth Amendment and the cruel and unusual punishment provision of the Eighth Amendment. . . .

To determine whether or not the execution of the petitioner may fairly take place after the experience through which he passed, we shall examine the circumstances under the assumption, but without so deciding, that violation of the principles of the Fifth and Eighth Amendments, as to double jeopardy and cruel and unusual punishment, would be violative of the due process clause of the Fourteenth Amendment. . . .

As this is a prosecution under state law, so far as double jeopardy is concerned, the Palko case is decisive. For we see no difference from a constitutional point of view between a new trial for error of law at the instance of the state that results in a death sentence instead of imprisonment for life and an execution that follows a failure of equipment. . . . We find no double jeopardy here which can be said to amount to a denial of federal due process in the proposed execution.

Second. We find nothing in what took place here which amounts to cruel and unusual punishment in the constitutional sense. The case before us does not call for an examination into any punishment except that of death. The traditional humanity of modern Anglo-American law forbids the infliction of unnecessary pain in the execution of the death sentence. . . . Even the fact that petitioner has already been subjected to a current of electricity does not make his subsequent execution any more cruel in the constitutional sense than any other execution. The cruelty against which the Constitution protects a convicted man is cruelty inherent in the method of punishment, not the necessary suffering involved in any method employed to extinguish life humanely. The fact that an unforeseeable accident prevented the prompt consummation of the sentence cannot, it seems to us, add an element of cruelty to a subsequent execution. There is no purpose to inflict unnecessary pain nor any unnecessary pain involved in the proposed execution. . . .

There is nothing in any of these papers to show any violation of petitioner's constitutional rights. . . .

MR. JUSTICE FRANKFURTER, concurring.

. . . The Fourteenth Amendment placed no specific restraints upon the States in the formulation of the administration of their criminal law. It restricted the freedom of the States generally, so that States thereafter could not "abridge the privileges or immunities of citizens of the United States," or "deprive any person of life, liberty, or property, without due process of law," or "deny to any person within its jurisdiction the equal protection of the laws."

These are broad, inexplicit clauses of the Constitution, unlike specific provisions of the first eight amendments formulated by the Founders to guard against recurrence of well-defined historic grievances. . . .

The notion that the Privileges or Immunities Clause of the Fourteenth Amendment absorbed, as it is called, the provisions of the Bill of Rights that limit the Federal Government has never been given countenance by this Court. . . .

The Fourteenth Amendment did not mean to imprison the States into the limited experience of the eighteenth century. It did mean to withdraw from the States the right to act in ways that are offensive to a decent respect for the dignity of man, and heedless of his freedom. . . .

In an impressive body of decisions this Court has decided that the Due Process Clause of the Fourteenth Amendment expresses a demand for civilized standards which are not defined by the specifically enumerated guarantees of the Bill of Rights. They neither contain the particularities of the first eight amendments nor are they confined to them. . . . Insofar as due process under the Fourteenth Amendment requires the States to observe any of the immunities . . . it does so because they "have been found to be implicit in the concept of ordered liberty, and thus, through the Fourteenth Amendment become valid as against the states." . . .

Once we are explicit in stating the problem before us in terms defined by an unbroken series of decisions, we cannot escape acknowledging that it involves the application of standards of fairness and justice very broadly conceived. They are not the application of merely personal standards but the impersonal standards of society which alone judges, as the organs of Law, are empowered to enforce. . . .

I cannot bring myself to believe that for Louisiana to leave to executive clemency, rather than to require, mitigation of a sentence of death duly pronounced upon conviction for murder because a first attempt to carry it out was an innocent misadventure offends principles of justice "rooted in the traditions and conscience of our people." . . .

Since I cannot say that it would be "repugnant to the conscience of mankind," for Louisiana to exercise the power on which she here stands, I cannot say that the Constitution withholds it.

MR. JUSTICE BURTON, with whom MR. JUSTICE DOUGLAS, MR. JUSTICE MURPHY and MR. JUSTICE RUTLEDGE concur, dissenting.

. . . We believe that . . . this cause be remanded for further proceedings. . . . Those proceedings should include the determination of certain material facts not previously determined, including the extent, if any, to which electric current was applied to the relator during his attempted electrocution on May 3, 1946. Where life is to be taken, there must be no avoidable error of law or uncertainty of fact. . . .

When this [the Fourteenth Amendment] was adopted in 1868, there long had been imbedded deeply in the standards of this nation a revulsion against subjecting guilty persons to torture culminating in death. . . .

The capital case before us presents an instance of the violation of the constitutional due process that is more clear than would be presented by many lesser punishments prohibited by the Eighth Amendment or its state counterparts. Taking human life by unnecessarily cruel means shocks the most fundamental instincts of civilized man. . . . It is unthinkable that any state legislature in modern times would enact a statute expressly authorizing capital punishment by repeated applications of an electric current separated by intervals of days or hours until finally death shall result. The Legislature of Louisiana did not do so. The Supreme Court of Louisiana did not say that it did. The Supreme Court of Louisiana said merely that the pending petitions for relief in this case presented an executive rather than a judicial question and, by that mistake of law, it precluded itself from discussing the constitutional issue before us.

In determining whether the proposed procedure is unconstitutional, we must measure it against a lawful electrocution. The contrast is that between instantaneous death and death by installments—caused by electric shocks administered after one or more intervening periods of complete consciousness of the victim. Electrocution, when instantaneous, can be inflicted by a state in conformity with due process of law. . . .

The all-important consideration is that the execution shall be so instantaneous and substantially painless that the punishment shall be reduced, as nearly as possible, to no more than that of death itself. . . .

Although the failure of the first attempt, in the present case, was unintended, the reapplication of the electric current will be intentional. How many deliberate and intentional reapplications of electric current does it take to produce a cruel, unusual and unconstitutional punishment? . . .

The petition contains the unequivocal allegation that the official electrocutioner "turned on the switch and a current of electricity was caused to pass through the body of the relator, all in the presence of the official witnesses." This allegation must be read in light of the Louisiana statute which authorized the electocutioner to apply . . . only such an electric current as was of "sufficient intensity to cause death." . . . It exceeds any punishment prescribed by law. There is no precedent for it. What then is it, if it be not cruel, unusual and unlawful? . . . We believe that if the facts are as alleged by the relator the proposed action is unconstitutional. We believe also that the Supreme Court of Louisiana should provide for the determination of the facts and then proceed in a manner not inconsistent with this opinion. . . .

It means merely that the courts of Louisiana must examine the facts, both as to the actual nature of the punishment already inflicted and that proposed to be inflicted and, if the proposed punishment amounts to a violation of due process of law under the Constitution of the United States, then the State must find some means of disposing of this case that will not violate that Constitution. . . .

Source: Louisiana ex. rel Francis v. Resweber, 329 U.S. 459 (1947), at 462–466, 467–481.

Document 2.8
Justice Felix Frankfurter Reviews Georgia's System for Determining the Sanity of the Accused, February 20, 1950

In Solesbee v. Balkcom *(1950), the Supreme Court affirmed a death sentence under a Georgia statute that gave the governor, after consultation with three physicians, the exclusive authority to determine whether a condemned prisoner was sane. Georgia state law prohibits execution of the insane. Justice Felix Frankfurter dissented in an opinion that made copious reference to the procedures in other states, foreshadowing an approach later adopted by the Court when interpreting the meaning of cruel and unusual punishment.*

MR. JUSTICE FRANKFURTER, dissenting.

. . . The question is this: may a State without offending the Due Process Clause of the Fourteenth Amendment put to death one on whose behalf it is claimed that he became insane while awaiting execution, if all opportunity to have his case put is denied and the claim of supervening insanity is rejected on the basis of an ex parte inquiry by the Governor of the State? . . .

If taking life under such circumstances [insanity] is forbidden by the Constitution, then it is not within the benevolent discretion of Georgia to determine how it will ascertain sanity. Georgia must afford the rudimentary safeguards for establishing the fact. If Georgia denies them she transgresses the substance of the limits that the Constitution places upon her. . . .

Due process is that which comports with the deepest notions of what is fair and right and just. . . .

If, as was held only the other day, due process saves a man from being sent to jail for sixty days on a charge of contempt because he was tried in secret, due process ought also to vindicate the self-respect of society by not sending a man to his death on the basis of a proceeding as to his sanity in which all opportunity on his behalf has been denied to show that he is in fact in that condition of insanity which bars the State from killing him. . . .

The risk of an undue delay is hardly comparable to the grim risk of the barbarous execution of an insane man because of a hurried, one-sided, untested determination of the question of insanity, the answers to which are as yet so wrapped in confusion and conflict and so dependent on elucidation by more than one-sided partisanship.

To deny all opportunity to make the claim . . . is in my view a denial of due process of law.

Source: Solesbee v. Balkcom, 339 U.S. 9 (1950), at 14–26.

Document 2.9
Justice Arthur Goldberg Examines the Constitutionality of Capital Punishment in Cases of Rape, October 21, 1963

In 1963 the Supreme Court declined to review the conviction of Frank Lee Rudolph, then under sentence of death in Alabama for the crime of rape. Justice Arthur Goldberg, joined by Justices William Brennan and William O. Douglas, dissented from that denial of certiorari and urged consideration of three questions relating to the death penalty and rape.

MR. JUSTICE GOLDBERG, with whom MR. JUSTICE DOUGLAS and MR. JUSTICE BRENNAN join, dissenting.

I would grant certiorari in the case . . . to consider whether the Eighth and Fourteenth Amendments . . . permit the imposition of the death penalty on a convicted rapist who has neither taken nor endangered human life. . . .

The following questions, *inter alia*, seem relevant and worthy of argument and consideration:

> In light of the trend both in this country and throughout the world against punishing rape by death, does the imposition of the death penalty by those States which retain it for rape violate "evolving standards of decency that mark the progress of our maturing society," or "standards of decency more or less universally accepted"?
>
> Is the taking of human life to protect a value other than human life consistent with the constitutional proscription against "punishments which by their excessive . . . severity are greatly disproportioned to the offenses charged"?
>
> Can the permissible aims of punishment (e.g. deterrence, isolation, rehabilitation) be achieved as effectively by punishing rape less severely than by death (e.g. by life imprisonment), if so, does the imposition of the death penalty for rape constitute "unnecessary cruelty"?

Source: Rudolph v. Alabama, 375 U.S. 889 (1963), at 889–891.

Document 2.10
The Law Firm of Jenner & Block Discusses Its Client, William Witherspoon, and the Case of *Witherspoon v. Illinois,* Fall 2001

In 1968 the Supreme Court reversed the murder conviction and death sentence of William Witherspoon on grounds that the Illinois statute under which he had been convicted permitted the prosecution to exclude from the jury all potential members who expressed conscientious or religious scruples against capital punishment. The result, the Court ruled, was to deprive Witherspoon of a fair trial mandated by the

Sixth Amendment and the Fourteenth. The decision led to the reversal of 350 death sentences in the United States, including Witherspoon's, as noted in this article from the newsletter of the law firm Jenner & Block, which represented the plaintiff pro bono.

While in prison, Bill Witherspoon became an author, writing magazine articles about social reform and the justice system and publishing a 1968 book, *Death Row,* based on interviews with nine other men on Death Row.

He also organized the "Voice of Youth" program to deter troubled youths from criminal activities by means of audiotapes and pamphlets produced in Cook County Jail. The program won commendations from Michigan Gov. George Romney, who said it "restores my faith that the social outcast does indeed make the best social worker."

In 1972, [Jenner & Block] Partner Daniel Murray joined Jerry Solovy's campaign to win parole for Mr. Witherspoon. The two lawyers gathered support from the warden of the Cook County Jail, several Quaker organizations, and noted author Nelson Algren, among many others, and organized a petition signed by every guard at Old Joliet Prison. In 1979, after many parole hearings, their efforts bore fruit and Mr. Witherspoon won his freedom.

Upon leaving prison, he returned to his native Detroit and worked for the next ten years with Project Start, a non-profit agency that finds jobs for ex-convicts. His work also involved lecturing groups including high school students, law students and Jenner & Block lawyers, calling for criminal justice reform and arguing against the death penalty.

He died March 4, 1990 after a long battle with cancer, survived by his wife, Luz Angela.

Source: Jenner & Block, *The Heart of the Matter: Pro Bono and Community Service News,* Vol. 1, no. 1 (Fall 2001): 4, available at www.jenner.com/news/pubs_item.asp?id=000001700001 (accessed February 16, 2009).

Document 2.11

The Arkansas Supreme Court Makes Its Case on the Exclusion of Jurors Based on the Jurors' Views of Capital Punishment, May 5, 1969

While some state courts scrupulously followed the rules laid down by the Supreme Court in the Witherspoon *case by reversing convictions in which courts had excluded jurors who expressed conscientious or religious scruples against capital punishment, other state courts found ways around the standards. This was true of the Arkansas supreme court's decision in* Davis v. State *(1969).*

JUSTICE CONLEY BYRD delivered the opinion of the Court.

. . . Appellant [Davis] contends here that the trial court erred, under the holding in *Witherspoon v. Illinois,* in excluding jurors who had conscientious scruples against capital punishment. A subsidiary argument is that the trial court insured the prosecution's request for a conviction and death sentence by excluding all prospective jurors who said they opposed the death sentence or had religious or conscientious scruples against the death penalty. We do not believe that the record sustains appellant's argument.

As we read the record, the trial courts followed the *Witherspoon* case, excluding Justice Douglas's concurrence, and our own case of *Atkins v. State.* In the latter case we pointed out:

"Whatever may be a man's view of capital punishment as a question of policy, the jury box is not a proper place for him to consider such a policy. There he is obliged, by his oath, to try the guilt or innocence of the accused, according to law and evidence, and not to set up his own private opinion against the policy of the law, which he is bound, as a good citizen, to abide by and administer, so long as it is in force, and until it is repealed by the constituted authority. . . ."

To follow appellant's argument to its logical conclusion would create a kind of anarchy in our system of government whereby the minority will always hold a veto over any established public policy. For instance, since the holding in *Bloom v. Illinois,* it would be almost impossible to enforce some provisions of the 1964 Civil Rights Act, if a court were forced to accept jurors whose private opinions are contrary to the policy of the law. For these reasons we find this point without merit. . . .

Source: Davis v. State, 246 Ark. 838 (1969), at 841–842.

Document 2.12
The NAACP Legal Defense Fund and the National Office for the Rights of the Indigent Broadly Attack the Death Penalty on Behalf of Edward Boykin, October Term 1968

Edward Boykin Jr., who had pleaded guilty to charges stemming from armed robbery, had been sentenced to death in Alabama. Jack Greenberg and Anthony Amsterdam, lawyers for the NAACP Legal Defense and Educational Fund, Inc., and the National Office for the Rights of the Indigent filed an amici curiae (friends of the court) brief in the case of Boykin v. Alabama *(1969). Greenberg and Amsterdam argued that Boykin's guilty plea had not been voluntary, that the state's capital sentencing rules offended due process, that Boykin's sentence constituted cruel and unusual punishment, and that the administration of the death penalty in Alabama and other Southern states was infected with racial discrimination. The Supreme Court ultimately reversed Boykin's conviction only on the issue of his guilty plea.*

. . . The issues of widest importance in this case . . . are the questions whether Edward Boykin's sentence of death for simple robbery violates the Eighth and Fourteenth Amendment prohibition against cruel and unusual punishments and whether its imposition in the unfettered discretion of a jury, which was empowered by Alabama law to choose between the penalties of death and imprisonment arbitrarily, capriciously, for any reason, or for no reason, violates the rule of law basic to the Due Process Clause. We must note at the outset however, that in our view the judgment of conviction and sentence below cannot be sustained on this record consistently with the Constitution, and that reversal is required for a reason quite independent of the two important issues presented relating to the validity of the death penalty. That reason may be briefly stated: the record below does not show compliance with requirements of the Fifth and Fourteenth Amendments in the taking of Boykin's guilty plea.

Three days after the first appointment of counsel, this indigent defendant was arraigned on five separate capital charges and pleaded guilty to all of them. These circumstances alone are cause for gravest concern. . . . The record contains not one word concerning the circumstances of the plea. . . . No inquiry was put on the record as to whether the plea was entered understandingly or ignorantly, freely or under inducement. . . . For aught that appears, the judicial confessions by which his life became forfeit were made on his behalf without his personal participation. . . .

We submit that the Constitution will brook no such summary procedure for the taking of a guilty plea in a capital case; Boykin's plea constituted, of course, a waiver of his rights to contest guilt and to insist that the prosecution prove him guilty at a trial. . . .

It is no accident that this Court has repeatedly stressed the affirmative duty of a trial judge to make adequate inquiry of the accused before accepting a waiver of counsel. . . .

We submit that it is plainly relevant where a judge takes an accused's guilty plea to five capital charges with no more concern for his protection than would attend a plea for a vehicle-code violation. . . .

We come [next] to the question whether Edward Boykin's sentence of death by electrocution for simple robbery violates the Eighth Amendment prohibition of cruel and unusual punishment. . . .

We venture to suggest that the answer to that question would appear easy enough to a student of Anglo-American history and contemporary culture, untrained in the law. If he were told that the Eighth Amendment contained a "basic prohibition against inhuman treatment," that its underlying concept was "nothing less than the dignity of man," that "the Amendment must draw its meaning from the evolving standards of decency that mark the progress of a maturing society," we submit that he could only conclude the Eighth Amendment forbade court-ordered killings of human beings, long after their apprehension and incarceration, as a punishment for the crime of robbery in Twentieth Century America. . . .

Our scholar would look first at history; and, accustomed to the adage that the lessons of history are never clear, he would be surprised. For the lesson of Anglo-American history is clear beyond all mistaking that the advance of civilization has been marked precisely by the progressive abandonment of the death penalty. . . .

For we cannot believe that the Eighth Amendment is not a restriction upon inhuman penal legislation rightfully enforceable by this Court. Nor do we believe that the Amendment's prohibition is restricted to drawing and quartering, and similar antiquated butcheries. . . . The Weems-Trop test, is, we submit, the proper one. Common standards of decency in our contemporary society do set limits of punishment allowable under the Eighth Amendment. . . .

But we have said enough, at this point, to enable us to state our major submission on behalf of Edward Boykin. His sentence of death for simple robbery is, we think, a cruel and unusual punishment because it affronts contemporary standards of decency, universally felt, that would condemn the use of death as a penalty for the crime of robbery if such a penalty were uniformly, regularly, and even-handedly applied either to all robbers or to any non-arbitrarily selected subclass of robbers. . . .

Since 1960, at the least, executions in the United States for any crime have been rare. During the last few years they have been freakishly rare. Executions for robbery-like crimes in the United States have been freakishly rare since 1930. In the nine years from and including 1960 until today, there were two of them. At the last reported count, four men in the Nation were on death row for crimes in the nature of robbery: Edward Boykin and three others. Boykin alone was on the row for simple robbery. . . .

[T]he principle legal device by which Alabama (like most States) permits the arbitrary administration of capital punishment is unrestricted jury discretion. . . . The discretion given Alabama jurors to sentence men whom they convict of robbery to live or die is absolute. It is totally unguided, unprincipled, unconstrained, uncontrolled, and unreviewable. . . . The trial judge simply gave the jurors two forms—a form for life and a form for death—and told them: "You can use either one form or the other when you arrive at your verdict." . . .

We think there can be no doubt about the unconstitutionality of such a procedure. . . .

The issues to which it speaks could not be more important or more fundamental. For, whatever else "due process of law" may encompass, it has always
been thought to impose some demand of fundamental procedural regularity in
decision-making, some insistence upon the rule of law, some adherence to the
principle established by Magna Carta that life and liberty of the subject should
not be taken but by the law of the land. . . .

We do not contend here that the Due Process Clause forbids entirely the exercise
of discretion in sentencing—even by a jury and even in a capital case. Ways may be
found to delimit and guide discretion, narrow its scope, and subject it to review; and
these may bring a grant of discretion within constitutionally tolerable limits. . . .

We submit that . . . the unfettered discretion of a jury violates the rule of law
that is fundamental to Due Process. . . .

Whatever the disposition . . . we would hope that courts will not universally
and perpetually decline to hear constitutionally relevant evidence. . . .

Boykin's petition for certiorari presents as a distinct question a claim of racial
discrimination in the application of the death penalty for Alabama Negroes. . . .
We agree that the apparent racial discrimination in the selection of the few, otherwise arbitrarily chosen men sentenced to die for robbery in Alabama and the
handful of Southern States which retain capital punishment for this crime is
highly relevant to the claim of cruel and unusual punishment. . . .

Finally, Boykin's petition for certiorari presents a constitutional challenge to
the "unitary" or single-verdict method of trying the issues of guilt and punishment in a capital case. On a proper record, that question would be a very substantial one. . . .

Source: Brief for the NAACP Legal Defense and Educational Fund, Inc., and the National Office for
the Rights of the Indigent, as Amici Curiae, *Boykin v. Alabama,* 395 U.S. 238 (1969), at 11–69.

Document 2.13
Distinguished Lawyers File Amicus Curiae Brief in Opposition to Single-Verdict Procedures in Capital Cases, October Term 1968

*Led by William Coleman, the first African American law clerk at the Supreme
Court; Whitney North Seymour, a former solicitor general of the United States; and
Cyrus Vance, former secretary of state, fifteen American lawyers filed an amicus
curiae brief in the case of* Maxwell v. Bishop *(1968). In their brief the lawyers
challenged on constitutional grounds Arkansas's single-verdict procedures in capital
cases that gave one jury the authority to determine both guilt and punishment. They
also made a frontal attack on racial disparities in application of the death penalty
by claiming that unguided jury discretion opens the door to racial discrimination in
sentencing and that African Americans were disproportionately executed for the*

crime of rape when the victim was white. The Supreme Court decided the Maxwell *case on other grounds, but later struck down similar single-verdict procedures and the death penalty for rape.*

The death penalty for a "capital" offense has become the exception, rather [than] the rule, and this accentuates the need for standards to determine the occasions on which it is to be inflicted if administration of the death penalty is to meet Due Process requirements. The current rarity of the death penalty also destroys the support of tradition for the Arkansas practice. . . .

The disappearance of the death penalty as a normal consequence of conviction for even the most heinous offenses has not only enlarged the operational content of jury "discretion," and created the necessity for standards, it has eliminated tradition as a ground for perpetuating the Arkansas practice. The issue now before the Court is vastly different from what it might have been even a few decades ago, though it remains clothed in the same conceptual garments.

The Arkansas procedure is tantamount to an instruction that race may be taken into account and is thus a deprivation of Equal Protection of the Laws. . . .

In simply submitting the issue of life or death, without comment, the trial court, in the context and under the circumstances, conveyed a gross misconception which deprived petitioner of Equal Protection of the laws and necessarily voided his death sentence.

Even if it be assumed, against all the evidence, that the death penalty was not discriminatorily inflicted upon petitioner, Due Process compels the introduction of protections against the apparent risk of such discrimination.

Petitioner abundantly proved in the District Court that "Negro defendants who rape white victims have been disproportionately sentenced to death by reason of race, during the years 1945–1965 in the State of Arkansas," . . . and the Court of Appeals seemed to agree. The statistics for the nation at large strongly imply that what is true in Arkansas is true in the entire South. Accumulated experience and professional opinion is virtually unanimous, moreover, that throughout the nation, "the death sentence is disproportionately imposed and carried out on the poor, the Negro, and members of unpopular groups." . . .

A system which authorizes predominately white, middle-class juries to mete out a death sentence to anyone they convict of a so-called capital offense, for any reason or for no reason, and which promises those juries that they will never be compelled to reveal or to articulate their reasons or lack of reasons, and which results in the disproportionate infliction of the death penalty on Negroes, plainly fails in its duty both to be and to appear fair. Due Process in its most elemental sense is glaringly denied. . . .

As petitioner has amply shown, a defendant in a capital case in Arkansas is faced with a grisly choice. He is permitted to adduce mitigating evidence on the penalty question only at the price of surrendering his right to a full and fair trial on the issue of guilt and his right not to incriminate himself. This is enough to invalidate the procedure. Yet the choices are even grislier than petitioner suggests. If an Arkansas rape defendant really fears that his life will be forfeit and is bent on saving it, he may be well advised not merely to surrender his right not to testify, and to forgo the defense of consent and other trial rights, but also to yield his very right to be tried. Only by pleading guilty can he maximize his chances of saving his life. . . .

The decision of the Court of Appeals for the Eighth Circuit [affirming Maxwell's conviction and sentence] should be reversed.

Source: Brief for Berl I. Bernhard, William Coleman, Samuel Dash, John W. Douglas, Steven Duke, William T. Gossett, John Griffiths, Rita Hauser, George N. Lindsay, Burke Marshall, Monrad S. Paulsen, Steven R. Rivkin, Whitney North Seymour, Jerome J. Shestack, and Cyrus Vance, as Amici Curiae, in *Maxwell v. Bishop*, 398 U.S. 262 (1970), at 3–18.

Document 2.14
The Supreme Court Examines Due Process and the Death Penalty in *McGautha v. California*, May 3, 1971

In McGautha v. California *(1971), a majority of the Supreme Court all but abandoned judicial intervention into capital punishment sentencing standards under the due process clause of the Fourteenth Amendment. Justice John M. Harlan's opinion argued that the quest for such rules would prove fruitless and deprive juries of the necessary discretion to mitigate death sentences. In dissent, Justice William Brennan accused the majority of sanctioning legislative negligence and unbridled state power unprecedented in other areas of constitutional law.*

MR. JUSTICE HARLAN delivered the opinion of the Court.

. . . In each case the decision whether the defendant should live or die was left to the absolute discretion of the jury. In McGautha's case the jury, in accordance with California law, determined punishment in a separate proceeding following the trial on the issue of guilt. In Crampton's case, in accordance with Ohio law, the jury determined guilt and punishment after a single trial and in a single verdict. . . .

Our function is not to impose on the States, ex cathedra, what might seem to us a better system for dealing with capital cases. Rather, it is to decide whether the Federal Constitution proscribes the present procedures of these two States in such cases. . . .

To fit their arguments within a constitutional frame of reference petitioners contend that to leave the jury completely at large to impose or withhold the death penalty as it sees fit is fundamentally lawless and therefore violates the basic command of the Fourteenth Amendment that no state shall deprive a person of his life without due process of law. Despite the undeniable surface appeal of the proposition, we conclude that the courts below correctly rejected it. . . .

In recent years academic and professional sources have suggested that jury sentencing discretion should be controlled by standards of some sort. . . .

In our view, such force as this argument has derives largely from its generality. Those who have come to grips with the hard task of actually attempting to draft means of channeling capital sentencing discretion have confirmed the lesson taught by the history recounted above. To identify before the fact those characteristics of criminal homicides and their perpetrators which call for the death penalty, and to express these characteristics in language which can be fairly understood and applied by the sentencing authority, appear to be tasks which are beyond present human ability. . . .

In light of history, experience, and the present limitations of human knowledge, we find it quite impossible to say that committing to the untrammeled discretion of the jury the power to pronounce life or death in capital cases is offensive to anything in the Constitution. . . .

MR. JUSTICE BRENNAN, with whom MR. JUSTICE DOUGLAS and MR. JUSTICE MARSHALL join, dissenting.

These cases test the viability of principles whose roots draw strength from the very core of the Due Process Clause. The question that petitioners present for our decision is whether the rule of law, basic to our society and binding upon the States by virtue of the Due Process Clause of the Fourteenth Amendment, is fundamentally inconsistent with capital sentencing procedures that are purposely constructed to allow the maximum possible variation from one case to the next, and provide no mechanism to prevent that consciously maximized variation from reflecting merely random or arbitrary choice. . . . With the issue so polarized, the Court is led to conclude that the rule of law and the power of the States to kill are in irreconcilable conflict. This conflict the Court resolves in favor of the States' power to kill.

In my view the Court errs at all points from its premises to its conclusions. Unlike the Court, I do not believe that the legislatures of the 50 States are so devoid of wisdom and the power of rational thought that they are unable to face the problem of capital punishment directly, and to determine for themselves the criteria under which convicted capital felons should be chosen to live or die. . . .

The Due Process Clause . . . does not limit the power of the States to choose among competing social and economic theories in the ordering of life within their respective jurisdictions. But it does require that, if state power is to be exerted, these choices must be made by a responsible organ of state government. For if they are not, the very best that may be hoped for is that state power will be exercised, not upon the basis of any social choice made by the people of the State, but instead merely on the basis of social choices made at the whim of the particular state official wielding the power. . . . Government by whim is the very antithesis of due process. . . .

We are not presented with the slightest attempt to bring the power of reason to bear on the considerations relevant to capital sentencing. We are faced with nothing more than stark legislative abdication. Not once in the history of this Court, until today, have we sustained against a due process challenge such an unguided, unbridled, unreviewable exercise of naked power. Almost a century ago, we found an almost identical California procedure constitutionally inadequate to license a laundry. Today we hold it adequate to license a life. I would reverse petitioners' sentences of death. . . .

Source: McGautha v. California, 402 U.S. 183 (1971), at 185–186, 196, 203–205, 249–250, 252–253.

NOTES

1. *Moore v. Dempsey,* 261 U.S. 86 (1923).
2. *Furman v. Georgia,* 408 U.S. 238 (1972).
3. *McGautha v. California,* 402 U.S. 183 (1971).
4. *Ex parte Quirin,* 317 U.S. 1 (1942); and *In re Yamashita,* 327 U.S. 1 (1946).
5. *Louisiana ex rel. Francis v. Resweber,* 329 U.S. 459 (1947).
6. *Palko v. Connecticut,* 302 U.S. 319 (1937); and *Adamson v. California,* 332 U.S. 46 (1947).
7. *Rosenberg v. United States,* 346 U.S. 273 (1953).
8. Quoted in Michael E. Parrish, "Cold War Justice: The Supreme Court and the Rosenbergs," *American Historical Review* 82 (October 1977): 808.
9. *Brown v. Allen,* 344 U.S. 443 (1953).
10. *Frank v. Mangum,* 237 U.S. 309 (1915).
11. *Chessman v. Teets,* 350 U.S. 3 (1955); and *Chessman v. Teets,* 354 U.S. 156 (1957).
12. See Theodore Hamm, *Rebel and a Cause: Caryl Chessman and the Politics of the Death Penalty in Postwar California 1948–1978* (Berkeley: University of California Press, 2001); Frank Parker, *Caryl Chessman: The Red Light Bandit* (Chicago: Burnham, 1975); Caryl Chessman, *Cell 2455, Death Row* (New York: Perma Books, 1960); and Caryl Chessman, *Trial by Ordeal* (Englewood Cliffs, N.J.: Prentice-Hall, 1955).
13. *Sheppard v. Maxwell,* 384 U.S. 333 (1966).
14. See James Neff, *The Wrong Man: The Final Verdict on the Dr. Sam Sheppard Murder Case* (New York: Random House, 2001); Jack Harrison Pollack, *Dr. Sam: An American Tragedy* (Chicago: Henry Regency, 1975); and Samuel H. Sheppard, *Endure and Conquer* (Cleveland: Cleveland World Publishing Co., 1966).
15. *Rudolph v. Alabama,* 375 U.S. 889 (1963).
16. Stuart Banner, *The Death Penalty: An American History* (Cambridge, Mass.: Harvard University Press, 2002), 140–141; Kenneth M. Stampp, *The Peculiar Institution: Slavery in the Ante-Bellum South* (New York: Knopf, 1956), 210–211; A. Leon Higginbotham Jr., *In the Matter of Color: Race and the American Legal Process—The*

Colonial Period (New York: Oxford University Press, 1978), 181–182, 256–257, 262–263; Randall Kennedy, *Race, Crime and the Law* (New York: Pantheon Books, 1997), 84–85; and U.S. Department of Justice, Bureau of Prisons, "National Prisoner Statistics, Bulletin No. 45," *Capital Punishment 1930–1968* (1969), 7.

17. See Herbert Shapiro, *White Violence and Black Response: From Reconstruction to Montgomery* (Amherst: University of Massachusetts Press, 1988), 395–401; and "Justice and the Communists," *Time*, May 14, 1951.

18. *Gaines v. Washington*, 277 U.S. 81 (1928).

19. *Bailey v. Alabama*, 211 U.S. 452 (1908).

20. *McCabe v. Atchinson, Topeka and Santa Fe Railroad*, 235 U.S. 151 (1914).

21. *Stromberg v. California*, 283 U.S. 359 (1931).

22. *Near v. Minnesota*, 283 U.S. 697 (1931).

23. The literature on the Scottsboro trials is voluminous. I have relied for this account on the following: James E. Goodman, *Stories of Scottsboro* (New York: Pantheon, 1994); Dan T. Carter, *Scottsboro: A Tragedy of the American South* (Baton Rouge: Louisiana State University Press, 1979); Haywood Patterson, *Scottsboro Boy* (Garden City, N.Y.: Doubleday, 1950); and the Famous Trials Web site created by Prof. Douglas O. Linder that can be found at www.law.umkc.edu/faculty/projects/ftrials/ftrials.htm.

24. The Alabama court voted 6–1 over a dissent by its chief justice to affirm the sentences, except for Eugene Williams, who, the court ruled, should not have been tried as an adult. "The record shows," wrote the majority, "that the defendants were represented by counsel who thoroughly cross-examined the state's witnesses, and presented such evidence as was available in their behalf, and no reason appears why the judgment should not be affirmed." *Weems, et al. v. State*, 224 Ala. 524 (1932).

25. *Gitlow v. New York*, 268 U.S. 652 (1925).

26. *Powell v. Alabama*, 287 U.S. 45 (1932).

27. Ibid., at 56–60.

28. *Hurtado v. California*, 110 U.S. 516 (1884).

29. Ibid., at 66–68. See also *Twining v. New Jersey*, 211 U.S. 78 (1908).

30. *Powell v. Alabama.*, at 71–72.

31. Ibid., at 72 (emphasis added).

32. Ibid., at 76.

33. In *McMann v. Richardson*, 397 U.S. 759 (1970), at 768–771, the Court held that effective counsel would be judged by whether the advice given at the time of the trial was "within the range of competence demanded of attorneys in criminal cases." In *Strickland v. Washington*, 466 U.S. 668 (1984), at 687–696, the Court placed the burden of proof on defendants to prove that their counsel's performance was "deficient" and that such a deficient performance prejudiced the defendant "so as to deprive the defendant of a fair trial."

34. *Norris v. Alabama*, 294 U.S. 587 (1935).

35. Ibid., at 590–596.

36. *Avery v. Alabama*, 308 U.S. 444 (1940).

37. *Betts v. Brady*, 316 U.S. 455 (1942). *Betts* was subsequently overruled by *Gideon v. Wainwright*, 372 U.S. 335 (1963).

38. *Akins v. Texas*, 325 U.S. 398 (1945).

39. *Batson v. Kentucky*, 476 U.S. 79 (1986). In *Batson* the Court held that prosecutors may not use race as a factor in making peremptory challenges and that defendants must only make a *prime facie* showing of evidence from the case to mount a challenge to race-based use of such challenges. *Miller-el v. Cockrell*, 537 U.S. 322

(2003), and *Snyder v. Louisiana*, 552 U.S. ____ (2008), extended *Batson* to permit the use of statistical and other evidence by defendants.

40. *Mooney v. Holohan*, 294 U.S. 103 (1935).
41. *Brown v. Mississippi*, 297 U.S. 278 (1936).
42. Ibid., at 284.
43. Ibid., at 285.
44. See *Chambers v. Florida*, 309 U.S. 227 (1940); and *White v. Texas*, 310 U.S. 530 (1940). In *White* an illiterate African American farm worker had been arrested with several others, taken to the woods, whipped by a Texas Ranger, and "with his mark" signed a confession later.
45. See, for example, *Haley v. Ohio*, 332 U.S. 596 (1948); and *Watts v. Indiana*, 338 U.S. 49 (1949).
46. See, for example, *Lisenba v. California*, 314 U.S. 219 (1941); and *Taylor v. Alabama*, 335 U.S. 252 (1948).
47. *Escobedo v. Illinois*, 378 U.S. 478 (1964); and *Miranda v. Arizona*, 384 U.S. 436 (1966).
48. *Snyder v. Massachusetts*, 291 U.S. 97 (1934).
49. Ibid., at 105–107.
50. Ibid,.at 116–117.
51. Ibid., at 122.
52. *Palko v. Connecticut*, 302 U.S. 319 (1937).
53. *Maxwell v. Dow*, 176 U.S. 581 (1900).
54. *Palko v. Connecticut*, at 328.
55. This account is based on Arthur S. Miller and Jeffrey H. Bowman, *Death by Installments: The Ordeal of Willie Francis* (New York: Greenwood Press, 1988); William M. Wiecek, "Felix Frankfurter, Incorporation, and the Willie Francis Case," *Journal of Supreme Court History* 26 (December 2002): 53–66; and *Louisiana ex rel. Francis v. Resweber*, 329 U.S. 459 (1947). Research by Miller, Bowman, and others indicates that the executioner, a state prison guard, was intoxicated at the time he pulled the switch.
56. Wiecek, "Felix Frankfurter," 55.
57. *Louisiana ex rel. Francis v. Resweber*, at 479–480. Affidavits submitted by witnesses to the execution lent credibility to Francis' claim: "Then the executioner turned on the switch and when he did Willie Francis' lips puffed out and he groaned and jumped so that the chair came off the floor." And, "I saw his lips puff out and swell, his body tensed and stretched." Finally, "This boy really got a shock when they turned that machine on." Burton also argued that a second execution attempt would deny Francis equal protection of the laws.
58. Wiecek, "Felix Frankfurter," 64.
59. *Louisiana ex rel. Francis v. Resweber*, at 471–472.
60. Wiecek, "Felix Frankfurter," 64.
61. *Louisiana ex rel. Francis v. Resweber*, at 462 (emphasis added).
62. Ibid., at 471.
63. *Adamson v. California*, 332 U.S. 46 (1947), at 56–57.
64. Ibid., at 57.
65. Black carefully avoided linking incorporation explicitly to the privileges and immunities clause in *Adamson* because it had become a constitutional derelict, except when used by the anti–New Deal justices in the late 1930s to strike down a state income tax provision, exacting the kind of judicial activism against economic policies that Black abhorred. See *Colgate v. Harvey*, 296 U.S. 404 (1935). In 1940 the

Court quickly overruled *Colgate* and buried further the privileges and immunities clause, even though it made more sense as a vehicle for incorporation than due process. See *Madden v. Kentucky*, 309 U.S. 83 (1940).

66. *Adamson v. California*, at 68.
67. Ibid., at 124–125.
68. *Nobles v. Georgia*, 168 U.S. 398 (1897), at 403 (emphasis added).
69. Ibid., at 406–407.
70. *Phyle v. Duffy*, 334 U.S. 431 (1948), at 434.
71. Ibid., at 440.
72. Ibid., at 444.
73. Ibid., at 445.
74. *Phyle v. Duffy*, 34 Cal. 2d 144 (1949). See also Howard C. Michaelsen Jr., "Post-Conviction Due Process Regarding Insanity Claim Prior to Execution," *Journal of Criminal Law and Criminology* (January–February 1951): 639–644.
75. *Solesbee v. Balkcom*, 339 U.S. 9 (1950), at 11–12.
76. Ibid., at 23.
77. *Weems v. United States*, 217 U.S. 349 (1910), at 380.
78. *Solesbee v. Balkcom*, at 25–26.
79. *Leland v. Oregon*, 343 U.S. 790 (1952).
80. Ibid., at 798–799.
81. Ibid., at 805.
82. On racial discrimination, see, for example, *Brown v. Board of Education of Topeka*, 347 U.S. 483 (1954); *Burton v. Wilmington Parking Authority*, 365 U.S. 715 (1961); and *Heart of Atlanta Motel v. United States*, 379 U.S. 241 (1964). On incorporation, see *Malloy v. Hogan*, 378 U.S. 1 (1964); and *Duncan v. Louisiana*, 391 U.S. 145 (1968), in which the Court extended Sixth Amendment jury trial provision to states in cases involving imprisonment for at least two years; and *Benton v. Maryland*, 395 U.S. 784 (1969). The retirement of Justice Frankfurter in 1963 hastened the Court's journey down the road of incorporation.
83. *Trop v. Dulles*, 356 U.S. 86 (1958).
84. Ibid., at 100–101.
85. Ibid., 102–103. Justices Black and Douglas joined Warren's opinion, but added that the denationalization provision failed the constitutional test by vesting unchecked discretion in military authorities with respect to dishonorable discharges that gave them the last word on citizenship.
86. Ibid., at 111–114.
87. *Robinson v. California*, 370 U.S. 660 (1962), at 662.
88. Ibid., at 666.
89. *Frank Lee Rudolph v. State of Alabama*, 275 Ala. 115 (1963).
90. See Herbert H. Haines, *Against Capital Punishment: The Anti-Death Penalty Movement in America, 1972–1994* (New York: Oxford University Press, 1996), 26–27.
91. *Rudolph v. Alabama*, 375 U.S. 889 (1963). According to Alan Dershowitz, Goldberg's law clerk, at least two members of the Court, Warren and Black, feared that the Court's intervention into the arena of capital punishment would endanger the progress already achieved in the areas of desegregation and racial equality. For similar reasons, the Warren Court declined to rule on miscegenation statutes until 1967, when it ruled in *Loving v. Virginia* (388 U.S. 1). See also Peter Wellerstein, "Race, Marriage, and the Law of Freedom: Alabama and Virginia, 1860's–1960's," *Chicago-Kent Law Review* 70 (1994): 371–437.

92. *Spencer v. Texas*, 385 U.S. 554 (1967).

93. Ibid., at 564–565, 568–569.

94. Ibid., at 569–588.

95. *United States v. Jackson*, 390 U.S. 570 (1968).

96. Ibid., at 572–573.

97. *Witherspoon v. Illinois*, 391 U.S. 510 (1968).

98. Ibid., at 513.

99. Ibid., at 523–524.

100. Ibid., at 528.

101. Ibid., at 539.

102. Ibid., at 541.

103. See, for example, *Spencer v. Beto*, 398 F.2d 500 (5th Cir. 1968), at 502; and *In re Anderson*, 69 Cal. 2d 613 (1968), at 617–619.

104. See *People v. Speck*, 41 Ill. 2d 177 (1968); and *People v. Mallet*, 45 Ill. 2d 388 (1970).

105. See also *State v. Mathis*, 52 N.J. 238 (1968).

106. See, for example, Faye Goldberg, "Toward Expansion of Witherspoon: Capital Scruples, Jury Bias, and the Use of Psychological Data to Raise Presumptions in the Law," *Harvard Civil Rights–Civil Liberties Review* 5 (1970): 53–69; and Craig Haney, "Juries and the Death Penalty," *Crime & Delinquency* 26 (1980): 512–527.

107. *Boykin v. Alabama*, 395 U.S. 238 (1969).

108. The trial court violated due process, Douglas wrote, when it accepted Boykin's guilty plea without first "canvassing the matter with the accused" with the "utmost solicitude." Ibid., at 242–244. On Federal Rule 11, respecting guilty pleas, see Federal Rules of Criminal Procedure, Rule 11, 383 U.S. 1097 (1966); and T.L.M., "Rule 11 of the Federal Rules of Criminal Procedure: The Case for Strict Compliance after *United States v. Dayton*," *Virginia Law Review* 66 (October 1980): 1169–1182.

109. *Maxwell v. Bishop*, 398 U.S. 262 (1970).

110. *Maxwell v. Bishop*, 398 F.2d 138 (8th Cir. 1968).

111. The cases were consolidated in *McGautha v. California*, 402 U.S. 183 (1971).

112. Ibid., at 195.

113. Ibid., at 204. In passing, Harlan noted that the California supreme court had narrowly rejected McGautha's claim that the state's standardless jury sentencing procedure violated the Constitution.

114. Ibid., at 226.

115. Ibid., at 229–230.

116. See *New York Times Co. v. Sullivan*, 376 U.S. 254 (1964); and *Baker v. Carr*, 369 U.S. 186 (1962).

117. *McGautha v. California*, at 249.

118. Ibid., at 252.

119. *Furman v. Georgia*, 403 U.S. 952 (1971); *Jackson v. Georgia*, 403 U.S. 952 (1971); *Branch v. Texas*, 403 U.S. 952 (1971); *Aikens v. California*, 403 U.S. 952 (1971); and *McKenzie v. Texas*, 403 U.S. 952 (1971).

120. *Furman v. Georgia*, 403 U.S. 952 (1971).

121. The California court would strike down the state's death penalty on February 18, 1972, a month after oral argument in *Furman*, which rendered moot the case of *Aikens v. California*. See *People v. Anderson*, 6 Cal.3d 628 (1972). The California constitutional provision departed from the Eighth Amendment by using "or" instead of "and," a conjunction that made a significant interpretative difference to the California high court.

CHAPTER 3

The Court and Popular Opinion
Moratorium and Reinstatement, 1972–1976

From the beginning of national life under the Constitution of the United States, political leaders, judges, lawyers, scholars, and ordinary citizens struggled to reconcile its republican commitments, premised on frequent elections and popular sovereignty, with a non-elected federal judiciary that served for good behavior and remained insulated from immediate electoral pressures, but that was nonetheless charged with deciding "all Cases, in Law and Equity, arising under this Constitution, the Laws of the United States, and Treaties made, or which shall be made, under their Authority."[1] The conundrum, sometimes described by critics of judicial power as "the counter-majoritarian problem," arises when the federal courts, especially the Supreme Court, resolve a particular case under the Constitution in a manner sharply at odds with the elected branches of government and the popular sentiments represented there.

Alexander Hamilton in *Federalist* No. 78 and Chief Justice John Marshall in *Marbury v. Madison* (1803) attempted to reconcile the problem of republicanism and a non-elected judiciary by arguing that when the judges decided a case arising under the Constitution adverse to elected officials they were simply enforcing the fundamental will of the people as expressed in the written Constitution. It was not the judges who imposed their will upon the people's representatives, this argument went, but the people themselves who had spoken in the form of the Constitution.[2] The intellectual effort to expunge subjective judicial values from the calculus of constitutional conflict never entirely succeeded as critics pointed out the difficulty of fixing a single meaning to such broad concepts as "due process of law," "commerce among the states," or "other high crimes and misdemeanors."

In the real world of institutional conflict, a judicial branch that strayed too far from popular opinion soon faced another of Hamilton's maxims: namely, that the judiciary was both the least dangerous branch of government and its weakest. Marshall discovered this fact when he rendered a decision strongly in support of the second Bank of the United States, which President Andrew Jackson nevertheless subsequently destroyed.[3] Chief Justice Roger Taney and his colleagues learned a similar lesson when they sanctioned the expansion of slavery into the nation's territories, as did the justices who joined Chief Justice Melville Fuller to strike down the federal income tax statute in 1895 and those of the depression-era Hughes Court who invalidated numerous laws intended to ease the nation's acute economic crisis.[4] All felt the wrath of a hostile public and eventual repudiation by the political branches.

Chastened by this historical experience, the post–New Deal Court adhered to the general philosophy of judicial restraint as articulated by the Harvard law professor James Bradley Thayer. Justices Oliver Wendell Holmes, Louis Brandeis, Benjamin Cardozo, and Felix Frankfurter each strongly championed deference to the value choices of the elected branches, avoided constitutional decisions whenever possible, and wielded the judicial veto only in the clearest cases. Even justices inclined to a more robust role found it difficult to openly repudiate this model of judicial deference and usually cloaked their value choices with the veil of inevitable constitutional mandate. In the early years of the Cold War, the Court practiced judicial deference with a vengeance, giving constitutional sanction to what many critics saw as serious political assaults on civil liberties.[5] But even the more activist Warren Court displayed considerable prudence when it avoided a decision on interracial marriages on two occasions during the same years it championed school desegregation.[6] By the time the justices finally invalidated miscegenation laws ten years later, they remained on the books in only sixteen of the states, the majority of those in the South.[7]

The miscegenation cases suggest a deeper truth about the Warren Court, which has too often been caricatured as the most egregious recent example of raw judicial power thwarting the popular will. Beginning with the segregation decisions and continuing through its rulings on reapportionment, school prayer, and criminal justice, the Court did become a lightning rod for vocal and sometimes violent protests by groups angered by those decisions. "Impeach Earl Warren" billboards sprang up along American highways. Members of Congress introduced numerous constitutional amendments to overturn particular decisions, notably those involving reapportionment and school prayer. In Warren's last term, presidential candidate Richard Nixon ran on a platform denouncing the Court's rulings.

Yet for all the anti-Court invective and agitation unleashed by its opponents, it is difficult to argue that the Warren Court lacked broad popular support for its decisions, including those that toppled segregation. The reapportionment decisions politically empowered the most rapidly growing and populous areas of urban and suburban America. The school prayer and criminal justice rulings brought outlying jurisdictions into conformity with a national consensus on the place of religion in public life and minimal standards of fairness due those accused of crimes. The Court's attack on racial segregation generated fierce resistance and horrific violence by white citizens in at least thirteen states, but this resistance inspired an even larger national backlash outside the South that produced three historic civil rights laws between 1964 and 1968. The Warren Court may not have been a model democratic institution, but it is difficult to claim that it flouted the will of the majority of the American people, a point made eloquently by several scholars, notably Jeffrey Rosen and Michael Klarman.[8]

The Warren Justices and the Idea of Progress

Five justices of the Warren era (Thurgood Marshall, William Brennan, William O. Douglas, Potter Stewart, and Byron White) remained on the bench to sit on the Burger Court in 1972. Stewart and White had often dissented from the Court's landmark criminal justice rulings in the 1960s, but even they could not avoid the knowledge that the Court had over the course of a decade begun to fulfill the vision first expressed by Justice Joseph McKenna in *Weems v. United States* (1910). McKenna had declared there that constitutional provisions related to crime and punishment such as the Eighth Amendment "may acquire meaning as public opinion becomes enlightened by a humane justice."[9] In *Trop v. Dulles* (1958), Chief Justice Warren echoed McKenna's view when he declared that the amendment "must draw its meaning from the evolving standards of decency that mark the progress of a maturing society."[10]

By 1972 at least three of the Warren justices (Brennan, Douglas, and Marshall) had good reason to believe that the Court's criminal justice decisions had confirmed enlightened public opinion and marked the progress of a maturing American society. In the 1960s, the Court had embedded into the criminal justice system new procedural protections from the time of arrest through legal appeals.[11] And despite the Court's 5–4 split in *McGautha v. California* (1971), in which unitary capital sentencing schemes where juries decided guilt and punishment in a single proceeding were sustained,[12] the American public appeared to be moving inexorably against state-sanctioned killing. During the 1960s, five state legislatures—Iowa, New York, Oregon, Vermont, and West Virginia—abolished the death penalty, bringing to thirteen the number of states that had put an end to the practice. That decade also saw a sharp drop in executions even in those states with death rows, from fifty-six in 1960 to zero executions in the five years between 1968 and 1972 (**Document 3.1**).

In their amici curiae ("friends of the court") brief filed on behalf of William Henry Furman, Lucious Jackson, and Elmer Branch, the Synagogue Council of America and the American Jewish Congress expressed the belief that "the steady decline in the number of persons executed during the past four decades can be explained only in terms of a widely held belief that the death penalty is basically cruel and morally unacceptable" (**Document 3.2**). But reading public opinion is a tricky business, as the Court quickly discovered. The notable decline in executions could be attributed in part to the Court's own criminal justice decisions, which had raised the costs of capital trials and appeals and slowed down the machinery of death. In response to the rise in political violence during the decade, Congress had shown no inclination to abolish capital punishment. The national legislature added new capital offenses to the federal criminal code, including air piracy and presidential and congressional assassinations.[13]

Confronting the *McGautha* Roadblock

Like all judges, Supreme Court justices usually pay solemn lip service to the doctrine of precedent, or *stare decisis* (stand by the decision). Simply put, the doctrine invokes the belief that like cases should be decided in like manner. The doctrine promotes stability and predictability in the legal system. At the same time, Supreme Court justices have never been too shy about overturning a prior decision, or making one irrelevant by distinguishing it from the case at hand. In 1870, for example, the Court ruled in *Hepburn v. Griswold* that the issuance of paper money by Congress during the Civil War had violated the Constitution.[14] A year later, with the addition of two new justices, the Court overruled *Hepburn* and sustained the constitutional validity of paper money in *Knox v. Lee* (1871).[15] The Hughes Court in *Minersville School District v. Gobitis* (1940) upheld the mandatory flag salute as a condition of attending public school.[16] Three years later the Stone Court struck down a similar requirement on First Amendment grounds in *West Virginia Board of Education v. Barnette* (1943).[17]

Furman v. Georgia (1972) presented the Burger Court with another problem of *stare decisis*. Justice Douglas, alone among those who would join the short per curiam opinion overturning the capital statutes in that case, stated the issue bluntly: "We are now imprisoned in the *McGautha* holding. Indeed, the seeds of the present case are in *McGautha*. Juries (or judges, as the case may be) have practically untrammeled discretion to let an accused live or insist that he die."[18] Justice John Marshall Harlan's opinion for the 5–4 majority in *McGautha* had slammed tight the door on Fourteenth Amendment due process challenges to unguided jury statutes in capital cases on two grounds: first, that "untrammeled discretion" in juries reflected a progressive, humane advance over mandatory death penalty laws, and, second, that any attempt by legislatures to define in advance the particular characteristics of homicide that merited death as opposed to a life sentence was doomed to fail as mere "boilerplate." The uniqueness of each homicide and each murder, Harlan concluded, made the quest for jury standards futile. Capital juries, like governors who exercised clemency, should be allowed to make these life or death judgments alone, guided only by their collective conscience.

As Douglas and other justices realized, Harlan's opinion raised a formidable roadblock for Furman, who, like Dennis McGautha, had committed homicide in the course of a robbery and had been convicted and sentenced under a Georgia statute that gave the jury "untrammeled discretion" to determine whether he would live or die. *McGautha,* of course, had been argued and decided on

Fourteenth Amendment due process grounds, while the Court had granted certiorari in *Furman* on an entirely different constitutional question. In *Furman* the question at hand was, "does the imposition and carrying out of the death penalty in [these cases] constitute cruel and unusual punishment in violation of the Eighth and Fourteenth Amendments?" But could an unguided capital sentencing scheme found to be constitutional against a due process challenge in *McGautha* still be struck down as a violation of the Eighth Amendment thirteen months later in *Furman?* The five Warren justices on the Burger Court, including Stewart and White, who had joined Harlan in *McGautha,* made that distinction when they joined in a per curiam (for the Court) opinion to overturn the death sentences in *Furman* and invalidate the death penalty statutes of the states and the federal government (**Document 3.3**). The five justices, however, could not agree upon a single rationale and wrote separate concurring opinions (**Document 3.4**). Their defenders argued that because each constitutional provision—due process and the Eighth Amendment—carried its own unique freight of case law, such distinctions were the very essence of judicial craftsmanship and integrity. Their critics, including the four new dissenting justices appointed by President Nixon, condemned the process as illogical and another example of judicial power run amok.[19]

Furman's two co-plaintiffs, Jackson and Branch, presented a lesser problem with respect to *McGautha*. They had been convicted and sentenced to death for the crime of rape, a capital offense in Georgia and Texas that had become vulnerable to constitutional attack on Eighth Amendment grounds since Justice Arthur Goldberg's dissent in *Rudolph v. Alabama* (1963) a decade earlier.[20] Not only had thirty-three states taken rape off their statute books as a capital offense, but those states where the penalty endured were, with the exception of Nevada, all Southern states where racial segregation had been mandated by law and where the penalty fell disproportionately upon African Americans. Like racial segregation itself, the death penalty for rape presented a classic instance of outlier states that remained indifferent to the "evolving standards of decency that mark the progress of a maturing society." In their amicus brief on behalf of Jackson and Branch, lawyers for the Synagogue Council of America stressed the disproportionality of the punishment for the crime of rape, capital punishment's vanishing incidence outside the South, and its racially discriminatory impact. Their brief prefigured themes articulated by justices in the majority, especially those authored by Douglas.

The Eighth Amendment as Equal Protection

Having identified the *McGautha* due process roadblock, Justice Douglas simply drove around it by another constitutional route. The Eighth Amendment, he argued, incorporated the equal protection mandate of the Fourteenth

Amendment. A death penalty would be "unusual," according to Douglas, if inflicted upon a defendant because of his race, religion, wealth, social position, or class "or under a procedure that gives room for the play of such prejudices." The record in the case did not prove that the defendants had been sentenced to death because of their race, Douglas wrote, but the uncontrolled discretion given to judges and juries by the statutes in Georgia and Texas invited such arbitrary and selective punishment upon "minorities whose numbers are few, who are outcasts of society, and who are unpopular, but whom society is willing to see suffer though it would not countenance general application of the same across the board."[21]

Douglas turned Harlan's *McGautha* argument upside down. Harlan had argued that discretionary capital sentencing statutes marked the progress of a maturing and humane society by vesting in juries the capacity to exercise mercy. Douglas viewed that same discretion as far more capable of unleashing baser motives, "feeding prejudices against the accused if he is poor and despised, and lacking political clout, or if he is a member of a suspect or unpopular minority, and saving those who by social position may be in a more protected position." The Eighth Amendment, read to incorporate the equal protection clause, required legislatures to write penal laws that are "evenhanded, nonselective, and non-arbitrary, and [required] judges to see to it that general laws are not applied sparsely, selectively, and spottily to unpopular groups."[22]

Douglas concluded his concurrence with the observation that even a capital statute that is nondiscriminatory on its face could be applied in such a way as to violate equal protection, but he left for another day the question of whether a mandatory death penalty law could withstand constitutional scrutiny.

Always Cruel and Unusual

Justice Brennan, who had dissented vigorously in *McGautha*, now moved in *Furman* a step further to becoming the first Supreme Court justice to find the death penalty per se unconstitutional because it violated four principles that together constituted "cruel and unusual punishment" prohibited by the Eighth Amendment.

First, for Brennan, death was the most unusual and the most severe of all punishments inflicted in the United States, as indicated by the complex legal rituals surrounding its implementation and by the fact that it remained the only punishment involving the conscious infliction of physical and mental pain. The punishment of death denied the executed person's humanity, it was irrevocable, and it was "uniquely degrading to human dignity." On those grounds alone, Brennan believed, the penalty in 1972 violated the Eighth Amendment.

Brennan's second principle trumped usage and acceptance, however, because the Eighth Amendment prohibited the *arbitrary infliction of severe punishment*. In fact, the most salient characteristic of the death penalty in 1972 was "the infrequency with which we resort to it." While population had grown, along with the incidents of murders and rapes committed over four decades, the number of persons executed for those offenses had fallen dramatically. "When the punishment of death is inflicted in a trivial number of the cases in which it is legally available," Brennan wrote, "the conclusion is virtually inescapable that it is being inflicted arbitrarily. Indeed, it smacks of little more than a lottery system." The discretionary procedures present in the existing capital statutes failed this constitutional test, according to Brennan, because they did not guard against "the totally capricious selection of criminals for the punishment of death."[23]

Third, history and present evidence indicated that the death penalty had been "almost totally rejected by contemporary society." Public executions had been banned as barbaric and brutalizing. The number of capital offenses had been reduced by statute; nine states had banned capital punishment entirely, and five authorized it only for rare crimes. Virtually all death sentences handed down in 1972 had been imposed by jury discretion. Taken together, Brennan concluded, these facts indicated that American society "questions the appropriateness of this punishment," exhibits "a deep-seated reluctance to inflict it," and "views this punishment with substantial doubt."[24]

Finally, Brennan argued, the Eighth Amendment prohibited this severe, unusual, and degrading punishment because it did not serve any penal purpose that could not be served equally by a less severe punishment. Available evidence indicated that the threat of death had no greater value as a deterrent to murder or rape than the threat of imprisonment, especially in light of the arbitrary process under which those who committed capital crimes would be convicted and sentenced. Under the present discretionary system, "the risk of death is remote and improbable; in contrast, the risk of long-term imprisonment is near and great." When death is so rarely and capriciously inflicted, Brennan concluded, it cannot provide an "emphatic denunciation for capital crimes" or provide "moral enforcement for the basic values of the community."[25]

Abhorrent to Currently Existing Moral Values

Justice Thurgood Marshall, the first African American confirmed to the Court and the legal architect of the NAACP's successful campaign against racial segregation in the public schools, joined Brennan to become only the second justice in the Court's history prepared to invalidate the death penalty in all cases on Eighth Amendment grounds. Like Brennan, Marshall pointed to four reasons why a court-imposed punishment might fall under a constitutional ban. Included were punishments so severe—for example, the rack and the thumbscrew—that a society could not tolerate them and punishments previously unknown as penalties that failed to meet a test of their humane purpose. Although the present capital statutes could not be challenged on those two grounds, they failed for other reasons already elaborated by Brennan. First, they were excessive and served no valid legislative or social purpose apart from retaliation, vengeance, and retribution, all reasons "roundly condemned as intolerable aspirations for a government in a free society." Second, they had become "morally unacceptable to the people of the United States at this time in their history."[26]

Marshall joined Brennan in concluding that the available evidence gave little support to the belief that the death penalty remained a better deterrent to capital crimes than life imprisonment. If that were so, the rates of homicide in states with the death penalty would be far lower than rates in states that had abolished it. But this was not the case. The homicide rate in Georgia, a death penalty state, was no lower than that in Michigan, which had been the first state to abolish the death penalty. Moreover, Marshall argued, most of the people who had committed capital crimes under the present discretionary statutes had never faced execution; even convicted murderers were unlikely to commit other crimes in prison or when released. The weakness of the deterrence argument left only the arguments for retribution or vengeance, both of which Marshall believed had been "consistently denigrated . . . as a permissible goal of punishment" under the Eighth Amendment.[27]

Finally, Marshall echoed Brennan's views that contemporary public opinion manifested grave doubts about the efficacy of the death penalty. To this Marshall added an important caveat: most Americans knew very little about how the states carried out the penalty. Broad opinion polls, then, could not adequately determine whether or not a punishment had become cruel and unusual. Only polls of those "people *who were fully informed* as to the purposes of the penalty and its liabilities [and who] would find the penalty shocking, unjust, and unacceptable" were valid.[28]

"Wantonly and So Freakishly Imposed"

Justice Stewart's concurring opinion in *Furman* became immortalized in the Court's official reports when he wrote, "these death sentences are cruel and unusual in the same way that being struck by lightning is cruel and unusual."[29] Stewart refused to endorse the "ultimate question" resolved by Brennan and Marshall: namely, that the death penalty could never be constitutionally sanctioned by the Eighth and Fourteenth Amendments. And he categorically rejected their belief that retribution was not a constitutionally permissible objective of the law. "The instinct for retribution is part of the nature of man, and channeling that instinct in the administration of criminal justice serves an important purpose in promoting the stability of a society governed by law."[30]

The sentences were cruel and unusual for Stewart because the penalty of death was infrequently imposed for murder and even less so for rape. And of all the people convicted of those crimes in 1967 and 1968, only the defendants in the case before them had become among "a capriciously selected random handful upon whom the sentence of death has in fact been imposed." While Stewart averred that racial discrimination had not been conclusively demonstrated in the three cases, he emphasized that regardless the Constitution could not permit the taking of life by states under procedures that allowed the penalty to be "so wantonly and so freakishly imposed."[31]

Stewart's concurrence deserves further discussion because he had joined Harlan's *McGautha* opinion, in which similar discretionary sentencing statutes challenged on due process grounds had been sustained. Stewart had often joined Harlan in dissent against many of the Warren Court's criminal justice decisions, but death penalty cases appear to have been different for him. Prior to *McGautha,* he had consistently supported new procedural limits in capital cases, notably in *Witherspoon v. Illinois* (1968), in which he authored the majority opinion, as well as in *United States v. Jackson* (1968), *Boykin v. Alabama* (1969), and *Maxwell v. Bishop* (1970).[32]

Stewart had also made a notable contribution to Eighth Amendment jurisprudence. He joined the Court after *Trop v. Dulles* (1958) had been decided, but he wrote the majority opinion in *Robinson v. California* (1962), in which the Court incorporated the Eighth Amendment into the Fourteenth and for the first time struck down a state law on Eighth Amendment grounds.[33] If a state could make heroin addiction alone a crime, he warned in *Robinson,* what would prevent criminal punishment for persons afflicted with mental illness, leprosy, or syphilis? The very randomness of death sentences for homicides and the severity of the death penalty for rape may have impressed Stewart as irrational as locking up an addict solely on the basis of his addiction. Finally, while noting that racial discrimination had not been proven in the *Furman* case, Stewart was not blind to that pathology. Stewart had authored a landmark civil rights decision at the end of the Warren era that gave new life to an old Reconstruction-era statute that permitted Congress to provide remedies for racial discrimination in the sale of real property.[34]

Unlike Stewart, Justice White had seldom been in the vanguard of judicial efforts to surround the death penalty with procedural protections. He had dissented in *Witherspoon* and joined Harlan's majority in *McGautha.* Logically, he should have joined the chief justice and the three other dissenters in *Furman,* but his concurrence was driven by a desire to maintain the death penalty, to eliminate so far as possible the random behavior of judges and juries that had been permitted to erode its consistent application, and to restore capital punishment as a credible deterrent to serious crime. Joining Stewart, he flatly rejected the position of Brennan and Marshall that no capital sentencing statute could pass constitutional muster in the future. Without saying so, he alone among the five-member majority believed the ultimate goal should be more executions, not fewer. Those executions should be carried out, however, under clearly defined legislative guidelines.

For at least three members of the majority, the decline in executions in the United States girded their belief that public opinion had turned against capital punishment. For White, by contrast, that decline signaled a broken mechanism that needed judicial and legislative overhaul in order to effectively fulfill its role in the criminal justice system. Harlan had argued in *McGautha* that discretionary statutes permitted juries and judges to engage in acts of mercy, but White now argued that such discretion had gone too far. "The short of it is that the policy of vesting sentencing authority primarily in juries—a decision largely motivated by the desire to mitigate the harshness of the law and to bring community judgment to bear on the sentence as well as guilt or innocence—has so effectively achieved its aims that capital punishment within the confines of the statutes now before us has for all practical purposes run its course."[35] White favored capital statutes that offered greater guidance for juries and judges in order to restore the efficacy of capital punishment as an effective deterrent.

Not Intolerably Cruel or Uncivilized

Led by Chief Justice Warren Burger, the four dissenters attacked the evidence and the logic of the concurring opinions (**Document 3.5**). Burger challenged the notion that the American public had turned against the death penalty by noting that over two-thirds of the states retained it and that Congress continued to add capital offenses to the statute books. Nor could the mere fact that juries did not impose the sentence in all cases where it was statutorily available be taken as evidence of widespread disapproval. Opponents could not have it both ways by arguing that juries displayed mercy and civilized values when they failed to recommend death, but acted capriciously and wantonly when they opted for execution. Juries knew the awesome life and death decisions they faced, Burger argued, and it was not surprising that they made them with care and discrimination. Of course there were prisoners on death row who would not be there had they been tried by a different jury or in a different jurisdiction, but their fate had been "controlled by a fortuitous circumstance" beyond the control of the law.[36]

The chief justice took special aim at Brennan's argument that the Eighth Amendment banned as "cruel and unusual" all punishments that did not efficiently accomplish the objective of deterring crime. The amendment clearly prohibited torturous and inhumane punishment, Burger wrote, but no decision of the Court had ever made efficacy of punishment a constitutional requirement. "I know of no convincing evidence that life imprisonment is a more effective deterrent than 20 years . . . or even that a $10 parking ticket is a more effective deterrent than a

$5 parking ticket. . . . [But] the questions raised by the necessity approach are beyond the pale of judicial inquiry under the Eighth Amendment."[37]

The concurring justices, Burger added, had all engaged in due process analysis and conclusions that the Court earlier resolved against any challenge in *McGautha* and that had no relevance in Eighth Amendment law. As a consequence of what had been decided, legislatures would likely move to strip juries of discretion and adopt mandatory death penalty statutes. "If this is the only alternative . . . I would have preferred that the Court opt for total abolition."[38]

"The Impoverished and Underprivileged Elements in Society"

Justice Lewis Powell, a courtly Virginian and former president of the American Bar Association, singled out Douglas, Brennan, and Marshall for special criticism in his dissent. Their claims of popular opposition to capital punishment, Powell declared, ignored the legislative record, state and federal, and the fact that juries had returned death sentences at a fairly stable rate of two per week over the course of the 1960s. He found it self-evident that the penalty fell more heavily on what he called "the relatively impoverished and underprivileged elements of society," because the "have-nots" in every society had been "subject to greater pressure to commit crimes and to fewer constraints than their more affluent fellow citizens." These "tragic by-products of social and economic deprivation" that had plagued humanity "since the beginning of recorded history" could not be cured by abolishing the system of criminal penalties.[39]

At the conclusion of his dissent, the chief justice observed that since no majority had been formed "on the ultimate issue" presented in *Furman*, "the future of capital punishment in this country has been left in limbo." But while lamenting that judicial power had been the vehicle for creating that limbo, Burger expressed pleasure that "legislative bodies have been given the opportunity . . . to make a thorough reassessment of the entire subject."[40] The five justices who constituted the majority in *Furman* had called, in effect, for a national referendum on capital punishment in America to either confirm or reverse their decision to strike down the existing statutes. Both they and the four dissenters had based key portions of their Eighth Amendment arguments on a reading of the public's attitude towards capital punishment as manifested in legislative choices, execution statistics, and opinion polls. An immediate answer to the question of the public's mood came quickly in the fall of 1972 in California.

The Supreme Court typically sets the agenda for the lower federal tribunals and for state courts as well, but in 1972 it was California's highest court that took the lead. On February 18, during the course of oral argument in *Furman*, the California supreme court, with one justice dissenting, issued its opinion in *People v. Anderson*,[41] in which a sentence of death was vacated. The court held that the death penalty in California violated the state's constitutional provision prohibiting "cruel or unusual punishment." Writing for the majority, Chief Justice Donald Wright pointed out that the California provision, using broader language than the Eighth Amendment, banned punishments that were either "cruel" or "unusual," and that the penalty offended contemporary standards of decency and that the state had failed to demonstrate it functioned as an effective deterrent to crime. The majority declined to rule on the Eighth Amendment question (**Document 3.6**).

In his dissent in *Furman* a few months later, Justice Harry Blackmun accused the per curiam majority of attempting to catch up with their California counterparts. "The Court, in my view," he wrote, "is somewhat propelled toward its result by the interim decision of the California Supreme Court . . . that the death penalty is violative of that state's constitution."[42] Blackmun's suspicions cannot be verified, but a portion of the California opinion on the ineffectiveness of deterrence did anticipate the arguments made by Brennan and Marshall in *Furman*. In addition, the California high court had obtained the reputation of being the most progressive and legally sophisticated among state tribunals, and its views could not be ignored—except, as it turned out, by the voters of California.

Soon after the decision in *Anderson*, pro-death penalty supporters in California, led by the state's attorney general, Evelle Younger, mounted an initiative campaign to overturn the California supreme court's decision through amendment of the California constitution. That proposal, Proposition 17, the Death Penalty Initiative, quickly gathered more than 1.25 million signatures and was placed on the state's November election ballot (**Document 3.7**). Its key provisions declared that all capital statutes in effect on February 17, 1972, remained in full force and that the death penalty "shall not be deemed to be, or to constitute, the infliction of cruel or unusual punishments . . . nor shall such punishments for such offenses be deemed to contravene any other provision of this Constitution."[43]

The state's law enforcement officials and its Republican Party establishment, headed by governor Ronald Reagan, actively promoted adoption of Proposition 17. State senator H. L. Richardson, for example, declared that murderers should die because they had violated God's law and because the death penalty was an effective deterrent (**Document 3.8**). "The average time served for murder in this state is 14 years; some murderers serve as few as seven years. Such is the going rate for human life these days. Life goes cheap in California." Opponents of the proposition were active too. Liberal newspapers such as the *Los Angeles Times* came out against Proposition 17.[44] *Furman* lawyer Amsterdam wrote an impassioned appeal to the voters of California in the *New York Times* (**Document 3.9**).

On November 7, 1972, the voters of California repudiated their state supreme court when they approved Proposition 17 by a 3 to 1 margin. In so doing, the citizens of California reinstituted the recently defunct death penalty statutes and

In September 1973 California governor Ronald Reagan signed into law legislation that reinstated the death penalty in the state for specific crimes. This legislation followed the Supreme Court's decision in Furman v. Georgia *and a successful state ballot initiative aimed at restoring capital punishment. In 1976, after the Court's ruling in* Gregg v. Georgia, *the California supreme court found the state's death penalty statute unconstitutional. It was once again reinstated, however, after the state passed legislation allowing for the presentation of mitigating evidence.*

authorized the legislature to add more capital crimes to the state's criminal code.[45] Legislatures in other states responded to *Furman* in much the same way. By 1976 thirty-five state legislatures had rewritten their death penalty statutes in an effort to conform to what they took to be the Court's *Furman* requirements. Congress also mandated a new federal death penalty for air piracy. Even President Nixon made an appeal for the restoration of the federal death penalty (**Document 3.10**).

The Death Penalty Revisited, July 2, 1976

Among the states, some—Louisiana and North Carolina notably—curtailed jury discretion entirely by mandating imposition of the death penalty for specific crimes, such as the murder of a police officer or homicide during the course of a robbery. While some states retained the penalty for kidnapping and rape, most narrowed the punishment only to homicides having certain characteristics, defined as constituting aggravating factors. States also required separate sentencing proceedings where defendants could introduce so-called mitigating factors relating to the crime itself, or to the characteristics of the defendant. Most provided for expedited review of all capital sentences to the state supreme court.

Two years after *Furman*, under these new statutes, juries had convicted and sentenced to death 254 persons; by 1976 the number of prisoners on the states' death rows had swollen to 460. On July 2, 1976, the justices decided five capital cases (*Gregg v. Georgia; Proffitt v. Florida; Jurek v. Texas; Woodson v. North Carolina*; and *Roberts, el al. v. Louisiana*), collectively know as *Gregg v. Georgia*, to determine whether the five state statutes had made revisions that avoided this ultimate penalty from being, as Justice Stewart had said in *Furman*, "so wantonly and so freakishly imposed."[46]

The Court that decided the July 2 cases contained one significant change from the bench that had ruled four years earlier in *Furman*. On November 12, 1975, an ailing Douglas resigned from the Court, having served longer (36 years and 7 months) than any justice in history. President Gerald Ford quickly nominated federal circuit court judge John Paul Stevens from Chicago to fill Douglas's seat. Unanimously confirmed by the Senate, Stevens took his seat in December and cast a decisive vote in the *Gregg* cases. The departure of Douglas meant that the Court lost its most potent voice with respect to equal protection arguments that had been the core of his concurring opinion in *Furman*. Douglas had concluded that the discretionary statutes gave too much room for discrimination on the grounds of race, religion, wealth, social position, or class and targeted those he described as "poor and despised." In one of their challenges to the revised Georgia statute, lawyers for Troy Gregg argued that it did nothing at all to curb the discretion still vested in prosecutors to determine who would be initially charged with capital murder, an argument that might have moved Douglas but that was categorically rejected by the seven justices who controlled the outcome in *Furman*.

The Stewart-Powell-Stevens Trio

With Brennan and Marshall maintaining their *Furman* posture—that capital punishment always constituted "cruel and unusual punishment" in violation of the Eighth Amendment—the fate of the five defendants and the state statutes in *Gregg* rested with the other seven members of the Court. In particular, it rested with Stewart, Powell, and Stevens, who voted as a bloc to determine the outcome in all five cases. In their combined opinion in *Gregg*, the trio categorically rejected the Brennan-Marshall position on the Eighth Amendment on several grounds (**Document 3.11**). First, they argued, the Constitution itself in its two due process clauses sanctioned death as a penalty, the death penalty was widely used at the time of the adoption of the Eighth Amendment, and no prior decision of the Court had held otherwise. Second, the California referendum and the decisions of thirty-five states and the federal government to reestablish the death penalty indicated that, contrary to Marshall and Brennan's claims, the penalty did not violate the evolving standards of decency test enunciated in *Weems* and *Trop*. Finally, the penalty could be justified on grounds of both its deterrent effect, where the evidence remained ambiguous, and retribution since "certain crimes are themselves so grievous an affront to humanity that the only adequate response may be the penalty of death."[47]

Because the death penalty did not, therefore, "invariably" violate the Constitution, the Stewart-Powell-Stevens trio addressed the central question in the five statutes: did the new procedures where discretion had been given to a sentencing body (jury or judge) provide, as *Furman* required, "that discretion . . . be suitably directed and limited so as to minimize the risk of wholly arbitrary and capricious action"? With respect to the Georgia, Florida, and Texas statutes, they and four concurring justices (Burger, White, William Rehnquist, and Blackmun) answered in the affirmative; with respect to the mandatory statutes of North Carolina and Louisiana, the trio and two concurring justices (Brennan and Marshall) answered in the negative.

The three statutes approved (Georgia's, Florida's, and Texas's) had different schemes, but the majority held that each sufficiently narrowed the criteria for imposing death and yet still retained broad discretion that permitted the exercise of mercy. In short, the Stewart-Powell-Stevens trio attempted to combine the dominant perspective of Justice Harlan's *McGautha* opinion (that discretion was an essential element in a civilized system of crime and punishment) with the requirement of explicit standards (which *Furman* had demanded and which Harlan had argued in *McGautha* would amount to little more than "boiler-plate"). The seeds of the Court's future death penalty conundrum about how to avoid capricious sentencing while maintaining discretion were sowed in *Gregg* and its companion cases.

Georgia's statute, under which Gregg had been convicted of armed robbery and murder, consisted of both a guilt stage and a sentencing stage. During the second sentencing stage, the jury could not sentence Gregg to death unless it found at least one of ten so-called aggravating factors, which included, for example, a previous felony conviction; the commission of a crime for the purpose of receiving money or anything else of value; the creation of a grave risk of death to others; the homicide of a police officer, prison guard, or fireman in the line of duty; or the commission of a crime that was "outrageously or wantonly vile, horrible, or inhuman in that it involves torture, depravity of mind, or an aggravated battery to the victim" (**Document 3.12**). At this stage, too, both defense and prosecution were permitted to introduce to the jury any mitigating evidence or aggravating evidence prior to its decision. But the aggravating evidence was not limited to the ten factors required for a death sentence, and the Georgia scheme did not require the jury to find that the aggravating evidence somehow outweighed the factors of mitigation.

The Georgia statute also required of all capital cases an expedited appeal to the state's supreme court, with that court required to determine whether the particular sentence was imposed "under the influence of passion, prejudice, or anything arbitrary . . . whether . . . the evidence supports the . . . finding of a statutory aggravating circumstance . . . and whether the sentence of death is excessive or disproportionate to the penalty imposed in similar cases, considering both the crime and the defendant."[48]

Unlike the statutes condemned in *Furman,* the Stewart-Powell-Stevens trio concluded, the Georgia revisions focused the jury's attention upon the particular circumstances of the crime and the particular characteristics of the individual defendant. While permitted to weigh mitigating and aggravating circumstances, the jury was required to find at least one aggravating factor before decreeing death. "In this way," they concluded, "the jury's discretion is channeled. No longer can a jury wantonly and freakishly impose the death sentence; it is always circumscribed by the legislative guidelines."[49]

The Stewart-Powell-Stevens trio argued that the bifurcated procedure in Georgia "is more likely to ensure elimination of the constitutional deficiencies identified in *Furman,*" but they did not make it a necessary condition of constitutionality. The Georgia system indicated that, contrary to *McGautha,* it was possible for legislatures to construct capital sentencing that measured up to the concerns in *Furman.* Whether they did so would be decided on a case-by-case basis.

The Florida and Texas Alternatives

The Court put a constitutional stamp of approval on the Georgia statute, despite criticism that at least one of its so-called aggravating factors (the crime was "outrageously or wantonly vile, horrible, or inhuman in that it involved torture, depravity of mind, or an aggravating battery of the victim") did little to guide a jury's decision and could still produce "wanton" and "freakish" imposition of the death penalty. On the same day, the coalition on the Court upheld the new Florida statute in *Proffitt v. Florida* (1976)[50] and the Texas statute in *Jurek v. Texas* (1976),[51] although both contained significant differences from the Georgia system.

Florida had sentenced William Proffitt to death for first-degree murder under a bifurcated procedure whereby the jury had to find at least one aggravating factor drawn from a list of eight similar to Georgia's (**Document 3.13**). In addition, the jury was required to weigh any of seven mitigating factors against the statutory aggravating factors before recommending death, an innovation that drew the approval of the Stewart-Powell-Stevens trio because it echoed recommendations made in the Model Penal Code.[52] The trio rejected the claim that at least one of the eight aggravating factors—that the crime was "especially heinous, atrocious and cruel"—was even vaguer than its Georgia counterpart and so broad as to invite arbitrary decisions about life or death (**Document 3.14**).

The Florida statute made the jury's recommendation only advisory. The trial judge could disregard it. If he imposed death against a jury recommendation, the judge had to weigh aggravating against mitigating factors and could do so only if "the facts suggesting a sentence of death should be so clear and convincing that virtually no reasonable person could differ."[53] The trio endorsed this broad judicial discretion with the curious argument that it "should lead, if anything, to even greater consistency in the imposition at the trial court level of capital punishment, since the trial judge is more experienced in sentencing than a jury."[54] In this case, the quest for standards through judicial discretion trumped the jury as the conscience of the community.

The Texas statute narrowly defined capital murder as that involving the murder of a peace officer or fireman; murder in the course of rape, kidnapping, arson, burglary, or robbery; or murder for hire. At the separate sentencing hearing, the jury had to answer in the affirmative three special questions before imposing death: Did the evidence establish beyond a reasonable doubt that the killing had been deliberate? Did the evidence establish beyond a reasonable doubt that the defendant would be a continuing threat to society? And, did the evidence suggest that the defendant's reaction to provocation was unreasonable? Stewart, Powell, and Stevens justified this obvious departure from the scheme of specific aggravating factors presented in Georgia and Florida by arguing that, by focusing upon the particularized nature of capital murder, Texas had accomplished the same objective of narrowing the criteria of those eligible for death. Moreover, they noted, this Texas formula might actually produce a smaller crop of death-eligible defendants (**Document 3.15**).

The Texas statute did not employ the language of aggravation or mitigation and asked the jury to consider only one aspect of the defendant's character before recommending death: his future risk to the community. Jurek's lawyers contended that this special issue was so fraught with subjectivity that it was essentially an invitation to "wanton" and "freakish" imposition of the death penalty and violated the Court's concern for individualizing punishment. The Stewart-Powell-Stevens trio brushed this concern aside by noting that the Texas court of criminal appeals had indicated that this special issue permitted a defendant to submit all mitigating evidence to the jury for consideration. "It is, of course, not easy to predict future behavior. The fact that such a determination is difficult, however, does not mean that it cannot be made. . . . For those sentenced to prison, these same predictions must be made by parole authorities. The task . . . in answering the statutory question in issue is thus basically no different from the task performed countless times each day throughout the American system of criminal justice."[55]

"Simply Papered Over"

The Stewart-Powell-Stevens trio, having joined the chief justice and four others to sustain the statutes and death sentences in Georgia, Florida, and Texas, next joined with Brennan and Marshall to strike down the mandatory statutes at issue in North Carolina (**Document 3.16**) and Louisiana. By invoking the language of "evolving standards of decency" and "the limits of civilized standards" from earlier Eighth Amendment cases such as *Weems* and *Trop,* the trio had been able to demonstrate by virtue of legislative decisions that the reenactment of capital punishment statutes like those in Georgia, Florida, and Texas after *Furman* provided powerful evidence that the death penalty did not violate the command of the Eighth Amendment. In the case of *Woodson v. North Carolina* (1976) and *Roberts v. Louisiana* (1976),[56] they turned this argument on its head to argue that mandatory death penalty statutes—even for premeditated killings in connection with arson, rape, robbery, kidnapping, burglary, or other felony—violated that amendment and the Court's mandate in *Furman* (**Document 3.17**).

The mandatory statutes in North Carolina and Louisiana, the majority ruled, crossed the Eighth Amendment line for three reasons that were rooted in history and in the *Furman* decision itself. Invoking *McGautha*, the majority argued that mandatory statutes had been repudiated by state legislatures in the nineteenth century both because of humanitarian reasons and because juries refused in many circumstances to convict defendants under such circumstances. Legislatures had adopted discretionary statutes in order to promote a renewed respect for the rule of law and to give juries latitude to distinguish those who deserved to die from those who did not. The state legislatures who responded to *Furman* had voted to repair the failed discretionary regimes, but not to restore the repudiated mandatory statutes as indicated by the examples of Georgia, Florida, Texas, and thirty other states.

North Carolina and Louisiana were exceptions in the post-*Furman* era, out of step with "civilized standards," and they had failed to comply with one of the decision's critical conclusions: death remained different from all other sanctions in kind rather than degree. Any sentencing procedures that neglected to consider "the character and record of the individual offender" excludes from the consideration of the sentencing authorities "the possibilities of compassionate or mitigating factors stemming from the diverse frailties of humankind."[57] North Carolina's mandatory statute, the plurality concluded, would turn back the clock and promote more lawlessness by juries unwilling to convict. Its solution had "simply papered over the problem of unguided and unchecked jury discretion" that the Court condemned in *Furman*.[58] Justice Rehnquist, nominated by President Nixon after serving in his Department of Justice, joined Burger, White, and Blackmun, but also filed a blistering dissent of his own in *Woodson*.

The majority, he wrote, had misread history. The behavior of juries who refused to convict defendants under mandatory death penalty statutes could not be taken as evidence of popular disapproval of such laws, but only the lawless acts of individuals. State legislatures, on the other hand, had continued to adopt such statutes, and their responses remained a better indicator of public sentiment. In adopting discretionary statutes, legislatures voted to make certain that some defendants who might otherwise have gone free endured some punishment, but that choice "hardly reflects the sort of an 'evolving standard of decency' to which the plurality professes obeisance."[59]

Rehnquist also chastised the decision for its emphasis upon individual considerations in sentencing, a concept he believed alien to Eighth Amendment law and its core value against "cruel and unusual punishment." Since Stewart, Powell, and Stevens had conceded that the North Carolina death penalty itself did not violate the Eighth Amendment, they had imported into it due process requirements that the Court had rejected in *McGautha*. "The Fourteenth Amendment," Rehnquist wrote, "giving the fullest scope to its 'majestic generalities' . . . is conscripted rather than interpreted when used to permit one but not another system for imposition of the death penalty."[60]

The July 2 Cases and the Future

In 1972 in *Furman* the Court ratified what had been in effect a national moratorium on the death penalty in the United States. In the process it essentially asked the American people to decide if they wished to see that moratorium continue or become permanent. From coast to coast the popular and legislative response to *Furman* was an overwhelming reaffirmation of the death penalty, which the Court itself ratified four years later in *Gregg* and its companion cases. It is worth speculating about what might have happened had the Court avoided a broad constitutional attack in *Furman*, decided those cases on much narrower grounds, and allowed the future of the death penalty to be resolved state by state through legislative and judicial decisions. Who is to say that the existing moratorium would not have continued, that other state courts would not have followed the example of California, or that more state legislatures would not have moved in the direction of abolition?

Without doubt, *Furman* focused public attention on the death penalty as never before, asking the baldest and most polarizing question: should state-sanctioned execution continue? The clearest answers came from states like North Carolina and Louisiana that adopted mandatory statutes. *Furman*, in short, aroused new enthusiasm for capital punishment in much the same way that the Court's 1973 abortion decision, *Roe v. Wade*, called forth a powerful national anti-abortion movement.[61] *Roe v. Wade* would provoke a similar legislative backlash, drawing the Court into decades of seemingly endless litigation and political controversy.

The July 2 cases had settled some constitutional questions, but also guaranteed that death penalty cases would crowd the justices' annual docket as never before. The seven votes affirming the constitutionality of the penalty in 1976 meant that total abolition would likely not come through a federal judicial decision. The Court would, as *Furman* required, insist on some legislative standards to determine which defendants were eligible for death. But those standards could not constrain sentencing discretion on an individual basis such that they destroyed the role of the jury as "the conscience of the community," the basic link between "contemporary community values and the penal system," without which punishment could not reflect "the evolving standards of decency that mark the progress of a maturing society."

Document 3.1
Brief Filed on Behalf of William Henry Furman by His Attorneys, September 9, 1971

Attorneys from the National Association for the Advancement of Colored People, led by Jack Greenberg, Michael Meltsner, and Anthony Amsterdam, filed the following brief emphasizing the rarity and randomness of state-sanctioned executions on behalf of William Henry Furman in the case of Furman v. Georgia.

. . . Summary of Argument

I. Petitioner's sentence of death is a rare, random and arbitrary infliction, prohibited by the Eighth Amendment principles briefed in *Aikens v. California*.

II. The Eighth Amendment forbids affirmance of a death sentence upon this record, which casts doubt upon petitioner's mental soundness. To relegate petitioner to the torments and vicissitudes of a death sentence without appropriate inquiry into his mental condition is to subject him to cruel and unusual punishment. . . .

The Brief for Petitioner in *Aikens v. California* fully develops the reasons why we believe that the death penalty is a cruel and unusual punishment for the crime of murder, as that penalty is administered in the United States today. At the heart of the argument is the principle that the Eighth Amendment condemns a penalty which is so oppressive that it can command public acceptance only by sporadic, exceedingly rare and arbitrary imposition.

Petitioner's case epitomizes that characteristic of the penalty of death for murder. His was a grave offense, but one no ways distinguishable from thousands of others for which the death penalty is not inflicted. Following a brief trial which told the jury nothing more than that petitioner had killed Mr. Micke by a single handgun shot through a closed door during an armed burglary attempt upon a dwelling—and which permitted his conviction whether or not the fatal shot was intentionally fired—he was condemned to die. The jury knew nothing else about the man they sentenced, except his age and race.

It is inconceivable to imagine contemporary acceptance of the general application of the death penalty upon such a basis. Only wholly random and arbitrary selection of a few, rare murder convicts makes capital punishment for murder tolerable to our society. For the reasons stated in the *Aikens* brief, it is not tolerable to the Eighth Amendment.

But there is an additional reason why the sentence of death imposed on this petitioner cannot constitutionally stand. The record in this case bears plain indications that petitioner is mentally ill. The imposition of a death sentence upon him without adequate inquiry concerning either his competency to be executed or his capacity to withstand the stress of such a sentence violates the Eighth Amendment. . . .

Source: Supreme Court of the United States, *William Henry Furman, Petitioner, v. Georgia, Respondent.* No. 71–5003, September 9, 1971, on writ of certiorari to the Supreme Court of Georgia brief for petitioner.

Document 3.2
Brief Filed on Behalf of the Synagogue Council of America and Its Constituents and the American Jewish Congress in *Furman v. Georgia*, September 9, 1971

The landmark Supreme Court case of Furman v. Georgia *drew many amici curiae (friends of the court) briefs from various organizations and individuals both supporting and opposing capital punishment. New York attorney Leo Pfeffer submitted the following amicus brief on behalf of the Synagogue Council of America, its constituent organizations, and the American Jewish Congress.*

. . . This brief seeks to introduce a factor which it is believed is not fully presented in the parties' briefs. It seeks to stress that the unacceptability of the death penalty, which establishes its invalidity under the Eighth Amendment, is not merely an American phenomenon but one expressing universal values. This is manifested by the expressions ranging from the *de facto* abolition of the death penalty by the Rabbis in Talmudic times two thousand years ago to the current studies and reports of the United Nations. We argue that a decent respect for the opinions of mankind impels a constitutional declaration by this Court that the law of the land is consistent with the universal unacceptability of the death penalty. . . .

All of the *amici* are opposed as a matter of principle to the imposition of the death penalty and supports its abolition. Their position is based on their judgment as to the demands of contemporary American democratic standards, but also has its roots in ancient Jewish tradition. This statement may seem surprising in view of the many references in the Hebrew Bible to the death penalty for such transgressions as adultery (Lev. 20:21), bestiality (Ex. 22:18), murder (Ex. 21:12) and rape of a betrothed woman (Deut. 22:15). Indeed, these Scriptural provisions are often invoked by defenders of capital punishment.

These statements, however, reflect an unfamiliarity with the full Jewish tradition, and specifically with the fact that Rabbinic Judaism during the Talmudic period, some two thousand years ago, represents the interpretation and implementation of the Scriptural command. We can fully understand the Scriptures only through their presentation by the Oral Law, of which Talmud is the prime exponent. . . .

To take a human life, the Rabbis said, is a matter of the gravest seriousness. Execution is not reversible. If a mistake is made what has been done cannot be undone. One who takes a human life, they pointed out, diminishes the Divine Image. On occasions, this extreme means may be necessary to protect society. But it may be carried out only when there can be absolutely no doubt concerning the guilt of the accused and of his freely chosen, deliberate and knowing act. In view of human fallibility which is so pervasive a factor in all judgments, a drastic step such as terminating a human life was as a practical matter not defensible. . . .

Under the Eighth Amendment to the Federal Constitution, made applicable to the states by the Fourteenth, a state may not impose punishment which is cruel or unusual. The ultimate responsibility of determining whether punishment is cruel or unusual rests not with the legislature but with the courts, and ultimately of course this Court. In discharging this responsibility the Court is not restricted to standards prevailing in 1789 when the Amendment was framed but should apply contemporary standards. Nor should these standards be limited by considerations of geographic regionalism, but should give weight to national and even international judgments. Moreover, it should consider the efficacy or inefficacy of the death penalty as a deterrent and should give weight to the usual if not inevitable concomitants of imposition of the death penalty, such as unequal and racially discriminatory imposition. Measured by these standards the death penalty constitutes cruel and unusual punishment within the meaning of the Eighth Amendment, and certainly so in cases of non-homicidal rape. . . .

We have suggested that local or regional standards are not the appropriate measure to determine whether the death penalty constitutes cruel and unusual punishment within the purview of the Eighth Amendment, and that fundamental rights secured by the national constitution must be applied nationally. We submit that viewed nationally "the evolving standards of decency that mark the progress of a maturing society" clearly point to the elimination of the death penalty in the United States.

Although general public opinion has fluctuated over the years, the trend is strongly toward abolition. Where an informed public opinion is concerned, opposition to capital punishment is overwhelming (with the exception of professional law enforcement officials, but not correction officials). . . .

Legislative action reflects this trend. In the past several years, five states (Iowa, New York, Oregon, West Virginia and Vermont) have abolished the death penalty. In addition, the United States Department of Justice has urged Congress to abolish the death penalty in places under its jurisdiction. . . .

An examination of what actually has been happening shows clearly that the death penalty has really become an "unusual" punishment. The number of persons executed within the United States in the years 1930, 1940, 1950 and from 1960 to the present as reported by the Federal Bureau of Prisons are shown in the following table:

1930 = 155
1940 = 124
1950 = 82
1960 = 56
1961 = 42
1962 = 47
1963 = 21
1964 = 15
1965 = 7
1966 = 1
1967 = 2
1968 = 0
1969 = 0
1970 = 0

. . . Nevertheless, the steady decline in the number of persons executed during the past four decades can be explained only in terms of a widely held belief that the death penalty is basically cruel and morally unacceptable. . . .

All the evidence points to the conclusion that capital punishment is on its way out. It is but a matter of time before the laws authorizing it are repealed or become dead letters. The reason for this is that it no longer comports with "the evolving standards of decency that mark the progress of a maturing society," and this will become increasingly obvious in the coming years.

Source: Supreme Court of the United States, *Earnest James Aikens, Petitioner v. State of California, Respondent; William Henry Furman, Petitioner v. State of Georgia, Respondent; Lucious Jackson, Petitioner v. State of Georgia, Respondent; Elmer Branch, Petitioner v. State of Texas, Respondent* [October Term 1971], September 9, 1971, Brief Amici Curiae and Motion for Leave to File Brief Amici Curiae of the Synagogue Council of America and Its Constituents (the Central Conference of American Rabbis, the Rabbinical Assembly of America, the Rabbinical Council of America, the Union of American Hebrew Congregations, the Union of Orthodox Jewish Congregations of America, The United Synagogue of America) and the American Jewish Congress.

Document 3.3
The Supreme Court Declares Existing Death Penalty Statutes Unconstitutional, but Five Justices in the Majority Cannot Agree on the Grounds, June 29, 1972

In Furman v. Georgia *(1972), the Supreme Court for the first time in U.S. history declared the death penalty cruel and unusual punishment prohibited by the Eighth Amendment. The decision voided the capital statutes of the states and the federal government. Five members of the Court agreed only on a short per curiam (for the Court) opinion, but then each wrote a separate concurring opinion expressing different views justifying their decisions. Four justices, led by Chief Justice Warren Burger, dissented.*

PER CURIAM.

Petitioner in No. 69–5003 [William Henry Furman] was convicted of murder in Georgia and was sentenced to death. . . . Petitioner in No. 69–5030 [Lucious Jackson] was convicted of rape in Georgia and was sentenced to death. . . . Petitioner in No. 69–5031 [Elmer Branch] was convicted of rape in Texas and was sentenced to death. . . . Certiorari was granted limited to the following question: "Does the imposition and carrying out of the death penalty in [these cases] constitute cruel and unusual punishment in violation of the Eighth and Fourteenth Amendments?" The Court holds that the imposition and carrying out of the death penalty in these cases constitute cruel and unusual punishment in violation of the Eighth and Fourteenth Amendments. The judgment in each case is therefore reversed insofar as it leaves undisturbed the death sentences imposed, and the cases are remanded for further proceedings.

So ordered.

Source: Furman v. Georgia, 408 U.S. 238 (1972), at 240–241.

Document 3.4
Five Justices Endorse the Per Curiam in *Furman*, June 29, 1972

Justices William O. Douglas, Potter Stewart, Byron White, William Brennan, and Thurgood Marshall constituted the majority who supported the per curiam opinion in Furman, *but each authored a separate concurring opinion. Douglas, for example, read the Eighth Amendment as incorporating the Fourteenth Amendment's requirement of equal protection of the law. Brennan and Marshall alone held that the death penalty had become per se unconstitutional as cruel and unusual punishment. Stewart advocated more guided statutory provisions in an effort to narrow the category of death-eligible capital defendants, while White likewise insisted on statutory guidance in order to restore confidence in the penalty. The concurring opinion of Justice Marshall, which largely echoed the views expressed in Justice Brennan's opinion, has been omitted.*

MR. JUSTICE DOUGLAS, concurring.

. . . It would seem to be incontestable that the death penalty inflicted on one defendant is "unusual" if it discriminates against him by reason of his race, religion, wealth, social position, or class, or if it is imposed under a procedure that gives room for the play of such prejudices. . . .

There is increasing recognition of the fact that the basic theme of equal protection is implicit in "cruel and unusual" punishments. "A penalty . . . should be considered 'unusually' imposed if it is administered arbitrarily or discriminatorily." . . .

We cannot say from facts disclosed in these records that these defendants were sentenced to death because they were black. Yet our task is not restricted to an effort to divine what motives impelled these death penalties. Rather, we deal with a system of law and of justice that leaves to the uncontrolled discretion of judges or juries the determination whether defendants committing these crimes should die or be imprisoned. Under these laws no standards govern the selection of the penalty. People live or die, dependent on the whim of 1 man or of 12. . . .

The high service rendered by the "cruel and unusual" punishment clause of the Eighth Amendment is to require legislatures to write penal laws that are evenhanded, nonselective, and nonarbitrary, and to require judges to see to it that general laws are not applied sparsely, selectively, and spottily to unpopular groups.

A law that stated that anyone making more than $50,000 would be exempt from the death penalty would plainly fall, as would a law that in terms said that blacks, those who never went beyond the fifth grade in school, those who made less than $3,000 a year, or those who were unpopular or unstable should be the only people executed. A law which in the overall view reaches that result in practice has no more sanctity than a law which in terms provides the same.

Thus, these discretionary statutes are unconstitutional in their operation. They are pregnant with discrimination and discrimination is an ingredient not compatible with the idea of equal protection of the laws that is implicit in the ban of "cruel and unusual" punishments. . . .

Whether a mandatory death penalty would otherwise be constitutional is a question I do not reach.

I concur in the judgments of the Court.

MR. JUSTICE BRENNAN, concurring.

. . . There are, then, four principles by which we may determine whether a particular punishment is "cruel and unusual." The primary principle, which I believe supplies the essential predicate for the application of the others, is that a punishment must not by its severity be degrading to human dignity. The paradigm violation of this principle would be the infliction of a torturous punishment of the type that the Clause has always prohibited. Yet "[i]t is unlikely that any State at this moment in history," . . . would pass a law providing for the infliction of such a punishment. Indeed, no such punishment has ever been before this Court. The same may be said of the other principles. It is unlikely that this Court will confront a severe punishment that is obviously inflicted in wholly arbitrary fashion; no State would engage in a reign of blind terror. Nor is it likely that this Court will be called upon to review a severe punishment that is clearly and totally rejected throughout society; no legislature would be able even to authorize the infliction of such a punishment. Nor, finally, is it likely that this Court will have to consider a severe punishment that is patently unnecessary; no State today would inflict a severe punishment knowing that there was no reason whatever for doing so. In short, we are unlikely to have occasion to determine that a punishment is fatally offensive under any one principle.

. . . If a punishment is unusually severe, if there is a strong probability that it is inflicted arbitrarily, if it is substantially rejected by contemporary society, and if there is no reason to believe that it serves any penal purpose more effectively than some less severe punishment, then the continued infliction of that punishment violates the command of the Clause that the State may not inflict inhuman and uncivilized punishments upon those convicted of crimes. . . .

The only explanation for the uniqueness of death is its extreme severity. Death is today an unusually severe punishment, unusual in its pain, in its finality, and in its enormity. . . . Since the discontinuance of flogging as a constitutionally permissible punishment, death remains as the only punishment that may involve the conscious infliction of physical pain. . . .

The unusual severity of death is manifested most clearly in its finality and enormity. Death, in these respects, is in a class by itself. . . .

The outstanding characteristic of our present practice of punishing criminals by death is the infrequency with which we resort to it. . . .

When a country of over 200 million people inflicts an unusually severe punishment no more than 50 times a year, the inference is strong that the punishment is not being regularly and fairly applied. . . .

When the punishment of death is inflicted in a trivial number of the cases in which it is legally available, the conclusion is virtually inescapable that it is being inflicted arbitrarily. Indeed, it smacks of little more than a lottery system. . . .

An examination of the history and present operation of the American practice of punishing criminals by death reveals that this punishment has been almost totally rejected by contemporary society. . . .

The progressive decline in, and the current rarity of, the infliction of death demonstrate that our society seriously questions the appropriateness of this punishment today. . . . At the very least, I must conclude that contemporary society views this punishment with substantial doubt. . . .

A rational person contemplating a murder or rape is confronted, not with the certainty of a speedy death, but with the slightest possibility that he will be executed in the distant future. The risk of death is remote and improbable; in contrast, the risk of long-term imprisonment is near and great. . . .

There is, then, no substantial reason to believe that the punishment of death, as currently administered, is necessary for the protection of society. . . .

When the overwhelming number of criminals who commit capital crimes go to prison, it cannot be concluded that death serves the purpose of retribution more effectively than imprisonment. The asserted public belief that murderers and rapists deserve to die is flatly inconsistent with the execution of a random few. . . .

In sum, the punishment of death is inconsistent with all four principles: Death is an unusually severe and degrading punishment; there is a strong probability that it is inflicted arbitrarily; its rejection by contemporary society is virtually total; and there is no reason to believe that it serves any penal purpose more effectively than the less severe punishment of imprisonment. The function of these principles is to enable a court to determine whether a punishment comports with human dignity. Death, quite simply, does not. . . .

MR. JUSTICE STEWART, concurring.

The penalty of death differs from all other forms of criminal punishment, not in degree but in kind. It is unique in its total irrevocability. It is unique in its rejection of rehabilitation of the convict as a basic purpose of criminal justice. And it is unique, finally, in its absolute renunciation of all that is embodied in our concept of humanity.

For these and other reasons, at least two of my Brothers have concluded that the infliction of the death penalty is constitutionally impermissible in all circumstances under the Eighth and Fourteenth Amendments. Their case is a strong one. But I find it unnecessary to reach the ultimate question they would decide. . . .

In the first place, it is clear that these sentences are "cruel" in the sense that they excessively go beyond, not in degree but in kind, the punishments that the state legislatures have determined to be necessary. In the second place, it is equally clear that these sentences are "unusual" in the sense that the penalty of death is infrequently imposed for murder, and that its imposition for rape is extraordinarily rare. But I do not rest my conclusion upon these two propositions alone.

These death sentences are cruel and unusual in the same way that being struck by lightning is cruel and unusual. For, of all the people convicted of rapes and murders in 1967 and 1968, many just as reprehensible as these, the petitioners are among a capriciously selected random handful upon whom the sentence of death has in fact been imposed. My concurring Brothers have demonstrated that, if any basis can be discerned for the selection of these few to be sentenced to die, it is the constitutionally impermissible basis of race. But racial discrimination has not been proved, and I put it to one side. I simply conclude that the Eighth and Fourteenth Amendments cannot tolerate the infliction of a sentence of death under legal systems that permit this unique penalty to be so wantonly and so freakishly imposed.

For these reasons, I concur in the judgments of the Court.

MR. JUSTICE WHITE, concurring.

. . . In joining the Court's judgments, therefore, I do not at all intimate that the death penalty is unconstitutional *per se* or that there is no system of capital punishment that would comport with the Eighth Amendment. That question, ably argued by several of my Brethren, is not presented by these cases and need not be decided. . . .

Most important, a major goal of the criminal law—to deter others by punishing the convicted criminal—would not be substantially served where the penalty is so seldom invoked that it ceases to be a credible threat essential to influence the conduct of others. For present purposes I accept the morality and utility of punishing one person to influence another. I accept also the effectiveness of punishment generally and need not reject the death penalty as a more effective deterrent than a lesser punishment. But common sense and experience tell us that seldom-enforced laws become ineffective measures for controlling human conduct and that the death penalty, unless imposed with sufficient frequency, will make little contribution to deterring those crimes for which it may be exacted. . . .

The imposition and execution of the death penalty are obviously cruel in the dictionary sense. But the penalty has not been considered cruel and unusual punishment in the constitutional sense because it was thought justified by the social ends it was deemed to serve. At the moment that it ceases realistically to further these purposes, however, the emerging question is whether its imposition in such circumstances would violate the Eighth Amendment. It is my view that it would, for its imposition would then be the pointless and needless extinction of life with only marginal contributions to any discernible social or public purposes. . . .

It is also my judgment that this point had been reached with respect to capital punishment as it is presently administered under the statutes involved in these cases. . . . I cannot avoid the conclusion that the statutes before us are now administered, the penalty is so infrequently imposed that the threat of execution is too attenuated to be of substantial service to criminal justice. . . .

The short of it is that the policy of vesting sentencing authority primarily in juries—a decision largely motivated by the desire to mitigate the harshness of the law and to bring community judgment to bear on the sentence as well as guilt or innocence—has so effectively achieved its aims that capital punishment within the confines of the statutes now before us has for all practical purposes run its course. . . .

Source: *Furman v. Georgia*, 408 U.S. 238 (1972), at 241–257, 258–306, 307–310, 311–314.

Document 3.5
Four Justices Dissent in *Furman v. Georgia*, June 29, 1972

Led by Chief Justice Warren Burger, four members of the Supreme Court dissented in the Furman *case. They averred that the existing death penalty statutes did not violate the Eighth Amendment. The main dissents were written by the chief justice, Justice Harry Blackmun, and Justice Lewis Powell. All rejected the argument that the penalty had been renounced by public opinion as contrary to evolving standards of decency and criticized the majority for engaging in judicial activism by overturning a policy choice made by elected officials.*

MR. CHIEF JUSTICE BURGER, with whom MR. JUSTICE BLACKMUN, MR. JUSTICE POWELL, and MR. JUSTICE REHNQUIST join, dissenting. . . .

There are no obvious indications that capital punishment offends the conscience of society to such a degree that our traditional deference to the legislative judgment must be abandoned. It is not a punishment such as burning at the stake that everyone would ineffably find to be repugnant to all civilized standards. Nor is it a punishment so roundly condemned that only a few aberrant legislatures have retained it on the statute books. Capital punishment is authorized by statute in 40 States, the District of Columbia, and in the federal courts for the commission of certain crimes. On four occasions in the last 11 years Congress has added to the list of federal crimes punishable by death. In looking for reliable indicia of contemporary attitude, none more trustworthy has been advanced. . . .

It cannot be gainsaid that by the choice of juries—and sometimes judges—the death penalty is imposed in far fewer than half the cases in which it is available. To go further and characterize the rate of imposition as "freakishly rare," as petitioners insist, is unwarranted hyperbole. And regardless of its characterization, the rate of imposition does not impel the conclusion that capital punishment is now regarded as intolerably cruel or uncivilized. . . .

The selectivity of juries in imposing the punishment of death is properly viewed as a refinement on, rather than a repudiation of, the statutory authorization for that penalty. Legislatures prescribe the categories of crimes for which the death penalty should be available, and, acting as "the conscience of the community," juries are entrusted to determine in individual cases that the ultimate punishment is warranted. . . . Given the general awareness that death is no longer a routine punishment for the crimes for which it is made available, it is hardly surprising that juries have been increasingly meticulous in their imposition of the penalty. But to assume from the mere fact of relative infrequency that only [a] random assortment of pariahs are sentenced to death, is to cast grave doubt on the basic integrity of our jury system. . . .

There are doubtless prisoners on death row who would not be there had they been tried before a different jury or in a different State. In this sense their fate has been controlled by a fortuitous circumstance. However, this element of fortuity does not stand as an indictment either of the general functioning of juries in capital cases or of the integrity of jury decisions in individual cases. There is no empirical basis for concluding that juries have generally failed to discharge in good faith the responsibility described in *Witherspoon*—that of choosing between life and death in individual cases according to the dictates of community values. . . .

The Eighth Amendment, as I have noted, was included in the Bill of Rights to guard against the use of torturous and inhuman punishments, not those of limited efficacy. . . .

The decisive grievance of the opinions—not translated into Eighth Amendment terms—is that the present system of discretionary sentencing in capital cases has failed to produce evenhanded justice; the problem is not that too few have been sentenced to die, but that the selection process has followed no rational pattern. This claim of arbitrariness is not only lacking in empirical support, but also it manifestly fails to establish that the death penalty is a "cruel and unusual" punishment. The Eighth Amendment was included in the Bill of Rights to assure that certain types of punishment would never be imposed, not to channelize the sentencing process. The approach of these concurring opinions has no antecedent in the Eighth Amendment cases. It is essentially and exclusively a procedural due process argument.

This ground of decision is plainly foreclosed as well as misplaced. Only one year ago, in *McGautha v. California*, the Court upheld the prevailing system of sentencing in capital cases. . . .

Real change could clearly be brought about if legislatures provided mandatory death sentences in such a way as to deny juries the opportunity to bring in a verdict on a lesser charge; under such a system, the death sentence could only be avoided by a verdict of acquittal. If this is the only alternative that the legislatures can safely pursue under today's ruling, I would have preferred that the Court opt for total abolition. . . .

MR. JUSTICE BLACKMUN, dissenting. . . .

Cases such as these provide for me an excruciating agony of the spirit. I yield to no one in the depth of my distaste, antipathy, and, indeed, abhorrence, for the death penalty, with all its aspects of physical distress and fear and of moral judgment exercised by finite minds. That distaste is buttressed by a belief that capital punishment serves no useful purpose that can be demonstrated. For me, it violates childhood's training and life's experiences, and is not compatible with the philosophical convictions I have been able to develop. It is antagonistic to any sense of "reverence for life." Were I a legislator, I would vote against the death penalty for the policy reasons argued by counsel for the respective petitioners and expressed and adopted in the several opinions filed by the Justices who vote to reverse these judgments. . . .

I do not sit on these cases, however, as a legislator, responsible, at least in part, to the will of constituents. Our task here, as must so frequently be emphasized and re-emphasized, is to pass upon the constitutionality of legislation that has been enacted and that is challenged. This is the sole task for judges. We should not allow our personal preferences as to the wisdom of legislative and congressional action, or our distaste for such action, to guide our judicial decision in cases such as these. The temptations to cross that policy line are very great. In fact, as today's decision reveals, they are almost irresistible.

The Court, in my view, is somewhat propelled toward its result by the interim decision of the California Supreme Court, with one justice dissenting, that the death penalty is violative of that State's constitution. So far as I am aware, that was the first time the death penalty in its entirely has been nullified by judicial decision. California's moral problem was a profound one, for more prisoners were on death row there than in any other State. California, of course, has the right to construe its constitution as it will. Its construction, however, is hardly a precedent for federal adjudication. . . .

Although personally I may rejoice at the Court's result, I find it difficult to accept or to justify as a matter of history, of law, or of constitutional pronouncement. I fear the Court has overstepped. It has sought and has achieved an end.

MR. JUSTICE POWELL, with whom THE CHIEF JUSTICE, MR. JUSTICE BLACKMUN, and MR. JUSTICE REHNQUIST join, dissenting.

The Court granted certiorari in these cases to consider whether the death penalty is any longer a permissible form of punishment. It is the judgment of five

Justices that the death penalty, as customarily prescribed and implemented in this country today, offends the constitutional prohibition against cruel and unusual punishments. The reasons for that judgment are stated in five separate opinions, expressing as many separate rationales. In my view, none of these opinions provides a constitutionally adequate foundation for the Court's decision.

MR. JUSTICE DOUGLAS concludes that capital punishment is incompatible with notions of "equal protection" that he finds to be "implicit" in the Eighth Amendment. MR. JUSTICE BRENNAN bases his judgment primarily on the thesis that the penalty "does not comport with human dignity." MR. JUSTICE STEWART concludes that the penalty is applied in a "wanton" and "freakish" manner. For MR. JUSTICE WHITE it is the "infrequency" with which the penalty is imposed that renders its use unconstitutional. MR. JUSTICE MARSHALL finds that capital punishment is an impermissible form of punishment because it is "morally unacceptable" and "excessive."

Although the central theme of petitioners' presentations in these cases is that the imposition of the death penalty is per se unconstitutional, only two of today's opinions explicitly conclude that so sweeping a determination is mandated by the Constitution. Both MR. JUSTICE BRENNAN and MR. JUSTICE MARSHALL call for the abolition of all existing state and federal capital punishment statutes. They intimate as well that no capital statute could be devised in the future that might comport with the Eighth Amendment. While the practical consequences of the other three opinions are less certain, they at least do not purport to render impermissible every possible statutory scheme for the use of capital punishment that legislatures might hereafter devise. Insofar as these latter opinions fail, at least explicitly, to go as far as petitioners' contentions would carry them, their reservations are attributable to a willingness to accept only a portion of petitioners' thesis. For the reasons cogently set out in the CHIEF JUSTICE'S dissenting opinion, and for reasons stated elsewhere in this opinion, I find my Brothers' less-than-absolute-abolition judgments unpersuasive. Because those judgments are, for me, not dispositive, I shall focus primarily on the broader ground upon which the petitions in these cases are premised. The foundations of my disagreement with that broader thesis are equally applicable to each of the concurring opinions. I will therefore not endeavor to treat each one separately. Nor will I attempt to predict what forms of capital statutes, if any, may avoid condemnation in the future under the variety of views expressed by the collective majority today. That difficult task, not performed in any of the controlling opinions, must go unanswered until other cases presenting these more limited inquiries arise.

Whatever uncertainties may hereafter surface, several of the consequences of today's decision are unmistakably clear. The decision is plainly one of the greatest importance. The Court's judgment removes the death sentences previously imposed on some 600 persons awaiting punishment in state and federal prisons throughout the country. At least for the present, it also bars the States and the Federal Government from seeking sentences of death for defendants awaiting trial on charges for which capital punishment was heretofore a potential alternative. The happy event for these countable few constitutes, however, only the most visible consequence of this decision. Less measurable, but certainly of no less significance, is the shattering effect this collection of views has on the root principles of stare decisis, federalism, judicial restraint and—most importantly—separation of powers.

The Court rejects as not decisive the clearest evidence that the Framers of the Constitution and the authors of the Fourteenth Amendment believed that those documents posed no barrier to the death penalty. The Court also brushes aside an unbroken line of precedent reaffirming the heretofore virtually unquestioned constitutionality of capital punishment. Because of the pervasiveness of the constitutional ruling sought by petitioners, and accepted in varying degrees by five members of the Court, today's departure from established precedent invalidates a staggering number of state and federal laws. The capital punishment laws of no less than 39 States and the District of Columbia are nullified. In addition, numerous provisions of the Criminal Code of the United States and of the Uniform Code of Military Justice also are voided. The Court's judgment not only wipes out laws presently in existence, but denies to Congress and to the legislatures of the 50 States the power to adopt new policies contrary to the policy selected by the Court. Indeed, it is the view of two of my Brothers that the people of each State must be denied the prerogative to amend their constitutions to provide for capital punishment even selectively for the most heinous crime.

In terms of the constitutional role of this Court, the impact of the majority's ruling is all the greater because the decision encroaches upon an area squarely within the historic prerogative of the legislative branch—both state and federal—to protect the citizenry through the designation of penalties for prohibitable conduct. It is the very sort of judgment that the legislative branch is competent to make and for which the judiciary is ill-equipped. Throughout our history, Justices of this Court have emphasized the gravity of decisions invalidating legislative judgments, admonishing the nine men who sit on this bench of the duty of self-restraint, especially when called upon to apply the expansive due process and cruel and unusual punishment rubrics. I can recall no case in which, in the name of deciding constitutional questions, this Court has subordinated national and local democratic processes to such an extent. . . .

The Constitution itself poses the first obstacle to petitioners' argument that capital punishment is per se unconstitutional. The relevant provisions are the Fifth, Eighth, and Fourteenth Amendments. The first of these provides in part:

"No person shall be held to answer for a capital, or otherwise infamous crime, unless on a presentment or indictment of a Grand Jury . . . ; nor shall any person be subject for the same offence to be twice put in jeopardy of life or limb; . . . nor be deprived of life, liberty, or property, without due process of law. . . ."

Thus, the Federal Government's power was restricted in order to guarantee those charged with crimes that the prosecution would have only a single opportunity to seek imposition of the death penalty and that the death penalty could not be exacted without due process and a grand jury indictment. The Fourteenth Amendment, adopted about 77 years after the Bill of Rights, imposed the due process limitation of the Fifth Amendment upon the States' power to authorize capital punishment.

The Eighth Amendment, adopted at the same time as the Fifth, proscribes "cruel and unusual" punishments. In an effort to discern its meaning, much has been written about its history in the opinions of this Court and elsewhere. That history need not be restated here since, whatever punishments the Framers of the Constitution may have intended to prohibit under the "cruel and unusual" language, there cannot be the slightest doubt that they intended no absolute bar on the Government's authority to impose the death penalty. As much is made clear by the three references to capital punishment in the Fifth Amendment. Indeed, the same body that proposed the Eighth Amendment also provided, in the first Crimes Act of 1790, for the death penalty for a number of offenses.

Of course, the specific prohibitions within the Bill of Rights are limitations on the exercise of power; they are not an affirmative grant of power to the Government. I, therefore, do not read the several references to capital punishment as foreclosing this Court from considering whether the death penalty in a particular case offends the Eighth and Fourteenth Amendments. Nor are "cruel and unusual punishments" and "due process of law" static concepts whose meaning and scope were sealed at the time of their writing. They were designed to be dynamic and to gain meaning through application to specific circumstances, many of which were not contemplated by their authors. While flexibility in the application of these broad concepts is one of the hallmarks of our system of government, the Court is not free to read into the Constitution a meaning that is plainly at variance with its language. Both the language of the Fifth and Fourteenth Amendments and the history of the Eighth Amendment confirm beyond doubt that the death penalty was considered to be a constitutionally permissible punishment. It is, however, within the historic process of constitutional adjudication to challenge the imposition of the death penalty in some barbaric manner or as a penalty wholly disproportionate to a particular criminal act. And in making such a judgment in a case before it, a court may consider contemporary standards to the extent they are relevant. While this weighing of a punishment against the Eighth

Amendment standard on a case-by-case basis is consonant with history and precedent, it is not what petitioners demand in these cases. They seek nothing less than the total abolition of capital punishment by judicial fiat. . . .

The plurality opinion in *Trop v. Dulles*, supra, is of special interest since it is this opinion, in large measure, that provides the foundation for the present attack on the death penalty. It is anomalous that the standard urged by petitioners—"evolving standards of decency that mark the progress of a maturing society"—should be derived from an opinion that so unqualifiedly rejects their arguments. Chief Justice Warren, joined by Justices Black, DOUGLAS, and Whittaker, stated flatly:

> "At the outset, let us put to one side the death penalty as an index of the constitutional limit on punishment. Whatever the arguments may be against capital punishment, both on moral grounds and in terms of accomplishing the purposes of punishment—and they are forceful—the death penalty has been employed throughout our history, and, in a day when it is still widely accepted, it cannot be said to violate the constitutional concept of cruelty." . . .

Perhaps enough has been said to demonstrate the unswerving position that this Court has taken in opinions spanning the last hundred years. On virtually every occasion that any opinion has touched on the question of the constitutionality of the death penalty, it has been asserted affirmatively, or tacitly assumed, that the Constitution does not prohibit the penalty. No Justice of the Court, until today, has dissented from this consistent reading of the Constitution. The petitioners in these cases now before the Court cannot fairly avoid the weight of this substantial body of precedent merely by asserting that there is no prior decision precisely in point. Stare decisis, if it is a doctrine founded on principle, surely applies where there exists a long line of cases endorsing or necessarily assuming the validity of a particular matter of constitutional interpretation. While these oft-repeated expressions of unchallenged belief in the constitutionality of capital punishment may not justify a summary disposition of the constitutional question before us, they are views expressed and joined in over the years by no less than 29 Justices of this Court and therefore merit the greatest respect. Those who now resolve to set those views aside indeed have a heavy burden. . . .

Any attempt to discern contemporary standards of decency through the review of objective factors must take into account several overriding considerations which petitioners choose to discount or ignore. In a democracy the first indicator of the public's attitude must always be found in the legislative judgments of the people's chosen representatives. MR. JUSTICE MARSHALL'S opinion today catalogues the salient statistics. Forty States, the District of Columbia, and the Federal Government still authorize the death penalty for a wide variety of crimes. That number has remained relatively static since the end of World War I. That does not mean, however, that capital punishment has become a forgotten issue in the legislative arena. As recently as January, 1971, Congress approved the death penalty for congressional assassination. In 1965 Congress added the death penalty for presidential and vice presidential assassinations. Additionally, the aircraft piracy statute passed in 1961 also carries the death penalty. MR. JUSTICE BLACKMUN'S dissenting opinion catalogues the impressive ease with which each of these statutes was approved. On the converse side, a bill proposing the abolition of capital punishment for all federal crimes was introduced in 1967 but failed to reach the Senate floor. . . .

Certainly the claim is justified that this criminal sanction falls more heavily on the relatively impoverished and underprivileged elements of society. The "have-nots" in every society always have been subject to greater pressure to commit crimes and to fewer constraints than their more affluent fellow citizens. This is, indeed, a tragic byproduct of social and economic deprivation, but it is not an argument of constitutional proportions under the Eighth or Fourteenth Amendment. The same discriminatory impact argument could be made with equal force and logic with respect to those sentenced to prison terms. The Due Process Clause admits of no distinction between the deprivation of "life" and the deprivation of "liberty." If discriminatory impact renders capital punishment cruel and unusual, it likewise renders invalid most of the prescribed penalties for crimes of violence. The root causes of the higher incidence of criminal penalties on "minorities and the poor" will not be cured by abolishing the system of penalties. Nor, indeed, could any society have a viable system of criminal justice if sanctions were abolished or ameliorated because most of those who commit crimes happen to be underprivileged. The basic problem results not from the penalties imposed for criminal conduct but from social and economic factors that have plagued humanity since the beginning of recorded history, frustrating all efforts to create in any country at any time the perfect society in which there are no "poor," no "minorities" and no "underprivileged." The causes underlying this problem are unrelated to the constitutional issue before the Court. . . .

I agree that discriminatory application of the death penalty in the past, admittedly indefensible, is no justification for holding today that capital punishment is invalid in all cases in which sentences were handed out to members of the class discriminated against. . . .

A final comment on the racial discrimination problem seems appropriate. The possibility of racial bias in the trial and sentencing process has diminished in recent years. The segregation of our society in decades past, which contributed substantially to the severity of punishment for interracial crimes, is now no longer prevalent in this country. Likewise, the day is past when juries do not represent the minority group elements of the community. The assurance of fair trials for all citizens is greater today than at any previous time in our history. Because standards of criminal justice have "evolved" in a manner favorable to the accused, discriminatory imposition of capital punishment is far less likely today than in the past. . . .

I now return to the overriding question in these cases: whether this Court, acting in conformity with the Constitution, can justify its judgment to abolish capital punishment as heretofore known in this country. It is important to keep in focus the enormity of the step undertaken by the Court today. Not only does it invalidate hundreds of state and federal laws, it deprives those jurisdictions of the power to legislate with respect to capital punishment in the future, except in a manner consistent with the cloudily outlined views of those Justices who do not purport to undertake total abolition. Nothing short of an amendment to the United States Constitution can reverse the Court's judgments. Meanwhile, all flexibility is foreclosed. The normal democratic process, as well as the opportunities for the several States to respond to the will of their people expressed through ballot referenda (as in Massachusetts, Illinois, and Colorado), is now shut off. . . .

With deference and respect for the views of the Justices who differ, it seems to me that all these studies—both in this country and elsewhere—suggest that, as a matter of policy and precedent, this is a classic case for the exercise of our oft-announced allegiance to judicial restraint. I know of no case in which greater gravity and delicacy have attached to the duty that this Court is called on to perform whenever legislation—state or federal—is challenged on constitutional grounds. It seems to me that the sweeping judicial action undertaken today reflects a basic lack of faith and confidence in the democratic process. Many may regret, as I do, the failure of some legislative bodies to address the capital punishment issue with greater frankness or effectiveness. Many might decry their failure either to abolish the penalty entirely or selectively, or to establish standards for its enforcement. But impatience with the slowness, and even the unresponsiveness, of legislatures is no justification for judicial intrusion upon their historic powers. . . .

Source: Furman v. Georgia, 408 U.S. 238 (1972), at 376–405, 406–414, 415–465.

Document 3.6

California's Supreme Court Declares That the Death Penalty Violates California's Constitution, February 18, 1972

Between January 17, 1972, when the Supreme Court heard oral arguments in Furman v. Georgia, *and June 29, 1972, when its opinions came down in that case, the California supreme court declared its death penalty law unconstitutional in the case of* People v. Anderson *on the grounds that the penalty violated the state's constitution, which prohibited "cruel or unusual punishments." As Justice Harry Blackmun noted in his dissent in* Furman, *the California decision likely influenced the thinking of some members on the U.S. Supreme Court. The voters of California ultimately rejected their supreme court's decision and reinstated capital punishment through the state's initiative process.*

CHIEF JUSTICE WRIGHT wrote the opinion for the Court:

A jury found Robert Page Anderson guilty of first degree murder, the attempted murder of three men, and first degree robbery, and fixed the penalty at death for the murder. . . .

Defendant contends that error was committed in selecting the jury, that certain evidence was improperly admitted, that the prosecutor was guilty of prejudicial misconduct, and that the death penalty constitutes both cruel and unusual punishment and, as such, contravenes the Eighth Amendment to the United States Constitution and article I, section 6, of the Constitution of California. We have concluded that capital punishment is both cruel and unusual as those terms are defined under article I, section 6, of the California Constitution, and that therefore death may not be exacted as punishment for crime in this state. Because we have determined that the California Constitution does not permit the continued application of capital punishment, we need not consider whether capital punishment may also be proscribed by the Eighth Amendment to the United States Constitution.

Before undertaking to examine the constitutionality of capital punishment in light of contemporary standards, it is instructive to note that article I, section 6, of the California Constitution, unlike the Eighth Amendment to the United States Constitution prohibits the infliction of cruel or unusual punishments. Thus, the California Constitution prohibits imposition of the death penalty if, judged by contemporary standards, it is either cruel or has become an unusual punishment.

Some commentators have suggested that the reach of the Eighth Amendment and that of Article I, section 6, are coextensive, and that the use of the disjunctive form in the latter is significant. Our view of the history of the California provision persuades us, however, that the delegates to the Constitutional Convention of 1849, who first adopted the section which was later incorporated into the Constitution of 1879, were aware of the significance of the disjunctive form and that its use was purposeful. . . .

The fact that the majority of constitutional models to which the delegates had access prohibited cruel or unusual punishment, and that many of these models reflected a concern on the part of their drafter not only that cruel punishments be prohibited, but that disproportionate and unusual punishments also be independently proscribed, persuades us that the delegates modified the California provision before adoption to substitute the disjunctive "or" for the conjunctive "and" in order to establish their intent that both cruel punishments and unusual punishments we outlawed. . . .

Respondent [California officials], while conceding the power and responsibility of the court to review penal statutes in light of article I, section 6, urges that we must accept as controlling indicia of contemporary civilized standards of decency both legislative acts creating new capital crimes and legislative acquiescence in the continuation of capital punishment. Although we accord great deference to the judgment of the Legislature in this respect, we would abdicate our responsibility to examine independently the question were our inquiry to begin and end with the fact that statutory provisions authorizing imposition of the death penalty have been recently enacted or continue to exist. . . .

Well over a century has now passed since the day when vigilante justice and public hangings made executions an acceptable practice of California life. We cannot today assume, as it was assumed in early opinions of this court, that capital punishment is not so cruel as to offend contemporary standards of decency. Appellant [Anderson] has asked that we not only reexamine the validity of the prior bases upon which the death penalty has been upheld, but that we independently examine its cruelty applying contemporary standards. . . . We have done so and have concluded that capital punishment is "cruel" as that term is understood in its constitutional sense. We have also . . . reexamined the bases upon which capital punishment has been upheld heretofore. . . . We have concluded that the death penalty cannot be justified as furthering any of the accepted purposes of punishment. Moreover, we have concluded that it can no longer escape characterization as an "unusual" punishment. . . .

Were the standards of another age the constitutional measure of "cruelty" today, whipping, branding, pillorying, severing or nailing ears, and boring of tongue, all of which were once practiced as forms of punishment in this country, might escape constitutional proscription, but none today would argue that they are not "cruel" punishments. . . . Our responsibility demands that we must construe that provision in accordance with contemporary standards. We have recognized before that our Constitution is a progressive document. . . . In reality, however, we think the dispute as to the standard to be more apparent than real for the standard today is the standard of 1849 and 1879—whether the punishment affronts contemporary standards of decency. The framers of our Constitution, like those who drafted the Bill of Rights, anticipated that interpretation of the cruel or unusual punishments clause would not be static but that the clause would be applied consistently with the standards of the age in which the questioned punishment was sought to be inflicted. . . .

We have . . . noted that the death sentence is rarely imposed in California today and that it is even more rarely carried out. But even adopting the broader test of widespread acceptance among civilized peoples, capital punishment can no longer withstand constitutional proscription. Respondent [California officials] seek to avoid this conclusion by suggesting that a punishment is not unusual in the constitutional sense unless it is unusual as to form, or method by which it is imposed. We cannot accept this limitation of the meaning of "unusual," however, for to do so would ignore the fact that execution is a form or method of punishment and would embroil us in future semantic disputes as to whether innovative types of punishment were unconstitutionally "unusual" forms of punishment. . . .

We have concluded that capital punishment is unconstitutionally cruel and that under article I, section 6, a cruel punishment is proscribed irrespective of whether it is excessive. If any doubt remained as to its cruelty, however, we could no longer uphold capital punishment on the ground that it is commonly accepted, for the repudiation of the death penalty in this country is reflected in a world-wide trend towards abolition.

Source: People v. Anderson, 6 Cal. 3d 628, 493 P.2d 880 (February 18, 1972), at 634–657.

Document 3.7
Californians Respond to State Court's Decision on Death Penalty with Proposition 17, November 7, 1972

In People v. Anderson, *decided in February 1972, the Supreme Court of California declared the state's existing death penalty law a violation of the California constitution's ban on "cruel or unusual punishments." Led by the state's attorney general and many law enforcement officials, California voters placed an initiative on the ballot, Proposition 17, to overturn the court's decision. In November 1973 the California electorate overwhelmingly adopted Proposition 17.*

Proposition 17

Section 27 is added to Article 1, to read:

Sec. 27. All statutes of this state in effect on February 17, 1972, requiring, authorizing, imposing or relating to the death penalty are in full force and effect, subject to legislative amendment or repeal by statute, initiative, or referendum. The death penalty provided for under those statutes shall not be deemed to be, or to constitute, the infliction of cruel or unusual punishments within the meaning of Article 1, Section 6, nor shall such punishment for such offenses be deemed to contravene any other provision of this Constitution.

Source: White v. Brown, 468 F.2d 301 (1972).

Document 3.8
State Senator H. L. Richardson Writes in Favor of Restoring California's Death Penalty, October 31, 1972

Following the California supreme court's decision in People v. Anderson *(1972), which struck down capital punishment in the state, proponents of the death penalty organized an initiative campaign to overrule the court and restore capital punishment. The initiative, known as Proposition 17, was approved by a 2–1 margin in November 1972. Prior to the vote, both proponents and opponents offered their views in major California newspapers such as the* Los Angeles Times. *Here, H. L. Richardson, a California state senator, argues in favor of Proposition 17.*

. . . The evidence is clear that capital punishment works. The rise in willful homicides all over California is closely linked with the decline in enforcement of the death penalty. Since 1963 there has been only one execution in our state. In that year the willful homicide rate per 100,000 population was 3.7%—a total of 656 murders. By 1971, the rate was 8.1% per 100,000 population—1,636 murders, or two and a half times as many.

To say that capital punishment does not deter all murderers is true. But neither do traffic laws deter all speeders. So to conclude that the death penalty should be abolished because the criminal still kills is as fatuous as arguing that speed limits should be abolished to stop traffic deaths.

Why should the murderer die? Not only because he has broken God's law—"Thou shalt not kill" (Exodus 20:13)—but also as a deterrent—"so those who will remain will hear and be afraid and they will never do anything bad like this in your midst" (Deuteronomy 19:19–20).

In recent years there have been many attempts to repeal the death penalty. Each time they were repelled by the citizens or their legislators.

In August, 1971, the California Poll found that 58% of the voters favored retention.

Six months later, nevertheless, six justices of the State Supreme Court declared capital punishment unconstitutional, thereby stripping the people of a protection designed to secure life and the blessing of liberty.

In his majority opinion, Chief Justice Donald Wright called the death sentence an affront to contemporary standards. Public opinion may be relevant, he wrote, but it is not the controlling factor in determining what is consonant with contemporary standards of decency. In other words, said the chief justice of California, public opinion be damned.

Justice Marshall McComb was the lone dissenter. "It is the duty of the electorate, and not the judiciary," he argued, "to decide whether it is sound public policy to impose the death penalty. If a change is to be made, it should be made through the legislative process or by the people through the initiative process."

The people agreed—and went to work. Never before have so many citizens signed petitions to qualify an initiative. More than 1.25 million persons signed up, assuring the people the right to make the final decision.

Here is the real question we must face when we consider the death penalty: Just how much value do we place on the life of a law-abiding citizen? The average time served for murder in this state is 14 years; some murderers serve as few as seven years. Such is the going rate for a human life these days. Life goes cheap in California.

The great lawyer, Blackstone, said: "The main strength and force of law consists in the penalty attached to it." Society's need to protect life and property ought to be considered absolute. With carnage of the innocents mounting, we have surely heard enough about the "rights" of a murderer. By his fatal assault on a fellow human being, he has lost the rights to dignity and privacy and freedom, even to life itself.

Source: "Is the Death Penalty Appropriate in a Modern Society?" *Los Angeles Times,* October 31, 1972, B7.

Document 3.9
Anthony Amsterdam Writes in Opposition to California's Proposition 17, November 4, 1972

Anthony Amsterdam, one of the attorneys who argued the case of Furman v. Georgia, *wrote the following piece in the* New York Times, *urging California's citizens to vote against Proposition 17, which was aimed at reinstating the death penalty.*

STANFORD, Calif.—On Nov. 7, California voters will decide whether to amend their state constitution to restore the death penalty. The proposed amendment, Proposition 17, has implications reaching beyond California and beyond even the question of capital punishment.

Proposition 17 was written to nullify a decision of the California Supreme Court, delivered last February, declaring that death is a "cruel or unusual punishment" forbidden by the California Constitution's Bill of Rights. Within days after that decision became final, initiative petitions seeking to overturn it were put into circulation. They accumulated enough signatures to qualify Proposition 17 for the ballot prior to June 29, the date on which the Supreme Court of the United States held that most forms of capital punishment also violated the Federal Constitution. The impact of the High Court's decision upon Proposition 17 is unclear: proponents of the proposition say that, if adopted, it will still succeed in killing some criminals, although neither they nor the voters can be sure which ones.

Proposition 17 represents a use of the amending process hitherto virtually unknown in this country. Its sponsorship by self-styled "conservatives" is ironic, since it breaks with venerable American traditions insofar as it cuts down a fundamental Bill of Rights guarantee in a hasty reaction to a judicial decision interpreting that guarantee.

As every schoolchild knows, the basis of our free American society is a government of limited powers in which minorities and isolated individuals are protected against oppression at the will of even an overwhelming majority. Majorities change, sometimes with frightening rapidity; our form of government therefore recognizes the need of every one of us to have our fundamental rights secured—including the right to decent treatment at the hands of those in power—whether or not we happen to be in the prevailing majority of the moment. We commonly think of the source of this security as the written guarantees of the Constitution: the Bill of Rights, due process of law, the equal protection of the laws. But because these guarantees are amendable, the real source of our security lies deeper. It lies in the unwritten principle that the written guarantees will not be triflingly amended—that they will not be amended except after the most mature experience and reflection have convincingly demonstrated that a guarantee is unserviceable in some important way. Without this principle, only very large minorities would remain safe for only very small periods of time.

Proposition 17, designed to overrule a California Supreme Court decision before the public had any experience under it or the slightest time to consider its effects, is a dangerous departure from this principle. The way the proposition got on the ballot underlies the gravity of the danger.

It was drafted by the California Attorney General, Evelle Younger, still smarting from defeat in the court. (Younger was so angry that he filed a rehearing petition which insulted the court instead of reasoning with it and he took the unprecedented step of asking the lone dissenting justice to incorporate Younger's insulting petition in his dissent.) Younger then organized a statewide machine of district attorneys and law enforcement officers to gather signatures for the proposition. District attorneys served as temporary and permanent chairmen of the initiative campaign in most counties; throughout the state, the proposition was disseminated through the offices of district attorneys and sheriffs and police stations; their switchboards supplied information to prospective signers; police officers and deputies were given quotas of signatures to obtain. By these and other means which flouted California laws forbidding the use of public facilities for political purposes, the state's law enforcement machinery was twisted into an instrument to undo a constitutional guarantee.

Unsurprisingly, the requisite number of signatures was gathered in record time. For it is a political truism that almost any proposal can be qualified for the ballot with the right kind of organization; and a pre-organized, militaristically-disciplined, cost-free apparatus reaching into every corner of the state has to be any constitution-amender's dream. Only for those of us who believe that the Bill of Rights deserves to endure, and that American democracy excludes the notion of a political police, the dream is something of a nightmare.

Source: "The Death Penalty and a Free Society," *New York Times,* November 4, 1972, 33.

Document 3.10
President Richard Nixon Urges Restoration of the Federal Death Penalty, March 14, 1973

In his State of the Union address to Congress on March 14, 1973, following his reelection in November 1972, President Richard Nixon urged Congress to reinstitute capital punishment for specific federal offenses in response to the Supreme Court's decision in Furman v. Georgia, *which had nullified federal as well as state laws.*

To the Congress of the United States:

This sixth message to the Congress on the State of the Union concerns our Federal system of criminal justice. It discusses both the progress we have made in improving that system and the additional steps we must take to consolidate our accomplishments and to further our efforts to achieve a safe, just, and law-abiding society.

In the period from 1960 to 1968 serious crime in the United States increased by 122 percent according to the FBI's Uniform Crime Index. The rate of increase accelerated each year until it reached a peak of 17 percent in 1968.

In 1968 one major public opinion poll showed that Americans considered lawlessness to be the top domestic problem facing the Nation. Another poll showed that four out of five Americans believed that "Law and order has broken down in this country." There was a very real fear that crime and violence were becoming a threat to the stability of our society.

The decade of the 1960s was characterized in many quarters by a growing sense of permissiveness in America—as well intentioned as it was poorly reasoned—in which many people were reluctant to take the steps necessary to control crime. It is no coincidence that within a few years' time, America experienced a crime wave that threatened to become uncontrollable.

This administration came to office in 1969 with the conviction that the integrity of our free institutions demanded stronger and firmer crime control. I promised that the wave of crime would not be the wave of the future. An all-out attack was mounted against crime in the United States. . . .

DEATH PENALTY

The sharp reduction in the application of the death penalty was a component of the more permissive attitude toward crime in the last decade.

I do not contend that the death penalty is a panacea that will cure crime. Crime is the product of a variety of different circumstances—sometimes social, sometimes psychological—but it is committed by human beings and at the point of commission it is the product of that individual's motivation. If the incentive not to commit crime is stronger than the incentive *to* commit it, then logic suggests that crime will be reduced. It is in part the entirely justified feeling of the prospective criminal that he will not suffer for his deed which, in the present circumstances, helps allow those deeds to take place.

Federal crimes are rarely "crimes of passion." Airplane hi-jacking is not done in a blind rage; it has to be carefully planned. The use of incendiary devices and bombs is not a crime of passion, nor is kidnapping; all these must be thought out in advance. At present those who plan these crimes do not have to include in their deliberations the possibility that they will be put to death for their deeds. I believe that in making their plans, they should have to consider the fact that if a death results from their crime, they too may die.

Under those conditions, I am confident that the death penalty can be a valuable deterrent. By making the death penalty available, we will provide Federal enforcement authorities with additional leverage to dissuade those individuals who may commit a Federal crime from taking the lives of others in the course of committing that crime.

Hard experience has taught us that with due regard for the rights of all—including the right to life itself we must return to a greater concern with protecting those who might otherwise be the innocent victims of violent crime than with protecting those who have committed those crimes. The society which fails to recognize this as a reasonable ordering of its priorities must inevitably find itself, in time, at the mercy of criminals.

America was heading in that direction in the last decade, and I believe that we must not risk returning to it again. Accordingly, I am proposing the re-institution of the death penalty for war-related treason, sabotage, and espionage, and for all specifically enumerated crimes under Federal jurisdiction from which death results.

The Department of Justice has examined the constitutionality of the death penalty in the light of the Supreme Court's recent decision in *Furman v. Georgia*. It is the Department's opinion that *Furman* holds unconstitutional the imposition of the death penalty only insofar as it is applied arbitrarily and capriciously. I believe the best way to accommodate the reservations of the Court is to authorize the automatic imposition of the death penalty where it is warranted.

Under the proposal drafted by the Department of Justice, a hearing would be required after the trial for the purpose of determining the existence or nonexistence of certain rational standards which delineate aggravating factors or mitigating factors.

Among those mitigating factors which would preclude the imposition of a death sentence are the youth of the defendant, his or her mental capacity, or the fact that the crime was committed under duress. Aggravating factors include the creation of a grave risk of danger to the national security, or to the life of another person, or the killing of another person during the commission of one of a circumscribed list of serious offenses, such as treason, kidnapping, or aircraft piracy.

The hearing would be held before the judge who presided at the trial and before either the same jury, or, if circumstances require, a jury specially impaneled. Imposition of the death penalty by the judge would be mandatory if the jury returns a special verdict finding the existence of one or more aggravating factors and the absence of any mitigating factor. The death sentence is *prohibited* if the jury finds the existence of one or more mitigating factors.

Current statutes containing the death penalty would be amended to eliminate the requirement for jury recommendation, thus limiting the imposition of the death penalty to cases in which the legislative guidelines for its imposition clearly require it, and eliminating arbitrary and capricious application of the death penalty which the Supreme Court has condemned in the *Furman* case. . . .

Source: "State of the Union Message to the Congress on Law Enforcement and Drug Abuse Prevention," March 14, 1973, Richard Nixon Library and Birthplace Foundation, available at www.nixonlibraryfoundation.org/clientuploads/directory/archive/1973_pdf_files/1973_0079.pdf.

Document 3.11
The Supreme Court Upholds the Revised Death Penalty Statutes in *Gregg v. Georgia*, July 2, 1976

In a trio of cases, known collectively as Gregg v. Georgia *(1976), the Supreme Court upheld revised death penalty statutes in cases from Georgia, Florida, and Texas. In the* Gregg *case, Justice Potter Stewart, joined by Justices Lewis Powell and John Paul Stevens, wrote the lead opinion. A concurring opinion was written by Justice Byron White, joined by Chief Justice Warren Burger and Justices William Rehnquist and Harry Blackmun. Justices William Brennan and Thurgood Marshall dissented.*

Judgment of the Court, and opinion of MR. JUSTICE STEWART, MR. JUSTICE POWELL, and MR. JUSTICE STEVENS, announced by MR. JUSTICE STEWART. . . .

The petitioner, Troy Gregg, was charged with committing armed robbery and murder. In accordance with Georgia procedure in capital cases, the trial was in two stages, a guilt stage and a sentencing stage. . . . The jury found the petitioner guilty of two counts of armed robbery and two counts of murder.

At the penalty stage, which took place before the same jury, neither the prosecution nor the petitioner's lawyer offered any additional evidence. . . . The trial judge instructed the jury that it could recommend either a death sentence or a life prison sentence on each count. The judge further charged the jury that in determining what sentence was appropriate the jury was free to consider the facts and circumstances, if any, presented by the parties in mitigation or aggravation.

Finally, the judge instructed the jury that it "would not be authorized to consider [imposing] the penalty of death" unless it first found beyond a reasonable doubt one of these aggravating circumstances:

One—That the offense of murder was committed while the offender was engaged in the commission of two other capital felonies, to-wit the armed robbery. . . .

Two—That the offender committed the offense of murder for the purpose of receiving money and the automobile described in the indictment.

Three—The offense of murder was outrageously and wantonly vile, horrible and inhuman, in that they [sic] involved the depravity of mind of the defendant.

Finding the first and second of these circumstances, the jury returned verdicts of death on each count. . . .

In addition to the conventional appellate process available in all criminal cases, provision is made for special expedited direct review by the Supreme Court of Georgia of the appropriateness of imposing the sentence of death in the particular case. The court is directed to consider "the punishment as well as any errors enumerated by way of appeal," and to determine:

> Whether the sentence of death was imposed under the influence of passion, prejudice, or any other arbitrary factor, and
> Whether, in cases other than treason or aircraft hijacking, the evidence supports the jury's or judge's finding of a statutory aggravating circumstance . . . and,
> Whether the sentence of death is excessive or disproportionate to the penalty imposed in similar cases, considering both the crime and the defendant. . . .
> We address initially the basic contention that the punishment of death for the crime of murder is, under all circumstances, "cruel and unusual" in violation of the Eighth and Fourteenth Amendments of the Constitution. . . .

The petitioners in the capital cases before the court today renew the "standard of decency" argument, but developments during the four years since *Furman* have undercut substantially the assumptions upon which their argument rested. Despite the continuing debate, dating back to the 19th century, over the morality and utility of capital punishment, it is now evident that a large proportion of American society continues to regard it as an appropriate and necessary criminal sanction.

The most marked indication of society's endorsement of the death penalty for murder is the legislative response to *Furman*. The legislatures of at least 35 States have enacted new statutes that provide for the death penalty for at least some crimes that result in the death of another person. . . .

The death penalty is said to serve two principal social purposes: retribution and deterrence of capital crimes by prospective offenders.

In part, capital punishment is an expression of society's moral outrage at particular offensive conduct. This function may be unappealing to many, but it is essential in any ordered society that asks its citizens to rely on legal processes rather than self-help to vindicate their wrongs. . . .

"Retribution is no longer the dominant objective of the criminal law, but neither is it a forbidden objective nor one inconsistent with our respect for the dignity of men," *Williams v. New York*. . . . Indeed, the decision that capital punishment may be the appropriate sanction in extreme cases is an expression of the community's belief that certain crimes are themselves so grievous an affront to humanity that the only adequate response may be the penalty of death.

Statistical attempts to evaluate the worth of the death penalty as a deterrent to crimes by potential offenders have occasioned a great deal of debate. The results simply have been inconclusive. . . . [But] the value of capital punishment as a deterrent of crime is a complex factual issue the resolution of which properly rests with the legislatures, which can evaluate the results of statistical studies in terms of their own local conditions and with a flexibility of approach that is not available to the courts. . . .

In sum, we cannot say that the judgment of the Georgia legislature that capital punishment may be necessary in some cases is clearly wrong. Considerations of federalism, as well as respect for the ability of a legislature to evaluate, in terms of its particular State, the moral consensus concerning the death penalty and its social utility as a sanction, require us to conclude, in the absence of more convincing evidence, that the infliction of death as a punishment for murder is not without justification and thus is not unconstitutionally severe. . . .

Because of the uniqueness of the death penalty, *Furman* held that it could not be imposed under sentencing procedures that created a substantial risk that it would be inflicted in an arbitrary and capricious manner. . . .

Furman mandates that where discretion is afforded a sentencing body on a matter so grave as the determination of whether a human life should be taken or spared, that discretion must be suitably directed and limited so as to minimize the risk of wholly arbitrary and capricious action. . . .

Those who have studied the question suggest that a bifurcated procedure—one in which the question of sentence is not considered until the determination of guilt has been made—is the best answer. . . . When a human life is at stake and when the jury must have information prejudicial to the question of guilt but relevant to the question of penalty in order to impose a rational sentence, a bifurcated system is more likely to ensure elimination of the constitutional deficiencies identified in *Furman*. . . .

In summary, the concerns expressed in *Furman* that the penalty of death not be imposed in an arbitrary or capricious manner can be met by a carefully drafted statute that ensures that the sentencing authority is given adequate information and guidance. As a general proposition these concerns are best met by a system that provides for a bifurcated proceeding at which the sentencing authority is apprised of the information relevant to the imposition of sentence and provided with standards to guide its use of the information. . . .

The new Georgia sentencing procedures . . . focus the jury's attention on the particularized nature of the crime and the particularized characteristics of the individual defendant. While the jury is permitted to consider any aggravating or mitigating circumstances, it must find and identify at least one statutory aggravating factor before it may impose a penalty of death. In this way the jury's discretion is channeled. No longer can a jury wantonly and freakishly impose the death sentence; it is always circumscribed by the legislative guidelines. In addition, the review function of the Supreme Court of Georgia affords additional assurance that the concerns that prompted our decision in *Furman* are not present to any significant degree in the Georgia procedure applied here.

For the reasons expressed in this opinion, we hold that the statutory system under which Gregg was sentenced to death does not violate the Constitution. Accordingly, the judgment of the Georgia Supreme Court is affirmed.

It is so ordered.

MR. JUSTICE WHITE, with whom THE CHIEF JUSTICE and MR. JUSTICE REHNQUIST join, concurring in the judgment.

. . . Petitioner's argument that there is an unconstitutional amount of discretion in the system which separates those suspects who receive the death penalty from those who receive life imprisonment, a lesser penalty, or are acquitted or never charged, seems to be in final analysis an indictment of our entire system of justice. Petitioner has argued in effect that no matter how effective the death penalty may be as a punishment, government, created and run as it must be by humans, is inevitably incompetent to administer it. This cannot be accepted as a proposition of constitutional law. Imposition of the death penalty is surely an awesome responsibility for any system of justice and those who participate in it. Mistakes will be made and discriminations will occur which will be difficult to explain. However, one of society's most basic tasks is that of protecting the lives of its citizens and one of the most basic ways in which it achieves the task is through criminal laws against murder. I decline to interfere with the manner in which Georgia has chosen to enforce such laws on what is simply an assertion of lack of faith in the ability of the system of justice to operate in a fundamentally fair manner.

MR. JUSTICE BRENNAN, dissenting.

. . . In *Furman v. Georgia*, I read "evolving standards of decency" as requiring focus upon the essence of the death penalty itself and not primarily or solely upon the procedures under which the determination to inflict the penalty upon a particular person was made. . . . That continues to be my view. . . .

My opinion in *Furman* . . . concluded that our civilization and the law had progressed to this point and that therefore the punishment of death, for whatever crime and under all circumstances, is "cruel and unusual" in violation of the Eighth and Fourteenth Amendments of the Constitution. I shall not again canvass the reasons that led to that conclusion. I emphasize only that foremost among the "moral concepts" recognized in our cases and inherent in the Clause is the primary moral principle that the State, even as it punishes, must treat its citizens in a manner consistent with their intrinsic worth as human beings—a punishment must not be so severe as to be degrading to human dignity. . . .

MR. JUSTICE MARSHALL, dissenting.

In *Furman v. Georgia*, I set forth at some length my views on the basic issue presented to the Court in these cases. The death penalty, I concluded, is a cruel and unusual punishment prohibited by the Eighth and Fourteenth Amendments. That continues to be my view. . . .

Since the decision in *Furman*, the legislatures of 35 States have enacted new statutes authorizing the imposition of the death penalty for certain crimes, and Congress has enacted a law providing the death penalty for air piracy resulting in death. I would be less than candid if I did not acknowledge that these developments have a significant bearing on a realistic assessment of the moral acceptability of the death penalty to the American people. But if the constitutionality of the death penalty turns, as I have urged, on the opinion of an *informed citizenry*, then even the enactment of new death statutes cannot be viewed as conclusive. . . . A recent study . . . has confirmed that the American people know little about the death penalty, and that the opinions of an informed public would differ significantly from those of a public unaware of the consequences and effects of the death penalty.

Even assuming, however, that the post-*Furman* enactment of statutes authorizing the death penalty renders the prediction of the views of an informed citizenry an uncertain basis for a constitutional decision, the enactment of those statutes has no bearing whatsoever on the conclusion that the death penalty is unconstitutional because it is excessive. An excessive penalty is invalid under the Cruel and Unusual Punishment Clause. . . . The inquiry there, then, is simply whether the death penalty is necessary to accomplish the legitimate legislative purposes in punishment, or whether a less severe penalty—life imprisonment—would do as well. . . .

In *Furman*, I canvassed the relevant data on the deterrent effect of capital punishment. . . . The available evidence, I concluded . . . was convincing that "capital punishment is not necessary as a deterrent to crime in our society."

The other principal purpose said to be served by the death penalty is retribution. The notion that retribution can serve as a moral justification for the sanction of death finds credence in the opinion of my Brothers Stewart, Powell, and Stevens. . . . It is this notion that I find to be the most disturbing aspect of today's unfortunate decisions. . . .

It simply defies belief to suggest that the death penalty is necessary to prevent the American people from taking the law into their own hands. . . .

There remains . . . what might be termed the purely retributive justification for the death penalty—that the death penalty is appropriate, not because of its beneficial effect on society, but because the taking of the murderer's life is itself morally good. Some of the language of the opinion of my Brothers Stewart, Powell, and Stevens . . . appears positively to embrace this notion of retribution for its own sake as a justification for capital punishment. . . .

The mere fact that the community demands the murderer's life in return for the evil he has done cannot sustain the death penalty, for as Justices Stewart, Powell, and Stevens remind us, "the Eighth Amendment demands more than that a challenged punishment be acceptable to contemporary society." To be sustained under the Eighth Amendment, the death penalty must "compor[t] with the basic concept of human dignity at the core of the Amendment [and must be] consistent with our respect for the dignity of [other] men." Under these standards, the taking of life "because the wrongdoer deserves it" surely must fall, for such a punishment has as its very basis the total denial of the wrong-doer's dignity and worth. . . .

The death penalty, unnecessary to promote the goal of deterrence or to further any legitimate notion of retribution, is an excessive penalty forbidden by the Eighth and Fourteenth Amendments. I respectfully dissent from the Court's judgment upholding the sentences of death imposed upon the petitioners in these cases.

Source: Gregg v. Georgia, 428 U.S. 153 (1976), at 159–207, 222–227, 228–231, 232–241.

Document 3.12
Georgia's Revised Capital Punishment Statute, 1976

Following the Supreme Court's decision in Furman v. Georgia *(1972), which struck down the state's death penalty law and those of other states, the Georgia legislature revised its capital punishment statute. The Court upheld a death sentence under the revised law in* Gregg v. Georgia *(1976), the relevant portions of which are printed below.*

Georgia Code Ann. 26–1101 (1972) provides:

"(a) A person commits murder when he unlawfully and with malice aforethought, either express or implied, causes the death of another human being. Express malice is that deliberate intention unlawfully to take away the life of a fellow creature, which is manifested by external circumstances capable of proof. Malice shall be implied where no considerable provocation appears, and where all the circumstances of the killing show an abandoned and malignant heart.

"(b) A person also commits the crime of murder when in the commission of a felony he causes the death of another human being, irrespective of malice.

"(c) A person convicted of murder shall be punished by death or by imprisonment for life."

Section 26–1902 (1972) provides:

"A person commits armed robbery when, with intent to commit theft, he takes property of another from the person or the immediate presence of another by use of an offensive weapon. The offense robbery by intimidation shall be a lesser included offense in the offense of armed robbery. A person convicted of armed robbery shall be punished by death or imprisonment for life, or by imprisonment for not less than one nor more than 20 years."

The statute provides in part:

"(a) The death penalty may be imposed for the offenses of aircraft hijacking or treason, in any case.

"(b) In all cases of other offenses for which the death penalty may be authorized, the judge shall consider, or he shall include in his instructions to the jury for it to consider, any mitigating circumstances or aggravating circumstances otherwise authorized by law and any of the following statutory aggravating circumstances which may be supported by the evidence:

"(1) The offense of murder, rape, armed robbery, or kidnapping was committed by a person with a prior record of conviction for a capital felony, or the offense of murder was committed by a person who has a substantial history of serious assaultive criminal convictions.

"(2) The offense of murder, rape, armed robbery, or kidnapping was committed while the offender was engaged in the commission of another capital felony, or aggravated battery, or the offense of murder was committed while the offender was engaged in the commission of burglary or arson in the first degree.

"(3) The offender by his act of murder, armed robbery, or kidnapping knowingly created a great risk of death to more than one person in a public place by means of a weapon or device which would normally be hazardous to the lives of more than one person.

"(4) The offender committed the offense of murder for himself or another, for the purpose of receiving money or any other thing of monetary value.

"(5) The murder of a judicial officer, former judicial officer, district attorney or solicitor or former district attorney or solicitor during or because of the exercise of his official duty.

"(6) The offender caused or directed another to commit murder or committed murder as an agent or employee of another person.

"(7) The offense of murder, rape, armed robbery, or kidnapping was outrageously or wantonly vile, horrible or inhuman in that it involved torture, depravity of mind, or an aggravated battery to the victim.

"(8) The offense of murder was committed against any peace . . . officer, corrections employee or fireman while engaged in the performance of his official duties.

"(9) The offense of murder was committed by a person in, or who has escaped from, the lawful custody of a peace officer or place of lawful confinement.

"(10) The murder was committed for the purpose of avoiding, interfering with, or preventing a lawful arrest or custody in a place of lawful confinement, of himself or another.

"(c) The statutory instructions as determined by the trial judge to be warranted by the evidence shall be given in charge and in writing to the jury for its deliberation. The jury, if its verdict be a recommendation of death, shall designate in writing, signed by the foreman of the jury, the aggravating circumstance or circumstances which it found beyond a reasonable doubt. In non-jury cases the judge shall make such designation. Except in cases of treason or aircraft hijacking, unless at least one of the statutory aggravating circumstances enumerated in section 27–2534.1 (b) is so found, the death penalty shall not be imposed."

Source: Gregg v. Georgia, 428 U.S. 153 (1976), footnotes 3–9.

Document 3.13
Florida's Death Penalty Statute, 1976

In Proffitt v. Florida *(1976), a companion case to* Gregg v. Georgia *(1976), the Supreme Court upheld Florida's revised death penalty statute, the relevant portions of which are printed below.*

The murder statute under which petitioner was convicted reads as follows:

"(1)(a) The unlawful killing of a human being, when perpetrated from a premeditated design to effect the death of the person killed or any human being, or when committed by a person engaged in the perpetration of, or in the attempt to perpetrate, any arson, involuntary sexual battery, robbery, burglary, kidnapping, aircraft piracy, or unlawful throwing, placing, or discharging of a destructive device or bomb, or which resulted from the unlawful distribution of heroin by a person 18 years of age or older when such drug is proven to be the proximate cause of the death of the user, shall be murder in the first degree and shall constitute a capital felony, punishable as provided in s. 775.082."

"(b) In all cases under this section, the procedure set forth in s.921.141 shall be followed in order to determine sentence of death or life imprisonment."

The aggravating circumstances are:

"(a) The capital felony was committed by a person under sentence of imprisonment."

"(b) The defendant was previously convicted of another capital felony or of a felony involving the use or threat of violence to the person."

"(c) The defendant knowingly created a great risk of death to many persons."

"(d) The capital felony was committed while the defendant was engaged, or was an accomplice, in the commission of, or an attempt to commit, or flight after committing or attempting to commit, any robbery, rape, arson, burglary, kidnapping, or aircraft piracy or the unlawful throwing, placing, or discharging of a destructive device or bomb."

"(e) The capital felony was committed for the purpose of avoiding or preventing a lawful arrest or effecting an escape from custody."

"(f) The capital felony was committed for pecuniary gain."

"(g) The capital felony was committed to disrupt or hinder the lawful exercise of any governmental function or the enforcement of laws."

"(h) The capital felony was especially heinous, atrocious, or cruel."

The mitigating circumstances are:

"(a) The defendant has no significant history of prior criminal activity."

"(b) The capital felony was committed while the defendant was under the influence of extreme mental or emotional disturbance."

"(c) The victim was a participant in the defendant's conduct or consented to the act."

"(d) The defendant was an accomplice in the capital felony committed by another person and his participation was relatively minor."

"(e) The defendant acted under extreme duress or under the substantial domination of another person."

"(f) The capacity of the defendant to appreciate the criminality of his conduct or to conform his conduct to the requirements of law was substantially impaired."

"(g) The age of the defendant at the time of the crime."

Source: Proffitt v. Florida, 428 U.S. 242 (1976), footnotes 4–6.

Document 3.14
The Supreme Court Upholds the Revised Florida Statute on Capital Punishment in *Proffitt v. Florida*, July 2, 1976

On the same day that it upheld Georgia's revised death penalty law, the Supreme Court also sustained Florida's revised death penalty law in the case of Proffitt v. Florida. *Justices William Brennan and Thurgood Marshall dissented in this case on the same grounds as in* Gregg v. Georgia.

Judgment of the Court, and opinion of MR. JUSTICE STEWART, MR. JUSTICE POWELL, and MR. JUSTICE STEVENS, announced by MR. JUSTICE POWELL.

The petitioner argues that the imposition of the death penalty under any circumstances is cruel and unusual punishment in violation of the Eighth and Fourteenth Amendments. We reject this argument for the reasons stated today in *Gregg v. Georgia.*

In response to *Furman v. Georgia,* the Florida Legislature adopted new statutes that authorize the imposition of the death penalty on those convicted of first-degree murder. At the same time Florida adopted a new capital-sentencing procedure, patterned in large part on the Model Penal Code. Under the new statute, if a defendant is found guilty of a capital offense, a separate evidentiary hearing is held before the trial judge and jury to determine his sentence. Evidence may be presented on any matter the judge deems relevant to sentencing and must include matters relating to certain legislatively specified aggravating and mitigating circumstances. Both the prosecution and the defense may present argument on whether the death penalty shall be imposed.

At the conclusion of the hearing the jury is directed to consider

[w]hether sufficient mitigating circumstances exist . . . which outweigh the aggravating circumstances found to exist; and . . . [b]ased on these considerations, whether the defendant should be sentenced to life [imprisonment] or death.

The jury's verdict is determined by majority vote. It is only advisory; the actual sentence is determined by the trial judge. The Florida Supreme Court has stated, however, that

[i]n order to sustain a sentence of death following a jury recommendation of life, the facts suggesting a sentence of death should be so clear and convincing that virtually no reasonable person could differ.

The trial judge is also directed to weigh the statutory aggravating and mitigating circumstances when he determines the sentence to be imposed on a defendant. The statute requires that if the trial court imposes a sentence of death,

it shall set forth in writing its findings upon which the sentence of death is based as to the facts: (a) [t]hat sufficient [statutory] aggravating circumstances exist . . . and (b) [t]hat there are insufficient [statutory] mitigating circumstances . . . to outweigh the aggravating circumstances.

The statute provides for automatic review by the Supreme Court of Florida of all cases in which a death sentence has been imposed. The law differs from that of Georgia in that it does not require the court to conduct any specific form of review. Since, however, the trial judge must justify the imposition of a death sentence with written findings, meaningful appellate review of each such sentence is made possible, and the Supreme Court of Florida, like its Georgia counterpart, considers its function to be to

"[guarantee] that the [aggravating and mitigating] reasons present in one case will reach a similar result to that reached under similar circumstances in another case. . . . If a defendant is sentenced to die, this Court can review that case in light of the other decisions and determine whether or not the punishment is too great."

On their face these procedures, like those used in Georgia, appear to meet the constitutional deficiencies identified in *Furman*. The sentencing authority in Florida, the trial judge, is directed to weigh eight aggravating factors against seven mitigating factors to determine whether the death penalty shall be imposed. This determination requires the trial judge to focus on the circumstances of the crime and the character of the individual defendant. He must, inter alia, consider whether the defendant has a prior criminal record, whether the defendant acted under duress or under the influence of extreme mental or emotional disturbance, whether the defendant's role in the crime was that of a minor accomplice, and whether the defendant's youth argues in favor of a more lenient sentence than might otherwise be imposed. The trial judge must also determine whether the crime was committed in the course of one of several enumerated felonies, whether it was committed for pecuniary gain, whether it was committed to assist in an escape from custody or to prevent a lawful arrest, and whether the crime was especially heinous, atrocious, or cruel. To answer these questions, which are not unlike those considered by a Georgia sentencing jury, the sentencing judge must focus on the individual circumstances of each homicide and each defendant.

The basic difference between the Florida system and the Georgia system is that in Florida the sentence is determined by the trial judge rather than by the jury. This Court has pointed out that jury sentencing in a capital case can perform an important societal function, but it has never suggested that jury sentencing is constitutionally required. And it would appear that judicial sentencing should lead, if anything, to even greater consistency in the imposition at the trial court level of capital punishment, since a trial judge is more experienced in sentencing than a jury, and therefore is better able to impose sentences similar to those imposed in analogous cases.

The Florida capital-sentencing procedures thus seek to assure that the death penalty will not be imposed in an arbitrary or capricious manner. Moreover, to the extent that any risk to the contrary exists, it is minimized by Florida's appellate review system, under which the evidence of the aggravating and mitigating circumstances is reviewed and reweighed by the Supreme Court of Florida "to determine independently whether the imposition of the ultimate penalty is warranted." The Supreme Court of Florida, like that of Georgia, has not hesitated to vacate a death sentence when it has determined that the sentence should not have been imposed. Indeed, it has vacated 8 of the 21 death sentences that it has reviewed to date.

Under Florida's capital-sentencing procedures, in sum, trial judges are given specific and detailed guidance to assist them in deciding whether to impose a death penalty or imprisonment for life. Moreover, their decisions are reviewed to ensure that they are consistent with other sentences imposed in similar circumstances. Thus, in Florida, as in Georgia, it is no longer true that there is "no meaningful basis for distinguishing the few cases in which [the death penalty] is imposed from the many cases in which it is not." On its face the Florida system thus satisfies the constitutional deficiencies identified in *Furman*.

As in *Gregg*, the petitioner contends, however, that, while perhaps facially acceptable, the new sentencing procedures in actual effect are merely cosmetic, and that arbitrariness and caprice still pervade the system under which Florida imposes the death penalty.

The petitioner first argues that arbitrariness is inherent in the Florida criminal justice system because it allows discretion to be exercised at each stage of a criminal proceeding—the prosecutor's decision whether to charge a capital offense in the first place, his decision whether to accept a plea to a lesser offense, the jury's consideration of lesser included offenses, and, after conviction and unsuccessful appeal, the Executive's decision whether to commute a death sentence. As we noted in *Gregg*, this argument is based on a fundamental misinterpretation of *Furman*, and we reject it for the reasons expressed in *Gregg*.

The petitioner next argues that the new Florida sentencing procedures in reality do not eliminate the arbitrary infliction of death that was condemned in *Furman*. Basically he contends that the statutory aggravating and mitigating circumstances are vague and overbroad, and that the statute gives no guidance as to how the mitigating and aggravating circumstances should be weighed in any specific case.

Initially the petitioner asserts that the enumerated aggravating and mitigating circumstances are so vague and so broad that virtually "any capital defendant becomes a candidate for the death penalty. . . ." In particular, the petitioner attacks the eighth and third statutory aggravating circumstances, which authorize the death penalty to be imposed if the crime is "especially heinous, atrocious, or cruel," or if "[t]he defendant knowingly created a great risk of death to many persons." These provisions must be considered as they have been construed by the Supreme Court of Florida.

That court has recognized that while it is arguable

> "that all killings are atrocious, . . . [s]till, we believe that the Legislature intended something 'especially' heinous, atrocious or cruel when it authorized the death penalty for first degree murder."

As a consequence, the court has indicated that the eighth statutory provision is directed only at "the conscienceless or pitiless crime which is unnecessarily torturous to the victim." We cannot say that the provision, as so construed, provides inadequate guidance to those charged with the duty of recommending or imposing sentences in capital cases. . . .

The directions given to judge and jury by the Florida statute are sufficiently clear and precise to enable the various aggravating circumstances to be weighed against the mitigating ones. As a result, the trial court's sentencing discretion is guided and channeled by a system that focuses on the circumstances of each individual homicide and individual defendant in deciding whether the death penalty is to be imposed.

Finally, the Florida statute has a provision designed to assure that the death penalty will not be imposed on a capriciously selected group of convicted defendants. The Supreme Court of Florida reviews each death sentence to ensure that similar results are reached in similar cases.

Nonetheless the petitioner attacks the Florida appellate review process because the role of the Supreme Court of Florida in reviewing death sentences is necessarily subjective and unpredictable. While it may be true that that court has not chosen to formulate a rigid objective test as its standard of review for all cases, it does not follow that the appellate review process is ineffective or arbitrary. In fact, it is apparent that the Florida court has undertaken responsibly to perform its function of death sentence review with a maximum of rationality and consistency. For example, it has several times compared the circumstances of a case under review with those of previous cases in which it has assessed the imposition of death sentences. By following this procedure the Florida court has in effect adopted the type of proportionality review mandated by the Georgia statute. And any suggestion that the Florida court engages in only cursory or rubber-stamp review of death penalty cases is totally controverted by the fact that it has vacated over one-third of the death sentences that have come before it.

Florida, like Georgia, has responded to *Furman* by enacting legislation that passes constitutional muster. That legislation provides that after a person is convicted of first-degree murder, there shall be an informed, focused, guided, and objective inquiry into the question whether he should be sentenced to death. If a death sentence is imposed, the sentencing authority articulates in writing the statutory reasons that led to its decision. Those reasons, and the evidence supporting them, are conscientiously reviewed by a court which, because of its statewide jurisdiction, can assure consistency, fairness, and rationality in the evenhanded operation of the state law. As in Georgia, this system serves to assure that sentences of death will not be "wantonly" or "freakishly" imposed. Accordingly, the judgment before us is affirmed.

It is so ordered.

Source: Proffitt v. Florida, 428 U.S. 242 (1976), at 247–259.

Document 3.15
The Supreme Court Upholds the Revised Texas Death Penalty Statute in *Jurek v. Texas*, July 2, 1976

In addition to upholding the revised death penalty statutes in Georgia and Florida on July 2, 1976, the Supreme Court also sustained the revised statute of Texas in the case of Jurek v. Texas. Justices William Brennan and Thurgood Marshall dissented on the same grounds stated in Gregg v. Georgia.

Judgment of the Court, and opinion of MR. JUSTICE STEWART, MR. JUSTICE POWELL, and MR. JUSTICE STEVENS, announced by MR. JUSTICE STEVENS.

The issue in this case is whether the imposition of the sentence of death for the crime of murder under the law of Texas violates the Eighth and Fourteenth Amendments to the Constitution.

The petitioner in this case, Jerry Lane Jurek, was charged by indictment with the killing of Wendy Adams "by choking and strangling her with his hands, and by drowning her in water by throwing her into a river . . . in the course of committing and attempting to commit kidnapping of and forcible rape upon the said Wendy Adams."

At the conclusion of the trial the jury returned a verdict of guilty.

Texas law requires that if a defendant has been convicted of a capital offense, the trial court must conduct a separate sentencing proceeding before the same jury that tried the issue of guilt. Any relevant evidence may be introduced at this proceeding, and both prosecution and defense may present argument for or against the sentence of death. The jury is then presented with two (sometimes three) questions, the answers to which determine whether a death sentence will be imposed.

During the punishment phase of the petitioner's trial, several witnesses for the State testified to the petitioner's bad reputation in the community. The petitioner's father countered with testimony that the petitioner had always been steadily employed since he had left school and that he contributed to his family's support.

The jury then considered the two statutory questions relevant to this case: (1) whether the evidence established beyond a reasonable doubt that the murder of the deceased was committed deliberately and with the reasonable expectation that the death of the deceased or another would result, and (2) whether the evidence established beyond a reasonable doubt that there was a probability that the defendant would commit criminal acts of violence that would constitute a continuing threat to society. The jury unanimously answered "yes" to both questions, and the judge, therefore, in accordance with the statute, sentenced the petitioner to death. The Court of Criminal Appeals of Texas affirmed the judgment.

The petitioner argues that the imposition of the death penalty under any circumstances is cruel and unusual punishment in violation of the Eighth and Fourteenth Amendments. We reject this argument for the reasons stated today in *Gregg v. Georgia*.

The new Texas Penal Code limits capital homicides to intentional and knowing murders committed in five situations: murder of a peace officer or fireman; murder committed in the course of kidnapping, burglary, robbery, forcible rape, or arson; murder committed for remuneration; murder committed while escaping or attempting to escape from a penal institution; and murder committed by a prison inmate when the victim is a prison employee.

In addition, Texas adopted a new capital-sentencing procedure. That procedure requires the jury to answer three questions in a proceeding that takes place subsequent to the return of a verdict finding a person guilty of one of the above categories of murder. The questions the jury must answer are these:

"(1) whether the conduct of the defendant that caused the death of the deceased was committed deliberately and with the reasonable expectation that the death of the deceased or another would result;

"(2) whether there is a probability that the defendant would commit criminal acts of violence that would constitute a continuing threat to society; and

"(3) if raised by the evidence, whether the conduct of the defendant in killing the deceased was unreasonable in response to the provocation, if any, by the deceased."

If the jury finds that the State has proved beyond a reasonable doubt that the answer to each of the three questions is yes, then the death sentence is imposed. If the jury finds that the answer to any question is no, then a sentence of life imprisonment results. The law also provides for an expedited review by the Texas Court of Criminal Appeals.

While Texas has not adopted a list of statutory aggravating circumstances the existence of which can justify the imposition of the death penalty as have Georgia and Florida, its action in narrowing the categories of murders for which a death sentence may ever be imposed serves much the same purpose. In fact, each of the five classes of murders made capital by the Texas statute is encompassed in Georgia and Florida by one or more of their statutory aggravating circumstances. For example, the Texas statute requires the jury at the guilt-determining stage to consider whether the crime was committed in the course of a particular felony, whether it was committed for hire, or whether the defendant was an inmate of a penal institution at the time of its commission. Thus, in essence, the Texas statute requires that the jury find the existence of a statutory aggravating circumstance before the death penalty may be imposed. So far as consideration of aggravating circumstances is concerned, therefore, the principal difference between Texas and the other two States is that the death penalty is an available sentencing option—even potentially—for a smaller class of murders in Texas. Otherwise the statutes are similar. Each requires the sentencing authority to focus on the particularized nature of the crime.

But a sentencing system that allowed the jury to consider only aggravating circumstances would almost certainly fall short of providing the individualized sentencing determination that we today have held in *Woodson v. North Carolina* to be required by the Eighth and Fourteenth Amendments. For such a system would approach the mandatory laws that we today hold unconstitutional in *Woodson* and *Roberts v. Louisiana*. A jury must be allowed to consider on the basis of all relevant evidence not only why a death sentence should be imposed, but also why it should not be imposed.

Thus, in order to meet the requirement of the Eighth and Fourteenth Amendments, a capital-sentencing system must allow the sentencing authority to consider mitigating circumstances. In *Gregg v. Georgia,* we today hold constitutionally valid a capital-sentencing system that directs the jury to consider any mitigating factors, and in *Proffitt v. Florida* we likewise hold constitutional a system that directs the judge and advisory jury to consider certain enumerated mitigating circumstances. The Texas statute does not explicitly speak of mitigating circumstances; it directs only that the jury answer three questions. Thus, the constitutionality of the Texas procedures turns on whether the enumerated questions allow consideration of particularized mitigating factors.

Thus, Texas law essentially requires that one of five aggravating circumstances be found before a defendant can be found guilty of capital murder, and that in considering whether to impose a death sentence the jury may be asked to consider whatever evidence of mitigating circumstances the defense can bring before it. It thus appears that, as in Georgia and Florida, the Texas capital-sentencing procedure guides and focuses the jury's objective consideration of the particularized circumstances of the individual offense and the individual offender before it can impose a sentence of death.

As in the Georgia and Florida cases, however, the petitioner contends that the substantial legislative changes that Texas made in response to this Court's *Furman* decision are no more than cosmetic in nature and have in fact not eliminated the arbitrariness and caprice of the system held in *Furman* to violate the Eighth and Fourteenth Amendments.

The petitioner first asserts that arbitrariness still pervades the entire criminal justice system of Texas—from the prosecutor's decision whether to charge a capital offense in the first place and then whether to engage in plea bargaining, through the jury's consideration of lesser included offenses, to the Governor's ultimate power to commute death sentences. This contention fundamentally misinterprets the *Furman* decision, and we reject it for the reasons set out in our opinion today in *Gregg v. Georgia*.

Focusing on the second statutory question that Texas requires a jury to answer in considering whether to impose a death sentence, the petitioner argues that it is impossible to predict future behavior and that the question is so vague as to be meaningless. It is, of course, not easy to predict future behavior. The fact that such a determination is difficult, however, does not mean that it cannot be made. Indeed, prediction of future criminal conduct is an essential element in many of the decisions rendered throughout our criminal justice system. The decision whether to admit a defendant to bail, for instance, must often turn on a judge's prediction of the defendant's future conduct. And any sentencing authority must predict a convicted person's probable future conduct when it engages in the process of determining what punishment to impose. For those sentenced to prison, these same predictions must be made by parole authorities. The task that a Texas jury must perform in answering the statutory question in issue is thus basically no different from the task performed countless times each day throughout the American system of criminal justice. What is essential is that the jury have before it all possible relevant information about the individual defendant whose fate it must determine. Texas law clearly assures that all such evidence will be adduced.

We conclude that Texas' capital-sentencing procedures, like those of Georgia and Florida, do not violate the Eighth and Fourteenth Amendments. By narrowing its definition of capital murder, Texas has essentially said that there must be at least one statutory aggravating circumstance in a first-degree murder case before a death sentence may even be considered. By authorizing the defense to bring before the jury at the separate sentencing hearing whatever mitigating circumstances relating to the individual defendant can be adduced, Texas has ensured that the sentencing jury will have adequate guidance to enable it to perform its sentencing function. By providing prompt judicial review of the jury's decision in a court with statewide jurisdiction, Texas has provided a means to promote the evenhanded, rational, and consistent imposition of death sentences under law. Because this system serves to assure that sentences of death will not be "wantonly" or "freakishly" imposed, it does not violate the Constitution. Accordingly, the judgment of the Texas Court of Criminal Appeals is affirmed.

It is so ordered.

Source: Jurek v. Texas, 428 U.S. 262 (1976), at 268–276.

Document 3.16
North Carolina Adopts Mandatory Death Penalty Statute, 1974

Following the Supreme Court's decision in Furman v. Georgia *(1972), the North Carolina General Assembly revised the state's death penalty law in 1974 to make the penalty mandatory under prescribed circumstances. This provision was struck down by the Court in* Woodson v. North Carolina *(1976). The key section of the statute is included here.*

Murder in the first and second degree defined; punishment—A murder which shall be perpetrated by means of poison, lying in wait, imprisonment, starving, torture, or by any other kind of willful, deliberate and premeditated killing, or which shall be committed in the perpetration or attempt to perpetrate any arson, rape, robbery, kidnapping, burglary or other felony, shall be deemed to be murder in the first degree and shall be punished with death. All other kinds of murder shall be deemed murder in the second degree, and shall be punished by imprisonment for a term of not less than two years nor more than life imprisonment in the State's prison.

Source: North Carolina General Statutes, Sections 14–17 (Cum Supp. 1975).

Document 3.17
The Supreme Court in *Woodson v. North Carolina* Claims That Mandatory Death Penalty Statutes Constitute Cruel and Unusual Punishment, July 2, 1976

While upholding revised capital punishment laws from Georgia, Florida, and Texas, the Supreme Court on the same day, July 2, 1976, struck down mandatory death sentence laws as a violation of the Eighth Amendment. The Court argued that such laws stripped juries and judges of all discretion and thus denied defendants an individualized judgment. In the lead case, Woodson v. North Carolina, *Justices Potter Stewart, Lewis Powell, and John Paul Stevens joined in the majority opinion. Dissenting opinions were written by Justices Byron White, Warren Burger, Harry Blackmun, and William Rehnquist.*

Judgment of the Court, and opinion of MR. JUSTICE STEWART, MR. JUSTICE POWELL, and MR. JUSTICE STEVENS, announced by MR. JUSTICE STEWART.

The question in this case is whether the imposition of a death sentence for the crime of first-degree murder under the law of North Carolina violates the Eighth and Fourteenth Amendments.

The petitioners were convicted of first-degree murder as the result of their participation in an armed robbery of a convenience food store, in the course of which the cashier was killed and a customer was seriously wounded. There were four participants in the robbery: the petitioners James Tyrone Woodson and Luby Waxton and two others, Leonard Tucker and Johnnie Lee Carroll. At the petitioners' trial Tucker and Carroll testified for the prosecution after having been permitted to plead guilty to lesser offenses; the petitioners testified to plead own defense.

The petitioners were found guilty on all charges, and, as was required by statute, sentenced to death. The Supreme Court of North Carolina affirmed. We granted certiorari to consider whether the imposition of the death penalties in this case comports with the Eighth and Fourteenth Amendments to the United States Constitution.

The petitioners argue that the imposition of the death penalty under any circumstances is cruel and unusual punishment in violation of the Eighth and Fourteenth Amendments. We reject this argument for the reasons stated today in *Gregg v. Georgia*, ante, at 168–187.

At the time of this Court's decision in *Furman v. Georgia*, North Carolina law provided that in cases of first-degree murder, the jury in its unbridled discretion could choose whether the convicted defendant should be sentenced to death or to life imprisonment. After the *Furman* decision the Supreme Court of North Carolina in *State v. Waddell* held unconstitutional the provision of the death penalty statute that gave the jury the option of returning a verdict of guilty without capital punishment, but held further that this provision was severable so that the statute survived as a mandatory death penalty law.

The North Carolina General Assembly in 1974 followed the court's lead and enacted a new statute that was essentially unchanged from the old one except that it made the death penalty mandatory. The statute now reads as follows:

> "Murder in the first and second degree defined; punishment—A murder which shall be perpetrated by means of poison, lying in wait, imprisonment, starving, torture, or by any other kind of willful, deliberate and premeditated killing, or which shall be committed in the perpetration or attempt to perpetrate any arson, rape, robbery, kidnapping, burglary or other felony, shall be deemed to be murder in the first degree and shall be punished with death. All other kinds of murder shall be deemed murder in the second degree, and shall be punished by imprisonment for a term of not less than two years nor more than life imprisonment in the State's prison." N.C. Gen. Stat. 14–17 (Cum. Supp. 1975).

It was under this statute that the petitioners, who committed their crime on June 3, 1974, were tried, convicted, and sentenced to death.

North Carolina, unlike Florida, Georgia, and Texas, has thus responded to the *Furman* decision by making death the mandatory sentence for all persons convicted of first-degree murder. In ruling on the constitutionality of the sentences imposed on the petitioners under this North Carolina statute, the Court now addresses for the first time the question whether a death sentence returned pursuant to a law imposing a mandatory death penalty for a broad category of homicidal offenses constitutes cruel and unusual punishment within the meaning of the Eighth and Fourteenth Amendments. The issue, like that explored in *Furman,* involves the procedure employed by the State to select persons for the unique and irreversible penalty of death.

The Eighth Amendment stands to assure that the State's power to punish is "exercised within the limits of civilized standards." Central to the application of the Amendment is a determination of contemporary standards regarding the infliction of punishment. As discussed in *Gregg v. Georgia,* indicia of societal values identified in prior opinions include history and traditional usage, legislative enactments, and jury determinations.

In order to provide a frame for assessing the relevancy of these factors in this case we begin by sketching the history of mandatory death penalty statutes in the United States. At the time the Eighth Amendment was adopted in 1791, the States uniformly followed the common-law practice of making death the exclusive and mandatory sentence for certain specified offenses. Although the range of capital offenses in the American Colonies was quite limited in comparison to the more than 200 offenses then punishable by death in England, the Colonies at the time of the Revolution imposed death sentences on all persons convicted of any of a considerable number of crimes, typically including at a minimum, murder, treason, piracy, arson, rape, robbery, burglary, and sodomy. As at common law, all homicides that were not involuntary, provoked, justified, or excused constituted murder and were automatically punished by death. Almost from the outset jurors reacted unfavorably to the harshness of mandatory death sentences. The States initially responded to this expression of public dissatisfaction with mandatory statutes by limiting the classes of capital offenses.

The history of mandatory death penalty statutes in the United States thus reveals that the practice of sentencing to death all persons convicted of a particular offense has been rejected as unduly harsh and unworkably rigid. The two crucial indicators of evolving standards of decency respecting the imposition of punishment in our society—jury determinations and legislative enactments—both point conclusively to the repudiation of automatic death sentences. At least since the Revolution, American jurors have, with some regularity, disregarded their oaths and refused to convict defendants where a death sentence was the automatic consequence of a guilty verdict. As we have seen, the initial movement to reduce the number of capital offenses and to separate murder into degrees was prompted in part by the reaction of jurors as well as by reformers who objected to the imposition of death as the penalty for any crime. Nineteenth century journalists, statesmen, and jurists repeatedly observed that jurors were often deterred from convicting palpably guilty men of first-degree murder under mandatory statutes. Thereafter, continuing evidence of jury reluctance to convict persons of capital offenses in mandatory death penalty jurisdictions resulted in legislative authorization of discretionary jury sentencing—by Congress for federal crimes in 1897, by North Carolina in 1949, and by Congress for the District of Columbia in 1962.

As we have noted today in *Gregg v. Georgia,* legislative measures adopted by the people's chosen representatives weigh heavily in ascertaining contemporary standards of decency. The consistent course charted by the state legislatures and by Congress since the middle of the past century demonstrates that the aversion of jurors to mandatory death penalty statutes is shared by society at large.

Still further evidence of the incompatibility of mandatory death penalties with contemporary values is provided by the results of jury sentencing under discretionary statutes. In *Witherspoon v. Illinois,* the Court observed that "one of the most important functions any jury can perform" in exercising its discretion to choose "between life imprisonment and capital punishment" is "to maintain a link between contemporary community values and the penal system." Various studies indicate that even in first-degree murder cases juries with sentencing discretion do not impose the death penalty "with any great frequency." The actions of sentencing juries suggest that under contemporary standards of decency death is viewed as an inappropriate punishment for a substantial portion of convicted first-degree murderers.

Although the Court has never ruled on the constitutionality of mandatory death penalty statutes, on several occasions dating back to 1899 it has commented upon our society's aversion to automatic death sentences. In *Winston v. United States* (1899), the Court noted that the "hardship of punishing with death every crime coming within the definition of murder at common law, and the reluctance of jurors to concur in a capital conviction, have induced American legislatures, in modern times, to allow some cases of murder to be punished by imprisonment, instead of by death."

More recently, the Court in *McGautha v. California* (1971), detailed the evolution of discretionary imposition of death sentences in this country, prompted by what it termed the American "rebellion against the common-law rule imposing a mandatory death sentence on all convicted murderers." Perhaps the one important factor about evolving social values regarding capital punishment upon which the Members of the *Furman* Court agreed was the accuracy of *McGautha*'s assessment of our Nation's rejection of mandatory death sentences.

It is now well established that the Eighth Amendment draws much of its meaning from "the evolving standards of decency that mark the progress of a maturing society." As the above discussion makes clear, one of the most significant developments in our society's treatment of capital punishment has been the rejection of the common-law practice of inexorably imposing a death sentence upon every person convicted of a specified offense. North Carolina's mandatory death penalty statute for first-degree murder departs markedly from contemporary standards respecting the imposition of the punishment of death and thus cannot be applied consistently with the Eighth and Fourteenth Amendments' requirement that the State's power to punish "be exercised within the limits of civilized standards."

A separate deficiency of North Carolina's mandatory death sentence statute is its failure to provide a constitutionally tolerable response to *Furman*'s rejection of unbridled jury discretion in the imposition of capital sentences. Central to the limited holding in *Furman* was the conviction that the vesting of standardless sentencing power in the jury violated the Eighth and Fourteenth Amendments. It is argued that North Carolina has remedied the inadequacies of the death penalty statutes held unconstitutional in *Furman* by withdrawing all sentencing discretion from juries in capital cases. But when one considers the long and consistent American experience with the death penalty in first-degree murder cases, it becomes evident that mandatory statutes enacted in response to *Furman* have simply papered over the problem of unguided and unchecked jury discretion.

A third constitutional shortcoming of the North Carolina statute is its failure to allow the particularized consideration of relevant aspects of the character and record of each convicted defendant before the imposition upon him of a sentence of death. In *Furman,* members of the Court acknowledged what cannot fairly be denied—that death is a punishment different from all other sanctions in kind rather than degree. A process that accords no significance to relevant facets of the character and record of the individual offender or the circumstances of the particular offense excludes from consideration in fixing the ultimate punishment of death the possibility of compassionate or mitigating factors stemming from the diverse frailties of humankind. It treats all persons convicted of a designated offense not as uniquely individual human beings, but as members of a faceless, undifferentiated mass to be subjected to the blind infliction of the penalty of death.

While the prevailing practice of individualizing sentencing determinations generally reflects simply enlightened policy rather than a constitutional imperative, we believe that in capital cases the fundamental respect for humanity underlying the Eighth Amendment, requires consideration of the character and record of the individual offender and the circumstances of the particular offense as a constitutionally indispensable part of the process of inflicting the penalty of death.

This conclusion rests squarely on the predicate that the penalty of death is qualitatively different from a sentence of imprisonment, however long. Death, in its finality, differs more from life imprisonment than a 100-year prison term difference from one of only a year or two. Because of that qualitative difference, there is a corresponding difference in the need for reliability in the determination that death is the appropriate punishment in a specific case.

For the reasons stated, we conclude that the death sentences imposed upon the petitioners under North Carolina's mandatory death sentence statute violated the Eighth and Fourteenth Amendments and therefore must be set aside. The judgment of the Supreme Court of North Carolina is reversed insofar as it upheld the death sentences imposed upon the petitioners, and the case is remanded for further proceedings not inconsistent with this opinion.

MR. JUSTICE BRENNAN, concurring in the judgment.

For the reasons stated in my dissenting opinion in *Gregg v. Georgia,* I concur in the judgment that sets aside the death sentence imposed under the North Carolina death sentence statute as violative of the Eighth and Fourteenth Amendments.

MR. JUSTICE MARSHALL, concurring in the judgment.

For the reasons stated in my dissenting opinion in *Gregg v. Georgia,* I am of the view that the death penalty is a cruel and unusual punishment forbidden by the Eighth and Fourteenth Amendments. I therefore concur in the Court's judgment.

MR. JUSTICE REHNQUIST, dissenting.

The difficulties which attend the plurality's explanation for the result it reaches tend at first to obscure difficulties at least as significant which inhere in the unarticulated premises necessarily underlying that explanation. I advert to the latter only briefly, in order to devote the major and following portion of this dissent to those issues which the plurality actually considers.

As an original proposition, it is by no means clear that the prohibition against cruel and unusual punishments embodied in the Eighth Amendment, and made applicable to the States by the Fourteenth Amendment, was not limited to those punishments deemed cruel and unusual at the time of the adoption of the Bill of Rights. If *Weems v. United States,* dealing not with the Eighth Amendment but with an identical provision contained in the Philippine Constitution, and the plurality opinion in *Trop v. Dulles* are to be taken as indicating the contrary, they should surely be weighed against statements in cases such as *Wilkerson v. Utah,* (1878); *In re Kemmler,* (1890); *Louisiana ex rel. Francis v. Resweber,* and the plurality opinion in *Trop* itself, that the infliction of capital punishment is not in itself violative of the Cruel and Unusual Punishments Clause. Thus for the plurality to begin its analysis with the assumption that it need only demonstrate that "evolving standards of decency" show that contemporary "society" has rejected such provisions is itself a somewhat shaky point of departure. But even if the assumption be conceded, the plurality opinion's analysis nonetheless founders.

The plurality relies first upon its conclusion that society has turned away from the mandatory imposition of death sentences, and second upon its conclusion that the North Carolina system has "simply papered over" the problem of unbridled jury discretion which two of the separate opinions in *Furman v. Georgia,* identified as the basis for the judgment rendering the death sentences there reviewed unconstitutional. The third "constitutional shortcoming" of the North Carolina statute is said to be "its failure to allow the particularized consideration of relevant aspects of the character and record of each convicted defendant before the imposition upon him of a sentence of death."

I do not believe that any one of these reasons singly, or all of them together, can withstand careful analysis. Contrary to the plurality's assertions, they would import into the Cruel and Unusual Punishments Clause procedural requirements which find no support in our cases. Their application will result in the invalidation of a death sentence imposed upon a defendant convicted of first-degree murder under the North Carolina system, and the upholding of the same sentence imposed on an identical defendant convicted on identical evidence of first-degree murder under the Florida, Georgia, or Texas systems—a result surely as "freakish" as that condemned in the separate opinions in *Furman.*

The plurality is simply mistaken in its assertion that "[t]he history of mandatory death penalty statutes in the United States thus reveals that the practice of sentencing to death all persons convicted of a particular offense has been rejected as unduly harsh and unworkably rigid." This conclusion is purportedly based on two historic developments: the first a series of legislative decisions during the 19th century narrowing the class of offenses punishable by death; the second a series of legislative decisions during both the 19th and 20th centuries, through which mandatory imposition of the death penalty largely gave way to jury discretion in deciding whether or not to impose this ultimate sanction. The first development may have some relevance to the plurality's argument in general but has no bearing at all upon this case. The second development, properly analyzed, has virtually no relevance even to the plurality's argument.

There can be no question that the legislative and other materials discussed in the plurality's opinion show a widespread conclusion on the part of state legislatures during the 19th century that the penalty of death was being required for too broad a range of crimes, and that these legislatures proceeded to narrow the range of crimes for which such penalty could be imposed. If this case involved the imposition of the death penalty for an offense such as burglary or sodomy, the virtually unanimous trend in the legislatures of the States to exclude such offenders from liability for capital punishment might bear on the plurality's Eighth Amendment argument. But petitioners were convicted of first-degree murder, and there is not the slightest suggestion in the material relied upon by the plurality that there had been any turning away at all, much less any such unanimous turning away, from the death penalty as a punishment for those guilty of first-degree murder. The legislative narrowing of the spectrum of capital crimes, therefore, while very arguably representing a general societal judgment since the trend was so widespread, simply never reached far enough to exclude the sort of aggravated homicide of which petitioners stand convicted.

The second string to the plurality's analytical bow is that legislative change from mandatory to discretionary imposition of the death sentence likewise evidences societal rejection of mandatory death penalties. The plurality simply does not make out this part of its case, however, in large part because it treats as being of equal dignity with legislative judgments the judgments of particular juries and of individual jurors.

There was undoubted dissatisfaction, from more than one sector of 19th century society, with the operation of mandatory death sentences. One segment of that society was totally opposed to capital punishment, and was apparently willing to accept the substitution of discretionary imposition of that penalty for its mandatory imposition as a halfway house on the road to total abolition. Another segment was equally unhappy with the operation of the mandatory system, but for an entirely different reason. As the plurality recognizes, this second segment of society was unhappy with the operation of the mandatory system, not because of the death sentences imposed under it, but because people obviously guilty of criminal offenses were not being convicted under it. Change to a discretionary system was accepted by these persons not because they thought mandatory imposition of the death penalty was cruel and unusual, but because they thought that if jurors were permitted to return a sentence other than death upon the conviction of a capital crime, fewer guilty defendants would be acquitted.

So far as the action of juries is concerned, the fact that in some cases juries operating under the mandatory system refused to convict obviously guilty defendants does not reflect any "turning away" from the death penalty, or the mandatory death penalty, supporting the proposition that it is "cruel and unusual." Given the requirement of unanimity with respect to jury verdicts in capital cases, a requirement which prevails today in States which accept a nonunanimous verdict in the case of other crimes, see *Johnson v. Louisiana,* it is apparent that a single juror could prevent a jury from returning a verdict of conviction. Occasional refusals to convict, therefore, may just as easily have represented the intransigence of only a small minority of 12 jurors as well as the unanimous judgment of all 12. The fact that the presence of such jurors could prevent conviction in a given case, even though the majority of society, speaking through legislatures, had decreed that it should be imposed, certainly does not indicate that society as a whole rejected mandatory punishment for such offenders; it does not even indicate that those few members of society who serve on juries, as a whole, had done so.

The second constitutional flaw which the plurality finds in North Carolina's mandatory system is that it has simply "papered over" the problem of unchecked jury discretion. The plurality states, that "there is general agreement that American juries have persistently refused to convict a significant portion of persons charged with first-degree murder of that offense under mandatory death penalty statutes." The plurality also states, that "as a matter of historic fact, juries operating under discretionary sentencing statutes have consistently returned death sentences in only a minority of first degree murder cases." The basic factual assumption of the plurality seems to be that for any given number of first-degree murder defendants subject to capital punishment, there will be a certain number of jurors who will be unwilling to impose the death penalty even though they are entirely satisfied that the necessary elements of the substantive offense are made out.

In North Carolina jurors unwilling to impose the death penalty may simply hang a jury or they may so assert themselves that a verdict of not guilty is brought in; in Louisiana they will have a similar effect in causing some juries to bring in a verdict of guilty of a lesser included offense even though all the jurors are satisfied that the elements of the greater offense are made out. Such jurors, of course, are violating their oath, but such violation is not only consistent with the majority's hypothesis; the majority's hypothesis is bottomed on its occurrence.

For purposes of argument, I accept the plurality's hypothesis; but it seems to me impossible to conclude from it that a mandatory death sentence statute such as North Carolina enacted is any less sound constitutionally than are the systems enacted by Georgia, Florida, and Texas which the Court upholds.

The plurality seems to believe, that provision for appellate review will afford a check upon the instances of juror arbitrariness in a discretionary system. But it is not at all apparent that appellate review of death sentences, through a process of comparing the facts of one case in which a death sentence was imposed with the facts of another in which such a sentence was imposed, will afford any meaningful protection against whatever arbitrariness results from jury discretion. All that such review of death sentences can provide is a comparison of fact situations which must in their nature be highly particularized if not unique, and the only relief which it can afford is to single out the occasional death sentence which in the view of the reviewing court does not conform to the standards established by the legislature.

Appellate review affords no correction whatever with respect to those fortunate few who are the beneficiaries of random discretion exercised by juries, whether under an admittedly discretionary system or under a purportedly mandatory system. It may make corrections at one end of the spectrum, but cannot at the other. It is even less clear that any provision of the Constitution can be read to require such appellate review. If the States wish to undertake such an effort, they are undoubtedly free to do so, but surely it is not required by the United States Constitution.

The plurality's insistence on "standards" to "guide the jury in its inevitable exercise of the power to determine which . . . murderers shall live and which shall die" is squarely contrary to the Court's opinion in *McGautha v. California*, written by Mr. Justice Harlan and subscribed to by five other Members of the Court only five years ago. So is the plurality's latter-day recognition, some four years after the decision of the case, that *Furman* requires "objective standards to guide, regularize, and make rationally reviewable the process for imposing a sentence of death." Its abandonment of stare decisis in this repudiation of *McGautha* is a far lesser mistake than its substitution of a superficial and contrived constitutional doctrine for the genuine wisdom contained in *McGautha*.

The plurality's insistence on individualized consideration of the sentencing, therefore, does not depend upon any traditional application of the prohibition against cruel and unusual punishment contained in the Eighth Amendment. The punishment here is concededly not cruel and unusual, and that determination has traditionally ended judicial inquiry in our cases construing the Cruel and Unusual Punishments Clause. What the plurality opinion has actually done is to import into the Due Process Clause of the Fourteenth Amendment what it conceives to be desirable procedural guarantees where the punishment of death, concededly not cruel and unusual for the crime of which the defendant was convicted, is to be imposed. This is squarely contrary to *McGautha*, and unsupported by any other decision of this Court. . . .

Source: Woodson v. North Carolina, 428 U.S. 280 (1976), at 283–306, 308–325.

NOTES

1. U.S. Constitution, Article III, Section 2.
2. See *The Federalist Papers*, No. 78: The Judiciary Department, *Independent Journal*, June 14, 1788 [Alexander Hamilton]; and *Marbury v. Madison*, 5 U.S. (1 Cranch) 137 (1803), 176–180.
3. *McCulloch v. Maryland*, 17 U.S. (4 Wheat.) 316 (1819).
4. See, respectively, *Dred Scott v. Sandford*, 60 U.S. (19 How.) 393 (1856); *Pollock v. Farmer's Loan and Trust Co.*, 157 U.S. 429 (1895), on rehearing 158 U.S. 601 (1895); and *United States v. Butler*, 297 U.S. 1 (1936), in which the Court overturned the first Agricultural Adjustment Act aimed at farm relief; and *Morehead v. New York ex rel. Tipaldo*, 298 U.S. 587 (1936), in which the Court struck down a New York minimum wage law.
5. See, for example, *Dennis v. United States*, 341 U.S. 494 (1951), in which the Court upheld the convictions of Communist Party leaders under the Smith Act; and *Communist Party v. Subversive Activities Control Board*, 367 U.S. 1 (1961), in which the Court upheld the registration provisions of the anti-communist McCarren Act.
6. In *Jackson v. State*, 348 U.S. 888 (1954), the Court declined to hear an appeal from the Alabama supreme court affirming the conviction of Linnie Jackson for violating the state's miscegenation statute, and in *Naim v. Naim*, 350 U.S. 891 and 895 (1956), it dismissed a similar Virginia case because it was "devoid of a properly presented federal question."
7. *Loving v. Virginia*, 388 U.S. 1 (1967).
8. See Jeffrey Rosen, *The Most Democratic Branch: How the Courts Serve America* (New York: Oxford University Press, 2006); and Michael Klarman, *Brown v. Board of Education and the Civil Rights Movement* (New York: Oxford University Press, 2007).
9. *Weems v. United States*, 217 U.S. 349 (1910), at 378.
10. *Trop v. Dulles*, 356 U.S. 86 (1958), at 101.
11. See, for example, *Griffin v. Illinois*, 351 U.S. 12 (1956); *Douglas v. California*, 372 U.S. 353 (1963); and *Miranda v. Arizona*, 384 U.S. 436 (1966).
12. *McGautha v. California*, 402 U.S. 183 (1971).
13. See 49 U.S.C. 1472; 18 U.S.C. 1751; and 18 U.S.C. 351.
14. *Hepburn v. Griswold*, 75 U.S. (8 Wall.) 603 (1870).
15. *Knox v. Lee*, 79 U.S. 457 (1871).
16. *Minersville School District v. Gobitis*, 310 U.S. 586 (1940).
17. *West Virginia Board of Education v. Barnette*, 319 U.S. 624 (1943).
18. *Furman v. Georgia*, 408 U.S. 238 (1972), at 248–249.
19. See, for example, Daniel D. Polsby, "The Death of Capital Punishment? *Furman v. Georgia*," *The Supreme Court Review* 1972 (1972): 1–40.
20. *Rudolph v. Alabama*, 375 U.S. 889 (1963).
21. *Furman v. Georgia*, at 242–245.
22. Ibid., at 253–256.
23. Ibid., at 270–278.
24. Ibid., at 292–296.
25. Ibid., at 301–305.
26. Ibid., at 324, 331–332.
27. Ibid., at 344–345.
28. Ibid., at 363–364 (emphasis added).

29. Ibid., at 310.
30. Ibid., at 308.
31. Ibid., at 310.
32. *Witherspoon v. Illinois*, 391 U.S. 510 (1968); *United States v. Jackson*, 390 U.S. 570 (1968); *Boykin v. Alabama*, 395 U.S. 238 (1969); and *Maxwell v. Bishop*, 398 U.S. 262 (1970).
33. *Trop v. Dulles*, 356 U.S. 86 (1958); and *Robinson v. California*, 370 U.S. 660 (1962).
34. *Jones v. Alfred H. Mayer, Co.*, 392 U.S. 409 (1968).
35. *Furman v. Georgia*, at 313.
36. Ibid., at 386–390.
37. Ibid., at 396.
38. Ibid., at 402.
39. Ibid., at 446–448.
40. Ibid., at 403.
41. *People v. Anderson*, 6 Cal. 3d 628, 493 P.2d 880 (1972).
42. *Furman v. Georgia*, at 411.
43. A legal challenge to the initiative was rejected by the federal Ninth Circuit Court of Appeals in *White v. Brown*, 468 F.2d 301 (1972).
44. "NO on the Death Penalty," *Los Angeles Times*, October 20, 1972, B6.
45. "Death Penalty Ok'd but Its Use Could Be Years in Future," *Los Angeles Times*, November 9, 1972, A20.
46. *Gregg v. Georgia*, 428 U.S. 153 (1976).
47. Ibid., at 168–187.
48. Ibid., at 198.
49. Ibid., at 206–207.
50. *Proffitt v. Florida*, 428 U.S. 242 (1976).
51. *Jurek v. Texas*, 428 U.S. 262 (1976).
52. *Proffitt v. Florida*, at 248. The Model Penal Code, developed by the American Law Institute, represents an ongoing effort to update and standardize U.S. penal law.
53. Ibid., at 249–250.
54. Ibid., at 252–253.
55. *Jurek v. Texas*, at 272. The Court would revisit and reconsider this provision of the Texas law in *Penry v. Lynaugh*, 492 U.S. 302 (1989), and *Penry v. Johnson*, 531 U.S. 34 (2001), with specific reference to mitigating factors concerning mental retardation. See chapter 4.
56. *Woodson v. North Carolina*, 428 U.S. 280 (1976); and *Roberts v. Louisiana*, 428 U.S. 325 (1976). The defendant in *Roberts* was Stanislaus Roberts. A year later, the Court reversed the conviction of one Harry Roberts, who had been sentenced to die under the same Louisiana statute for the killing of a police officer. See *Roberts v. Louisiana*, 431 U.S. 633 (1977).
57. *Woodson v. North Carolina*, at 304.
58. Ibid., at 302.
59. Ibid., at 313.
60. Ibid., at 324.
61. *Roe v. Wade*, 410 U.S. 113 (1973).

CHAPTER 4

Delegating Death
The White-Rehnquist Court, 1976–1989

In the years between the *Furman* decision (1972) and the late 1980s, the Supreme Court struggled to reconcile two strands of its death penalty jurisprudence that remained in tension. *Furman* had overturned capital sentencing statutes that left juries and judges with almost unlimited discretion to determine who, among murderers, should live or die.[1] *Furman* in effect ordered legislatures to provide capital sentencers with statutory guidelines. *Gregg* and its companion opinions (*Proffitt* and *Jurek*) gave the states a green light to commence executions under revised statutes that more narrowly defined the circumstances under which capital defendants could be put to death.[2] At the same time, a plurality of the justices in *Woodson* rejected mandatory death penalty laws on the grounds that they constituted cruel and unusual punishment by stripping juries of the discretion necessary to individualize punishment.[3] Over the next two decades, its membership shifting rapidly, the Court attempted without great success to reconcile these two constitutional commands.

At least two justices, William Brennan and Thurgood Marshall, rejected from the start the search for what might be called guided discretion in capital cases and voted consistently that capital punishment was per se unconstitutional as cruel and unusual punishment. They were joined in the late 1980s by Justice Harry Blackmun, a dissenter in *Furman* and *Woodson,* who came to believe that the quest for a constitutional death penalty statute remained beyond the Court's wisdom. Led by Justices Byron White and William Rehnquist, who became chief justice in 1986, a majority of the justices rejected these extreme positions and continued the jurisprudential journey to reconcile guidance with discretion while generally granting the states broad latitude in structuring the capital sentencing process.

These were also years of resurgent conservatism in American political life following the social upheavals arising from the civil rights movement, the Vietnam War, and the Watergate scandal that forced the resignation of President Richard Nixon and the imprisonment of his top advisers. In Georgia governor Jimmy Carter the country elected in 1976 the most conservative Democrat since the 1920s. Carter failed to secure a single appointment to the Court during his term in office. The election of Ronald Reagan in 1980 ushered in a decade of conservative domination of the executive branch that saw the appointment of the first female justice (Sandra Day O' Connor) and the elevation of Rehnquist to the center chair. Rehnquist was joined on the bench by another Reagan appointee, Antonin Scalia, with whom he shared the belief that the Eighth Amendment and its reference to cruel and unusual punishment should be viewed by the Court in terms of its "original" (1790) meaning.

"Let's Do It"

In one of the more ironic twists in the history of the Court's engagement with the death penalty, none of the three defendants whose sentences were upheld in the landmark July 2, 1976, cases—Troy Leon Gregg, William Proffitt, and Jerry Lane Jurek—were ever executed by the states of Georgia, Florida, and Texas. One of four death row inmates who staged a daring escape from Georgia's Reidsville prison on July 29, 1980, Gregg placed two telephone calls to a reporter for the *Albany* (Georgia) *Herald* while on the run, telling him: "We had to get out. We couldn't stand it any longer. We all decided we'd rather be dead than stay here another day. Conditions here are inhuman." A day later, Gregg's body was found floating in a North Carolina lake twelve miles from a house where local police and FBI agents captured the three other inmates. Gregg had been beaten to death. Georgia authorities said they had no other details.[4]

In 1982 the Federal Court of Appeals for the Eleventh Circuit sent Proffitt's case back to the Florida trial court when it ruled that the judge had violated the defendant's Sixth Amendment rights during the sentencing phase by denying his counsel the opportunity to cross-examine testimony and reports by court-appointed psychologists. In addition, the judge was faulted with having misconstrued the statutory aggravating factors in the Florida law and impermissibly considering nonstatutory aggravating factors.[5] When the trial court again sentenced Proffitt to die, the Florida supreme court reversed on the grounds that under recent Florida decisions the penalty of death for murder during the course of a burglary would be disproportionate and that mitigating circumstances, including the fact that Proffitt had no prior criminal record and voluntarily surrendered following the crime, outweighed the aggravating factors. The court reduced Proffitt's sentence to life without the opportunity for parole for twenty-five years.[6]

In a habeas corpus proceeding in 1980, the Fifth U.S. Circuit Court of Appeals reversed a district court and overturned Jurek's conviction on the grounds that the second of two confessions introduced at his trial had not been voluntary. The Supreme Court's refusal to review that decision drew an angry dissent from Justice Rehnquist, who described the ruling as "a procedural nicety" that "renders Texas' death penalty statute an ineffective deterrent . . . [and] frustrates society's compelling interest in having its constitutionally valid laws swiftly and surely carried out."[7] At his retrial a year later, Jurek reached a plea-bargain agreement with prosecutors. In exchange for his guilty plea to a count of capital murder, prosecutors agreed not to seek the death penalty and dropped the initial rape charge. He was sentenced to life in prison.[8]

Gary Gilmore, whose criminal record began at age fourteen with car theft, had the dubious honor of being the first person put to death in the United States following the *Gregg* decision. Gilmore robbed and murdered a gas station attendant and a motel manager during a two-day crime spree in Utah in July 1976. Tried, convicted, and sentenced to death in October 1976, Gilmore chose the firing squad rather than hanging, twice attempted suicide while awaiting execution, waived all appeals by his lawyers, and, when asked for any last words before the bullets tore into him on January 17, 1977, said: "Let's do it!"

The five-man firing squad did a far more effective job than Wallace Wilkerson's had done a century earlier (**Document 4.1**). Gilmore donated his eyes for transplant purposes and became immortalized in novelist Norman Mailer's book *The Executioner's Song,* which won for its author the Pulitzer Prize in 1979. American pop culture took notice of the execution too. The television film version of Mailer's book won an Emmy Award for actor Tommy Lee Jones, who played Gilmore. Gilmore's brother wrote a memoir, entitled *Shot Through the Heart,* that was turned into an HBO movie. The cast of NBC's comedy hit show, *Saturday Night Live,* performed a holiday medley entitled, "Let's Kill Gary Gilmore for Christmas," and the pop singing group The Adverts hit the top 20 on the charts in England with "Gary Gilmore's Eyes." This troubled son of a dysfunctional family quickly became the most recognized death row prisoner since Caryl Chessman, the so-called red light bandit who had been gassed in California in the 1960s.

Two years after the media attention swirling around Gilmore's execution, Florida carried out its first execution after *Gregg* when it electrocuted a thirty-year-old drifter and work camp escapee, John Spenkelink, convicted of shooting his traveling companion in a Tallahassee hotel room. Although Spenkelink claimed he had been sodomized and forced to play "russian roulette," and that he shot his victim in self-defense, he was convicted and sentenced under the statute upheld by the Court in *Proffitt.*

Spenkelink's long journey through the state and federal courts prior to his execution on the morning of May 25, 1979, was, unlike Gilmore's uncontested (Gilmore had dropped all final appeals) execution, a harbinger of what lay ahead for those sentenced to die in the wake of the Court's July 2, 1976 decisions, as well as for those charged with judging them. After the Florida trial court and the state supreme court twice rejected Spenkelink's claims, he sought relief two times through habeas corpus proceedings in the federal district court and the Fifth Circuit Court of Appeals, but was rebuffed on both occasions. The Fifth Circuit also lifted a stay of execution from a district judge that had delayed the execution one day. Despite three separate requests, the Court declined full review of Spenkelink's case, with Justices Brennan and Marshall dissenting. On two occasions

Gary Gilmore, whose legal battle and ultimate execution were chronicled in Norman Mailer's The Executioner's Song, *is shown here leaving his third sentencing hearing on December 16, 1976. Gilmore was sentenced to death and executed by firing squad on January 17, 1977, for the murder of two people in the summer of 1976. He was the first person put to death in the United States after the* Gregg *decision.*

the Court vacated stays of execution, one of which had been granted by Marshall. On the morning of May 25, the Court again turned down by a vote of 6–2 a final petition for a new stay presented by Ramsey Clark, a former attorney general of the United States and the son of former Supreme Court justice Tom Clark (**Document 4.2**). Five hours later, Spenkelink's execution marked the end of his long, tortuous journey.[9]

The Balance of Power

The 1980s brought significant changes to the makeup of the Court that determined in large measure the direction of its death penalty jurisprudence. With the retirement of Potter Stewart in 1983, only three members of the Warren Court continued to sit—Brennan, Marshall, and White. Stewart, a critical part of the key plurality of the justices in *Furman, Gregg,* and *Woodson,* seldom wavered from the middle course he had charted in those cases: capital statutes must eliminate arbitrariness, but not eliminate discretion by mandating death for certain crimes. He believed that the death penalty comported with the Constitution and popular opinion, but had to be surrounded with the full panoply of procedural protections from arrest through appeals. He also believed it could be sufficiently rationalized and limited to a diminishing number of defendants through a judicious combination of explicit statutory guidelines that required judges and juries to carefully weigh aggravating and mitigating circumstances in each case.

Stewart was prepared to live with the inherent contradiction between explicit standards and discretion and to redraw the balance at the Court between the two if he thought the legislatures, the judges, and the juries strayed too far in either direction. Justices Lewis Powell and John Paul Stevens, who had joined him in *Gregg* and *Woodson*, tended to follow Stewart's lead, and O'Connor, his replacement, adopted a similar posture after 1983. The Powell-Stevens-O'Connor trio, when joined by Brennan and Marshall and occasionally by Blackmun, held the balance of power on the Court until the late 1980s. Reagan's appointment of Scalia in 1986 and Anthony Kennedy in 1988, however, combined with his elevation of Rehnquist to chief justice, significantly diminished the influence of the trio.

The last Warren justices, Brennan, Marshall, and White, represented opposite poles on capital punishment. For Brennan and Marshall, no statute could pass the Eighth Amendment barrier, an absolutist position they tirelessly advocated alone until joined in 1994 by Blackmun, who had dissented in *Furman* and endorsed a mandatory death penalty in *Woodson*. Unlike Stewart, White had endorsed *Furman*'s demand for standards in the hope of fine-tuning the machinery of death to the point where more convictions and death sentences would be carried out with dispatch. A firm believer in the death penalty as an effective instrument of crime deterrence, White also favored broad deference to the statutory and judicial judgments of state legislatures and courts. And because he remained on the Court longer than either Brennan or Marshall (until 1993), his views carried more weight on the constitutional scales, especially when they were joined with the similar outlooks of Rehnquist and, later, Scalia and Kennedy.

Narrowing the Death Eligible: Rape

Prior to Stewart's retirement and sandwiched between the executions of Gilmore and Spenkelink, the justices who endorsed more restrictions on the death penalty (Stewart, Powell, Stevens, Brennan, and Marshall) achieved notable victories by limiting the types of crimes eligible for the death penalty and imposing new substantive limits even on states that had adopted guided and separate penalty trials in response to *Furman*. In the seven-year period between 1976 and 1983, the majority decided fifteen out of sixteen capital cases in favor of the defendant.

In 1977 the Court's plurality, led by White, who wrote the opinion, struck down Georgia's statutory death penalty for the rape of an adult woman, citing orthodox Eighth Amendment law, including *Weems* and *Trop,* that the penalty was disproportionate to the offense.[10] "Rape is without doubt deserving of serious punishment," White wrote, "but in terms of moral depravity and of the injury to the person and public, it does not compare with murder, which does involve the taking of human life."[11] *Coker* was not an easy case for someone like White, disposed to affirm capital sentences, since the circumstances of the defendant's crime included two of Georgia's aggravating conditions: Erlich Coker had a previous felony conviction and committed the rape in the course of an armed robbery (**Document 4.3**).

White's vote can be explained by the issue not directly confronted by the majority: race. He noted, for example, that only Georgia and Florida of all the states continued to mandate death for rape (and in Florida's case only for the rape of a child) and that in nine out of ten rape cases in Georgia since 1973 juries had not imposed the death sentence. He did not mention another statistic: between 1930 and the early 1980s, out of 455 persons put to death in the United States for the crime of rape, 405 were African Americans and close to 90 percent of those had been convicted of raping a white woman.[12] Apart from Rehnquist, White was the most vigorous defender of the death penalty on the Burger Court, but he had also displayed a high degree of sensitivity to racial discrimination, both as a member of the Kennedy justice department under Robert Kennedy and later on the Court.[13]

Although both White and Powell, who wrote a separate concurrence, took pains to narrow the decision to cases involving the rape of an adult, Chief Justice Warren Burger and Rehnquist saw the larger implications of the ruling. "The clear implication of today's holding appears to be that the death penalty may be properly imposed only as to crimes resulting in the death of the victim," Burger wrote in dissent. "This casts serious doubt upon the constitutional validity of statutes imposing the death penalty for a variety of conduct which, though dangerous, may not necessarily result in any immediate death, e.g., treason, airplane hijacking, and kidnapping."[14]

Taking Mitigation Seriously

A year after *Coker,* the Stewart and Stevens–led coalition, absent White but joined by Burger, dramatically reaffirmed the Court's opposition to mandatory death penalty statutes when it overturned the death sentence of Sandra Lockett, who had been convicted for her role as the getaway driver in an armed robbery that ended in a homicide.[15] The ringleader of the robbery, who had also fired the fatal shots, received only a life sentence. The plurality opinion, written by Burger, overturned the Ohio statute on Eighth and Fourteenth Amendment grounds for failing to sufficiently individualize the capital sentencing decision by restricting the list of mitigating factors that a trial judge could weigh before imposing death (**Document 4.4**). While Ohio enumerated seven aggravating factors that made a defendant death eligible, its list of allowable mitigating factors included only that the crime had been "induced or facilitated" by the victim, the defendant had been acting under duress, or the defendant had acted under psychosis or mental deficiency.

Ohio's restricted list of mitigating factors, Burger wrote, violated the historic constitutional mandate for individualized sentencing, especially in capital cases, a mandate that had doctrinal roots in *McGautha*.[16] It therefore came perilously close to the mandatory law struck down in *Woodson*. Lockett had been condemned without any consideration of her age, her previous criminal record, or her marginal role in the robbery and homicide. The Constitution procedurally required, the chief justice concluded, "in all but the rarest kind of capital cases" that judge or jury not be precluded from considering as a mitigating factor *"any aspect of a defendant's character or record and any of the circumstances of the offense that the defendant proffers as a basis for a sentence less than death."*[17]

The Court did not say in *Lockett* that the Eighth Amendment now required state judges and juries to weigh mitigation against aggravation and only condemn those defendants where aggravation tipped the balance, but that seemed to be the clear implication of the decision. It brought dissents from White and Rehnquist, who argued that the plurality had done more than reaffirm *Woodson* by giving mitigation such broad constitutional status and protection. They judged that *Lockett* had backtracked from *Furman* and threatened to restore the discredited regime of sentencing discretion. "This [decision] invites a return to the pre-*Furman* days when the death penalty was generally reserved for those very few for whom society has least consideration," White wrote, expressing both concern for the equal protection issues in capital cases and his fear that more juries would use the broad mitigation command to weaken the deterrent value of the penalty.[18] Rehnquist believed the new constitutional rule "will not eliminate arbitrariness or freakishness in the imposition of sentences, but will codify and institutionalize it."[19]

Rebalancing Aggravation and Mitigation

Lockett left open the question of how judges and juries were to weigh aggravating versus mitigating factors before imposing death, and to what extent the Court itself, as opposed to state appellate courts, would police these judgments. *Godfrey v. Georgia* (1980) and *Eddings v. Oklahoma* (1982) began to offer some answers to those questions when the Court overturned death sentences in both cases.[20] Threatened with divorce by his estranged wife who had moved in with her mother after a long period of family acrimony, Godfrey killed them both with a shotgun before turning himself in to the local sheriff. The jury sentenced him to death after finding that the homicides constituted an aggravating circumstance as defined by Georgia law as "outrageously or wantonly vile, horrible and inhuman."[21]

Again led by Stewart, joined by Stevens, Powell, and Blackmun, the Court threw out the sentence on the grounds that the statutory language was too vague to distinguish one aggravating circumstance from another, a point conceded by the Georgia supreme court, which had nonetheless affirmed the sentence. But because the Georgia high court had not indicated a narrowing of the language in its decision, Godfrey could not be put to death as the justices reevaluated the aggravating circumstances to hold that "[his] crimes cannot be said to have reflected more 'depravity' than that of any person guilty of murder."[22]

The Court's rebalancing of aggravating factors drew a sharp rebuke from White and also from Rehnquist. The latter recited the gruesome details of the shotgun deaths of Godfrey's wife and mother-in-law to suggest that the trial court and the Georgia supreme court had ample reason in finding the homicides exhibited "torture" and "depravity of the mind," but his main objection focused on the Court's eagerness to second-guess the state court and to forget that the criminal law would always be administered by fallible human beings. "Our mandate does not extend to interfering with fact finders in state criminal proceedings or with state courts that are responsible and consistently interpreting state law," White wrote, but "today, a majority of this Court . . . informs the Georgia Supreme Court that, to some extent, its efforts have been outside the Constitution."[23]

In *Eddings*, decided two years later, the majority reaffirmed *Lockett* and indicated an equal willingness to rebalance a state court's assessment of mitigating circumstances. The sixteen-year-old defendant, Monty Lee Eddings, had shotgunned a highway patrolman who stopped him for a traffic offense, telling his riding companion that "if the motherfucking pig tried to stop him he was going to blow him away."[24] The Oklahoma statute allowed trial courts and appellate courts to consider "any mitigating circumstances," but they had narrowed their consideration of mitigation only to Eddings' age at the time of the crime, while ignoring other circumstances of his life, including violent treatment at the hands of his parents and his impaired emotional development. Justice Powell's majority opinion concluded that Eddings' "unfortunate childhood" should have been given greater explicit weight by the state court in its instructions to the jury as a mitigating factor, a conclusion that drew from Chief Justice Burger and the dissenters only the assumption that the Oklahoma appellate courts had probably done so (**Document 4.5**).

Felony Murder

At the very end of its 1982 term, again dividing 5–4, the Court sharply restricted the conditions under which a person who participated in a felony that involved a homicide could be put to death, even though he did not do the killing and had no intention of killing. Earl Enmund and two confederates, Samson and Jeanette

Armstrong, planned to rob an elderly couple, Thomas and Eunice Kersey, at their Florida farmhouse in the spring of 1975, with Enmund driving the getaway car while the Armstrongs carried out the actual robbery. When Eunice Kersey, aged 74, foiled their plan by wounding Jeanette Armstrong, Samson Armstrong shot and killed both husband and wife before stealing their money and driving off with Enmund who had been parked 200 yards away from the farmhouse.

Samson Armstrong, the trigger man, was convicted of first-degree murder and sentenced to death. Under Florida's felony-murder statute, Enmund's role was enough to make him a constructive aider and abettor, a principal in first-degree murder, upon whom the death penalty could be imposed. Under the statute the prosecution did not have to prove that Enmund had a culpable mental state (mens rea); it was also irrelevant that he did not kill the Kerseys, was not present during the killing, did not intend to kill the Kerseys, or anticipate that lethal force would be used during the robbery. Writing for the majority, Justice White concluded that the Eighth and Fourteenth Amendments barred Enmund's execution under the statute and the circumstances of the case, which made *Enmund v. Florida* another constitutional landmark with respect to criminal liability (**Document 4.6**).

Drawing upon the methodology he used in *Coker v. Georgia,* White invoked evidence from other state statutes as well as decisions by juries and prosecutors to argue that the Florida law was an outlier in punishing felony murder in addition to first-degree murder with death, especially in the absence of some culpable mental state that both the trial court and the Florida supreme court had ignored. "We are not aware of a single person convicted of felony murder over the past quarter century who did not kill or attempt to kill, and did not intend the death of the victim, who has been executed, and that only three persons in that category are presently sentenced to die."[25] The death penalty for one in Enmund's category would be disproportionate.

White made it clear, however, that statistics alone did not drive the majority's decision because the Court had engaged in its own independent constitutional analysis: "It is for us ultimately to judge whether the Eighth Amendment permits the imposition of the death penalty on one such as Enmund . . . who does not himself kill, attempt to kill, or intend that a killing take place or that lethal force will be employed. We have concluded, along with most legislatures and juries, that it does not."[26]

Finally, White argued, executing Enmund under the Florida statute would not serve either the purpose of deterrence or retribution, the two principal social purposes of the death penalty upheld in *Gregg v. Georgia.* Since a tiny percentage of robberies resulted in homicides and juries had displayed a strong reluctance to invoke the death penalty on those only vicariously guilty of murder, these facts attenuated the penalty's utility as an effective deterrence. And in the absence of his moral guilt "putting Enmund to death to avenge two killings that he did not commit and had no intention of committing or causing does not measurably contribute to the retributive end of ensuring that the criminal gets his just deserts."[27]

The four dissenters in *Enmund,* led by Justice O'Connor, criticized the majority for reaching the Eighth Amendment question and again imposing a new criminal law requirement upon the states. They questioned White's statistical evidence and rejected his argument on proportionality, but even they would have overturned the death sentence on procedural grounds that stressed the absence of mitigation factors required by *Lockett* and *Eddings.* The sentencing judge had erroneously concluded that Enmund fired the fatal shots, a mistake corrected by the Florida supreme court on appeal, which observed properly that Enmund had been "a few hundred feet away" in the getaway car at the time of the killings. But the Florida high court still echoed the sentencing judge in finding "no mitigating circumstances" that would justify a lesser penalty than death. O'Connor seized on these points to argue that at least one mitigating factor had been present—Enmund's "relatively minor" role in the murders—and that consideration of this factor would likely have produced a different sentence.[28]

Although reluctant to reach constitutional issues in *Enmund,* O'Connor had expressed the need for heightened procedural protections in all capital cases, especially when judges and juries weighed aggravating and mitigating circumstances. Writing a concurrence in *Eddings,* she urged the Court to adopt "extraordinary measures" to insure "as much as humanly possible," that death sentences were not imposed by "whim, passion, prejudice, or mistake."[29]

New Procedural Protections

While the Court's critical death penalty decisions in the early 1980s focused on which crimes qualified as death eligible (*Coker* and *Enmund*) or on appropriate sentencing procedures (*Lockett, Godfrey,* and *Eddings*), the justices also mandated new constitutional requirements on state courts during both the guilt and sentencing stages of death penalty cases. In *Beck v. Alabama* (1980), for example, Justice Stevens and the majority ruled that trial court judges must inform jurors in any capital case that they can vote for a lesser offense in order to avoid the stark choice between guilty and complete acquittal.[30] The same year, with only Rehnquist dissenting, the justices reaffirmed in *Adams v. Texas* the essentials of the *Witherspoon* decision, which had established that a capital defendant was entitled to a neutrally selected jury.[31] The Texas statute struck down in *Adams* excluded jurors who could not take an oath that the mandatory death penalty or imprisonment for life would not "affect [their] deliberations on any issue of fact."[32]

A year later, in *Bullington v. Missouri,* a sharply divided Court held that the Constitution's double jeopardy clause prohibited a death sentence on retrial if a first jury imposed a life sentence.[33] And during that same term in *Estelle v. Smith* the Court ruled that the Fifth Amendment right against self-incrimination barred the states from forcing a defendant to submit to a psychiatric examination solely for the purposes of sentencing.[34]

Rehnquist's Complaint

The Court's death penalty decisions from *Coker* to *Estelle* provoked a stinging rebuke in 1981 from Justice Rehnquist, who had found himself on the dissenting side in most of them. He used the occasion of the Court's refusal for the second time to hear the appeal of Wayne Carl Coleman to write a dissent from the denial of certiorari. Under sentence of death in Georgia for murdering six members of a family in 1973, Coleman had exhausted his direct appeals in the state courts and had been denied relief through habeas corpus in Georgia based on his claims of prejudicial pre-trial publicity. When the Court declined to hear his appeal, Justices Marshall and Brennan dissented on the grounds that Coleman should be granted the assistance of compulsory process to call witnesses, including the original members of the jury. Rehnquist filed his own dissent, also urging the Court to hear the case. His objective, however, was the opposite of Marshall and Brennan's. Rehnquist sought to definitively end all further litigation and speed Coleman's execution (**Document 4.7**).

The Court's refusal to grant certiorari, Rehnquist argued, would not begin to end the case. Coleman's lawyers would now raise these same issues or others with a single-judge federal habeas court; if that failed, he could appeal to the federal circuit court of appeals. Throughout this process, any single judge having jurisdiction could stay the execution pending further review. "Given so many bites at the apple," Rehnquist noted, "the odds favor petitioner finding some court willing to vacate his death sentence because in its view his trial or sentence was not free from constitutional error."[35] Although the Court had upheld the death penalty in *Gregg,* and states had enacted the requisite statutes, Rehnquist complained, "the death penalty in this country is virtually an illusion. Since 1976, hundreds of juries have sentenced hundreds of persons to death . . . yet virtually nothing happens except endlessly drawn out legal proceedings."[36]

He placed the blame squarely on his colleagues for "this mockery" of the criminal justice system:

Out of a desire to avoid even the possibility of a "Bloody Assizes," this Court and the lower federal courts have converted the constitutional limits upon imposition of the death penalty by the States and the Federal government into arcane niceties which parallel the equity court practices described in Charles Dickens' *Bleak House.* Even though we have upheld the constitutionality of capital punishment statutes, I fear that by our recent actions we have mistakenly sent a signal to the lower state and federal courts that the actual imposition of the death sentence is to be avoided at all costs.[37]

Rehnquist's dissent "to expedite the administration of the death penalty" drew a retort from Justice Stevens, who noted that ninety such petitions for certiorari had been filed in the past ten months. To grant review and decide the merits of every capital case would consume half the justices' calendar. Furthermore, "death cases are indeed different from all other litigation. The penalty, once imposed, is irrevocable. In balance, therefore, I think the Court wisely declines to select this group of cases in which to experiment with accelerated procedures."[38]

Stevens staked out a far different position from Rehnquist's in *Smith v. North Carolina* (1982), when in another dissent from the denial of certiorari in three capital cases he proposed that in all death penalty sentencing the Court adopt the standard of "beyond a reasonable doubt" recently articulated by the Utah supreme court. Judges or juries would be required to weigh "the totality of the aggravating and mitigating circumstances" in each case and be persuaded "beyond a reasonable doubt" that the totality of aggravation outweighed total mitigation. Further, the sentencing authority would have to be persuaded "beyond a reasonable doubt" that the death penalty was justified and appropriate in the circumstances of the case.[39]

The Tide Turns

Between the winter of 1982 and the spring of 1983, the landscape of the Court's capital punishment law changed as dramatically as at any time since the *Furman* decision a decade earlier. And the change reflected the new demographics of death row, the growing backlog of appeals on the justices' docket, and the triumph of Justice Rehnquist. The Court sanctioned expedited decisions by federal appeals courts in capital cases, displayed greater deference to interpretations of state law by state courts, and vacated stays of execution that allowed death sentences to be carried out. As the death row population rose, especially in Texas, Florida, Georgia, and California, and condemned prisoners exhausted their state and federal appeals, the justices were increasingly the last exit on the road to the death chamber. Only Justices Brennan and Marshall, steadfast opponents of capital punishment, consistently dissented from what they regarded as the Court's efforts to shorten the federal appeals process, defer to the state courts, and hasten executions.

On December 7, 1982, Charles Brooks Jr., became the first person put to death in Texas since 1964 and the first in the United States to die by lethal injection when the Court denied a stay of execution previously turned down by the Fifth Circuit Court of Appeals. The Court's action was the climax to nine separate hearings and review by twenty-three judges, state and federal.[40]

Three months later, the justices vacated a lower court stay to allow the third contested execution since Gary Gilmore's. The execution in Alabama of John Evans III, however, did not go smoothly:

> The 1,900 volts lasted 30 seconds. Smoke and steam rose from [Evans'] head. A fiery arc shot from beneath the mask that covered his face. Smoke poured from the electrode on his left leg. . . . But Evans was not dead. The electrode on his leg had burned through the straps and popped off. His body was motionless, but as the wires were reattached, he moved as if he were trying to draw a breath. Then came the second jolt, again for 30 seconds. Still the doctors were unsure that Evans had expired. His lawyers made a final appeal, conveyed by phone to Governor George Wallace, on the ground that the punishment had become intolerably cruel and unusual. Wallace said no. It took one more jolt, another 30 seconds, to make sure that John Evans, 33, had finally been put to death.[41]

The macabre details of Evans' execution were overshadowed by the substance of the Court's next decisions in the cases of Thomas Barefoot, Marcelino Ramos, Alpha Stephens, and Elwood Barclay. In *Barefoot v. Estelle* (1983), speaking through Justice White, the majority upheld a very compressed schedule adopted by the Fifth Circuit for the review of a district court denial of habeas corpus for a capital prisoner. A circuit court, White wrote, need not grant stays of execution in order to decide an appeal according to its full briefing and argument procedures. Instead, it can summarily decide the appeal at the same time it considers and denies the stay, provided the court gives notice, opportunity for argument, and addresses the merits of the petitioner's claim. "Federal courts are not forums in which to relitigate state trials," White declared. "Even less is federal habeas corpus a means by which a defendant is entitled to delay an execution indefinitely."[42]

By telling the circuit courts to develop local procedures for summarily deciding the merits of death penalty appeals on motions for stays of execution, the Court gave lawyers for capital petitioners a smaller window through which to file their appeals and stop the executions. *Barefoot* gave the states another victory as well when it dramatically opened up the types of evidence a jury might hear during the penalty phase of a trial. The *Barefoot* jury had been allowed to hear expert psychiatric testimony that the defendant was likely to commit further criminal acts of violence if not executed, although the Texas psychiatrists had not examined Barefoot and his lawyers argued that such testimony was inherently unreliable according to other professional opinions and likely to sway the jury in favor of death.[43]

Lockett had given defendants broad discretion with respect to the introduction of mitigating evidence during the penalty phase. *Barefoot* decisively tipped the scales back to prosecutors on the question of aggravation. In *California v. Ramos* (1983) the Court made certain everybody got the message. An amendment to California's death penalty statute required trial judges at the penalty phase to inform juries that a sentence of life imprisonment without the possibility of parole could be commuted by the governor to a sentence that included the possibility of parole; they were not required, however, to tell juries that the governor can commute a death sentence. The California supreme court struck down the provision as a violation of the Eighth Amendment, agreeing with Ramos' lawyers that the instruction was unfair and misleading because the jury could believe that only death would prevent the defendant from ever reentering society.[44]

Although twenty-five other state courts had agreed with California and overturned similar instructions that mentioned the possibility of commutation or parole, the Burger Court majority, led by Justice O' Connor, reversed the California supreme court and found no Eighth Amendment violation (**Document 4.8**). State legislatures should be given broad scope to determine what evidence sentencing juries hear. Disclosing the governor's general power to commute a death sentence might operate to a defendant's disadvantage, O'Connor wrote, while the contested instruction "alone does not impermissibly impel the jury toward voting for the death sentence. This information is relevant and factually accurate, and was properly before the jury."[45]

In their dissent, Marshall and Brennan argued that if there were compelling reasons for not informing the jury about the governor's power to commute, "the solution is not to permit the misleading instruction, but to prohibit altogether any instruction concerning commutation."[46] *Barefoot* permitted juries to base their life or death decision on speculation concerning "future dangerousness." *Ramos* now invited similar speculation about what governors might or might not do with respect to commuting death sentences. Justice Stevens chastised the majority for even accepting the appeal from California prosecutors, eager to remove another obstacle to the state's gas chamber. "No rule of law commanded the Court to grant certiorari," he complained. "No other state would have been required to follow the California precedent if it had been permitted to stand. Nothing more than an interest in facilitating the imposition of the death penalty in California justified this Court's exercise of its discretion to review the judgment of the California Supreme Court."[47]

Georgia and Florida Revisited

Barefoot and *Ramos* represented a significant departure from the Court's post-*Furman* agenda to surround both the trial and sentencing phases of capital proceedings with sufficient explicit rules to guarantee "guided discretion," with the emphasis upon "guided." That is what Justice O'Connor meant in *Eddings* when she wrote that the law demanded "extraordinary measures" in capital cases to insure that death sentences did not reflect "whim, passion, prejudice, or mistake." Her opinion in *Ramos,* however, reversing the highest court in California on jury instructions condemned by many as dishonest and confusing, seemed to invite these very mistakes. *Zant v. Stephens* and *Barclay v. Florida*, decided the same year as *Ramos*, soon made it clear that when mistakes of law were made in capital cases, the remedy should be found at the level of state courts, not the Supreme Court of the United States.[48]

In both *Zant* and *Barclay*, trial judges had made either a constitutional or state-law error by admitting certain aggravating evidence during the penalty stage of trials that ultimately resulted in death sentences for Alpha Stephens and Elwood Barclay. In both cases, the Georgia and Florida supreme courts had nonetheless refused to overturn the sentences and require new penalty trials. The jury in Stephens' case had found three statutory aggravating circumstances that moved it into the penalty phase, although only one was required under the statute to make the defendant death eligible. Once the penalty phase began, however, the statute permitted the Georgia jury to weigh all aggravating and mitigating evidence without specific limitations.

During the time of Stephens' appeal, the Georgia supreme court had struck down one of the three aggravating circumstances as unconstitutionally vague: that the defendant "ha[d] a substantial history of serious assaultive [sic] criminal convictions." The Georgia high court nonetheless sustained Stephens' death sentence on the basis of the remaining, valid aggravating circumstances: that he had escaped from lawful imprisonment at the time of the homicide and that he had a prior conviction for capital murder.[49]

The justices had to decide two basic questions: had the invalid aggravating circumstance tipped the scales against Stephens during the jury's trial phase, and did the open-ended penalty structure comply with the "guided discretion" requirements of *Gregg* and its progeny? Justice Stevens and the majority answered "no" to the first question when they agreed with the Georgia supreme court that the trial error had been "harmless" and "yes" to the second question on the grounds that the Georgia high court's review of all capital cases protected defendants against jury verdicts that departed too far from the statutory norm.

In order to find the error in Stephens' case "harmless," Justice Stevens had to distinguish a significant line of decisions, especially *Stromberg v. California* (1931) and *Street v. New York* (1969), where the Court had ruled that a conviction resting on several statutory grounds, one of which is held to violate a constitutional right, must be reversed to insure protection of the right and that the conviction had not been tainted by the constitutional violation.[50] In *Chapman v. California* (1967), moreover, the Court held that no constitutional error is "harmless" unless an appellate court concludes "beyond a reasonable doubt" that the error did not affect the result.[51] But Stevens limited the reach of *Stromberg* and *Street* to their specific facts—a violation of the First Amendment—and ignored *Chapman* entirely.

Finally, Stevens endorsed the conclusion of the Georgia supreme court that the risk to the defendant had been "inconsequential," and he accepted its assurance that the state high court reviewed sentencing patterns in all similar capital cases in order to protect against "arbitrariness and to assure proportionality."[52] Having once upheld the Georgia statute in 1976 in *Gregg*, the Court now expressed an eagerness to leave its monitoring and fine-tuning to the Georgia supreme court, a clear victory for Justices White and Rehnquist who had been urging exactly such deference since 1976.

In his concurring opinion in *Zant*, Rehnquist told the Court that its on-again, off-again search for finely calibrated rules to guide the penalty phase of capital trials would never succeed because these decisions would always remain controlled by "countless facts and circumstances," another reminder from him that Justice John Marshall Harlan had been essentially right in *McGautha* when he argued in favor of discretionary capital statutes and his brethren wrong in *Furman*. Rehnquist drove home the point again when he wrote for the plurality in *Barclay*. There, he affirmed a death sentence based on non-statutory aggravating evidence, even though Florida's more structured law limited the sentencing judge or jury to aggravating circumstances set out in the statute. Despite the grotesque nature of Barclay's homicide (shooting a white victim at random in the hope of triggering an urban rebellion), his Florida jury recommended a life sentence, but the trial judge sentenced Barclay to death under the provision in the state law that required him to uphold the jury "unless the facts suggesting a sentence of death are so clear and convincing that no reasonable person could differ."[53]

The trial judge's inventory of the aggravating factors in Barclay's penalty trial had been a hodgepodge of legal errors and mistakes of fact, interlaced with personal reflections on his own experiences with racial discord during the Second World War. Chief among Barclay's aggravating circumstances, according to the trial judge, was his prior record of breaking and entering with intent to commit grand larceny. But the Florida statute and the Florida supreme court had restricted the definition of prior crimes only to those involving violence. The judge claimed that the homicide had been committed in the course of a kidnapping, which was dubious, and that Barclay had been under a prison sentence when he killed, which was flatly incorrect.

The Florida supreme court had dismissed these errors as "harmless" under state law in affirming Barclay's death sentence, the same conclusion reached by Rehnquist, with a concurrence by Stevens and Powell. "The Constitution does not require that the sentencing process be transformed into a rigid and mechanical parsing of statutory aggravating factors," Rehnquist wrote. As for the trial judge's comparison of Barclay's racial motivation with his own experience at a Nazi concentration camp, that struck Rehnquist as "entirely fitting for the moral, factual, and legal judgment of judges and juries to play a meaningful role in sentencing."[54]

Stevens and Powell reaffirmed that the Constitution required consistent and rational application of the death penalty, which, they argued, Florida had provided by its explicit statutory narrowing of aggravating factors and through "meaningful appellate review" of death sentences by the state supreme court.

Blackmun's dissent ridiculed those conclusions. The Florida courts, trial as well as appellate, had made a "mockery" of the state's death penalty statute. "The procedures by which Barclay was condemned to die cannot pass constitutional muster. . . . This case illustrates the capital sentencing process gone awry. Relying on factors not mentioned in Florida law and statutory factors distorted beyond recognition, Judge Olliff overrode the jury. . . . The Florida Supreme Court failed to conduct any meaningful review, and instead showered the trial judge with praise for his performance."[55]

Blackmun had dissented with Rehnquist in *Furman,* but his dissent in *Barclay* as well as in *Barefoot* and *Ramos* suggested that he had become a prime candidate to join Brennan and Marshall in their broader condemnation of capital punishment. But for the moment, the *Barclay* plurality, led by Rehnquist, looked back beyond *Furman* to *McGautha,* or, as Stevens had put it in *Zant:* "What is important is an individualized determination on the basis of the character of the individual and the circumstances of the crime."[56] Discretion and delegation to lower courts, state and federal, seemed to rule the law of capital punishment.

Disciplining the Ninth Circuit

When federal circuit courts such as the Fifth Circuit accelerated the process of considering stays of execution and appeals, they found support from majorities on the Supreme Court. But when judges on the Ninth Circuit delayed California's execution of Robert Alton Harris in 1992, the state's first in twenty-five years, they met extraordinary opposition from the nation's highest court. Harris and his bother, Daniel, stole a car from two teenagers in San Diego in 1978 in preparation for holding up a bank. Before the robbery, however, Robert Harris shot and killed the teenagers. Despite what he described as a "dismal childhood," including a mother convicted of bank robbery and a father who committed incest with his sister and often beat him, a jury found Harris guilty and sentenced him to die in the state's gas chamber.[57]

After twice declining to review Harris' conviction, the Court's hand was forced by a decision of the Ninth Circuit a year after *Zant* and *Ramos* on the substantive issue of whether prior decisions had made it mandatory that state appellate courts conduct a comparative review of each death sentence to determine if the punishment was proportional in relation to similar cases—what the justices called "comparative proportionality review." In both *Zant* and *Barclay,* the majority had expressed the view that such comparative review by the Georgia and Florida

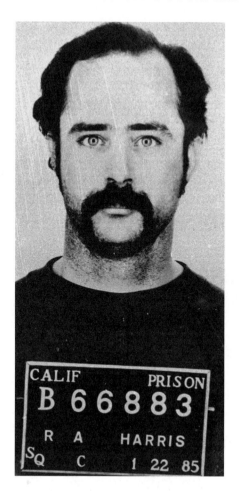

Robert Harris was sentenced to death for killing two teenagers and robbing a bank in 1978. On appeal, the Ninth Circuit Court overturned his death sentence saying that his sentencing violated the Eighth Amendment. The Supreme Court subsequently overruled the Ninth Circuit Court. This began a series of extraordinary legal maneuvers and last-minute attempts at relief. In the end, the Supreme Court admonished the lower courts, telling them: "No further stays of Robert Alton Harris' execution shall be entered by the federal courts except upon order of this Court."

supreme courts had protected the defendants against arbitrary imposition of the death penalty.

Relying on that language, the Ninth Circuit Court of Appeals granted Harris relief on a habeas petition, overturned his sentence, and ruled that California's failure to provide comparative proportionality review in its capital sentencing law violated the Eighth Amendment.[58]

With only Brennan and Marshall dissenting, the Supreme Court, speaking through Justice White, reversed the Ninth Circuit and held that such comparative proportionality review was not a constitutional requirement. "Any capital sentencing scheme may occasionally produce aberrational outcomes," White intoned. "[But] such inconsistencies are a far cry from the major systemic defects identified in *Furman*. As we have acknowledged in the past, 'there can be no perfect procedure for deciding in which cases governmental authority should be used to impose death.'"[59] That was only the beginning of Harris' journey through the federal courts.

During Harris' penalty trial in California, a psychiatrist who testified for the state described the defendant as a sociopath, but court-appointed experts who examined him found no evidence suggesting mental impairment and his original counsel did not pursue that issue further. A new attorney, however, found psychiatric evidence that Harris suffered organic brain damage, likely the result of fetal alcohol syndrome from his alcoholic mother. A federal district court refused to order a hearing at which this evidence could be introduced and cross-examined and a panel of the Ninth Circuit upheld that decision by a 2–1 vote in the late summer of 1990.[60]

Four days before Harris' scheduled execution, federal district judge Marilyn Patel stayed the execution for ten days to hear new arguments from Harris' lawyers that the use of lethal gas constituted cruel and unusual punishment. Only three states including California continued to use this method of execution, and one, Arizona, had begun to debate revising its laws after a recent execution provoked a legislative backlash. Lawyers for California immediately asked the Ninth Circuit to overturn Patel's stay, which a three-judge panel did, 2–1, with its dissenting judge, John T. Noonan, protesting that his colleagues had violated the circuit's own rules of procedure. If the stay had remained in effect for the hearing scheduled by Patel, Harris' death warrant would have expired and delayed his execution for more than a month.

On Monday evening, April 20, hours before Harris' execution, circuit court judge Betty Binns Fletcher issued another stay of execution on a claim of new evidence, but it was rejected at 2:30 a.m. (Washington, D.C., time) by the Supreme Court. On the West Coast, however, ten judges of the Ninth Circuit issued a separate stay on the lethal gas issue and an eleventh, Judge William A. Norris, did the same a few minutes later. In a telephone conference call after 3:00 a.m. in Washington, the Supreme Court dissolved these two stays by a vote of 7–2. As prison guards strapped Harris into the San Quentin gas chamber shortly before 6 a.m., circuit court judge Harry Pregerson issued a fourth stay and contended that Harris should be given an opportunity to litigate the lethal gas issue in the California courts. Harris was removed from the gas chamber briefly. Then, over dissents by Justices Stevens and Blackmun, an angry Supreme Court majority vacated Pregerson's stay with an extraordinary command to all federal judges: "No further stays of Robert Alton Harris' execution shall be entered by the federal courts except upon order of this Court" (**Document 4.9**). Harris died inhaling cyanide gas fourteen minutes later (**Document 4.10**).[61]

Harris was put to death in 1992; the murders that propelled him to that point were committed in 1979. Over the course of those thirteen years the Supreme Court had seen significant changes in its composition: Brennan and Marshall had retired, the former replaced by David Souter, a relatively unknown federal appeals judge from New Hampshire, and the latter by Clarence Thomas, a conservative African American who had been groomed as Marshall's replacement since the administration of President Reagan. Of more significance, Rehnquist had replaced Burger as chief justice after a bruising confirmation battle in 1986; he had been joined by two additional Reagan nominees, both federal appeals judges, Antonin Scalia and Anthony Kennedy. Scalia, possessed of a keen intelligence and acerbic pen, espoused the doctrine of "originalism," which held that decisions should be based on the understanding of the Constitution's meaning in 1789. Like Souter, Kennedy had yet to stake out a firm position on either side of the Court's old ideological divide between Brennan-Marshall and Rehnquist-White. Justices O'Connor and Powell, firm admirers of each other's prudence, held the balance of power on the Rehnquist Court, with the Stevens-Blackmun duo now taking up a consistent role as dissenters in capital cases.

The final days and hours of the Harris case represented a clear victory for Rehnquist and White, who had long feared the potential legal chaos in the federal system where individual judges retained the power to stay executions through habeas corpus petitions and where the Court itself would be dragged into every last minute execution drama unless greater deference and finality could be given to lower-level actors such as state juries, judges, and appellate courts. For White, Rehnquist, and the justices who joined them, the ordeal of the Harris litigation vindicated what the Court had done to off-load final capital decision making in cases such as *Barefoot, Ramos, Zant,* and *Barclay.*

More Executions, More Limits

Between the lethal injection of Thomas Barefoot in 1984 and the gassing of Robert Harris eight years later, three hundred men and one woman, Velma Barfield, were put to death in the United States as the Court generally adopted the White-Rehnquist approach of deference and delegation in capital cases. The vast majority of these executions took place in the so-called death belt stretching from Virginia to Texas through the South. During those same years, state judges and juries meted out death sentences to 2,259 additional defendants; courts, state and federal, reversed the convictions of 217 persons sentenced to death and overturned the sentences of 419 more defendants. Governors commuted death sentences in 35 cases. Support for capital punishment reached new levels of approval in public opinion polls, moving from 72 percent in 1985 to 80 percent in 1994.

Despite a general posture of delegating final judgments in most capital cases, the justices continued in the last years of the Burger Court and the early years of the Rehnquist Court to make new death penalty law wholesale, sometimes at the procedural level, sometimes narrowing the category of the death eligible, but usually affirming the policy judgments made by state legislatures and courts. Reflecting the general public mood that overwhelmingly favored capital punishment, the most critical decisions, such as *McCleskey v. Kemp* (1987) and *Stanford v. Kentucky* (1989), rejected claims advanced by lawyers for capital defendants that racial discrimination fatally infected capital sentencing and that executing juveniles violated contemporary standards of decency.[62]

In a long line of cases the Court had praised capital juries as the "conscience of the community" in the making of death penalty decisions, but in *Spaziano v. Florida* (1984), decided the same term with *Harris,* the Court sustained a Florida statute that gave judges the power to impose death despite a jury recommendation for mercy.[63] The decision also departed from the Court's oft-voiced belief that "death was different" when it came to sentencing and its Eighth Amendment methodology of making a legislative head count to measure "contemporary standards of decency." Florida was one of three states out of the thirty-seven maintaining capital punishment that gave judges override power. Blackmun, who wrote the Court's opinion, appears to have been motivated in part by the belief that judges would be better able than juries to ensure comparative proportionality in capital sentencing, a requirement the Court had rejected earlier in *Harris.* Six years later, with White writing for the majority and Blackmun now dissenting, the Court also sustained an Arizona statute in *Walton v. Arizona* (1990) that gave judges the authority to determine the existence of aggravating and mitigating circumstances and impose a death sentence.[64]

Capital defendants did gain one notable victory in the *Harris-Spaziano* term when the Court reaffirmed that a sentencing decision of life imprisonment constituted an "implied acquittal" under the double jeopardy clause, thereby barring imposition of a death sentence when the defendant won a new trial on appeal. The case, *Arizona v. Rumsey* (1984), involved an Arizona sentencing provision later upheld in *Walton* but built upon an earlier decision in which the second trial and death sentence had been imposed by a jury rather than a single judge.[65]

In two companion decisions in 1986, *Lockhart v. McCree* and *Turner v. Murray,* the Court reached contrasting conclusions regarding the composition of juries in capital cases.[66] The historic *Witherspoon* decision by the Warren Court barred a prosecutor from removing for cause a prospective juror who simply voiced doubts about the death penalty unless the reservations appeared so strong that they would prevent the juror from making a decision based on the evidence at the guilt phase of the trial. In *Adams v. Texas* (1980), the Court held that a juror's refusal to take an oath declaring that a "mandatory penalty of death . . . will not affect his deliberations" was not sufficient grounds for exclusion.[67] In *Wainwright v. Witt* (1985), however, the Court permitted the removal of a juror who did not voice unequivocal opposition to the death penalty, but sufficient opposition to strongly suggest it would impair her ability to carry out her duties "in accordance with her instructions and her oath."[68]

These decisions left open the question of how much opposition to the death penalty would impair a juror's functioning during the sentencing phase of a capital case. Ardia McCree's lawyers had argued that jurors excluded solely because of their opposition to capital punishment (the so-called Witherspoon-excludables) permitted Arkansas and other states to create "death qualification" panels that deprived their client of his Sixth Amendment rights to a jury that reflected a cross-section of the community. A federal district court and the Eighth Circuit Court of Appeals had agreed with that argument, based in part on a battery of social science studies that concluded that "death qualification" produced "conviction-prone" juries.

After challenging the conclusions of those studies, Rehnquist and the majority assumed their methodological validity, but nonetheless held that such "death qualifying" juries in capital cases did not violate the Constitution because the exclusion was based on "shared attitudes," not "some immutable characteristic such as race, gender, or ethnic background" that stripped the members of those groups of their basic rights of citizenship. In contrast, the "Witherspoon-excludables," Rehnquist wrote, would retain their rights to participate as jurors in all other criminal and civil trials.[69]

Noting that all the documented studies supported the conclusion of the district court and the appeals court, Justice Marshall argued that "the true impact of death qualification on the fairness of a trial is likely even more devastating that the studies show. . . . Faced with the near unanimity of authority supporting respondent's claim . . . the majority here makes but a weak effort to contest that proposition. . . . This disregard for the clear import of the evidence tragically misconstrues the settled constitutional principles that guarantee a defendant the right to a fair trial and an impartial jury whose composition is not biased toward the prosecution."[70] Justice Rehnquist's concerns about race exclusion in *McCree* did not carry over into *Turner v. Murray,* in which the issue focused on a defendant's right in capital trials to interrogate prospective jurors about racial prejudice. In 1976 in a non-capital case, *Ristaino v. Ross,* the Court ruled that the Constitution did not require an inquiry into questions of bias simply because the defendant and victims were of different races.[71] The Court reaffirmed this position in a federal prosecution of a Mexican American convicted of smuggling aliens into the United States,[72] but the Court carved out an exception in *Turner* for death penalty cases, with White authoring the opinion and Rehnquist dissenting. Without overturning the conviction, White and the majority held that a capital defendant accused of an interracial crime is entitled to have prospective jurors informed of the race of the victim and questioned on the issue of racial bias.[73]

In the only Eighth Amendment decision of Burger's last term—and the first since *Enmund v. Florida* four years earlier—a narrow 5–4 majority ruled in *Ford v. Wainwright* (1986) that executing an insane person constituted "cruel and unusual punishment." Alvin Bernard Ford had been convicted of murder and sentenced to death in Florida in 1974, but at the time of his pending execution he referred to himself as "Pope John Paul III," claimed to have appointed nine new justices to the state's supreme court, and believed he was free to leave death row any time he chose to do so. A panel of three psychiatrists appointed by Gov. Robert Graham found him suffering from various mental disorders, but still capable of understanding the nature of the death penalty. On their judgment alone, the governor signed Ford's death warrant.

Although no state statute in the country, including Florida's, permitted the execution of the insane, Justice Marshall's opinion for the Court invoked both the common law and "evolving standards of decency" to constitutionalize the protection under the Eighth Amendment and hold that Florida's statute failed to provide Ford an adversarial hearing where experts other than those selected by the governor could testify with respect to the sanity issue. "Whether its aim be to protect the condemned from fear and pain without comfort of understanding, or to protect the dignity of society itself from the barbarity of exacting mindless vengeance, the restriction finds enforcement in the Eighth Amendment," Marshall wrote (**Document 4.11**).

Justices O'Connor, White, Rehnquist, and Chief Justice Burger found no Eighth Amendment bar to executing the insane and criticized the majority for reaching that constitutional question. O'Connor and White, however, agreed that the Florida statute lacked essential elements of due process, and they would have vacated the sentence on that ground and required Florida to hold a new competency hearing consistent with the Fourteenth Amendment. Rehnquist and Burger objected to both the Eighth and Fourteenth Amendment conclusions and would have left the insanity issue to both state common law and statutory remedies with the additional observation that under the former, the executive judged the insanity of the condemned, not the courts.[74] Florida never executed Ford.

The Rehnquist Era Begins

Ford v. Wainwright formally restricted a category of the death eligible while articulating due process standards for determining insanity in similar cases. Early decisions of the Rehnquist Court looked in the opposite direction, beginning with *Tison v. Arizona* (1987) in which the justices revisited the question of felony murder and the Eighth Amendment. The Tison brothers, Raymond and Rickey, joined by other family members, had planned and executed a daring armed prison break for their father, Gary, and his cellmate, Randy Greenawalt, in the course of which a family of four, including two children, was robbed, kidnapped, and eventually murdered by Gary Tison and Greenawalt. Raymond and Rickey watched the shotgun-style executions and fled with the others until their arrests during another shoot-out at a police roadblock.

Although Raymond and Rickey had not intended the death of the family or pulled the trigger, they were both sentenced to death by a judge under Arizona's felony-murder and accomplice liability statute, and the Arizona supreme court affirmed, holding that consistent with *Enmund v. Florida* the brothers "intended, contemplated, or anticipated that lethal force would or might be used, or that life would or might be taken."[75] Justice O'Connor's opinion for the Court over-turned the Arizona court's reading of *Enmund* as erroneous, but announced a new felony-murder standard to resolve cases such as that of the Tison brothers, who fell somewhere between the minor role played by the defendant in *Enmund* and the felony murderer who actually killed, attempted to kill, or intended to kill. The Eighth Amendment, O'Connor wrote, did not bar a death sentence as dis-proportionate for those who, like the Tison brothers, were "major participants in a felony" and who also displayed "reckless indifference to human life."[76]

In addition to challenging the majority's conclusions that the brothers had displayed a "reckless indifference to human life," Justice Brennan and the dis-senters pointed out that the majority had taken a giant step backwards from *Enmund:* not a single person had been put to death in the United States since 1955 for felony murder who had not actually killed, attempted to kill, or intended to kill his victim. Furthermore, every other felony-murder defendant on Arizona's death row who had raised a similar challenge had been found either to have killed or intended to kill. "Thus, like *Enmund,* the Tisons' sentence appears to be an aberration within Arizona itself as well as nationally and inter-nationally," Brennan concluded.[77] *Tison v. Arizona* significantly expanded death eligibility for felony murder, but the Tison brothers escaped the ultimate penalty when at their re-sentencing trial the judge ruled that their statements to author-ities that placed them at the murder scene could not be used by the prosecution. Both received life sentences. Randy Greenawalt, one of the trigger men, was executed in 1997.[78]

Christopher Burger was not as fortunate as the Tison brothers. Convicted of murder and sentenced to death in Georgia in 1978, in *Burger v. Kemp* (1987) he raised the claim that his attorney had denied him "effective counsel" required by the Sixth Amendment by failing to pursue an investigation into mitigating circum-stances, especially to require a psychological examination and explore Burger's troubled childhood and family history.[79] Writing for the majority that rejected these claims, Justice Stevens applied the rigorous standard for determining "effective counsel" articulated three years earlier in another capital case, *Strickland v. Washington* (1984).[80]

Strickland insisted that "every effort be made to eliminate the distorting effects of hindsight, to reconstruct the circumstances of counsel's challenged conduct, and to evaluate the conduct from counsel's perspective at the time."[81] In order to prevail under *Strickland,* therefore, a plaintiff had to jump over two hurdles. First, he had to demonstrate that his trial lawyer's performance included serious legal errors, inconsistent with reasonable professional standards, and, second, that those errors had been so egregious that they deprived the plaintiff of a fair trial. Applying that standard to the mitigation stage of Burger's trial, the Court concluded that his counsel's decision not to mount "an all-out investigation into [Burger's] background in search of mitigating circumstances was supported by reasonable professional judgment."[82] Justice Blackmun, finding the facts of *Burger* consistent with the *Strickland* standards, dissented for himself, Powell, Marshall, and Brennan.[83]

Revisiting Race

From the perspective of anti–death penalty advocates, the worst was yet to come. In 1987 and 1989 the Rehnquist Court decided three cases with significant ramifications for the future of capital punishment: *McCleskey v. Kemp, Penry v. Lynaugh,* and *Stanford v. Kentucky.* In *McCleskey* the majority effectively barred the door to claims that the death penalty was fatally infected with racial discrimination; in *Penry* the Court sanctioned the death penalty for mentally retarded offenders; and in *Stanford* it rejected the argument that the Eighth Amendment prohibited the execution of a juvenile who had committed murder at the age of sixteen or seventeen.[84] This last decision in particular met with strong protests from leaders of the European Union, who noted that such executions violated international treaties to which the United States was a signatory.

In 1986, overruling the Warren Court decision in *Swain v. Alabama* (1965), the Burger Court in *Batson v. Kentucky* placed the burden of proof on prosecutors to demonstrate that their use of peremptory challenges to exclude jurors had not been based solely on the jurors' race, thereby denying defendants a jury drawn from a cross-section of the community in violation of the Sixth and Fourteenth Amendments.[85] A defendant has no constitutional right to a jury made up in whole or in part by persons of his own race, wrote Justice Powell, but the state violates equal protection when it tries him before a jury from which members of his race have been intentionally excluded by the use of peremptory challenges. That same term the Court had also ruled in *Turner v. Murray* that capital defendants had the right to question prospective jurors about racial prejudice in interracial murder cases.

The Court's concern for racial discrimination reached its limit a year later in the case of Warren McCleskey, a black man convicted and sentenced to die in Georgia for the murder of a white policeman during an armed robbery. Lawyers for McCleskey presented the Court with two statistical studies of over two thousand murder cases in Georgia during the 1970s completed by Professor David Baldus and his associates. The Baldus study demonstrated a large disparity in the imposition of the death sentence in Georgia based on the race of the murder victim and, to some extent, the race of the defendant (**Document 4.12**). Defendants who killed white victims received the death penalty in 11 percent of the cases, but defendants charged with killing blacks received the death penalty in only 1 percent of the cases. In short, the murder of a white victim in Georgia was four and half times more likely to provoke a death sentence than the otherwise identical murder of a black victim.

The Court of Appeals for the Eleventh Circuit accepted the Baldus findings as valid, but rejected McCleskey's claim that it proved racial discrimination in his particular case in violation of the equal protection clause. Writing for the Court, Justice Powell, who had dissented in *Furman* on the grounds that rigorous scientific evidence had failed to demonstrate wholly arbitrary death verdicts, agreed with the circuit court that the Baldus study was "statistically valid," but nonetheless affirmed McCleskey's sentence (**Document 4.13**). The Baldus study demonstrated a pattern of arbitrary sentencing in Georgia that could not be explained by any factor other than race, Powell conceded, but that did not prove unconstitutional discrimination against McCleskey because myriad considerations must have entered the jury's sentencing decision. *Furman* stood for the requirement of objective standards, but Powell and the majority now took refuge in "the discretion that is fundamental to our criminal process [and] we decline to assume that what is unexplained is invidious."[86]

Powell predicted a parade of horrors that would follow in the wake of overturning the sentence. McCleskey's claim "taken to its logical conclusion," he wrote, "throws into serious question the principles that underlie our entire criminal justice system." If the Court accepted his claim that racial bias has impermissibly tainted the capital sentencing decision, the justices would soon be faced with similar claims as to other types of penalty and the claim that his sentence rests on the irrelevant factor of race "easily could be extended to apply to claims based on unexplained discrepancies that correlate to membership in other minority groups, and even to gender." With respect to capital punishment, the Constitution of the United States, he concluded, "does not place totally unrealistic conditions on its use."[87]

In the leading dissent, Justice Brennan began with the observation that the majority "finds no fault in a system in which lawyers must tell their clients that race casts a large shadow on the capital sentencing process." That the Baldus study and McCleskey's lawyers could not prove the influence of race on his sentencing decision was irrelevant, according to Brennan, because *Furman* and all its progeny had placed the emphasis on the risk of an arbitrary sentence, not the proven fact of one. He drove the point home by citing *Furman*, noting that the death penalty "may not be imposed under sentencing procedures that create a substantial risk that the punishment will be inflicted in an arbitrary and capricious manner." And he marked the contradiction at the core of Powell's opinion, which accepted the validity of the Baldus study but then dismissed the probability of prejudice as insufficient. "Close analysis of the Baldus study . . . in light of both statistical principles and human experience reveals that the risk that race influenced McCleskey's sentence is intolerable by any imaginable standard."[88]

McCleskey fought a second round before the Court that became another death penalty landmark. In his third habeas corpus petition to U.S. District Judge J. Owen Forrester in 1990, McCleskey claimed that Georgia prosecutors had used a jail house informant's testimony during his trial in violation of the Sixth Amendment as interpreted by the Warren Court in *Massiah v. United States* (1964).[89] Forrester overturned McCleskey's conviction on those grounds, but the Eleventh Circuit Court reversed, finding that McCleskey would have been convicted without the tainted evidence and also ruling that this habeas petition constituted an abuse of the writ. In affirming the circuit court, the Supreme Court in *McCleskey v. Zant* (1991) raised the bar for death row defendants who had failed to raise such claims in earlier petitions for the writ. A defendant would have to show that the failure to raise the claim resulted from factors beyond his control and that the error was so fundamental that conviction resulted "despite the petitioner's factual innocence."[90] Georgia electrocuted McCleskey on September 25, 1991, after seven separate stays of execution had been lifted in eight hours and the condemned man made two trips to the electric chair.[91] After his retirement from the Court, when asked by his biographer which of his many votes he would change, Justice Powell said, "McCleskey."[92]

The Rehnquist-White Court

On the final day of their regular term in 1989, seventeen years after *Furman* had invalidated the existing death penalty statutes, the Court gave a powerful indication that Justices Rehnquist and White, dissenters in 1972, had won the fundamental constitutional debate over capital punishment in the United States. On June 29, the Court handed down both *Penry v. Lynaugh* and *Stanford v. Kentucky*. In *Penry*, although ordering a new sentencing trial in Texas for Johnny Paul Penry because the state statute had not allowed the jury to give consideration to his mental retardation, Justice O'Connor's majority opinion determined that executing the mentally retarded did not cross the Eighth Amendment threshold of "cruel and unusual punishment."[93] Once again taking a head count of state laws and abandoning an independent judicial determination, O'Connor found that only two states had prohibited such executions. When combined with the fourteen states that banned capital punishment, this total was insufficient to establish a national consensus (**Document 4.14**).

In dissent, Justice Brennan reminded his brethren of their duty to do more than count noses when applying the amendment. At its core, he argued, had always been the question of proportionality in punishment, including both the injury caused and also the defendant's moral culpability. "Execution of the mentally retarded is unconstitutional under both these strands of the Eighth Amendment," he concluded.[94]

On the same day, with Justice Scalia writing for the majority, the justices upheld the death sentences of Kevin Stanford and Heath Wilkins for murders committed in Kentucky and Missouri when they were under the age of eighteen (**Document 4.15**). A year earlier the Court had ruled in *Thompson v. Oklahoma* that the execution of a fifteen-year-old capital offender violated the Eighth Amendment, with Scalia, Rehnquist, and White dissenting.[95] In *Stanford v. Kentucky*, those dissenters, joined by Justice Kennedy, prevailed.

Stanford and Wilkins could not argue that such punishment was illegal at the time of the adoption of the Eighth Amendment, Scalia argued, because the common law then set the time of incapacity at age fourteen. And a review of state laws indicated "neither a historical nor a modern societal consensus forbidding the imposition of capital punishment on any person who murders at 16 or 17 years of age." In order to reach this conclusion, Scalia and the majority had to eliminate from their count the fourteen states and the District of Columbia that banned capital punishment entirely and only count the fifteen that specifically prohibited the execution of those under eighteen. Counting those fourteen non-executing states, he claimed, would be like including in a consensus against cockfighting all states that prohibited wagering.

The use of foreign case law and statutes in briefs for Stanford and Wilkins drew Scalia's condemnation as he dismissed all references to the laws of nations other than the United States. And finally, he narrowed the scope of proportionality review under the Eighth Amendment by asserting it had never been invoked independently to determine a societal consensus, but had always relied upon "objective evidence" found in state laws and jury verdicts.[96]

Justice Brennan could only protest that Scalia's methodology for determining the scope of "cruel and unusual punishment" bore little resemblance to the Court's precedents, that his head count of state laws ignored an obvious societal consensus against executing juveniles, and that the Court should pay attention to "organizations with expertise in relevant fields and the choices of governments elsewhere in the world."[97] The United States was one of six countries that permitted such executions.

A Rehnquist majority now dominated the Court's constitutional jurisprudence with respect to the death penalty, but it did not ultimately decide the fate of either Kevin Stanford or Heath Wilkins. Kentucky governor Paul Patton commuted Stanford's sentence in 2003. After a federal judge overturned Wilkins' guilty plea in 1995 on the grounds that he had suffered from psychiatric disorders when attempting to represent himself, Missouri accepted a new guilty plea from him for second-degree murder and he was sentenced in 1999 to three consecutive life terms.[98]

By affirming McCleskey's conviction and rejecting the Baldus study on racial discrimination, the Rehnquist Court eliminated one of the final constitutional barriers to the continued imposition of the death penalty in the United States. *Penry* and *Stanford* threatened to close other doors for the condemned as well. For opponents of capital punishment, therefore, the path to abolition had been decisively narrowed to four areas of litigation: continued piecemeal attacks on procedural defects in individual trials, further restrictions on death-eligible categories, the invocation of international law as a component of evolving standards of decency, and litigation over the newest method of executions, lethal injections. On these issues, the struggle over capital punishment remained open.

Document 4.1
Norman Mailer Recounts the Execution of Gary Gilmore, 1979

Gary Gilmore became the first person put to death following the restoration of capital punishment in 1976. He was executed by firing squad in Utah on January 17, 1977. This account of his execution comes from Norman Mailer's book, The Executioner's Song, *which won the Pulitzer Prize.*

Ron Stranger's first impression was how many people were in the room. God, the number of spectators. Executions must be spectator sport. It really hit him even before his first look at Gary, and then he was thankful the hood was not on yet. That was a relief. Gilmore was still a human being, not a hooded, grotesque thing, and Ron realized he had been preparing himself for the shock of seeing Gary with his face concealed in a black bag. But, no, there was Gary staring at the crowd with an odd humor in his face. Stranger knew what he was thinking. "Anybody who knows somebody is going to get an invite to the turkey shoot." . . . [Bob] Moody also felt anger at all the people who had been invited. Sam Smith had given them such fuss whether it would be five or seven guests. Now there were all these needless people pressed behind the line, and the executioners back of the screen talking. You couldn't hear what they were saying, but you could hear them, and it incensed Bob that Ernie Wright, Director of Corrections, was dancing around greeting people, practically gallivanting with his big white cowboy hat, looking like a Texas bureaucrat.

Moody had the feeling the riflemen behind the blind were purposely not looking at Gary, but keeping their backs to him, chatting away in a group, and would only turn around in the last minute when given the order. . . .

Cline Campbell's first thought when he walked into the room was, my goodness, do they sell tickets to this? All the same, Campbell could feel how everybody was scared to death. It hung over the execution. . . .

As soon as Ron returned to his position behind the line, a prison official came up to ask if he wanted cotton for his ears. Then Ron noticed that everybody was taking cotton, so he stuffed some into his head, and watched Sam Smith walk over to the back of the room where a red telephone was on a chair. Then Sam Smith made a phone call, and walked back and came up to Gary and started to read a declaration.

. . . All the while, Gary was not looking at the Warden, but rather, leaning in his chair from side to side in order to stare around the large body of Sam Smith, practically tipping that chair over trying to see the faces behind the executioner's blind, catch a glint of their expression.

Then the Warden said, "Do you have anything you'd like to say?" and Gary looked up at the ceiling and hesitated, then said, "Let's do it." That was it. . . .

The way Stranger heard it, it came out like Gary wanted to say something good and dignified and clever, but couldn't think of anything profound. The drugs had left him too dead. Rather than say nothing, he did his best to say it very clear, "Let's do it."

Three or four men in red coats came up and put a hood on Gilmore's head. Nothing was said after that.

Absolutely nothing said. They put a waist strap on Gilmore, and a head strap. . . . Now the doctor was beside him, pinning a white circle on Gilmore's black shirt, and the doctor stepped back. . . . Ron and Bob Moody and Cline Campbell heard a countdown begin, and Norall Wootton put his fingers in his ears on top of the cotton, and Gary's body looked calm to Campbell. . . .

Stranger said to himself, "I hope I don't fall down." He had his hand up to protect his head somehow. Right through the cotton, he heard the sound of heavy breathing and saw the barrels of the rifles projecting from the slits of the blind. He was shocked at how close those muzzles were to the victim. They sure didn't want to miss. Then it all got so quiet your attention was called to it. Right through the cotton, Ron heard these whispers. "One," and "Two," and they never got to say, "Three" before the guns went, "Bam. Bam. Bam." So loud it was terrifying. . . .

Schiller heard three shots, expecting four. Gary's body did not jerk nor the chair move, and Schiller waited for the fourth shot and found out later that two must have come out simultaneously. . . .

Vern just heard a great big *WHAM!* When it happened, Gary never raised a finger. Didn't quiver at all. His left hand never moved, and then, after he was shot, his head went forward, but the strap held his head up, and then the right hand slowly rose in the air and slowly went down as if to say, "That did it, gentlemen." Schiller thought his movement was as delicate as the fingers of a pianist raising his hand before he puts it down on the keys. The blood started to flow through the black shirt and came out onto the white pants and started to drop on the floor between Gary's legs, and the smell of gunpowder was everywhere. . . .

Ron closed his eyes and when he opened them again, the blood was a pool in Gary's lap, running to his feet and covering his tennis shoes, those crazy red, white and blue tennis shoes he always wore in Maximum. The shoelaces were now blooded over. . . .

An officer finally came around and said to the people standing behind the line, "Time for you to leave." Schiller walked out saying to himself, "What have we accomplished? There aren't going to be less murders."

All the while Father Meersman and Cline Campbell were unbuckling Gilmore's arms and legs. Campbell kept thinking of the importance of the eyes. He said to himself. "Why doesn't somebody move? We've got to save the eyes."

Source: Norman Mailer, *The Executioner's Song* (New York: Little, Brown, 1979; New York: Vintage Books, reprint edition, 1994), 980–988. Citations are to the Vintage edition.

Document 4.2
The Supreme Court Denies Stay of Execution for John Spenkelink, May 22, 1979

On May 22, 1979, Justice William Rehnquist denied a stay of execution for John Spenkelink, under sentence of death in Florida. Spenkelink became the first person put to death after lengthy appeals in the wake of Gregg v. Georgia. *Rehnquist's opinion details the extent of that prolonged four years of litigation. Florida electrocuted Spenkelink on May 25, 1979.*

Mr. Justice REHNQUIST, Circuit Justice.

This application for stay has come to me by reason of the unavailability of Mr. Justice POWELL. On December 20, 1973, following a trial and jury verdict, applicant was sentenced to death pursuant to the Florida statute that we upheld in *Proffitt v. Florida,* for a murder committed in February 1973. On applicant's appeal, the Supreme Court of Florida affirmed both the conviction and sentence, and this Court denied certiorari. Applicant next sought executive clemency from the Governor of Florida, but his request for that relief was denied on September 12, 1977, and at the same time the Governor signed a death warrant setting applicant's execution for 8:30 a.m. on September 19, 1977. The following day, applicant filed a motion collateral relief in the Florida trial court that had convicted him; this motion, too, was denied, the Supreme Court of Florida affirmed its denial, and we again denied certiorari.

One day after he filed his petition for collateral relief in state court, however, applicant filed a petition for federal habeas corpus in the United States District Court for the Middle District of Florida, which transferred the case to the Northern District of Florida. That court stayed the execution and scheduled an evidentiary hearing for September 21, 1977. At that time a hearing was held, which lasted from the late morning into the evening and produced over 300 pages of testimony. On September 23, the District Court dismissed the petition and ordered that the stay of execution previously issued by it terminate at noon on September 30. But the District Court also granted applicant a certificate of probable cause to appeal, and the Court of Appeals for the Fifth Circuit then stayed applicant's execution pending its decision of his appeal.

On August 21, 1978, a panel of the Court of Appeals for the Fifth Circuit affirmed the judgment of the District Court. In an opinion comprising 39 pages in the Federal Reporter, the Court of Appeals for the Fifth Circuit dealt at length with all of applicant's claims, which had previously been rejected by the United States District Court and by the Supreme Court of Florida. It affirmed the judgment of the District Court, and we again denied certiorari on March 26, 1979, with Mr. Justice BRENNAN and Mr. Justice MARSHALL dissenting on the basis of their views set forth in *Gregg v. Georgia*.

According to the application now before me, the Governor of Florida again denied executive clemency on Friday, May 18, 1979, and signed a death warrant authorizing the execution of applicant on Wednesday, May 23, 1979, at 7 a.m., e.d.t. On Monday, May 21, applicant filed a petition for a writ of habeas corpus in the United States District Court for the Northern District of Florida requesting the court to stay his execution pending consideration and final determination of the petition. According to the applicant, the only point he seeks to preserve in his application to me for a stay is that under this Court's decision in *Presnell v. Georgia,* "the failure to accord petitioner adequate advance notice of the aggravating circumstances alleged by the prosecution as the basis for seeking the death penalty" denied applicant rights secured to him by the Eighth and Fourteenth Amendments to the Constitution of the United States. In *Presnell,* this Court held that the "fundamental principles of procedural fairness" enunciated in *Cole v. Arkansas,* "apply with no less force at the penalty phase of a trial in a capital case than they do in the guilt-determining phase of any criminal trial." *Cole,* in turn, had held that "[t]o conform to due process of law, petitioners were entitled to have the validity of their convictions appraised on consideration of the case as it was tried and as the issues were determined in the trial court."

This claim was submitted to and denied by the District Court for the Northern District of Florida on Monday, May 21, 1979. The District Court simultaneously entered a second order refusing certification of the appeal under both local and statutory rules, and denying a stay of execution pending appeal. Today, a panel of the Court of Appeals for the Fifth Circuit has, by a divided vote, denied applicant a certificate of probable cause, a certificate for leave to appeal in forma pauperis, and his motion for a stay of execution. Throughout these many hearings, appeals, and applications, there has been virtually no dispute that substantial evidence supported the jury's verdict that applicant was guilty of first-degree murder, or that the Florida state trial judge had ample basis for following the jury's recommendation that the death penalty be imposed. The Supreme Court of Florida in its opinion affirming applicant's conviction stated:

> As more fully set out above the record shows this crime to be premeditated, especially cruel, atrocious, and heinous and in connection with robbery of the victim to secure return of money claimed by Appellant. The aggravating circumstances justify imposition of the death sentence. Both Appellant and his victim were career criminals and Appellant showed no mitigating factors to require a more lenient sentence.

The Court of Appeals for the Fifth Circuit, in affirming the denial of federal habeas relief, said:

> On February 4, 1973, petitioner John A. Spenkelink, a 24-year-old white male and twice convicted felon, who had escaped from a California correctional camp, murdered his traveling companion, Joseph J. Szymankiewicz, a white male, in their Tallahassee, Florida motel room. Spenkelink shot Szymankiewicz, who was asleep in bed, once in the head just behind the left ear and a second time in the back, which fragmented the spine, ruptured the aorta, and resulted in the victim's death. [Spenkelink] then recounted a cover story to the motel proprietor in order to delay discovery of the body and left.

When I granted an application for stay of execution as Circuit Justice in *Evans v. Bennett,* I referred to the oft-repeated rule that a Circuit Justice must act as surrogate for the entire Court when acting on a stay application. Even though he would deny the application if he were to consider only his own views as to its merits, he is obligated to consider the views that each Member of the Court may have as to its merits, and if he believes that four Members of the Court would vote to grant certiorari to review the applicant's claims, he is obligated to grant the application, provided it meets the other requirements for a stay. In *Evans,* supra, although I would not have voted to grant certiorari to consider applicant's claims, I was satisfied that there was a reasonable probability that four other Members of the Court would have voted differently. I therefore granted the application pending referral to the next scheduled Conference of the full Court.

In this case, by contrast, I have consulted all of my colleagues who are available, and am confident that four of them would not vote to grant certiorari to hear any of the numerous constitutional claims previously presented by applicant in his three earlier petitions for certiorari to this Court. It devolves upon me, however, as a single Justice, to answer as best I can whether four Members of the Court would grant certiorari to consider applicant's new claim that his death sentence was imposed in violation of our opinion in *Presnell v. Georgia.* The easiest way to find out, of course, would be to have the necessary copies of applicant's papers circulated to all eight of my colleagues in order to obtain their firsthand assessment of this contention at the next regularly scheduled Conference of the

Court on Thursday. Even if I were only marginally convinced that there were four Justices who might vote to grant certiorari in order to hear this claim presented, in view of the fact that applicant's life is at stake, I would probably follow that course. But evaluating applicant's "new" claim as best I can, it does not impart to me even that degree of conviction. As I understand it, he contends that *Presnell,* which required that a state appellate court affirm a capital sentence on the same theory under which it had been imposed by the trial court, be extended to require that the defendant receive some sort of formal notice, perhaps in the form of a specification in the indictment or information, of each and every one of the statutorily prescribed aggravating circumstances upon which the prosecution intends to rely for the imposition of the death penalty. I do not believe that four Members of this Court would find that claim either factually or legally sufficient to persuade them to vote to grant certiorari in order to review its denial in the federal habeas proceeding.

Applicant has conceded in his memorandum of law in support of the present federal habeas action that "defense counsel could properly have been expected to know that the State might seek a death sentence on the grounds that the offense was (1) committed by a defendant previously convicted of a felony involving the use or threat of violence or (2) committed by a defendant under sentence of imprisonment." But the memorandum goes on to state that "a homicide caused by a single gun shot wound to the heart is not self-evidently 'especially heinous, atrocious, or cruel.' And it was not until the sentencing hearing itself that petitioner was appraised that the State would seek the death penalty on this ground."

Cole v. Arkansas, which *Presnell* simply extended to the sentencing phase of a capital trial, was after all decided in 1948, and was not then thought to embody any novel principle of constitutional law. Applicant concedes that there was adequate notice at the sentencing stage of the hearing for the State to seek the death penalty on two of the statutorily defined aggravating circumstances, and the fact that it has required six years for him to discover that he did not have adequate notice as to the other grounds upon which it was sought, and was thereby prejudiced, tends to detract from the substantiality of his contention.

Applicant has had not merely one day in court. He has had many, many days in court. It has been the conclusion of the Supreme Court of Florida that the death sentence was imposed in accordance with the requirements of Florida law as well as those of the United States Constitution, and it has been the conclusion of the United States District Court for the Northern District of Florida and the Court of Appeals for the Fifth Circuit that there was no federal constitutional error in the process by which applicant was sentenced to death. Three times this Court has refused to review the determinations of these state

and federal courts. I do not believe that the claim presented in the present application would be any more successful than the claims presented in the preceding three petitions for certiorari. The application for stay of execution of John A. Spenkelink, presently scheduled for Wednesday, May 23, 1979, at 7 a.m., e.d.t., is accordingly
  Denied.

Source: *Spenkelink v. Wainwright* 442 U.S. 1301 (1979), 1301–1307.

Document 4.3
The Supreme Court Strikes Down the Death Penalty in Cases of Rape of Adult Women in *Coker v. Georgia*, June 29, 1977

Four members of the Court (Justices Byron White, Potter Stewart, Harry Blackmun, and John Paul Stevens), joined in concurrences by Justices William Brennan and Thurgood Marshall, declared the death penalty for the rape of an adult woman unconstitutional as cruel and unusual punishment in the 1977 case of Coker v. Georgia. *Justices Lewis Powell and William Rehnquist and Chief Justice Warren Burger dissented.*

MR. JUSTICE WHITE announced the judgment of the Court and filed an opinion in which MR. JUSTICE STEWART, MR. JUSTICE BLACKMUN, and MR. JUSTICE STEVENS, joined.

Georgia Code Ann. 26–2001 (1972) provides that "[a] person convicted of rape shall be punished by death or by imprisonment for life, or by imprisonment for not less than one nor more than 20 years."

Punishment is determined by a jury in a separate sentencing proceeding in which at least one of the statutory aggravating circumstances must be found before the death penalty may be imposed. Petitioner Coker was convicted of rape and sentenced to death. Both the conviction and the sentence were affirmed by the Georgia Supreme Court. Coker was granted a writ of certiorari, limited to the single claim, rejected by the Georgia court, that the punishment of death for rape violates the Eighth Amendment, which proscribes "cruel and unusual punishments" and which must be observed by the States as well as the Federal Government.

I

While serving various sentences for murder, rape, kidnaping [sic], and aggravated assault, petitioner escaped from the Ware Correctional Institution near Waycross, Ga., on September 2, 1974. At approximately 11 o'clock that night, petitioner entered the house of Allen and Elnita Carver through an unlocked kitchen door. Threatening the couple with a "board," he tied up Mr. Carver in the bathroom, obtained a knife from the kitchen, and took Mr. Carver's money and the keys to the family car. Brandishing the knife and saying "you know what's going to happen to you if you try anything, don't you," Coker then raped Mrs. Carver. Soon thereafter, petitioner drove away in the Carver car, taking Mrs. Carver with him. Mr. Carver, freeing himself, notified the police; and not long thereafter petitioner was apprehended. Mrs. Carver was unharmed.

Petitioner was charged with escape, armed robbery, motor vehicle theft, kidnapping, and rape. Counsel was appointed to represent him. Having been found competent to stand trial, he was tried. The jury returned a verdict of guilty, rejecting his general plea of insanity. A sentencing hearing was then conducted in accordance with the procedures dealt with at length in *Gregg v. Georgia,* where this Court sustained the death penalty for murder when imposed pursuant to the statutory procedures. The jury's verdict on the rape count was death by electrocution. Both aggravating circumstances on which the court instructed were found to be present by the jury. . . .

. . . It is now settled that the death penalty is not invariably cruel and unusual punishment within the meaning of the Eighth Amendment; it is not inherently barbaric or an unacceptable mode of punishment for crime; neither is it always disproportionate to the crime for which it is imposed. It is also established that imposing capital punishment, at least for murder, in accordance with the procedures provided under the Georgia statutes saves the sentence from the infirmities which led the Court to invalidate the prior Georgia capital punishment statute in *Furman v. Georgia.*

In sustaining the imposition of the death penalty in *Gregg,* however, the Court firmly embraced the holdings and dicta from prior cases to the effect that the Eighth Amendment bars not only those punishments that are "barbaric" but also those that are "excessive" in relation to the crime committed. Under *Gregg,* a punishment is "excessive" and unconstitutional if it (1) makes no measurable contribution to acceptable goals of punishment and hence is nothing more than the purposeless and needless imposition of pain and suffering; or (2) is grossly out of proportion to the severity of the crime. A punishment might fail the test on either ground. Furthermore, these Eighth Amendment judgments should not be, or appear to be, merely the subjective views of individual Justices; judgment should be informed by objective factors to the maximum possible extent. To this end, attention must be given to the public attitudes concerning a particular sentence—history and precedent, legislative attitudes, and the response of juries reflected in their sentencing decisions are to be consulted. In *Gregg,* after giving due regard to such sources, the Court's judgment was that the death penalty for deliberate murder was neither the purposeless imposition of severe punishment nor a punishment grossly disproportionate to the crime. But the Court reserved the question of the constitutionality of the death penalty when imposed for other crimes. . . .

III

That question, with respect to rape of an adult woman, is now before us. We have concluded that a sentence of death is grossly disproportionate and excessive punishment for the crime of rape and is therefore forbidden by the Eighth Amendment as cruel and unusual punishment.

A

As advised by recent cases, we seek guidance in history and from the objective evidence of the country's present judgment concerning the acceptability of death as a penalty for rape of an adult woman. At no time in the last 50 years have a majority of the States authorized death as a punishment for rape. In 1925, 18 States, the District of Columbia, and the Federal Government authorized capital punishment for the rape of an adult female. By 1971 just prior to the decision in *Furman v. Georgia,* that number had declined, but not substantially, to 16 States plus the Federal Government. *Furman* then invalidated most of the capital punishment statutes in this country, including the rape statutes, because, among other reasons, of the manner in which the death penalty was imposed and utilized under those laws.

With their death penalty statutes for the most part invalidated, the States were faced with the choice of enacting modified capital punishment laws in an attempt to satisfy the requirements of *Furman* or of being satisfied with life imprisonment as the ultimate punishment for any offense. Thirty-five States immediately reinstituted the death penalty for at least limited kinds of crime. This public judgment as to the acceptability of capital punishment, evidenced by the immediate, post-*Furman* legislative reaction in a large majority of the States, heavily influenced the Court to sustain the death penalty for murder in *Gregg v. Georgia.*

. . . In reviving death penalty laws to satisfy *Furman*'s mandate, none of the States that had not previously authorized death for rape chose to include rape among capital felonies. Of the 16 States in which rape had been a capital offense, only three provided the death penalty for rape of an adult woman in their revised statutes—Georgia, North Carolina, and Louisiana. In the latter two States, the death penalty was mandatory for those found guilty, and those laws were invalidated by *Woodson* and *Roberts.* When Louisiana and North Carolina, responding to those decisions, again revised their capital punishment laws, they re-enacted the death penalty for murder but not for rape; none of the seven other legislatures that to our knowledge have amended or replaced their death penalty statutes since July 2, 1976, including four States (in addition to Louisiana and North Carolina) that had authorized the death sentence for rape prior to 1972 and had reacted to *Furman* with mandatory statutes, included rape among the crimes for which death was an authorized punishment. . . .

The current judgment with respect to the death penalty for rape is not wholly unanimous among state legislatures, but it obviously weighs very heavily on the side of rejecting capital punishment as a suitable penalty for raping an adult woman.

B

It was also observed in *Gregg* that "[t]he jury . . . is a significant and reliable objective index of contemporary values because it is so directly involved," and that it is thus important to look to the sentencing decisions that juries have made in the course of assessing whether capital punishment is an appropriate penalty for the crime being tried. Of course, the jury's judgment is meaningful only where the jury has an appropriate measure of choice as to whether the death penalty is to be imposed. As far as execution for rape is concerned, this is now true only in Georgia and in Florida; and in the latter State, capital punishment is authorized only for the rape of children.

According to the factual submissions in this Court, out of all rape convictions in Georgia since 1973—and that total number has not been tendered—63 cases had been reviewed by the Georgia Supreme Court as of the time of oral argument; and of these, 6 involved a death sentence, 1 of which was set aside, leaving 5 convicted rapists now under sentence of death in the State of Georgia. Georgia juries have thus sentenced rapists to death six times since 1973. This obviously is not a negligible number; and the State argues that as a practical matter juries simply reserve the extreme sanction for extreme cases of rape and that recent experience surely does not prove that jurors consider the death penalty to be a disproportionate punishment for every conceivable instance of rape, no matter how aggravated. Nevertheless, it is true that in the vast majority of cases, at least 9 out of 10, juries have not imposed the death sentence.

IV

These recent events evidencing the attitude of state legislatures and sentencing juries do not wholly determine this controversy, for the Constitution contemplates that in the end our own judgment will be brought to bear on the question of the acceptability of the death penalty under the Eighth Amendment. Nevertheless, the legislative rejection of capital punishment for rape strongly confirms our own judgment, which is that death is indeed a disproportionate penalty for the crime of raping an adult woman. . . .

Rape is without doubt deserving of serious punishment; but in terms of moral depravity and of the injury to the person and to the public, it does not compare with murder, which does involve the unjustified taking of human life. Although it may be accompanied by another crime, rape by definition does not include the death of or even the serious injury to another person. The murderer kills; the rapist, if no more than that, does not. Life is over for the victim of the murderer; for the rape victim, life may not be nearly so happy as it was, but it is not over and normally is not beyond repair. We have the abiding conviction that the death penalty, which "is unique in its severity and irrevocability," is an excessive penalty for the rapist who, as such, does not take human life.

This does not end the matter; for under Georgia law, death may not be imposed for any capital offense, including rape, unless the jury or judge finds one of the statutory aggravating circumstances and then elects to impose that sentence. For the rapist to be executed in Georgia, it must therefore be found not only that he committed rape but also that one or more of the following aggravating circumstances were present: (1) that the rape was committed by a person with a prior record of conviction for a capital felony; (2) that the rape was committed while the offender was engaged in the commission of another capital felony, or aggravated battery; or (3) the rape "was outrageously or wantonly vile, horrible or inhuman in that it involved torture, depravity of mind, or aggravated battery to the victim." Here, the first two of these aggravating circumstances were alleged and found by the jury.

Neither of these circumstances, nor both of them together, change our conclusion that the death sentence imposed on Coker is a disproportionate punishment for rape. Coker had prior convictions for capital felonies—rape, murder, and kidnapping—but these prior convictions do not change the fact that the instant crime being punished is a rape not involving the taking of life.

It is also true that the present rape occurred while Coker was committing armed robbery, a felony for which the Georgia statutes authorize the death penalty. But Coker was tried for the robbery offense as well as for rape and received a separate life sentence for this crime; the jury did not deem the robbery itself deserving of the death penalty, even though accompanied by the aggravating circumstance, which was stipulated, that Coker had been convicted of a prior capital crime.

We note finally that in Georgia a person commits murder when he unlawfully and with malice aforethought, either express or implied, causes the death of another human being. He also commits that crime when in the commission of a felony he causes the death of another human being, irrespective of malice. But even where the killing is deliberate, it is not punishable by death absent proof of aggravating circumstances. It is difficult to accept the notion, and we do not, that the rapist, with or without aggravating circumstances, should be punished more heavily than the deliberate killer as long as the rapist does not himself take the life of his victim. The judgment of the Georgia Supreme Court upholding the death sentence is reversed, and the case is remanded to that court for further proceedings not inconsistent with this opinion.

So ordered.

MR. JUSTICE BRENNAN, concurring in the judgment.

Adhering to my view that the death penalty is in all circumstances cruel and unusual punishment prohibited by the Eighth and Fourteenth Amendments, I concur in the judgment of the Court setting aside the death sentence imposed under the Georgia rape statute.

MR. JUSTICE MARSHALL, concurring in the judgment.

In *Gregg v. Georgia*, . . . I stated: "In *Furman v. Georgia*, . . . I set forth at some length my views on the basic issue presented to the Court in these cases. The death penalty, I concluded, is a cruel and unusual punishment prohibited by the Eighth and Fourteenth Amendments. That continues to be my view.". . . I continue to adhere to those views in concurring in the judgment of the Court in this case.

MR. JUSTICE POWELL, concurring in the judgment in part and dissenting in part.

I concur in the judgment of the Court on the facts of this case, and also in the plurality's reasoning supporting the view that ordinarily death is disproportionate punishment for the crime of raping an adult woman. Although rape invariably is a reprehensible crime, there is no indication that petitioner's offense was committed with excessive brutality or that the victim sustained serious or lasting injury. The plurality, however, does not limit its holding to the case before us or to similar cases. Rather, in an opinion that ranges well beyond what is necessary, it holds that capital punishment always—regardless of the circumstances—is a disproportionate penalty for the crime of rape. . . .

Today, in a case that does not require such an expansive pronouncement, the plurality draws a bright line between murder and all rapes—regardless of the degree of brutality of the rape or the effect upon the victim. I dissent because I am not persuaded that such a bright line is appropriate. The deliberate viciousness of the rapist may be greater than that of the murderer. Rape is never an act committed accidentally. Rarely can it be said to be unpremeditated. There also is wide variation in the effect on the victim. The plurality opinion says that "[l]ife is over for the victim of the murderer; for the rape victim, life may not be nearly so happy as it was, but it is not over and normally is not beyond repair." But there is indeed "extreme variation" in the crime of rape. Some victims are so grievously injured physically or psychologically that life is beyond repair.

Thus, it may be that the death penalty is not disproportionate punishment for the crime of aggravated rape. Final resolution of the question must await careful inquiry into objective indicators of society's "evolving standards of decency," particularly legislative enactments and the responses of juries in capital cases. The plurality properly examines these indicia, which do support the conclusion that society finds the death penalty unacceptable for the crime of rape in the absence of excessive brutality or severe injury. But it has not been shown that society finds the penalty disproportionate for all rapes. In a proper case a more discriminating inquiry than the plurality undertakes well might discover that both juries and legislatures have reserved the ultimate penalty for the case of an outrageous rape resulting in serious, lasting harm to the victim. I would not prejudge the issue. To this extent, I respectfully dissent.

MR. CHIEF JUSTICE BURGER, with whom MR. JUSTICE REHNQUIST joins, dissenting.

In a case such as this, confusion often arises as to the Court's proper role in reaching a decision. Our task is not to give effect to our individual views on capital punishment; rather, we must determine what the Constitution permits a State to do under its reserved powers. In striking down the death penalty imposed upon the petitioner in this case, the Court has overstepped the bounds of proper constitutional adjudication by substituting its policy judgment for that of the state legislature. I accept that the Eighth Amendment's concept of disproportionality bars the death penalty for minor crimes. But rape is not a minor crime; hence the Cruel and Unusual Punishments Clause does not give the Members of this Court license to engraft their conceptions of proper public policy onto the considered legislative judgments of the States. Since I cannot agree that Georgia lacked the constitutional power to impose the penalty of death for rape, I dissent from the Court's judgment. . . .

The Court today holds that the State of Georgia may not impose the death penalty on Coker. In so doing, it prevents the State from imposing any effective punishment upon Coker for his latest rape. The Court's holding, moreover, bars Georgia from guaranteeing its citizens that they will suffer no further attacks by this habitual rapist. In fact, given the lengthy sentences Coker must serve for the crimes he has already committed, the Court's holding assures that petitioner—as well as others in his position—will henceforth feel no compunction whatsoever about committing further rapes as frequently as he may be able to escape from confinement and indeed even within the walls of the prison itself. To what extent we have left States "elbowroom" to protect innocent persons from depraved human beings like Coker remains in doubt. . . .

The question of whether the death penalty is an appropriate punishment for rape is surely an open one. It is arguable that many prospective rapists would be deterred by the possibility that they could suffer death for their offense; it is also arguable that the death penalty would have only minimal deterrent effect. It may well be that rape victims would become more willing to report the crime and aid in the apprehension of the criminals if they knew that community disapproval of rapists was sufficiently strong to inflict the extreme penalty; or perhaps they would be reluctant to cooperate in the prosecution of rapists if they knew that a conviction might result in the imposition of the death penalty. Quite possibly, the occasional, well-publicized execution of egregious rapists may cause citizens to feel greater security in their daily lives; or, on the contrary, it may be that members of a civilized community will suffer the pangs of a heavy conscience because such punishment will be perceived as excessive. We cannot know which among this range of possibilities is correct, but today's holding forecloses the very exploration we have said federalism was intended to foster. . . .

Rape thus is not a crime "light years" removed from murder in the degree of its heinousness; it certainly poses a serious potential danger to the life and safety of innocent victims—apart from the devastating psychic consequences. It would seem to follow therefore that, affording the States proper leeway under the broad standard of the Eighth Amendment, if murder is properly punishable by death, rape should be also, if that is the considered judgment of the legislators. . . .

Whatever our individual views as to the wisdom of capital punishment, I cannot agree that it is constitutionally impermissible for a state legislature to make the "solemn judgment" to impose such penalty for the crime of rape. Accordingly, I would leave to the States the task of legislating in this area of the law.

Source: Coker v. Georgia, 433 U.S. 584 (1977), at 587–604, 605–622.

Document 4.4
The Supreme Court Decides That States May Not Limit Mitigating Evidence in Capital Cases, July 3, 1978

In Woodson v. North Carolina *(1976) the Supreme Court struck down mandatory death sentence statutes on the grounds that they failed to give juries and judges the opportunity to individualize sentencing by considering mitigating evidence. The decision left open the question of whether a state might by statute seek to limit the types of mitigating evidence introduced during the sentencing portion of a capital trial. Sandra Lockett, a twenty-one-year-old African American, was sentenced to death under an Ohio law that made such restrictions. The Court reversed her sentence in* Lockett v. Ohio *and voided the law in an opinion written by Chief Justice Warren Burger. Justice William Rehnquist dissented in part.*

MR. CHIEF JUSTICE BURGER delivered the opinion of the Court with respect to the constitutionality of petitioner's conviction, together with an opinion in which MR. JUSTICE STEWART, MR. JUSTICE POWELL, and MR. JUSTICE STEVENS joined, on the constitutionality of the statute under which petitioner was sentenced to death, and announced the judgment of the Court.

We granted certiorari in this case to consider, among other questions, whether Ohio violated the Eighth and Fourteenth Amendments by sentencing Sandra Lockett to death pursuant to a statute that narrowly limits the sentencer's discretion to consider the circumstances of the crime and the record and character of the offender as mitigating factors.

I

Lockett was charged with aggravated murder with the aggravating specifications (1) that the murder was "committed for the purpose of escaping detection, apprehension, trial, or punishment" for aggravated robbery, and (2) that the murder was "committed while . . . committing, attempting to commit, or fleeing immediately after committing or attempting to commit . . . aggravated robbery." That offense was punishable by death in Ohio. She was also charged with aggravated robbery. The State's case against her depended largely upon the testimony of a coparticipant, one Al Parker. . . .

Someone, apparently Lockett's brother, suggested a plan for robbing a pawnshop. No one planned to kill the pawnshop operator in the course of the robbery. Because she knew the owner, Lockett was not to be among those entering the pawnshop, though she did guide the others to the shop that night. The robbery proceeded according to plan until the pawnbroker grabbed the gun when Parker announced the "stickup." The gun went off with Parker's finger on the trigger, firing a fatal shot into the pawnbroker.

Parker went back to the car where Lockett waited with the engine running. While driving away from the pawnshop, Parker told Lockett what had happened. She took the gun from the pawnshop and put it into her purse. Lockett and Parker drove to Lockett's aunt's house and called a taxicab. Shortly thereafter, while riding away in a taxicab, they were stopped by the police, but by this time Lockett had placed the gun under the front seat. Lockett told the police that Parker rented a room from her mother and lived with her family. After verifying this story with Lockett's parents, the police released Lockett and Parker. Lockett hid Dew and Parker in the attic when the police arrived at the Lockett household later that evening.

Parker was subsequently apprehended and charged with aggravated murder with specifications, an offense punishable by death, and aggravated robbery. Prior to trial, he pleaded guilty to the murder charge and agreed to testify against Lockett, her brother, and Dew. In return, the prosecutor dropped the aggravated robbery charge and the specifications to the murder charge, thereby eliminating the possibility that Parker could receive the death penalty. . . .

The court instructed the jury that, before it could find Lockett guilty, it had to find that she purposely had killed the pawnbroker while committing or attempting to commit aggravated robbery. The jury was further charged that one who "purposely aids, helps, associates himself or herself with another for the purpose of committing a crime is regarded as if he or she were the principal offender and is just as guilty as if the person performed every act constituting the offense. . . ."

Regarding the intent requirement, the court instructed:

A person engaged in a common design with others to rob by force and violence an individual or individuals of their property is presumed to acquiesce in whatever may reasonably be necessary to accomplish the object of their enterprise. . . .

If the conspired robbery and the manner of its accomplishment would be reasonably likely to produce death, each plotter is equally guilty with the principal offender as an aider and abettor in the homicide. . . . An intent to kill by an aider and abettor may be found to exist beyond a reasonable doubt under such circumstances. . . .

The jury found Lockett guilty as charged.

Once a verdict of aggravated murder with specifications had been returned, the Ohio death penalty statute required the trial judge to impose a death sentence unless, after "considering the nature and circumstances of the offense" and Lockett's "history, character, and condition," he found by a preponderance of the evidence that (1) the victim had induced or facilitated the offense, (2) it was unlikely that Lockett would have committed the offense but for the fact that she "was under duress, coercion, or strong provocation," or (3) the offense was "primarily the product of [Lockett's] psychosis or mental deficiency."

In accord with the Ohio statute, the trial judge requested a presentence report as well as psychiatric and psychological reports. The reports contained detailed information about Lockett's intelligence, character, and background. The psychiatric and psychological reports described her as a 21-year-old with low-average or average intelligence, and not suffering from a mental deficiency. One of the psychologists reported that "her prognosis for rehabilitation" if returned to society was favorable. The presentence report showed that Lockett had committed no major offenses although she had a record of several minor ones as a juvenile and two minor offenses as an adult. It also showed that she had once used heroin but was receiving treatment at a drug abuse clinic and seemed to be "on the road to success" as far as her drug problem was concerned. It concluded that Lockett suffered no psychosis and was not mentally deficient.

After considering the reports and hearing argument on the penalty issue, the trial judge concluded that the offense had not been primarily the product of psychosis or mental deficiency. Without specifically addressing the other two statutory mitigating factors, the judge said that he had "no alternative, whether [he] like[d] the law or not" but to impose the death penalty. He then sentenced Lockett to death. . . .

III

Lockett challenges the constitutionality of Ohio's death penalty statute on a number of grounds. We find it necessary to consider only her contention that her death sentence is invalid because the statute under which it was imposed did not permit the sentencing judge to consider, as mitigating factors, her character, prior record, age, lack of specific intent to cause death, and her relatively minor part in the crime. To address her contention from the proper perspective, it is helpful to review the developments in our recent cases where we have applied the Eighth and Fourteenth Amendments to death penalty statutes. We do not write on a "clean slate." . . .

In the last decade, many of the States have been obliged to revise their death penalty statutes in response to the various opinions supporting the judgments in *Furman* and *Gregg* and its companion cases. The signals from this Court have not, however, always been easy to decipher. The States now deserve the clearest guidance that the Court can provide; we have an obligation to reconcile previously differing views in order to provide that guidance. . . .

B

With that obligation in mind we turn to Lockett's attack on the Ohio statute. Essentially she contends that the Eighth and Fourteenth Amendments require that the sentencer be given a full opportunity to consider mitigating circumstances in capital cases and that the Ohio statute does not comply with that requirement. She relies, in large part, on the plurality opinions in *Woodson* and the joint opinion in *Jurek,* but she goes beyond them.

We begin by recognizing that the concept of individualized sentencing in criminal cases generally, although not constitutionally required, has long been accepted in this country. Consistent with that concept, sentencing judges traditionally have taken a wide range of factors into account. That States have authority to make aiders and abettors equally responsible, as a matter of law, with principals, or to enact felony-murder statutes is beyond constitutional challenge. But the definition of crimes generally has not been thought automatically to dictate what should be the proper penalty. And where sentencing discretion is granted, it generally has been agreed that the sentencing judge's "possession of the fullest information possible concerning the defendant's life and characteristics" is "[h]ighly relevant—if not essential—[to the] selection of an appropriate sentence." . . .

Although legislatures remain free to decide how much discretion in sentencing should be reposed in the judge or jury in noncapital cases, the plurality opinion in *Woodson* . . . concluded that "in capital cases the fundamental respect for humanity underlying the Eighth Amendment . . . requires consideration of the character and record of the individual offender and the circumstances of the particular offense as a constitutionally indispensable part of the process of inflicting the penalty of death."

That declaration rested "on the predicate that the penalty of death is qualitatively different" from any other sentence. We are satisfied that this qualitative difference between death and other penalties calls for a greater degree of reliability when the death sentence is imposed. The mandatory death penalty statute in *Woodson* was held invalid because it permitted no consideration of "relevant facets of the character and record of the individual offender or the circumstances of the particular offense." The plurality did not attempt to indicate, however, which facets of an offender or his offense it deemed "relevant" in capital sentencing or what degree of consideration of "relevant facets" it would require.

We are now faced with those questions and we conclude that the Eighth and Fourteenth Amendments require that the sentencer, in all but the rarest kind of capital case, not be precluded from considering, as a mitigating factor, any aspect of a defendant's character or record and any of the circumstances of the offense that the defendant proffers as a basis for a sentence less than death. . . .

There is no perfect procedure for deciding in which cases governmental authority should be used to impose death. But a statute that prevents the sentencer in all capital cases from giving independent mitigating weight to aspects of the defendant's character and record and to circumstances of the offense proffered in mitigation creates the risk that the death penalty will be imposed in spite of factors which may call for a less severe penalty. When the choice is between life and death, that risk is unacceptable and incompatible with the commands of the Eighth and Fourteenth Amendments.

The Ohio death penalty statute does not permit the type of individualized consideration of mitigating factors we now hold to be required by the Eighth and Fourteenth Amendments in capital cases. Its constitutional infirmities can best be understood by comparing it with the statutes upheld in *Gregg, Proffitt,* and *Jurek.* The limited range of mitigating circumstances which may be considered by the sentencer under the Ohio statute is incompatible with the Eighth and Fourteenth Amendments. To meet constitutional requirements, a death penalty statute must not preclude consideration of relevant mitigating factors.

C

Accordingly, the judgment under review is reversed to the extent that it sustains the imposition of the death penalty, and the case is remanded for further proceedings. . . .

MR. JUSTICE MARSHALL, concurring in the judgment.

I continue to adhere to my view that the death penalty is, under all circumstances, a cruel and unusual punishment prohibited by the Eighth Amendment . . . This case, as well, serves to reinforce my view.

When a death sentence is imposed under the circumstances presented here, I fail to understand how any of my Brethren—even those who believe that the death penalty is not wholly inconsistent with the Constitution—can disagree that it must be vacated. Under the Ohio death penalty statute, this 21-year-old Negro woman was sentenced to death for a killing that she did not actually commit or intend to commit. She was convicted under a theory of vicarious liability. The imposition of the death penalty for this crime totally violates the principle of proportionality embodied in the Eighth Amendment's prohibition, it makes no distinction between a willful and malicious murderer and an accomplice to an armed robbery in which a killing unintentionally occurs.

Permitting imposition of the death penalty solely on proof of felony murder, moreover, necessarily leads to the kind of "lightning bolt," "freakish," and "wanton" executions that persuaded other Members of the Court to join MR. JUSTICE BRENNAN and myself in *Furman* in holding Georgia's death penalty statute unconstitutional. Whether a death results in the course of a felony (thus giving rise to felony-murder liability) turns on fortuitous events that do not distinguish the intention or moral culpability of the defendants. . . .

MR. JUSTICE REHNQUIST, concurring in part and dissenting in part. . . .

I

Whether out of a sense of judicial responsibility or a less altruistic sense of futility, there are undoubtedly circumstances which require a Member of this Court "to bow to the authority" of an earlier case despite his "original and continuing belief that the decision was constitutionally wrong." The Court has most assuredly not adopted the dissenting views which I expressed in the previous capital punishment cases. It has just as surely not cloven to a principled doctrine either holding the infliction of the death penalty to be unconstitutional per se or clearly and understandably stating the terms under which the Eighth and Fourteenth Amendments permit the death penalty to be imposed. Instead, as I believe the Court has gone from pillar to post, with the result that the sort of reasonable predictability upon which legislatures, trial courts, and appellate courts must of necessity rely has been all but completely sacrificed.

THE CHIEF JUSTICE states: "We do not write on a 'clean slate.'" But it can scarcely be maintained that today's decision is the logical application of a

coherent doctrine first espoused by the opinions leading to the Court's judgment in *Furman,* and later elaborated in the *Woodson* series of cases decided
two Terms ago. Indeed, it cannot even be responsibly maintained that it is a
principled application of the plurality and lead opinions in the *Woodson* series of
cases, without regard to *Furman.* The opinion strives manfully to appear as a
logical exegesis of those opinions, but I believe that it fails in the effort. We are
now told, in effect, that in order to impose a death sentence the judge or jury
must receive in evidence whatever the defense attorney wishes them to hear. I
do not think THE CHIEF JUSTICE'S effort to trace this quite novel constitutional principle back to the plurality and lead opinions in the *Woodson* cases
succeeds. . . .

It seems to me indisputably clear from today's opinion that, while we may not
be writing on a clean slate, the Court is scarcely faithful to what has been written
before. Rather, it makes a third distinct effort to address the same question, an
effort which derives little support from any of the various opinions in *Furman* or
from the prevailing opinions in the *Woodson* cases. As a practical matter, I doubt
that today's opinion will make a great deal of difference in the manner in which
trials in capital cases are conducted, since I would suspect that it has been the
practice of most trial judges to permit a defendant to offer virtually any sort of
evidence in his own defense as he wished. By encouraging defendants in capital
cases, and presumably sentencing judges and juries, to take into consideration
anything under the sun as a "mitigating circumstance," it will not guide sentencing discretion but will totally unleash it. . . .

. . . I trust that I am not insensitive to THE CHIEF JUSTICE'S expressed
concern in his opinion that "[t]he States now deserve the clearest guidance that
the Court can provide" on capital punishment. Given the posture of my colleagues in this case, however, there does not seem to me to be any way in which
I can assist in the discharge of that obligation. I am frank to say that I am uncertain whether today's opinion represents the seminal case in the exposition by this
Court of the Eighth and Fourteenth Amendments as they apply to capital punishment, or whether instead it represents the third false start in this direction
within the past six years. . . .

I finally reject the proposition which the plurality finds it unnecessary to
reach. That claim is that the death penalty, as applied to one who participated in
this murder as Lockett did, is "disproportionate" and therefore violative of the
Eighth and Fourteenth Amendments. I know of no principle embodied in those
Amendments, other than perhaps one's personal notion of what is a fitting punishment for a crime, which would allow this Court to hold the death penalty
imposed upon her unconstitutional because under the judge's charge to the jury
the latter were not required to find that she intended to cause the death of her
victim. . . . Centuries of common-law doctrine establishing the felony-murder

doctrine, dealing with the relationship between aiders and abettors and princi-pals, would have to be rejected to adopt this view. Just as surely as many thoughtful moralists and penologists would reject the Biblical notion of "an eye for an eye, a tooth for a tooth," as a guide for minimum sentencing, there is nothing in the prohibition against cruel and unusual punishments contained in the Eighth Amendment which sets that injunction as a limitation on the maxi-mum sentence which society may impose.

Since all of petitioner's claims appear to me to be without merit, I would affirm the judgment of the Supreme Court of Ohio.

Source: Lockett v. Ohio, 438 U.S. 586 (1978), at 597–609, 629–636.

Document 4.5
The Supreme Court Requires Individualized Consideration of Mitigating Factors in *Eddings v. Oklahoma*, January 19, 1982

In a prelude to its later decisions barring the death penalty for juvenile offenders, the Supreme Court in Eddings v. Oklahoma *(1982) ordered a new trial for Monty Lee Eddings, who had been convicted of killing a highway patrol officer at the age of sixteen. Without reaching the specific issue of Eddings's sage, the Court ruled that the trial judge's instructions to the sentencing jury had not specifically called members' attention to the defendant's youth as a mitigating factor, thus violating the Eighth and Fourteenth Amendments.*

JUSTICE POWELL delivered the opinion of the Court.

Petitioner Monty Lee Eddings was convicted of first-degree murder and sen-tenced to death. Because this sentence was imposed without "the type of indi-vidualized consideration of mitigating factors . . . required by the Eighth and Fourteenth Amendments in capital cases," *Lockett v. Ohio,* we reverse.

I

On April 4, 1977, Eddings, a 16-year-old youth, and several younger com-panions ran away from their Missouri homes. They traveled in a car owned by Eddings' brother, and drove without destination or purpose in a southwest-erly direction eventually reaching the Oklahoma Turnpike. Eddings had in the car a shotgun and several rifles he had taken from his father. After he momentarily lost control of the car, he was signalled to pull over by Officer Crabtree of the Oklahoma Highway Patrol. Eddings did so, and when the offi-cer approached the car, Eddings stuck a loaded shotgun out of the window and fired, killing the officer.

Because Eddings was a juvenile, the State moved to have him certified to stand trial as an adult. Finding that there was prosecutive merit to the complaint and that Eddings was not amenable to rehabilitation within the juvenile system, the trial court granted the motion. The ruling was affirmed on appeal. Eddings was then charged with murder in the first degree, and the District Court of Creek County found him guilty upon his plea of nolo contendere.

The Oklahoma death penalty statute provides in pertinent part:

> Upon conviction . . . of guilt of a defendant of murder in the first degree, the court shall conduct a separate sentencing proceeding to determine whether the defendant should be sentenced to death or life imprisonment. . . . In the sentencing proceeding, evidence may be presented as to *any mitigating circumstances* or as to any of the aggravating circumstances enumerated in this act. [Okla.Stat., Tit. 21, § 701.10 (1980) (emphasis added).]

Section 701.12 lists seven separate aggravating circumstances; the statute nowhere defines what is meant by "any mitigating circumstances."

At the sentencing hearing, the State alleged three of the aggravating circumstances enumerated in the statute: that the murder was especially heinous, atrocious, or cruel, that the crime was committed for the purpose of avoiding or preventing a lawful arrest, and that there was a probability that the defendant would commit criminal acts of violence that would constitute a continuing threat to society.

In mitigation, Eddings presented substantial evidence at the hearing of his troubled youth. The testimony of his supervising Juvenile Officer indicated that Eddings had been raised without proper guidance. His parents were divorced when he was 5 years old, and until he was 14 Eddings lived with his mother without rules or supervision. There is the suggestion that Eddings' mother was an alcoholic and possibly a prostitute. By the time Eddings was 14 he no longer could be controlled, and his mother sent him to live with his father. But neither could the father control the boy. Attempts to reason and talk gave way to physical punishment. The Juvenile Officer testified that Eddings was frightened and bitter, that his father overreacted and used excessive physical punishment: "Mr. Eddings found the only thing that he thought was effectful with the boy was actual punishment, or physical violence—hitting with a strap or something like this." Testimony from other witnesses indicated that Eddings was emotionally disturbed in general and at the time of the crime, and that his mental and emotional development were at a level several years below his age. A state psychologist stated that Eddings had a sociopathic or antisocial personality and that approximately 30% of youths suffering from such a disorder grew out of it as they aged. A sociologist specializing in juvenile offenders testified that Eddings was treatable. A psychiatrist testified that Eddings could be rehabilitated by intensive therapy over a 15- to 20-year period. He testified further that Eddings "did pull the trigger, he did kill someone, but I don't even think he knew that he was doing it." The psychiatrist suggested that, if treated, Eddings would no longer pose a serious threat to society.

At the conclusion of all the evidence, the trial judge weighed the evidence of aggravating and mitigating circumstances. He found that the State had proved each of the three alleged aggravating circumstances beyond a reasonable doubt. Turning to the evidence of mitigating circumstances, the judge found that Eddings' youth was a mitigating factor of great weight: "I have given very serious consideration to the youth of the Defendant when this particular crime was committed. Should I fail to do this, I think I would not be carrying out my duty." But he would not consider in mitigation the circumstances of Eddings' unhappy upbringing and emotional disturbance: "[T]he Court cannot be persuaded entirely by the . . . fact that the youth was sixteen years old when this heinous crime was committed. Nor can the Court in following the law, in my opinion, consider the fact of this young man's violent background." Finding that the only mitigating circumstance was Eddings' youth and finding further that this circumstance could not outweigh the aggravating circumstances present, the judge sentenced Eddings to death.

The Court of Criminal Appeals affirmed the sentence of death. It found that each of the aggravating circumstances alleged by the State had been present. It recited the mitigating evidence presented by Eddings in some detail, but in the end it agreed with the trial court that only the fact of Eddings' youth was properly considered as a mitigating circumstance:

> [Eddings] also argues his mental state at the time of the murder. He stresses his family history in saying he was suffering from severe psychological and emotional disorders, and that the killing was in actuality an inevitable product of the way he was raised. There is no doubt that the petitioner has a personality disorder. But all the evidence tends to show that he knew the difference between right and wrong at the time he pulled the trigger, and that is the test of criminal responsibility in this State. For the same reason, the petitioner's family history is useful in explaining why he behaved the way he did, but it does not excuse his behaviour.

II

In *Lockett v. Ohio,* CHIEF JUSTICE BURGER, writing for the plurality, stated the rule that we apply today:

> [W]e conclude that the Eighth and Fourteenth Amendments require that the sentencer . . . not be precluded from considering, *as a mitigating factor,* any aspect of a defendant's character or record and any of the circumstances of the offense that the defendant proffers as a basis for a sentence less than death. . . .

As THE CHIEF JUSTICE explained, the rule in *Lockett* is the product of a considerable history reflecting the law's effort to develop a system of capital punishment at once consistent and principled but also humane and sensible to the uniqueness of the individual. Since the early days of the common law, the legal system has struggled to accommodate these twin objectives. Thus, the common law began by treating all criminal homicides as capital offenses, with a mandatory sentence of death. Later it allowed exceptions, first through an exclusion for those entitled to claim benefit of clergy and then by limiting capital punishment to murders upon "malice prepensed." In this country we attempted to soften the rigor of the system of mandatory death sentences we inherited from England, first by grading murder into different degrees of which only murder of the first degree was a capital offense and then by committing use of the death penalty to the absolute discretion of the jury. By the time of our decision in *Furman v. Georgia*, the country had moved so far from a mandatory system that the imposition of capital punishment frequently had become arbitrary and capricious. . . .

Thus, the rule in *Lockett* followed from the earlier decisions of the Court and from the Court's insistence that capital punishment be imposed fairly, and with reasonable consistency, or not at all. By requiring that the sentencer be permitted to focus "on the characteristics of the person who committed the crime," the rule in *Lockett* recognizes that "justice . . . requires . . . that there be taken into account the circumstances of the offense together with the character and propensities of the offender." By holding that the sentencer in capital cases must be permitted to consider any relevant mitigating factor, the rule in *Lockett* recognizes that a consistency produced by ignoring individual differences is a false consistency.

III

We now apply the rule in *Lockett* to the circumstances of this case. The trial judge stated that "in following the law," he could not "consider the fact of this young man's violent background." There is no dispute that by "violent background" the trial judge was referring to the mitigating evidence of Eddings' family history. From this statement it is clear that the trial judge did not evaluate the evidence in mitigation and find it wanting as a matter of fact; rather he found that as a matter of law he was unable even to consider the evidence.

The Court of Criminal Appeals took the same approach. It found that the evidence in mitigation was not relevant because it did not tend to provide a legal excuse from criminal responsibility. Thus the court conceded that Eddings had a "personality disorder," but cast this evidence aside on the basis that "he knew the difference between right and wrong . . . and that is the test of criminal responsibility." Similarly, the evidence of Eddings' family history was "useful in explaining" his behavior, but it did not "excuse" the behaviour. From these statements it appears that the Court of Criminal Appeals also considered only that evidence to be mitigating which would tend to support a legal excuse from criminal liability.

We find that the limitations placed by these courts upon the mitigating evidence they would consider violated the rule in *Lockett*. Just as the State may not by statute preclude the sentencer from considering any mitigating factor, neither may the sentencer refuse to consider, as a matter of law, any relevant mitigating evidence. In this instance, it was as if the trial judge had instructed a jury to disregard the mitigating evidence Eddings proffered on his behalf. The sentencer, and the Court of Criminal Appeals on review, may determine the weight to be given relevant mitigating evidence. But they may not give it no weight by excluding such evidence from their consideration.

Nor do we doubt that the evidence Eddings offered was relevant mitigating evidence. Eddings was a youth of 16 years at the time of the murder. Evidence of a difficult family history and of emotional disturbance is typically introduced by defendants in mitigation. In some cases, such evidence properly may be given little weight. But when the defendant was 16 years old at the time of the offense there can be no doubt that evidence of a turbulent family history, of beatings by a harsh father, and of severe emotional disturbance is particularly relevant. . . .

On remand, the state courts must consider all relevant mitigating evidence and weigh it against the evidence of the aggravating circumstances. We do not weight the evidence for them. Accordingly, the judgment is reversed to the extent that it sustains the imposition of the death penalty, and the case is remanded for further proceedings not inconsistent with this opinion.

So ordered.

JUSTICE O'CONNOR, concurring.

I write separately to address more fully the reasons why this case must be remanded in light of *Lockett v. Ohio*, which requires the trial court to consider and weigh all of the mitigating evidence concerning the petitioner's family background and personal history. . . .

In order to ensure that the death penalty was not erroneously imposed, the *Lockett* plurality concluded that "the Eighth and Fourteenth Amendments require that the sentencer, in all but the rarest kind of capital case, not be precluded from considering, as a mitigating factor, any aspect of a defendant's character or record and any of the circumstances of the offense that the defendant proffers as a basis for a sentence less than death."

In the present case, of course, the relevant Oklahoma statute permits the defendant to present evidence of any mitigating circumstance. Nonetheless, in sentencing the petitioner (which occurred about one month before *Lockett* was decided), the judge remarked that he could not "in following the law . . . consider the fact of this young man's violent background." Although one can reasonably argue that these extemporaneous remarks are of no legal significance, I believe that the reasoning of the plurality opinion in *Lockett* compels a remand so that we do not "risk that the death penalty will be imposed in spite of factors which may call for a less severe penalty."

I disagree with the suggestion in the dissent that remanding this case may serve no useful purpose. Even though the petitioner had an opportunity to present evidence in mitigation of the crime, it appears that the trial judge believed that he could not consider some of the mitigating evidence in imposing sentence. In any event, we may not speculate as to whether the trial judge and the Court of Criminal Appeals actually considered all of the mitigating factors and found them insufficient to offset the aggravating circumstances, or whether the difference between this Court's opinion and the trial court's treatment of the petitioner's evidence is "purely a matter of semantics," as suggested by the dissent. *Woodson* and *Lockett* require us to remove any legitimate basis for finding ambiguity concerning the factors actually considered by the trial court. . . .

CHIEF JUSTICE BURGER, with whom JUSTICE WHITE, JUSTICE BLACKMUN, and JUSTICE REHNQUIST join, dissenting.

It is important at the outset to remember—as the Court does not—the narrow question on which we granted certiorari. We took care to limit our consideration to whether the Eighth and Fourteenth Amendments prohibit the imposition of a death sentence on an offender because he was 16 years old in 1977 at the time he committed the offense; review of all other questions raised in the petition for certiorari was denied. Yet the Court today goes beyond the issue on which review was sought—and granted—to decide the case on a point raised for the first time in petitioner's brief to this Court. This claim was neither presented to the Oklahoma courts nor presented to this Court in the petition for certiorari. Relying on this "11th-hour" claim, the Court strains to construct a plausible legal theory to support its mandate for the relief granted. . . .

We held in *Lockett* that the "Eighth and Fourteenth Amendments require that the sentencer . . . not be precluded from considering, as a mitigating factor, any aspect of a defendant's character or record and any of the circumstances of the offense that the defendant proffers as a basis for a sentence less than death." We therefore found the Ohio statute flawed, because it did not permit individualized consideration of mitigating circumstances—such as the defendant's comparatively minor role in the offense, lack of intent to kill the victim, or age. We did not, however, undertake to dictate the weight that a sentencing court must ascribe to the various factors that might be categorized as "mitigating," nor did we in any way suggest that this Court may substitute its sentencing judgment for that of state courts in capital cases. . . .

In its attempt to make out a violation of *Lockett*, the Court relies entirely on a single sentence of the trial court's opinion delivered from the bench at the close of the sentencing hearing. After discussing the aggravated nature of petitioner's offense, and noting that he had "given very serious consideration to the youth of the Defendant when this particular crime was committed," the trial judge said that he could not "be persuaded entirely by the . . . fact that the youth was sixteen years old when this heinous crime was committed. Nor can the Court in following the law, in my opinion, consider the fact of this young man's violent background."

From this statement, the Court concludes "it is clear that the trial judge did not evaluate the evidence in mitigation and find it wanting as a matter of fact, rather he found that as a matter of law he was unable even to consider the evidence." This is simply not a correct characterization of the sentencing judge's action.

In its parsing of the trial court's oral statement, the Court ignores the fact that the judge was delivering his opinion extemporaneously from the bench, and could not be expected to frame each utterance with the specificity and precision that might be expected of a written opinion or statute. Extemporaneous court-room statements are not often models of clarity. Nor does the Court give any weight to the fact that the trial court had spent considerable time listening to the testimony of a probation officer and various mental health professionals who described Eddings' personality and family history—an obviously meaningless exercise if, as the Court asserts, the judge believed he was barred "as a matter of law" from "considering" their testimony. Yet even examined in isolation, the trial court's statement is at best ambiguous; it can just as easily be read to say that, while the court had taken account of Eddings' unfortunate childhood, it did not consider that either his youth or his family background was sufficient to offset the aggravating circumstances that the evidence revealed. Certainly nothing in *Lockett* would preclude the court from making such a determination. . . .

II

It can never be less than the most painful of our duties to pass on capital cases, and the more so in a case such as this one. However, there comes a time in every case when a court must "bite the bullet."

Whether the Court's remand will serve any useful purpose remains to be seen, for petitioner has already been given an opportunity to introduce whatever evidence he considered relevant to the sentencing determination. Two Oklahoma courts have weighed that evidence and found it insufficient to offset the aggravating circumstances shown by the State. The Court's opinion makes clear that some Justices who join it would not have imposed the death penalty had they sat as the sentencing authority. Indeed, I am not sure I would have done so. But the Constitution does not authorize us to determine whether sentences imposed by state courts are sentences we consider "appropriate"; our only authority is to decide whether they are constitutional under the Eight [sic] Amendment. The Court stops far short of suggesting that there is any constitutional proscription against imposition of the death penalty on a person who was under age 18 when the murder was committed. In the last analysis, the Court is forced to conclude that it is "the state courts [which] must consider [petitioner's mitigating evidence] and weigh it against the evidence of the aggravating circumstances. We do not weigh the evidence for them."

Because the sentencing proceedings in this case were in no sense inconsistent with *Lockett*, I would decide the sole issue on which we granted certiorari, and affirm the judgment.

Source: Eddings v. Oklahoma, 455 U.S. 104 (1982), at 110–117, 120–128.

Document 4.6
The Supreme Court Overturns Felony Murder Sentence as Cruel and Unusual Punishment, July 2, 1982

The Supreme Court narrowed the category of the death eligible in Enmund v. Florida *(1982) by overturning a sentence for felony murder in which the defendant had not killed or intended to kill in the course of a robbery. Justice Byron White, writing for the Court, engaged in what had become orthodox methodology for determining "contemporary standards of decency" by counting legislative statutes and jury decisions with respect to the crime and the punishment. White also stressed that the Court made an independent judgment and rejected the argument that death for felony murder could not be justified either on grounds of deterrence or retribution. Justice Sandra Day O'Connor's dissent contested White's method of counting legislative noses and jury verdicts.*

JUSTICE WHITE delivered the opinion of the Court.

I

The facts of this case, taken principally from the opinion of the Florida Supreme Court, are as follows. On April 1, 1975, at approximately 7:45 a.m., Thomas and Eunice Kersey, aged 86 and 74, were robbed and fatally shot at their farmhouse in central Florida. The evidence showed that Sampson and Jeanette Armstrong had gone to the back door of the Kersey house and asked for water for an overheated car. When Mr. Kersey came out of the house, Sampson Armstrong grabbed him, pointed a gun at him, and told Jeanette Armstrong to take his money. Mr. Kersey cried for help, and his wife came out of the house with a gun and shot Jeanette Armstrong, wounding her. Sampson Armstrong, and perhaps Jeanette Armstrong, then shot and killed both of the Kerseys, dragged them into the kitchen, and took their money and fled.

Two witnesses testified that they drove past the Kersey house between 7:30 and 7:40 a.m. and saw a large cream- or yellow-colored car parked beside the road about 200 yards from the house and that a man was sitting in the car. Another witness testified that at approximately 6:45 a.m. he saw Ida Jean Shaw, petitioner's common-law wife and Jeanette Armstrong's mother, driving a yellow Buick with a vinyl top which belonged to her and petitioner Earl Enmund. Enmund was a passenger in the car along with an unidentified woman. At about 8 a.m. the same witness saw the car return at a high rate of speed. Enmund was driving, Ida Jean Shaw was in the front seat, and one of the other two people in the car was lying down across the back seat.

Enmund, Sampson Armstrong, and Jeanette Armstrong were indicted for the first-degree murder and robbery of the Kerseys. Enmund and Sampson Armstrong were tried together. The prosecutor maintained in his closing argument that "Sampson Armstrong killed the old people." The judge instructed the jury that "[t]he killing of a human being while engaged in the perpetration of or in the attempt to perpetrate the offense of robbery is murder in the first degree even though there is no premeditated design or intent to kill."

He went on to instruct them that

[i]n order to sustain a conviction of first degree murder while engaging in the perpetration of or in the attempted perpetration of the crime of robbery, the evidence must establish beyond a reasonable doubt that the defendant was actually present and was actively aiding and abetting the robbery or attempted robbery, and that the unlawful killing occurred in the perpetration of or in the attempted perpetration of the robbery.

The jury found both Enmund and Sampson Armstrong guilty of two counts of first-degree murder and one count of robbery. A separate sentencing hearing was held and the jury recommended the death penalty for both defendants under the Florida procedure whereby the jury advises the trial judge whether to impose the death penalty. . . . The trial judge then sentenced Enmund to death on the two counts of first-degree murder. Enmund appealed, and the Florida Supreme Court remanded for written findings. The trial judge found four statutory aggravating circumstances: the capital felony was committed while Enmund was engaged in or was an accomplice in the commission of an armed robbery, the capital felony was committed for pecuniary gain, it was especially heinous, atrocious, or cruel, and Enmund was previously convicted of a felony involving the use or threat of violence. The court found that "none of the statutory mitigating circumstances applied" to Enmund and that the aggravating circumstances outweighed the mitigating circumstances. Enmund was therefore sentenced to death on each of the murder counts.

The Florida Supreme Court affirmed Enmund's conviction and sentences. It found that "[t]here was no direct evidence at trial that Earl Enmund was present at the back door of the Kersey home when the plan to rob the elderly couple led to their being murdered."

However, it rejected petitioner's argument that at most he could be found guilty of second-degree murder under Florida's felony-murder rule. The court explained that the interaction of the "'felony murder rule and the law of principals combine to make a felon generally responsible for the lethal acts of his co-felon.'" . . .

. . . In so doing, the court expressly rejected Enmund's submission that because the evidence did not establish that he intended to take life, the death penalty was barred by the Eighth Amendment of the United States Constitution.

We granted Enmund's petition for certiorari, presenting the question whether death is a valid penalty under the Eighth and Fourteenth Amendments for one who neither took life, attempted to take life, nor intended to take life.

II

As recounted above, the Florida Supreme Court held that the record supported no more than the inference that Enmund was the person in the car by the side of the road at the time of the killings, waiting to help the robbers escape. This was enough under Florida law to make Enmund a constructive aider and abettor and hence a principal in first-degree murder upon whom the death penalty could be imposed. It was thus irrelevant to Enmund's challenge to the death sentence that he did not himself kill and was not present at the killings; also beside the point was whether he intended that the Kerseys be killed or anticipated that lethal force would or might be used if necessary to effectuate the robbery or a safe escape. We have concluded that imposition of the death penalty in these circumstances is inconsistent with the Eighth and Fourteenth Amendments.

A

The Cruel and Unusual Punishments Clause of the Eighth Amendment is directed, in part, "'against all punishments which by their excessive length or severity are greatly disproportioned to the offenses charged.'" This Court most recently held a punishment excessive in relation to the crime charged in *Coker v. Georgia* (1977). There the plurality opinion concluded that the imposition of the death penalty for the rape of an adult woman "is grossly disproportionate and excessive punishment for the crime of rape and is therefore forbidden by the Eighth Amendment as cruel and unusual punishment." In reaching this conclusion, it was stressed that our judgment "should be informed by objective factors to the maximum possible extent." Accordingly, the Court looked to the historical development of the punishment at issue, legislative judgments, international opinion, and the sentencing decisions juries have made before bringing its own judgment to bear on the matter. We proceed to analyze the punishment at issue in this case in a similar manner. . . .

Thirty-six state and federal jurisdictions presently authorize the death penalty. Of these, only eight jurisdictions authorize imposition of the death penalty solely for participation in a robbery in which another robber takes life. Of the remaining 28 jurisdictions, in 4 felony murder is not a capital crime. Eleven States require some culpable mental state with respect to the homicide as a prerequisite to conviction of a crime for which the death penalty is authorized. Of these 11 States, 8 make knowing, intentional, purposeful, or premeditated killing an element of capital murder. Three other States require proof of a culpable mental state short of intent, such as recklessness or extreme indifference to human life, before the death penalty may be imposed. In these 11 States, therefore, the actors in a felony murder are not subject to the death penalty without proof of their mental state, proof which was not required with respect to Enmund either under the trial court's instructions or under the law announced by the Florida Supreme Court.

Four additional jurisdictions do not permit a defendant such as Enmund to be put to death. Of these, one State flatly prohibits capital punishment in cases where the defendant did not actually commit murder. Two jurisdictions preclude the death penalty in cases such as this one where the defendant "was a principal in the offense, which was committed by another, but his participation was relatively minor, although not so minor as to constitute a defense to prosecution." One other State limits the death penalty in felony murders to narrow circumstances not involved here.

Nine of the remaining States deal with the imposition of the death penalty for a vicarious felony murder in their capital sentencing statutes. In each of these States, a defendant may not be executed solely for participating in a felony in which a person was killed if the defendant did not actually cause the victim's death. For a defendant to be executed in these States, typically the statutory aggravating circumstances which are present must outweigh mitigating factors. To be sure, a vicarious felony murderer may be sentenced to death in these jurisdictions absent an intent to kill if sufficient aggravating circumstances are present. However, six of these nine States make it a statutory mitigating circumstance that the defendant was an accomplice in a capital felony committed by another person and his participation was relatively minor. By making minimal participation in a capital felony committed by another person a mitigating circumstance, these sentencing statutes reduce the likelihood that a person will be executed for vicarious felony murder. The remaining three jurisdictions exclude felony murder from their lists of aggravating circumstances that will support a death sentence. In each of these nine States, a nontriggerman guilty of felony murder cannot be sentenced to death for the felony murder absent aggravating circumstances above and beyond the felony murder itself.

Thus only a small minority of jurisdictions—eight—allow the death penalty to be imposed solely because the defendant somehow participated in a robbery in the course of which a murder was committed. While the current legislative judgment with respect to imposition of the death penalty where a defendant did not take life, attempt to take it, or intend to take life is neither "wholly unanimous among state legislatures," nor as compelling as the legislative judgments considered in *Coker,* it nevertheless weighs on the side of rejecting capital punishment for the crime at issue. . . .

C

Society's rejection of the death penalty for accomplice liability in felony murders is also indicated by the sentencing decisions that juries have made. As we have previously observed, "[t]he jury . . . is a significant and reliable objective index of contemporary values because it is so directly involved." The evidence is overwhelming that American juries have repudiated imposition of the death penalty for crimes such as petitioner's. First, according to the petitioner, a search of all reported appellate court decisions since 1954 in cases where a defendant was executed for homicide shows that of the 362 executions, in 339 the person executed personally committed a homicidal assault. In 2 cases the person executed had another person commit the homicide for him, and in 16 cases the facts were not reported in sufficient detail to determine whether the person executed committed the homicide. The survey revealed only 6 cases out of 362 where a nontriggerman felony murderer was executed. All six executions took place in 1955. By contrast, there were 72 executions for rape in this country between 1955 and this Court's decision in *Coker v. Georgia* in 1977.

That juries have rejected the death penalty in cases such as this one where the defendant did not commit the homicide, was not present when the killing took place, and did not participate in a plot or scheme to murder is also shown by petitioner's survey of the Nation's death-row population. As of October 1, 1981, there were 796 inmates under sentences of death for homicide. Of the 739 for whom sufficient data are available, only 41 did not participate in the fatal assault on the victim. Of the 40 among the 41 for whom sufficient information was available, only 16 were not physically present when the fatal assault was committed. These 16 prisoners included only 3, including petitioner, who were sentenced to die absent a finding that they hired or solicited someone else to kill the victim or participated in a scheme designed to kill the victim. The figures for Florida are similar. . . .

. . . The fact remains that we are not aware of a single person convicted of felony murder over the past quarter century who did not kill or attempt to kill, and did not intend the death of the victim, who has been executed, and that only three persons in that category are presently sentenced to die. Nor can these figures be discounted by attributing to petitioner the argument that "death is an unconstitutional penalty absent an intent to kill," and observing that the statistics are incomplete with respect to intent. Petitioner's argument is that because he did not kill, attempt to kill, and he did not intend to kill, the death penalty is disproportionate as applied to him, and the statistics he cites are adequately tailored to demonstrate that juries—and perhaps prosecutors as well—consider death a disproportionate penalty for those who fall within his category.

III

Although the judgments of legislatures, juries, and prosecutors weigh heavily in the balance, it is for us ultimately to judge whether the Eighth Amendment permits imposition of the death penalty on one such as Enmund who aids and abets a felony in the course of which a murder is committed by others but who does not himself kill, attempt to kill, or intend that a killing take place or that lethal force will be employed. We have concluded, along with most legislatures and juries, that it does not. . . .

In *Gregg v. Georgia* the opinion announcing the judgment observed that "[t]he death penalty is said to serve two principal social purposes: retribution and deterrence of capital crimes by prospective offenders." Unless the death penalty when applied to those in Enmund's position measurably contributes to one or both of these goals, it "is nothing more than the purposeless and needless imposition of pain and suffering," and hence an unconstitutional punishment. We are quite unconvinced, however, that the threat that the death penalty will be imposed for murder will measurably deter one who does not kill and has no intention or purpose that life will be taken. Instead, it seems likely that "capital punishment can serve as a deterrent only when murder is the result of premeditation and deliberation," for if a person does not intend that life be taken or contemplate that lethal force will be employed by others, the possibility that the death penalty will be imposed for vicarious felony murder will not "enter into the cold calculus that precedes the decision to act." . . .

As for retribution as a justification for executing Enmund, we think this very much depends on the degree of Enmund's culpability—what Enmund's intentions, expectations, and actions were. American criminal law has long considered a defendant's intention—and therefore his moral guilt—to be critical to "the degree of [his] criminal culpability," and the Court has found criminal penalties to be unconstitutionally excessive in the absence of intentional wrongdoing. . . .

For purposes of imposing the death penalty, Enmund's criminal culpability must be limited to his participation in the robbery, and his punishment must be tailored to his personal responsibility and moral guilt. Putting Enmund to death to avenge two killings that he did not commit and had no intention of committing or causing does not measurably contribute to the retributive end of ensuring that the criminal gets his just deserts. This is the judgment of most of the legislatures that have recently addressed the matter, and we have no reason to disagree with that judgment for purposes of construing and applying the Eighth Amendment.

Because the Florida Supreme Court affirmed the death penalty in this case in the absence of proof that Enmund killed or attempted to kill, and regardless of whether Enmund intended or contemplated that life would be taken, we reverse the judgment upholding the death penalty and remand for further proceedings not inconsistent with this opinion.

So ordered.

JUSTICE O'CONNOR, with whom THE CHIEF JUSTICE, JUSTICE POWELL, and JUSTICE REHNQUIST join, dissenting.

Today the Court holds that the Eighth Amendment prohibits a State from executing a convicted felony murderer. I dissent from this holding not only because I believe that it is not supported by the analysis in our previous cases, but also because today's holding interferes with state criteria for assessing legal guilt by recasting intent as a matter of federal constitutional law. . . .

The Eighth Amendment concept of proportionality was first fully expressed in *Weems v. United States* (1910). In that case, defendant Weems was sentenced to 15 years at hard labor for falsifying a public document. After remarking that "it is a precept of justice that punishment for crime should be graduated and proportioned to offense," and after comparing Weems' punishment to the punishments for other crimes, the Court concluded that the sentence was cruel and unusual.

Not until two-thirds of a century later, in *Coker v. Georgia,* did the Court declare another punishment to be unconstitutionally disproportionate to the crime. Writing for himself and three other Members of the Court, JUSTICE WHITE concluded that death is a disproportionate penalty for the crime of raping an adult woman. In reaching this conclusion, the plurality was careful to inform its judgment "by objective factors to the maximum possible extent [by giving attention] to the public attitudes concerning a particular sentence—history and precedent, legislative attitudes, and the response of juries reflected in their sentencing decisions." The plurality's resort to objective factors was no doubt an effort to derive "from the evolving standards of decency that mark the progress of a maturing society" the meaning of the requirement of proportionality contained within the Eighth Amendment.

The plurality noted that within the previous 50 years a majority of the States had never authorized death as a punishment for rape. More significantly to the plurality, only 3 of the 35 States that immediately reinstituted the death penalty following the Court's judgment in *Furman v. Georgia,* (1972) (invalidating nearly all state capital punishment statutes), defined rape as a capital offense. The plurality also considered "the sentencing decisions that juries have made in the course of assessing whether capital punishment is an appropriate penalty for the crime being tried." ("The jury also is a significant and reliable objective index of contemporary values because it is so directly involved.") From the available data, the plurality concluded that in at least 90% of the rape convictions since 1973, juries in Georgia had declined to impose the death penalty.

Thus, the conclusion reached in *Coker* rested in part on the Court's observation that both legislatures and juries firmly rejected the penalty of death for the crime of rape. In addition to ascertaining "contemporary standards," the plurality opinion also considered qualitative factors bearing on the question whether the death penalty was disproportionate, for "the Constitution contemplates that in the end our own judgment will be brought to bear on the question of the acceptability of the death penalty under the Eighth Amendment."

Coker teaches, therefore, that proportionality—at least as regards capital punishment—not only requires an inquiry into contemporary standards as expressed by legislators and jurors, but also involves the notion that the magnitude of the punishment imposed must be related to the degree of the harm inflicted on the victim, as well as to the degree of the defendant's blameworthiness. Moreover, because they turn on considerations unique to each defendant's case, these latter factors underlying the concept of proportionality are reflected in this Court's conclusion in *Lockett v. Ohio,* that "individualized consideration [is] a constitutional requirement in imposing the death sentence."

In sum, in considering the petitioner's challenge, the Court should decide not only whether the petitioner's sentence of death offends contemporary standards as reflected in the responses of legislatures and juries, but also whether it is disproportionate to the harm that the petitioner caused and to the petitioner's involvement in the crime, as well as whether the procedures under which the petitioner was sentenced satisfied the constitutional requirement of individualized consideration set forth in *Lockett.* . . .

B

Following the analysis set forth in *Coker,* the petitioner examines the historical development of the felony-murder rule, as well as contemporary legislation and jury verdicts in capital cases, in an effort to show that imposition of the death penalty on him would violate the Eighth Amendment. This effort fails, however, for the available data do not show that society has rejected conclusively the death penalty for felony murderers. . . .

. . . The Court's curious method of counting the States that authorize imposition of the death penalty for felony murder cannot hide the fact that 23 States permit a sentencer to impose the death penalty even though the felony murderer has neither killed nor intended to kill his victim. While the Court acknowledges that eight state statutes follow the Florida death penalty scheme, it also concedes that 15 other statutes permit imposition of the death penalty where the defendant neither intended to kill or actually killed the victims. Not all of the statutes list the same aggravating circumstances. Nevertheless, the question before the Court is not whether a particular species of death penalty statute is unconstitutional, but whether a scheme that permits imposition of the death penalty, absent a finding that the defendant either killed or intended to kill the victims, is unconstitutional. In short, the Court's peculiar statutory analysis cannot withstand closer scrutiny.

Thus, in nearly half of the States, and in two-thirds of the States that permit the death penalty for murder, a defendant who neither killed the victim nor specifically intended that the victim die may be sentenced to death for his participation in the robbery-murder. Far from "weigh[ing] very heavily on the side of rejecting capital punishment as a suitable penalty for" felony murder, these legislative judgments indicate that our "evolving standards of decency" still embrace capital punishment for this crime. For this reason, I conclude that the petitioner has failed to meet the standards in *Coker* and *Woodson* that the "two crucial indicators of evolving standards of decency . . . —jury determinations and legislative enactments—both point conclusively to the repudiation" of capital punishment for felony murder. In short, the death penalty for felony murder does not fall short of our national "standards of decency."

Source: Enmund v. Florida, 458 U.S. 782 (1982), at 788–831.

Document 4.7
The Case of *Coleman v. Balkcom* Yields Lively Debate on the Supreme Court Regarding Death Penalty Appeals, April 27, 1981

In Coleman v. Balkcom *(1981), the Supreme Court declined to review a denial of habeas corpus by the Georgia courts in the case of a death row inmate who claimed that a state statute had prevented him from calling certain witnesses who could testify regarding pre-trial publicity that had prejudiced his case. Justices William Brennan and Thurgood Marshall dissented from this denial of certiorari (discretionary review) on the grounds that the petition raised important constitutional questions in a capital case. Justice William Rehnquist also filed a dissent urging the Court to hear the case, but his argument focused on what he regarded as intolerable delays in death penalty cases and he blamed the Court for frustrating the effective restoration of capital punishment in America. Justice John Paul Stevens endorsed the Court's denial of review, but wrote a strong criticism of Rehnquist's proposal to hear more capital cases, which he interpreted as an effort to speed up executions.*

The petition for a writ of certiorari is denied.

JUSTICE STEVENS, concurring.

The Court's management of its discretionary docket is a subject that merits reexamination from time to time in the light of changes that affect the business of the federal judiciary. Opinions dissenting from the denial of certiorari sometimes create the impression that we review fewer cases than we should; I hold the opposite view. Today JUSTICE REHNQUIST advances the proposition, as I understand his dissenting opinion, that we should promptly grant certiorari and decide the merits of every capital case coming from the state courts in order to expedite the administration of the death penalty.

In my judgment, the Court wisely rejects this proposal. In the last 10 months, over 90 certiorari petitions have been filed in capital cases. If we were to hear even a substantial percentage of these cases on the merits, they would consume over half of this Court's argument calendar. Although the interest in protecting the constitutional rights of persons sentenced to death is properly characterized as a federal interest, the interest in imposing the death sentence is essentially a state interest. Because the persons on death row are concentrated in only a few States, because some States have no capital punishment at all, and because the range of capital offenses differs in different States, it is quite clear that all States do not share the same interest in accelerating the execution rate. This Court's primary function is to adjudicate federal questions. To make the primary mission of this Court the vindication of certain States' interests in carrying out the death penalty would be an improper allocation of the Court's limited resources.

Moreover, one may also question whether JUSTICE REHNQUIST's proposal would accomplish its intended purpose. As I understand his proposal, it would preclude the federal district courts from granting writs of habeas corpus in any capital cases on any ground that had been presented to and rejected by this Court. Because this Court is not equipped to process all of these cases as expeditiously as the several district courts, it is most unlikely that this innovative proposal would dramatically accelerate the execution of the persons on death row.

One of the causes of delay in the conclusion of litigation in capital cases has been the fact that the enactment of new state legislation after this Court's decision in *Furman v. Georgia* generated a number of novel constitutional questions. Although those questions have not been difficult for three Members of the

Court, other Justices have found a number of these questions sufficiently important and difficult to justify the delays associated with review in this Court. The principal delay—a matter of four years—was the period between the entry of the stays in the *Furman* litigation in 1972, and the decisions in July, 1976, in *Gregg v. Georgia, Proffitt v. Florida,* and *Jurek v. Texas,* 428 U.S. 262, in which the constitutionality of the death penalty was ultimately sustained. Following that basic holding, the Court has also decided several other cases presenting substantial constitutional issues relating to capital punishment statutes; presumably those issues will no longer detain the state or federal courts in their consideration of cases in which the death penalty has been imposed. One therefore should not assume that the delays of the past few years will necessarily be reflected in the future if the various state authorities act with all possible diligence. The deterrent value of any punishment is, of course, related to the promptness with which it is inflicted. In capital cases, however, the punishment is inflicted in two stages. Imprisonment follows immediately after conviction; but the execution normally does not take place until after the conclusion of post-trial proceedings in the trial court, direct and collateral review in the state judicial system, collateral review in the federal judicial system, and clemency review by the executive department of the State. However critical one may be of these protracted post-trial procedures, it seems inevitable that there must be a significant period of incarceration on death row during the interval between sentencing and execution. If the death sentence is ultimately set aside or its execution delayed for a prolonged period, the imprisonment during that period is nevertheless a significant form of punishment. Indeed, the deterrent value of incarceration during that period of uncertainty may well be comparable to the consequences of the ultimate step itself. In all events, what is at stake in this procedural debate is the length of that period of incarceration, rather than the question whether the offender shall be severely punished.

How promptly a diligent prosecutor can complete all of the proceedings necessary to carry out a death sentence is still uncertain. Much of the delay associated with past litigation should not reoccur in cases that merely raise issues that have now been resolved. As is true of all other types of litigation as well, however, inevitably new issues arise that will be sufficiently important and difficult to require deliberation before they are fully resolved. This Court should endeavor to conclude capital cases—like all other litigation—as promptly as possible. We must, however, also be as sure as possible that novel procedural shortcuts have not permitted error of a constitutional magnitude to occur. For, after all, death cases are indeed different in kind from all other litigation. The penalty, once imposed, is irrevocable. In balance, therefore, I think the Court wisely declines to select this group of cases in which to experiment with accelerated procedures. Accordingly, I concur in the order denying certiorari.

JUSTICE MARSHALL, with whom JUSTICE BRENNAN joins, dissenting.

Petitioner was convicted of first-degree murder and sentenced to death. After exhausting his direct appeals, petitioner filed this action in the Superior Court of Tattnall County, Ga., seeking a writ of habeas corpus. One of petitioner's claims was that prejudicial publicity had created an atmosphere in which a fair trial was impossible. Petitioner's counsel asserted in an affidavit that the jurors in his original trial, if called as witnesses, would "testify as to the widespread discussion of the [offense] in Seminole County . . . and to the fact that they, as jurors, were affected in their statutory decision-making process by the adverse pre-trial publicity." The affidavit further alleged that the county jury commissioners, members of the jury panels, and numerous reporters and expert witnesses would offer testimony to similar effect. In order to prove these allegations, petitioner sought compulsory process to require the witnesses to testify.

At that point, petitioner's efforts were thwarted by Ga.Code § 38–801(e) (1978). Although that statute has since been amended, at the time of petitioner's habeas hearing, it provided that subpoenas in habeas cases could be served only in the county in which the hearing was held or within 150 miles of that county. None of the witnesses petitioner wished to summon lived so close. As one would expect, most of them lived in or near Seminole County, where the offense was committed. Petitioner was further constrained by the provisions of Ga.Code § 50–127 (1978) to file his habeas petition in the county where he was incarcerated. In sum, only the State's procedural requirement threatened to prevent petitioner from calling the witnesses who he alleged would testify in support of his claim. Consequently, petitioner asked the trial court to declare § 38–801(e) unconstitutional and to permit him to perfect service anywhere in the State. The trial court sustained the statute and denied the petition for habeas corpus on the merits. The Georgia Supreme Court declined to grant leave to appeal. Because the availability of compulsory process to an individual challenging his death penalty raises important questions under the Due Process Clause, I would grant the petition for certiorari.

A habeas corpus proceeding is, of course, civil, rather than criminal, in nature, and consequently the ordinary Sixth Amendment guarantee of compulsory process, which is made applicable to the States by the Fourteenth Amendment, does not apply. Nevertheless, when the death penalty is in issue, the Constitution may impose unusual limitations on the States. As we emphasized just last Term "there is a significant constitutional difference between the death penalty and lesser punishments." If an individual is imprisoned for an offense he did not commit, the error can to some extent be rectified. But if he is executed, the wrong that has been done can never be corrected. That is just one reason that I, of course, adhere to my view that the State may never put an individual to death without imposing a cruel and unusual punishment prohibited by the Eighth and

Fourteenth Amendments. Yet surely those among my Brethren who believe that there are circumstances in which the State may legitimately impose this ultimate sanction would not want to see an innocent individual put to death. Certainly no Member of this Court would countenance a conviction obtained in violation of the Constitution. Because of the unique finality of the death penalty, its imposition must be the result of careful procedures and must survive close scrutiny on post-trial review. I do not believe that this rigorous scrutiny is possible when, as here, procedural rules ultimately abandoned by the State are all that stand between the convicted individual and the chance to prove his claims.

Petitioner offered to call as witnesses the jurors, who, he alleged, would testify not merely to the atmosphere surrounding the trial, but to the actual effect of that atmosphere on their deliberations. The only obstacle to calling those witnesses was the State's failure to provide him with a means of serving compulsory process. In order to agree with petitioner that this failure amounts to a violation of the Due Process Clause, it would not be necessary to hold that compulsory process is constitutionally required in any other civil, or indeed, in any other habeas proceeding. It would instead be sufficient to recognize the unique character of the death penalty and of the restraints required by the Constitution before the State may impose it. Granting the assistance of compulsory process to an individual under sentence of death but ready and willing to demonstrate the unconstitutionality of the manner of his conviction might well be among those restraints. Accordingly, I would grant the petition for certiorari to consider that question.

JUSTICE REHNQUIST, dissenting.

Ordinarily I would have no hesitation joining the majority of my colleagues in denying the petition for certiorari in this case. The questions presented in the petition are of importance only to petitioner himself, and therefore are not suitable candidates for the exercise of our discretionary jurisdiction. But, in a larger sense, the case raises significant issues about the administration of capital punishment statutes in this country, and reflects the increasing tendency to postpone or delay the enforcement of those constitutionally valid statutes. Because I think stronger measures are called for than the mere denial of certiorari in a case such as this, I would grant the petition for certiorari so that the case can be fully briefed and argued.

A mere recital of the facts of this case illustrates the delay to which I have referred. Petitioner was convicted by a jury in 1973 of murdering six members of a family, after raping and torturing some members of that family. He was sentenced to death under Georgia's capital punishment statute, a statute expressly held constitutional in *Gregg v. Georgia* (1976). The sentence was affirmed by the Supreme Court of Georgia, and this Court denied the first petition for certiorari. Petitioner subsequently sought state collateral relief, which was denied by the state habeas court. The Georgia Supreme Court then denied his application for a writ of probable cause to appeal. Petitioner has now filed his second petition for certiorari in this Court. Because petitioner has had a full opportunity to have his claims considered on direct review by both the Supreme Court of Georgia and this Court and on collateral review by the state courts of Georgia, and because the issues presented are not substantial, it is not surprising that the majority of the Court votes to deny the petition for certiorari.

I dissent not because I believe that petitioner has made any showing in the Georgia courts that he was deprived of any rights secured to him by the United States Constitution, but rather because our mere denial of certiorari will not in all likelihood end the already protracted litigation in this case. If petitioner follows the path of many of his predecessors, he will now turn to a single-judge federal habeas court, alleging anew some or all of the reasons which he urges here for granting the petition for certiorari. If he fails to impress the particular United States District Court in which his habeas petition is filed, he may upon the issuance of a certificate of probable cause appeal to a United States Court of Appeals. And throughout this exhaustive appeal process, any single judge having jurisdiction over the case may of course stay the execution of the penalty pending further review. Given so many bites at the apple, the odds favor petitioner finding some court willing to vacate his death sentence because in its view his trial or sentence was not free from constitutional error.

It seems to me that we have thus reached a stalemate in the administration of federal constitutional law. Although this Court has determined that capital punishment statutes do not violate the Constitution, and although 30-odd States have enacted such statutes, apparently in the belief that they constitute sound social policy, the existence of the death penalty in this country is virtually an illusion. Since 1976, hundreds of juries have sentenced hundreds of persons to death, presumably in the belief that the death penalty in those circumstances is warranted, yet virtually nothing happens except endlessly drawn out legal proceedings such as those adverted to above. Of the hundreds of prisoners condemned to die who languish on the various "death rows," few of them appear to face any imminent prospect of their sentence being executed. Indeed, in the five years since *Gregg v. Georgia,* there has been only one execution of a defendant who has persisted in his attack upon his sentence. My in-chambers opinion in that case describes some of the many avenues of relief which can be pursued by one sentenced to death.

I do not think that this Court can continue to evade some responsibility for this mockery of our criminal justice system. Perhaps out of a desire to avoid even the possibility of a "Bloody Assizes," this Court and the lower federal courts have converted the constitutional limits upon imposition of the death penalty by the States and the Federal Government into arcane niceties which parallel the equity court practices described in Charles Dickens' "Bleak House." Even though we have upheld the constitutionality of capital punishment statutes, I fear that by our recent actions we have mistakenly sent a signal to the lower state and federal courts that the actual imposition of the death sentence is to be avoided at all costs.

That surely was not the intent of the opinion of JUSTICES STEWART, POWELL, and STEVENS in *Gregg v. Georgia*. That opinion recognized that capital punishment is said to serve two principal social purposes—retribution and the deterrence of capital crimes by prospective offenders. It went on to explain:

"The value of capital punishment as a deterrent of crime is a complex factual issue the resolution of which properly rests with the legislatures, which can evaluate the results of statistical studies in terms of their own local conditions and with a flexibility of approach that is not available to the courts. . . ."

"In sum, we cannot say that the judgment of the Georgia Legislature that capital punishment may be necessary in some cases is clearly wrong. Considerations of federalism, as well as respect for the ability of a legislature to evaluate, in terms of its particular State, the moral consensus concerning the death penalty and its social utility as a sanction, require us to conclude, in the absence of more convincing evidence, that the infliction of death as a punishment for murder is not without justification and thus is not unconstitutionally severe."

What troubles me is that this Court, by constantly tinkering with the principles laid down in the five death penalty cases decided in 1976, together with the natural reluctance of state and federal habeas judges to rule against an inmate on death row, has made it virtually impossible for States to enforce with reasonable promptness their constitutionally valid capital punishment statutes. When society promises to punish by death certain criminal conduct, and then the courts fail to do so, the courts not only lessen the deterrent effect of the threat of capital punishment, they undermine the integrity of the entire criminal justice system. To be sure, the importance of procedural protections to an accused should not be minimized, particularly in light of the irreversibility of the death sentence. But it seems to me that when this Court surrounds capital defendants with numerous procedural protections unheard of for other crimes and then pristinely denies a petition for certiorari in a case such as this, it in effect all but prevents the States from imposing a death sentence on a defendant who has been fairly tried by a jury of peers. As Justice Jackson stated in *Stein v. New York*, "The petitioners have had fair trial and fair review. The people of the State are also entitled to due process of law."

The other principal purpose of capital punishment is retribution. The testimony of Lord Justice Denning, then Master of the Rolls of the Court of Appeal in England, before the Royal Commission on Capital Punishment answers those who insist that respect for the "sanctity of life" compels the end of the death sentence for any crime, no matter how heinous. He explained:

"Punishment is the way in which society expresses its denunciation of wrongdoing, and, in order to maintain respect for law, it is essential that the punishment inflicted for grave crimes should adequately reflect the revulsion felt by the great majority of citizens for them. It is a mistake to consider the objects of punishment as being deterrent or reformative or preventive and nothing else. . . . The truth is that some crimes are so outrageous that society insists on adequate punishment, because the wrongdoer deserves it, irrespective of whether it is a deterrent or not."

There can be little doubt that delay in the enforcement of capital punishment frustrates the purpose of retribution. As the opinion in *Gregg* stated, "[W]hen people begin to believe that organized society is unwilling or unable to impose upon criminal offenders the punishment they *'deserve' then there are sown the seeds of anarchy-of self-help, vigilante justice, and lynch law."* San Francisco experienced vigilante justice during the Gold Rush in the middle part of the last century; the mining towns of Montana experienced it a short time later; and it is still with us as a result of the series of unsolved slayings of Negro children in Atlanta.

In thinking about capital punishment, it is important to remember that the preservation of some degree of liberty for all demands that government restrain the few who kill law-abiding members of the community. As Judge Learned Hand long ago recognized:

"And what is this liberty which must lie in the hearts of men and women? It is not the ruthless, the unbridled will; it is not freedom to do as one likes. That is the denial of liberty, and leads straight to its overthrow. A society in which men recognize no check upon their freedom soon becomes a society where freedom is the possession of only a savage few; as we have learned to our sorrow."

James Madison made the same point in this now famous passage from Federalist Paper No. 51:

"But what is government itself but the greatest of all reflections on human nature? If men were angels, no government would be necessary. If angels were to govern men, neither external nor internal controls on government would be necessary. In framing a government which is to be administered by men over men, the great difficulty lies in this: *you must first enable the government to control the governed,* and in the next place oblige it to control itself."

I believe we have in our judicial decisions focused so much on controlling the government that we have lost sight of the equally important objective of enabling the government to control the governed. When our systems of administering criminal justice cannot provide security to our people in the streets or in their homes, we are rapidly approaching the state of savagery which Learned Hand describes. In Atlanta, we cannot protect our small children at play. In the Nation's Capital, law enforcement authorities cannot protect the lives of employees of this very Court who live four blocks from the building in which we sit and deliberate the constitutionality of capital punishment. In light of the foregoing, I do not believe it is a responsible exercise of our certiorari jurisdiction to blithely deny petitions for certiorari in cases where petitioners have been sentenced to death and present for review claims which seem on their face to have little merit, and which have been extensively considered by state and federal courts on both direct and collateral review. The 5-year history of death sentences, as opposed to execution of those sentences, is a matter with respect to which no Member of this Court can be unaware. If capital punishment is indeed constitutional when imposed for the taking of the life of another human being, we cannot responsibly discharge our duty by pristinely denying a petition such as this, realizing full well that our action will simply further protect the litigation.

Accordingly, I believe that the petition should be granted in order that this Court may deal with all of petitioner's claims on their merits. If, after full briefing and argument, the Court decides to affirm, the provisions of 28 U.S.C. § 2244(c) would come into operation. That section provides in pertinent part:

> "In a habeas corpus proceeding brought in behalf of a person in custody pursuant to the judgment of a State court, a prior judgment of the Supreme Court of the United States on an appeal or review by a writ of certiorari at the instance of the prisoner of the decision of such State court shall be conclusive as to all issues of fact or law with respect to an asserted denial of a Federal right which constitutes ground for discharge in a habeas corpus proceeding, actually adjudicated by the Supreme Court therein. . . ."

Thus, the jurisdiction of the federal courts over petitioner's sentence of death would be at an end, and unless the appropriate state officials commuted petitioner's sentence, it would presumably be carried out. In any event, the decision would then be in the hands of the State which had initially imposed the death penalty, not in the hands of the federal courts.

Source: Coleman v. Balkcom, 451 U.S. 949 (1981), at 950–964.

Document 4.8
The Justices Reverse California Supreme Court on Eighth Amendment, July 6, 1983

The so-called Briggs initiative in California revised the state's capital sentencing rules to require judges to inform juries that a sentence of life imprisonment without parole could be commuted by the governor to life with parole, although it did not require judges to also inform juries of the governor's even broader power to commute a death sentence. The California supreme court, following the example of twenty-five other state courts, struck down the Briggs instruction as a violation of the Eighth Amendment. The Burger Court granted review to the California attorney general and reversed the California supreme court on the constitutional issue in an opinion written by Justice Sandra Day O'Connor in California v. Ramos. *The Court found the instruction consistent with prior decisions that encouraged juries to hear a wide range of evidence. Citing other precedents, Justices William Brennan, Thurgood Marshall, and Harry Blackmun argued in dissent that the Briggs instruction tipped the scales unfairly on the side of death. Justice John Paul Stevens's dissent criticized the Court for granting review to the state's attorney general, which he saw as another attempt to hasten executions in California and elsewhere.*

JUSTICE O'CONNOR delivered the opinion of the Court.

This case requires us to consider the constitutionality under the Eighth and Fourteenth Amendments of instructing a capital sentencing jury regarding the Governor's power to commute a sentence of life without possibility of parole. Finding no constitutional defect in the instruction, we reverse the decision of the Supreme Court of California and remand for further proceedings.

I

On the night of June 2, 1979, respondent Marcelino Ramos participated in the robbery of a fast-food restaurant where he was employed as a janitor. As respondent's codefendant placed a food order, respondent entered the restaurant, went behind the front counter into the work area, ostensibly for the purpose of checking his work schedule, and emerged with a gun. Respondent directed the two employees working that night into the restaurant's walk-in refrigerator and ordered them to face the back wall. Respondent entered and emerged from the refrigerator several times, inquiring at one point about the keys to the restaurant safe. When he entered for the last time, he instructed the two employees to kneel on the floor of the refrigerator, to remove their hats, and to pray. Respondent struck both on the head and then shot them, wounding one and killing the other.

Respondent was charged with robbery, attempted murder, and first-degree murder. Defense counsel presented no evidence at the guilt phase of respondent's trial, and the jury returned a verdict of guilt on all counts. Under California law, first-degree murder is punishable by death or life imprisonment without the possibility of parole where an alleged "special circumstance" is found true by the jury at the guilt phase. At the separate penalty phase, respondent presented extensive evidence in an attempt to mitigate punishment. In addition to requiring jury instructions on aggravating and mitigating circumstances, California law requires that the trial judge inform the jury that a sentence of life imprisonment without the possibility of parole may be commuted by the Governor to a sentence that includes the possibility of parole. At the penalty phase of respondent's trial, the judge delivered the following instruction:

"You are instructed that, under the State Constitution, a Governor is empowered to grant a reprieve, pardon, or commutation of a sentence following conviction of a crime. Under this power, a Governor may in the future commute or modify a sentence of life imprisonment without possibility of parole to a lesser sentence that would include the possibility of parole."

The jury returned a verdict of death.

On appeal, the Supreme Court of California affirmed respondent's conviction, but reversed the death sentence, concluding that the Briggs Instruction required by Cal. Penal Code Ann. § 190.3 violated the Federal Constitution. The court found two constitutional flaws in the instruction. First, it invites the jury to consider factors that are foreign to its task of deciding whether the defendant should live or die. According to the State Supreme Court, instead of assuring that this decision rests on "consideration of the character and record of the individual offender and the circumstances of the particular offense," the instruction focuses the jury's attention on the Governor's power to render the defendant eligible for parole if the jury does not vote to execute him, and injects an entirely speculative element into the capital sentencing determination. Second, the court concluded that, because the instruction does not also inform the jury that the Governor possesses the power to commute a death sentence, it leaves the jury with the mistaken belief that the only way to keep the defendant off the streets is to condemn him to death. Accordingly, the court remanded for a new penalty phase.

We granted certiorari, and now reverse and remand.

II

In challenging the constitutionality of the Briggs Instruction, respondent presses upon us the two central arguments advanced by the Supreme Court of California in its decision. He contends (1) that a capital sentencing jury may not constitutionally consider possible commutation, and (2) that the Briggs Instruction unconstitutionally misleads the jury by selectively informing it of the Governor's power to commute one of its sentencing choices but not the other. Respondent's first argument raises two related but distinct concerns—*viz.*, that the power of commutation is so speculative a factor that it injects an unacceptable level of unreliability into the capital sentencing determination, and that consideration of this factor deflects the jury from its constitutionally mandated task of basing the penalty decision on the character of the defendant and the nature of the offense. We address these points and respondent's second argument. . . .

B

Addressing respondent's specific arguments, we find unpersuasive the suggestion that the possible commutation of a life sentence must be held constitutionally irrelevant to the sentencing decision and that it is too speculative an element for the jury's consideration. On this point, we find *Jurek v. Texas,* controlling.

The Texas capital sentencing system upheld in *Jurek* limits capital homicides to intentional and knowing murders committed in five situations. The jury finds the defendant guilty of one of these five categories of murder, the jury must answer three statutory questions. If the jury concludes that the State has proved beyond a reasonable doubt that each question is answered in the affirmative, then the death sentence is imposed. In approving this statutory scheme, the joint opinion in *Jurek* rejected the contention that the second statutory question—requiring consideration of the defendant's future dangerousness—was unconstitutionally vague because it involved prediction of human behavior. . . .

By bringing to the jury's attention the possibility that the defendant may be returned to society, the Briggs Instruction invites the jury to assess whether the defendant is someone whose probable future behavior makes it undesirable that he be permitted to return to society. Like the challenged factor in Texas' statutory scheme, then, the Briggs Instruction focuses the jury on the defendant's probable future dangerousness. The approval in *Jurek* of explicit consideration of this factor in the capital sentencing decision defeats respondent's contention that, because of the speculativeness involved, the State of California may not constitutionally permit consideration of commutation.

. . . The Briggs Instruction gives the jury accurate information of which both the defendant and his counsel are aware, and it does not preclude the defendant from offering any evidence or argument regarding the Governor's power to commute a life sentence.

C

Closely related to, yet distinct from, respondent's speculativeness argument is the contention that the Briggs Instruction is constitutionally infirm because it deflects the jury's focus from its central task. Respondent argues that the commutation instruction diverts the jury from undertaking the kind of individualized sentencing determination that, under *Woodson v. North Carolina,* is "a constitutionally indispensable part of the process of inflicting the penalty of death."

As we have already noted as a functional matter, the Briggs Instruction focuses the jury's attention on whether this particular defendant is one whose possible return to society is desirable. In this sense, then, the jury's deliberation is individualized. The instruction invites the jury to predict not so much what some future Governor might do, but more what the defendant himself might do if released into society.

Any contention that injecting this factor into the jury's deliberations constitutes a departure from the kind of individualized focus required in capital sentencing decisions was implicitly rejected by the decision in *Jurek.* . . .

Finally, we emphasize that informing the jury of the Governor's power to commute a sentence of life without possibility of parole was merely an accurate statement of a potential sentencing alternative. To describe the sentence as "life imprisonment *without possibility* of parole" is simply inaccurate when, under state law, the Governor possesses authority to commute that sentence to a lesser sentence that includes the possibility of parole. The Briggs Instruction thus corrects a misconception and supplies the jury with accurate information for its deliberation in selecting an appropriate sentence. . . .

C

Having concluded that a capital sentencing jury's consideration of the Governor's power to commute a life sentence is not prohibited by the Federal Constitution, we now address respondent's contention that the Briggs Instruction must be held unconstitutional because it fails to inform jurors also that a death sentence may be commuted. In essence, respondent complains that the Briggs Instruction creates the misleading impression that the jury can prevent the defendant's return to society only by imposing the death sentence, thus biasing the jury in favor of death.

Thus, according to respondent, if the Federal Constitution permits the jury to consider possible commutation of a life sentence, the Federal Constitution requires that the jury also be instructed that a death sentence may be commuted. We find respondent's argument puzzling. If, as we must assume, respondent's principal objection is that the impact of the Briggs Instruction is to skew the jury toward imposing death, we fail to see how an instruction on the Governor's power to commute death sentences as well as life sentences restores the situation to one of "neutrality." Although such an instruction would be "neutral" in the sense of giving the jury complete and factually accurate information about the commutation power, it would not "balance" the impact of the Briggs Instruction, even assuming, *arguendo,* that the current instruction has any impermissible skewing effect. Disclosure of the complete nature of the commutation power would not eliminate any skewing in favor of death or increase the reliability of the sentencing choice. A jury concerned about preventing the defendant's potential return to society will not be any less inclined to vote for the death penalty upon learning that even a death sentence may not have such an effect. In fact, advising jurors that a death verdict is theoretically modifiable, and thus not "final," may incline them to approach their sentencing decision with less appreciation for the gravity of their choice and for the moral responsibility reposed in them as sentencers.

In short, an instruction disclosing the Governor's power to commute a death sentence may operate to the defendant's distinct disadvantage. It is precisely this perception that the defendant is prejudiced by an instruction on the possible commutation of a death sentence that led the California Supreme Court to prohibit the giving of such an instruction. Thus, state law at the time of respondent Ramos' trial precluded the giving of the "other half " of the commutation instruction that respondent now argues is constitutionally required.

Moreover, we are not convinced by respondent's argument that the Briggs Instruction alone impermissibly impels the jury toward voting for the death sentence. Any aggravating factor presented by the prosecution has this impact. . . .

IV

In sum, the Briggs Instruction does not violate any of the substantive limitations this Court's precedents have imposed on the capital sentencing process. It does not preclude individualized sentencing determinations or consideration of mitigating factors, nor does it impermissibly inject an element too speculative for the jury's deliberation. Finally, its failure to inform the jury also of the Governor's power to commute a death sentence does not render it constitutionally infirm. Therefore, we defer to the State's identification of the Governor's power to commute a life sentence as a substantive factor to be presented for the sentencing jury's consideration. . . .

The judgment of the Supreme Court of California is reversed, and the case is remanded for further proceedings not inconsistent with this opinion.

It is so ordered.

JUSTICE MARSHALL, with whom JUSTICE BRENNAN joins, and with whom JUSTICE BLACKMUN joins as to Parts II, III, IV, and V, dissenting.

Even if I accepted the prevailing view that the death penalty may constitutionally be imposed under certain circumstances, I could not agree that a State may tip the balance in favor of death by informing the jury that the defendant may eventually be released if he is not executed. In my view, the Briggs Instruction is unconstitutional for three reasons. It is misleading. It invites speculation and guesswork. And it injects into the capital sentencing process a factor that bears no relation to the nature of the offense or the character of the offender.

I

I continue to adhere to my view that the death penalty is in all circumstances cruel and unusual punishment forbidden by the Eighth and Fourteenth Amendments. I would vacate the death sentence on this basis alone. However, even if I could accept the prevailing view that the death penalty may constitutionally be imposed under certain circumstances, I would vacate the death sentence in this case.

II

Apart from the permissibility of ever instructing a jury to consider the possibility of commutation, the Briggs Instruction is unconstitutional because it misleads the jury about the scope of the Governor's clemency power. By upholding that instruction, the majority authorizes "state-sanctioned fraud and deceit in the most serious of all state actions: the taking of a human life."

The Briggs Instruction may well mislead the jury into believing that it can eliminate any possibility of commutation by imposing the death sentence. It indicates that the Governor can commute a life sentence without possibility of parole, but not that the Governor can also commute a death sentence. The instruction thus erroneously suggests to the jury that a death sentence will assure the defendant's permanent removal from society, whereas the alternative sentence will not.

Presented with this choice, a jury may impose the death sentence to prevent the Governor from exercising his power to commute a life sentence without possibility of parole. Yet such a sentencing decision would be based on a grotesque mistake, for the Governor also has the power to commute a death sentence. The possibility of this mistake is deliberately injected into the sentencing process by the Briggs Instruction. In my view, the Constitution simply does not permit a State to "stac[k] the deck" against a capital defendant in this manner. . . .

JUSTICE STEVENS, dissenting.

No rule of law required the Court to hear this case. We granted certiorari only because at least four Members of the Court determined—as a matter of discretion—that review of the constitutionality of the so-called Briggs Instruction would represent a wise use of the Court's scarce resources.

When certiorari was granted in this case, the Court had been informed by the respondent that the Briggs Instruction is unique: "Only California requires that juries be instructed selectively on the Governor's power to commute life without parole sentences." Further, the Court had been informed, accurately, that the overwhelming number of jurisdictions condemn any comment whatsoever in a capital case on the Governor's power to commute. That statement was followed by a half-page list of citations to state court decisions. These facts shed an illuminating light on the Court's perception of how its discretion should be exercised.

Even if one were to agree with the Court's conclusion that the instruction does not violate the defendant's procedural rights, it would nevertheless be fair to ask what harm would have been done to the administration of justice by state courts if the California court had been left undisturbed in its determination. It is clear that omission of the instruction could not conceivably prejudice the prosecutor's legitimate interests. Surely if the character of an offense and the character of the offender are such that death is the proper penalty, the omission of a comment on the Governor's power to commute a life sentence would not preclude the jury from returning the proper verdict. If it were true that this instruction may make the difference between life and death in a case in which the scales are otherwise evenly balanced, that is a reason why the instruction should not be given—not a reason for giving it. For the existence of the rarely exercised power of commutation has absolutely nothing to do with the defendant's culpability or his capacity for rehabilitation. The Governor's power to commute is entirely different from any relevant aggravating circumstance that may legitimately impel the jury toward voting for the death penalty. The Briggs Instruction has no greater justification than an instruction to the jury that, if the scales are evenly balanced, you should remember that more murders have been committed by people whose names begin with the initial "S" than with any other letter.

No matter how trivial the impact of the instruction may be, it is fundamentally wrong for the presiding judge at the trial—who should personify the evenhanded administration of justice—to tell the jury, indirectly to be sure, that doubt concerning the proper penalty should be resolved in favor of the most certain method of preventing the defendant from ever walking the streets again.

The Court concludes its opinion by solemnly noting that we "sit as judges, not as legislators, and the wisdom of the decision to permit juror consideration of possible commutation is best left to the States." Why, I ask with all due respect, did not the Justices who voted to grant certiorari in this case allow the wisdom of state judges to prevail in California, especially when they have taken a position consistent with those of state judges in Alabama, Arkansas, Colorado, Delaware, Florida, Georgia, Illinois, Kentucky, Louisiana, Maryland, Missouri, Nebraska, Nevada, New Jersey, North Carolina, Oklahoma, Oregon, Pennsylvania, South Carolina, Tennessee, Texas, Virginia, Washington, West Virginia, and Wyoming?

I repeat, no rule of law commanded the Court to grant certiorari. No other State would have been required to follow the California precedent if it had been permitted to stand. Nothing more than an interest in facilitating the imposition of the death penalty in California justified this Court's exercise of its discretion to review the judgment of the California Supreme Court. That interest, in my opinion, is not sufficient to warrant this Court's review of the validity of a jury instruction when the wisdom of giving that instruction is plainly a matter that is best left to the States.

. . . I disagree with the Court's decision on the merits. But even if the Court were correct on the merits, I would still firmly disagree with its decision to grant certiorari. I therefore respectfully dissent.

Source: California v. Ramos, 463 U.S. 992 (1983), at 997–1014, 1016–1029, 1030–1031.

Document 4.9
The Supreme Court Reprimands Ninth Circuit on the Execution of Robert Harris, April 21, 1992

Expressing its displeasure with the continued intervention by judges on the Ninth Circuit Court of Appeals who delayed the pending execution of Robert Alton Harris in California, the Supreme Court finally brought an end to all future stays with this most unusual order. Justices Harry Blackmun and John Paul Stevens dissented and would have allowed the existing stay to remain in effect.

Application to vacate the stay of execution of sentence of death, presented to Justice O'Connor, and by her referred to the Court, granted, and it is ordered that the order staying the execution entered by the United States Court of Appeals for the Ninth Circuit of April 21, 1992, is vacated. No further stays of Robert Alton Harris's execution shall be entered by the federal courts except upon order of this Court. Justice Blackmun and Justice Stevens would deny the application.

Source: Vasquez v. Harris, 503 U.S. 1000 (1992).

Document 4.10
California Executes Robert Alton Harris after Long Legal Battle, April 22, 1992

Robert Alton Harris died in California's gas chamber on April 21, 1992, after a long legal battle between lower federal courts and the Supreme Court of the United States. Harriet Chiang and William Carlsen filed this report for the San Francisco Chronicle.

Robert Alton Harris became the first person executed in California in 25 years yesterday after a grueling night of legal moves that are expected to clear the way for numerous executions in the years to come.

Only minutes after he was pronounced dead at 6:21 a.m., the word was flashed throughout the world. The execution in California, a trend-setter in a nation where executions have largely been confined to the South, was widely condemned in the international press.

"Double killer Robert Alton Harris went to his death in California's gas chamber yesterday in a grotesque ritual that shamed and sickened America," said London's Daily Express.

In the Bay Area, hundreds of protesters called for an end to the death penalty, the American Civil Liberties Union was mourning what it described as a tragic death, and prosecutors across the state were hopeful that it would be easier now to carry out the death penalty.

Charles Weisselberg, who teaches criminal law at the University of Southern California's Law Center, said that Harris' execution was an "emotional and legal milestone."

Harris' execution "is the beginning of a time when we're going to execute dozens of inmates over the next five years," he predicted.

Yesterday's execution came after a night of frantic legal maneuvering involving the U.S. Court of Appeals, the Harris defense team, the state attorney general and the U.S. Supreme Court. Four times, the appellate court ordered a stay of the execution—and each time, the high court put the execution back on track.

At one point Monday evening, Harris' lawyers asked the California Supreme Court to block the execution and review the lawyers' claim that execution by means of lethal injection is cruel and unusual punishment.

But the court, which had ruled against Harris six times in the past 13 years, turned him down for the last time. The order was signed by Chief Justice Malcolm Lucas, with a lone dissent by Justice Stanley Mosk, the court's only liberal.

While the courts were juggling Harris' fate, protesters outside San Quentin were singing, chanting and unleashing boisterous cheers over each stay. Harris waited in his cell for word on whether he would live or die.

Had Harris not been executed before midnight yesterday, his death warrant would have expired, forcing state officials to wait at least 40 days before another warrant could have been carried out.

The final stay came at 3:49 a.m., with Harris strapped to the gas chamber chair. He waited for 10 minutes after a federal judge issued a last-minute stay. He seemed perplexed and at one point said, "Let's pull it," referring to the lever that releases the cyanide.

Finally, Harris was taken out of the chamber by three guards and was returned to his cell. The reprieve by Judge Harry Pregerson of the U.S. Court of Appeals, a former Marine who had received a purple heart during World War II, lasted less than two hours.

As dawn approached, the Supreme Court put an end to the legal roller coaster. Any more stays would have to come from the high court itself, seven of the nine justices declared.

Justices John Paul Stevens and Harry A. Blackmun dissented, saying that death by lethal gas is unconstitutional.

"The barbaric use of cyanide gas in the Holocaust, the development of cyanide agents as chemical weapons, our contemporary understanding of execution by lethal gas and the development of less cruel methods of execution all demonstrate that execution by cyanide gas is unnecessarily cruel," Stevens wrote for the two justices.

At San Quentin, the witnesses were immediately summoned to the viewing room outside the pale green gas chamber.

Prison officials rushed Harris to the gas chamber the second time. Witnesses say the condemned man seemed composed as he was strapped in shortly before 6 a.m.

His last words before entering the chamber were: "You can be a king or a street sweeper, but everyone dances with the Grim Reaper," a line taken from the teen comedy film "Bill and Ted's Bogus Journey."

Among the witnesses were four relatives of the two San Diego teenagers killed by Harris on July 5, 1978.

Steven Baker, the father of Michael Baker, one of the slain boys, stood a few feet away from Harris during the execution. Baker said he thought he saw the killer mouth the words "I'm sorry" to him just before the deadly gas fumes filled the chamber.

According to prison officials, it took at least 10 minutes from the time the cyanide vapors reached Harris' face until he was pronounced dead.

Department of Corrections spokesman Tip Kindel said the Harris family took possession of the body for burial. No other details were given.

Hours before his death, a federal judge ordered that Harris' execution be videotaped as evidence in a pending class-action lawsuit challenging the use of lethal gas as cruel and unusual punishment.

The videotape has been placed under seal by U.S. District Judge Marilyn Hall Patel, who is considering the constitutionality of California's use of the gas chamber.

Harris had consented to the taping of his last few moments.

Dorothy Ehrlich, director of the American Civil Liberties Union, which is bringing the lawsuit, called Harris' execution "a tragedy."

In a statement yesterday, she called the gas chamber "an excruciatingly painful and unnecessarily prolonged method of death."

California legislators are considering changing the law and replacing the gas chamber with lethal injection as the state's means of execution.

Supreme Court Rebuke

The chaotic last-minute appeals in the Harris case, which delayed his execution for six hours, prompted an unprecedented reaction from the U.S. Supreme Court.

"There is no good reason for this abusive delay, which has been compounded by last-minute attempts to manipulate the judicial process," the court wrote in an unsigned opinion minutes before Harris died.

The families of the two slain 16-year-old boys, Michael Baker and John Mayeski, had long voiced frustration and anger over Harris' 13 years of appeals that had spared him from four execution dates.

William Stalder, uncle of Mayeski, felt no sympathy for Harris. "It's all over, it's a relief," he said.

At a press conference yesterday, Attorney General Dan Lungren looked somber and tired.

He showed reporters a list of inmates who are far enough along in the legal system to be considered next in line for execution. Legal experts said it may be at least a year before the next execution.

The next person who may follow Harris to the gas chamber is Edgar Hendricks, facing execution for the killing of two San Francisco men in 1980. After Hendricks is Melvin Meffrey Wade, sentenced to die for the 1981 torture-beating death of his 10-year-old stepdaughter, and Bernard Lee Hamilton, convicted of the 1979 murder of Eleanor Buchanan in San Diego.

"I said some prayers, not only for the victims of crime, but for Mr. Harris' soul," Lungren said. "It was a difficult thing to understand, when you believe in the possible redemption of every soul, how we can continue to do what we must do to protect the innocent in our society."

Protesters' Response

More than 200 death penalty opponents resumed their demonstrations after the execution during lunch-hour protests in San Francisco, vowing to "stop the killing."

The protesters, representing some seven organizations, marched to the Federal Building on Golden Gate Avenue, where they chanted, "U.S., you know, death penalty's got to go."

"We have been betrayed," said Ali Miller, national director of Amnesty International's death penalty program.

She decried the "bitter lesson" administered by the U.S. Supreme Court when, in an extraordinary move, it overturned the last stay and forbade any lower federal court from granting any more delays of Harris' execution.

"I'm not proud to be a Californian today," said Claudia King, death penalty coordinator for Humanitas. "We're angry at you (the state and federal governments) for killing in our name. . . . But above all, we're not going to go away."

Source: San Francisco Chronicle, April 22, 1992, A1.

Document 4.11
The Supreme Court Decides That the Eighth Amendment Bars Execution of the Insane, June 26, 1986

Invoking both the history of the common law and the Eighth Amendment, the Supreme Court ruled in Ford v. Wainwright (1986) that the Constitution prohibits the execution of persons who become insane after trial and sentence. The plurality opinion of Justice Thurgood Marshall found Florida's procedure for determining insanity inadequate because it vested absolute discretion in the governor and did not afford the condemned an opportunity to be heard. Justice William Rehnquist dissented, joined by Chief Justice Warren Burger.

JUSTICE MARSHALL announced the judgment of the Court with respect to Parts I and II and an opinion with respect to Parts III, IV, and V, in which JUSTICE BRENNAN, JUSTICE BLACKMUN, and JUSTICE STEVENS join.

For centuries no jurisdiction has countenanced the execution of the insane, yet this Court has never decided whether the Constitution forbids the practice. Today we keep faith with our common-law heritage in holding that it does.

I

Alvin Bernard Ford was convicted of murder in 1974 and sentenced to death. There is no suggestion that he was incompetent at the time of his offense, at trial, or at sentencing. In early 1982, however, Ford began to manifest gradual changes in behavior. They began as an occasional peculiar idea or confused perception, but became more serious over time. After reading in the newspaper that the Ku Klux Klan had held a rally in nearby Jacksonville, Florida, Ford developed an obsession focused upon the Klan. His letters to various people reveal endless brooding about his "Klan work," and an increasingly pervasive delusion that he had become the target of a complex conspiracy, involving the Klan and assorted others, designed to force him to commit suicide. He believed that the prison guards, part of the conspiracy, had been killing people and putting the bodies in the concrete enclosures used for beds. Later, he began to believe that his women relatives were being tortured and sexually abused somewhere in the prison. This notion developed into a delusion that the people who were tormenting him at the prison had taken members of Ford's family hostage. The hostage delusion took firm hold and expanded, until Ford was reporting that 135 of his friends and family were being held hostage in the prison, and that only he could help them. By "day 287" of the "hostage crisis," the list of hostages had expanded to include "senators, Senator Kennedy, and many other leaders." In a letter to the Attorney General of Florida, written in 1983, Ford appeared to assume authority for ending the "crisis," claiming to have fired a number of prison officials. He began to refer to himself as "Pope John Paul, III," and reported having appointed nine new justices to the Florida Supreme Court.

Counsel for Ford asked a psychiatrist who had examined Ford earlier, Dr. Jamal Amin, to continue seeing him and to recommend appropriate treatment. On the basis of roughly 14 months of evaluation, taped conversations between

Ford and his attorneys, letters written by Ford, interviews with Ford's acquaintances, and various medical records, Dr. Amin concluded in 1983 that Ford suffered from "a severe, uncontrollable, mental disease which closely resembles 'Paranoid Schizophrenia With Suicide Potential'"—a "major mental disorder . . . severe enough to substantially affect Mr. Ford's present ability to assist in the defense of his life."

Ford subsequently refused to see Dr. Amin again, believing him to have joined the conspiracy against him, and Ford's counsel sought assistance from Dr. Harold Kaufman, who interviewed Ford in November 1983. Ford told Dr. Kaufman that "I know there is some sort of death penalty, but I'm free to go whenever I want because it would be illegal and the executioner would be executed." When asked if he would be executed, Ford replied: "I can't be executed because of the landmark case. I won. *Ford v. State* will prevent executions all over." These statements appeared amidst long streams of seemingly unrelated thoughts in rapid succession. Dr. Kaufman concluded that Ford had no understanding of why he was being executed, made no connection between the homicide of which he had been convicted and the death penalty, and indeed sincerely believed that he would not be executed because he owned the prisons and could control the Governor through mind waves. Dr. Kaufman found that there was "no reasonable possibility that Mr. Ford was dissembling, malingering or otherwise putting on a performance. . . ." The following month, in an interview with his attorneys, Ford regressed further into nearly complete incomprehensibility, speaking only in a code characterized by intermittent use of the word "one," making statements such as "Hands one, face one. Mafia one. God one, father one, Pope one. Pope one. Leader one."

Counsel for Ford invoked the procedures of Florida law governing the determination of competency of a condemned inmate. Following the procedures set forth in the statute, the Governor of Florida appointed a panel of three psychiatrists to evaluate whether Ford had "the mental capacity to understand the nature of the death penalty and the reasons why it was imposed upon him." At a single meeting, the three psychiatrists together interviewed Ford for approximately 30 minutes. Each doctor then filed a separate two- or three-page report with the Governor, to whom the statute delegates the final decision. One doctor concluded that Ford suffered from "psychosis with paranoia" but had "enough cognitive functioning to understand the nature and the effects of the death penalty, and why it is to be imposed on him." Another found that, although Ford was "psychotic," he did "know fully what can happen to him." The third concluded that Ford had a "severe adaptational disorder," but did "comprehend his total situation including being sentenced to death, and all of the implications of that penalty." He believed that Ford's disorder, "although severe, seem[ed] contrived and recently learned." Thus, the interview produced three different diagnoses, but accord on the question of sanity as defined by state law.

The Governor's decision was announced on April 30, 1984, when, without explanation or statement, he signed a death warrant for Ford's execution. Ford's attorneys unsuccessfully sought a hearing in state court to determine anew Ford's competency to suffer execution. Counsel then filed a petition for habeas corpus in the United States District Court for the Southern District of Florida, seeking an evidentiary hearing on the question of Ford's sanity, proffering the conflicting findings of the Governor-appointed commission and subsequent challenges to their methods by other psychiatrists. The District Court denied the petition without a hearing. The Court of Appeals granted a certificate of probable cause and stayed Ford's execution, and we rejected the State's effort to vacate the stay of execution. The Court of Appeals then addressed the merits of Ford's claim and a divided panel affirmed the District Court's denial of the writ. This Court granted Ford's petition for certiorari in order to resolve the important issue whether the Eighth Amendment prohibits the execution of the insane and, if so, whether the District Court should have held a hearing on petitioner's claim.

II

Since this Court last had occasion to consider the infliction of the death penalty upon the insane, our interpretations of the Due Process Clause and the Eighth Amendment have evolved substantially. Now that the Eighth Amendment has been recognized to affect significantly both the procedural and the substantive aspects of the death penalty, the question of executing the insane takes on a wholly different complexion. The adequacy of the procedures chosen by a State to determine sanity, therefore, will depend upon an issue that this Court has never addressed: whether the Constitution places a substantive restriction on the State's power to take the life of an insane prisoner.

There is now little room for doubt that the Eighth Amendment's ban on cruel and unusual punishment embraces, at a minimum, those modes or acts of punishment that had been considered cruel and unusual at the time that the Bill of Rights was adopted.

> Although the Framers may have intended the Eighth Amendment to go beyond the scope of its English counterpart, their use of the language of the English Bill of Rights is convincing proof that they intended to provide at least the same protection.

Moreover, the Eighth Amendment's proscriptions are not limited to those practices condemned by the common law in 1789. Not bound by the sparing humanitarian concessions of our forebears, the Amendment also recognizes the "evolving standards of decency that mark the progress of a maturing society." In addition to considering the barbarous methods generally outlawed in the 18th century, therefore, this Court takes into account objective evidence of contemporary values

before determining whether a particular punishment comports with the fundamental human dignity that the Amendment protects.

A

We begin, then, with the common law. The bar against executing a prisoner who
has lost his sanity bears impressive historical credentials; the practice consistently
has been branded "savage and inhuman." Blackstone explained:

> [I]diots and lunatics are not chargeable for their own acts, if committed when under these
> incapacities: no, not even for treason itself. Also, if a man in his sound memory commits a
> capital offence, and before arraignment for it, he becomes mad, he ought not to be
> arraigned for it: because he is not able to plead to it with that advice and caution that he
> ought. And if, after he has pleaded, the prisoner becomes mad, he shall not be tried: for
> how can he make his defence? If, after he be tried and found guilty, he loses his senses
> before judgment, judgment shall not be pronounced; and if, after judgment, he becomes
> of nonsane memory, execution shall be stayed: for peradventure, says the humanity of the
> English law, had the prisoner been of sound memory, he might have alleged something in
> stay of judgment or execution.

Sir Edward Coke had earlier expressed the same view of the common law of
England:

> [B]y intendment of Law the execution of the offender is for example, . . . but so it is not
> when a mad man is executed, but should be a miserable spectacle, both against Law, and
> of extream inhumanity and cruelty, and can be no example to others.

Other recorders of the common law concurred.

As is often true of common-law principles, the reasons for the rule are less
sure and less uniform than the rule itself. One explanation is that the execution of an insane person simply offends humanity, another, that it provides no
example to others and thus contributes nothing to whatever deterrence value
is intended to be served by capital punishment. Other commentators postu-
late religious underpinnings: that it is uncharitable to dispatch an offender
"into another world, when he is not of a capacity to fit himself for it." It is
also said that execution serves no purpose in these cases because madness is its
own punishment: furiosus solo furore punitur. More recent commentators
opine that the community's quest for "retribution"—the need to offset a
criminal act by a punishment of equivalent "moral quality"—is not served by
execution of an insane person, which has a "lesser value" than that of the
crime for which he is to be punished. Unanimity of rationale, therefore, we do
not find. "But whatever the reason of the law is, it is plain the law is so." We
know of virtually no authority condoning the execution of the insane at
English common law. . . .

B

This ancestral legacy has not outlived its time. Today, no State in the Union permits the execution of the insane. It is clear that the ancient and humane limitation upon the State's ability to execute its sentences has as firm a hold upon the jurisprudence of today as it had centuries ago in England. The various reasons put forth in support of the common-law restriction have no less logical, moral, and practical force than they did when first voiced. For today, no less than before, we may seriously question the retributive value of executing a person who has no comprehension of why he has been singled out and stripped of his fundamental right to life. Similarly, the natural abhorrence civilized societies feel at killing one who has no capacity to come to grips with his own conscience or deity is still vivid today. And the intuition that such an execution simply offends humanity is evidently shared across this Nation. Faced with such wide spread evidence of a restriction upon sovereign power, this Court is compelled to conclude that the Eighth Amendment prohibits a State from carrying out a sentence of death upon a prisoner who is insane. Whether its aim be to protect the condemned from fear and pain without comfort of understanding, or to protect the dignity of society itself from the barbarity of exacting mindless vengeance, the restriction finds enforcement in the Eighth Amendment.

III

The Eighth Amendment prohibits the State from inflicting the penalty of death upon a prisoner who is insane. Petitioner's allegation of insanity in his habeas corpus petition, if proved, therefore, would bar his execution. The question before us is whether the District Court was under an obligation to hold an evidentiary hearing on the question of Ford's sanity. In answering that question, we bear in mind that, while the underlying social values encompassed by the Eighth Amendment are rooted in historical traditions, the manner in which our judicial system protects those values is purely a matter of contemporary law. Once a substantive right or restriction is recognized in the Constitution, therefore, its enforcement is in no way confined to the rudimentary process deemed adequate in ages past. . . .

C

Florida law directs the Governor, when informed that a person under sentence of death may be insane, to stay the execution and appoint a commission of three psychiatrists to examine the prisoner. "The examination of the convicted person shall take place with all three psychiatrists present at the same time." After receiving the report of the commission, the Governor must determine whether "the convicted person has the mental capacity to understand the nature of the death penalty and the reasons why it was imposed on him." If the Governor finds that the prisoner has that capacity, then a death warrant is issued; if not, then the prisoner is committed to a mental health facility. The procedure is conducted wholly within the executive branch, ex parte, and provides the exclusive means for determining sanity.

Petitioner received the statutory process. The Governor selected three psychiatrists, who together interviewed Ford for a total of 30 minutes, in the presence of eight other people, including Ford's counsel, the State's attorneys, and correctional officials. The Governor's order specifically directed that the attorneys should not participate in the examination in any adversarial manner. This order was consistent with the present Governor's "publicly announced policy of excluding all advocacy on the part of the condemned from the process of determining whether a person under a sentence of death is insane."

After submission of the reports of the three examining psychiatrists, reaching conflicting diagnoses but agreeing on the ultimate issue of competency, Ford's counsel attempted to submit to the Governor some other written materials, including the reports of the two other psychiatrists who had examined Ford at greater length, one of whom had concluded that the prisoner was not competent to suffer execution. The Governor's office refused to inform counsel whether the submission would be considered. The Governor subsequently issued his decision in the form of a death warrant. That this most cursory form of procedural review fails to achieve even the minimal degree of reliability required for the protection of any constitutional interest, and thus falls short of adequacy is self-evident.

IV

The first deficiency in Florida's procedure lies in its failure to include the prisoner in the truth-seeking process. Notwithstanding this Court's longstanding pronouncement that "[t]he fundamental requisite of due process of law is the opportunity to be heard," state practice does not permit any material relevant to the ultimate decision to be submitted on behalf of the prisoner facing execution. In all other proceedings leading to the execution of an accused, we have said that the factfinder must "have before it all possible relevant information about the individual defendant whose fate it must determine." And we have forbidden States to limit the capital defendant's submission of relevant evidence in mitigation of the sentence. It would be odd were we now to abandon our insistence upon unfettered presentation of relevant information, before the final fact antecedent to execution has been found. . . .

B

A related flaw in the Florida procedure is the denial of any opportunity to challenge or impeach the state-appointed psychiatrists' opinions. "[C]ross-examination . . . is beyond any doubt the greatest legal engine ever invented for the discovery of truth." Cross-examination of the psychiatrists, or perhaps a less formal equivalent, would contribute markedly to the process of seeking truth in sanity disputes by bringing to light the bases for each expert's beliefs, the precise factors underlying those beliefs, any history of error or caprice of the examiner, any personal bias with respect to the issue of capital punishment, the expert's degree of certainty about his or her own conclusions, and the precise meaning of ambiguous words used in the report. Without some questioning of the experts concerning their technical conclusions, a factfinder simply cannot be expected to evaluate the various opinions, particularly when they are themselves inconsistent. The failure of the Florida procedure to afford the prisoner's representative any opportunity to clarify or challenge the state experts' opinions or methods creates a significant possibility that the ultimate decision made in reliance on those experts will be distorted.

C

Perhaps the most striking defect in the procedures as noted earlier, is the State's placement of the decision wholly within the executive branch. Under this procedure, the person who appoints the experts and ultimately decides whether the State will be able to carry out the sentence that it has long sought is the Governor, whose subordinates have been responsible for initiating every stage of the prosecution of the condemned from arrest through sentencing. The commander of the State's corps of prosecutors cannot be said to have the neutrality that is necessary for reliability in the factfinding proceeding. . . .

Having identified various failings of the Florida scheme, we must conclude that the State's procedures for determining sanity are inadequate to preclude federal redetermination of the constitutional issue. We do not here suggest that only a full trial on the issue of sanity will suffice to protect the federal interests; we leave to the State the task of developing appropriate ways to enforce the constitutional restriction upon its execution of sentences. It may be that some high threshold showing on behalf of the prisoner will be found a necessary means to control the number of nonmeritorious or repetitive claims of insanity. Other legitimate pragmatic considerations may also supply the boundaries of the procedural safeguards that feasibly can be provided. . . .

B

Today we have explicitly recognized in our law a principle that has long resided there. It is no less abhorrent today than it has been for centuries to exact in penance the life of one whose mental illness prevents him from comprehending the reasons for the penalty or its implications. In light of the clear need for trustworthiness in any factual finding that will prevent or permit the carrying out of an execution, we hold that Florida provides inadequate assurances of accuracy to satisfy the requirements of the Constitution. Having been denied a factfinding procedure "adequate to afford a full and fair hearing" on the critical issue, petitioner is entitled to an evidentiary hearing in the District Court, de novo, on the question of his competence to be executed.

The judgment of the Court of Appeals is reversed, and the case is remanded for further proceedings consistent with this opinion.

It is so ordered.

JUSTICE REHNQUIST, with whom THE CHIEF JUSTICE joins, dissenting.

The Court today holds that the Eighth Amendment prohibits a State from carrying out a lawfully imposed sentence of death upon a person who is currently insane. This holding is based almost entirely on two unremarkable observations. First, the Court states that it "know[s] of virtually no authority condoning the execution of the insane at English common law." Ante, at 408. Second, it notes that "[t]oday, no State in the Union permits the execution of the insane." Ibid. Armed with these facts, and shielded by the claim that it is simply "keep[ing] faith with our common-law heritage," ante, at 401, the Court proceeds to cast aside settled precedent and to significantly alter both the common-law and current practice of not executing the insane. It manages this feat by carefully ignoring the fact that the Florida scheme it finds unconstitutional, in which the Governor is assigned the ultimate responsibility of deciding whether a condemned prisoner is currently insane, is fully consistent with the "common-law heritage" and current practice on which the Court purports to rely.

The Court places great weight on the "impressive historical credentials" of the common-law bar against executing a prisoner who has lost his sanity. What it fails to mention, however, is the equally important and unchallenged fact that at common law it was the executive who passed upon the sanity of the condemned. So when the Court today creates a constitutional right to a determination of sanity outside of the executive branch, it does so not in keeping with but at the expense of "our common-law heritage." . . .

Since no State sanctions execution of the insane, the real battle being fought in this case is over what procedures must accompany the inquiry into sanity. The Court reaches the result it does by examining the common law, creating a constitutional right that no State seeks to violate, and then concluding that the common-law procedures are inadequate to protect the newly created but common-law based right. I find it unnecessary to "constitutionalize" the already uniform view that the insane should not be executed, and inappropriate to "selectively incorporate" the common-law practice. I therefore dissent.

Source: Ford v. Wainwright, 477 U.S. 399 (1986), at 402–418, 432–436.

Document 4.12
Baldus Study on Race and the Death Penalty in Georgia

David Baldus, a professor of law at the University of Iowa, and his co-researchers, George Woodworth, an associate professor of statistics at the University of Wisconsin, and Charles A. Pulaski Jr., a law professor at Arizona State University, conducted two studies in Georgia between 1974 and 1979 to determine the level of disparities attributable to race in the rate of the imposition of death sentences. Known collectively as the Baldus study (Procedural Reform Study and Charging and Sentencing Study), their findings were advanced by attorneys for Warren McCleskey in his attempt to reverse his death sentence. The major conclusions of the Baldus study were summarized by Judge Thomas Alonzo Clark of the Eleventh Circuit Court of Appeals in his dissenting opinion in McCleskey v. Kemp, *753 F.2d 877 (11th Cir. 1985).*

CLARK, Circuit Judge, dissenting in part and concurring in part,

We are challenged to determine how much racial discrimination, if any, is tolerable in the imposition of the death penalty. Although I also join in Judge Johnson's dissent, this dissent is directed to the majority's erroneous conclusion that the evidence in this case does not establish a prima facie Fourteenth Amendment violation.

The Study

The Baldus study, which covers the period 1974 to 1979, is a detailed study of over 2,400 homicide cases. From these homicides, 128 persons received the death penalty. Two types of racial disparity are established—one based on the race of the victim and one based on the race of the defendant. If the victim is white, a defendant is more likely to receive the death penalty. If the defendant is black, he is more likely to receive the death penalty. One can only conclude that in the operation of this system the life of a white is dearer, the life of a black cheaper.

Before looking at a few of the figures, a perspective is necessary. Race is a factor in the system only where there is room for discretion, that is, where the decision maker has a viable choice. In the large number of cases, race has no effect. These are cases where the facts are so mitigated the death penalty is not even considered as a possible punishment. At the other end of the spectrum are the tremendously aggravated murder cases where the defendant will very probably receive the death penalty, regardless of his race or the race of the victim. In between is the mid-range of cases where there is an approximately 20% racial disparity.

The Baldus study was designed to determine whether like situated cases are treated similarly. As a starting point, an unanalyzed aritithmetic comparison of all of the cases reflected the following:

Death Sentencing Rates by Defendant/Victim Racial Combination

A Black Defendant/ White Victim	B White Defendant/ White Victim	C Black Defendant/ Black Victim	D White Defendant/ Black Victim
.22 (50/228)	.08 (58/745)	.01 (18/1438)	.03 (2/64)
.11 (108/973)		.013 (20/1502)	

These figures show a gross disparate racial impact—that where the victim was white there were 11% death sentences, compared to only 1.3 percent death sentences when the victim was black. Similarly, only 8% of white defendants compared to 22% of black defendants received the death penalty when the victim was white. The Supreme Court has found similar gross disparities to be sufficient proof of discrimination to support a Fourteenth Amendment violation.

The Baldus study undertook to determine if this racial sentencing disparity was caused by considerations of race or because of other factors or both. In order to find out, it was necessary to analyze and compare each of the potential death penalty cases and ascertain what relevant factors were available for consideration by the decision makers. There were many factors such as prior capital record, contemporaneous offense, motive, killing to avoid arrest or for hire, as well as race. The study showed that race had as much or more impact than any other single factor. Stated another way, race influences the verdict just as much as any one of the aggravating circumstances listed in Georgia's death penalty statute. Therefore, in the application of the statute in Georgia, race of the defendant and of the victim, when it is black/white, functions as if it were an aggravating circumstance in a discernible number of cases.

Another part of the study compared the disparities in death penalty sentencing according to race of the defendant and race of the victim and reflected the differences in the sentencing depending upon the predicted chance of death, i.e., whether the type of case was or was not one where the death penalty would be given.

Table 43

Race of Defendant Disparities in Death Sentencing Rates Controlling for the Predicted Likelihood of a Death Sentence and the Race Victim

A Predicted Chance of a Death Sentence 1 (least) to 8 (highest)	B Average Actual Sentencing Rate for the Cases at Each Level	C Death Sentencing Rates for White Victim Cases Involving		D	E Arithmetic Difference Race of Defendant Rates (Col. C- Col. D)
		Black Defendants	White Defendants		
1	.0 (0/33)	.0 (0/9)	.0 (0/5)		.0
2	.0 (0/56)	.0 (0/8)	.0 (0/19)		.0
3	.08 (6/77)	.30 (3/10)	.03 (1/39)		.27
4	.07 (4/57)	.23 (3/13)	.04 (1/29)		.19
5	.27 (15/58)	.35 (9/26)	.20 (4/20)		.15
6	.18 (11/63)	.38 (3/8)	.16 (5/32)		.22
7	.41 (29/70)	.64 (9/14)	.39 (15/39)		.25
8	.88 (51/58)	.91 (20/22)	.89 (25/28)		.02

Table Continued

F Ratio of Race of the Defendant Rates (Col. C/Col. D)	G Death Sentencing Rates for Black Victim Cases Involving	H	I Arithmetic Differences in Race of the Defendant Rates (Col. G- Col. H)	J Ratio of Race of the Defendant Rates (Col. G- Col. H)
	Black Defendants	White Defendants		
—	.0 (0/19)	—	—	0
—	.0 (0/27)	.0	.0	0

(Continued)

F	G		H	I	J
Ratio of Race of the Defendant Rates (Col. C/Col. D)	Death Sentencing Rates for Black Victim Cases Involving			Arithmetic Differences in Race of the Defendant Rates (Col. G- Col. H)	Ratio of Race of the Defendant Rates (Col. G- Col. H)
	Black Defendants	White Defendants			
10.	.11 (2/18)	.0		.11	0
5.75	.0 (0/15)	—		—	—
1.75	.17 (2/12)	—		—	—
2.38	.05 (1/20)	.50		−.45	.10
1.64	.39 (5/13)	.0		.39	.0
1.02	.75 (6/8)	—		—	—

Columns A and B reflect the step progression of least aggravated to most aggravated cases. Table 43, DB, Ex. 91. Columns C an D compare sentencing rates of black defendants to white defendants when the victim is white and reflect that in Steps 1 and 2 no death penalty was given in those 41 cases. In Step 8, 45 death penalties were given in 50 cases, only two blacks and three whites escaping the death penalty—this group obviously representing the most aggravated cases. By comparing Steps 3 through 7, one can see that in each group black defendants received death penalties disproportionately to white defendants by differences of .27, .19, .15, .22, and .25. This indicates that unless the murder is so vile as to almost certainly evoke the death penalty (Step 8), blacks are approximately 20% more likely to get the death penalty.

The right side of the chart reflects how unlikely it is that any defendant, but more particularly white defendants, will receive the death penalty when the victim is black. . . .

Source: McCleskey v. Kemp, 753 F.2d 877 (11th Cir. 1985), at 921–923.

Document 4.13

Justices Reject Statistical Study on Racial Disparities in Death Penalty Cases, April 22, 1987

In the most important constitutional challenge to the death penalty since Furman *(1972), the Supreme Court affirmed the conviction and death sentence of Warren McCleskey in 1987 when it rejected a sophisticated statistical study by David Baldus and his associates that established the existence of racial disparity in capital sentencing. Writing for the Court, Justice Lewis Powell conceded the validity of the Baldus study, but rejected McCleskey's claims on the grounds that the statistics could not prove intentional racial discrimination in McCleskey's specific case. Powell also argued that accepting McCleskey's argument would undermine the entire criminal justice system. Among the four dissenters, Justice William Brennan pointed out that the Court has historically accepted such statistical evidence in discrimination cases and that Powell's arguments undermined his own conclusions.*

JUSTICE POWELL delivered the opinion of the Court.

This case presents the question whether a complex statistical study that indicates a risk that racial considerations enter into capital sentencing determinations proves that petitioner McCleskey's capital sentence is unconstitutional under the Eighth or Fourteenth Amendment.

I

McCleskey, a black man, was convicted of two counts of armed robbery and one count of murder in the Superior Court of Fulton County, Georgia, on October 12, 1978. McCleskey's convictions arose out of the robbery of a furniture store and the killing of a white police officer during the course of the robbery. The evidence at trial indicated that McCleskey and three accomplices planned and carried out the robbery. All four were armed. McCleskey entered the front of the store while the other three entered the rear. McCleskey secured the front of the store by rounding up the customers and forcing them to lie face down on the floor. The other three rounded up the employees in the rear and tied them up with tape. The manager was forced at gunpoint to turn over the store receipts, his watch, and $6. During the course of the robbery, a police officer, answering a silent alarm, entered the store through the front door. As he was walking down the center aisle of the store, two shots were fired. Both struck the officer. One hit him in the face and killed him.

Several weeks later, McCleskey was arrested in connection with an unrelated offense. He confessed that he had participated in the furniture store robbery, but denied that he had shot the police officer. At trial, the State introduced evidence that at least one of the bullets that struck the officer was fired from a .38 caliber Rossi revolver. This description matched the description of the gun that

McCleskey had carried during the robbery. The State also introduced the testimony of two witnesses who had heard McCleskey admit to the shooting.

The jury convicted McCleskey of murder. . . . McCleskey offered no mitigating evidence. The jury recommended that he be sentenced to death on the murder charge and to consecutive life sentences on the armed robbery charges. The court followed the jury's recommendation and sentenced McCleskey to death.

On appeal, the Supreme Court of Georgia affirmed the convictions and the sentences. This Court denied a petition for a writ of certiorari. . . .

McCleskey next filed a petition for a writ of habeas corpus in the Federal District Court for the Northern District of Georgia. His petition raised 18 claims, one of which was that the Georgia capital sentencing process is administered in a racially discriminatory manner in violation of the Eighth and Fourteenth Amendments to the United States Constitution. In support of his claim, McCleskey proffered a statistical study performed by Professors David C. Baldus, Charles Pulaski, and George Woodworth (the Baldus study) that purports to show a disparity in the imposition of the death sentence in Georgia based on the race of the murder victim and, to a lesser extent, the race of the defendant. The Baldus study is actually two sophisticated statistical studies that examine over 2,000 murder cases that occurred in Georgia during the 1970's. The raw numbers collected by Professor Baldus indicate that defendants charged with killing white persons received the death penalty in 11% of the cases, but defendants charged with killing blacks received the death penalty in only 1% of the cases. The raw numbers also indicate a reverse racial disparity according to the race of the defendant: 4% of the black defendants received the death penalty, as opposed to 7% of the white defendants.

Baldus also divided the cases according to the combination of the race of the defendant and the race of the victim. He found that the death penalty was assessed in 22% of the cases involving black defendants and white victims; 8% of the cases involving white defendants and white victims; 1% of the cases involving black defendants and black victims; and 3% of the cases involving white defendants and black victims. Similarly, Baldus found that prosecutors sought the death penalty in 70% of the cases involving black defendants and white victims; 32% of the cases involving white defendants and white victims; 15% of the cases involving black defendants and black victims; and 19% of the cases involving white defendants and black victims.

Baldus subjected his data to an extensive analysis, taking account of 230 variables that could have explained the disparities on nonracial grounds. One of his models concludes that, even after taking account of 39 nonracial variables, defendants charged with killing white victims were 4.3 times as likely to receive a death sentence as defendants charged with killing blacks. According to this model, black defendants were 1.1 times as likely to receive a death sentence as other defendants. Thus, the Baldus study indicates that black defendants, such as

McCleskey, who kill white victims have the greatest likelihood of receiving the death penalty.

The District Court held an extensive evidentiary hearing on McCleskey's petition. Although it believed that McCleskey's Eighth Amendment claim was foreclosed, it nevertheless considered the Baldus study with care. It concluded that McCleskey's "statistics do not demonstrate a prima facie case in support of the contention that the death penalty was imposed upon him because of his race, because of the race of the victim, or because of any Eighth Amendment concern." As to McCleskey's Fourteenth Amendment claim, the court found that the methodology of the Baldus study was flawed in several respects. Because of these defects, the court held that the Baldus study "fail[ed] to contribute anything of value" to McCleskey's claim. Accordingly, the court denied the petition insofar as it was based upon the Baldus study.

The Court of Appeals for the Eleventh Circuit, sitting en banc, carefully reviewed the District Court's decision on McCleskey's claim. It assumed the validity of the study itself and addressed the merits of McCleskey's Eighth and Fourteenth Amendment claims. That is, the court assumed that the study

> showed that systematic and substantial disparities existed in the penalties imposed upon homicide defendants in Georgia based on race of the homicide victim, that the disparities existed at a less substantial rate in death sentencing based on race of defendants, and that the factors of race of the victim and defendant were at work in Fulton County.

Even assuming the study's validity, the Court of Appeals found the statistics "insufficient to demonstrate discriminatory intent or unconstitutional discrimination in the Fourteenth Amendment context, [and] insufficient to show irrationality, arbitrariness and capriciousness under any kind of Eighth Amendment analysis."

The court noted:

> The very exercise of discretion means that persons exercising discretion may reach different results from exact duplicates. Assuming each result is within the range of discretion, all are correct in the eyes of the law. It would not make sense for the system to require the exercise of discretion in order to be facially constitutional, and at the same time hold a system unconstitutional in application where that discretion achieved different results for what appear to be exact duplicates, absent the state showing the reasons for the difference. . . .

> The Baldus approach . . . would take the cases with different results on what are contended to be duplicate facts, where the differences could not be otherwise explained, and conclude that the different result was based on race alone. . . . This approach ignores the realities. . . . There are, in fact, no exact duplicates in capital crimes and capital defendants. The type of research submitted here tends to show which of the directed factors were effective, but is of restricted use in showing what undirected factors control the exercise of constitutionally required discretion.

The court concluded:

> Viewed broadly, it would seem that the statistical evidence presented here, assuming its validity, confirms rather than condemns the system. . . . The marginal disparity based on the race of the victim tends to support the state's contention that the system is working far differently from the one which *Furman* condemned. In pre-*Furman* days, there was no rhyme or reason as to who got the death penalty and who did not. But now, in the vast majority of cases, the reasons for a difference are well documented. That they are not so clear in a small percentage of the cases is no reason to declare the entire system unconstitutional.

The Court of Appeals affirmed the denial by the District Court of McCleskey's petition for a writ of habeas corpus insofar as the petition was based upon the Baldus study, with three judges dissenting as to McCleskey's claims based on the Baldus study. We granted certiorari, and now affirm.

II

McCleskey's first claim is that the Georgia capital punishment statute violates the Equal Protection Clause of the Fourteenth Amendment. He argues that race has infected the administration of Georgia's statute in two ways: persons who murder whites are more likely to be sentenced to death than persons who murder blacks, and black murderers are more likely to be sentenced to death than white murderers. As a black defendant who killed a white victim, McCleskey claims that the Baldus study demonstrates that he was discriminated against because of his race and because of the race of his victim. In its broadest form, McCleskey's claim of discrimination extends to every actor in the Georgia capital sentencing process, from the prosecutor who sought the death penalty and the jury that imposed the sentence, to the State itself that enacted the capital punishment statute and allows it to remain in effect despite its allegedly discriminatory application. We agree with the Court of Appeals, and every other court that has considered such a challenge, that this claim must fail.

A

Our analysis begins with the basic principle that a defendant who alleges an equal protection violation has the burden of proving "the existence of purposeful discrimination." A corollary to this principle is that a criminal defendant must prove that the purposeful discrimination "had a discriminatory effect" on him. Thus, to prevail under the Equal Protection Clause, McCleskey must prove that the decisionmakers in his case acted with discriminatory purpose. He offers no evidence specific to his own case that would support an inference that racial considerations played a part in his sentence. Instead, he relies solely on the Baldus study. McCleskey argues that the Baldus study compels an inference that his sentence rests on purposeful discrimination. McCleskey's claim that these statistics are sufficient proof of discrimination, without regard to the facts of a particular case, would extend to all capital cases in Georgia, at least where the victim was white and the defendant is black.

The Court has accepted statistics as proof of intent to discriminate in certain limited contexts. First, this Court has accepted statistical disparities as proof of an equal protection violation in the selection of the jury venire in a particular district. Although statistical proof normally must present a "stark" pattern to be accepted as the sole proof of discriminatory intent under the Constitution, "[b]ecause of the nature of the jury-selection task, . . . we have permitted a finding of constitutional violation even when the statistical pattern does not approach [such] extremes." Second, this Court has accepted statistics in the form of multiple-regression analysis to prove statutory violations under Title VII of the Civil Rights Act of 1964.

But the nature of the capital sentencing decision, and the relationship of the statistics to that decision, are fundamentally different from the corresponding elements in the venire-selection or Title VII cases. Most importantly, each particular decision to impose the death penalty is made by a petit jury selected from a properly constituted venire. Each jury is unique in its composition, and the Constitution requires that its decision rest on consideration of innumerable factors that vary according to the characteristics of the individual defendant and the facts of the particular capital offense. Thus, the application of an inference drawn from the general statistics to a specific decision in a trial and sentencing simply is not comparable to the application of an inference drawn from general statistics to a specific venire-selection or Title VII case. In those cases, the statistics relate to fewer entities, and fewer variables are relevant to the challenged decisions.

Another important difference between the cases in which we have accepted statistics as proof of discriminatory intent and this case is that, in the venire-selection and Title VII contexts, the decisionmaker has an opportunity to explain the statistical disparity. Here, the State has no practical opportunity to rebut the Baldus study. "[C]ontrolling considerations of . . . public policy," dictate that jurors "cannot be called . . . to testify to the motives and influences that led to their verdict." Similarly, the policy considerations behind a prosecutor's traditionally "wide discretion" suggest the impropriety of our requiring prosecutors to defend their decisions to seek death penalties, "often years after they were made." Moreover, absent far stronger proof, it is unnecessary to seek such a rebuttal, because a legitimate and unchallenged explanation for the decision is apparent from the record: McCleskey committed an act for which the United States Constitution and Georgia laws permit imposition of the death penalty.

Finally, McCleskey's statistical proffer must be viewed in the context of his challenge. McCleskey challenges decisions at the heart of the State's criminal justice system. "[O]ne of society's most basic tasks is that of protecting the lives of its citizens and one of the most basic ways in which it achieves the task is through criminal laws against murder." Implementation of these laws necessarily requires discretionary judgments. Because discretion is essential to the criminal justice process, we would demand exceptionally clear proof before we would infer that the discretion has been abused. The unique nature of the decisions at issue in this case also counsels against adopting such an inference from the disparities indicated by the Baldus study. Accordingly, we hold that the Baldus study is clearly insufficient to support an inference that any of the decisionmakers in McCleskey's case acted with discriminatory purpose.

B

McCleskey also suggests that the Baldus study proves that the State as a whole has acted with a discriminatory purpose. He appears to argue that the State has violated the Equal Protection Clause by adopting the capital punishment statute and allowing it to remain in force despite its allegedly discriminatory application. But

> "[d]iscriminatory purpose" . . . implies more than intent as volition or intent as awareness of consequences. It implies that the decisionmaker, in this case a state legislature, selected or reaffirmed a particular course of action at least in part 'because of,' not merely 'in spite of,' its adverse effects upon an identifiable group."

For this claim to prevail, McCleskey would have to prove that the Georgia Legislature enacted or maintained the death penalty statute because of an anticipated racially discriminatory effect. In *Gregg v. Georgia,* this Court found that the Georgia capital sentencing system could operate in a fair and neutral manner. There was no evidence then, and there is none now, that the Georgia Legislature enacted the capital punishment statute to further a racially discriminatory purpose. Nor has McCleskey demonstrated that the legislature maintains the capital punishment statute because of the racially disproportionate impact suggested by the Baldus study. As legislatures necessarily have wide discretion in the choice of criminal laws and penalties, and as there were legitimate reasons for the Georgia Legislature to adopt and maintain capital punishment, we will not infer a discriminatory purpose on the part of the State of Georgia. Accordingly, we reject McCleskey's equal protection claims.

III

McCleskey also argues that the Baldus study demonstrates that the Georgia capital sentencing system violates the Eighth Amendment. We begin our analysis of this claim by reviewing the restrictions on death sentences established by our prior decisions under that Amendment.

A

The Eighth Amendment prohibits infliction of "cruel and unusual punishments." This Court's early Eighth Amendment cases examined only the "particular methods of execution to determine whether they were too cruel to pass constitutional muster." Subsequently, the Court recognized that the constitutional prohibition against cruel and unusual punishments "is not fastened to the obsolete but may acquire meaning as public opinion becomes enlightened by a humane justice." In *Weems,* the Court identified a second principle inherent in the Eighth Amendment, "that punishment for crime should be graduated and proportioned to offense." . . .

B

Two principal decisions guide our resolution of McCleskey's Eighth Amendment claim. In *Furman v. Georgia,* the Court concluded that the death penalty was so irrationally imposed that any particular death sentence could be presumed excessive. Under the statutes at issue in *Furman,* there was no basis for determining in any particular case whether the penalty was proportionate to the crime: "[T]he death penalty [was] exacted with great infrequency even for the most atrocious crimes and . . . there [was] no meaningful basis for distinguishing the few cases in which it [was] imposed from the many cases in which it [was] not."

In *Gregg,* the Court specifically addressed the question left open in *Furman*—whether the punishment of death for murder is "under all circumstances, 'cruel and unusual' in violation of the Eighth and Fourteenth Amendments of the Constitution." We noted that the imposition of the death penalty for the crime of murder "has a long history of acceptance both in the United States and in England." "The most marked indication of society's endorsement of the death penalty for murder [was] the legislative response to *Furman.*" During the 4-year period between *Furman* and *Gregg,* at least 35 States had reenacted the death penalty, and Congress had authorized the penalty for aircraft piracy. . . .

Finally, where the objective indicia of community values have demonstrated a consensus that the death penalty is disproportionate as applied to a certain class of cases, we have established substantive limitations on its application. In *Coker v. Georgia,* the Court held that a State may not constitutionally sentence an individual to death for the rape of an adult woman. In *Enmund v. Florida,* the Court prohibited imposition of the death penalty on a defendant convicted of felony murder absent a showing that the defendant possessed a sufficiently culpable mental state. Most recently, in *Ford v. Wainwright,* we prohibited execution of prisoners who are insane. . . .

D

In sum, our decisions since *Furman* have identified a constitutionally permissible range of discretion in imposing the death penalty. First, there is a required threshold below which the death penalty cannot be imposed. In this context, the State must establish rational criteria that narrow the decisionmaker's judgment as to whether the circumstances of a particular defendant's case meet the threshold. Moreover, a societal consensus that the death penalty is disproportionate to a particular offense prevents a State from imposing the death penalty for that offense. Second, States cannot limit the sentencer's consideration of any relevant circumstance that could cause it to decline to impose the penalty. In this respect, the State cannot channel the sentencer's discretion, but must allow it to consider any relevant information offered by the defendant.

IV

A

In light of our precedents under the Eighth Amendment, McCleskey cannot argue successfully that his sentence is "disproportionate to the crime in the traditional sense." He does not deny that he committed a murder in the course of a planned robbery, a crime for which this Court has determined that the death penalty constitutionally may be imposed. His disproportionality claim "is of a different sort." McCleskey argues that the sentences in his case is disproportionate to the sentences in other murder cases.

On the one hand, he cannot base a constitutional claim on an argument that his case differs from other cases in which defendants did receive the death penalty. On automatic appeal, the Georgia Supreme Court found that McCleskey's death sentence was not disproportionate to other death sentences imposed in the State. The court supported this conclusion with an appendix containing citations to 13 cases involving generally similar murders. Moreover, where the statutory procedures adequately channel the sentencer's discretion, such proportionality review is not constitutionally required.

On the other hand, absent a showing that the Georgia capital punishment system operates in an arbitrary and capricious manner, McCleskey cannot prove a constitutional violation by demonstrating that other defendants who may be similarly situated did not receive the death penalty. In *Gregg*, the Court confronted the argument that "the opportunities for discretionary action that are inherent in the processing of any murder case under Georgia law," specifically the opportunities for discretionary leniency, rendered the capital sentences imposed arbitrary and capricious. We rejected this contention. . . .

Because McCleskey's sentence was imposed under Georgia sentencing procedures that focus discretion "on the particularized nature of the crime and the particularized characteristics of the individual defendant," id., at 206, we lawfully may presume that McCleskey's death sentence was not "wantonly and freakishly" imposed, id., at 207, and thus that the sentence is not disproportionate within any recognized meaning under the Eighth Amendment.

Although our decision in *Gregg* as to the facial validity of the Georgia capital punishment statute appears to foreclose McCleskey's disproportionality argument, he further contends that the Georgia capital punishment system is arbitrary and capricious in application, and therefore his sentence is excessive, because racial considerations may influence capital sentencing decisions in Georgia. We now address this claim. . . .

To evaluate McCleskey's challenge, we must examine exactly what the Baldus study may show. Even Professor Baldus does not contend that his statistics prove that race enters into any capital sentencing decisions or that race was a factor in McCleskey's particular case. Statistics at most may show only a likelihood that a particular factor entered into some decisions. There is, of course, some risk of racial prejudice influencing a jury's decision in a criminal case. There are similar risks that other kinds of prejudice will influence other criminal trials. The question "is at what point that risk becomes constitutionally unacceptable." McCleskey asks us to accept the likelihood allegedly shown by the Baldus study as the constitutional measure of an unacceptable risk of racial prejudice influencing capital sentencing decisions. This we decline to do.

Because of the risk that the factor of race may enter the criminal justice process, we have engaged in "unceasing efforts" to eradicate racial prejudice from our criminal justice system. Our efforts have been guided by our recognition that "the inestimable privilege of trial by jury . . . is a vital principle, underlying the whole administration of criminal justice." Thus, it is the jury that is a criminal defendant's fundamental "protection of life and liberty against race or color prejudice." Specifically, a capital sentencing jury representative of a criminal defendant's community assures a "diffused impartiality," in the jury's task of "express[ing] the conscience of the community on the ultimate question of life or death."

Individual jurors bring to their deliberations "qualities of human nature and varieties of human experience, the range of which is unknown and perhaps unknowable." The capital sentencing decision requires the individual jurors to focus their collective judgment on the unique characteristics of a particular criminal defendant. It is not surprising that such collective judgments often are difficult to explain. But the inherent lack of predictability of jury decisions does not justify their condemnation. On the contrary, it is the jury's function to make the difficult and uniquely human judgments that defy codification and that "buil[d] discretion, equity, and flexibility into a legal system."

McCleskey's argument that the Constitution condemns the discretion allowed decisionmakers in the Georgia capital sentencing system is antithetical to the fundamental role of discretion in our criminal justice system. Discretion in the criminal justice system offers substantial benefits to the criminal defendant. Not only can a jury decline to impose the death sentence, it can decline to convict or choose to convict of a lesser offense. Whereas decisions against a defendant's interest may be reversed by the trial judge or on appeal, these discretionary exercises of leniency are final and unreviewable. Similarly, the capacity of prosecutorial discretion to provide individualized justice is "firmly entrenched in American law." As we have noted, a prosecutor can decline to charge, offer a plea bargain, or decline to seek a death sentence in any particular case. Of course, "the power to be lenient [also] is the power to discriminate," but a capital punishment system that did not allow for discretionary acts of leniency "would be totally alien to our notions of criminal justice." . . .

C

At most, the Baldus study indicates a discrepancy that appears to correlate with race. Apparent disparities in sentencing are an inevitable part of our criminal justice system. The discrepancy indicated by the Baldus study is "a far cry from the major systemic defects identified in *Furman*." As this Court has recognized, any mode for determining guilt or punishment "has its weaknesses and the potential for misuse." Specifically, "there can be 'no perfect procedure for deciding in which cases governmental authority should be used to impose death.'" Despite these imperfections, our consistent rule has been that constitutional guarantees are met when "the mode [for determining guilt or punishment] itself has been surrounded with safeguards to make it as fair as possible." Where the discretion that is fundamental to our criminal process is involved, we decline to assume that what is unexplained is invidious. In light of the safeguards designed to minimize racial bias in the process, the fundamental value of jury trial in our criminal justice system, and the benefits that discretion provides to criminal defendants, we hold that the Baldus study does not demonstrate a constitutionally significant risk of racial bias affecting the Georgia capital sentencing process.

V

Two additional concerns inform our decision in this case. First, McCleskey's claim, taken to its logical conclusion, throws into serious question the principles that underlie our entire criminal justice system. The Eighth Amendment is not limited in application to capital punishment, but applies to all penalties. Thus, if we accepted McCleskey's claim that racial bias has impermissibly tainted the capital sentencing decision, we could soon be faced with similar claims as to other types of penalty. Moreover, the claim that his sentence rests on the irrelevant factor of race easily could be extended to apply to claims based on unexplained discrepancies that correlate to membership in other minority groups, even to gender. Similarly, since McCleskey's claim relates to the race of his victim, other claims could apply with equally logical force to statistical disparities that correlate with the race or sex of other actors in the criminal justice system, such as defense attorneys or judges. Also, there is no logical reason that such a claim need be limited to racial or sexual bias. If arbitrary and capricious punishment is the touchstone under the Eighth Amendment, such a claim could—at least in theory—be based upon any arbitrary variable, such as the defendant's facial characteristics, or the physical attractiveness of the defendant or the victim, that some statistical study indicates may be influential in jury decisionmaking. As these examples illustrate, there is no limiting principle to the type of challenge brought by McCleskey. The Constitution does not require that a State eliminate any demonstrable disparity that correlates with a potentially irrelevant factor in order to operate a criminal justice system that includes capital punishment. As we have stated specifically in the context of capital punishment, the Constitution does not "plac[e] totally unrealistic conditions on its use."

Second, McCleskey's arguments are best presented to the legislative bodies. It is not the responsibility—or indeed even the right—of this Court to determine the appropriate punishment for particular crimes. It is the legislatures, the elected representatives of the people, that are "constituted to respond to the will and consequently the moral values of the people." Legislatures also are better qualified to weigh and "evaluate the results of statistical studies in terms of their own local conditions and with a flexibility of approach that is not available to the courts." Capital punishment is now the law in more than two-thirds of our States. It is the ultimate duty of courts to determine on a case-by-case basis whether these laws are applied consistently with the Constitution. Despite McCleskey's wide-ranging arguments that basically challenge the validity of capital punishment in our multiracial society, the only question before us is whether in his case, the law of Georgia was properly applied. We agree with the District Court and the Court of Appeals for the Eleventh Circuit that this was carefully and correctly done in this case.

Accordingly, we affirm the judgment of the Court of Appeals for the Eleventh Circuit.

It is so ordered.

JUSTICE BRENNAN, with whom JUSTICE MARSHALL joins, and with whom JUSTICE BLACKMUN and JUSTICE STEVENS join in all but Part I, dissenting.

I

Adhering to my view that the death penalty is in all circumstances cruel and unusual punishment forbidden by the Eighth and Fourteenth Amendments, I would vacate the decision below insofar as it left undisturbed the death sentence imposed in this case. The Court observes that "[t]he *Gregg*-type statute imposes unprecedented safeguards in the special context of capital punishment," which "ensure a degree of care in the imposition of the death penalty that can be described only as unique." Notwithstanding these efforts, murder defendants in Georgia with white victims are more than four times as likely to receive the death sentence as are defendants with black victims. Nothing could convey more powerfully the intractable reality of the death penalty: "that the effort to eliminate arbitrariness in the infliction of that ultimate sanction is so plainly doomed to failure that it—and the death penalty—must be abandoned altogether."

Even if I did not hold this position, however, I would reverse the Court of Appeals, for petitioner McCleskey has clearly demonstrated that his death sentence was imposed in violation of the Eighth and Fourteenth Amendments. I write separately to emphasize how conclusively McCleskey has also demonstrated precisely the type of risk of irrationality in sentencing that we have consistently condemned in our Eighth Amendment jurisprudence.

II

At some point in this case, Warren McCleskey doubtless asked his lawyer whether a jury was likely to sentence him to die. A candid reply to this question would have been disturbing. First, counsel would have to tell McCleskey that few of the details of the crime or of McCleskey's past criminal conduct were more important than the fact that his victim was white. Furthermore, counsel would feel bound to tell McCleskey that defendants charged with killing white victims in Georgia are 4.3 times as likely to be sentenced to death as defendants charged with killing blacks. In addition, frankness would compel the disclosure that it was more likely than not that the race of McCleskey's victim would determine whether he received a death sentence: 6 of every 11 defendants convicted of killing a white person would not have received the death penalty if their victims had been black, while, among defendants with aggravating and mitigating factors comparable to McCleskey's, 20 of every 34 would not have been sentenced to die if their victims had been black. Finally, the assessment would not be complete without the information that cases involving black defendants and white victims are more likely to result in a death sentence than cases featuring any other racial combination of defendant and victim. The story could be told in a variety of ways, but McCleskey could not fail to grasp its essential narrative line: there was a significant chance that race would play a prominent role in determining if he lived or died.

The Court today holds that Warren McCleskey's sentence was constitutionally imposed. It finds no fault in a system in which lawyers must tell their clients that race casts a large shadow on the capital sentencing process. The Court arrives at this conclusion by stating that the Baldus study cannot "prove that race enters into any capital sentencing decisions or that race was a factor in McCleskey's particular case." Since, according to Professor Baldus, we cannot say "to a moral certainty" that race influenced a decision, we can identify only "a likelihood that a particular factor entered into some decisions," and "a discrepancy that appears to correlate with race." This "likelihood" and "discrepancy," holds the Court, is insufficient to establish a constitutional violation. The Court reaches this conclusion by placing four factors on the scales opposite McCleskey's evidence: the desire to encourage sentencing discretion, the existence of "statutory safeguards" in the Georgia scheme, the fear of encouraging widespread challenges to other sentencing decisions, and the limits of the judicial role. The Court's evaluation of the significance of petitioner's evidence is fundamentally at odds with our consistent concern for rationality in capital sentencing, and the considerations that the majority invokes to discount that evidence cannot justify ignoring its force.

III

A

It is important to emphasize at the outset that the Court's observation that McCleskey cannot prove the influence of race on any particular sentencing decision is irrelevant in evaluating his Eighth Amendment claim. Since *Furman v. Georgia,* the Court has been concerned with the risk of the imposition of an arbitrary sentence, rather than the proven fact of one. *Furman* held that the death penalty "may not be imposed under sentencing procedures that create a substantial risk that the punishment will be inflicted in an arbitrary and capricious manner." As JUSTICE O'CONNOR observed in *Caldwell v. Mississippi,* a death sentence must be struck down when the circumstances under which it has been imposed "creat[e] an unacceptable risk that 'the death penalty [may have been] meted out arbitrarily or capriciously' or through 'whim or mistake.'" This emphasis on risk acknowledges the difficulty of divining the jury's motivation in an individual case. In addition, it reflects the fact that concern for arbitrariness focuses on the rationality of the system as a whole, and that a system that features a significant probability that sentencing decisions are influenced by impermissible considerations cannot be regarded as rational. As we said in *Gregg v. Georgia,* "the petitioner looks to the sentencing system as a whole (as the Court did in *Furman* and we do today)": a constitutional violation is established if a plaintiff demonstrates a "pattern of arbitrary and capricious sentencing."

As a result, our inquiry under the Eighth Amendment has not been directed to the validity of the individual sentences before us. In Godfrey, for instance, the Court struck down the petitioner's sentence because the vagueness of the statutory definition of heinous crimes created a risk that prejudice or other impermissible influences might have infected the sentencing decision. In vacating the sentence, we did not ask whether it was likely that Godfrey's own sentence reflected the operation of irrational considerations. Nor did we demand a demonstration that such considerations had actually entered into other sentencing decisions involving heinous crimes. Similarly, in *Roberts v. Louisiana* and *Woodson v. North Carolina* we struck down death sentences in part because mandatory imposition of the death penalty created the risk that a jury might rely on arbitrary considerations in deciding which persons should be convicted of capital crimes. Such a risk would arise, we said, because of the likelihood that jurors reluctant to impose capital punishment on a particular defendant would refuse to return a conviction, so that the effect of mandatory sentencing would be to recreate the unbounded sentencing discretion condemned in *Furman*. We did not ask whether the death sentences in the cases before us could have reflected the jury's rational consideration and rejection of mitigating factors. Nor did we require proof that juries had actually acted irrationally in other cases.

Defendants challenging their death sentences thus never have had to prove that impermissible considerations have actually infected sentencing decisions. We have required instead that they establish that the system under which they were sentenced posed a significant risk of such an occurrence. McCleskey's claim does differ, however, in one respect from these earlier cases: it is the first to base a challenge not on speculation about how a system might operate, but on empirical documentation of how it *does* operate.

The Court assumes the statistical validity of the Baldus study, and acknowledges that McCleskey has demonstrated a risk that racial prejudice plays a role in capital sentencing in Georgia. Nonetheless, it finds the probability of prejudice insufficient to create constitutional concern. Close analysis of the Baldus study, however, in light of both statistical principles and human experience, reveals that the risk that race influenced McCleskey's sentence is intolerable by any imaginable standard. . . .

McCleskey's statistics have particular force because most of them are the product of sophisticated multiple-regression analysis. Such analysis is designed precisely to identify patterns in the aggregate, even though we may not be able to reconstitute with certainty any individual decision that goes to make up that pattern. Multiple-regression analysis is particularly well suited to identify the influence of impermissible considerations in sentencing, since it is able to control for permissible factors that may explain an apparent arbitrary pattern. While the decisionmaking process of a body such as a jury may be complex, the Baldus study provides a massive compilation of the details that are most relevant to that decision. As we held in the context of Title VII of the Civil Rights Act of 1964 last Term, a multiple-regression analysis need not include every conceivable variable to establish a party's case, as long as it includes those variables that account for the major factors that are likely to influence decisions. In this case, Professor Baldus in fact conducted additional regression analyses in response to criticisms and suggestions by the District Court, all of which confirmed, and some of which even strengthened, the study's original conclusions.

The statistical evidence in this case thus relentlessly documents the risk that McCleskey's sentence was influenced by racial considerations. This evidence shows that there is a better than even chance in Georgia that race will influence the decision to impose the death penalty: a majority of defendants in white-victim crimes would not have been sentenced to die if their victims had been black. In determining whether this risk is acceptable, our judgment must be shaped by the awareness that "[t]he risk of racial prejudice infecting a capital sentencing proceeding is especially serious in light of the complete finality of the death sentence." In determining the guilt of a defendant, a State must prove its case beyond a reasonable doubt. That is, we refuse to convict if the chance of error is simply less likely than not. Surely, we should not be willing to take a person's life if the chance that his death sentence was irrationally imposed is more likely than not. In light of the gravity of the interest at stake, petitioner's statistics on their face are a powerful demonstration of the type of risk that our Eighth Amendment jurisprudence has consistently condemned.

C

Evaluation of McCleskey's evidence cannot rest solely on the numbers themselves. We must also ask whether the conclusion suggested by those numbers is consonant with our understanding of history and human experience. Georgia's legacy of a race-conscious criminal justice system, as well as this Court's own recognition of the persistent danger that racial attitudes may affect criminal proceedings, indicates that McCleskey's claim is not a fanciful product of mere statistical artifice.

For many years, Georgia operated openly and formally precisely the type of dual system the evidence shows is still effectively in place. The criminal law expressly differentiated between crimes committed by and against blacks and whites, distinctions whose lineage traced back to the time of slavery. During the colonial period, black slaves who killed whites in Georgia, regardless of whether in self-defense or in defense of another, were automatically executed.

By the time of the Civil War, a dual system of crime and punishment was well established in Georgia. The state criminal code contained separate sections for "Slaves and Free Persons of Color," and for all other persons. The code provided, for instance, for an automatic death sentence for murder committed by blacks, but declared that anyone else convicted of murder might receive life imprisonment if the conviction were founded solely on circumstantial testimony or simply if the jury so recommended. The code established that the rape of a free white female by a black "shall be" punishable by death. However, rape by anyone else of a free white female was punishable by a prison term not less than 2 nor more than 20 years. The rape of blacks was punishable "by fine and imprisonment, at the discretion of the court." A black convicted of assaulting a free white person with intent to murder could be put to death at the discretion of the court, but the same offense committed against a black, slave or free, was classified as a "minor" offense whose punishment lay in the discretion of the court, as long as such punishment did not "extend to life, limb, or health." Assault with intent to murder by a white person was punishable by a prison term of from 2 to 10 years. While sufficient provocation could reduce a charge of murder to manslaughter, the code provided that "[o]bedience and submission being the duty of a slave, much greater provocation is necessary to reduce a homicide of a white person by him to voluntary manslaughter, than is prescribed for white persons."

In more recent times, some 40 years ago, Gunnar Myrdal's epochal study of American race relations produced findings mirroring McCleskey's evidence:

> As long as only Negroes are concerned and no whites are disturbed, great leniency will be shown in most cases. . . . The sentences for even major crimes are ordinarily reduced when the victim is another Negro.

*****

> For offenses which involve any actual or potential danger to whites, however, Negroes are punished more severely than whites.

*****

> On the other hand, it is quite common for a white criminal to be set free if his crime was against a Negro.

This Court has invalidated portions of the Georgia capital sentencing system three times over the past 15 years. The specter of race discrimination was acknowledged by the Court in striking down the Georgia death penalty statute in *Furman*. Justice Douglas cited studies suggesting imposition of the death penalty in racially discriminatory fashion, and found the standardless statutes before the Court "pregnant with discrimination." JUSTICE MARSHALL pointed to statistics indicating that "Negroes [have been] executed far more often than whites in proportion to their percentage of the population. Studies indicate that while the higher rate of execution among Negroes is partially due to a higher rate of crime, there is evidence of racial discrimination." Although Justice Stewart declined to conclude that racial discrimination had been plainly proved, he stated that "[m]y concurring Brothers have demonstrated that, if any basis can be discerned for the selection of these few to be sentenced to die, it is the constitutionally impermissible basis of race." . . . It is clear that the Court regarded the opportunity for the operation of racial prejudice a particularly troublesome aspect of the unbounded discretion afforded by the Georgia sentencing scheme. . . .

This historical review of Georgia criminal law is not intended as a bill of indictment calling the State to account for past transgressions. Citation of past practices does not justify the automatic condemnation of current ones. But it would be unrealistic to ignore the influence of history in assessing the plausible implications of McCleskey's evidence. . . .

History and its continuing legacy thus buttress the probative force of McCleskey's statistics. Formal dual criminal laws may no longer be in effect, and intentional discrimination may no longer be prominent. The conclusions drawn from McCleskey's statistical evidence are therefore consistent with the lessons of social experience. . . .

It has now been over 13 years since Georgia adopted the provisions upheld in *Gregg*. Professor Baldus and his colleagues have compiled data on almost 2,500 homicides committed during the period 1973–1979. They have taken into account the influence of 230 nonracial variables, using a multitude of data from the State itself, and have produced striking evidence that the odds of being sentenced to death are significantly greater than average if a defendant is black or his or her victim is white. The challenge to the Georgia system is not speculative or theoretical; it is empirical. As a result, the Court cannot rely on the statutory safeguards in discounting McCleskey's evidence, for it is the very effectiveness of those safeguards that such evidence calls into question. . . .

The Court next states that its unwillingness to regard petitioner's evidence as sufficient is based in part on the fear that recognition of McCleskey's claim would open the door to widespread challenges to all aspects of criminal sentencing. Taken on its face, such a statement seems to suggest a fear of too much justice. Yet surely the majority would acknowledge that if striking evidence indicated that other minority groups, or women, or even persons with blond hair, were disproportionately sentenced to death, such a state of affairs would be repugnant to deeply rooted conceptions of fairness. The prospect that there may be more widespread abuse than McCleskey documents may be dismaying, but it does not justify complete abdication of our judicial role. The Constitution was framed fundamentally as a bulwark against governmental power, and preventing the arbitrary administration of punishment is a basic ideal of any society that purports to be governed by the rule of law.

In fairness, the Court's fear that McCleskey's claim is an invitation to descend a slippery slope also rests on the realization that any humanly imposed system of penalties will exhibit some imperfection. Yet to reject McCleskey's powerful evidence on this basis is to ignore both the qualitatively different character of the death penalty and the particular repugnance of racial discrimination, considerations which may properly be taken into account in determining whether various punishments are "cruel and unusual." Furthermore, it fails to take account of the unprecedented refinement and strength of the Baldus study. . . .

The Court also maintains that accepting McCleskey's claim would pose a threat to all sentencing because of the prospect that a correlation might be demonstrated between sentencing outcomes and other personal characteristics. Again, such a view is indifferent to the considerations that enter into a determination whether punishment is "cruel and unusual." Race is a consideration whose influence is expressly constitutionally proscribed. We have expressed a moral commitment, as embodied in our fundamental law, that this specific characteristic should not be the basis for allotting burdens and benefits. Three constitutional amendments, and numerous statutes, have been prompted specifically by the desire to address the effects of racism. Furthermore, we have explicitly acknowledged the illegitimacy of race as a consideration in capital sentencing. That a decision to impose the death penalty could be influenced by race is thus a particularly repugnant prospect, and evidence that race may play even a modest role in levying a death sentence should be enough to characterize that sentence as "cruel and unusual." . . .

The Court's projection of apocalyptic consequences for criminal sentencing is thus greatly exaggerated. The Court can indulge in such speculation only by ignoring its own jurisprudence demanding the highest scrutiny on issues of death and race. As a result, it fails to do justice to a claim in which both those elements are intertwined—an occasion calling for the most sensitive inquiry a court can conduct. Despite its acceptance of the validity of Warren McCleskey's evidence, the Court is willing to let his death sentence stand because it fears that we cannot successfully define a different standard for lesser punishments. This fear is baseless.

Finally, the Court justifies its rejection of McCleskey's claim by cautioning against usurpation of the legislatures' role in devising and monitoring criminal punishment. The Court is, of course, correct to emphasize the gravity of constitutional intervention and the importance that it be sparingly employed. The fact that "[c]apital punishment is now the law in more than two thirds of our States," however, does not diminish the fact that capital punishment is the most awesome act that a State can perform. The judiciary's role in this society counts for little if the use of governmental power to extinguish life does not elicit close scrutiny. . . .

V

At the time our Constitution was framed 200 years ago this year, blacks "had for more than a century before been regarded as beings of an inferior order, and altogether unfit to associate with the white race, either in social or political relations; and so far inferior, that they had no rights which the white man was bound to respect." Only 130 years ago, this Court relied on these observations to deny American citizenship to blacks. A mere three generations ago, this Court sanctioned racial segregation, stating that "[i]f one race be inferior to the other socially, the Constitution of the United States cannot put them upon the same plane."

In more recent times, we have sought to free ourselves from the burden of this history. Yet it has been scarcely a generation since this Court's first decision striking down racial segregation, and barely two decades since the legislative prohibition of racial discrimination in major domains of national life. These have been honorable steps, but we cannot pretend that in three decades we have completely escaped the grip of a historical legacy spanning centuries. Warren McCleskey's evidence confronts us with the subtle and persistent influence of the past. His message is a disturbing one to a society that has formally repudiated racism, and a frustrating one to a Nation accustomed to regarding its destiny as the product of its own will. Nonetheless, we ignore him at our peril, for we remain imprisoned by the past as long as we deny its influence in the present.

It is tempting to pretend that minorities on death row share a fate in no way connected to our own, that our treatment of them sounds no echoes beyond the chambers in which they die. Such an illusion is ultimately corrosive, for the reverberations of injustice are not so easily confined. "The destinies of the two races in this country are indissolubly linked together," and the way in which we choose those who will die reveals the depth of moral commitment among the living.

The Court's decision today will not change what attorneys in Georgia tell other Warren McCleskeys about their chances of execution. Nothing will soften the harsh message they must convey, nor alter the prospect that race undoubtedly will continue to be a topic of discussion. McCleskey's evidence will not have obtained judicial acceptance, but that will not affect what is said on death row. However many criticisms of today's decision may be rendered, these painful conversations will serve as the most eloquent dissents of all.

Source: McCleskey v. Kemp, 481 U.S. 279 (1987), at 283–320, 321–345.

Document 4.14

Justice Sandra Day O'Connor on Executing the Mentally Retarded, June 26, 1989

In Penry v. Lynaugh *(1989),* the Supreme Court ordered a new sentencing trial for Johnny Paul Penry on the grounds that the Texas procedure had not provided the jury with sufficient clarity to consider his mental retardation as a mitigating circumstance. At the same time, Justice O'Connor's opinion for the Court rejected the categorical claim that the mentally retarded could never be executed.

JUSTICE O'CONNOR delivered the opinion of the Court except as to Part IV-C

In this case, we must decide whether petitioner, Johnny Paul Penry, was sentenced to death in violation of the Eighth Amendment because the jury was not instructed that it could consider and give effect to his mitigating evidence in imposing its sentence. We must also decide whether the Eighth Amendment categorically prohibits Penry's execution because he is mentally retarded.

I

On the morning of October 25, 1979, Pamela Carpenter was brutally raped, beaten, and stabbed with a pair of scissors in her home in Livingston, Texas. She died a few hours later in the course of emergency treatment. Before she died, she described her assailant. Her description led two local sheriff's deputies to suspect Penry, who had recently been released on parole after conviction on another rape charge. Penry subsequently gave two statements confessing to the crime and was charged with capital murder.

At a competency hearing held before trial, a clinical psychologist, Dr. Jerome Brown, testified that Penry was mentally retarded. As a child, Penry was diagnosed as having organic brain damage, which was probably caused by trauma to the brain at birth. Penry was tested over the years as having an IQ between 50 and 63, which indicates mild to moderate retardation. Dr. Brown's own testing before the trial indicated that Penry had an IQ of 54. Dr. Brown's evaluation also revealed that Penry, who was 22 years old at the time of the crime, had the mental age of a 6 1/2-year-old, which means that "he has the ability to learn and the learning or the knowledge of the average 6 1/2 year old kid." Penry's social maturity, or ability to function in the world, was that of a 9- or 10-year-old. Dr. Brown testified that "there's a point at which anyone with [Penry's] IQ is always incompetent, but, you know, this man is more in the borderline range."

The jury found Penry competent to stand trial. The guilt-innocence phase of the trial began on March 24, 1980. The trial court determined that Penry's confessions were voluntary, and they were introduced into evidence. At trial, Penry raised an insanity defense and presented the testimony of a psychiatrist, Dr. Jose Garcia. Dr. Garcia testified that Penry suffered from organic brain damage and moderate retardation, which resulted in poor impulse control and an inability to learn from experience. Dr. Garcia indicated that Penry's brain damage was probably caused at birth, but may have been caused by beatings and multiple injuries to the brain at an early age. In Dr. Garcia's judgment, Penry was suffering from an organic brain disorder at the time of the offense which made it impossible for him to appreciate the wrongfulness of his conduct or to conform his conduct to the law.

Penry's mother testified at trial that Penry was unable to learn in school and never finished the first grade. Penry's sister testified that their mother had frequently beaten him over the head with a belt when he was a child. Penry was also routinely locked in his room without access to a toilet for long periods of time. As a youngster, Penry was in and out of a number of state schools and hospitals, until his father removed him from state schools altogether when he was 12. Penry's aunt subsequently struggled for over a year to teach Penry how to print his name.

The State introduced the testimony of two psychiatrists to rebut the testimony of Dr. Garcia. Dr. Kenneth Vogtsberger testified that although Penry was a person of limited mental ability, he was not suffering from any mental illness or defect at the time of the crime, and that he knew the difference between right and wrong and had the potential to honor the law. In his view, Penry had characteristics consistent with an antisocial personality, including an inability to learn from experience and a tendency to be impulsive and to violate society's norms. He testified further that Penry's low IQ scores under-estimated his alertness and understanding of what went on around him.

Dr. Felix Peebles also testified for the State that Penry was legally sane at the time of the offense and had a "full-blown anti-social personality." In addition, Dr. Peebles testified that he personally diagnosed Penry as being mentally retarded in 1973 and again in 1977, and that Penry "had a very bad life generally, bringing up." In Dr. Peebles' view, Penry "had been socially and emotionally deprived and he had not learned to read and write adequately." Although they disagreed with the defense psychiatrist over the extent and cause of Penry's mental limitations, both psychiatrists for the State acknowledged that Penry was a person of extremely limited mental ability, and that he seemed unable to learn from his mistakes.

The jury rejected Penry's insanity defense and found him guilty of capital murder. The following day, at the close of the penalty hearing, the jury decided the sentence to be imposed on Penry by answering three "special issues":

(1) whether the conduct of the defendant that caused the death of the deceased was committed deliberately and with the reasonable expectation that the death of the deceased or another would result;

(2) whether there is a probability that the defendant would commit criminal acts of violence that would constitute a continuing threat to society; and

(3) if raised by the evidence, whether the conduct of the defendant in killing the deceased was unreasonable in response to the provocation, if any, by the deceased.

If the jury unanimously answers "yes" to each issue submitted, the trial court must sentence the defendant to death. Otherwise, the defendant is sentenced to life imprisonment.

Defense counsel raised a number of objections to the proposed charge to the jury. With respect to the first special issue, he objected that the charge failed to define the term "deliberately." With respect to the second special issue, he objected that the charge failed to define the terms "probability," "criminal acts of violence," and "continuing threat to society." Defense counsel also objected to the charge because it failed to "authorize a discretionary grant of mercy based upon the existence of mitigating circumstances" and because it "fail[ed] to require as a condition to the assessment of the death penalty that the State show beyond a reasonable doubt that any aggravating circumstances found to exist outweigh any mitigating circumstances." In addition, the charge failed to instruct the jury that it may take into consideration all of the evidence whether aggravating or mitigating in nature which was submitted in the full trial of the case. Defense counsel also objected that, in light of Penry's mental retardation, permitting the jury to assess the death penalty in this case amounted to cruel and unusual punishment prohibited by the Eighth Amendment.

These objections were overruled by the trial court. The jury was then instructed that the State bore the burden of proof on the special issues, and that before any issue could be answered "yes," all 12 jurors must be convinced by the evidence beyond a reasonable doubt that the answer to that issue should be "yes." The jurors were further instructed that in answering the three special issues, they could consider all the evidence submitted in both the guilt-innocence phase and the penalty phase of the trial. The jury charge then listed the three questions, with the names of the defendant and the deceased inserted.

The jury answered "yes" to all three special issues, and Penry was sentenced to death. The Texas Court of Criminal Appeals affirmed his conviction and sentence on direct appeal. The court concluded that Penry was allowed to present all relevant mitigating evidence at the punishment hearing, and that there was no constitutional infirmity in failing to require the jury to find that aggravating circumstances outweighed mitigating ones or in failing to authorize a discretionary grant of mercy based upon the existence of mitigating circumstances. The court also held that imposition of the death penalty was not prohibited by virtue of Penry's mental retardation. This Court denied certiorari on direct review.

Penry then filed this federal habeas corpus petition challenging his death sentence. Among other claims, Penry argued that he was sentenced in violation of the Eighth Amendment because the trial court failed to instruct the jury on how to weigh mitigating factors in answering the special issues and failed to define the term "deliberately." Penry also argued that it was cruel and unusual punishment to execute a mentally retarded person. The District Court denied relief, and Penry appealed to the Court of Appeals for the Fifth Circuit.

The Court of Appeals affirmed the District Court's judgment. . . .

We granted certiorari to resolve two questions. First, was Penry sentenced to death in violation of the Eighth Amendment because the jury was not adequately instructed to take into consideration all of his mitigating evidence and because the terms in the Texas special issues were not defined in such a way that the jury could consider and give effect to his mitigating evidence in answering them? Second, is it cruel and unusual punishment under the Eighth Amendment to execute a mentally retarded person with Penry's reasoning ability? . . .

Penry does not challenge the facial validity of the Texas death penalty statute, which was upheld against an Eighth Amendment challenge in *Jurek v. Texas*. Nor does he dispute that some types of mitigating evidence can be fully considered by the sentencer in the absence of special jury instructions. Instead, Penry argues that, on the facts of this case, the jury was unable to fully consider and give effect to the mitigating evidence of his mental retardation and abused background in answering the three special issues. In our view, the relief Penry seeks does not "impos[e] a new obligation" on the State of Texas. Rather, Penry simply asks the State to fulfill the assurance upon which *Jurek* was based: namely, that the special issues would be interpreted broadly enough to permit the sentencer to consider all of the relevant mitigating evidence a defendant might present in imposing sentence. . . .

Our decisions subsequent to *Jurek* have reaffirmed that the Eighth Amendment mandates an individualized assessment of the appropriateness of the death penalty. In *Lockett v. Ohio*, a plurality of this Court held that the Eighth and Fourteenth Amendments require that the sentencer "not be precluded from considering, as a mitigating factor, any aspect of a defendant's character or record and any of the circumstances of the offense that the defendant proffers as a basis for a sentence less than death." Thus, the Court held unconstitutional the Ohio death penalty statute which mandated capital punishment upon a finding of one aggravating circumstance unless one of three statutory mitigating factors were present. . . .

Thus, at the time Penry's conviction became final, it was clear that a State could not, consistent with the Eighth and Fourteenth Amendments, prevent the sentencer from considering and giving effect to evidence relevant to the defendant's background or character or to the circumstances of the offense that mitigate against imposing the death penalty. Moreover, the facial validity of the Texas death penalty statute had been upheld in *Jurek* on the basis of assurances that the special issues would be interpreted broadly enough to enable sentencing juries to consider all of the relevant mitigating evidence a defendant might present. Penry argues that those assurances were not fulfilled in his particular case because, without appropriate instructions, the jury could not fully consider and give effect to the mitigating evidence of his mental retardation and abused childhood in rendering its sentencing decision. The rule Penry seeks—that when such mitigating evidence is presented, Texas juries must, upon request, be given jury instructions that make it possible for them to give effect to that mitigating evidence in determining whether the death penalty should be imposed—is not a "new rule" because it is dictated by *Lockett*. Moreover, in light of the assurances upon which *Jurek* was based, we conclude that the relief Penry seeks does not "impos[e] a new obligation" on the State of Texas. . . .

Although Penry offered mitigating evidence of his mental retardation and abused childhood as the basis for a sentence of life imprisonment rather than death, the jury that sentenced him was only able to express its views on the appropriate sentence by answering three questions: Did Penry act deliberately when he murdered Pamela Carpenter? Is there a probability that he will be dangerous in the future? Did he act unreasonably in response to provocation? The jury was never instructed that it could consider the evidence offered by Penry as mitigating evidence and that it could give mitigating effect to that evidence in imposing sentence. . . .

Penry's mental retardation was relevant to the question whether he was capable of acting "deliberately," but it also "had relevance to [his] moral culpability beyond the scope of the special verdict questio[n]." Personal culpability is not solely a function of a defendant's capacity to act "deliberately." A rational juror at the penalty phase of the trial could have concluded, in light of Penry's confession, that he deliberately killed Pamela Carpenter to escape detection. Because Penry was mentally retarded, however, and thus less able than a normal adult to control his impulses or to evaluate the consequences of his conduct, and because of his history of childhood abuse, that same juror could also conclude that Penry was less morally "culpable than defendants who have no such excuse," but who acted "deliberately" as that term is commonly understood.

In the absence of jury instructions defining "deliberately" in a way that would clearly direct the jury to consider fully Penry's mitigating evidence as it bears on his personal culpability, we cannot be sure that the jury was able to give effect to the mitigating evidence of Penry's mental retardation and history of abuse in answering the first special issue. Without such a special instruction, a juror who believed that Penry's retardation and background diminished his moral culpability and made imposition of the death penalty unwarranted would be unable to give effect to that conclusion if the juror also believed that Penry committed the crime "deliberately." Thus, we cannot be sure that the jury's answer to the first special issue reflected a "reasoned moral response" to Penry's mitigating evidence.

The second special issue asks "whether there is a probability that the defendant would commit criminal acts of violence that would constitute a continuing threat to society." The mitigating evidence concerning Penry's mental retardation indicated that one effect of his retardation is his inability to learn from his mistakes. Although this evidence is relevant to the second issue, it is relevant only as an aggravating factor because it suggests a "yes" answer to the question of future dangerousness. The prosecutor argued at the penalty hearing that there was "a very strong probability, based on the history of this defendant, his previous criminal record, and the psychiatric testimony that we've had in this case, that the defendant will continue to commit acts of this nature." Even in a prison setting, the prosecutor argued, Penry could hurt doctors, nurses, librarians, or teachers who worked in the prison.

Penry's mental retardation and history of abuse is thus a two-edged sword: it may diminish his blameworthiness for his crime even as it indicates that there is a probability that he will be dangerous in the future. . . .

The State conceded at oral argument in this Court that if a juror concluded that Penry acted deliberately and was likely to be dangerous in the future, but also concluded that because of his mental retardation he was not sufficiently culpable to deserve the death penalty, that juror would be unable to give effect to that mitigating evidence under the instructions given in this case. The State contends, however, that to instruct the jury that it could render a discretionary grant of mercy, or say "no" to the death penalty, based on Penry's mitigating evidence, would be to return to the sort of unbridled discretion that led to *Furman v. Georgia*. We disagree. . . .

In this case, in the absence of instructions informing the jury that it could consider and give effect to the mitigating evidence of Penry's mental retardation and abused background by declining to impose the death penalty, we conclude that the jury was not provided with a vehicle for expressing its "reasoned moral response" to that evidence in rendering its sentencing decision. Our reasoning in *Lockett* thus compels a remand for resentencing so that we do not "risk that the death penalty will be imposed in spite of factors which may call for a less severe penalty." . . .

IV

Penry's second claim is that it would be cruel and unusual punishment, prohibited by the Eighth Amendment, to execute a mentally retarded person like himself with the reasoning capacity of a 7-year-old. He argues that because of their mental disabilities, mentally retarded people do not possess the level of moral culpability to justify imposing the death sentence. He also argues that there is an emerging national consensus against executing the mentally retarded. The State responds that there is insufficient evidence of a national consensus against executing the retarded, and that existing procedural safeguards adequately protect the interests of mentally retarded persons such as Penry. . . .

B

The Eighth Amendment categorically prohibits the infliction of cruel and unusual punishments. At a minimum, the Eighth Amendment prohibits punishment considered cruel and unusual at the time the Bill of Rights was adopted. The prohibitions of the Eighth Amendment are not limited, however, to those practices condemned by the common law in 1789. The prohibition against cruel and unusual punishments also recognizes the "evolving standards of decency that mark the progress of a maturing society." In discerning those "evolving standards," we have looked to objective evidence of how our society views a particular punishment today. The clearest and most reliable objective evidence of contemporary values is the legislation enacted by the country's legislatures. We have also looked to data concerning the actions of sentencing juries.

It was well settled at common law that "idiots," together with "lunatics," were not subject to punishment for criminal acts committed under those incapacities. . . .

There was no one definition of idiocy at common law, but the term "idiot" was generally used to describe persons who had a total lack of reason or understanding, or an inability to distinguish between good and evil. Hale wrote that a person who is deaf and mute from birth "is in presumption of law an ideot . . . because he hath no possibility to understand what is forbidden by law to be done, or under what penalties: but if it can appear, that he hath the use of understanding, . . . then he may be tried, and suffer judgment and execution." . . .

The common law prohibition against punishing "idiots" for their crimes suggests that it may indeed be "cruel and unusual" punishment to execute persons who are profoundly or severely retarded and wholly lacking the capacity to appreciate the wrongfulness of their actions. Because of the protections afforded by the insanity defense today, such a person is not likely to be convicted or face the prospect of punishment. Moreover, under *Ford v. Wainwright,* someone who is "unaware of the punishment they are about to suffer and why they are to suffer it" cannot be executed.

Such a case is not before us today. Penry was found competent to stand trial. In other words, he was found to have the ability to consult with his lawyer with a reasonable degree of rational understanding, and was found to have a rational as well as factual understanding of the proceedings against him. In addition, the jury rejected his insanity defense, which reflected their conclusion that Penry knew that his conduct was wrong and was capable of conforming his conduct to the requirements of the law.

Penry argues, however, that there is objective evidence today of an emerging national consensus against execution of the mentally retarded, reflecting the "evolving standards of decency that mark the progress of a maturing society." The federal Anti-Drug Abuse Act of 1988 prohibits execution of a person who is mentally retarded. Only one State, however, currently bans execution of retarded persons who have been found guilty of a capital offense. Maryland has enacted a similar statute which will take effect on July 1, 1989.

In contrast, in *Ford v. Wainwright*, which held that the Eighth Amendment prohibits execution of the insane, considerably more evidence of a national consensus was available. No State permitted the execution of the insane, and 26 States had statutes explicitly requiring suspension of the execution of a capital defendant who became insane. Other States had adopted the common law prohibition against executing the insane. Moreover, in examining the objective evidence of contemporary standards of decency in *Thompson v. Oklahoma*, the plurality noted that 18 States expressly established a minimum age in their death penalty statutes, and all of them required that the defendant have attained at least the age of 16 at the time of the offense. In our view, the two state statutes prohibiting execution of the mentally retarded, even when added to the 14 States that have rejected capital punishment completely, do not provide sufficient evidence at present of a national consensus.

Penry does not offer any evidence of the general behavior of juries with respect to sentencing mentally retarded defendants, nor of decisions of prosecutors. He points instead to several public opinion surveys that indicate strong public opposition to execution of the retarded. For example, a poll taken in Texas found that 86% of those polled supported the death penalty, but 73% opposed its application to the mentally retarded. A Florida poll found 71% of those surveyed were opposed to the execution of mentally retarded capital defendants, while only 12% were in favor. A Georgia poll found 66% of those polled opposed to the death penalty for the retarded, 17% in favor, with 16% responding that it depends how retarded the person is. In addition, the AAMR, the country's oldest and largest organization of professionals working with the mentally retarded, opposes the execution of persons who are mentally retarded. The public sentiment expressed in these and other polls and resolutions may ultimately find expression in legislation, which is an objective indicator of contemporary values upon which we can rely. But at present, there is insufficient evidence of a national consensus against executing mentally retarded people convicted of capital offenses for us to conclude that it is categorically prohibited by the Eighth Amendment. . . .

On the record before the Court today, however, I cannot conclude that all mentally retarded people of Penry's ability—by virtue of their mental retardation alone, and apart from any individualized consideration of their personal responsibility—inevitably lack the cognitive, volitional, and moral capacity to act with the degree of culpability associated with the death penalty. Mentally retarded persons are individuals whose abilities and experiences can vary greatly. . . .

In addition to the varying degrees of mental retardation, the consequences of a retarded person's mental impairment, including the deficits in his or her adaptive behavior, "may be ameliorated through education and habilitation." In light of the diverse capacities and life experiences of mentally retarded persons, it cannot be said on the record before us today that all mentally retarded people, by definition, can never act with the level of culpability associated with the death penalty. . . .

In sum, mental retardation is a factor that may well lessen a defendant's culpability for a capital offense. But we cannot conclude today that the Eighth Amendment precludes the execution of any mentally retarded person of Penry's ability convicted of a capital offense simply by virtue of his or her mental retardation alone. So long as sentencers can consider and give effect to mitigating evidence of mental retardation in imposing sentence, an individualized determination whether "death is the appropriate punishment" can be made in each particular case. While a national consensus against execution of the mentally retarded may someday emerge reflecting the "evolving standards of decency that mark the progress of a maturing society," there is insufficient evidence of such a consensus today.

Accordingly, the judgment below is affirmed in part and reversed in part, and the case is remanded for further proceedings consistent with this opinion.

It is so ordered.

Source: Penry v. Lynaugh, 492 U.S. 302 (1989), at 313–335.

Document 4.15
The Supreme Court Rules That States May Execute Juvenile Murderers in *Stanford v. Kentucky*, June 26, 1989

In the same term that it rejected the argument that the mentally retarded could not be executed consistent with the Eighth Amendment, the Supreme Court turned down a similar claim regarding defendants under the age of eighteen who committed murder. Writing for a plurality of the justices, Antonin Scalia argued that neither state legislation nor jury verdicts indicated a national consensus against capital punishment for minors. Justice William Brennan dissented for himself and four others in an opinion that questioned Scalia's methodology and also invoked international legal norms.

JUSTICE SCALIA announced the judgment of the Court and delivered the opinion of the Court with respect to Parts I, II, III, and IV-A, and an opinion with respect to Parts IV-B and V, in which THE CHIEF JUSTICE, JUSTICE WHITE, and JUSTICE KENNEDY join.

These two consolidated cases require us to decide whether the imposition of capital punishment on an individual for a crime committed at 16 or 17 years of age constitutes cruel and unusual punishment under the Eighth Amendment.

I

The first case, No. 87–5765, involves the shooting death of 20-year-old Barbel Poore in Jefferson County, Kentucky. Petitioner Kevin Stanford committed the murder on January 7, 1981, when he was approximately 17 years and 4 months of age. Stanford and his accomplice repeatedly raped and sodomized Poore during and after their commission of a robbery at a gas station where she worked as an attendant. They then drove her to a secluded area near the station, where Stanford shot her pointblank in the face and then in the back of her head. The proceeds from the robbery were roughly 300 cartons of cigarettes, two gallons of fuel, and a small amount of cash. A corrections officer testified that petitioner explained the murder as follows: "[H]e said, I had to shoot her, [she] lived next door to me and she would recognize me. . . . I guess we could have tied her up or something or beat [her up] . . . and tell her if she tells, we would kill her. . . . Then after he said that he started laughing."

After Stanford's arrest, a Kentucky juvenile court conducted hearings to determine whether he should be transferred for trial as an adult. The statute provided that juvenile court jurisdiction could be waived and an offender tried as an adult if he was either charged with a Class A felony or capital crime, or was over 16 years of age and charged with a felony. Stressing the seriousness of petitioner's offenses and the unsuccessful attempts of the juvenile system to treat him for numerous instances of past delinquency, the juvenile court found certification for trial as an adult to be in the best interest of petitioner and the community.

Stanford was convicted of murder, first-degree sodomy, first-degree robbery, and receiving stolen property, and was sentenced to death and 45 years in prison. The Kentucky Supreme Court affirmed the death sentence, rejecting Stanford's "deman[d] that he has a constitutional right to treatment." Finding that the record clearly demonstrated that "there was no program or treatment appropriate for the appellant in the juvenile justice system," the court held that the juvenile court did not err in certifying petitioner for trial as an adult. The court also stated that petitioner's "age and the possibility that he might be rehabilitated were mitigating factors appropriately left to the consideration of the jury that tried him."

The second case before us today involves the stabbing death of Nancy Allen, a 26-year-old mother of two who was working behind the sales counter of the convenience store she and David Allen owned and operated in Avondale, Missouri. Petitioner Heath Wilkins committed the murder on July 27, 1985, when he was approximately 16 years and 6 months of age. The record reflects that Wilkins' plan was to rob the store and murder "whoever was behind the counter" because "a dead person can't talk." While Wilkins' accomplice, Patrick Stevens, held Allen, Wilkins stabbed her, causing her to fall to the floor. When Stevens had trouble operating the cash register, Allen spoke up to assist him, leading Wilkins to stab her three more times in her chest. Two of these wounds penetrated the victim's heart. When Allen began to beg for her life, Wilkins stabbed her four more times in the neck, opening her carotid artery. After helping themselves to liquor, cigarettes, rolling papers, and approximately $450 in cash and checks, Wilkins and Stevens left Allen to die on the floor.

Because he was roughly six months short of the age of majority for purposes of criminal prosecution, Wilkins could not automatically be tried as an adult under Missouri law. Before that could happen, the juvenile court was required to terminate juvenile court jurisdiction and certify Wilkins for trial as an adult under Missouri law, which permits individuals between 14 and 17 years of age who have committed felonies to be tried as adults. Relying on the "viciousness, force and violence" of the alleged crime, petitioner's maturity, and the failure of the juvenile justice system to rehabilitate him after previous delinquent acts, the juvenile court made the necessary certification.

Wilkins was charged with first-degree murder, armed criminal action, and carrying a concealed weapon. After the court found him competent, petitioner entered guilty pleas to all charges. A punishment hearing was held, at which both the State and petitioner himself urged imposition of the death sentence. Evidence at the hearing revealed that petitioner had been in and out of juvenile facilities since the age of eight for various acts of burglary, theft, and arson, had attempted to kill his mother by putting insecticide into Tylenol capsules, and had killed several animals in his neighborhood. Although psychiatric testimony indicated that Wilkins had "personality disorders," the witnesses agreed that Wilkins was aware of his actions and could distinguish right from wrong.

Determining that the death penalty was appropriate, the trial court entered the following order:

"[T]he court finds beyond reasonable doubt that the following aggravating circumstances exist:

"1. The murder in the first degree was committed while the defendant was engaged in the perpetration of the felony of robbery, and

"2. The murder in the first degree involved depravity of mind and that as a result thereof, it was outrageously or wantonly vile, horrible or inhuman."

On mandatory review of Wilkins' death sentence, the Supreme Court of Missouri affirmed, rejecting the argument that the punishment violated the Eighth Amendment. We granted certiorari in these cases to decide whether the Eighth Amendment precludes the death penalty for individuals who commit crimes at 16 or 17 years of age.

II

The thrust of both Wilkins' and Stanford's arguments is that imposition of the death penalty on those who were juveniles when they committed their crimes falls within the Eighth Amendment's prohibition against "cruel and unusual punishments." Wilkins would have us define juveniles as individuals 16 years of age and under; Stanford would draw the line at 17.

Neither petitioner asserts that his sentence constitutes one of "those modes or acts of punishment that had been considered cruel and unusual at the time that the Bill of Rights was adopted." Nor could they support such a contention. At that time, the common law set the rebuttable presumption of incapacity to commit any felony at the age of 14, and theoretically permitted capital punishment to be imposed on anyone over the age of 7. In accordance with the standards of this common-law tradition, at least 281 offenders under the age of 18 have been executed in this country, and at least 126 under the age of 17.

Thus petitioners are left to argue that their punishment is contrary to the "evolving standards of decency that mark the progress of a maturing society." They are correct in asserting that this Court has "not confined the prohibition embodied in the Eighth Amendment to 'barbarous' methods that were generally outlawed in the 18th century," but instead has interpreted the Amendment "in a flexible and dynamic manner." In determining what standards have "evolved," however, we have looked not to our own conceptions of decency, but to those of modern American society as a whole. As we have said, "Eighth Amendment judgments should not be, or appear to be, merely the subjective views of individual Justices; judgment should be informed by objective factors to the maximum possible extent." This approach is dictated both by the language of the Amendment—which proscribes only those punishments that are both "cruel and unusual"—and by the "deference we owe to the decisions of the state legislatures under our federal system." . . .

Since a majority of the States that permit capital punishment authorize it for crimes committed at age 16 or above, petitioners' cases are more analogous to *Tison v. Arizona* than *Coker.* In *Tison,* which upheld Arizona's imposition of the death penalty for major participation in a felony with reckless indifference to human life, we noted that only 11 of those jurisdictions imposing capital punishment rejected its use in such circumstances. As we noted earlier, here the number is 15 for offenders under 17, and 12 for offenders under 18. We think the same conclusion as in *Tison* is required in these cases.

Petitioners make much of the recently enacted federal statute providing capital punishment for certain drug-related offenses, but limiting that punishment to offenders 18 and over. That reliance is entirely misplaced. To begin with, the statute in question does not embody a judgment by the Federal Legislature that no murder is heinous enough to warrant the execution of such a youthful offender, but merely that the narrow class of offense it defines is not. The congressional judgment on the broader question, if apparent at all, is to be found in the law that permits 16- and 17-year-olds (after appropriate findings) to be tried and punished as adults for all federal offenses, including those bearing a capital penalty that is not limited to 18-year-olds. Moreover, even if it were true that no federal statute permitted the execution of persons under 18, that would not remotely establish—in the face of a substantial number of state statutes to the contrary—a national consensus that such punishment is inhumane, any more than the absence of a federal lottery establishes a national consensus that lotteries are socially harmful. To be sure, the absence of a federal death penalty for 16- or 17-year-olds (if it existed) might be evidence that there is no national consensus in favor of such punishment. It is not the burden of Kentucky and Missouri, however, to establish a national consensus approving what their citizens have voted to do; rather, it is the "heavy burden" of petitioners to establish a national consensus against it. As far as the primary and most reliable indication of consensus is concerned—the pattern of enacted laws—petitioners have failed to carry that burden. . . .

IV

A

Wilkins and Stanford argue, however, that even if the laws themselves do not establish a settled consensus, the application of the laws does. That contemporary society views capital punishment of 16- and 17-year-old offenders as inappropriate is demonstrated, they say, by the reluctance of juries to impose, and prosecutors to seek, such sentences. Petitioners are quite correct that a far smaller number of offenders under 18 than over 18 have been sentenced to death in this country. From 1982 through 1988, for example, out of 2,106 total death sentences, only 15 were imposed on individuals who were 16 or under when they committed their crimes, and only 30 on individuals who were 17 at the time of the crime. And it appears that actual executions for crimes committed under age 18 accounted for only about two percent of the total number of executions that occurred between 1642 and 1986. As Wilkins points out, the last execution of a person who committed a crime under 17 years of age occurred in 1959. These statistics, however, carry little significance. Given the undisputed fact that a far smaller percentage of capital crimes are committed by persons under 18 than over 18, the discrepancy in treatment is much less than might seem. Granted, however, that a substantial discrepancy exists, that does not establish the requisite proposition that the death sentence for offenders under 18 is categorically unacceptable to prosecutors and juries. To the contrary, it is not only possible, but overwhelmingly probable, that the very considerations which induce petitioners and their supporters to believe that death should never be imposed on offenders under 18 cause prosecutors and juries to believe that it should rarely be imposed.

B

This last point suggests why there is also no relevance to the laws cited by petitioners and their amici which set 18 or more as the legal age for engaging in various activities, ranging from driving to drinking alcoholic beverages to voting. It is, to begin with, absurd to think that one must be mature enough to drive carefully, to drink responsibly, or to vote intelligently, in order to be mature enough to understand that murdering another human being is profoundly wrong, and to conform one's conduct to that most minimal of all civilized standards. But even if the requisite degrees of maturity were comparable, the age statutes in question would still not be relevant. They do not represent a social judgment that all persons under the designated ages are not responsible enough to drive, to drink, or to vote, but at most a judgment that the vast majority are not. These laws set the appropriate ages for the operation of a system that makes its determinations in gross, and that does not conduct individualized maturity tests for each driver, drinker, or voter. The criminal justice system, however, does provide individualized testing. In the realm of capital punishment in particular, "individualized consideration [is] a constitutional requirement." Twenty-nine States, including both Kentucky and Missouri, have codified this constitutional requirement in laws specifically designating the defendant's age as a mitigating factor in capital cases. Moreover, the determinations required by juvenile transfer statutes to certify a juvenile for trial as an adult ensure individualized consideration of the maturity and moral responsibility of 16- and 17-year-old offenders before they are even held to stand trial as adults. The application of this particularized system to the petitioners can be declared constitutionally inadequate only if there is a consensus, not that 17 or 18 is the age at which most persons, or even almost all persons, achieve sufficient maturity to be held fully responsible for murder; but that 17 or 18 is the age before which no one can reasonably be held fully responsible. What displays society's views on this latter point are not the ages set forth in the generalized system of driving, drinking, and voting laws cited by petitioners and their amici, but the ages at which the States permit their particularized capital punishment systems to be applied.

V

Having failed to establish a consensus against capital punishment for 16- and 17-year-old offenders through state and federal statutes and the behavior of prosecutors and juries, petitioners seek to demonstrate it through other indicia, including public opinion polls, the views of interest groups, and the positions adopted by various professional associations. We decline the invitation to rest constitutional law upon such uncertain foundations. A revised national consensus so broad, so clear, and so enduring as to justify a permanent prohibition upon all units of democratic government must appear in the operative acts (laws and the application of laws) that the people have approved.

We also reject petitioners' argument that we should invalidate capital punishment of 16- and 17-year-old offenders on the ground that it fails to serve the legitimate goals of penology. According to petitioners, it fails to deter because juveniles, possessing less developed cognitive skills than adults, are less likely to fear death; and it fails to exact just retribution because juveniles, being less mature and responsible, are also less morally blameworthy. In support of these claims, petitioners and their supporting amici marshal an array of socioscientific evidence concerning the psychological and emotional development of 16- and 17-year-olds.

If such evidence could conclusively establish the entire lack of deterrent effect and moral responsibility, resort to the Cruel and Unusual Punishments Clause would be unnecessary; the Equal Protection Clause of the Fourteenth Amendment would invalidate these laws for lack of rational basis. But as the adjective "socioscientific" suggests (and insofar as evaluation of moral responsibility is concerned perhaps the adjective "ethicoscientific" would be more apt), it is not demonstrable that no 16-year-old is "adequately responsible" or significantly deterred. It is rational, even if mistaken, to think the contrary. The battle must be fought, then, on the field of the Eighth Amendment; and in that struggle socioscientific, ethicoscientific, or even purely scientific evidence is not an available weapon. The punishment is either "cruel and unusual" (i. e., society has set its face against it) or it is not. The audience for these arguments, in other words, is not this Court but the citizenry of the United States. It is they, not we, who must be persuaded. For as we stated earlier, our job is to identify the "evolving standards of decency"; to determine, not what they should be, but what they are. We have no power under the Eighth Amendment to substitute our belief in the scientific evidence for the society's apparent skepticism. In short, we emphatically reject petitioner's suggestion that the issues in this case permit us to apply our "own informed judgment." Brief for Petitioner in No. 87–6026, p. 23, regarding the desirability of permitting the death penalty for crimes by 16- and 17-year-olds. . . .

While the dissent is correct that several of our cases have engaged in so-called "proportionality" analysis, examining whether "there is a disproportion 'between the punishment imposed and the defendant's blameworthiness,'" and whether a punishment makes any "measurable contribution to acceptable goals of punishment," see post, at 393, we have never invalidated a punishment on this basis alone. All of our cases condemning a punishment under this mode of analysis also found that the objective indicators of state laws or jury determinations evidenced a societal consensus against that penalty. In fact, the two methodologies blend into one another, since "proportionality" analysis itself can only be conducted on the basis of the standards set by our own society; the only alternative, once again, would be our personal preferences.

* * *

We discern neither a historical nor a modern societal consensus forbidding the imposition of capital punishment on any person who murders at 16 or 17 years of age. Accordingly, we conclude that such punishment does not offend the Eighth Amendment's prohibition against cruel and unusual punishment.

The judgments of the Supreme Court of Kentucky and the Supreme Court of Missouri are therefore

Affirmed.

JUSTICE BRENNAN, with whom JUSTICE MARSHALL, JUSTICE BLACK-MUN, and JUSTICE STEVENS join, dissenting.

I believe that to take the life of a person as punishment for a crime committed when below the age of 18 is cruel and unusual and hence is prohibited by the Eighth Amendment.

The method by which this Court assesses a claim that a punishment is unconstitutional because it is cruel and unusual is established by our precedents, and it bears little resemblance to the method four Members of the Court apply in this case. To be sure, we begin the task of deciding whether a punishment is unconstitutional by reviewing legislative enactments and the work of sentencing juries relating to the punishment in question to determine whether our Nation has set its face against a punishment to an extent that it can be concluded that the punishment offends our "evolving standards of decency." The Court undertakes such an analysis in this case. But JUSTICE SCALIA, in his plurality opinion on this point, would treat the Eighth Amendment inquiry as complete with this investigation. I agree with JUSTICE O'CONNOR that a more searching inquiry is mandated by our precedents interpreting the Cruel and Unusual Punishments Clause. In my view, that inquiry must in these cases go beyond age-based statutory classifications relating to matters other than capital punishment, and must also encompass what JUSTICE SCALIA calls, with evident but misplaced disdain, "ethicoscientific" evidence. Only then can we be in a position to judge, as our cases require, whether a punishment is unconstitutionally excessive, either because it is disproportionate given the culpability of the offender, or because it serves no legitimate penal goal.

I

Our judgment about the constitutionality of a punishment under the Eighth Amendment is informed, though not determined by an examination of contemporary attitudes toward the punishment, as evidenced in the actions of legislatures and of juries. The views of organizations with expertise in relevant fields and the choices of governments elsewhere in the world also merit our attention as indicators whether a punishment is acceptable in a civilized society.

A

The Court's discussion of state laws concerning capital sentencing gives a distorted view of the evidence of contemporary standards that these legislative determinations provide. Currently, 12 of the States whose statutes permit capital punishment specifically mandate that offenders under age 18 not be sentenced to death. When one adds to these 12 States the 15 (including the District of Columbia) in which capital punishment is not authorized at all, it appears that the governments in fully 27 of the States have concluded that no one under 18 should face the death penalty. A further three States explicitly refuse to authorize sentences of death for those who committed their offense when under 17, making a total of 30 States that would not tolerate the execution of petitioner Wilkins. Congress' most recent enactment of a death penalty statute also excludes those under 18.

In 19 States that have a death penalty, no minimum age for capital sentences is set in the death penalty statute. The notion that these States have consciously authorized the execution of juveniles derives from the congruence in those jurisdictions of laws permitting state courts to hand down death sentences, on the one hand, and, on the other, statutes permitting the transfer of offenders under 18 from the juvenile to state court systems for trial in certain circumstances. I would not assume, however, in considering how the States stand on the moral issue that underlies the constitutional question with which we are presented, that a legislature that has never specifically considered the issue has made a conscious moral choice to permit the execution of juveniles. On a matter of such moment that most States have expressed an explicit and contrary judgment, the decisions of legislatures that are only implicit, and that lack the "earmarks of careful consideration that we have required for other kinds of decisions leading to the death penalty," must count for little. I do not suggest, of course, that laws of these

States cut against the constitutionality of the juvenile death penalty—only that accuracy demands that the baseline for our deliberations should be that 27 States refuse to authorize a sentence of death in the circumstances of petitioner Stanford's case, and 30 would not permit Wilkins' execution; that 19 States have not squarely faced the question; and that only the few remaining jurisdictions have explicitly set an age below 18 at which a person may be sentenced to death.

B

The application of these laws is another indicator the Court agrees to be relevant. The fact that juries have on occasion sentenced a minor to death shows, the Court says, that the death penalty for adolescents is not categorically unacceptable to juries. This, of course, is true; but it is not a conclusion that takes Eighth Amendment analysis very far. Just as we have never insisted that a punishment have been rejected unanimously by the States before we may judge it cruel and unusual, so we have never adopted the extraordinary view that a punishment is beyond Eighth Amendment challenge if it is sometimes handed down by a jury.

Both in absolute and in relative terms, imposition of the death penalty on adolescents is distinctly unusual. Adolescent offenders make up only a small proportion of the current death-row population: 30 out of a total of 2,186 inmates, or 1.37 percent. Eleven minors were sentenced to die in 1982; nine in 1983; six in 1984; five in 1985; seven in 1986; and two in 1987. Forty-one, or 2.3 percent, of the 1,813 death sentences imposed between January 1, 1982, and June 30, 1988, were for juvenile crimes. And juvenile offenders are significantly less likely to receive the death penalty than adults. During the same period, there were 97,086 arrests of adults for homicide, and 1,772 adult death sentences, or 1.8 percent; and 8,911 arrests of minors for homicide, compared to 41 juvenile death sentences, or 0.5 percent. . . .

C

Further indicators of contemporary standards of decency that should inform our consideration of the Eighth Amendment question are the opinions of respected organizations. Where organizations with expertise in a relevant area have given careful consideration to the question of a punishment's appropriateness, there is no reason why that judgment should not be entitled to attention as an indicator of contemporary standards. There is no dearth of opinion from such groups that the state-sanctioned killing of minors is unjustified. A number, indeed, have filed briefs amicus curiae in these cases, in support of petitioners. The American Bar Association has adopted a resolution opposing the imposition of capital punishment upon any person for an offense committed while under age 18, as has the National Council of Juvenile and Family Court Judges. The American Law

Institute's Model Penal Code similarly includes a lower age limit of 18 for the death sentence. And the National Commission on Reform of the Federal Criminal Laws also recommended that 18 be the minimum age.

Our cases recognize that objective indicators of contemporary standards of decency in the form of legislation in other countries is also of relevance to Eighth Amendment analysis. Many countries, of course—over 50, including nearly all in Western Europe—have formally abolished the death penalty, or have limited its use to exceptional crimes such as treason. Of the nations that retain capital punishment, a majority—65—prohibit the execution of juveniles. Sixty-one countries retain capital punishment and have no statutory provision exempting juveniles, though some of these nations are ratifiers of international treaties that do prohibit the execution of juveniles. Since 1979, Amnesty International has recorded only eight executions of offenders under 18 throughout the world, three of these in the United States. The other five executions were carried out in Pakistan, Bangladesh, Rwanda, and Barbados. In addition to national laws, three leading human rights treaties ratified or signed by the United States explicitly prohibit juvenile death penalties. Within the world community, the imposition of the death penalty for juvenile crimes appears to be overwhelmingly disapproved.

D

Together, the rejection of the death penalty for juveniles by a majority of the States, the rarity of the sentence for juveniles, both as an absolute and a comparative matter, the decisions of respected organizations in relevant fields that this punishment is unacceptable, and its rejection generally throughout the world, provide to my mind a strong grounding for the view that it is not constitutionally tolerable that certain States persist in authorizing the execution of adolescent offenders. It is unnecessary, however, to rest a view that the Eighth Amendment prohibits the execution of minors solely upon a judgment as to the meaning to be attached to the evidence of contemporary values outlined above, for the execution of juveniles fails to satisfy two well-established and independent Eighth Amendment requirements—that a punishment not be disproportionate, and that it make a contribution to acceptable goals of punishment. . . .

III

There can be no doubt at this point in our constitutional history that the Eighth Amendment forbids punishment that is wholly disproportionate to the blameworthiness of the offender. "The constitutional principle of proportionality has been recognized explicitly in this Court for almost a century." . . .

Proportionality analysis requires that we compare "the gravity of the offense," understood to include not only the injury caused, but also the defendant's culpability, with "the harshness of the penalty." In my view, juveniles so generally lack the degree of responsibility for their crimes that is a predicate for the constitutional imposition of the death penalty that the Eighth Amendment forbids that they receive that punishment.

A

Legislative determinations distinguishing juveniles from adults abound. These age-based classifications reveal much about how our society regards juveniles as a class, and about societal beliefs regarding adolescent levels of responsibility. . . .

B

There may be exceptional individuals who mature more quickly than their peers, and who might be considered fully responsible for their actions prior to the age of 18, despite their lack of the experience upon which judgment depends. In my view, however, it is not sufficient to accommodate the facts about juveniles that an individual youth's culpability may be taken into account in the decision to transfer him or her from the juvenile to the adult court system for trial, or that a capital sentencing jury is instructed to consider youth and other mitigating factors. I believe that the Eighth Amendment requires that a person who lacks that full degree of responsibility for his or her actions associated with adulthood not be sentenced to death. Hence it is constitutionally inadequate that a juvenile offender's level of responsibility be taken into account only along with a host of other factors that the court or jury may decide outweigh that want of responsibility. . . .

C

Juveniles very generally lack that degree of blameworthiness that is, in my view, a constitutional prerequisite for the imposition of capital punishment under our precedents concerning the Eighth Amendment proportionality principle. The individualized consideration of an offender's youth and culpability at the transfer stage and at sentencing has not operated to ensure that the only offenders under 18 singled out for the ultimate penalty are exceptional individuals whose level of responsibility is more developed than that of their peers. In that circumstance, I believe that the same categorical assumption that juveniles as a class are insufficiently mature to be regarded as fully responsible that we make in so many other areas is appropriately made in determining whether minors may be subjected to the death penalty. . . . I would hold that the Eighth Amendment prohibits the execution of any person for a crime committed below the age of 18.

Source: Stanford v. Kentucky, 492 U.S. 361 (1989), at 365–380, 383–405.

Notes

1. *Furman v. Georgia,* 408 U.S. 238 (1976).
2. *Gregg v. Georgia,* 428 U.S. 153 (1972); *Proffitt v. Florida,* 428 U.S. 242 (1976); and *Jurek v. Texas,* 428 U.S. 262 (1976).
3. *Woodson v. North Carolina,* 428 U.S. 280 (1976).
4. "4 in Death Row in Georgia Flee Jail in Disguise," *New York Times,* July 29, 1980, A10; "3 Convicted Killers Recaptured in North Carolina; 4th Is Found Dead," *New York Times,* July 31, 1980, A12; and "Jurors Told of Escape Try as Isaacs Awaits Sentence," *Atlanta Journal* and *Atlanta Constitution,* January 27, 1988, A9.
5. *Proffitt v. Wainwright,* 685 F.2d 1227 (1982).
6. *Proffitt v. State of Florida,* 510 So. 2d 896 (1987). See also "Justices Commute Killer's Historic Death Sentence," *Miami Herald,* July 10, 1987, 8A.
7. *Jurek v. Estelle,* 623 F.2d 929 (1980); and *Estelle v. Jurek,* 450 U.S. 1014 (1981), at 1015–1021.
8. "A Deadly Distinction Case That Revised the Death Penalty Ended Ironically—With Life," *Houston Chronicle,* February 4, 2001, 28.
9. See *Spenkelink v. State,* 313 So. 2d 666 (Fla. 1975); *Spenkelink v. Florida,* 428 U.S. 911 (1976); *Spenkelink v. State,* 350 So. 2d 85 (1977); *Spenkelink v. Florida,* 434 U.S. 960 (1977); *Spenkelink v. Wainwright,* 578 F. 2d 582 (5th Cir. 1978); and *Spenkelink v. Wainwright,* 442 U.S. 1301 (1979). See also "Florida Executed Killer As Plea Fails," *New York Times,* May 26, 1979, 1.
10. *Coker v. Georgia,* 433 U.S. 584 (1977); see also *Weems v. United States,* 217 U.S. 349 (1910), and *Trop v. Dulles,* 356 U.S. 86 (1958).
11. *Coker v. Georgia,* at 598.
12. Jack Greenberg, "Capital Punishment as a System," *Yale Law Journal,* 90 (1982): 912, n.3.
13. See, for example, *Reitman v. Mulkey,* 387 U.S. 369 (1967), in which the Court overturned a California voter–approved initiative that voided a state law barring racial discrimination in the sale and rental of housing.
14. *Coker v. Georgia,* at 622.
15. *Lockett v. Ohio,* 438 U.S. 586 (1978).
16. See *McGautha v. California,* 402 U.S. 183 (1971).
17. *Lockett v. Ohio,* at 603–605 (emphasis added).
18. Ibid., at 623.
19. Ibid., at 631.
20. *Godfrey v. Georgia,* 446 U.S. 420 (1980); and *Eddings v. Oklahoma,* 455 U.S. 104 (1982).
21. *Godfrey v. Georgia,* at 426.
22. Ibid., at 433.

23. Ibid., at 451, 457.
24. *Eddings v. Oklahoma,* at 125 n.7.
25. *Enmund v. Florida,* 458 U.S. 782 (1982), at 796.
26. Ibid., at 797.
27. Ibid., at 801.
28. Ibid., at 829–831.
29. *Eddings v. Oklahoma,* at 118.
30. *Beck v. Alabama,* 447 U.S. 625 (1980).
31. *Adams v. Texas,* 448 U.S. 38 (1980). See *Witherspoon v. Illinois,* 391 U.S. 510 (1968).
32. *Adams v. Texas,* at 45–46.
33. *Bullington v. Missouri,* 451 U.S. 430 (1981).
34. *Estelle v. Smith,* 451 U.S. 454 (1981).
35. *Coleman v. Balkcom,* 451 U.S. 949 (1981), at 957.
36. Ibid., at 958.
37. Ibid. The notorious "Bloody Assizes" were a series of criminal trials in England conducted by Lord Chief Justice George Jeffreys following the unsuccessful rebellion by the Duke of Monmouth against King James II in 1685. Over 1,400 persons alleged to be involved in the conspiracy were eventually tried, with 400 put to death, including one Elizabeth Gaunt, the last woman burned at the stake in England.
38. Ibid., at 949, 953.
39. *Smith v. North Carolina,* 459 U.S. 1056 (1982). Stevens quoted from the Utah decision *State v. Wood,* 648 P.2d 71, 9 (Utah 1982).
40. *Brooks v. Estelle,* 697 F. 2d 586, 588 (5th Cir 1982), stay and certiorari denied, 459 U.S. 1061 (1982).
41. "Final Judgment," *Time,* May 2, 1983, 23.
42. *Barefoot v. Estelle,* 463 U.S. 880 (1983), at 887.
43. Ibid., at 887–888, 896.
44. *People v. Ramos,* 30 Cal. 3d. 553, 639 P.2d 908 (1982).
45. *California v. Ramos,* 463 U.S. 992 (1983), at 1010–1012.
46. Ibid., at 1017–1018.
47. Ibid., at 1031.
48. *Zant v. Stephens,* 462 U.S. 862 (1983); and *Barclay v. Florida,* U.S. 463 U.S. 939 (1983).
49. *Zant v. Stephens,* at 871.
50. *Stromberg v. California,* 283 U.S. 359 (1931); and *Street v. New York,* 394 U.S. 576 (1969).
51. *Chapman v. California,* 386 U.S. 18 (1967).
52. *Zant v. Stephens,* at 883–885, 890.
53. *Barclay v. Florida,* at 944.
54. Ibid., at 948–951.
55. Ibid., at 984, 990–991.
56. *Zant v. Stephens,* at 879.
57. *People v. Harris,* 171 Cal. Rptr. 679 (Cal. 1981).
58. *Harris v. Pulley,* 692 F.2d 1789, 1196–1197 (9th Cir. 1982).
59. *Pulley v. Harris,* 465 U.S. 37 (1984), at 45, 50 (White, J., for the Court; Stevens, J., concurring; Marshall, J., and Brennan, J., dissenting).
60. *Harris v. Vasquez,* 949 F. 2d 1497 (9th Cir. 1990).

61. Even after this final stay had been lifted, the California supreme court entered the fray one last time when it refused to hear arguments on the lethal gas issue, with one justice, Stanley Mosk, dissenting. The California legislature soon revised its capital punishment statute to offer the condemned a choice between lethal injection or gas. For full details on the Harris case, see John T. Noonan, "Horses of the Night: *Harris v. Vasquez*," *Stanford Law Review* 45 (April 1993): 1011–1025; Evan Caminker and Erwin Chemerinsky, "The Lawless Execution of Robert Alton Harris," *Yale Law Journal* 102 (1992): 225–236; and "Legal Chaos Over Harris Reveals a Clash of Views Execution," *Los Angeles Times*, April 23, 1992, 1.

62. *McCleskey v. Kemp*, 481 U.S. 279 (1987); and *Stanford v. Kentucky*, 492 U.S. 361 (1989).

63. *Spaziano v. Florida*, 468 U.S. 447 (1984).

64. *Walton v. Arizona*, 497 U.S. 639 (1990).

65. *Arizona v. Rumsey*, 467 U.S. 203 (1984). The earlier decision was *Bullington v. Missouri*, 451 U.S. 430 (1981).

66. *Lockhart v. McCree*, 476 U.S. 162 (1986); and *Turner v. Murray*, 476 U.S. 28 (1986).

67. *Adams v. Texas*, 448 U.S. 38 (1980).

68. *Wainwright v. Witt*, 469 U.S. 412 (1985), at 430–435.

69. *Lockhart v. McCree*, at 163, 173–177.

70. Ibid., at 191–193.

71. *Ristaino v. Ross*, 424 U.S. 589 (1976).

72. *Rosales-Lopez v. United States*, 451 U.S. 182 (1981).

73. *Turner v. Murray*, at 33–36.

74. *Ford v. Wainwright*, 477 U.S. 399 (1986), at 432.

75. *Tison v. Arizona*, 481 U.S. 137 (1987), at 139.

76. Ibid., at 150–158.

77. Ibid., at 178–179.

78. "Prosecutor Says High Court Ruling Shields Tisons from Death Penalty," *Arizona Daily Star*, April 11, 1992; "Ricky Tison is Resentenced to Life for His Role in 4 Slayings," *Arizona Daily Star*, July 11, 1992; and "Greenawalt Dies for '78 Crime Spree," *Arizona Daily Star*, January 23, 1997.

79. *Burger v. Kemp*, 483 U.S. 776 (1987).

80. *Strickland v. Washington*, 466 U.S. 668 (1984).

81. Ibid., at 689.

82. Ibid., at 794–795.

83. Ibid., at 797–817.

84. *McCleskey v. Kemp*, 481 U.S. 279 (1987); *Penry v. Lynaugh*, 492 U.S. 302 (1989); and *Stanford v. Kentucky*, 492 U.S. 361 (1989).

85. *Batson v. Kentucky*, 476 U.S. 79 (1986); see also *Swain v. Alabama*, 380 U.S. 202 (1965).

86. *McCleskey v. Kemp*, at 314.

87. Ibid., at 313–319.

88. Ibid., at 322–325.

89. *Massiah v. United States*, 377 U.S. 201 (1964).

90. *McCleskey v. Zant*, 499 U.S. 467 (1991).

91. "Execution of McCleskey Spurs Outrage," *Atlanta Journal* and *Atlanta Constitution*, September 25, 1991, A1.

92. See John C. Jeffries Jr., *Justice Lewis F. Powell: A Biography* (New York: Scribner's, 1994), 451.

93. A clinical psychologist believed Penry, twenty-two years old at the time of the crime, had the mental age of a six-and-a-half-year-old. A psychiatrist testified that he suffered from organic brain damage, either caused at birth or due to the frequent beatings on the head by his mother when he was a child.

94. *Penry v. Lynaugh*, at 343.

95. *Thompson v. Oklahoma*, 487 U.S. 815 (1988).

96. *Stanford v. Kentucky*, at 377–380.

97. Ibid., at 383–384.

98. "Youngest Ever Sent to Death Row Gets Three Life Sentences," *St. Louis Post-Dispatch*, May 22, 1999, 17.

CHAPTER 5

Tinkering with the Machinery
Limiting Death, Reaffirming Death, 1989–2009

In the thirty-three years between the Supreme Court's 1976 decision in *Gregg v. Georgia*, which restored capital punishment in the United States,[1] and the execution of Johnny Johnson by the state of Texas in early February 2009, a total of 1,149 persons were put to death. Of those total executions, 1,047, or 91 percent, took place between Chief Justice William Rehnquist's first term in 1987 and his last in 2005. In the years from 1997 to 2002, moreover, executions reached their highest annual levels since the early 1950s, with 98 death sentences carried out in 1999 and 85 the following year; the number of executions annually did not fall below 50 until 2007. Today, public opinion in favor of capital punishment remains steady between 60 and 70 percent.[2] With statistics such as these, any thought nursed by capital punishment abolitionists that the Court's decision in *Furman v. Georgia* would lead eventually to the extinction of state-sanctioned death has all but vanished.[3]

In the wake of the Oklahoma City bombing in 1995, Congress passed and President Bill Clinton signed into law the Antiterrorism and Effective Death Penalty Act (AEDPA) of 1996 (**Document 5.1**). The act sharply curtailed habeas corpus review by placing significant restrictions on prisoners' ability to file successive federal habeas corpus petitions.[4] The AEDPA habeas provisions, for example, barred federal courts from reconsidering legal and factual issues passed upon by state courts in most instances; imposed a general one-year statute of limitations within which habeas petitions had to be filed after the completion of a direct appeal; and required federal appeals courts to grant approval for repetitious habeas petitions. The Court had already imposed restrictions of its own on habeas review, and it unanimously upheld the AEDPA in *Felker v. Turpin*, finding that these new limitations did not suspend the writ in violation of Article I, Section 9 of the Constitution, which says "the Privilege of the Writ of Habeas corpus shall not be suspended, unless when in Cases of Rebellion or Invasion the public Safety may require it."[5] Ironically, during these same years of restricted habeas review and rising executions, the justices also imposed new constitutional restrictions on the death penalty by affording defendants additional procedural protections and once again narrowing the category of those eligible for the supreme penalty.

Prior to her retirement in January 2006, Justice Sandra Day O'Connor moved cautiously away from the Rehnquist-White block to become a frequent voice for restriction along with Justice John Paul Stevens. Justices Anthony Kennedy, David Souter, Stephen Breyer, and Ruth Bader Ginsburg joined them upon occasion, while Justice Harry Blackmun became the third member after Justice William Brennan and Justice Thurgood Marshall to abandon all hope for a constitutional solution eliminating the arbitrary imposition of the death penalty. Justices Antonin Scalia and Clarence Thomas, on the other hand, continued to endorse the views of the chief justice and Justice Byron White and to bemoan these judicial interventions. Scalia and Thomas took refuge in their understanding of the original meaning of the Eighth Amendment. According to their reading of history and the constitutional text, the Fifth Amendment's due process clause sanctioned the death penalty and the Eighth Amendment only barred specific types of barbaric punishments. Scalia expressed his feelings cogently in *Atkins v. Virginia* (2002) when the Court overruled *Penry v. Lynaugh* (1989) to hold that the Constitution prohibited the execution of the mentally retarded: "Today's opinion adds one more to the long list of substantive and procedural requirements impeding imposition of the death penalty imposed under this Court's assumed power to invent a death-is-different jurisprudence. None of those requirements existed when the Eighth Amendment was adopted, and some of them were not even supported by current moral consensus. . . . There is something to be said for popular abolition of the death penalty; there is nothing to be said for its incremental abolition by this Court."[6]

Abstention and Intervention

A sextet of cases decided between 1990 and 1993 revealed both the shifting coalitions that determined the Court's death penalty jurisprudence in these years and its inability to sustain a consistent course of either intervention or abstention. In *Blystone v. Pennsylvania* (1990), a Rehnquist-led majority, joined by O'Connor and Kennedy, upheld Pennsylvania's statute that mandated death "if the jury unanimously finds at least one aggravating circumstance . . . and no mitigating circumstance or if the jury unanimously finds one or more aggravating circumstances or if the jury unanimously finds one or more aggravating circumstances which outweigh any mitigating circumstances."[7] Scott Blystone had been found guilty and sentenced to death for a homicide perpetrated in the course of a $13 robbery, a felony and an aggravating circumstance under the statute. He challenged the statute on the grounds that it constituted a mandatory death penalty prohibited by the Court's decision in *Woodson v. North Carolina* (1976) and *Sumner v. Shuman* (1987) because it restricted the discretion of the jury and deprived him of an individualized sentencing hearing.[8] In *Sumner,* the Court had overturned a Nevada statute that mandated the death penalty for homicides committed while the defendant was serving a life sentence without the possibility of parole.

Rehnquist and the majority distinguished the impermissible "mandatory" statutes struck down earlier on the grounds that the Pennsylvania legislature did not impose death automatically for certain types of crimes, but still required the jury to determine that an aggravating circumstance outweighed mitigating circumstances present in a particular crime, committed by a particular defendant.[9] The dissenters accused the majority of ignoring the distinction between a statute that only defined a class of death-eligible defendants and one, such as Pennsylvania's, which stripped juries of the ultimate decision and mandated death for a category of murderers. Although Pennsylvania asked juries to weigh aggravation against mitigation, it clearly tilted the scales in favor of death by precluding the jury from distinguishing levels of aggravation.[10]

In *Clemons v. Mississippi* (1990) that same term, with O'Connor and Kennedy again joining the majority, the Court continued on its path of delegating final capital decisions to state appellate courts and reaffirming the "harmless error" doctrine that generally held that convictions and sentences were not to be overturned unless the particular procedural error alone would have led to a different outcome.[11] Moreover, the decisions of state supreme courts on state procedural law were binding on the federal courts. In *Clemons* the Court held that the Mississippi supreme court could salvage a death sentence by performing its own weighing of aggravating and mitigating circumstances in a case where the jury's initial verdict rested in part upon a finding that the homicide had been "especially heinous, atrocious or cruel," an aggravating circumstance held to be unconstitutional. A Scalia-led majority nationalized the "harmless error" rule and reaffirmed its delegation to state courts in *Brown v. Sanders* (2006) by holding that a jury's reliance on an invalid aggravating circumstance raised a constitutional problem only insofar as it allowed the jury to take into account facts and circumstances that "would not otherwise have been before it."[12] But if that evidence admitted under an invalid factor was also admissible in support of "one of the other [valid sentencing] factors" no constitutional violation occurred. Four dissenters (Stevens, Breyer, Souter, and Ginsburg) denounced the decision for, as Breyer put it, putting "a thumb on death's side of the scale."[13]

With Justices White and Kennedy switching sides, the Marshall-Brennan-Stevens-Blackmun coalition gained one minor victory that term in *McKoy v. North Carolina* when the Court overturned a North Carolina capital sentencing scheme that required the jury to reach a unanimous decision on each mitigating factor when deciding whether to impose the death penalty.[14] That rule, wrote Marshall, prevented the jury from considering all mitigating evidence and passing an individualized judgment on the defendant. Justice O'Connor, who had authored the foundational mitigation decision in *Lockett v. Ohio,* joined Scalia and Rehnquist in dissent, one of the last times she would do so. Four years later in *Simmons v. South Carolina* (1994), the Court required states that provided the alternative of life in prison without parole to inform juries specifically of the defendant's ineligibility for parole in sentencing proceedings when prosecutors argued for the death penalty on the grounds that the defendant posed a future danger to society.[15] Only Scalia and Thomas found this modest procedural ruling an intolerable burden on the states attempting to enforce their capital statutes. "I fear we have read today the first page of a whole new chapter in the 'death-is-different' jurisprudence which this Court is in the apparently continuous process of composing," the former wrote. "The heavily outnumbered opponents of capital punishment have successfully opened yet another front in their guerilla war to make this unquestionably constitutional sentence a practical impossibility."[16]

But apart from *McKoy* and *Simmons,* the proponents of "death-is-different" jurisprudence hardly dominated the Court in this period, as demonstrated by *Payne v. Tennessee* (1991) and *Herrera v. Collins* (1993).[17] In the former, the Court revisited the question of whether the Eighth Amendment prohibited the states from introducing at the time of capital sentencing statements by the survivors of the victim, so-called victim-impact statements. Twice before, in *Booth v. Maryland* (1987) and *South Carolina v. Gathers* (1989), the Court had banned such statements on the grounds that sentencing judgments should focus exclusively on the circumstances of the crime and the nature of the defendant.[18] In *Payne,* however, the arrival of Justices Kennedy and Souter to replace retiring justices Lewis Powell and Brennan gave Rehnquist a 6–3 majority to overrule both *Booth* and *Gathers* on the grounds that evidence about the victim and the impact of a murder upon the victim's family were relevant to a jury's ultimate decision and "there is no reason to treat such evidence differently than other relevant evidence is treated."

In dissent Justice Stevens ridiculed the majority's claim that even-handed justice required the introduction of victim-impact evidence to balance the scales with mitigating evidence. The defense, he pointed out, would not be permitted to introduce evidence regarding the moral delinquencies of a murder victim. "This argument is a classic non sequitur," he responded. "The victim is not on trial: her character, whether good or bad, cannot therefore constitute either an aggravating or a mitigating circumstance."[19]

Two years later in 1993 Leonel Torres Herrera, under sentence of death in Texas for the killing of two police officers in 1982, brought before the justices a complicated case filled with difficult substantive and procedural issues. Herrera attempted to raise via a second habeas corpus petition a claim of actual innocence based on four new affidavits that asserted the crimes had actually been committed by his brother, who had died in 1984. Herrera's lawyers asked the Court to decide two questions: Did the Eighth and Fourteenth Amendments bar the execution of the innocent? And, could such a claim of actual innocence be raised, even ten years after a trial, in a federal habeas action that presented newly discovered evidence?

Herrera was not the ideal plaintiff to raise such a claim. In addition to physical evidence linking him to the crime scenes and eye-witness testimony that identified him as the shooter, Herrera had initially written a letter confessing to one of the killings. The affidavits, in addition to their hearsay quality, contained numerous contradictions. In addition, even the liberal Warren Court had restricted habeas claims to violations of the Constitution and rejected the idea that the writ could grant relief to state prisoners on the grounds of newly discovered evidence.[20] The federal district court and the court of appeals had turned Herrera down on those grounds.

Herrera provoked a number of sharp exchanges among the justices (**Document 5.2**). No member of the Court disputed Chief Justice Rehnquist's conclusion for the majority that executing an innocent person was inconsistent with the Constitution of the United States. Justices Scalia and Thomas did reject the claim that the document created any right to demand "judicial consideration of newly discovered evidence of innocence brought forward after conviction," and would have left such decisions to executive clemency.[21]

Rehnquist's opinion reaffirmed emphatically that habeas could grant relief only for constitutional violations, which Herrera had not raised, but he admitted "for the sake of argument" that "a truly persuasive demonstration of 'actual innocence' after trial" could warrant habeas relief "if there were no state avenue open to process such a claim." In short, Rehnquist argued, such a "persuasive demonstration" might trigger "the sort of constitutional claim . . . we have assumed, arguendo [for the sake of argument], to exist," but the threshold requirements for such a showing would "necessarily be extraordinarily high." Herrera's affidavits did not come close to that standard.[22]

While Rehnquist's opinion conceded too much for Scalia and Thomas, it drew a sharp dissent from Blackmun, joined in part by Stevens and Souter, who did not find any bar in previous habeas decisions to considering a claim of actual innocence and who would have remanded the case to the district court for a full hearing on the new affidavits. Blackmun also challenged the conclusion that Herrera had not raised a constitutional claim by pointing out that the Fourteenth Amendment prohibited the deprivation of life without due process. If the Eighth Amendment prohibited the death penalty for rape and the mere participation in a robbery where a homicide occurred, it surely prohibited the execution of the innocent. "The execution of a person who can show that he is innocent," he concluded, "comes perilously close to simple murder."[23] Texas executed Herrera four months later in 1993.

Herrera, and the long line of cases leading up to it, brought Blackmun to a critical point. A year later, in *Callins v. Collins,* he announced that "from this day forward, I no longer shall tinker with the machinery of death" (**Document 5.3**).

O'Connor's Defection

Justice O'Connor, joined by Justice Kennedy, had concurred separately in *Herrera,* pointing out that the Court had not ruled that the Constitution permitted the execution of the actually innocent and that the question remained open whether such "convincing claims" could be entertained in the federal courts. "If the Constitution's guarantees of fair procedure and the safeguards of clemency and pardon fulfill their historical mission," she concluded, "it may never require resolution at all."[24] The O'Connor-Kennedy concurrence gave some indication that the two justices would soon part ways with the Rehnquist-led majority on capital cases and even more decisively with Scalia and Thomas.

In another Texas case, *Johnson v. Texas* (1993), decided the same term with *Herrera,* the Court upheld the death sentence of Dorsie Lee Johnson, who at age 19 had killed a convenience store clerk in the course of a robbery.[25] The trial judge asked the jury to answer two special questions prescribed by Texas law: Was the death committed deliberately and with the reasonable expectation it would result in death? And, was there a probability that Johnson would commit future violent acts that made him a continuing threat to society? The jury answered yes to both questions and Johnson was sentenced to death. On appeal, rejected by the Texas courts, Johnson argued that the second question did not allow the jury to specifically consider his age as a mitigating factor bearing upon his culpability. In fact, the instruction would have led the jury to weigh his age only as an aggravating factor.

Writing for the majority, Justice Kennedy distinguished this case from the mental retardation at issue in *Penry* on the grounds that Johnny Paul Penry's disability rendered him unable to learn from his youthful mistakes, whereas the ill effects of Johnson's youth were "readily comprehended as a mitigating factor" when the jury answered the second question. O'Connor's dissent for herself, joined by Blackmun, Souter, and Stevens, argued that in all probability the Texas instruction encouraged the jury to consider Johnson's age as an aggravating factor and did not give effect to "the most relevant mitigating aspect of youth: its relation to the young offender's moral culpability and responsibility for the crime."[26] Texas executed Johnson four years later.

When other capital cases from Texas reached the justices in O'Connor's final years on the bench, she commanded the majorities. First, in *Penry v. Johnson* (2001) (known as *Penry II*) O'Connor and the Court, which now included Justice Kennedy, saved Penry a second time from lethal injection when they sent his case back to Texas for resentencing on the grounds that the trial judge in his second trial had failed to comply with the Court's initial ruling in the first *Penry* case, which required a specific jury instruction with respect to mitigating circumstances—in Penry's case his mental retardation and abusive childhood. "*Penry I* did not hold that the mere mention of 'mitigating circumstances' . . . satisfies the Eighth Amendment," O'Connor affirmed. "Nor does it stand for the proposition that it is constitutionally sufficient to inform the jury that it may 'consider' mitigating circumstances. . . . Rather, the key . . . is that the jury be able to 'consider and *give effect* to [a defendant's mitigating] evidence in imposing sentence."[27] The Texas judge's instructions on mitigation had been so confusing that they made it impossible, O'Connor wrote, for the jury to treat Penry as "a uniquely individual human being" when making its life or death decision.

O'Connor's opinion in *Penry II* gave new momentum to revisiting *Penry I*, in which the justice herself thirteen years earlier had rejected an Eighth Amendment attack on executing the mentally retarded. But now in 2002, led by Stevens and joined by O'Connor and Kennedy, the Court held in *Atkins v. Virginia* (2002) that executing the retarded did constitute "cruel and unusual punishment," although it left it up to the individual states to provide the framework for determining the extent of retardation (**Document 5.4**). By the time of *Atkins,* eighteen states had already enacted a similar prohibition, but this was fewer than the twenty death penalty states that had failed to adopt such a ban, a statistic that drew a pungent dissent from Scalia, Rehnquist, and Thomas, who claimed the opinion "rested so obviously upon nothing but the personal views of its [the Court's] members."[28]

Penry II and *Atkins* finally spared Johnny Paul Penry when the Texas Court of Criminal Appeals overturned his third death sentence on grounds of improper jury instructions on mitigation and ordered a new trial in 2005. Texas prosecutors declined to pursue a fourth trial in 2008, and Penry accepted a plea bargain to serve a life term without parole. The district attorney who had prosecuted Penry three times had died by 2008, taking much institutional knowledge of the case with him. If a new jury failed to bring in a death sentence, Penry would have been eligible for immediate parole under Texas law. Finally, prosecutors doubted that a new jury instruction on mitigation could survive scrutiny at the appellate level.[29]

Texas prosecutors had abandoned a fourth trial for Penry as a result of O'Connor's mitigation opinion in *Tennard v. Dretke* (2004) and a per curiam in *Smith v. Texas* (2004) that rested largely on *Tennard* and *Penry II.*[30] In *Tennard* O'Connor and the majority reversed the Fifth Circuit Court of Appeals, which had ruled that the Texas jury was not required to give full constitutional effect to mitigating evidence unless it demonstrated a "uniquely severe permanent handicap with which the defendant was burdened through no fault of his own," and then only if the crime could be "attributable" to the handicap.[31] In *Smith*, with Scalia and Thomas dissenting, the Court rejected other Texas instructions that allowed the jury to consider mitigating factors only if those factors suggested the defendant would not be a danger in the future and required the jury to swear to impose death if they thought he was a future danger.

Effective Counsel

The Court reinforced its expansive opinions on mitigation in these years with a pair of decisions that imposed new obligations on defense attorneys to conduct more thorough investigations into factors that might bear upon a defendant's background during the sentencing phase of a capital trial. In *Wiggins v. Smith* (2003), with O'Connor again taking the lead, the Court defined the meaning of "effective assistance" of legal counsel left vague in *Strickland v. Washington* (1984) by adopting the American Bar Association Guidelines for the Appointment and Performance of Defense Counsel in Death Penalty Cases as the standard for purposes of the Sixth Amendment.[32] Reversing the Fourth Circuit Court of Appeals and granting Kevin Wiggins a new sentencing hearing, the Court noted that his attorney presented no mitigating evidence to the jury during the sentencing phase and failed to adequately investigate his client's personal history, which included severe physical and sexual abuse.

Two years later in *Rompilla v. Beard* (2005) the justices reversed the Third Circuit and again ordered a new capital sentencing hearing when the defendant's trial attorney accepted his client's and family member's claim that no mitigating evidence was available and then failed to conduct an independent investigation that later revealed organic brain damage and childhood problems probably related to fetal alcohol syndrome. Justice Souter's opinion for the majority was joined by O'Connor, Stevens, Breyers and Ginsburg.[33]

Kennedy's Reconsideration

In 1988, the year he took his seat on the Court but arrived too late to consider the issues, Justice Kennedy did not participate when the justices ruled that "evolving standards of decency that mark the progress of a maturing society" prohibited the execution of William Thompson, who had committed his crime at the age of fifteen.[34] A year later, however, Kennedy joined Scalia's majority opinion in *Stanford v. Kentucky* (1989) holding that the same Eighth Amendment and "evolving standards of decency" did not bar the death penalty for offenders who were at least sixteen years old at the time of the crime.[35] Like O'Connor, however, Kennedy displayed a growing reluctance to march with the chief justice, Scalia, and Thomas during Rehnquist's final years. *Roper v. Simmons* (2005) became his declaration of independence when his opinion for the majority overruled *Stanford* to hold that the Eighth Amendment barred the execution of those who committed their crime while under the age of eighteen (**Document 5.5**).

At the age of seventeen Christopher Simmons and a younger friend carried out a plot to break into the Missouri home of Shirley Crook, who had been involved in an auto accident with him, and kidnap her. They tied Mrs. Crook up with electrical wire, drove her out of town, and threw her off a bridge into a river where she drowned. There was no doubt about premeditation, and Simmons confessed to the crime. Despite his lack of a criminal record and his age, the jury sentenced him to die. The Missouri supreme court initially upheld Simmons' sentence, but in 2003, following the Supreme Court decision in *Atkins v. Virginia* voiding death sentences for the mentally retarded, the state high court heard a further appeal and overturned the sentence on the grounds that a national consensus had formed against the execution of juveniles. Missouri prosecutors sought to reverse that judgment before Rehnquist's court.

In one respect, Kennedy's opinion for the majority tracked the Missouri supreme court and traditional Eighth Amendment doctrine by counting legislative heads and jury verdicts to demonstrate that "evolving standards of decency" had produced a national consensus against the death penalty for those who, like Simmons, had committed homicide under the age of eighteen. While twenty states continued to have the death penalty for juveniles on their statute books, only three (Oklahoma, Texas, and Virginia) had executed such minors in the past decade; five other states had abolished the sanction since 1989 when the Court handed down *Stanford*.

In addition, Kennedy cited sociological and medical research demonstrating that juveniles generally lacked good judgment, were prone to engage in reckless behavior, and possessed a limited sense of responsibility that explained why virtually every state prohibited them from voting, serving on juries, or getting married without the consent of an adult. And to the great displeasure of Justice Scalia, Kennedy also invoked the legal decisions made by foreign governments. Kennedy regularly attended annual meetings of international jurists in Salzburg, Germany, and kept abreast of judicial decisions rendered by European courts. He drew upon this experience in his *Stanford* opinion. While countries such as Iran, China, and Saudi Arabia had taken a stand against the execution of juveniles since 1990, the United States continued to engage in the practice and had refused to sign Article 37 of the United Nations Convention on the Rights of the Child (1990), which prohibited the punishment. The only other country that failed to sign the convention was Somalia.[36]

Missouri death row inmate Christopher Simmons was seventeen when he committed murder. In October 2004 the Supreme Court heard arguments on whether it is constitutional under the Eighth Amendment to execute people whose crimes were committed when they were juveniles. In Roper v. Simmons *the Court found that executing juveniles violates the Eighth Amendment's ban on cruel and unusual punishment.*

The dissenters, including the chief justice, O'Connor, Scalia, and Thomas, questioned Kennedy's arithmetic by pointing out that only eighteen of the thirty-eight states that continued to sanction capital punishment had abolished the penalty for juveniles. Scalia reaffirmed his long-standing devotion to what he called the original intent of the Constitution's Framers by pointing out that states executed people under the age of eighteen at the time the Eighth Amendment had been ratified. Foreign laws were irrelevant to interpreting the Constitution, he concluded, and he accused Kennedy and others of citing them only when the particular foreign laws endorsed their own moral preferences.[37]

End of the Rehnquist Era

Chief Justice Rehnquist, who had been diagnosed with thyroid cancer in 2004, missed forty-four oral arguments between late 2004 and early 2005. He did not appear on the bench when the Court decided *Simmons* on March 1, 2005, and only returned briefly on March 21. Justice O'Connor, nursing a husband ailing with Alzheimer's disease, announced her retirement on July 1, 2005. Two months later, on September 3, the chief justice died, bringing to an end an era in the Court's history and its death penalty jurisprudence. On December 2, 2005, North Carolina put to death Kenneth Boyd, the one-thousandth person executed since the Court restored capital punishment in 1976, a landmark that indicated that despite the harsh criticism leveled by Justice Scalia against decisions such as *Atkins* and *Simmons,* the Court had not significantly reduced the incidence of the death penalty in America.

Since 1976 the justices had reduced the pool of the death-eligible by banning the penalty for rapists, many felony-murderers, the mentally retarded, and juveniles, in addition to imposing new procedural safeguards on capital trials with respect to mitigating evidence and the competence of defense lawyers. But opponents of capital punishment, who otherwise applauded these individual rulings, also pointed out that the sum total of the Court's efforts had been to reassure the American public that those who would continue to be executed were indeed the worst of the worst, who deserved the supreme penalty. By narrowing the categories of those eligible for execution and surrounding capital trials with greater procedural safeguards, the Court soothed the public's conscience and legitimated the death penalty.

Beyond the Court

During the last of the Rehnquist years, opponents of capital punishment often found comfort in decisions made by other actors away from the nine justices in Washington. In the fall of 2001, for example, the Supreme Court of Georgia declared the use of the state's electric chair "cruel and unusual punishment" under the state's constitution, an interpretation that rejected federal precedents and mandated lethal injection instead. Utah's legislature and governor put an end to the state's use of the firing squad in 2004. In 2006 the American Medical Association, the National Association of Emergency Medical Technicians, and the American Society of Anesthesiologists all declared it a violation of medical ethics for their members to participate in lethal injections.

Most dramatic of all, Illinois governor George H. Ryan emptied the state's death row by commuting the sentences of 171 individuals on January 11, 2003, after the legislature failed to adopt any of his proposals for reforming the state's capital sentencing statute (**Document 5.6**). Echoing the late Justice Blackmun, Ryan told reporters that a three-year study by his task force had found more and more questions about the fairness of the system that led him to conclude that the Illinois death penalty system "is arbitrary and capricious—and therefore immoral—I no longer shall tinker with the machinery of death." "The legislature refused to reform it or repeal it," Ryan said. "But I will not stand for it."[38]

The Roberts Era Begins

Noting that he had clerked for Justice Rehnquist in 1980–1981 and seldom displayed a penchant for judicial activism on the D.C. Circuit Court of Appeals, opponents of capital punishment did not nurse the illusion that the new chief justice, John Glover Roberts Jr., would fundamentally alter the Court's death penalty jurisprudence. Moreover, Roberts had been nominated two days after

Rehnquist's death by President George W. Bush, who, as governor of Texas between 1995 and 2000, had signed more death warrants than any state chief executive during those years.

Brown v. Sanders (2006), the first capital case where Roberts sat as chief justice, demonstrated continuity with the Rehnquist era. The California supreme court had affirmed Ronald Sanders's death sentence although that court had invalidated two of the four special aggravating circumstances submitted to the jury during his sentencing trial. The Ninth Circuit Court of Appeals reversed the California court on the grounds that allowing the jury to consider the invalid circumstances had substantially affected the outcome of the sentencing decision and constituted an Eighth Amendment violation. The California court should have determined whether the invalid circumstances constituted harmless error "beyond a reasonable doubt."

As it had often done in the past, the Supreme Court overturned the Ninth Circuit on the Eighth Amendment question and articulated a new, narrow rule with respect to invalid aggravating circumstances; they affirmed Sanders's death sentence. Roberts joined Scalia's opinion for the 5–4 majority that drew dissents from Stevens, Souter, Breyer, and Ginsburg. Invalid aggravating circumstances would not amount to a constitutional violation, Scalia wrote, when "other sentencing factors" enabled the jury to give similar weight to "the same facts and circumstances" found invalid. In Sanders's case, a catch-all "circumstances of the crime" aggravating factor provided that similar weight and had not skewed the jury's decision for death.[39]

A month later, with Breyer writing the opinion, the justices agreed in *Oregon v. Guzek* (2006) that the Eighth Amendment did not require the states to admit evidence of a defendant's innocence during the sentencing phase of his trial if that evidence had not been introduced during the trial phase itself.[40] The Oregon supreme court had so ruled in overturning Randy Lee Guzek's death sentence for a third time. Roberts signed on with Breyer's opinion, which still prompted a concurrence from Scalia and Justice Thomas, who feared that Breyer and the majority had left too large an opening in the door of further appeals by remanding the case to the Oregon courts for consideration whether its state law permitted Guzek to introduce alibi evidence to impeach the testimony of other witnesses during his sentencing trial.

The Court's newest member, Justice Samuel Alito, who filled O' Connor's seat in January 2006, sat on the bench during *Guzek* but had not participated in the decision. Alito did, however, cast a decisive vote in June 2006 when the Court decided *Kansas v. Marsh,* one of the most contentious death penalty decisions since *Herrera v. Collins.*[41] Michael Lee Marsh II had been convicted and sentenced to death for the murder of a mother and her young child. The Kansas capital punishment statute allowed juries to impose death in circumstances where they found that aggravating and mitigating circumstances weighed equally. Making such a judgment of equipoise, the jury sentenced Marsh to die. Following Marsh's sentencing, however, the Kansas supreme court declared the state statute unconstitutional on grounds that it violated the Eighth Amendment, a ruling that brought an instant appeal by Kansas officials to the Supreme Court (**Document 5.7**).

As a general rule, the Rehnquist Court had delegated broad discretion and delegation to state courts in capital cases, especially when decisions turned on interpretations of the state's substantive and procedural law. *Marsh*, however, like *Oregon v. Guzek*, involved a state court's interpretation of the Eighth Amendment and it suffered the same fate. Writing for the 5–4 majority that now included Alito, Justice Thomas' opinion reversed the Kansas supreme court and upheld the state's death penalty statute, finding it consistent with both the Eighth Amendment and prior decisions. So long as juries are permitted to hear all mitigating and aggravating evidence, Thomas wrote, states are permitted to impose death when these factors are equally balanced. Justice Stevens protested that the Court should not have heard the Kansas appeal. Justice Souter, joined by Stevens, Breyer, and Ginsburg denounced the statute as a violation of the Eighth Amendment, finding it to be "morally absurd" and "obtuse by any moral or social measure."

But broad deference to state courts enjoyed a renaissance at the end of 2007 in *Uttecht v. Brown*, when the same 5–4 majority (including Roberts and Alito) reversed the Ninth Circuit to hold that state judges in capital trials should be given the benefit of the doubt when they excluded for cause potential jurors whom they believed would not be able to follow the law due to their doubts about the death penalty.[42] The dissenters argued that once again the Court majority had tilted the scales in favor of death.

With Justice Kennedy assuming the role often played earlier by O'Connor, the liberal wing of the Court secured one predictable victory a few weeks after *Uttecht*, when in *Panetti v. Quarterman* the Court reaffirmed *Ford v. Wainwright* (1986) that the Eighth Amendment prohibited the execution of insane persons and defendants could litigate their compentency through a habeas petition once their execution date had been set.[43] Kennedy's opinion was notable for finding that the AEDPA did not bar Scott Panetti's habeas action and that neither the Texas courts nor the Fifth Circuit Court of Appeals had afforded him procedural protections or a definition of incompetence consistent with *Ford*. Thomas, writing for himself, Roberts, Scalia, and Alito, dissented from all those conclusions. *Panetti* indicated that without Kennedy, the Roberts-Scalia-Thomas-Alito wing of the Court could not control its death penalty jurisprudence. Any doubts about that were laid to rest in the battle over lethal injection.

A Fatal Cocktail

Early in 2008, for only the third time in its history, the Court confronted the question of whether a particular method of executing persons sentenced to death in the United States violated the constitutional prohibition in the Eighth Amendment against "cruel and unusual punishment."[44] On January 7, 2008, the Court heard oral arguments on behalf of Ralph Baze and Thomas Bowling, death row inmates in Kentucky, against John Rees, commissioner of the state's department of corrections. Baze and Bowling had each been convicted of two counts of capital murder and sentenced to death.

Kentucky intended to execute the convicted murderers with a lethal injection of three drugs—sodium thiopental, pancuronium bromide, and potassium chloride—a fatal cocktail used by thirty of the thirty-six states and the federal government that employed this method for carrying out the death penalty. Lawyers for Baze and Bowling sought to block their execution by arguing that the specific protocol adopted by Kentucky for administering the drugs exposed their clients to an unnecessary risk of excruciating pain, thus violating the constitutional ban on "cruel and unusual punishment."

If prison personnel improperly administered the first drug, a powerful barbiturate sedative, these lawyers argued, their clients would suffer unbearable pain from the second and third drugs intended to stop respiration and induce cardiac arrest. The second drug, a paralytic agent, would mask the pain experienced by the condemned before death. Further, they claimed, the use of the first drug alone in a significant dose would be sufficient to induce death and avoid the risk of such a painful demise, although they had not raised this issue in the Kentucky courts.

After a lengthy trial involving dozens of experts for the state and the condemned pair, the trial court rejected their lawyers' arguments and the Kentucky supreme court affirmed that ruling. When the Supreme Court subsequently agreed to hear the case, its grant of certiorari effectively imposed a nationwide moratorium on lethal injection as a method of execution, although Texas carried out one execution after the justices had acted in Washington.[45]

The justices voiced considerable skepticism about both arguments put forward by the attorneys for Baze and Bowling. The first drug, the lawyers argued, might fail to completely anesthetize the condemned due to improper setting of an IV or the incorrect mixing of the sodium pentothal. To which Justice Kennedy observed: "Well, if it were properly administered, would you have a case here? Let's assume 100 percent of cases are properly administered."

In his oral argument, Donald Verrilli, Baze's attorney stated: "If there were a way to guarantee that the procedure worked every time, then we wouldn't have substantial risk. . . . [But] you cannot assure that there is going to be a guarantee of . . . successful administration of the anesthetic. And that is why the monitoring part of the process is so critical."[46]

Kentucky's protocol failed the test of proper monitoring of anesthetic death, Verrilli argued, because its execution team lacked medical expertise, including the setting of the catheters through visual observation of the condemned by the warden and his deputy inside the execution chamber. Such expert monitoring, Justice Scalia pointed out, could only be provided by a medical doctor, "and medical doctors, according to the Code of Ethics of the American Medical Association, can't participate [in executions.]"[47]

Verrilli's second line of attack on the availability of an alternative, one-drug lethal dose of thiopental drew a challenge from Justice Alito, who disputed that the issue had been properly raised in the Kentucky courts. Justice Breyer, although less concerned with that procedural point, questioned whether any of the expert studies by the British medical journal *Lancet* or a Netherlands task force on euthanasia demonstrated the efficacy of the single drug in producing a painless death. "And I ended up thinking of course there is a risk of human error," he concluded. "There is a risk of human error generally where you're talking about the death penalty, and this may be one extra problem. But the question here is can we say that there is a more serious problem here than with other execution methods?"[48]

Justice Souter suggested remanding issues back to the trial court for further fact-finding, including the availability of medical personnel and their training and a comparative analysis of the three- versus one-drug method of inducing death. Souter's comment brought a sharp rebuke from Scalia, who predicted it would produce another "nationwide cessation of all executions while the trial court finishes its work and then it goes to another appeal to the state supreme court and ultimately, well, it could take years."[49]

Justices Souter and Stevens finally questioned Kentucky's use of the second drug in the protocol, the paralytic agent Pavulon that inhibited all muscular-skeletal movements and finally stopped respiration. Kentucky law prohibited the use of such drugs by veterinarians when killing animals in favor of a single dose of a barbiturate, but the state's penal officials defended its use on the grounds that it provided a more dignified death for the condemned, spared the feelings of witnesses who might be otherwise upset by muscular or skeletal movements, and shortened the actual time of death.

When Kentucky's lawyers argued that successful use of the first drug avoided the risk of excruciating pain by the paralytic agent, Stevens observed: "The dignity of the process outweighs the risk of excruciating pain?" When the attorney for Kentucky replied in the negative, Justice Stevens continued: "But then the risk of excruciating pain outweighs the risk of an undignified death. . . . Everyone who goes through the process knows there is some risk of excruciating pain that could be avoided by a single-drug protocol. Would he prefer to say, I want to die in a dignified way. . . . I am terribly troubled by the fact that the second drug is what seems to cause all the risk of excruciating pain, and seems to be almost totally unnecessary in terms of any rational basis for a requirement. . . . The interest in protecting the dignity of the inmate and of the observers is the justification for the second drug."[50]

These concerns about alternative methods of lethal injection brought a final tart rejoinder from Scalia. "If that's part of the analysis, this never ends. . . . There will always be some claim that there is some new method that's been devised, and once again executions are stayed throughout the country."[51]

Three months after oral argument, the justices in *Baze v. Rees* by a vote of 7–2 rejected the plaintiff's claims and ruled Kentucky's lethal injection protocol consistent with the requirements of the Eighth Amendment (**Document 5.8**). Chief Justice Roberts, writing for himself and two other justices, Kennedy and Alito, disposed of the "substantial risk of pain" argument by noting that the use of sodium thiopental in the three-drug combination had been adopted by every state and the federal government, a widely accepted practice which made it impossible to label the procedure "objectively intolerable." Kentucky had taken reasonable steps to insure an adequate dose of sodium thiopental and to monitor the inmate's reactions throughout the procedure and, further, the state had a legitimate interest in using a neuromuscular paralytic and rejecting a one-drug, barbiturate-only solution in order to provide a speedy and certain death. The Constitution, the chief justice concluded, prohibited only "wanton infliction of pain," not simply the possibility of pain.[52]

Justice Stevens, while concurring in the judgment on the basis of past decisions, hinted that he now believed capital punishment unconstitutional on Eighth Amendment grounds, and he predicted that the *Baze* case would generate further litigation over the three-drug protocol, the specific use of the neuromuscular paralytic, and the justification for the death penalty itself. Quoting the late Justice White, he concluded that the penalty violated the Eighth Amendment because it represented "the pointless and needless extinction of life with only marginal contributions to any discernible social or public purposes."[53]

In their joint concurring opinion, Justices Thomas and Scalia reprimanded the plurality for crafting a needless standard that found no support in the original understanding of the Eighth Amendment or past decisions that prohibited only methods of execution intentionally designed to inflict pain. Kentucky and other states had adopted the three-drug protocol with the intention of making capital punishment more humane. Justice Breyer, also concurring, noted that the death penalty's lawfulness had not been raised and that neither the trial record nor available scientific literature demonstrated that Kentucky's procedures created a significant risk of "unnecessary suffering" by the condemned.[54]

The two dissenters, Ginsburg and Souter, would have remanded the case to the Kentucky courts for further inquiry into the state's monitoring procedures and its continued use of sodium thiopental to insure that its protocol did not create what they called "an untoward, readily avoidable risk of inflicting severe and unnecessary pain."[55]

By the end of the Court's 2007 term in June, six states had resumed executions, all but one with lethal injection protocols similar to Kentucky's. A total of twenty-three executions had been scheduled for the remainder of 2008. On the other hand, one Ohio judge, James Burge, ordered the state to halt its method of lethal injections using the three-drug cocktail because the possibility of improper administration of sodium thiopental raised the risk that the protocol would violate Ohio's statute requiring a "sufficient dosage to quickly and painlessly cause death."[56]

The Ohio ruling appeared to confirm the views of many death penalty scholars and lawyers that *Baze,* instead of ending litigation and debate, had simply opened the door to more challenges, especially where state protocols diverged from Kentucky's. Because of the divided opinion in *Baze,* said Deborah W. Denno, a law professor at Fordham University, "attorneys are in pretty good shape for further litigation."[57]

Capital Punishment and Child Rape

At the very end of their 2007 term, the justices again addressed the issue of the Eighth Amendment and capital punishment in *Kennedy v. Louisiana,* in which by a vote of 5–4 they declared unconstitutional a Louisiana statute that imposed death for the rape of a child under twelve years of age.[58] Justice Kennedy, writing for the majority, invoked in part the same rationale of a national consensus that the Court had used with respect to lethal injection in *Baze* to hold that the Louisiana statute imposed a penalty disproportionate to the crime itself. In every death penalty case since *Gregg* and *Coker v. Georgia* (1977),[59] Kennedy argued, the Court had never sustained a statute where the crime had not resulted in the death of the victim. Only six states out of the thirty-six that imposed capital punishment authorized it for child rape. Child rape cases also imposed high emotional and psychological costs on any child called to testify and often proved unreliable, thereby raising the risk of convicting the innocent.[60]

Justice Alito, joined by Scalia, Thomas, and the chief justice, dissented on the grounds that the *Coker* decision prohibiting the death penalty for the rape of an adult woman had led many states to believe erroneously that the Eighth Amendment barred the penalty for child rape as well. The Court's earlier ruling had thus prevented the development of a larger state consensus on child rape. The dissenters also chastised the majority for engaging in "policy arguments" that were irrelevant to the question of whether the death penalty for child rape constituted "cruel and unusual punishment." The Eighth Amendment did not authorize the Court to strike down state criminal laws "on the ground that they are not in the best interests of crime victims or the broader society."[61]

The decision in *Kennedy* also drew sharp rebukes from both presumptive presidential nominees, Senators John McCain and Barack Obama. "That there is a judge anywhere in America who does not believe that the rape of a child represents the most heinous of crimes, which is deserving of the most serious of punishments, is profoundly disturbing," McCain told reporters. Obama condemned the Court's "blanket prohibition" and argued that under narrow, limited, well-defined circumstances, the death penalty would be appropriate for such "a heinous crime."[62]

The Challenges of Implementing the Death Penalty

While the Court in 2008 gave a limited green light to one method of carrying out the death penalty in *Baze* and restricted its application in *Kennedy,* the California Commission on the Fair Administration of Justice issued a report and recommendations on that state's death penalty regime that echoed Justice Stevens' grim assessment in *Baze*. The commission's 145-page document described California's system, now the largest in the nation with 670 inmates awaiting execution, as dysfunctional, unmanageable, and on the brink of collapse. Since capital punishment was restored in 1978, only 12 prisoners had been put to death in California amid a staggering backlog in post-conviction appeals.

Robert Bell shot and killed a store clerk during a failed robbery attempt in 1978. At age fifty-seven he is the state of California's longest-serving death row inmate; his appeals remain before the courts. In order to clear the present backlog, the commission noted, the state would have to execute five prisoners each month for the next twelve years. Instead of that unlikely scenario, the commission recommended additional funds of $95 million to hire and train qualified attorneys to handle appeals and consideration of more life sentences instead of death. "The time has come to address death penalty reform in a frank and honest way," the commission concluded.[63]

At the same time California's report was made public, officials in Georgia were attempting to navigate their way through a series of Supreme Court mandates in an effort to bring to trial Brian Nichols, whose bloody rampage in an Atlanta courtroom on March 11, 2005, appeared to be one of the most open-and-shut cases of capital murder in the nation's history.

Nichols, a thirty-three-year-old African American, was being retried on a charge of rape in Atlanta's Fulton County Courthouse when he overpowered his guard in a holding cell, took her gun, and stormed into the courtroom of Judge Rowland Barnes. There he shot and killed Judge Barnes and a court reporter, Julie Ann Brandau, before fleeing the building; outside on the street he gunned down a deputy sheriff, Hoyt Teasley. Before he took refuge in the apartment of a total stranger and surrendered hours later, Nichols also shot and killed a federal customs agent, David Wilhelm. Several witnesses saw the courtroom shootings and Nichols himself confessed to all four killings when interrogated by the Atlanta police.

To no one's surprise at the time, the district attorney of Fulton County sought the death penalty. But by the summer of 2008, three years after Nichols' murder spree, jury selection had been placed on hold as a result of financial conflicts and the resignation of Nichols' initial defense team, one member of which had allowed his bar membership to lapse. The state, attempting to comply with Supreme Court rulings on the right to counsel and a defendant's access to expert testimony, had paid Nichols' new defense team, headed by Henderson Hill of North Carolina, about $1.2 million, with no end in sight. The Georgia Public Defenders Standards Council, created in 2003 to unify and make coherent the state's decentralized system of providing legal assistance to the poor, remained locked for months in a financial battle with the Georgia legislature over additional funding for the Nichols case and others. Alarmed over the rising costs of Nichols' defense, the council attempted unsuccessfully to remove Hill and his team from the case, a gambit the trial judge rejected and which Nichols' defenders claimed would be a gross violation of the right to counsel.

In an effort to move the trial out of the Fulton County Courthouse where Nichols launched his murder spree, the county engaged in prolonged negotiations with Atlanta officials over use of facilities in the city's new municipal courthouse. Nichols meanwhile had entered a plea of not guilty by reason of a "delusional compulsion," one version of the state's insanity defense. His lawyers challenged the state's right to have its own experts examine his mental condition and they moved to bar an "enhanced" audio recording of the gunshots fired at the judge and court reporter. They also asked the trial judge to throw out the entire case against Nichols on the grounds that the chief prosecutor had at his rape trial engaged in criminal misconduct before the trial that impaired her judgment and that the district attorney withheld this information from the defendant's lawyers.[64]

After District Attorney Paul Howard turned down an agreement under which Nichols would plead guilty in exchange for a life sentence without parole, the case finally went to trial in August 2008. It required many weeks to select a jury that finally included six African American women, two African American men, two white women, a white man, and one Asian American man, who listened to three months of testimony from 144 witnesses, including defense psychologists who claimed that Nichols was insane at the time he stormed into Judge Barnes' courtroom. They reviewed more than 1,200 pieces of evidence. Fulton County officials estimated the trial cost to the government at $3 million. On November

7, 2008, after rejecting Nichols' insanity defense, the jury found him guilty of killing Barnes, Brandau, Teasley, and Wilhelm.

On December 13, however, after three days of debate the jury announced it was hopelessly deadlocked over the death penalty, with nine in favor and three against. Judge James Bodiford kept them deliberating for extra hours on Friday, December 14, before accepting the fact that they would never be unanimous as required under Georgia law before imposing death. That same day Bodiford sentenced Nichols to eleven life sentences, plus 485 years in prison without parole.[65] Predictably, the jury verdict sparked criticism and outrage in Georgia, even among opponents of capital punishment. Michael Mears, a law professor who had defended many death penalty cases, pointed out that under Georgia and federal precedents that require sentences to be proportional to penalties given for similar murders the Nichols verdict raised serious problems. "If Brian Nichols does not receive the death penalty, how is the Georgia Supreme Court going to allow any other death penalty to stand that involves the murder of a police officer or court official?" Many state legislators in Georgia vowed to introduce new legislation to eliminate the requirement of unanimity in capital cases, a change that would make Georgia the only state with such a requirement and which opponents charged would violate both the Eighth and Fourteenth Amendments. District Attorney Howard suggested that Nichols might still be tried and sentenced to death in federal court for the murder of Wilhelm.

The Nichols case led observers to point out a slight downward trend in death sentences between 1998 and 2007, from 306 in the former year to 115 in the latter, a result, some argued, of growing public distrust in the penalty, the number of sentences overturned as a result of new DNA testing, and increased reliance on the life-without-parole sentencing option. "To get 12 people to decide to kill somebody is a difficult undertaking," said Stephen Bright of the Southern Center for Human Rights shortly after the Nichols verdict. "People are overwhelmingly in favor of the death penalty when the Gallup poll calls. But when you ask them in a courtroom to actually impose the death penalty, a lot of people feel very uncomfortable."[66]

At the Supreme Court in 2008, *Baze v. Rees* indicated that the death penalty continued to pass muster under the U.S. Constitution, despite the limitations imposed on the crime of child rape in *Kennedy v. Louisiana*. Between *Baze* and the winter of 2009, twenty-four executions had been carried out by lethal injection, all in the South and one-third in Texas alone. But four months before the *Baze* decision, without an execution since 1963, the state of New Jersey abolished capital punishment (**Document 5.9** and **Document 5.10**). New Jersey was the first state to do so since the Court's 1972 *Furman* decision.[67] It was soon followed, however, by New Mexico, which on March 18, 2009 became the fifteenth state to abolish the death penalty when Gov. Bill Richardson signed a bill ending

New Mexico governor Bill Richardson signs a bill into law on March 18, 2009, that repealed the state's death penalty. New Mexico joins Alaska, Massachusetts, Michigan, and others as a state in which capital punishment has been abolished.

capital punishment and substituting life without parole in future cases (**Document 5.11** and **Document 5.12**). New Mexico had not carried out an execution in thirty years and had only two persons on death row at the time.

While the Supreme Court put its stamp of constitutional approval on lethal injection in 2008, the Nebraska supreme court almost simultaneously declared the use of the electric chair in that state "cruel and unusual punishment" in violation of the Nebraska constitution.[68] On February 8 that court issued a ruling prohibiting its use (**Document 5.13**). That same month the state of Mississippi freed death-row inmate Kennedy Brewer as a result of DNA tests that proved he had not murdered a child. Brewer, who had been on death row for twelve years, became the 127th death-row inmate exonerated as a result of DNA testing since 2000.[69]

In March 2009 the Maryland legislature approved new legislation requiring specific evidence of guilt such as DNA evidence in all cases in which prosecutors seek the death penalty. The Virginia legislature at the same time upheld Gov. Tim Kaine's veto of a bill that would have expanded capital punishment in that state to murder accomplices. "We execute enough people in Virginia," Kaine remarked after the vote. "We don't need to expand it." Similar legislative debates over abolition were taking place in Connecticut and South Dakota. The Hartford *Courant* urged Connecticut legislators to act soon on abolition and condemned the penalty as "unworkable, not to mention expensive, unfair and risky."[70]

Document 5.1
Congress Limits Federal Habeas Corpus Appeals, April 24, 1996

In 1996 Congress passed and President Bill Clinton signed into law the Antiterrorism and Effective Death Penalty Act, which sharply curtailed access to habeas corpus review in the federal courts by state prisoners, especially those under sentence of death. While the Supreme Court itself had imposed certain procedural limitations on the lower federal courts before 1996, the new law realized the objectives of those like Chief Justice William Rehnquist, who sought further restrictions on death penalty appeals.

Antiterrorism and Effective Death Penalty Act of 1996 (Enrolled as Agreed to or Passed by Both House and Senate)

TITLE I—HABEAS CORPUS REFORM

SEC. 101. FILING DEADLINES.

Section 2244 of title 28, United States Code, is amended by adding at the end the following new subsection:

'(d)(1)   A 1-year period of limitation shall apply to an application for a writ of habeas corpus by a person in custody pursuant to the judgment of a State court. The limitation period shall run from the latest of—

'(A)   the date on which the judgment became final by the conclusion of direct review or the expiration of the time for seeking such review;

'(B)   the date on which the impediment to filing an application created by State action in violation of the Constitution or laws of the United States is removed, if the applicant was prevented from filing by such State action;

'(C)   the date on which the constitutional right asserted was initially recognized by the Supreme Court, if the right has been newly recognized by the Supreme Court and made retroactively applicable to cases on collateral review; or

'(D)   the date on which the factual predicate of the claim or claims presented could have been discovered through the exercise of due diligence.

'(2)   The time during which a properly filed application for State post-conviction or other collateral review with respect to the pertinent judgment or claim is pending shall not be counted toward any period of limitation under this subsection.'.

SEC. 102. APPEAL.

Section 2253 of title 28, United States Code, is amended to read as follows:

'Sec. 2253. Appeal

'(a)   In a habeas corpus proceeding or a proceeding under section 2255 before a district judge, the final order shall be subject to review, on appeal, by the court of appeals for the circuit in which the proceeding is held.

'(b)   There shall be no right of appeal from a final order in a proceeding to test the validity of a warrant to remove to another district or place for commitment or trial a person charged with a criminal offense against the United States, or to test the validity of such person's detention pending removal proceedings.

'(c)(1)   Unless a circuit justice or judge issues a certificate of appealability, an appeal may not be taken to the court of appeals from—

'(A)   the final order in a habeas corpus proceeding in which the detention complained of arises out of process issued by a State court; or

'(B)   the final order in a proceeding under section 2255.

'(2)   A certificate of appealability may issue under paragraph (1) only if the applicant has made a substantial showing of the denial of a constitutional right.

'(3)   The certificate of appealability under paragraph (1) shall indicate which specific issue or issues satisfy the showing required by paragraph (2).'.

SEC. 103. AMENDMENT OF FEDERAL RULES OF APPELLATE PROCEDURE.

Rule 22 of the Federal Rules of Appellate Procedure is amended to read as follows:

'Rule 22. Habeas corpus and section 2255 proceedings

'(a)   APPLICATION FOR THE ORIGINAL WRIT—An application for a writ of habeas corpus shall be made to the appropriate district court. If application is made to a circuit judge, the application shall be transferred to the appropriate district court. If an application is made to or transferred to the district court and denied, renewal of the application before a circuit judge shall not be permitted. The applicant may, pursuant to section 2253 of title 28, United States Code, appeal to the appropriate court of appeals from the order of the district court denying the writ.

'(b)   CERTIFICATE OF APPEALABILITY—In a habeas corpus proceeding in which the detention complained of arises out of process issued by a

State court, an appeal by the applicant for the writ may not proceed unless a district or a circuit judge issues a certificate of appealability pursuant to section 2253(c) of title 28, United States Code. If an appeal is taken by the applicant, the district judge who rendered the judgment shall either issue a certificate of appealability or state the reasons why such a certificate should not issue. The certificate or the statement shall be forwarded to the court of appeals with the notice of appeal and the file of the proceedings in the district court. If the district judge has denied the certificate, the applicant for the writ may then request issuance of the certificate by a circuit judge. If such a request is addressed to the court of appeals, it shall be deemed addressed to the judges thereof and shall be considered by a circuit judge or judges as the court deems appropriate. If no express request for a certificate is filed, the notice of appeal shall be deemed to constitute a request addressed to the judges of the court of appeals. If an appeal is taken by a State or its representative, a certificate of appealability is not required.'.

SEC. 104. SECTION 2254 AMENDMENTS.

Section 2254 of title 28, United States Code, is amended—

(1) by amending subsection (b) to read as follows:

'(b)(1) An application for a writ of habeas corpus on behalf of a person in custody pursuant to the judgment of a State court shall not be granted unless it appears that—

'(A)   the applicant has exhausted the remedies available in the courts of the State; or

'(B)(i) there is an absence of available State corrective process; or

'(ii) circumstances exist that render such process ineffective to protect the rights of the applicant.

'(2) An application for a writ of habeas corpus may be denied on the merits, notwithstanding the failure of the applicant to exhaust the remedies available in the courts of the State.

'(3) A State shall not be deemed to have waived the exhaustion requirement or be estopped from reliance upon the requirement unless the State, through counsel, expressly waives the requirement.';

(2) by redesignating subsections (d), (e), and (f) as subsections (e), (f), and (g), respectively;

(3) by inserting after subsection (c) the following new subsection:

'(d) An application for a writ of habeas corpus on behalf of a person in custody pursuant to the judgment of a State court shall not be granted with respect to any claim that was adjudicated on the merits in State court proceedings unless the adjudication of the claim—

'(1) resulted in a decision that was contrary to, or involved an unreasonable application of, clearly established Federal law, as determined by the Supreme Court of the United States; or

'(2) resulted in a decision that was based on an unreasonable determination of the facts in light of the evidence presented in the State court proceeding.';

(4) by amending subsection (e), as redesignated by paragraph (2), to read as follows:

'(e)(1) In a proceeding instituted by an application for a writ of habeas corpus by a person in custody pursuant to the judgment of a State court, a determination of a factual issue made by a State court shall be presumed to be correct. The applicant shall have the burden of rebutting the presumption of correctness by clear and convincing evidence.

'(2) If the applicant has failed to develop the factual basis of a claim in State court proceedings, the court shall not hold an evidentiary hearing on the claim unless the applicant shows that—

'(A) the claim relies on—

'(i) a new rule of constitutional law, made retroactive to cases on collateral review by the Supreme Court, that was previously unavailable; or

'(ii) a factual predicate that could not have been previously discovered through the exercise of due diligence; and

'(B) the facts underlying the claim would be sufficient to establish by clear and convincing evidence that but for constitutional error, no reasonable factfinder would have found the applicant guilty of the underlying offense.'; and

(5) by adding at the end the following new subsections:

'(h) Except as provided in section 408 of the Controlled Substances Act, in all proceedings brought under this section, and any subsequent proceedings on review, the court may appoint counsel for an applicant who is or becomes financially unable to afford counsel, except as provided by a rule promulgated by the Supreme Court pursuant to statutory authority. Appointment of counsel under this section shall be governed by section 3006A of title 18.

'(i)   The ineffectiveness or incompetence of counsel during Federal or State collateral post-conviction proceedings shall not be a ground for relief in a proceeding arising under section 2254.'.

SEC. 105. SECTION 2255 AMENDMENTS.

Section 2255 of title 28, United States Code, is amended—

(1)   by striking the second and fifth undesignated paragraphs; and

(2)   by adding at the end the following new undesignated paragraphs:
'A 1-year period of limitation shall apply to a motion under this section. The limitation period shall run from the latest of—
'(1)   the date on which the judgment of conviction becomes final;
'(2)   the date on which the impediment to making a motion created by governmental action in violation of the Constitution or laws of the United States is removed, if the movant was prevented from making a motion by such governmental action;

'(3)   the date on which the right asserted was initially recognized by the Supreme Court, if that right has been newly recognized by the Supreme Court and made retroactively applicable to cases on collateral review; or

'(4)   the date on which the facts supporting the claim or claims presented could have been discovered through the exercise of due diligence.

'Except as provided in section 408 of the Controlled Substances Act, in all proceedings brought under this section, and any subsequent proceedings on review, the court may appoint counsel, except as provided by a rule promulgated by the Supreme Court pursuant to statutory authority. Appointment of counsel under this section shall be governed by section 3006A of title 18.

'A second or successive motion must be certified as provided in section 2244 by a panel of the appropriate court of appeals to contain—

'(1)   newly discovered evidence that, if proven and viewed in light of the evidence as a whole, would be sufficient to establish by clear and convincing evidence that no reasonable factfinder would have found the movant guilty of the offense; or

'(2)   a new rule of constitutional law, made retroactive to cases on collateral review by the Supreme Court, that was previously unavailable.'.

SEC. 106. LIMITS ON SECOND OR SUCCESSIVE APPLICATIONS.

(a)   CONFORMING AMENDMENT TO SECTION 2244(a)—Section 2244(a) of title 28, United States Code, is amended by striking 'and the petition' and all that follows through 'by such inquiry.' and inserting ', except as provided in section 2255.'.

(b)   LIMITS ON SECOND OR SUCCESSIVE APPLICATIONS—Section 2244(b) of title 28, United States Code, is amended to read as follows:

'(b)(1) A claim presented in a second or successive habeas corpus application under section 2254 that was presented in a prior application shall be dismissed.

'(2) A claim presented in a second or successive habeas corpus application under section 2254 that was not presented in a prior application shall be dismissed unless—

'(A) the applicant shows that the claim relies on a new rule of constitutional law, made retroactive to cases on collateral review by the Supreme Court, that was previously unavailable; or

'(B)(i) the factual predicate for the claim could not have been discovered previously through the exercise of due diligence; and

'(ii) the facts underlying the claim, if proven and viewed in light of the evidence as a whole, would be sufficient to establish by clear and convincing evidence that, but for constitutional error, no reasonable factfinder would have found the applicant guilty of the underlying offense.

'(3)(A) Before a second or successive application permitted by this section is filed in the district court, the applicant shall move in the appropriate court of appeals for an order authorizing the district court to consider the application.

'(B) A motion in the court of appeals for an order authorizing the district court to consider a second or successive application shall be determined by a three-judge panel of the court of appeals.

'(C) The court of appeals may authorize the filing of a second or successive application only if it determines that the application makes a prima facie showing that the application satisfies the requirements of this subsection.

'(D) The court of appeals shall grant or deny the authorization to file a second or successive application not later than 30 days after the filing of the motion.

'(E) The grant or denial of an authorization by a court of appeals to file a second or successive application shall not be appealable and shall not be the subject of a petition for rehearing or for a writ of certiorari.

'(4) A district court shall dismiss any claim presented in a second or successive application that the court of appeals has authorized to be filed unless the applicant shows that the claim satisfies the requirements of this section.'.

SEC. 107. DEATH PENALTY LITIGATION PROCEDURES.

(a) ADDITION OF CHAPTER TO TITLE 28, UNITED STATES CODE-
Title 28, United States Code, is amended by inserting after chapter 153 the following new chapter:

'CHAPTER 154—SPECIAL HABEAS CORPUS PROCEDURES IN CAPITAL CASES

'Sec.

'2261. Prisoners in State custody subject to capital sentence; appointment of counsel; requirement of rule of court or statute; procedures for appointment.

'2262. Mandatory stay of execution; duration; limits on stays of execution; successive petitions.

'2263. Filing of habeas corpus application; time requirements; tolling rules.

'2264. Scope of Federal review; district court adjudications.

'2265. Application to State unitary review procedure.

'2266. Limitation periods for determining applications and motions.

'Sec. 2261. Prisoners in State custody subject to capital sentence; appointment of counsel; requirement of rule of court or statute; procedures for appointment

'(a)   This chapter shall apply to cases arising under section 2254 brought by prisoners in State custody who are subject to a capital sentence. It shall apply only if the provisions of subsections (b) and (c) are satisfied.

'(b)   This chapter is applicable if a State establishes by statute, rule of its court of last resort, or by another agency authorized by State law, a mechanism for the appointment, compensation, and payment of reasonable litigation expenses of competent counsel in State postconviction proceedings brought by indigent prisoners whose capital convictions and sentences have been upheld on direct appeal to the court of last resort in the State or have otherwise become final for State law purposes. The rule of court or statute must provide standards of competency for the appointment of such counsel.

'(c)   Any mechanism for the appointment, compensation, and reimbursement of counsel as provided in subsection (b) must offer counsel to all State prisoners under capital sentence and must provide for the entry of an order by a court of record—

'(1)   appointing one or more counsels to represent the prisoner upon a finding that the prisoner is indigent and accepted the offer or is unable competently to decide whether to accept or reject the offer;

'(2)   finding, after a hearing if necessary, that the prisoner rejected the offer of counsel and made the decision with an understanding of its legal consequences; or

'(3)   denying the appointment of counsel upon a finding that the prisoner is not indigent.

'(d)   No counsel appointed pursuant to subsections (b) and (c) to represent a State prisoner under capital sentence shall have previously represented the prisoner at trial or on direct appeal in the case for which the appointment is made unless the prisoner and counsel expressly request continued representation.

'(e)   The ineffectiveness or incompetence of counsel during State or Federal post-conviction proceedings in a capital case shall not be a ground for relief in a proceeding arising under section 2254. This limitation shall not preclude the appointment of different counsel, on the court's own motion or at the request of the prisoner, at any phase of State or Federal post-conviction proceedings on the basis of the ineffectiveness or incompetence of counsel in such proceedings.

'Sec. 2262. Mandatory stay of execution; duration; limits on stays of execution; successive petitions

'(a)   Upon the entry in the appropriate State court of record of an order under section 2261(c), a warrant or order setting an execution date for a State prisoner shall be stayed upon application to any court that would have jurisdiction over any proceedings filed under section 2254. The application shall recite that the State has invoked the post-conviction review procedures of this chapter and that the scheduled execution is subject to stay.

'(b)   A stay of execution granted pursuant to subsection (a) shall expire if—

'(1)   a State prisoner fails to file a habeas corpus application under section 2254 within the time required in section 2263;

'(2)   before a court of competent jurisdiction, in the presence of counsel, unless the prisoner has competently and knowingly waived such counsel, and after having been advised of the consequences, a State prisoner under capital sentence waives the right to pursue habeas corpus review under section 2254; or

'(3)   a State prisoner files a habeas corpus petition under section 2254 within the time required by section 2263 and fails to make a substantial showing of the denial of a Federal right or is denied relief in the district court or at any subsequent stage of review.

'(c)   If one of the conditions in subsection (b) has occurred, no Federal court thereafter shall have the authority to enter a stay of execution in the case, unless the court of appeals approves the filing of a second or successive application under section 2244(b).

'Sec. 2263. Filing of habeas corpus application; time requirements; tolling rules

'(a)   Any application under this chapter for habeas corpus relief under section 2254 must be filed in the appropriate district court not later than 180 days after final State court affirmance of the conviction and sentence on direct review or the expiration of the time for seeking such review.

'(b)   The time requirements established by subsection (a) shall be tolled—

   '(1)   from the date that a petition for certiorari is filed in the Supreme Court until the date of final disposition of the petition if a State prisoner files the petition to secure review by the Supreme Court of the affirmance of a capital sentence on direct review by the court of last resort of the State or other final State court decision on direct review;

   '(2)   from the date on which the first petition for post-conviction review or other collateral relief is filed until the final State court disposition of such petition; and

   '(3)   during an additional period not to exceed 30 days, if—

      '(A)   a motion for an extension of time is filed in the Federal district court that would have jurisdiction over the case upon the filing of a habeas corpus application under section 2254; and

      '(B)   a showing of good cause is made for the failure to file the habeas corpus application within the time period established by this section.

'Sec. 2264. Scope of Federal review; district court adjudications

'(a)   Whenever a State prisoner under capital sentence files a petition for habeas corpus relief to which this chapter applies, the district court shall only consider a claim or claims that have been raised and decided on the merits in the State courts, unless the failure to raise the claim properly is—

   '(1)   the result of State action in violation of the Constitution or laws of the United States;

   '(2)   the result of the Supreme Court's recognition of a new Federal right that is made retroactively applicable; or

   '(3)   based on a factual predicate that could not have been discovered through the exercise of due diligence in time to present the claim for State or Federal post-conviction review.

'(b)   Following review subject to subsections (a), (d), and (e) of section 2254, the court shall rule on the claims properly before it.

'Sec. 2265. Application to State unitary review procedure

'(a)   For purposes of this section, a 'unitary review' procedure means a State procedure that authorizes a person under sentence of death to raise, in the course of direct review of the judgment, such claims as could be raised on collateral attack. This chapter shall apply, as provided in this section, in relation to a State unitary review procedure if the State establishes by rule of its court of last resort or by statute a mechanism for the appointment, compensation, and payment of reasonable litigation expenses of competent counsel in the unitary review proceedings, including expenses relating to the litigation of collateral claims in the proceedings. The rule of court or statute must provide standards of competency for the appointment of such counsel.

'(b)   To qualify under this section, a unitary review procedure must include an offer of counsel following trial for the purpose of representation on unitary review, and entry of an order, as provided in section 2261(c), concerning appointment of counsel or waiver or denial of appointment of counsel for that purpose. No counsel appointed to represent the prisoner in the unitary review proceedings shall have previously represented the prisoner at trial in the case for which the appointment is made unless the prisoner and counsel expressly request continued representation.

'(c)   Sections 2262, 2263, 2264, and 2266 shall apply in relation to cases involving a sentence of death from any State having a unitary review procedure that qualifies under this section. References to State 'postconviction review' and 'direct review' in such sections shall be understood as referring to unitary review under the State procedure. The reference in section 2262(a) to 'an order under section 2261(c)' shall be understood as referring to the post-trial order under subsection (b) concerning representation in the unitary review proceedings, but if a transcript of the trial proceedings is unavailable at the time of the filing of such an order in the appropriate State court, then the start of the 180-day limitation period under section 2263 shall be deferred until a transcript is made available to the prisoner or counsel of the prisoner.

'Sec. 2266. Limitation periods for determining applications and motions

'(a)   The adjudication of any application under section 2254 that is subject to this chapter, and the adjudication of any motion under section 2255 by a person under sentence of death, shall be given priority by the district court and by the court of appeals over all noncapital matters.

'(b)(1)(A)   A district court shall render a final determination and enter a final judgment on any application for a writ of habeas corpus brought under this chapter in a capital case not later than 180 days after the date on which the application is filed.

'(B)   A district court shall afford the parties at least 120 days in which to complete all actions, including the preparation of all pleadings and briefs, and if necessary, a hearing, prior to the submission of the case for decision.

'(C)(i)   A district court may delay for not more than one additional 30-day period beyond the period specified in subparagraph (A), the rendering of a determination of an application for a writ of habeas corpus if the court issues a written order making a finding, and stating the reasons for the finding, that the ends of justice that would be served by allowing the delay outweigh the best interests of the public and the applicant in a speedy disposition of the application.

'(ii)   The factors, among others, that a court shall consider in determining whether a delay in the disposition of an application is warranted are as follows:

'(I)   Whether the failure to allow the delay would be likely to result in a miscarriage of justice.

'(II)   Whether the case is so unusual or so complex, due to the number of defendants, the nature of the prosecution, or the existence of novel questions of fact or law, that it is unreasonable to expect adequate briefing within the time limitations established by subparagraph (A).

'(III)   Whether the failure to allow a delay in a case that, taken as a whole, is not so unusual or so complex as described in subclause (II), but would otherwise deny the applicant reasonable time to obtain counsel, would unreasonably deny the applicant or the government continuity of counsel, or would deny counsel for the applicant or the government the reasonable time necessary for effective preparation, taking into account the exercise of due diligence.

'(iii)   No delay in disposition shall be permissible because of general congestion of the court's calendar.

'(iv)   The court shall transmit a copy of any order issued under clause (i) to the Director of the Administrative Office of the United States Courts for inclusion in the report under paragraph (5).

'(2)   The time limitations under paragraph (1) shall apply to—

'(A)   an initial application for a writ of habeas corpus;

'(B)   any second or successive application for a writ of habeas corpus; and

'(C)   any redetermination of an application for a writ of habeas corpus following a remand by the court of appeals or the Supreme Court for further proceedings, in which case the limitation period shall run from the date the remand is ordered.

'(3)(A)   The time limitations under this section shall not be construed to entitle an applicant to a stay of execution, to which the applicant would otherwise not be entitled, for the purpose of litigating any application or appeal.

'(B)   No amendment to an application for a writ of habeas corpus under this chapter shall be permitted after the filing of the answer to the application, except on the grounds specified in section 2244(b).

'(4)(A)   The failure of a court to meet or comply with a time limitation under this section shall not be a ground for granting relief from a judgment of conviction or sentence.

'(B)   The State may enforce a time limitation under this section by petitioning for a writ of mandamus to the court of appeals. The court of appeals shall act on the petition for a writ of mandamus not later than 30 days after the filing of the petition.

'(5)(A)   The Administrative Office of the United States Courts shall submit to Congress an annual report on the compliance by the district courts with the time limitations under this section.

'(B)   The report described in subparagraph (A) shall include copies of the orders submitted by the district courts under paragraph (1)(B)(iv).

'(C)(1)(A)   A court of appeals shall hear and render a final determination of any appeal of an order granting or denying, in whole or in part, an application brought under this chapter in a capital case not later than 120 days after the date on which the reply brief is filed, or if no reply brief is filed, not later than 120 days after the date on which the answering brief is filed.

'(B)(i)   A court of appeals shall decide whether to grant a petition for rehearing or other request for rehearing en banc not later than 30 days after the date on which the petition for rehearing is filed unless a responsive pleading is required, in which case the court shall decide whether to grant the petition not later than 30 days after the date on which the responsive pleading is filed.

'(ii)   If a petition for rehearing or rehearing en banc is granted, the court of appeals shall hear and render a final determination of the appeal not later than 120 days after the date on which the order granting rehearing or rehearing en banc is entered.

'(2) The time limitations under paragraph (1) shall apply to—

'(A)   an initial application for a writ of habeas corpus;

'(B)   any second or successive application for a writ of habeas corpus; and

'(C)   any redetermination of an application for a writ of habeas corpus or related appeal following a remand by the court of appeals en banc or the Supreme Court for further proceedings, in which case the limitation period shall run from the date the remand is ordered.

'(3)   The time limitations under this section shall not be construed to entitle an applicant to a stay of execution, to which the applicant would otherwise not be entitled, for the purpose of litigating any application or appeal.

'(4)(A)   The failure of a court to meet or comply with a time limitation under this section shall not be a ground for granting relief from a judgment of conviction or sentence.

'(B)   The State may enforce a time limitation under this section by applying for a writ of mandamus to the Supreme Court.

'(5)   The Administrative Office of the United States Courts shall submit to Congress an annual report on the compliance by the courts of appeals with the time limitations under this section.'.

(b) TECHNICAL AMENDMENT—The part analysis for part IV of title 28, United States Code, is amended by adding after the item relating to chapter 153 the following new item:
2261.'.

(c) EFFECTIVE DATE—Chapter 154 of title 28, United States Code (as added by subsection (a)) shall apply to cases pending on or after the date of enactment of this Act.

Source: U.S. Senate, "S.735, Antiterrorism and Effective Death Penalty Act of 1996," 104th Cong., 1st sess. Available at THOMAS (Library of Congress) at http://thomas.loc.gov/cgi-bin/query/F?c104:4:./temp/~c104Je4p7q:e12000: (accessed May 13, 2009).

Document 5.2
The Justices Debate "Actual Innocence" and the Death Penalty, January 25, 1993

In Herrera v. Collins *(1993), the Supreme Court was called upon to decide whether the Eighth Amendment and/or the Fourteenth barred the execution of a person who alleged in a habeas corpus petition, ten years after his conviction for murder, that he was "actually innocent" of the crime. Chief Justice William Rehnquist's opinion for the Court rejected Leonel Torres Herrera's specific claim, but at the same time held that the Constitution did not sanction the execution of the innocent. The case was complicated by difficult substantive and procedural issues, including the fact that Herrera's claims rested largely on dubious affidavits, that Texas law imposed strict limitations on the submission of newly discovered evidence, and that prior Court rulings even by the liberal Warren Court narrowed the claims that could be raised through habeas corpus. Few decisions provoked sharper debate among the justices. Justices Sandra Day O'Connor and Anthony Kennedy took pains to point out that the Court had not said innocent persons could be put to death; Justices Antonin Scalia and Clarence Thomas complained that the chief justice had not slammed the door tightly enough against such claims; and the dissenters (Harry Blackmun, John Paul Stevens, and David Souter) argued that the Court should have affirmed clearly that such an execution would come "perilously close to simple murder."*

CHIEF JUSTICE REHNQUIST delivered the opinion of the Court.

Petitioner Leonel Torres Herrera was convicted of capital murder and sentenced to death in January, 1982. He unsuccessfully challenged the conviction on direct appeal and state collateral proceedings in the Texas state courts, and in a federal habeas petition. In February, 1992—10 years after his conviction—he urged in a second federal habeas petition that he was "actually innocent" of the murder for which he was sentenced to death, and that the Eighth Amendment's prohibition against cruel and unusual punishment and the Fourteenth Amendment's guarantee of due process of law therefore forbid his execution. He supported this claim with affidavits tending to show that his now-dead brother, rather than he, had been the perpetrator of the crime. Petitioner urges us to hold that this showing of innocence entitles him to relief in this federal habeas proceeding. We hold that it does not.

Shortly before 11 p.m. on an evening in late September, 1981, the body of Texas Department of Public Safety Officer David Rucker was found by a passerby on a stretch of highway about six miles east of Los Fresnos, Texas, a few miles north of Brownsville in the Rio Grande Valley. Rucker's body was lying beside his patrol car. He had been shot in the head.

At about the same time, Los Fresnos Police Officer Enrique Carrisalez observed a speeding vehicle traveling west towards Los Fresnos, away from the place where Rucker's body had been found, along the same road. Carrisalez, who was accompanied in his patrol car by Enrique Hernandez, turned on his flashing red lights and pursued the speeding vehicle. After the car had stopped briefly at a red light, it signaled that it would pull over and did so. The patrol car pulled up behind it. Carrisalez took a flashlight and walked toward the car of the speeder. The driver opened his door and exchanged a few words with Carrisalez before firing at least one shot at Carrisalez' chest. The officer died nine days later.

Petitioner Herrera was arrested a few days after the shootings and charged with the capital murder of both Carrisalez and Rucker. He was tried and found guilty of the capital murder of Carrisalez in January, 1982, and sentenced to death. In July, 1982, petitioner pleaded guilty to the murder of Rucker.

At petitioner's trial for the murder of Carrisalez, Hernandez, who had witnessed Carrisalez' slaying from the officer's patrol car, identified petitioner as the person who had wielded the gun. A declaration by Officer Carrisalez to the same effect, made while he was in the hospital, was also admitted. Through a license plate check, it was shown that the speeding car involved in Carrisalez' murder was registered to petitioner's "live-in" girlfriend. Petitioner was known to drive this car, and he had a set of keys to the car in his pants pocket when he was arrested. Hernandez identified the car as the vehicle from which the murderer had emerged to fire the fatal shot. He also testified that there had been only one person in the car that night.

The evidence showed that Herrera's Social Security card had been found alongside Rucker's patrol car on the night he was killed. Splatters of blood on the car identified as the vehicle involved in the shootings, and on petitioner's blue jeans and wallet were identified as type A blood—the same type which Rucker had. (Herrera has type O blood.) Similar evidence with respect to strands of hair found in the car indicated that the hair was Rucker's, and not Herrera's. A handwritten letter was also found on the person of petitioner when he was arrested, which strongly implied that he had killed Rucker.

Petitioner appealed his conviction and sentence, arguing, among other things, that Hernandez' and Carrisalez' identifications were unreliable and improperly admitted. The Texas Court of Criminal Appeals affirmed, and we denied certiorari. Petitioner's application for state habeas relief was denied. Petitioner then filed a federal habeas petition, again challenging the identifications offered against him at trial. This petition was denied, and we again denied certiorari. . . .

In February, 1992, petitioner lodged the instant habeas petition—his second—in federal court, alleging, among other things, that he is innocent of the murders of Rucker and Carrisalez, and that his execution would thus violate the Eighth and Fourteenth Amendments. In addition to proffering the above affidavits, petitioner presented the affidavits of Raul Herrera Jr., Raul Senior's son, and Jose Ybarra Jr., a schoolmate of the Herrera brothers. Raul, Junior, averred that he had witnessed his father shoot Officers Rucker and Carrisalez, and petitioner was not present. Raul, Junior, was nine years old at the time of the killings. Ybarra alleged that Raul Senior, told him one summer night in 1983 that he had shot the two police officers. Petitioner alleged that law enforcement officials were aware of this evidence, and had withheld it in violation of *Brady v. Maryland* (1963).

The District Court dismissed most of petitioner's claims as an abuse of the writ. However, "in order to ensure that Petitioner can assert his constitutional claims and out of a sense of fairness and due process," the District Court granted petitioner's request for a stay of execution so that he could present his claim of actual innocence, along with the Raul, Junior, and Ybarra affidavits, in state court. Although it initially dismissed petitioner's Brady claim on the ground that petitioner had failed to present "any evidence of withholding exculpatory material by the prosecution," the District Court also granted an evidentiary hearing on this claim after reconsideration, id., at 54.

The Court of Appeals vacated the stay of execution. It agreed with the District Court's initial conclusion that there was no evidentiary basis for petitioner's Brady claim, and found disingenuous petitioner's attempt to couch his claim of actual innocence in *Brady* terms. Absent an accompanying constitutional violation, the Court of Appeals held that petitioner's claim of actual innocence was not cognizable because, under *Townsend v. Sain* (1963), "the existence merely of newly discovered evidence relevant to the guilt of a state prisoner is not a ground for relief on federal habeas corpus." We granted certiorari, and the Texas Court of Criminal Appeals stayed petitioner's execution. We now affirm.

Petitioner asserts that the Eighth and Fourteenth Amendments to the United States Constitution prohibit the execution of a person who is innocent of the crime for which he was convicted. This proposition has an elemental appeal, as would the similar proposition that the Constitution prohibits the imprisonment of one who is innocent of the crime for which he was convicted. After all, the central purpose of any system of criminal justice is to convict the guilty and free the innocent. But the evidence upon which petitioner's claim of innocence rests was not produced at his trial, but rather eight years later. In any system of criminal justice, "innocence" or "guilt" must be determined in some sort of a judicial proceeding. Petitioner's showing of innocence, and indeed his constitutional claim for relief based upon that showing, must be evaluated in the light of the previous proceedings in this case, which have stretched over a span of 10 years.

A person when first charged with a crime is entitled to a presumption of innocence, and may insist that his guilt be established beyond a reasonable doubt. Other constitutional provisions also have the effect of ensuring against the risk of convicting an innocent person. In capital cases, we have required additional protections because of the nature of the penalty at stake. All of these constitutional safeguards, of course, make it more difficult for the State to rebut and finally overturn the presumption of innocence which attaches to every criminal defendant. But we have also observed that "[d]ue process does not require that every conceivable step be taken, at whatever cost, to eliminate the possibility of convicting an innocent person." To conclude otherwise would all but paralyze our system for enforcement of the criminal law.

Once a defendant has been afforded a fair trial and convicted of the offense for which he was charged, the presumption of innocence disappears. Here, it is not disputed that the State met its burden of proving at trial that petitioner was guilty of the capital murder of Officer Carrisalez beyond a reasonable doubt. Thus, in the eyes of the law, petitioner does not come before the Court as one who is "innocent," but, on the contrary, as one who has been convicted by due process of law of two brutal murders.

Based on affidavits here filed, petitioner claims that evidence never presented to the trial court proves him innocent notwithstanding the verdict reached at his trial. Such a claim is not cognizable in the state courts of Texas. For to obtain a new trial based on newly discovered evidence, a defendant must file a motion within 30 days after imposition or suspension of sentence.

Claims of actual innocence based on newly discovered evidence have never been held to state a ground for federal habeas relief absent an independent constitutional violation occurring in the underlying state criminal proceeding. Chief Justice Warren made this clear in *Townsend v. Sain:*

> Where newly discovered evidence is alleged in a habeas application, evidence which could not reasonably have been presented to the state trier of facts, the federal court must grant an evidentiary hearing. Of course, such evidence must bear upon the constitutionality of the applicant's detention; the existence merely of newly discovered evidence relevant to the guilt of a state prisoner is not a ground for relief on federal habeas corpus.

This rule is grounded in the principle that federal habeas courts sit to ensure that individuals are not imprisoned in violation of the Constitution—not to correct errors of fact.

More recent authority construing federal habeas statutes speaks in a similar vein. "Federal courts are not forums in which to relitigate state trials." The guilt or innocence determination in state criminal trials is "a decisive and portentous event. . . . Society's resources have been concentrated at that time and place in order to decide, within the limits of human fallibility, the question of guilt or innocence of one of its citizens." Few rulings would be more disruptive of our federal system than to provide for federal habeas review of freestanding claims of actual innocence.

Our decision in *Jackson v. Virginia* (1979) comes as close to authorizing evidentiary review of a state-court conviction on federal habeas as any of our cases. There, we held that a federal habeas court may review a claim that the evidence adduced at a state trial was not sufficient to convict a criminal defendant beyond a reasonable doubt. But in so holding, we emphasized:

> "[T]his inquiry does not require a court to 'ask itself whether *it* believes that the evidence at the trial established guilt beyond a reasonable doubt.' Instead, the relevant question is whether, after viewing the evidence in the light most favorable to the prosecution, *any* rational trier of fact could have found the essential elements of the crime beyond a reasonable doubt. This familiar standard gives full play to the responsibility of the trier of fact fairly to resolve conflicts in the testimony, to weigh the evidence, and to draw reasonable inferences from basic facts to ultimate facts." (emphasis in original) . . .

We specifically noted that "the standard announced . . . does not permit a court to make its own subjective determination of guilt or innocence." . . .

Petitioner is understandably imprecise in describing the sort of federal relief to which a suitable showing of actual innocence would entitle him. In his brief, he states that the federal habeas court should have "an important initial opportunity to hear the evidence and resolve the merits of Petitioner's claim." Acceptance of this view would presumably require the habeas court to hear testimony from the witnesses who testified at trial as well as those who made the statements in the affidavits which petitioner has presented, and to determine anew whether or not petitioner is guilty of the murder of Officer Carrisalez. Indeed, the dissent's approach differs little from that hypothesized here.

The dissent would place the burden on petitioner to show that he is "probably" innocent. Although petitioner would not be entitled to discovery "as a matter of right," the District Court would retain its "discretion to order discovery . . . when it would help the court make a reliable determination with respect to the prisoner's claim." And although the District Court would not be required to hear testimony from the witnesses who testified at trial or the affiants upon whom petitioner relies, the dissent would allow the District Court to do so "if the petition warrants a hearing." At the end of the day, the dissent would have the District Court "make a case-by-case determination about the reliability of the newly discovered evidence under the circumstances," and then "weigh the evidence in favor of the prisoner against the evidence of his guilt."

The dissent fails to articulate the relief that would be available if petitioner were to meets its "probable innocence" standard. Would it be commutation of petitioner's death sentence, new trial, or unconditional release from imprisonment? The typical relief granted in federal habeas corpus is a conditional order of release unless the State elects to retry the successful habeas petitioner, or in a capital case a similar conditional order vacating the death sentence. Were petitioner to satisfy the dissent's "probable innocence" standard, therefore, the District Court would presumably be required to grant a conditional order of relief, which would in effect require the State to retry petitioner 10 years after his first trial, not because of any constitutional violation which had occurred at the first trial, but simply because of a belief that, in light of petitioner's newfound evidence, a jury might find him not guilty at a second trial.

Yet there is no guarantee that the guilt or innocence determination would be any more exact. To the contrary, the passage of time only diminishes the reliability of criminal adjudications. Under the dissent's approach, the District Court would be placed in the even more difficult position of having to weigh the probative value of "hot" and "cold" evidence on petitioner's guilt or innocence.

This is not to say that our habeas jurisprudence casts a blind eye toward innocence. In a series of cases we have held that a petitioner otherwise subject to defenses of abusive or successive use of the writ may have his federal constitutional claim considered on the merits if he makes a proper showing of actual innocence. This rule, or fundamental miscarriage of justice exception, is grounded in the "equitable discretion" of habeas courts to see that federal constitutional errors do not result in the incarceration of innocent persons. But this body of our habeas jurisprudence makes clear that a claim of "actual innocence" is not itself a constitutional claim, but instead a gateway through which a habeas petitioner must pass to have his otherwise barred constitutional claim considered on the merits.

Petitioner in this case is simply not entitled to habeas relief based on the reasoning of this line of cases. For he does not seek excusal of a procedural error so that he may bring an independent constitutional claim challenging his conviction or sentence, but rather argues that he is entitled to habeas relief because newly discovered evidence shows that his conviction is factually incorrect. The fundamental miscarriage of justice exception is available "only where the prisoner supplements his constitutional claim with a colorable showing of factual innocence." We have never held that it extends to freestanding claims of actual innocence. Therefore, the exception is inapplicable here.

Petitioner asserts that this case is different because he has been sentenced to death. But we have "refused to hold that the fact that a death sentence has been imposed requires a different standard of review on federal habeas corpus." We have, of course, held that the Eighth Amendment requires increased reliability of the process by which capital punishment may be imposed. But petitioner's claim does not fit well into the doctrine of these cases, since, as we have pointed out, it is far from clear that a second trial 10 years after the first trial would produce a more reliable result. . . .

Petitioner also relies on *Johnson v. Mississippi,* where we held that the Eighth Amendment requires reexamination of a death sentence based in part on a prior felony conviction which was set aside in the rendering State after the capital sentence was imposed. There, the State insisted that it was too late in the day to raise this point. But we pointed out that the Mississippi Supreme Court had previously considered similar claims by writ of error coram nobis. Thus, there was no need to override state law relating to newly discovered evidence in order to consider Johnson's claim on the merits. Here, there is no doubt that petitioner seeks additional process—an evidentiary hearing on his claim of "actual innocence" based on newly discovered evidence—which is not available under Texas law more than 30 days after imposition or suspension of sentence.

Alternatively, petitioner invokes the Fourteenth Amendment's guarantee of due process of law in support of his claim that his showing of actual innocence entitles him to a new trial, or at least to a vacation of his death sentence. "[B]ecause the States have considerable expertise in matters of criminal procedure and the criminal process is grounded in centuries of common law tradition," we have "exercis[ed] substantial deference to legislative judgments in this area."

Thus, we have found criminal process lacking only where it "'offends some principle of justice so rooted in the traditions and conscience of our people as to be ranked as fundamental.'"

The Constitution itself, of course, makes no mention of new trials. New trials in criminal cases were not granted in England until the end of the 17th century. And even then, they were available only in misdemeanor cases, though the writ of error coram nobis was available for some errors of fact in felony cases. . . .

The early federal cases adhere to the common law rule that a new trial may be granted only during the term of court in which the final judgment was entered. . . .

. . . In 1945, we set a 2-year time limit for filing new trial motions based on newly discovered evidence and abolished the exception for capital cases. We have strictly construed the Rule 33 time limits. And the Rule's treatment of new trials based on newly discovered evidence has not changed since its adoption. . . .

The practice in the States today, while of limited relevance to our historical inquiry, is divergent. Texas is one of 17 States that requires a new trial motion based on newly discovered evidence to be made within 60 days of judgment. One State adheres to the common law rule and requires that such a motion be filed during the term in which judgment was rendered. Eighteen jurisdictions have time limits ranging between one and three years, with 10 States and the District of Columbia following the 2 year federal time limit. Only 15 States allow a new trial motion based on newly discovered evidence to be filed more than three years after conviction. Of these States, four have waivable time limits of less than 120 days, two have waivable time limits of more than 120 days, and nine States have no time limits.

In light of the historical availability of new trials, our own amendments to Rule 33, and the contemporary practice in the States, we cannot say that Texas' refusal to entertain petitioner's newly discovered evidence eight years after his conviction transgresses a principle of fundamental fairness "rooted in the traditions and conscience of our people." This is not to say, however, that petitioner is left without a forum to raise his actual innocence claim. For under Texas law, petitioner may file a request for executive clemency. Clemency is deeply rooted in our Anglo-American tradition of law, and is the historic remedy for preventing miscarriages of justice where judicial process has been exhausted. . . .

Executive clemency has provided the "fail-safe" in our criminal justice system. . . .

In Texas, the Governor has the power, upon the recommendation of a majority of the Board of Pardons and Paroles, to grant clemency. The board's consideration is triggered upon request of the individual sentenced to death, his or her representative, or the Governor herself. In capital cases, a request may be made for a full pardon. The Governor has the sole authority to grant one reprieve in any capital case not exceeding 30 days.

The Texas clemency procedures contain specific guidelines for pardons on the ground of innocence. The board will entertain applications for a recommendation of full pardon because of innocence upon receipt of the following: "(1) a written unanimous recommendation of the current trial officials of the court of conviction; and/or (2) a certified order or judgment of a court having jurisdiction accompanied by certified copy of the findings of fact (if any); and (3) affidavits of witnesses upon which the finding of innocence is based." In this case, petitioner has apparently sought a 30 day reprieve from the Governor, but has yet to apply for a pardon, or even a commutation, on the ground of innocence or otherwise.

As the foregoing discussion illustrates, in state criminal proceedings, the trial is the paramount event for determining the guilt or innocence of the defendant. Federal habeas review of state convictions has traditionally been limited to claims of constitutional violations occurring in the course of the underlying state criminal proceedings. Our federal habeas cases have treated claims of "actual innocence," not as an independent constitutional claim, but as a basis upon which a habeas petitioner may have an independent constitutional claim considered on the merits, even though his habeas petition would otherwise be regarded as successive or abusive. History shows that the traditional remedy for claims of innocence based on new evidence, discovered too late in the day to file a new trial motion, has been executive clemency.

We may assume, for the sake of argument in deciding this case, that, in a capital case, a truly persuasive demonstration of "actual innocence" made after trial would render the execution of a defendant unconstitutional, and warrant federal habeas relief if there were no state avenue open to process such a claim. But because of the very disruptive effect that entertaining claims of actual innocence would have on the need for finality in capital cases, and the enormous burden that having to retry cases based on often stale evidence would place on the States, the threshold showing for such an assumed right would necessarily be extraordinarily high. The showing made by petitioner in this case falls far short of any such threshold.

Petitioner's newly discovered evidence consists of affidavits. In the new trial context, motions based solely upon affidavits are disfavored, because the affiants' statements are obtained without the benefit of cross-examination and an opportunity to make credibility determinations. Petitioner's affidavits are particularly suspect in this regard because, with the exception of Raul Herrera Jr.'s affidavit, they consist of hearsay. Likewise, in reviewing petitioner's new evidence, we are mindful that defendants often abuse new trial motions "as a method of delaying enforcement of just sentences." Although we are not presented with a new trial motion per se, we believe the likelihood of abuse is as great—or greater—here.

Finally, the affidavits must be considered in light of the proof of petitioner's guilt at trial—proof which included two eyewitness identifications, numerous pieces of circumstantial evidence, and a handwritten letter in which petitioner apologized for killing the officers and offered to turn himself in under certain conditions. That proof, even when considered alongside petitioner's belated affidavits, points strongly to petitioner's guilt.

This is not to say that petitioner's affidavits are without probative value. Had this sort of testimony been offered at trial, it could have been weighed by the jury, along with the evidence offered by the State and petitioner, in deliberating upon its verdict. Since the statements in the affidavits contradict the evidence received at trial, the jury would have had to decide important issues of credibility. But coming 10 years after petitioner's trial, this showing of innocence falls far short of that which would have to be made in order to trigger the sort of constitutional claim which we have assumed, arguendo, to exist.

The judgment of the Court of Appeals is Affirmed.

JUSTICES O'CONNOR, with whom JUSTICE KENNEDY joins, concurring. . . .

The conclusion seems inescapable: petitioner is guilty. The dissent does not contend otherwise. Instead, it urges us to defer to the District Court's determination that petitioner's evidence was not "so insubstantial that it could be dismissed without any hearing at all." I do not read the District Court's decision as making any such determination. Nowhere in its opinion did the District Court question the accuracy of the jury's verdict. Nor did it pass on the sufficiency of the affidavits. The District Court did not even suggest that it wished to hold an evidentiary hearing on petitioner's actual innocence claims. Indeed, the District Court apparently believed that a hearing would be futile, because the court could offer no relief in any event. As the court explained, claims of "newly discovered evidence bearing directly upon guilt or innocence" are not cognizable on habeas corpus "unless the petition implicates a constitutional violation."

As the dissent admits, the District Court had an altogether different reason for entering a stay of execution. It believed, from a "sense of fairness and due process," that petitioner should have the chance to present his affidavits to the state courts. But the District Court did not hold that the state courts should hold a hearing either; it instead ordered the habeas petition dismissed and the stay lifted once the state court action was filed, without further condition. As the Court of Appeals recognized, that rationale was insufficient to support the stay order. Texas courts do not recognize new evidence claims on collateral review. Nor would they entertain petitioner's claim as a motion for a new trial; under Texas law, such motions must be made within 30 days of trial. Because petitioner could not have obtained relief—or even a hearing—through the state courts, it was error for the District Court to enter a stay permitting him to try.

Of course, the Texas courts would not be free to turn petitioner away if the Constitution required otherwise. But the District Court did not hold that the

Constitution required them to entertain petitioner's claim. On these facts, that would be an extraordinary holding. Petitioner did not raise his claim shortly after Texas' 30 day limit expired; he raised it eight years too late. Consequently, the District Court would have had to conclude not that Texas' 30 day limit for new evidence claims was too short to comport with due process, but that applying an 8-year limit to petitioner would be. As the Court demonstrates today, there is little in fairness or history to support such a conclusion. . . .

Ultimately, two things about this case are clear. First is what the Court does not hold. Nowhere does the Court state that the Constitution permits the execution of an actually innocent person. Instead, the Court assumes for the sake of argument that a truly persuasive demonstration of actual innocence would render any such execution unconstitutional, and that federal habeas relief would be warranted if no state avenue were open to process the claim. Second is what petitioner has not demonstrated. Petitioner has failed to make a persuasive showing of actual innocence. Not one judge—no state court judge, not the District Court Judge, none of the three judges of the Court of Appeals, and none of the Justices of this Court—has expressed doubt about petitioner's guilt. Accordingly, the Court has no reason to pass on, and appropriately reserves, the question whether federal courts may entertain convincing claims of actual innocence. That difficult question remains open. If the Constitution's guarantees of fair procedure and the safeguards of clemency and pardon fulfill their historical mission, it may never require resolution at all.

JUSTICE SCALIA, with whom JUSTICE THOMAS joins, concurring.

We granted certiorari on the question whether it violates due process or constitutes cruel and unusual punishment for a State to execute a person who, having been convicted of murder after a full and fair trial, later alleges that newly discovered evidence shows him to be "actually innocent." I would have preferred to decide that question, particularly since, as the Court's discussion shows, it is perfectly clear what the answer is: there is no basis in text, tradition, or even in contemporary practice (if that were enough) for finding in the Constitution a right to demand judicial consideration of newly discovered evidence of innocence brought forward after conviction. In saying that such a right exists, the dissenters apply nothing but their personal opinions to invalidate the rules of more than two thirds of the States, and a Federal Rule of Criminal Procedure for which this Court itself is responsible. If the system that has been in place for 200 years (and remains widely approved) "shock[s]" the dissenters' consciences, perhaps they should doubt the calibration of their consciences, or, better still, the usefulness of "conscience shocking" as a legal test.

I nonetheless join the entirety of the Court's opinion, because there is no legal error in deciding a case by assuming, arguendo, that an asserted constitutional right exists, and because I can understand, or at least am accustomed to, the reluctance of the present Court to admit publicly that Our Perfect Constitution lets stand any injustice, much less the execution of an innocent man who has received, though to no avail, all the process that our society has traditionally deemed adequate. With any luck, we shall avoid ever having to face this embarrassing question again, since it is improbable that evidence of innocence as convincing as today's opinion requires would fail to produce an executive pardon.

My concern is that, in making life easier for ourselves, we not appear to make it harder for the lower federal courts, imposing upon them the burden of regularly analyzing newly-discovered-evidence-of-innocence claims in capital cases (in which event, such federal claims, it can confidently be predicted, will become routine and even repetitive). A number of Courts of Appeals have hitherto held, largely in reliance on our unelaborated statement in *Townsend v. Sain* (1963), that newly discovered evidence relevant only to a state prisoner's guilt or innocence is not a basis for federal habeas corpus relief. I do not understand it to be the import of today's decision that those holdings are to be replaced with a strange regime that assumes permanently, though only "arguendo," that a constitutional right exists, and expends substantial judicial resources on that assumption. The Court's extensive and scholarly discussion of the question presented in the present case does nothing but support our statement in *Townsend* and strengthen the validity of the holdings based upon it.

JUSTICE BLACKMUN, with whom JUSTICE STEVENS and JUSTICE SOUTER join with respect to Parts I–IV, dissenting.

Nothing could be more contrary to contemporary standards of decency, or more shocking to the conscience than to execute a person who is actually innocent.

I therefore must disagree with the long and general discussion that precedes the Court's disposition of this case. That discussion, of course, is dictum, because the Court assumes, "for the sake of argument in deciding this case, that, in a capital case, a truly persuasive demonstration of 'actual innocence' made after trial would render the execution of a defendant unconstitutional." Without articulating the standard it is applying, however, the Court then decides that this petitioner has not made a sufficiently persuasive case. Because I believe that, in the first instance, the District Court should decide whether petitioner is entitled to a hearing and whether he is entitled to relief on the merits of his claim, I would reverse the order of the Court of Appeals and remand this case for further proceedings in the District Court.

The Court's enumeration of the constitutional rights of criminal defendants surely is entirely beside the point. These protections sometimes fail. We really are being asked to decide whether the Constitution forbids the execution of a person who has been validly convicted and sentenced, but who, nonetheless, can prove his innocence with newly discovered evidence. Despite the State of Texas' astonishing protestation to the contrary, I do not see how the answer can be anything but "yes." . . .

The protection of the Eighth Amendment does not end once a defendant has been validly convicted and sentenced. In *Johnson v. Mississippi* (1988), the petitioner had been convicted of murder and sentenced to death on the basis of three aggravating circumstances. One of those circumstances was that he previously had been convicted of a violent felony in the State of New York. After Johnson had been sentenced to death, the New York Court of Appeals reversed his prior conviction. Although there was no question that the prior conviction was valid at the time of Johnson's sentencing, this Court held that the Eighth Amendment required review of the sentence, because "the jury was allowed to consider evidence that has been revealed to be materially inaccurate." In *Ford v. Wainwright*, the petitioner had been convicted of murder and sentenced to death. There was no suggestion that he was incompetent at the time of his offense, at trial, or at sentencing, but subsequently he exhibited changes in behavior that raised doubts about his sanity. This Court held that Florida was required under the Eighth Amendment to provide an additional hearing to determine whether Ford was mentally competent, and that he could not be executed if he were incompetent. Both *Johnson* and *Ford* recognize that capital defendants may be entitled to further proceedings because of an intervening development even though they have been validly convicted and sentenced to death. . . .

The Court also suggests that allowing petitioner to raise his claim of innocence would not serve society's interest in the reliable imposition of the death penalty, because it might require a new trial that would be less accurate than the first. This suggestion misses the point entirely. The question is not whether a second trial would be more reliable than the first, but whether, in light of new evidence, the result of the first trial is sufficiently reliable for the State to carry out a death sentence. Furthermore, it is far from clear that a State will seek to retry the rare prisoner who prevails on a claim of actual innocence. I believe a prisoner must show not just that there was probably a reasonable doubt about his guilt, but that he is probably actually innocent. I find it difficult to believe that any State would choose to retry a person who meets this standard.

I believe it contrary to any standard of decency to execute someone who is actually innocent. Because the Eighth Amendment applies to questions of guilt or innocence, and to persons upon whom a valid sentence of death has been imposed, I also believe that petitioner may raise an Eighth Amendment challenge to his punishment on the ground that he is actually innocent.

Execution of the innocent is equally offensive to the Due Process Clause of the Fourteenth Amendment. The majority's discussion misinterprets petitioner's Fourteenth Amendment claim as raising a procedural, rather than a substantive, due process challenge. . . .

Petitioner's claim falls within our due process precedents. In *Rochin v. California* (1953), deputy sheriffs investigating narcotics sales broke into Rochin's room and observed him put two capsules in his mouth. The deputies attempted to remove the capsules from his mouth and, having failed, took Rochin to a hospital and had his stomach pumped. The capsules were found to contain morphine. . . . The Court held that the deputies' conduct "shock[ed] the conscience" and violated due process. "Illegally breaking into the privacy of the petitioner, the struggle to open his mouth and remove what was there, the forcible extraction of his stomach's contents—this course of proceeding by agents of government to obtain evidence is bound to offend even hardened sensibilities. They are methods too close to the rack and the screw to permit of constitutional differentiation." The lethal injection that petitioner faces as an allegedly innocent person is certainly closer to the rack and the screw than the stomach pump condemned in *Rochin*. Execution of an innocent person is the ultimate "arbitrary impositio[n]." It is an imposition from which one never recovers, and for which one can never be compensated. Thus, I also believe that petitioner may raise a substantive due process challenge to his punishment on the ground that he is actually innocent.

Given my conclusion that it violates the Eighth and Fourteenth Amendments to execute a person who is actually innocent, I find no bar in *Townsend v. Sain* to consideration of an actual-innocence claim. Newly discovered evidence of petitioner's innocence does bear on the constitutionality of his execution. Of course, it could be argued this is in some tension with *Townsend*'s statement that "the existence merely of newly discovered evidence relevant to the guilt of a state prisoner is not a ground for relief on federal habeas corpus." That statement, however, is no more than distant dictum here, for we never had been asked to consider whether the execution of an innocent person violates the Constitution.

The majority's discussion of petitioner's constitutional claims is even more perverse when viewed in the light of this Court's recent habeas jurisprudence. Beginning with a trio of decisions in 1986, this Court shifted the focus of federal habeas review of successive, abusive, or defaulted claims away from the preservation of constitutional rights to a fact-based inquiry into the habeas petitioner's guilt or innocence. The Court sought to strike a balance between the State's interest in the finality of its criminal judgments and the prisoner's interest in access to a forum to test the basic justice of his sentence. In striking this balance, the Court adopted the view that there should be an exception to the concept of finality when a prisoner can make a colorable claim of actual innocence. . . .

Having adopted an "actual innocence" requirement for review of abusive, successive, or defaulted claims, however, the majority would now take the position that "a claim of 'actual innocence' is not itself a constitutional claim, but instead a gateway through which a habeas petitioner must pass to have his otherwise barred constitutional claim considered on the merits." In other words, having held that a prisoner who is incarcerated in violation of the Constitution must show he is actually innocent to obtain relief, the majority would now hold that a prisoner who is actually innocent must show a constitutional violation to obtain relief. The only principle that would appear to reconcile these two positions is the principle that habeas relief should be denied whenever possible. . . .

Whatever procedures a State might adopt to hear actual-innocence claims, one thing is certain: the possibility of executive clemency is not sufficient to satisfy the requirements of the Eighth and Fourteenth Amendments. The majority correctly points out: "A pardon is an act of grace." The vindication of rights guaranteed by the Constitution has never been made to turn on the unreviewable discretion of an executive official or administrative tribunal. Indeed, in *Ford v. Wainwright,* we explicitly rejected the argument that executive clemency was adequate to vindicate the Eighth Amendment right not to be executed if one is insane. The possibility of executive clemency "exists in every case in which a defendant challenges his sentence under the Eighth Amendment. Recognition of such a bare possibility would make judicial review under the Eighth Amendment meaningless." . . .

The question that remains is what showing should be required to obtain relief on the merits of an Eighth or Fourteenth Amendment claim of actual innocence. I agree with the majority that, "in state criminal proceedings, the trial is the paramount event for determining the guilt or innocence of the defendant." I also think that "a truly persuasive demonstration of 'actual innocence' made after trial would render the execution of a defendant unconstitutional." The question is what "a truly persuasive demonstration" entails, a question the majority's disposition of this case leaves open. . . .

I think the standard for relief on the merits of an actual innocence claim must be higher than the threshold standard for merely reaching that claim or any other claim that has been procedurally defaulted or is successive or abusive. I would hold that, to obtain relief on a claim of actual innocence, the petitioner must show that he probably is innocent. This standard is supported by several considerations. First, new evidence of innocence may be discovered long after the defendant's conviction. Given the passage of time, it may be difficult for the State to retry a defendant who obtains relief from his conviction or sentence on an actual innocence claim. The actual innocence proceeding thus may constitute the final word on whether the defendant may be punished. In light of this fact, an otherwise constitutionally valid conviction or sentence should not be set aside lightly. Second, conviction after a constitutionally adequate trial strips the defendant of the presumption of innocence. The government bears the burden of proving the defendant's guilt beyond a reasonable doubt, but once the government has done so, the burden of proving innocence must shift to the convicted defendant. The actual innocence inquiry is therefore distinguishable from review for sufficiency of the evidence, where the question is not whether the defendant is innocent, but whether the government has met its constitutional burden of proving the defendant's guilt beyond a reasonable doubt. When a defendant seeks to challenge the determination of guilt after he has been validly convicted and sentenced, it is fair to place on him the burden of proving his innocence, not just raising doubt about his guilt.

In considering whether a prisoner is entitled to relief on an actual-innocence claim, a court should take all the evidence into account, giving due regard to its reliability. Because placing the burden on the prisoner to prove innocence creates a presumption that the conviction is valid, it is not necessary or appropriate to make further presumptions about the reliability of newly discovered evidence generally. Rather, the court charged with deciding such a claim should make a case-by-case determination about the reliability of the newly discovered evidence under the circumstances. The court then should weigh the evidence in favor of the prisoner against the evidence of his guilt. Obviously, the stronger the evidence of the prisoner's guilt, the more persuasive the newly discovered evidence of innocence must be. A prisoner raising an actual innocence claim in a federal habeas petition is not entitled to discovery as a matter of right. The district court retains discretion to order discovery, however, when it would help the court make a reliable determination with respect to the prisoner's claim.

It should be clear that the standard I would adopt would not convert the federal courts into "forums in which to relitigate state trials." It would not "require the habeas court to hear testimony from the witnesses who testified at trial," though, if the petition warrants a hearing, it may require the habeas court to hear the testimony of "those who made the statements in the affidavits which petitioner has presented." I believe that, if a prisoner can show that he is probably actually innocent, in light of all the evidence, then he has made "a truly persuasive demonstration," and his execution would violate the Constitution. I would so hold.

In this case, the District Court determined that petitioner's newly discovered evidence warranted further consideration. Because the District Court doubted its own authority to consider the new evidence, it thought that petitioner's claim of actual innocence should be brought in state court, but it clearly did not think that petitioner's evidence was so insubstantial that it could be dismissed without any hearing at all. I would reverse the order of the Court of Appeals and remand the case to the District Court to consider whether petitioner has shown, in light of all the evidence, that he is probably actually innocent. . . .

I have voiced disappointment over this Court's obvious eagerness to do away with any restriction on the States' power to execute whomever and however they please. I have also expressed doubts about whether, in the absence of such restrictions, capital punishment remains constitutional at all. Of one thing, however, I am certain. Just as an execution without adequate safeguards is unacceptable, so too is an execution when the condemned prisoner can prove that he is innocent. The execution of a person who can show that he is innocent comes perilously close to simple murder.

Source: Herrera v. Collins, 506 U.S. 390 (1993), at 394–446.

Document 5.3
Justice Harry Blackmun and Justice Antonin Scalia Debate the Death Penalty in *Callins v. Collins*, February 22, 1994

On February 22, 1994, the Supreme Court refused to hear the appeal of death row inmate Bruce Edwin Callins. That decision provoked a dissent by Justice Harry Blackmun, who declared he believed capital punishment could not be imposed consistently with the commands of the Constitution of the United States despite decades of Court attempts to do so. Blackmun said he would no longer "tinker with the machinery of death," but would in the future hold the death penalty unconstitutional in all cases. Blackmun's dissent drew a concurring opinion from Justice Antonin Scalia, who argued that his colleague was wrong about the Constitution and that the contradictions he perceived had resulted from the Court's own mistaken decisions.

The petition for a writ of certiorari is denied.

JUSTICE SCALIA, concurring.

JUSTICE BLACKMUN dissents from the denial of certiorari in this case with a statement explaining why the death penalty "as currently administered" is contrary to the Constitution of the United States. That explanation often refers to "intellectual, moral and personal" perceptions, but never to the text and tradition of the Constitution. It is the latter, rather than the former that ought to control. The Fifth Amendment provides that

> [n]o person shall be held to answer for a capital . . . crime, unless on a presentment or indictment of a Grand Jury, . . . nor be deprived of life . . . without due process of law.

This clearly permits the death penalty to be imposed, and establishes beyond doubt that the death penalty is not one of the "cruel and unusual punishments" prohibited by the Eighth Amendment.

As JUSTICE BLACKMUN describes, however, over the years since 1972, this Court has attached to the imposition of the death penalty two quite incompatible sets of commands: the sentencer's discretion to impose death must be closely confined, see *Furman v. Georgia*, but the sentencer's discretion not to impose death (to extend mercy) must be unlimited, see *Eddings v. Oklahoma, Lockett v.*

Ohio. These commands were invented without benefit of any textual or historical support; they are the product of just such "intellectual, moral, and personal" perceptions as JUSTICE BLACKMUN expresses today, some of which (viz., those that have been "perceived" simultaneously by five members of the Court) have been made part of what is called "the Court's Eighth Amendment jurisprudence," post.

Though JUSTICE BLACKMUN joins those of us who have acknowledged the incompatibility of the Court's *Furman* and Lockett-Eddings lines of jurisprudence, see *Graham v. Collins*, he unfortunately draws the wrong conclusion from the acknowledgment. He says:

> [T]he proper course when faced with irreconcilable constitutional commands is not to ignore one or the other, nor to pretend that the dilemma does not exist, but to admit the futility of the effort to harmonize them. This means accepting the fact that the death penalty cannot be administered in accord with our Constitution.

Surely a different conclusion commends itself—to wit, that at least one of these judicially announced irreconcilable commands which cause the Constitution to prohibit what its text explicitly permits must be wrong.

Convictions in opposition to the death penalty are often passionate and deeply held. That would be no excuse for reading them into a Constitution that does not contain them, even if they represented the convictions of a majority of Americans. Much less is there any excuse for using that course to thrust a minority's views upon the people. JUSTICE BLACKMUN begins his statement by describing with poignancy the death of a convicted murderer by lethal injection. He chooses, as the case in which to make that statement, one of the less brutal of the murders that regularly come before us—the murder of a man ripped by a bullet suddenly and unexpectedly, with no opportunity to prepare himself and his affairs, and left to bleed to death on the floor of a tavern. The death-by-injection which JUSTICE BLACKMUN describes looks pretty desirable next to that. It looks even better next to some of the other cases currently before us which JUSTICE BLACKMUN did not select as the vehicle for his announcement that the death penalty is always unconstitutional—for example, the case of the 11-year-old girl raped by four men and then killed by stuffing her panties down her throat. See *McCollum v. North Carolina* now pending before the Court. How enviable a quiet death by lethal injection compared with that! If the people conclude that such more brutal deaths may be deterred by capital punishment; indeed, if they merely conclude that justice requires such brutal deaths to be avenged by capital punishment; the creation of false, untextual and unhistorical contradictions within "the Court's Eighth Amendment jurisprudence" should not prevent them.

JUSTICE BLACKMUN, dissenting.

On February 23, 1994, at approximately 1:00 a.m., Bruce Edwin Callins will be executed by the State of Texas. Intravenous tubes attached to his arms will carry the instrument of death, a toxic fluid designed specifically for the purpose of killing human beings. The witnesses, standing a few feet away, will behold Callins, no longer a defendant, an appellant, or a petitioner, but a man, strapped to a gurney, and seconds away from extinction.

Within days, or perhaps hours, the memory of Callins will begin to fade. The wheels of justice will churn again, and somewhere another jury or another judge will have the unenviable task of determining whether some human being is to live or die. We hope, of course, that the defendant whose life is at risk will be represented by competent counsel—someone who is inspired by the awareness that a less-than-vigorous defense truly could have fatal consequences for the defendant. We hope that the attorney will investigate all aspects of the case, follow all evidentiary and procedural rules, and appear before a judge who is still committed to the protection of defendants' rights—even now, as the prospect of meaningful judicial oversight has diminished. In the same vein, we hope that the prosecution, in urging the penalty of death, will have exercised its discretion wisely, free from bias, prejudice, or political motive, and will be humbled, rather than emboldened, by the awesome authority conferred by the State.

But even if we can feel confident that these actors will fulfill their roles to the best of their human ability, our collective conscience will remain uneasy. Twenty years have passed since this Court declared that the death penalty must be imposed fairly, and with reasonable consistency, or not at all, see *Furman v. Georgia,* and, despite the effort of the States and courts to devise legal formulas and procedural rules to meet this daunting challenge, the death penalty remains fraught with arbitrariness, discrimination, caprice, and mistake. This is not to say that the problems with the death penalty today are identical to those that were present 20 years ago. Rather, the problems that were pursued down one hole with procedural rules and verbal formulas have come to the surface somewhere else, just as virulent and pernicious as they were in their original form. Experience has taught us that the constitutional goal of eliminating arbitrariness and discrimination from the administration of death, see *Furman v. Georgia,* can never be achieved without compromising an equally essential component of fundamental fairness—individualized sentencing.

It is tempting, when faced with conflicting constitutional commands, to sacrifice one for the other or to assume that an acceptable balance between them already has been struck. In the context of the death penalty, however, such jurisprudential maneuvers are wholly inappropriate. The death penalty must be imposed "fairly, and with reasonable consistency, or not at all." . . .

On their face, these goals of individual fairness, reasonable consistency, and absence of error appear to be attainable: courts are in the very business of erecting procedural devices from which fair, equitable, and reliable outcomes are presumed to flow. Yet, in the death penalty area, this Court, in my view, has engaged in a futile effort to balance these constitutional demands, and now is retreating not only from the *Furman* promise of consistency and rationality, but from the requirement of individualized sentencing as well. Having virtually conceded that both fairness and rationality cannot be achieved in the administration of the death penalty, see *McCleskey v. Kemp*, the Court has chosen to deregulate the entire enterprise, replacing, it would seem, substantive constitutional requirements with mere aesthetics, and abdicating its statutorily and constitutionally imposed duty to provide meaningful judicial oversight to the administration of death by the States.

From this day forward, I no longer shall tinker with the machinery of death. For more than 20 years, I have endeavored—indeed, I have struggled—along with a majority of this Court, to develop procedural and substantive rules that would lend more than the mere appearance of fairness to the death penalty endeavor. Rather than continue to coddle the Court's delusion that the desired level of fairness has been achieved and the need for regulation eviscerated, I feel morally and intellectually obligated simply to concede that the death penalty experiment has failed. It is virtually self-evident to me now that no combination of procedural rules or substantive regulations ever can save the death penalty from its inherent constitutional deficiencies. The basic question—does the system accurately and consistently determine which defendants "deserve" to die?—cannot be answered in the affirmative. It is not simply that this Court has allowed vague aggravating circumstances to be employed, see, e.g., *Arave v. Creech*, relevant mitigating evidence to be disregarded, see, e.g., *Johnson v. Texas*, and vital judicial review to be blocked, see, e.g., *Coleman v. Thompson*. The problem is that the inevitability of factual, legal, and moral error gives us a system that we know must wrongly kill some defendants, a system that fails to deliver the fair, consistent, and reliable sentences of death required by the Constitution. . . .

There is little doubt now that *Furman*'s essential holding was correct. Although most of the public seems to desire, and the Constitution appears to permit, the penalty of death, it surely is beyond dispute that, if the death penalty cannot be administered consistently and rationally, it may not be administered at all. I never have quarreled with this principle; in my mind, the real meaning of *Furman*'s diverse concurring opinions did not emerge until some years after *Furman* was decided. . . . Since *Gregg*, I faithfully have adhered to the *Furman* holding, and have come to believe that it is indispensable to the Court's Eighth Amendment jurisprudence.

Delivering on the *Furman* promise, however, has proved to be another matter. *Furman* aspired to eliminate the vestiges of racism and the effects of poverty in capital sentencing; it deplored the "wanton" and "random" infliction of death by a government with constitutionally limited power. *Furman* demanded that the sentencer's discretion be directed and limited by procedural rules and objective standards in order to minimize the risk of arbitrary and capricious sentences of death.

In the years following *Furman,* serious efforts were made to comply with its mandate. State legislatures and appellate courts struggled to provide judges and juries with sensible and objective guidelines for determining who should live and who should die. Some States attempted to define who is "deserving" of the death penalty through the use of carefully chosen adjectives, reserving the death penalty for those who commit crimes that are "especially heinous, atrocious, or cruel," or "wantonly vile, horrible or inhuman." Other States enacted mandatory death penalty statutes, reading *Furman* as an invitation to eliminate sentencer discretion altogether. Still other States specified aggravating and mitigating factors that were to be considered by the sentencer and weighed against one another in a calculated and rational manner.

Unfortunately, all this experimentation and ingenuity yielded little of what *Furman* demanded. It soon became apparent that discretion could not be eliminated from capital sentencing without threatening the fundamental fairness due a defendant when life is at stake. Just as contemporary society was no longer tolerant of the random or discriminatory infliction of the penalty of death, see *Furman,* evolving standards of decency required due consideration of the uniqueness of each individual defendant when imposing society's ultimate penalty.

This development in the American conscience would have presented no constitutional dilemma if fairness to the individual could be achieved without sacrificing the consistency and rationality promised in *Furman.* But over the past two decades, efforts to balance these competing constitutional commands have been to no avail. Experience has shown that the consistency and rationality promised in *Furman* are inversely related to the fairness owed the individual when considering a sentence of death. A step toward consistency is a step away from fairness. . . .

Thus, although individualized sentencing in capital cases was not considered essential at the time the Constitution was adopted, Woodson recognized that American standards of decency could no longer tolerate a capital sentencing process that failed to afford a defendant individualized consideration in the determination whether he or she should live or die.

The Court elaborated on the principle of individualized sentencing in *Lockett v. Ohio.* In that case, a plurality acknowledged that strict restraints on sentencer discretion are necessary to achieve the consistency and rationality promised in *Furman,* but held that, in the end, the sentencer must retain unbridled discretion to afford mercy. Any process or procedure that prevents the sentencer from considering as a mitigating factor, any aspect of a defendant's character or record and any circumstances of the offense that the defendant proffers as a basis for a sentence less than death, creates the constitutionally intolerable risk that "the death penalty will be imposed in spite of factors which may call for a less severe penalty." . . . The Court's duty under the Constitution therefore is to "develop a system of capital punishment at once consistent and principled but also humane and sensible to the uniqueness of the individual." . . .

C

I believe the *Woodson-Lockett* line of cases to be fundamentally sound, and rooted in American standards of decency that have evolved over time. In *California v. Brown,* I said in dissent:

> "The sentencer's ability to respond with mercy towards a defendant has always struck me as a particularly valuable aspect of the capital sentencing procedure. . . . [W]e adhere so strongly to our belief that a sentencer should have the opportunity to spare a capital defendant's life on account of compassion for the individual because, recognizing that the capital sentencing decision must be made in the context of "contemporary values," *Gregg v. Georgia,* we see in the sentencer's expression of mercy a distinctive feature of our society that we deeply value."

Yet, as several Members of the Court have recognized, there is real "tension" between the need for fairness to the individual and the consistency promised in *Furman.* On the one hand, discretion in capital sentencing must be "controlled by clear and objective standards so as to produce nondiscriminatory [and reasoned] application." On the other hand, the Constitution also requires that the sentencer be able to consider "any relevant mitigating evidence regarding the defendant's character or background, and the circumstances of the particular offense." The power to consider mitigating evidence that would warrant a sentence less than death is meaningless unless the sentencer has the discretion and authority to dispense mercy based on that evidence. Thus, the Constitution, by requiring a heightened degree of fairness to the individual, and also a greater degree of equality and rationality in the administration of death, demands sentencer discretion that is at once generously expanded and severely restricted.

This dilemma was laid bare in *Penry v. Lynaugh.* The defendant in *Penry* challenged the Texas death penalty statute, arguing that it failed to allow the sentencing jury to give full mitigating effect to his evidence of mental retardation and history of child abuse. The Texas statute required the jury, during the penalty phase, to answer three "special issues"; if the jury unanimously answered "yes" to each issue, the trial court was obligated to sentence the defendant to death. Only one of the three issues—whether the defendant posed a "continuing threat to society"—was related to the evidence Penry offered in mitigation. But Penry's evidence of mental retardation and child abuse was a two-edged sword as it related to that special issue: "it diminish[ed] his blameworthiness for his crime even as it indicate[d] that there [was] a probability that he [would] be dangerous in the future." The Court therefore reversed Penry's death sentence, explaining that a reasonable juror could have believed that the statute prohibited a sentence less than death based upon his mitigating evidence.

After *Penry,* the paradox underlying the Court's post-*Furman* jurisprudence was undeniable. Texas had complied with *Furman* by severely limiting the sentencer's discretion, but those very limitations rendered Penry's death sentence unconstitutional.

D

The theory underlying *Penry* and *Lockett* is that an appropriate balance can be struck between the *Furman* promise of consistency and the *Lockett* requirement of individualized sentencing if the death penalty is conceptualized as consisting of two distinct stages. In the first stage of capital sentencing, the demands of *Furman* are met by "narrowing" the class of death-eligible offenders according to objective, fact-bound characteristics of the defendant or the circumstances of the offense. Once the pool of death-eligible defendants has been reduced, the sentencer retains the discretion to consider whatever relevant mitigating evidence the defendant chooses to offer.

Over time, I have come to conclude that even this approach is unacceptable: it simply reduces, rather than eliminates, the number of people subject to arbitrary sentencing. It is the decision to sentence a defendant to death—not merely the decision to make a defendant eligible for death—that may not be arbitrary. While one might hope that providing the sentencer with as much relevant mitigating evidence as possible will lead to more rational and consistent sentences, experience has taught otherwise. It seems that the decision whether a human being should live or die is so inherently subjective—rife with all of life's understandings, experiences, prejudices, and passions—that it inevitably defies the rationality and consistency required by the Constitution.

E

The arbitrariness inherent in the sentencer's discretion to afford mercy is exacerbated by the problem of race. . . .

A renowned example of racism infecting a capital sentencing scheme is documented in *McCleskey v. Kemp.* Warren McCleskey, an African-American, argued that the Georgia capital sentencing scheme was administered in a racially discriminatory manner, in violation of the Eighth and Fourteenth Amendments. In support of his claim, he proffered a highly reliable statistical study (the Baldus study) which indicated that, after taking into account some 230 nonracial factors that might legitimately influence a sentencer, the jury more likely than not would have spared McCleskey's life had his victim been black. The Baldus study further demonstrated that blacks who kill whites are sentenced to death "at nearly 22 times the rate of blacks who kill blacks, and more than 7 times the rate of whites who kill blacks."

Despite this staggering evidence of racial prejudice infecting Georgia's capital sentencing scheme, the majority turned its back on *McCleskey*'s claims, apparently troubled by the fact that Georgia had instituted more procedural and substantive safeguards than most other States since *Furman*, but was still unable to stamp out the virus of racism. Faced with the apparent failure of traditional legal devices to cure the evils identified in *Furman*, the majority wondered aloud whether the consistency and rationality demanded by the dissent could ever be achieved without sacrificing the discretion which is essential to fair treatment of individual defendants. . . .

F

In the years since *McCleskey*, I have come to wonder whether there was truth in the majority's suggestion that discrimination and arbitrariness could not be purged from the administration of capital punishment without sacrificing the equally essential component of fairness—individualized sentencing. Viewed in this way, the consistency promised in *Furman* and the fairness to the individual demanded in *Lockett* are not only inversely related, but irreconcilable in the context of capital punishment. Any statute or procedure that could effectively eliminate arbitrariness from the administration of death would also restrict the sentencer's discretion to such an extent that the sentencer would be unable to give full consideration to the unique characteristics of each defendant and the circumstances of the offense. By the same token, any statute or procedure that would provide the sentencer with sufficient discretion to consider fully and act upon the unique circumstances of each defendant would "thro[w] open the back door to arbitrary and irrational sentencing." All efforts to strike an appropriate balance between these conflicting constitutional commands are futile because there is a heightened need for both in the administration of death.

But even if the constitutional requirements of consistency and fairness are theoretically reconcilable in the context of capital punishment, it is clear that this Court is not prepared to meet the challenge. In apparent frustration over its inability to strike an appropriate balance between the *Furman* promise of consistency and the *Lockett* requirement of individualized sentencing, the Court has retreated from the field, allowing relevant mitigating evidence to be discarded, vague aggravating circumstances to be employed, and providing no indication that the problem of race in the administration of death will ever be addressed. In fact, some members of the Court openly have acknowledged a willingness simply to pick one of the competing constitutional commands and sacrifice the other. These developments are troubling, as they ensure that death will continue to be meted out in this country arbitrarily and discriminatorily, and without that "degree of respect due the uniqueness of the individual." In my view, the proper course when faced with irreconcilable constitutional commands is not to ignore one or the other, nor to pretend that the dilemma does not exist, but to admit the futility of the effort to harmonize them. This means accepting the fact that the death penalty cannot be administered in accord with our Constitution. . . .

III

Perhaps one day this Court will develop procedural rules or verbal formulas that actually will provide consistency, fairness, and reliability in a capital sentencing scheme. I am not optimistic that such a day will come. I am more optimistic, though, that this Court eventually will conclude that the effort to eliminate arbitrariness while preserving fairness "in the infliction of [death] is so plainly doomed to failure that it—and the death penalty—must be abandoned altogether." I may not live to see that day, but I have faith that eventually it will arrive. The path the Court has chosen lessens us all. I dissent.

Source: Callins v. Collins, 510 U.S. 1141 (1994), at 1141–1145.

Document 5.4
The Supreme Court in *Atkins v. Virginia* Bans Execution of the Mentally Retarded, June 20, 2002

In Atkins v. Virginia *(2002), speaking through Justice John Paul Stevens, the Supreme Court overruled* Penry v. Lynaugh *(1989) to hold that the Eighth Amendment prohibited the execution of the mentally retarded, although the opinion left to the states the procedure for determining mental retardation. In dissent, Justice Antonin Scalia attacked the majority for imposing its own moral judgments upon the country and erecting another barrier to enforcement of capital statutes.*

JUSTICE STEVENS delivered the opinion of the Court.

Those mentally retarded persons who meet the law's requirements for criminal responsibility should be tried and punished when they commit crimes. Because of their disabilities in areas of reasoning, judgment, and control of their impulses, however, they do not act with the level of moral culpability that characterizes the most serious adult criminal conduct. Moreover, their impairments can jeopardize the reliability and fairness of capital proceedings against mentally retarded defendants.

Presumably for these reasons, in the 13 years since we decided *Penry v. Lynaugh,* the American public, legislators, scholars, and judges have deliberated over the question whether the death penalty should ever be imposed on a mentally retarded criminal. The consensus reflected in those deliberations informs our answer to the question presented by this case: whether such executions are "cruel and unusual punishments" prohibited by the Eighth Amendment to the Federal Constitution.

I

Petitioner, Daryl Renard Atkins, was convicted of abduction, armed robbery, and capital murder, and sentenced to death. At approximately midnight on August 16, 1996, Atkins and William Jones, armed with a semiautomatic handgun, abducted Eric Nesbitt, robbed him of the money on his person, drove him to an automated teller machine in his pickup truck where cameras recorded their withdrawal of additional cash, then took him to an isolated location where he was shot eight times and killed.

Jones and Atkins both testified in the guilt phase of Atkins' trial. Each confirmed most of the details in the other's account of the incident, with the important exception that each stated that the other had actually shot and killed Nesbitt. Jones' testimony, which was both more coherent and credible than Atkins', was obviously credited by the jury and was sufficient to establish Atkins' guilt. At the penalty phase of the trial, the State introduced victim impact evidence and proved two aggravating circumstances: future dangerousness and "vileness of the offense." To prove future dangerousness, the State relied on Atkins' prior felony convictions as well as the testimony of four victims of earlier robberies and assaults. To prove the second aggravator, the prosecution relied upon the trial record, including pictures of the deceased's body and the autopsy report.

In the penalty phase, the defense relied on one witness, Dr. Evan Nelson, a forensic psychologist who had evaluated Atkins before trial and concluded that he was "mildly mentally retarded." His conclusion was based on interviews with people who knew Atkins, a review of school and court records, and the administration of a standard intelligence test which indicated that Atkins had a full scale IQ of 59.

The jury sentenced Atkins to death, but the Virginia Supreme Court ordered a second sentencing hearing because the trial court had used a misleading verdict form. At the resentencing, Dr. Nelson again testified. The State presented an expert rebuttal witness, Dr. Stanton Samenow, who expressed the opinion that Atkins was not mentally retarded, but rather was of "average intelligence, at least," and diagnosable as having antisocial personality disorder. The jury again sentenced Atkins to death.

The Supreme Court of Virginia affirmed the imposition of the death penalty. Atkins did not argue before the Virginia Supreme Court that his sentence was disproportionate to penalties imposed for similar crimes in Virginia, but he did contend "that he is mentally retarded and thus cannot be sentenced to death." The majority of the state court rejected this contention, relying on our holding in *Penry*. The Court was "not willing to commute Atkins' sentence of death to life imprisonment merely because of his IQ score."

Justice Hassell and Justice Koontz dissented. They rejected Dr. Samenow's opinion that Atkins possesses average intelligence as "incredulous as a matter of law," and concluded that "the imposition of the sentence of death upon a criminal defendant who has the mental age of a child between the ages of 9 and 12 is excessive." In their opinion, "it is indefensible to conclude that individuals who are mentally retarded are not to some degree less culpable for their criminal acts. By definition, such individuals have substantial limitations not shared by the general population. A moral and civilized society diminishes itself if its system of justice does not afford recognition and consideration of those limitations in a meaningful way."

Because of the gravity of the concerns expressed by the dissenters, and in light of the dramatic shift in the state legislative landscape that has occurred in the past 13 years, we granted certiorari to revisit the issue that we first addressed in the *Penry* case.

II

The Eighth Amendment succinctly prohibits "excessive" sanctions. It provides: "Excessive bail shall not be required, nor excessive fines imposed, nor cruel and unusual punishments inflicted." In *Weems v. United States* we held that a punishment of 12 years jailed in irons at hard and painful labor for the crime of falsifying records was excessive. We explained "that it is a precept of justice that punishment for crime should be graduated and proportioned to the offense."

A claim that punishment is excessive is judged not by the standards that prevailed in 1685 when Lord Jeffreys presided over the "Bloody Assizes" or when the Bill of Rights was adopted, but rather by those that currently prevail. As Chief Justice Warren explained in his opinion in *Trop v. Dulles:* "The basic concept underlying the Eighth Amendment is nothing less than the dignity of man. . . . The Amendment must draw its meaning from the evolving standards of decency that mark the progress of a maturing society."

We have pinpointed that the "clearest and most reliable objective evidence of contemporary values is the legislation enacted by the country's legislatures." Relying in part on such legislative evidence, we have held that death is an impermissibly excessive punishment for the rape of an adult woman, *Coker v. Georgia,* or for a defendant who neither took life, attempted to take life, nor intended to take life, *Enmund v. Florida.*

We also acknowledged in *Coker* that the objective evidence, though of great importance, did not "wholly determine" the controversy, "for the Constitution contemplates that in the end our own judgment will be brought to bear on the question of the acceptability of the death penalty under the Eighth Amendment."

Thus, in cases involving a consensus, our own judgment is "brought to bear," by asking whether there is reason to disagree with the judgment reached by the citizenry and its legislators.

Guided by our approach in these cases, we shall first review the judgment of legislatures that have addressed the suitability of imposing the death penalty on the mentally retarded and then consider reasons for agreeing or disagreeing with their judgment.

III

The parties have not called our attention to any state legislative consideration of the suitability of imposing the death penalty on mentally retarded offenders prior to 1986. In that year, the public reaction to the execution of a mentally retarded murderer in Georgia apparently led to the enactment of the first state statute prohibiting such executions. In 1988, when Congress enacted legislation reinstating the federal death penalty, it expressly provided that a "sentence of death shall not be carried out upon a person who is mentally retarded." In 1989, Maryland enacted a similar prohibition. It was in that year that we decided *Penry*, and concluded that those two state enactments, "even when added to the 14 States that have rejected capital punishment completely, do not provide sufficient evidence at present of a national consensus."

Much has changed since then. Responding to the national attention received by the Bowden execution and our decision in *Penry*, state legislatures across the country began to address the issue. In 1990 Kentucky and Tennessee enacted statutes similar to those in Georgia and Maryland, as did New Mexico in 1991, and Arkansas, Colorado, Washington, Indiana, and Kansas in 1993 and 1994. In 1995, when New York reinstated its death penalty, it emulated the Federal Government by expressly exempting the mentally retarded. Nebraska followed suit in 1998. There appear to have been no similar enactments during the next two years, but in 2000 and 2001 six more States–South Dakota, Arizona, Connecticut, Florida, Missouri, and North Carolina–joined the procession. The Texas Legislature unanimously adopted a similar bill, and bills have passed at least one house in other States, including Virginia and Nevada.

It is not so much the number of these States that is significant, but the consistency of the direction of change. . . . Moreover, even in those States that allow the execution of mentally retarded offenders, the practice is uncommon. Some States, for example New Hampshire and New Jersey, continue to authorize executions, but none have been carried out in decades. Thus there is little need to pursue legislation barring the execution of the mentally retarded in those States. And it appears that even among those States that regularly execute offenders and that have no prohibition with regard to the mentally retarded, only five have executed offenders possessing a known IQ less than 70 since we decided *Penry*. The practice, therefore, has become truly unusual, and it is fair to say that a national consensus has developed against it.

To the extent there is serious disagreement about the execution of mentally retarded offenders, it is in determining which offenders are in fact retarded. In this case, for instance, the Commonwealth of Virginia disputes that Atkins suffers from mental retardation. Not all people who claim to be mentally retarded will be so impaired as to fall within the range of mentally retarded offenders about whom there is a national consensus. As was our approach in *Ford v. Wainwright*, with regard to insanity, "we leave to the State[s] the task of developing appropriate ways to enforce the constitutional restriction upon its execution of sentences."

IV

This consensus unquestionably reflects widespread judgment about the relative culpability of mentally retarded offenders, and the relationship between mental retardation and the penological purposes served by the death penalty. Additionally, it suggests that some characteristics of mental retardation undermine the strength of the procedural protections that our capital jurisprudence steadfastly guards.

. . . Mentally retarded persons frequently know the difference between right and wrong and are competent to stand trial, but, by definition they have diminished capacities to understand and process information, to communicate, to abstract from mistakes and learn from experience, to engage in logical reasoning, to control impulses, and to understand others' reactions. . . . There is no evidence that they are more likely to engage in criminal conduct than others, but there is abundant evidence that they often act on impulse rather than pursuant to a premeditated plan, and that in group settings they are followers rather than leaders. Their deficiencies do not warrant an exemption from criminal sanctions, but they do diminish their personal culpability.

In light of these deficiencies, our death penalty jurisprudence provides two reasons consistent with the legislative consensus that the mentally retarded should be categorically excluded from execution. First, there is a serious question as to whether either justification that we have recognized as a basis for the death penalty applies to mentally retarded offenders. *Gregg v. Georgia* identified "retribution and deterrence of capital crimes by prospective offenders" as the social purposes served by the death penalty. Unless the imposition of the death penalty on a mentally retarded person "measurably contributes to one or both of these goals, it 'is nothing more than the purposeless and needless imposition of pain and suffering,' and hence an unconstitutional punishment."

With respect to retribution–the interest in seeing that the offender gets his "just deserts"–the severity of the appropriate punishment necessarily depends on the culpability of the offender. Since *Gregg*, our jurisprudence has consistently confined the imposition of the death penalty to a narrow category of the most serious crimes. . . . If the culpability of the average murderer is insufficient to justify the most extreme sanction available to the State, the lesser culpability of the mentally retarded offender surely does not merit that form of retribution. Thus, pursuant to our narrowing jurisprudence, which seeks to ensure that only the most deserving of execution are put to death, an exclusion for the mentally retarded is appropriate.

With respect to deterrence–the interest in preventing capital crimes by prospective offenders–"it seems likely that 'capital punishment can serve as a deterrent only when murder is the result of premeditation and deliberation,'" *Enmund*. Exempting the mentally retarded from that punishment will not affect the "cold calculus that precedes the decision" of other potential murderers. Indeed, that sort of calculus is at the opposite end of the spectrum from behavior of mentally retarded offenders. The theory of deterrence in capital sentencing is predicated upon the notion that the increased severity of the punishment will inhibit criminal actors from carrying out murderous conduct. Yet it is the same cognitive and behavioral impairments that make these defendants less morally culpable–for example, the diminished ability to understand and process information, to learn from experience, to engage in logical reasoning, or to control impulses–that also make it less likely that they can process the information of the possibility of execution as a penalty and, as a result, control their conduct based upon that information. Nor will exempting the mentally retarded from execution lessen the deterrent effect of the death penalty with respect to offenders who are not mentally retarded. Such individuals are unprotected by the exemption and will continue to face the threat of execution. Thus, executing the mentally retarded will not measurably further the goal of deterrence. . . .

Our independent evaluation of the issue reveals no reason to disagree with the judgment of "the legislatures that have recently addressed the matter" and concluded that death is not a suitable punishment for a mentally retarded criminal. We are not persuaded that the execution of mentally retarded criminals will measurably advance the deterrent or the retributive purpose of the death penalty. Construing and applying the Eighth Amendment in the light of our "evolving standards of decency," we therefore conclude that such punishment is excessive and that the Constitution "places a substantive restriction on the State's power to take the life" of a mentally retarded offender.

The judgment of the Virginia Supreme Court is reversed and the case is remanded for further proceedings not inconsistent with this opinion.

It is so ordered.

JUSTICE SCALIA, with whom the CHIEF JUSTICE and JUSTICE THOMAS join, dissenting.

Today's decision is the pinnacle of our Eighth Amendment death-is-different jurisprudence. Not only does it, like all of that jurisprudence, find no support in the text or history of the Eighth Amendment; it does not even have support in current social attitudes regarding the conditions that render an otherwise just death penalty inappropriate. Seldom has an opinion of this Court rested so obviously upon nothing but the personal views of its members.

I

I begin with a brief restatement of facts that are abridged by the Court but important to understanding this case. After spending the day drinking alcohol and smoking marijuana, petitioner Daryl Renard Atkins and a partner in crime drove to a convenience store, intending to rob a customer. Their victim was Eric Nesbitt, an airman from Langley Air Force Base, whom they abducted, drove to a nearby automated teller machine, and forced to withdraw $200. They then drove him to a deserted area, ignoring his pleas to leave him unharmed. According to the co-conspirator, whose testimony the jury evidently credited, Atkins ordered Nesbitt out of the vehicle and, after he had taken only a few steps, shot him one, two, three, four, five, six, seven, eight times in the thorax, chest, abdomen, arms, and legs.

The jury convicted Atkins of capital murder. At resentencing (the Virginia Supreme Court affirmed his conviction but remanded for resentencing because the trial court had used an improper verdict form), the jury heard extensive evidence of petitioner's alleged mental retardation. A psychologist testified that petitioner was mildly mentally retarded with an IQ of 59, that he was a "slow learne[r]," who showed a "lack of success in pretty much every domain of his life," and that he had an "impaired" capacity to appreciate the criminality of his conduct and to conform his conduct to the law. Petitioner's family members offered additional evidence in support of his mental retardation claim (*e.g.,* that petitioner is a "follower"). The State contested the evidence of retardation and presented testimony of a psychologist who found "absolutely no evidence other than the IQ score . . . indicating that [petitioner] was in the least bit mentally retarded" and concluded that petitioner was "of average intelligence, at least." . . .

II

As the foregoing history demonstrates, petitioner's mental retardation was a *central issue* at sentencing. The jury concluded, however, that his alleged retardation was not a compelling reason to exempt him from the death penalty in light of the brutality of his crime and his long demonstrated propensity for violence. "In upsetting this particularized judgment on the basis of a constitutional absolute," the Court concludes that no one who is even slightly mentally retarded can have sufficient "moral responsibility to be subjected to capital punishment for any crime. As a sociological and moral conclusion that is implausible; and it is doubly implausible as an interpretation of the United States Constitution."

Under our Eighth Amendment jurisprudence, a punishment is "cruel and unusual" if it falls within one of two categories: "those modes or acts of punishment that had been considered cruel and unusual at the time that the Bill of Rights was adopted," *Ford v. Wainwright,* and modes of punishment that are inconsistent with modern "standards of decency," as evinced by objective indicia, the most important of which is "legislation enacted by the country's legislatures," *Penry v. Lynaugh.*

The Court makes no pretense that execution of the mildly mentally retarded would have been considered "cruel and unusual" in 1791. Only the *severely* or *profoundly* mentally retarded, commonly known as "idiots," enjoyed any special status under the law at that time. They, like lunatics, suffered a "deficiency in will" rendering them unable to tell right from wrong. . . . Due to their incompetence, idiots were "excuse[d] from the guilt, and of course from the punishment, of any criminal action committed under such deprivation of the senses." Instead, they were often committed to civil confinement or made wards of the State, thereby preventing them from "go[ing] loose, to the terror of the king's subjects." Mentally retarded offenders with less severe impairments–those who were not "idiots"–suffered criminal prosecution and punishment, including capital punishment.

The Court is left to argue, therefore, that execution of the mildly retarded is inconsistent with the "evolving standards of decency that mark the progress of a maturing society." Before today, our opinions consistently emphasized that Eighth Amendment judgments regarding the existence of social "standards" "should be informed by objective factors to the maximum possible extent" and "should not be, or appear to be, merely the subjective views of individual Justices." "First" among these objective factors are the "statutes passed by society's elected representatives," because it "will rarely if ever be the case that the Members of this Court will have a better sense of the evolution in views of the American people than do their elected representatives," *Thompson, supra.*

The Court pays lipservice to these precedents as it miraculously extracts a "national consensus" forbidding execution of the mentally retarded, *ante,* at 12, from the fact that 18 States–less than *half* (47%) of the 38 States that permit capital punishment (for whom the issue exists)–have very recently enacted legislation barring execution of the mentally retarded. Even that 47% figure is a distorted one. If one is to say, as the Court does today, that *all* executions of the mentally retarded are so morally repugnant as to violate our national "standards of decency," surely the "consensus" it points to must be one that has set its righteous face against *all* such executions. Not 18 States, but only seven–18% of death penalty jurisdictions–have legislation of that scope. Eleven of those that the Court counts enacted statutes prohibiting execution of mentally retarded defendants *convicted after, or convicted of crimes committed after, the effective date* of the legislation; those already on death row, or consigned there before the statute's effective date, or even (in those States using the date of the crime as the criterion of retroactivity) tried in the future for murders committed many years ago, could be put to death. That is not a statement of absolute moral repugnance, but one of current preference between two tolerable approaches. Two of these States permit execution of the mentally retarded in other situations as well: Kansas apparently permits execution of all except the *severely* mentally retarded; New York permits execution of the mentally retarded who commit murder in a correctional facility.

But let us accept, for the sake of argument, the Court's faulty count. That bare number of States alone–*18*–should be enough to convince any reasonable person that no "national consensus" exists. How is it possible that agreement among 47% of the death penalty jurisdictions amounts to "consensus"? Our prior cases have generally required a much higher degree of agreement before finding a punishment cruel and unusual on "evolving standards" grounds. What the Court calls evidence of "consensus" in the present case (a fudged 47%) more closely resembles evidence that we found *inadequate* to establish consensus in earlier cases. . . .

The Court attempts to bolster its embarrassingly feeble evidence of "consensus" with the following: "It is not so much the number of these States that is significant, but the *consistency* of the direction of change." But in what *other* direction *could we possibly* see change? Given that 14 years ago *all* the death penalty statutes included the mentally retarded, *any* change (except precipitate undoing of what had just been done) was *bound to be* in the one direction the Court finds significant enough to overcome the lack of real consensus. That is to say, to be accurate the Court's "*consistency*-of-the-direction-of-change" point should be recast into the following unimpressive observation: "No State has yet undone its exemption of the mentally retarded, one for as long as 14 whole years." In any event, reliance upon "trends," even those of much longer duration than a mere 14 years, is a perilous basis for constitutional adjudication. . . .

But the Prize for the Court's Most Feeble Effort to fabricate "national consensus" must go to its appeal (deservedly relegated to a footnote) to the views of assorted professional and religious organizations, members of the so-called "world community," and respondents to opinion polls. I agree with the Chief Justice that the views of professional and religious organizations and the results of opinion polls are irrelevant. Equally irrelevant are the practices of the "world community," whose notions of justice are (thankfully) not always those of our people. "We must never forget that it is a Constitution for the United States of America that we are expounding. . . . [W]here there is not first a settled consensus among our own people, the views of other nations, however enlightened the Justices of this Court may think them to be, cannot be imposed upon Americans through the Constitution."

III

Beyond the empty talk of a "national consensus," the Court gives us a brief glimpse of what really underlies today's decision: pretension to a power confined *neither* by the moral sentiments originally enshrined in the Eighth Amendment (its original meaning) *nor even* by the current moral sentiments of the American people. "[T]he Constitution," the Court says, "contemplates that in the end *our own judgment* will be brought to bear on the question of the acceptability of the death penalty under the Eighth Amendment." (The unexpressed reason for this unexpressed "contemplation" of the Constitution is presumably that really good lawyers have moral sentiments superior to those of the common herd, whether in 1791 or today.) The arrogance of this assumption of power takes one's breath away. And it explains, of course, why the Court can be so cavalier about the evidence of consensus. . . .

* * *

Today's opinion adds one more to the long list of substantive and procedural requirements impeding imposition of the death penalty imposed under this Court's assumed power to invent a death-is-different jurisprudence. None of those requirements existed when the Eighth Amendment was adopted, and some of them were not even supported by current moral consensus. They include prohibition of the death penalty for "ordinary" murder, for rape of an adult woman, and for felony murder absent a showing that the defendant possessed a sufficiently culpable state of mind, prohibition of the death penalty for any person under the age of 16 at the time of the crime, prohibition of the death penalty as the mandatory punishment for any crime, a requirement that the sentencer not be given unguided discretion, a requirement that the sentencer be empowered to take into account all mitigating circumstances, and a requirement that the accused receive a judicial evaluation of his claim of insanity before the sentence can be executed. There is something to be said for popular abolition of the death penalty; there is nothing to be said for its incre-mental abolition by this Court. . . .

Source: Atkins v. Virginia, 536 U.S. 304 (2002), at 311–321, 337–354.

Document 5.5
The Supreme Court Rules That the Eighth Amendment Prohibits Imposition of the Death Penalty on Persons under Eighteen, March 1, 2005

In Thompson v. Oklahoma *(1988), the Supreme Court ruled that the states could not execute a juvenile who committed murder at the age of fifteen, but in* Stanford v. Kentucky *(1989) a sharply divided Court upheld the death penalty for those who committed their crime between the ages of sixteen and seventeen. In 2005 the justices reconsidered* Stanford *in* Roper v. Simmons, *following their earlier decision in* Atkins v. Virginia, *which banned the execution of the mentally retarded. Justice Anthony Kennedy wrote for the majority in* Roper *in an opinion unusual for its vigorous citation of international legal precedents against executing juveniles, references that evoked criticism from Justice Antonin Scalia in his dissent.*

JUSTICE KENNEDY delivered the opinion of the Court.

This case requires us to address, for the second time in a decade and a half, whether it is permissible under the Eighth and Fourteenth Amendments to the Constitution of the United States to execute a juvenile offender who was older than 15 but younger than 18 when he committed a capital crime. In *Stanford v. Kentucky,* a divided Court rejected the proposition that the Constitution bars capital punishment for juvenile offenders in this age group. We reconsider the question.

I

At the age of 17, when he was still a junior in high school, Christopher Simmons, the respondent here, committed murder. About nine months later, after he had turned 18, he was tried and sentenced to death. There is little doubt that Simmons was the instigator of the crime. Before its commission Simmons said he wanted to murder someone. In chilling, callous terms he talked about his plan, discussing it for the most part with two friends, Charles Benjamin and John Tessmer, then aged 15 and 16 respectively. Simmons proposed to commit bur-glary and murder by breaking and entering, tying up a victim, and throwing the victim off a bridge. Simmons assured his friends they could "get away with it" because they were minors.

The three met at about 2 a.m. on the night of the murder, but Tessmer left before the other two set out. (The State later charged Tessmer with conspiracy, but dropped the charge in exchange for his testimony against Simmons.) Simmons and Benjamin entered the home of the victim, Shirley Crook, after reaching through an open window and unlocking the back door. Simmons turned on a hallway light. Awakened, Mrs. Crook called out, "Who's there?" In response Simmons entered Mrs. Crook's bedroom, where he recognized her from a previous car accident involving them both. Simmons later admitted this confirmed his resolve to murder her.

Using duct tape to cover her eyes and mouth and bind her hands, the two perpetrators put Mrs. Crook in her minivan and drove to a state park. They reinforced the bindings, covered her head with a towel, and walked her to a railroad trestle spanning the Meramec River. There they tied her hands and feet together with electrical wire, wrapped her whole face in duct tape and threw her from the bridge, drowning her in the waters below.

By the afternoon of September 9, Steven Crook had returned home from an overnight trip, found his bedroom in disarray, and reported his wife missing. On the same afternoon fishermen recovered the victim's body from the river. Simmons, meanwhile, was bragging about the killing, telling friends he had killed a woman "because the bitch seen my face."

The next day, after receiving information of Simmons' involvement, police arrested him at his high school and took him to the police station in Fenton, Missouri. They read him his *Miranda* rights. Simmons waived his right to an attorney and agreed to answer questions. After less than two hours of interrogation, Simmons confessed to the murder and agreed to perform a videotaped reenactment at the crime scene.

The State charged Simmons with burglary, kidnaping [sic], stealing, and murder in the first degree. As Simmons was 17 at the time of the crime, he was outside the criminal jurisdiction of Missouri's juvenile court system. He was tried as an adult. At trial the State introduced Simmons' confession and the videotaped reenactment of the crime, along with testimony that Simmons discussed the crime in advance and bragged about it later. The defense called no witnesses in the guilt phase. The jury having returned a verdict of murder, the trial proceeded to the penalty phase.

The State sought the death penalty. As aggravating factors, the State submitted that the murder was committed for the purpose of receiving money; was committed for the purpose of avoiding, interfering with, or preventing lawful arrest of the defendant; and involved depravity of mind and was outrageously and wantonly vile, horrible, and inhuman. The State called Shirley Crook's husband, daughter, and two sisters, who presented moving evidence of the devastation her death had brought to their lives.

In mitigation Simmons' attorneys first called an officer of the Missouri juvenile justice system, who testified that Simmons had no prior convictions and that no previous charges had been filed against him. Simmons' mother, father, two younger half brothers, a neighbor, and a friend took the stand to tell the jurors of the close relationships they had formed with Simmons and to plead for mercy on his behalf. Simmons' mother, in particular, testified to the responsibility Simmons demonstrated in taking care of his two younger half brothers and of his grandmother and to his capacity to show love for them.

During closing arguments, both the prosecutor and defense counsel addressed Simmons' age, which the trial judge had instructed the jurors they could consider as a mitigating factor. Defense counsel reminded the jurors that juveniles of Simmons' age cannot drink, serve on juries, or even see certain movies, because "the legislatures have wisely decided that individuals of a certain age aren't responsible enough." Defense counsel argued that Simmons' age should make "a huge difference to [the jurors] in deciding just exactly what sort of punishment to make." In rebuttal, the prosecutor gave the following response: "Age, he says. Think about age. Seventeen years old. Isn't that scary? Doesn't that scare you? Mitigating? Quite the contrary I submit. Quite the contrary."

The jury recommended the death penalty after finding the State had proved each of the three aggravating factors submitted to it. Accepting the jury's recommendation, the trial judge imposed the death penalty.

Simmons obtained new counsel, who moved in the trial court to set aside the conviction and sentence. One argument was that Simmons had received ineffective assistance at trial. To support this contention, the new counsel called as witnesses Simmons' trial attorney, Simmons' friends and neighbors, and clinical psychologists who had evaluated him.

Part of the submission was that Simmons was "very immature," "very impulsive," and "very susceptible to being manipulated or influenced." The experts testified about Simmons' background including a difficult home environment and dramatic changes in behavior, accompanied by poor school performance in adolescence. Simmons was absent from home for long periods, spending time using alcohol and drugs with other teenagers or young adults. The contention by Simmons' postconviction counsel was that these matters should have been established in the sentencing proceeding.

The trial court found no constitutional violation by reason of ineffective assistance of counsel and denied the motion for postconviction relief. In a consolidated appeal from Simmons' conviction and sentence, and from the denial of postconviction relief, the Missouri Supreme Court affirmed. The federal courts denied Simmons' petition for a writ of habeas corpus.

After these proceedings in Simmons' case had run their course, this Court held that the Eighth and Fourteenth Amendments prohibit the execution of a mentally retarded person. Simmons filed a new petition for state postconviction relief, arguing that the reasoning of *Atkins* established that the Constitution prohibits the execution of a juvenile who was under 18 when the crime was committed.

The Missouri Supreme Court agreed. It held that since *Stanford,*

"a national consensus has developed against the execution of juvenile offenders, as demonstrated by the fact that eighteen states now bar such executions for juveniles, that twelve other states bar executions altogether, that no state has lowered its age of execution below 18 since *Stanford,* that five states have legislatively or by case law raised or established the minimum age at 18, and that the imposition of the juvenile death penalty has become truly unusual over the last decade."

On this reasoning it set aside Simmons' death sentence and resentenced him to "life imprisonment without eligibility for probation, parole, or release except by act of the Governor."

We granted certiorari, and now affirm.

II

The Eighth Amendment provides: "Excessive bail shall not be required, nor excessive fines imposed, nor cruel and unusual punishments inflicted." The provision is applicable to the States through the Fourteenth Amendment. As the Court explained in *Atkins,* the Eighth Amendment guarantees individuals the right not to be subjected to excessive sanctions. The right flows from the basic "precept of justice that punishment for crime should be graduated and proportioned to [the] offense." By protecting even those convicted of heinous crimes, the Eighth Amendment reaffirms the duty of the government to respect the dignity of all persons.

The prohibition against "cruel and unusual punishments," like other expansive language in the Constitution, must be interpreted according to its text, by considering history, tradition, and precedent, and with due regard for its purpose and function in the constitutional design. To implement this framework we have established the propriety and affirmed the necessity of referring to "the evolving standards of decency that mark the progress of a maturing society" to determine which punishments are so disproportionate as to be cruel and unusual.

In *Thompson v. Oklahoma,* a plurality of the Court determined that our standards of decency do not permit the execution of any offender under the age of 16 at the time of the crime. The plurality opinion explained that no death penalty State that had given express consideration to a minimum age for the death penalty had set the age lower than 16. The plurality also observed that "[t]he conclusion that it would offend civilized standards of decency to execute a person who was less than 16 years old at the time of his or her offense is consistent with the views that have been expressed by respected professional organizations, by other nations that share our Anglo-American heritage, and by the leading members of the Western European community." The opinion further noted that juries imposed the death penalty on offenders under 16 with exceeding rarity; the last execution of an offender for a crime committed under the age of 16 had been carried out in 1948, 40 years prior.

Bringing its independent judgment to bear on the permissibility of the death penalty for a 15-year-old offender, the *Thompson* plurality stressed that "[t]he reasons why juveniles are not trusted with the privileges and responsibilities of an adult also explain why their irresponsible conduct is not as morally reprehensible as that of an adult." According to the plurality, the lesser culpability of offenders under 16 made the death penalty inappropriate as a form of retribution, while the low likelihood that offenders under 16 engaged in "the kind of cost-benefit analysis that attaches any weight to the possibility of execution" made the death penalty ineffective as a means of deterrence. With Justice O'Connor concurring in the judgment on narrower grounds, the Court set aside the death sentence that had been imposed on the 15-year-old offender.

The next year, in *Stanford v. Kentucky,* the Court, over a dissenting opinion joined by four Justices, referred to contemporary standards of decency in this country and concluded the Eighth and Fourteenth Amendments did not proscribe the execution of juvenile offenders over 15 but under 18. The Court noted that 22 of the 37 death penalty States permitted the death penalty for 16-year-old offenders, and, among these 37 States, 25 permitted it for 17-year-old offenders. These numbers, in the Court's view, indicated there was no national consensus "sufficient to label a particular punishment cruel and unusual." A plurality of the Court also "emphatically reject[ed]" the suggestion that the Court should bring its own judgment to bear on the acceptability of the juvenile death penalty.

The same day the Court decided *Stanford,* it held that the Eighth Amendment did not mandate a categorical exemption from the death penalty for the mentally retarded. In reaching this conclusion it stressed that only two States had enacted laws banning the imposition of the death penalty on a mentally retarded person convicted of a capital offense. According to the Court, "the two state statutes prohibiting execution of the mentally retarded, even when added to the 14 States that have rejected capital punishment completely, [did] not provide sufficient evidence at present of a national consensus."

Three Terms ago the subject was reconsidered in *Atkins.* We held that standards of decency have evolved since *Penry* and now demonstrate that the execution of the mentally retarded is cruel and unusual punishment. The Court noted objective indicia of society's standards, as expressed in legislative enactments and state practice with respect to executions of the mentally retarded. When *Atkins* was decided only a minority of States permitted the practice, and even in those

States it was rare. On the basis of these indicia the Court determined that executing mentally retarded offenders "has become truly unusual, and it is fair to say that a national consensus has developed against it." . . .

Just as the *Atkins* Court reconsidered the issue decided in *Penry,* we now reconsider the issue decided in *Stanford.* The beginning point is a review of objective indicia of consensus, as expressed in particular by the enactments of legislatures that have addressed the question. This data gives us essential instruction. We then must determine, in the exercise of our own independent judgment, whether the death penalty is a disproportionate punishment for juveniles.

III

A

The evidence of national consensus against the death penalty for juveniles is similar, and in some respects parallel, to the evidence *Atkins* held sufficient to demonstrate a national consensus against the death penalty for the mentally retarded. When *Atkins* was decided, 30 States prohibited the death penalty for the mentally retarded. This number comprised 12 that had abandoned the death penalty altogether, and 18 that maintained it but excluded the mentally retarded from its reach. By a similar calculation in this case, 30 States prohibit the juvenile death penalty, comprising 12 that have rejected the death penalty altogether and 18 that maintain it but, by express provision or judicial interpretation, exclude juveniles from its reach. *Atkins* emphasized that even in the 20 States without formal prohibition, the practice of executing the mentally retarded was infrequent. Since *Penry,* only five States had executed offenders known to have an IQ under 70. In the present case, too, even in the 20 States without a formal prohibition on executing juveniles, the practice is infrequent. Since *Stanford,* six States have executed prisoners for crimes committed as juveniles. In the past 10 years, only three have done so. . . . In December 2003 the Governor of Kentucky decided to spare the life of Kevin Stanford, and commuted his sentence to one of life imprisonment without parole, with the declaration that "[w]e ought not be executing people who, legally, were children." By this act the Governor ensured Kentucky would not add itself to the list of States that have executed juveniles within the last 10 years even by the execution of the very defendant whose death sentence the Court had upheld in *Stanford v. Kentucky.*

There is, to be sure, at least one difference between the evidence of consensus in *Atkins* and in this case. Impressive in *Atkins* was the rate of abolition of the death penalty for the mentally retarded. Sixteen States that permitted the execution of the mentally retarded at the time of *Penry* had prohibited the practice by the time we heard *Atkins.* By contrast, the rate of change in reducing the incidence of the juvenile death penalty, or in taking specific steps to abolish it, has been slower. Five States that allowed the juvenile death penalty at the time of *Stanford* have abandoned it in the intervening 15 years—four through legislative enactments and one through judicial decision.

. . . The number of States that have abandoned capital punishment for juvenile offenders since *Stanford* is smaller than the number of States that abandoned capital punishment for the mentally retarded after *Penry;* yet we think the same consistency of direction of change has been demonstrated. Since *Stanford,* no State that previously prohibited capital punishment for juveniles has reinstated it. This fact, coupled with the trend toward abolition of the juvenile death penalty, carries special force in light of the general popularity of anticrime legislation, and in light of the particular trend in recent years toward cracking down on juvenile crime in other respects. Any difference between this case and *Atkins* with respect to the pace of abolition is thus counterbalanced by the consistent direction of the change. . . .

Petitioner cannot show national consensus in favor of capital punishment for juveniles but still resists the conclusion that any consensus exists against it. Petitioner supports this position with, in particular, the observation that when the Senate ratified the International Covenant on Civil and Political Rights, it did so subject to the President's proposed reservation regarding Article 6(5) of that treaty, which prohibits capital punishment for juveniles. This reservation at best provides only faint support for petitioner's argument. First, the reservation was passed in 1992; since then, five States have abandoned capital punishment for juveniles. Second, Congress considered the issue when enacting the Federal Death Penalty Act in 1994, and determined that the death penalty should not extend to juveniles. The reservation to Article 6(5) of the ICCPR provides minimal evidence that there is not now a national consensus against juvenile executions. . . .

B

A majority of States have rejected the imposition of the death penalty on juvenile offenders under 18, and we now hold this is required by the Eighth Amendment. . . .

Three general differences between juveniles under 18 and adults demonstrate that juvenile offenders cannot with reliability be classified among the worst offenders. First, as any parent knows and as the scientific and sociological studies respondent and his *amici* cite tend to confirm, "[a] lack of maturity and an underdeveloped sense of responsibility are found in youth more often than in adults and are more understandable among the young. These qualities often result in impetuous and ill-considered actions and decisions." . . . In recognition of the comparative immaturity and irresponsibility of juveniles, almost every State prohibits those under 18 years of age from voting, serving on juries, or marrying without parental consent.

The second area of difference is that juveniles are more vulnerable or suscepti-ble to negative influences and outside pressures, including peer pressure. This is explained in part by the prevailing circumstance that juveniles have less control, or less experience with control, over their own environment.

The third broad difference is that the character of a juvenile is not as well formed as that of an adult. The personality traits of juveniles are more transitory, less fixed.

These differences render suspect any conclusion that a juvenile falls among the worst offenders. The susceptibility of juveniles to immature and irresponsible behavior means "their irresponsible conduct is not as morally reprehensible as that of an adult." Their own vulnerability and comparative lack of control over their immediate surroundings mean juveniles have a greater claim than adults to be forgiven for failing to escape negative influences in their whole environment. The reality that juveniles still struggle to define their identity means it is less sup-portable to conclude that even a heinous crime committed by a juvenile is evi-dence of irretrievably depraved character. From a moral standpoint it would be misguided to equate the failings of a minor with those of an adult, for a greater possibility exists that a minor's character deficiencies will be reformed. . . .

Once the diminished culpability of juveniles is recognized, it is evident that the penological justifications for the death penalty apply to them with lesser force than to adults. We have held there are two distinct social purposes served by the death penalty: "retribution and deterrence of capital crimes by prospective offenders." As for retribution, we remarked in *Atkins* that "[i]f the culpability of the average murderer is insufficient to justify the most extreme sanction available to the State, the lesser culpability of the mentally retarded offender surely does not merit that form of retribution." The same conclusions follow from the lesser culpability of the juvenile offender. Whether viewed as an attempt to express the community's moral outrage or as an attempt to right the balance for the wrong to the victim, the case for retribution is not as strong with a minor as with an adult. Retribution is not proportional if the law's most severe penalty is imposed on one whose culpability or blameworthiness is diminished, to a substantial degree, by reason of youth and immaturity.

As for deterrence, it is unclear whether the death penalty has a significant or even measurable deterrent effect on juveniles, as counsel for the petitioner acknowledged at oral argument. In general we leave to legislatures the assessment of the efficacy of various criminal penalty schemes. Here, however, the absence of evidence of deterrent effect is of special concern because the same characteristics that render juveniles less culpable than adults suggest as well that juveniles will be less susceptible to deterrence. In particular, as the plurality observed in *Thompson*, "[t]he likelihood that the teenage offender has made the kind of cost-benefit analysis that attaches any weight to the possibility of execution is so remote as to be virtually nonexistent." To the extent the juvenile death penalty might have residual deterrent effect, it is worth noting that the punishment of life imprisonment without the possibility of parole is itself a severe sanction, in particular for a young person. . . .

Drawing the line at 18 years of age is subject, of course, to the objections always raised against categorical rules. The qualities that distinguish juveniles from adults do not disappear when an individual turns 18. By the same token, some under 18 have already attained a level of maturity some adults will never reach. For the reasons we have discussed, however, a line must be drawn. The plurality opinion in *Thompson* drew the line at 16. In the intervening years the *Thompson* plurality's conclusion that offenders under 16 may not be executed has not been challenged. The logic of *Thompson* extends to those who are under 18. The age of 18 is the point where society draws the line for many purposes between childhood and adulthood. It is, we conclude, the age at which the line for death eligibility ought to rest.

These considerations mean *Stanford v. Kentucky* should be deemed no longer controlling on this issue. To the extent *Stanford* was based on review of the objective indicia of consensus that obtained in 1989, it suffices to note that those indicia have changed. It should be observed, furthermore, that the *Stanford* Court should have considered those States that had abandoned the death penalty altogether as part of the consensus against the juvenile death penalty, a State's decision to bar the death penalty altogether of necessity demonstrates a judgment that the death penalty is inappropriate for all offenders, including juveniles. Last, to the extent *Stanford* was based on a rejection of the idea that this Court is required to bring its independent judgment to bear on the proportionality of the death penalty for a particular class of crimes or offenders, it suffices to note that this rejection was inconsistent with prior Eighth Amendment decisions, *Thompson; Enmund; Coker.* It is also inconsistent with the premises of our recent decision in *Atkins.*

In holding that the death penalty cannot be imposed upon juvenile offenders, we take into account the circumstance that some States have relied on *Stanford* in seeking the death penalty against juvenile offenders. This consideration, however, does not outweigh our conclusion that *Stanford* should no longer control in those few pending cases or in those yet to arise.

IV

Our determination that the death penalty is disproportionate punishment for offenders under 18 finds confirmation in the stark reality that the United States is the only country in the world that continues to give official sanction to the juvenile death penalty. This reality does not become controlling, for the task of interpreting the Eighth Amendment remains our responsibility. Yet at least from the time of the Court's decision in *Trop,* the Court has referred to the laws of other countries and to international authorities as instructive for its interpretation of the Eighth Amendment's prohibition of "cruel and unusual punishments."

As respondent and a number of *amici* emphasize, Article 37 of the United Nations Convention on the Rights of the Child, which every country in the world has ratified save for the United States and Somalia, contains an express prohibition on capital punishment for crimes committed by juveniles under 18. No ratifying country has entered a reservation to the provision prohibiting the execution of juvenile offenders. Parallel prohibitions are contained in other significant international covenants.

Respondent and his *amici* have submitted, and petitioner does not contest, that only seven countries other than the United States have executed juvenile offenders since 1990: Iran, Pakistan, Saudi Arabia, Yemen, Nigeria, the Democratic Republic of Congo, and China. Since then each of these countries has either abolished capital punishment for juveniles or made public disavowal of the practice. In sum, it is fair to say that the United States now stands alone in a world that has turned its face against the juvenile death penalty. . . .

It is proper that we acknowledge the overwhelming weight of international opinion against the juvenile death penalty, resting in large part on the understanding that the instability and emotional imbalance of young people may often be a factor in the crime. The opinion of the world community, while not controlling our outcome, does provide respected and significant confirmation for our own conclusions.

Over time, from one generation to the next, the Constitution has come to earn the high respect and even, as Madison dared to hope, the veneration of the American people. The document sets forth, and rests upon, innovative principles original to the American experience, such as federalism; a proven balance in political mechanisms through separation of powers; specific guarantees for the accused in criminal cases; and broad provisions to secure individual freedom and preserve human dignity. These doctrines and guarantees are central to the American experience and remain essential to our present-day self-definition and national identity. Not the least of the reasons we honor the Constitution, then, is because we know it to be our own. It does not lessen our fidelity to the Constitution or our pride in its origins to acknowledge that the express affirmation of certain fundamental rights by other nations and peoples simply underscores the centrality of those same rights within our own heritage of freedom.

***

The Eighth and Fourteenth Amendments forbid imposition of the death penalty on offenders who were under the age of 18 when their crimes were committed. The judgment of the Missouri Supreme Court setting aside the sentence of death imposed upon Christopher Simmons is affirmed.

It is so ordered.

JUSTICE SCALIA, with whom THE CHIEF JUSTICE and JUSTICE THOMAS join, dissenting.

In urging approval of a constitution that gave life-tenured judges the power to nullify laws enacted by the people's representatives, Alexander Hamilton assured the citizens of New York that there was little risk in this, since "[t]he judiciary . . . ha[s] neither FORCE nor WILL but merely judgment." But Hamilton had in mind a traditional judiciary, "bound down by strict rules and precedents which serve to define and point out their duty in every particular case that comes before them." Bound down, indeed. What a mockery today's opinion makes of Hamilton's expectation, announcing the Court's conclusion that the meaning of our Constitution has changed over the past 15 years–not, mind you, that this Court's decision 15 years ago was *wrong*, but that the Constitution *has changed*. The Court reaches this implausible result by purporting to advert, not to the original meaning of the Eighth Amendment, but to "the evolving standards of decency," of our national society. It then finds, on the flimsiest of grounds, that a national consensus which could not be perceived in our people's laws barely 15 years ago now solidly exists. Worse still, the Court says in so many words that what our people's laws say about the issue does not, in the last analysis, matter: "[I]n the end our own judgment will be brought to bear on the question of the acceptability of the death penalty under the Eighth Amendment." The Court thus proclaims itself sole arbiter of our Nation's moral standards–and in the course of discharging that awesome responsibility purports to take guidance from the views of foreign courts and legislatures. Because I do not believe that the meaning of our Eighth Amendment, any more than the meaning of other provisions of our Constitution, should be determined by the subjective views of five Members of this Court and like-minded foreigners, I dissent.

I

In determining that capital punishment of offenders who committed murder before age 18 is "cruel and unusual" under the Eighth Amendment, the Court first considers, in accordance with our modern (though in my view mistaken) jurisprudence, whether there is a "national consensus," that laws allowing such executions contravene our modern "standards of decency." We have held that this determination should be based on "objective indicia that reflect the public attitude toward a given sanction"–namely, "statutes passed by society's elected representatives." As in *Atkins v. Virginia,* the Court dutifully recites this test and claims halfheartedly that a national consensus has emerged since our decision in *Stanford,* because 18 States–or 47% of States that permit capital punishment–now have legislation prohibiting the execution of offenders under 18, and because all of four States have adopted such legislation since *Stanford*.

Words have no meaning if the views of less than 50% of death penalty States can constitute a national consensus. Our previous cases have required overwhelming opposition to a challenged practice, generally over a long period of time. In *Coker v. Georgia*, a plurality concluded the Eighth Amendment prohibited capital punishment for rape of an adult woman where only one jurisdiction authorized such punishment. The plurality also observed that "[a]t no time in the last 50 years ha[d] a majority of States authorized death as a punishment for rape." In *Ford v. Wainwright*, we held execution of the insane unconstitutional, tracing the roots of this prohibition to the common law and noting that "no State in the union permits the execution of the insane." In *Enmund v. Florida*, we invalidated capital punishment imposed for participation in a robbery in which an accomplice committed murder, because 78% of all death penalty States prohibited this punishment. Even there we expressed some hesitation, because the legislative judgment was "neither 'wholly unanimous among state legislatures,' . . . nor as compelling as the legislative judgments considered in *Coker*." By contrast, agreement among 42% of death penalty States in *Stanford*, which the Court appears to believe was correctly decided at the time, was insufficient to show a national consensus.

In an attempt to keep afloat its implausible assertion of national consensus, the Court throws overboard a proposition well established in our Eighth Amendment jurisprudence. "It should be observed," the Court says, "that the *Stanford* Court should have considered those States that had abandoned the death penalty altogether as part of the consensus against the juvenile death penalty . . . ; a State's decision to bar the death penalty altogether of necessity demonstrates a judgment that the death penalty is inappropriate for all offenders, including juveniles." The insinuation that the Court's new method of counting contradicts only "the *Stanford* Court" is misleading. *None* of our cases dealing with an alleged constitutional limitation upon the death penalty has counted, as States supporting a consensus in favor of that limitation, States that have eliminated the death penalty entirely. And with good reason. Consulting States that bar the death penalty concerning the necessity of making an exception to the penalty for offenders under 18 is rather like including old-order Amishmen in a consumer-preference poll on the electric car. Of *course* they don't like it, but that sheds no light whatever on the point at issue. That 12 States favor *no* executions says something about consensus against the death penalty, but nothing–absolutely nothing–about consensus that offenders under 18 deserve special immunity from such a penalty. In repealing the death penalty, those 12 States considered *none* of the factors that the Court puts forth as determinative of the issue before us today–lower culpability of the young, inherent recklessness, lack of capacity for considered judgment, etc. What might be relevant, perhaps, is how many of those States permit 16- and 17-year-old offenders to be treated as adults with respect to noncapital offenses. (They all do, indeed, some even *require* that juveniles as young as 14 be tried as adults if they are charged with murder.) The attempt by the Court to turn its remarkable minority consensus into a faux majority by counting Amishmen is an act of nomological desperation. . . .

II

Of course, the real force driving today's decision is not the actions of four state legislatures, but the Court's "own judgment" that murderers younger than 18 can never be as morally culpable as older counterparts. The Court claims that this usurpation of the role of moral arbiter is simply a "retur[n] to the rul[e] established in decisions predating *Stanford*." That supposed rule–which is reflected solely in dicta and never once in a *holding* that purports to supplant the consensus of the American people with the Justices' views–was repudiated in *Stanford* for the very good reason that it has no foundation in law or logic. If the Eighth Amendment set forth an ordinary rule of law, it would indeed be the role of this Court to say what the law is. But the Court having pronounced that the Eighth Amendment is an ever-changing reflection of "the evolving standards of decency" of our society, it makes no sense for the Justices then to *prescribe* those standards rather than discern them from the practices of our people. On the evolving-standards hypothesis, the only legitimate function of this Court is to identify a moral consensus of the American people. By what conceivable warrant can nine lawyers presume to be the authoritative conscience of the Nation? . . .

Today's opinion provides a perfect example of why judges are ill equipped to make the type of legislative judgments the Court insists on making here. To support its opinion that States should be prohibited from imposing the death penalty on anyone who committed murder before age 18, the Court looks to scientific and sociological studies, picking and choosing those that support its position. It never explains why those particular studies are methodologically sound; none was ever entered into evidence or tested in an adversarial proceeding. . . .

In other words, all the Court has done today, to borrow from another context, is to look over the heads of the crowd and pick out its friends. . . .

Even putting aside questions of methodology, the studies cited by the Court offer scant support for a categorical prohibition of the death penalty for murderers under 18. At most, these studies conclude that, *on average,* or *in most cases,* persons under 18 are unable to take moral responsibility for their actions. Not one of the cited studies opines that all individuals under 18 are unable to appreciate the nature of their crimes. . . .

III

Though the views of our own citizens are essentially irrelevant to the Court's decision today, the views of other countries and the so-called international community take center stage.

The Court begins by noting that "Article 37 of the United Nations Convention on the Rights of the Child, which every country in the world has ratified *save for the United States* and Somalia, contains an express prohibition on capital punishment for crimes committed by juveniles under 18." The Court also discusses the International Covenant on Civil and Political Rights, which the Senate ratified only subject to a reservation that reads:

"The United States reserves the right, subject to its Constitutional restraints, to impose capital punishment on any person (other than a pregnant woman) duly convicted under existing or future laws permitting the imposition of capital punishment, including such punishment for crime committed by persons below eighteen years of age."

Unless the Court has added to its arsenal the power to join and ratify treaties on behalf of the United States, I cannot see how this evidence favors, rather than refutes, its position. That the Senate and the President–those actors our Constitution empowers to enter into treaties, see Art. II, §2–have declined to join and ratify treaties prohibiting execution of under-18 offenders can only suggest that *our country* has either not reached a national consensus on the question, or has reached a consensus contrary to what the Court announces. That the reservation to the ICCPR was made in 1992 does not suggest otherwise, since the reservation still remains in place today. It is also worth noting that, in addition to barring the execution of under-18 offenders, the United Nations Convention on the Rights of the Child prohibits punishing them with life in prison without the possibility of release. If we are truly going to get in line with the international community, then the Court's reassurance that the death penalty is really not needed, since "the punishment of life imprisonment without the possibility of parole is itself a severe sanction," gives little comfort. . . .

More fundamentally, however, the basic premise of the Court's argument–that American law should conform to the laws of the rest of the world–ought to be rejected out of hand. In fact the Court itself does not believe it. In many significant respects the laws of most other countries differ from our law–including not only such explicit provisions of our Constitution as the right to jury trial and grand jury indictment, but even many interpretations of the Constitution prescribed by this Court itself. The Court-pronounced exclusionary rule, for example, is distinctively American. . . . England, for example, rarely excludes evidence found during an illegal search or seizure and has only recently begun excluding evidence from illegally obtained confessions. Canada rarely excludes evidence and will only do so if admission will "bring the administration of justice into disrepute." The

European Court of Human Rights has held that introduction of illegally seized evidence does not violate the "fair trial" requirement in Article 6, §1, of the European Convention on Human Rights. . . .

And let us not forget the Court's abortion jurisprudence, which makes us one of only six countries that allow abortion on demand until the point of viability. Though the Government and *amici* in cases following *Roe v. Wade* urged the Court to follow the international community's lead, these arguments fell on deaf ears. . . .

The Court should either profess its willingness to reconsider all these matters in light of the views of foreigners, or else it should cease putting forth foreigners' views as part of the *reasoned basis* of its decisions. To invoke alien law when it agrees with one's own thinking, and ignore it otherwise, is not reasoned decisionmaking, but sophistry. . . .

IV

To add insult to injury, the Court affirms the Missouri Supreme Court without even admonishing that court for its flagrant disregard of our precedent in *Stanford*. Until today, we have always held that "it is this Court's prerogative alone to overrule one of its precedents." Today, however, the Court silently approves a state-court decision that blatantly rejected controlling precedent.

One must admit that the Missouri Supreme Court's action, and this Court's indulgent reaction, are, in a way, understandable. In a system based upon constitutional and statutory text democratically adopted, the concept of "law" ordinarily signifies that particular words have a fixed meaning. Such law does not change, and this Court's pronouncement of it therefore remains authoritative until (confessing our prior error) we overrule. The Court has purported to make of the Eighth Amendment, however, a mirror of the passing and changing sentiment of American society regarding penology. The lower courts can look into that mirror as well as we can; and what we saw 15 years ago bears no necessary relationship to what they see today. Since they are not looking at the same text, but at a different scene, why should our earlier decision control their judgment?

However sound philosophically, this is no way to run a legal system. We must disregard the new reality that, to the extent our Eighth Amendment decisions constitute something more than a show of hands on the current Justices' current personal views about penology, they purport to be nothing more than a snapshot of American public opinion at a particular point in time (with the timeframes now shortened to a mere 15 years). We must treat these decisions just as though they represented *real* law, *real* prescriptions democratically adopted by the American people, as conclusively (rather than sequentially) construed by this Court. Allowing lower courts to reinterpret the Eighth Amendment whenever they decide enough time has passed for a new snapshot leaves this Court's decisions without any force–especially since the "evolution" of our Eighth Amendment is no longer determined by objective criteria. To allow lower courts to behave as we do, "updating" the Eighth Amendment as needed, destroys stability and makes our case law an unreliable basis for the designing of laws by citizens and their representatives, and for action by public officials. The result will be to crown arbitrariness with chaos.

Source: Roper v. Simmons, 543 U.S. 551 (2005), at 555–578, 607–630.

Document 5.6
Illinois Governor George Ryan Commutes 167 Death Sentences, January 11, 2003

Forty-eight hours before his term of office ended in January 2003, Illinois governor George Ryan commuted all death sentences in the state to prison terms of life or less, the largest such emptying of death row in history. Ryan felt compelled to act after the Illinois legislature failed to adopt proposed reforms to the state's death penalty law. On January 11, Ryan explained the reasons for his action in a speech at the Northwestern University College of Law. The governor was later convicted of eighteen felony counts involving fraud and conspiracy and sentenced to six-and-a-half years in prison.

Four years ago I was sworn in as the 39th Governor of Illinois. That was just four short years ago; that's when I was a firm believer in the American System of Justice and the death penalty. I believed that the ultimate penalty for the taking of a life was administrated in a just and fair manner.

Today, 3 days before I end my term as Governor, I stand before you to explain my frustrations and deep concerns about both the administration and the penalty of death. It is fitting that we are gathered here today at Northwestern University with the students, teachers, lawyers and investigators who first shed light on the sorrowful condition of Illinois' death penalty system. . . .

During my time in public office I have always reserved my right to change my mind if I believed it to be in the best public interest, whether it be about taxes, abortions or the death penalty. But I must confess that the debate with myself has been the toughest concerning the death penalty. I suppose the reason the death penalty has been the toughest is because it is so final, the only public policy that determines who lives and who dies. In addition it is the only issue that attracts most of the legal minds across the country. I have received more advice on this issue than any other policy issue I have dealt with in my 35 years of public service. I have kept an open mind on both sides of the issues of commutation for life or death.

I have read, listened to and discussed the issue with the families of the victims as well as the families of the condemned. I know that any decision I make will not be accepted by one side or the other. I know that my decision will be just that— my decision, based on all the facts I could gather over the past 3 years. I may never be comfortable with my final decision, but I will know in my heart, that I did my very best to do the right thing. . . .

My responsibilities and obligations are more than my neighbors and my family. I represent all the people of Illinois, like it or not. The decision I make about our criminal justice system is felt not only here, but the world over.

The other day, I received a call from former South African President Nelson Mandela who reminded me that the United States sets the example for justice and fairness for the rest of the world. Today the United States is not in league with most of our major allies: Europe, Canada, Mexico, most of South and Central America. These countries rejected the death penalty. We are partners in death with several third world countries. Even Russia has called a moratorium.

The death penalty has been abolished in 12 states. In none of these states has the homicide rate increased. In Illinois last year we had about 1000 murders, only 2 percent of that 1000 were sentenced to death. Where is the fairness and equality in that? The death penalty in Illinois is not imposed fairly or uniformly because of the absence of standards for the 102 Illinois State Attorneys, who must decide whether to request the death sentence. Should geography be a factor in determining who gets the death sentence? I don't think so but in Illinois it makes a difference. You are 5 times more likely to get a death sentence for first degree murder in the rural area of Illinois than you are in Cook County. Where is the justice and fairness in that? Where is the proportionality?

The Most Reverend Desmond Tutu wrote to me this week stating that "to take a life when a life has been lost is revenge, it is not justice. He says justice allows for mercy, clemency and compassion. These virtues are not weakness."

"In fact the most glaring weakness is that no matter how efficient and fair the death penalty may seem in theory, in actual practice it is primarily inflicted upon the weak, the poor, the ignorant and against racial minorities." That was a quote from former California Governor Pat Brown. He wrote that in his book "Public Justice, Private Mercy" he wrote that nearly 50 years ago, nothing has changed in nearly 50 years.

I never intended to be an activist on this issue. I watched in surprise as freed death row inmate Anthony Porter was released from jail. A free man, he ran into the arms of Northwestern University Professor Dave Protess who poured his heart and soul into proving Porter's innocence with his journalism students.

He was 48 hours away from being wheeled into the execution chamber where the state would kill him.

It would all be so antiseptic and most of us would not have even paused, except that Anthony Porter was innocent of the double murder for which he had been condemned to die.

After Mr. Porter's case there was the report by *Chicago Tribune* reporters Steve Mills and Ken Armstrong documenting the systemic failures of our capital punishment system. Half of the nearly 300 capital cases in Illinois had been reversed for a new trial or resentencing.

Nearly Half!

33 of the death row inmates were represented at trial by an attorney who had later been disbarred or at some point suspended from practicing law.

Of the more than 160 death row inmates, 35 were African American defendants who had been convicted or condemned to die by all-white juries.

More than two-thirds of the inmates on death row were African American.

46 inmates were convicted on the basis of testimony from jailhouse informants.

I can recall looking at these cases and the information from the Mills/Armstrong series and asking my staff: How does that happen? How in God's name does that happen? I'm not a lawyer, so somebody explain it to me.

But no one could. Not to this day.

Then over the next few months there were three more exonerated men, freed because their sentence hinged on a jailhouse informant or new DNA technology proved beyond a shadow of doubt their innocence.

We then had the dubious distinction of exonerating more men than we had executed. 13 men found innocent, 12 executed.

As I reported yesterday, there is not a doubt in my mind that the number of innocent men freed from our Death Row stands at 17, with the pardons of Aaron Patterson, Madison Hobley, Stanley Howard and Leroy Orange.

That is an absolute embarrassment. 17 exonerated death row inmates is nothing short of a catastrophic failure. But the 13, now 17 men, is just the beginning of our sad arithmetic in prosecuting murder cases. During the time we have had capital punishment in Illinois, there were at least 33 other people wrongly convicted on murder charges and exonerated. Since we reinstated the death penalty there are also 93 people, 93, where our criminal justice system imposed the most severe sanction and later rescinded the sentence or even released them from custody because they were innocent.

How many more cases of wrongful conviction have to occur before we can all agree that the system is broken?

In the United States the overwhelming majority of those executed are psychotic, alcoholic, drug addicted or mentally unstable. They frequently are raised in an impoverished and abusive environment. . . .

Seldom are people with money or prestige convicted of capital offenses, even more seldom are they executed. . . .

Earlier this year, the U.S. Supreme Court held that it is unconstitutional and cruel and unusual punishment to execute the mentally retarded. It is now the law of the land. How many people have we already executed who were mentally retarded and are now dead and buried? Although we now know that they have been killed by the state unconstitutionally and illegally. Is that fair? Is that right?

This court decision was last spring. The General Assembly failed to pass any measure defining what constitutes mental retardation. We are a rudderless ship because they failed to act. . . .

Some people have assailed my power to commute sentences, a power that literally hundreds of legal scholars from across the country have defended. But prosecutors in Illinois have the ultimate commutation power, a power that is exercised every day. They decide who will be subject to the death penalty, who will get a plea deal or even who may get a complete pass on prosecution. By what objective standards do they make these decisions? We do not know, they are not public. There were more than 1000 murders last year in Illinois. There is no doubt that all murders are horrific and cruel. Yet, less than 2 percent of those murder defendants will receive the death penalty. That means more than 98% of victims families do not get, and will not receive whatever satisfaction can be derived from the execution of the murderer. Moreover, if you look at the cases, as I have done both individually and collectively—a killing with the same circumstances might get 40 years in one county and death in another county. I have also seen where co-defendants who are equally or even more culpable get sentenced to a term of years, while another less culpable defendant ends up on death row. . . .

How fair is that? . . .

I spent a good deal of time reviewing these death row cases. My staff, many of whom are lawyers, spent busy days and many sleepless nights answering my questions, providing me with information, giving me advice. It became clear to me that whatever decision I made, I would be criticized. It also became clear to me that it was impossible to make reliable choices about whether our capital punishment system had really done its job.

As I came closer to my decision, I knew that I was going to have to face the question of whether I believed so completely in the choice I wanted to make that I could face the prospect of even commuting the death sentence of Daniel Edwards, the man who had killed a close family friend of mine. I discussed it with my wife, Lura Lynn, who has stood by me all these years. She was angry and disappointed at my decision like many of the families of other victims will be. . . .

The fact is that the failure of the General Assembly to act is merely a symptom of the larger problem. Many people express the desire to have capital punishment. Few, however, seem prepared to address the tough questions that arise when the system fails. It is easier and more comfortable for politicians to be tough on crime and support the death penalty. It wins votes. But when it comes to admitting that we have a problem, most run for cover. Prosecutors across our state continue to deny that our death penalty system is broken, or they say if there is a problem, it is really a small one and we can fix it somehow. It is difficult to see how the system can be fixed when not a single one of the reforms proposed by my Capital Punishment Commission has been adopted. Even the reforms the prosecutors agree with haven't been adopted.

So when will the system be fixed? How much more risk can we afford? Will we actually have to execute an innocent person before the tragedy that is our capital punishment system in Illinois is really understood? This summer, a United States District court judge held the federal death penalty was unconstitutional and noted that with the number of recent exonerations based on DNA and new scientific technology we undoubtedly executed innocent people before this technology emerged.

As I prepare to leave office, I had to ask myself whether I could really live with the prospect of knowing that I had the opportunity to act, but that I failed to do so because I might be criticized. Could I take the chance that our capital punishment system might be reformed, that wrongful convictions might not occur, that enterprising journalism students might free more men from death row? A system that's so fragile that it depends on young journalism students is seriously flawed. . . .

Another issue that came up in my individual, case-by-case review was the issue of international law. The Vienna Convention protects U.S. citizens abroad and foreign nationals in the United States. It provides that if you are arrested, you should be afforded the opportunity to contact your consulate. There are five men on death row who were denied that internationally recognized human right. Mexico's President Vicente Fox contacted me to express his deep concern for the Vienna Convention violations. If we do not uphold international law here, we cannot expect our citizens to be protected outside the United States. . . .

In 1994, near the end of his distinguished career on the Supreme Court of the United States, Justice Harry Blackmun wrote an influential dissent in the body of law on capital punishment. 20 years earlier he was part of the court that issued the landmark *Furman* decision. The Court decided that the death penalty statutes in use throughout the country were fraught with severe flaws that rendered them unconstitutional. Quite frankly, they were the same problems we see here in Illinois. To many, it looked liked the *Furman* decision meant the end of the death penalty in the United States.

This was not the case. Many states responded to *Furman* by developing and enacting new and improved death penalty statutes. In 1976, four years after it had decided *Furman*, Justice Blackmun joined the majority of the United States Supreme Court in deciding to give the States a chance with these new and improved death penalty statutes. There was great optimism in the air.

This was the climate in 1977, when the Illinois legislature was faced with the momentous decision of whether to reinstate the death penalty in Illinois. I was a member of the General Assembly at that time and when I pushed the green button in favor of reinstating the death penalty in this great State, I did so with the belief that whatever problems had plagued the capital punishment system in the past were now being cured. I am sure that most of my colleagues who voted with me that day shared that view.

But 20 years later, after affirming hundreds of death penalty decisions, Justice Blackmun came to the realization, in the twilight of his distinguished career that the death penalty remains fraught with "arbitrariness, discrimination, caprice and mistake." He expressed frustration with a 20-year struggle to develop procedural and substantive safeguards. In a now famous dissent he wrote in 1994, "From this day forward, I no longer shall tinker with the machinery of death."

One of the few disappointments of my legislative and executive career is that the General Assembly failed to work with me to reform our deeply flawed system.

I don't know why legislators could not heed the rising voices of reform. I don't know how many more systemic flaws we needed to uncover before they would be spurred to action.

Three times I proposed reforming the system with a package that would restrict the use of jailhouse snitches, create a statewide panel to determine death eligible cases, and reduce the number of crimes eligible for death. These reforms would not have created a perfect system, but they would have dramatically reduced the chance for error in the administration of the ultimate penalty. . . .

Our systemic case-by-case review has found more cases of innocent men wrongfully sentenced to death row. Because our three year study has found only more questions about the fairness of the sentencing; because of the spectacular failure to reform the system; because we have seen justice delayed for countless death row inmates with potentially meritorious claims; because the Illinois death penalty system is arbitrary and capricious—and therefore immoral—I no longer shall tinker with the machinery of death.

I cannot say it more eloquently than Justice Blackmun.

The legislature couldn't reform it.

Lawmakers won't repeal it.

But I will not stand for it.

I must act.

Our capital system is haunted by the demon of error, error in determining guilt, and error in determining who among the guilty deserves to die. Because of all of these reasons today I am commuting the sentences of all death row inmates.

This is a blanket commutation. I realize it will draw ridicule, scorn and anger from many who oppose this decision. They will say I am usurping the decisions of judges and juries and state legislators. But as I have said, the people of our state have vested in me to act in the interest of justice. Even if the exercise of my power becomes my burden I will bear it. Our constitution compels it. I sought this office, and even in my final days of holding it I cannot shrink from the obligations to justice and fairness that it demands.

There have been many nights where my staff and I have been deprived of sleep in order to conduct our exhaustive review of the system. But I can tell you this: I will sleep well knowing I made the right decision.

As I said when I declared the moratorium, it is time for a rational discussion on the death penalty. While our experience in Illinois has indeed sparked a debate, we have fallen short of a rational discussion. Yet if I did not take this action, I feared that there would be no comprehensive and thorough inquiry into the guilt of the individuals on death row or of the fairness of the sentences applied.

To say it plainly one more time—the Illinois capital punishment system is broken. It has taken innocent men to a hair's breadth escape from their unjust execution. Legislatures past have refused to fix it. Our new legislature and our new Governor must act to rid our state of the shame of threatening the innocent with execution and the guilty with unfairness.

In the days ahead, I will pray that we can open our hearts and provide something for victims' families other than the hope of revenge. Lincoln once said: "I have always found that mercy bears richer fruits than strict justice." I can only hope that will be so. God bless you. And God bless the people of Illinois.

Source: Web site of the Oklahoma Coalition to Abolish the Death Penalty, at www.ocadp.org/educate/ryan_speech_commutations.htm (accessed May 13, 2009).

Document 5.7
The Justices Debate Kansas Death Penalty Statute, April 25, 2006

On April 25, 2006, the Supreme Court heard oral argument in the case of Kansas v. Marsh, *which focused on a provision in the state's capital sentencing law that mandated death if the jury found aggravating and mitigating circumstances to be equally balanced. The following colloquy took place between Kansas attorney general Phill Kline, defending the law, and Justices John Paul Stevens, David Souter, and Antonin Scalia. By a 5–4 vote the Court later upheld the statute.*

. . . JUSTICE STEVENS: May I just ask—. . .—this question and kind of cut through—is it a correct interpretation of the instructions, as a whole, to say, in effect, "If you find the aggravating and mitigating circumstances are equally balanced, you shall impose the death sentence"?

MR. KLINE: If a juror finds—that is correct, Justice Stevens—if the juror's decided conclusion and reasoned moral judgment is that the mitigating factors and the aggravating factors are in balance, and find that beyond a reasonable doubt, instruction number 10 clearly indicates that death is the appropriate sentence. So, it—

JUSTICE SOUTER: The difficulty I have is in the phrase that you have mentioned in the course of your argument a couple of times referring to the "reasoned moral response." And the difficulty I have in squaring "reasoned moral response" with the construction that the Kansas Court and we all agree is the proper construction of the–of the–of the equipoise kind of provision, is this. Kansas has a right, as I understand it, to define what it regards as the aggravating circumstances, those that support a death verdict. And Kansas has done so. Kansas is also saying that if a jury cannot find that the aggravators, as we've defined them, outweigh the mitigators—i.e., if the jury is in equipoise—the result must be death, anyway. And that does not seem to be a reasoned moral response. I'm assuming that a reasoned moral response would be: the death penalty should be imposed because the aggravators do outweigh—i.e., it's not equipoise—the aggravators are heavier. And because Kansas is saying, "Even though they're not, death is the result, anyway," it doesn't seem like a reasoned moral response. What is your answer to that?

MR. KLINE: Justice Souter, of course the State believes that it is. It is, first of all, consistent with this Court's precedent as what is required—

JUSTICE SOUTER: Well, that's the issue.

MR. KLINE: And in the—in the Walton case, this Court found that a functionally identical provision in Arizona, even though the burden remained on the defendant, was appropriate after the State had met the requirements of guided discretion, as well as the individualized sentencing requirement, in setting about a—proving that, "This defendant is more deserving of death than anybody else convicted of the same crime."

JUSTICE SOUTER: But here we have, it seems to me, to be a stark finding that it has not been proven. That is what "equipoise" means. If aggravators are the basis for a death sentence, the equipoise finding is, "Aggravators don't predominate. We cannot make that conclusion. We're right on the fence." And it seems to me that to call that a reasoned moral response—"We're on the fence, but execute anyway"—seems a total inconsistency.

MR. KLINE: The State maintains, Justice Souter, that the decision that the mitigating factors do not outweigh the aggravating factors is a decision, and it is a—

JUSTICE SOUTER: But it's a decision that says, "We don't know what should be done." If aggravators define the basis for execution, and mitigators define the basis for life, the equipoise verdict says, in so many words, "We don't know which is more important." And Kansas says, when the jury comes back and says, "We don't know," that the result should be death. And that is what seems to be inconsistent with the notion of a reasoned moral response.

MR. KLINE: The distinction, Justice Souter, that I believe, from your analogy, is that the Kansas Legislature has said they do know, and that death is appropriate once a defendant has been found guilty of capital murder, in a very narrow definition. And then, once the—

JUSTICE SCALIA: It seems to be it sounds different if you put it differently. Surely, it's a reasoned moral response to say, "We have found these horrible aggravating factors in this murder. It's not even your usual murder. There are these terrible aggravating factors. Three of them, we found. And we further find that there is no mitigating evidence to outweigh those aggravating factors." That seems to me a perfectly valid moral response.

MR. KLINE: That is correct, Justice Scalia.

JUSTICE SOUTER: But that is not our case, is it? Because our case is not, "We don't find that the mitigators outweigh." Our case is, "We find the mitigators are of equal weight." That's why you get to equipoise. It's not a question of the failure of mitigators to predominate.

JUSTICE SCALIA: No.

JUSTICE SOUTER: It is the sufficiency of mitigators to equal in weight. And that's what poses the problem, it seems to me.

JUSTICE SCALIA: But it seems to me that to be equal in weight is not to predominate. And that's all the jury is saying—

MR. KLINE: I would agree, Justice Scalia—

JUSTICE SCALIA:—if there's nothing to outweigh the aggravating factors.

JUSTICE SOUTER: Of course it is not to predominate, but it is something more precise than merely not predominating. It is a fact, in effect, that you don't know, if all you know is that they don't predominate. The fact that you know, here, is that they equal and—. . .

Source: Supreme Court of the United States, Oral Argument, *Kansas, Petitioner, v. Michael Lee Marsh, III,* April 25, 2006, 7–12. Available at www.supremecourtus.gov/oral_arguments/argument_transcripts/04–1170b.pdf (accessed May 13, 2009).

Document 5.8
The Supreme Court Upholds the Constitutionality of Lethal Injection in *Baze v. Rees,* April 16, 2008

The following are excerpts from the Supreme Court's decision in Baze v. Rees, *which sustained Kentucky's method of lethal injection against claims that it constituted cruel and unusual punishment prohibited by the Eighth Amendment. Chief Justice John Roberts, joined by Justices Anthony Kennedy and Samuel Alito, announced the judgment of the Court, concluding that Kentucky's lethal injection protocol satisfies the Eighth Amendment. Justices John Paul Stevens and Antonin Scalia also offered opinions concurring in the judgment of the Court.*

CHIEF JUSTICE ROBERTS announced the judgment of the Court and delivered an opinion, in which JUSTICE KENNEDY and JUSTICE ALITO join. . . .

Petitioners in this case—each convicted of double homicide—acknowledge that the lethal injection procedure, if applied as intended, will result in a humane death. They nevertheless contend that the lethal injection protocol is unconstitutional under the Eighth Amendment's ban on "cruel and unusual punishments," because of the risk that the protocol's terms might not be properly followed, resulting in significant pain. They propose an alternative protocol, one that they concede has not been adopted by any State and has never been tried.

. . . We too agree that petitioners have not carried their burden of showing that the risk of pain from maladministration of a concededly humane lethal injection protocol, and the failure to adopt untried and untested alternatives, constitute cruel and unusual punishment. The judgment below is affirmed.

. . . We begin with the principle, settled by *Gregg* [*v. Georgia*], that capital punishment is constitutional. It necessarily follows that there must be a means of carrying it out. Some risk of pain is inherent in any method of execution—no matter how humane—if only from the prospect of error in following the required procedure. It is clear, then, that the Constitution does not demand the avoidance of all risk of pain in carrying out executions. . . .

This Court has never invalidated a State's chosen procedure for carrying out a sentence of death as the infliction of cruel and unusual punishment. . . .

. . . [W]e observed that "[p]unishments are cruel when they involve torture or a lingering death; but the punishment of death is not cruel within the meaning of that word as used in the Constitution. It implies there something inhumane and barbarous, something more than the mere extinguishing of life." . . .

Permitting an Eighth Amendment violation to be established on such a showing would threaten to transform courts into boards of inquiry charged with determining "best practices" for executions, with each ruling supplanted by another round of litigation touting a new and improved methodology. Such an approach finds no support in our cases, would embroil the courts in ongoing scientific controversies beyond their expertise, and would substantially intrude on the role of state legislatures in implementing their execution procedures—a role that by all accounts the States have fulfilled with an earnest desire to provide for progressively more humane manner of death. . . .

. . . We agree with the state trial court and the State Supreme Court, however, that petitioners have not shown that the risk of an inadequate dose of the first drug is substantial. And we reject the argument that the Eighth Amendment requires Kentucky to adopt the untested alternative procedures petitioners have identified. . . .

A [future] stay of execution may not be granted on grounds such as those asserted here unless the condemned prisoner establishes that the State's lethal injection protocol creates a demonstrated risk of severe pain. He must show that the risk is substantial when compared to the known and available alternatives. A State with a lethal injection protocol substantially similar to the protocol we uphold today would not create a risk that meets this standard. . . .

JUSTICE STEVENS, concurring in the judgment. . . .

In *Gregg v. Georgia*, we explained that unless a criminal sanction serves a legitimate penological function, it constitutes "gratuitous infliction of suffering" in violation of the Eighth Amendment. We then identified three societal purposes for death as a sanction: incapacitation, deterrence, and retribution. In the past three decades, however, each of these rationales has been called into question. . . .

We are left, then, with retribution as the primary rationale for imposing the death penalty. And indeed, it is the retribution rationale that animates much of the remaining enthusiasm for the death penalty. . . .

. . . The time for a dispassionate, impartial comparison of the enormous costs that death penalty litigation impose on society with the benefits that it produces has surely arrived. . . .

In sum, just as Justice [Byron] White ultimately based his conclusion in *Furman* on his extensive exposure to countless cases for which death is the authorized penalty, I have relied on my own experience in reaching the conclusion that the imposition of the death penalty represents "the pointless and needless extinction of life with only marginal contributions to any discernable social or public purposes. A penalty with such negligible returns to the State [is] patently excessive and cruel and unusual punishment violative of the Eighth Amendment. . . .

JUSTICE SCALIA, with whom JUSTICE THOMAS joins, concurring in the judgment. . . .

This [JUSTICE STEVENS'] conclusion is insupportable as an interpretation of the Constitution, which generally leaves it to democratically elected legislatures rather than courts to decide what makes significant contribution to social or public purposes. Besides that more general proposition, the very text of the document recognizes that the death penalty is a permissible legislative choice. The

Fifth Amendment expressly requires a presentment or indictment of a grand jury to hold a person to answer for "a capital, or otherwise infamous crime," and prohibits deprivation of "life" without due process of law. . . . The same Congress that proposed the Eighth Amendment also enacted the Act of April 30, 1790, which made several offenses punishable by death. . . .

*****

I take no position on the desirability of the death penalty, except to say that its value is eminently debatable and the subject of deeply, indeed passionately, held views—which means, to me, that it is preeminently not a matter to be resolved here. And especially not when it is explicitly permitted by the Constitution.

Source: Baze v. Rees, 553 U.S. _____ (2008).

Document 5.9
New Jersey Commission Recommends Abolition of Death Penalty, January 2, 2007

In January 2006 the New Jersey legislature authorized the creation of a Death Penalty Study Commission. The thirteen members of the commission were tasked with studying all aspects of the death penalty as then administered in the state and to report their findings and any proposed legislation back to the legislature and the governor prior to November 2006. The commission issued its report in January 2007, recommending abolition of the death penalty. Following are the report's executive summary, findings, and recommendations.

Executive Summary

The New Jersey Death Penalty Study Commission was created by P.L.2005, c.321. The enactment directed the Commission to study all aspects of the death penalty as currently administered in New Jersey and to report its findings and recommendations, including any recommended legislation, to the Legislature and the Governor. The enactment also directed the Commission to study seven specific issues. The Commission's findings and recommendations are set out below.

Findings

(1) There is no compelling evidence that the New Jersey death penalty rationally serves a legitimate penological intent.

(2) The costs of the death penalty are greater than the costs of life in prison without parole, but it is not possible to measure these costs with any degree of precision.

(3) There is increasing evidence that the death penalty is inconsistent with evolving standards of decency.

(4) The available data do not support a finding of invidious racial bias in the application of the death penalty in New Jersey.

(5) Abolition of the death penalty will eliminate the risk of disproportionality in capital sentencing.

(6) The penological interest in executing a small number of persons guilty of murder is not sufficiently compelling to justify the risk of making an irreversible mistake.

(7) The alternative of life imprisonment in a maximum security institution without the possibility of parole would sufficiently ensure public safety and address other legitimate social and penological interests, including the interests of the families of murder victims.

(8) Sufficient funds should be dedicated to ensure adequate services and advocacy for the families of murder victims.

Recommendations

The Commission recommends that the death penalty in New Jersey be abolished and replaced with life imprisonment without the possibility of parole, to be served in a maximum security facility. The Commission also recommends that any cost savings resulting from the abolition of the death penalty be used for benefits and services for survivors of victims of homicide.

Source: New Jersey Death Penalty Study Commission, "New Jersey Death Penalty Study Commission Report," January 2, 2007. Available at www.njleg.state.nj.us/committees/dpsc_final.pdf (accessed May 13, 2009).

Document 5.10
New Jersey Governor Jon Corzine on the State's Repeal of the Death Penalty, December 17, 2007

On December 17, 2007, New Jersey became the first state since 1976 to end capital punishment when Gov. Jon Corzine signed legislation that shut down the state's execution chamber. Corzine commuted the sentences of those on death row to life imprisonment.

Good morning everyone.

Thank you all for being here. Today, December 17th 2007, is a momentous day—a day of progress—for the State of New Jersey and for the millions of people across our nation and around the globe who reject the death penalty as a moral or practical response to the grievous, even heinous, crime of murder.

Today, through my signature on this bill, New Jersey abolishes the death penalty as a policy of our state.

For the people of New Jersey, I sign this legislation with pride.

I want to thank so many of those who join us today for their thoughtfulness and courage in making today a reality.

First let me cite the Death Penalty Study Commission, chaired by Reverend Bill Howard, pastor of Bethany Baptist Church in Newark, a group that was made up of a diverse set of individuals representative of prosecutors, law-enforcement, victims, religious groups and others.

Let me just note, five of the Commissioners were directly impacted by the violence of murder in their families, directly.

The state legislature showed courageous leadership. I must say, incredible leadership not just by Senator Lesniak and Senator Martin, the sponsors or Assemblyman Caraballo, or Assemblyman Bateman, the leaders Roberts & Codey—but for all those that voted yes.

This is one of those conscience votes that individuals must actually weigh and balance their own sense of morality and I am very, very grateful to all of you. A number of you are here today who voted yes, Senator Gil, Senator Turner. I look forward to joining with all of you as I sign this bill.

It should be noted that because of the action of the legislature, this is the first state to legislatively end the death penalty since the U.S. Supreme Court reauthorized capital punishment in 1976.

I also want to thank advocacy groups, particularly New Jerseyans for Alternatives to the Death Penalty, which have created a fundamental grass roots groundswell that put pressure on those of us in public service to stand up and do the right thing. The New Jersey Catholic Conference, the ACLU and there are many other groups that joined in this process and I am eternally grateful.

I also want to recognize that other good people will describe today's actions in quite different terms—in terms of injustice—particularly for those who carry heavy hearts, broken hearts from their tragic losses.

While no one can imagine their pain, I will sign this law abolishing the death penalty because I and a bipartisan majority of our legislature—and I congratulate Senator Bateman and Senator Martin in particular for their leadership on this—believe a nonviolent sentence of life in prison without parole best captures our State's highest values and reflects our best efforts to search for true justice, rather than state-endorsed killing.

As Reverend King implored all mankind while accepting his Nobel Peace Prize—"Man must evolve, for all human conflict, a method of resolution which rejects revenge, aggression and retaliation."

Today, New Jersey is truly evolving.

We evolve, if you believe as I do, that government cannot provide a foolproof death penalty that precludes the possibility of executing the innocent.

Society must ask—Is it not morally superior to imprison 100 people for life than it is to execute all 100 when it is probable we execute an innocent?

We evolve, if you believe as I do, that because New Jersey has not executed anyone in 44 years, there is little collective will or appetite for our community to enforce this law and therefore the law has little deterrence value.

That is, if you ever accepted there was a deterrent value.

We evolve, if you believe as I do, that the loved ones of victims may be more deeply hurt by long delays and endless appeals than they would be if there were certainty of life in prison with no possibility of parole.

Our debate has brought forth victims' voices on both sides of this perspective.

We evolve, if you believe as I do, it is economic folly to expend more State resources on legal processes in an attempt to execute an inmate than keeping a criminal incarcerated for life.

It is estimated that it cost the State of New Jersey more than a quarter-billion dollars, above and beyond incarceration, to pursue the death penalty since it was reinstated in 1982—a significant sum that could have effectively be used in supporting and compensating victims' families.

Finally, we evolve, if you believe as I do, that it is difficult, if not impossible, to devise a humane technique of execution—one that is not cruel and unusual.

These are all thoughtful and logical arguments, and there are others, to abolish the death penalty—the Commission and the legislature gave weight to these arguments—but for me, the question is more fundamental.

I believe society must first determine if its endorsement of violence begets violence—and—if violence undermines our commitment to the sanctity of life.

To these questions, I answer "Yes," and therefore I believe we must evolve to ending that endorsement.

Now, make no mistake: by this action, society is not forgiving these heinous crimes or acts that have caused immeasurable pain to the families and brought fear to society.

The perpetrators of these actions deserve absolutely no sympathy and the criminals deserve the strictest punishment that can be imposed without imposing death.

That punishment is life in prison without parole.

The only exception, of course, is the determination that a convicted felon is in fact innocent beyond the shadow of a doubt.

Let me repeat: this bill does not forgive or in any way condone the unfathomable acts carried out by the eight men now on New Jersey's death row.

They will spend the rest of their lives in jail.

And to that end, last night, I signed an order commuting to life without parole the death sentences of the eight persons currently on death row.

This commutation action provides legal certainty that these individuals will never again walk free in our society.

These commutations, along with today's bill signing, brings to a close in New Jersey the protracted moral and practical debate on the death penalty.

Our collective decision is one for which we can be proud.

Thank you.

Source: New Jersey Office of the Governor, "Remarks—Elimination of the Death Penalty," December 17, 2007. Available at www.state.nj.us/governor/news/speeches/elimination_death_penalty.html (accessed May 13, 2009).

Document 5.11
New Mexico Abolishes the Death Penalty, March 18, 2009
On March 18, 2009, the state of New Mexico repealed the death penalty. The law, championed by Democratic state representative Gail Chasey, replaced capital punishment with life imprisonment without the possibility of parole. New Mexico was the second state to ban executions since the Supreme Court approved new capital punishment laws in 1976.

AN ACT

RELATING TO CAPITAL FELONY SENTENCING; ABOLISHING THE DEATH PENALTY; PROVIDING FOR LIFE IMPRISONMENT WITHOUT POSSIBILITY OF RELEASE OR PAROLE.

BE IT ENACTED BY THE LEGISLATURE OF THE STATE OF NEW MEXICO:

Section 1. Section 31–18–14 NMSA 1978 (being Laws 1979, Chapter 150, Section 1, as amended) is amended to read:

"31–18–14. SENTENCING AUTHORITY—CAPITAL FELONIES.—When a defendant has been convicted of a capital felony, the defendant shall be sentenced to life imprisonment or life imprisonment without possibility of release or parole."

Section 2. Section 31–18–23 NMSA 1978 (being Laws 1994, Chapter 24, Section 2, as amended) is amended to read:

"31–18–23. THREE VIOLENT FELONY CONVICTIONS—MANDATORY LIFE IMPRISONMENT—EXCEPTION.—

A. When a defendant is convicted of a third violent felony, and each violent felony conviction is part of a separate transaction or occurrence, and at least the third violent felony conviction is in New Mexico, the defendant shall, in addition to the sentence imposed for the third violent conviction, be punished by a sentence of life imprisonment. The life imprisonment sentence shall be subject to parole pursuant to the provisions of Section 31–21–10 NMSA 1978.

B. The sentence of life imprisonment shall be imposed after a sentencing hearing, separate from the trial or guilty plea proceeding resulting in the third violent felony conviction, pursuant to the provisions of Section 31–18–24 NMSA 1978.

C. For the purpose of this section, a violent felony conviction incurred by a defendant before the defendant reaches the age of eighteen shall not count as a violent felony conviction.

D. When a defendant has a felony conviction from another state, the felony conviction shall be considered a violent felony for the purposes of the Criminal Sentencing Act if that crime would be considered a violent felony in New Mexico.

E. As used in the Criminal Sentencing Act:

(1) "great bodily harm" means an injury to the person that creates a high probability of death or that causes serious disfigurement or that results in permanent loss or impairment of the function of any member or organ of the body; and

(2) "violent felony" means:

(a) murder in the first or second degree, as provided in Section 30–2–1 NMSA 1978;

(b) shooting at or from a motor vehicle resulting in great bodily harm, as provided in Subsection B of Section 30–3–8 NMSA 1978;

(c) kidnapping resulting in great bodily harm inflicted upon the victim by the victim's captor, as provided in Subsection B of Section 30–4–1 NMSA 1978;

(d) criminal sexual penetration, as provided in Subsection C or D or Paragraph (5) or (6) of Subsection E of Section 30–9–11 NMSA 1978; and

(e) robbery while armed with a deadly weapon resulting in great bodily harm as provided in Section 30–16–2 NMSA 1978 and Subsection A of Section 30–1–12 NMSA 1978."

Section 3. Section 31–20A-2 NMSA 1978 (being Laws 1979, Chapter 150, Section 3) is amended to read:

"31–20A-2. CAPITAL FELONY—DETERMINATION OF SENTENCE.—

If a jury finds, beyond a reasonable doubt, that one or more aggravating circumstances exist, as enumerated in Section 31–20A-5 NMSA 1978, the defendant shall be sentenced to life imprisonment without possibility of release or parole.

If the jury does not make the finding that one or more aggravating circumstances exist, the defendant shall be sentenced to life imprisonment."

Section 4. Section 31–21–10 NMSA 1978 (being Laws 1980, Chapter 28, Section 1, as amended) is amended to read:

"31–21–10. PAROLE AUTHORITY AND PROCEDURE.—

A. An inmate of an institution who was sentenced to life imprisonment becomes eligible for a parole hearing after the inmate has served thirty years of the sentence. Before ordering the parole of an inmate sentenced to life imprisonment, the board shall:

(1) interview the inmate at the institution where the inmate is committed;

(2) consider all pertinent information concerning the inmate, including:

(a) the circumstances of the offense;

(b) mitigating and aggravating circumstances;

(c) whether a deadly weapon was used in the commission of the offense;

(d) whether the inmate is a habitual offender;

(e) the reports filed under Section 31–21–9 NMSA 1978; and

(f) the reports of such physical and mental examinations as have been made while in an institution;

(3) make a finding that a parole is in the best interest of society and the inmate; and

(4) make a finding that the inmate is able and willing to fulfill the obligations of a law-abiding citizen.

If parole is denied, the inmate sentenced to life imprisonment shall again become entitled to a parole hearing at two-year intervals. The board may, on its own motion, reopen any case in which a hearing has already been granted and parole denied.

B. Unless the board finds that it is in the best interest of society and the parolee to reduce the period of parole, a person who was sentenced to life imprisonment shall be required to undergo a minimum period of parole of five years. During the period of parole, the person shall be under the guidance and supervision of the board.

C. An inmate of an institution who was sentenced to life imprisonment without possibility of release or parole is not eligible for parole and shall remain incarcerated for the entirety of the inmate's natural life.

D. Except for certain sex offenders as provided in Section 31–21–10.1 NMSA 1978, an inmate who was convicted of a first, second or third degree felony and who has served the sentence of imprisonment imposed by the court in an institution designated by the corrections department shall be required to undergo a two-year period of parole. An inmate who was convicted of a fourth degree felony and who has served the sentence of imprisonment imposed by the court in an institution designated by the corrections department shall be required to undergo a one-year period of parole. During the period of parole, the person shall be under the guidance and supervision of the board.

E. Every person while on parole shall remain in the legal custody of the institution from which the person was released, but shall be subject to the orders of the board. The board shall furnish to each inmate as a prerequisite to release under its supervision a written statement of the conditions of parole that shall be accepted and agreed to by the inmate as evidenced by the inmate's signature affixed to a duplicate copy to be retained in the files of the board. The board shall also require as a prerequisite to release the submission and approval of a parole plan. If an inmate refuses to affix the inmate's signature to the written statement of the conditions of parole or does not have an approved parole plan, the inmate shall not be released and shall remain in the custody of the institution in which the inmate has served the inmate's sentence, excepting parole, until such time as the period of parole the inmate was required to serve, less meritorious deductions, if any, expires, at which time the inmate shall be released from that institution without parole, or until such time that the inmate evidences acceptance and agreement to the conditions of parole as required or receives approval for the inmate's parole plan or both. Time served from the date that an inmate refuses to accept and agree to the conditions of parole or fails to receive approval for the inmate's parole plan shall reduce the period, if any, to be served under parole at a later date. If the district court has ordered that the inmate make restitution to a victim as provided in Section 31–17–1 NMSA 1978, the board shall include restitution as a condition of parole. The board shall also personally apprise the inmate of the conditions of parole and the inmate's duties relating thereto.

F. When a person on parole has performed the obligations of the person's release for the period of parole provided in this section, the board shall make a final order of discharge and issue the person a certificate of discharge.

G. Pursuant to the provisions of Section 31–18–15 NMSA 1978, the board shall require the inmate as a condition of parole:

(1) to pay the actual costs of parole services to the adult probation and parole division of the corrections department for deposit to the corrections department intensive supervision fund not exceeding one thousand eight hundred dollars ($1,800) annually to be paid in monthly installments of not less than twenty-five dollars ($25.00) and not more than one hundred fifty dollars ($150), as set by the appropriate district supervisor of the adult probation and parole division, based upon the financial circumstances of the defendant. The defendant's payment of the supervised parole costs shall not be waived unless the board holds an evidentiary hearing and finds that the defendant is unable to pay the costs. If the board waives the defendant's payment of the supervised parole costs and the defendant's financial circumstances subsequently change so that the defendant is able to pay the costs, the appropriate district supervisor of the adult probation and parole division shall advise the board and the board shall hold an evidentiary hearing to determine whether the waiver should be rescinded; and

(2) to reimburse a law enforcement agency or local crime stopper program for the amount of any reward paid by the agency or program for information leading to the inmate's arrest, prosecution or conviction.

H. The provisions of this section shall apply to all inmates except geriatric, permanently incapacitated and terminally ill inmates eligible for the medical and geriatric parole program as provided by the Parole Board Act."

Section 5. REPEAL.—Sections 31–14–1 through 31–14–16, Section 31–18–14.1, Section 31–20A-1, Sections 31–20A-2.1 through 31–20A-4 and Section 31–20A-6 NMSA 1978 (being Laws 1929, Chapter 69, Sections 1 through 10, Laws 1955, Chapter 127, Section 1, Laws 1979, Chapter 150, Section 9, Laws 1955, Chapter 127, Sections 3 and 4, Laws 1929, Chapter 69, Sections 12 and 13, Laws 2001, Chapter 128, Section 1, Laws 1979, Chapter 150, Section 2, Laws 1991, Chapter 30, Section 1 and Laws 1979, Chapter 150, Sections 4, 5 and 7, as amended) are repealed.

Section 6. APPLICABILITY.—The provisions of this act apply to crimes committed on or after July 1, 2009.

Section 7. EFFECTIVE DATE.—The effective date of the provisions of this act is July 1, 2009.

Source: New Mexico Legislature, "An Act Relating to Capital Felony Sentencing; Abolishing the Death Penalty; Providing for Life Imprisonment Without Possibility of Release or Parole," March 18, 2009. Available at www.nmlegis.gov/Sessions/09%20Regular/final/HB0285.pdf (accessed May 13, 2009).

Document 5.12
New Mexico Governor Bill Richardson Signs Repeal of the Death Penalty, March 18, 2009

On March 18, 2009, New Mexico governor Bill Richardson signed into law the repeal of the state's death penalty statute, making New Mexico the second state to ban executions since the Supreme Court approved new capital punishment laws in 1976. In his signatory statement, Governor Richardson outlined his own feelings about the death penalty and noted the "long, personal journey" he had experienced. Despite having supported capital punishment for most of his life, Richardson's time serving as governor altered his views by bringing to light key flaws in the criminal justice system that he felt warranted this action.

SANTA FE—Governor Bill Richardson today signed House Bill 285, Repeal of the Death Penalty. The Governor's remarks follow:

Today marks the end of a long, personal journey for me and the issue of the death penalty.

Throughout my adult life, I have been a firm believer in the death penalty as a just punishment—in very rare instances, and only for the most heinous crimes. I still believe that.

But six years ago, when I took office as Governor of the State of New Mexico, I started to challenge my own thinking on the death penalty.

The issue became more real to me because I knew the day would come when one of two things might happen: I would either have to take action on legislation to repeal the death penalty, or more daunting, I might have to sign someone's death warrant.

I'll be honest. The prospect of either decision was extremely troubling. But I was elected by the people of New Mexico to make just this type of decision.

So, like many of the supporters who took the time to meet with me this week, I have believed the death penalty can serve as a deterrent to some who might consider murdering a law enforcement officer, a corrections officer, a witness to a crime or kidnapping and murdering a child. However, people continue to commit terrible crimes even in the face of the death penalty and responsible people on both sides of the debate disagree—strongly—on this issue.

But what we cannot disagree on is the finality of this ultimate punishment. Once a conclusive decision has been made and executed, it cannot be reversed. And it is in consideration of this, that I have made my decision.

I have decided to sign legislation that repeals the death penalty in the state of New Mexico.

Regardless of my personal opinion about the death penalty, I do not have confidence in the criminal justice system as it currently operates to be the final arbiter when it comes to who lives and who dies for their crime. If the State is going to undertake this awesome responsibility, the system to impose this ultimate penalty must be perfect and can never be wrong.

But the reality is the system is not perfect—far from it. The system is inherently defective. DNA testing has proven that. Innocent people have been put on death row all across the country.

Even with advances in DNA and other forensic evidence technologies, we can't be 100-percent sure that only the truly guilty are convicted of capital crimes. Evidence, including DNA evidence, can be manipulated. Prosecutors can still abuse their powers. We cannot ensure competent defense counsel for all defendants. The sad truth is the wrong person can still be convicted in this day and age, and in cases where that conviction carries with it the ultimate sanction, we must have ultimate confidence—I would say certitude—that the system is without flaw or prejudice. Unfortunately, this is demonstrably not the case.

And it bothers me greatly that minorities are overrepresented in the prison population and on death row.

I have to say that all of the law enforcement officers, and especially the parents and spouses of murder victims, made compelling arguments to keep the death penalty. I respect their opinions and have taken their experiences to heart—which is why I struggled—even today—before making my final decision.

Yes, the death penalty is a tool for law enforcement. But it's not the only tool. For some would-be criminals, the death penalty may be a deterrent. But it's not, and never will be, for many, many others.

While today's focus will be on the repeal of the death penalty, I want to make clear that this bill I'm signing actually makes New Mexico safer. With my signature, we now have the option of sentencing the worst criminals to life in prison without the possibility of parole. They will never get out of prison.

Faced with the reality that our system for imposing the death penalty can never be perfect, my conscience compels me to replace the death penalty with a solution that keeps society safe.

The bill I am signing today, which was courageously carried for so many years by Representative Gail Chasey, replaces the death penalty with true life without the possibility of parole—a sentence that ensures violent criminals are locked away from society forever, yet can be undone if an innocent person is wrongfully convicted. More than 130 death row inmates have been exonerated in the past 10 years in this country, including four New Mexicans—a fact I cannot ignore.

From an international human rights perspective, there is no reason the United States should be behind the rest of the world on this issue. Many of the countries that continue to support and use the death penalty are also the most repressive nations in the world. That's not something to be proud of.

In a society which values individual life and liberty above all else, where justice and not vengeance is the singular guiding principle of our system of criminal law, the potential for wrongful conviction and, God forbid, execution of an innocent person stands as anathema to our very sensibilities as human beings. That is why I'm signing this bill into law.

Source: Office of New Mexico Governor Bill Richardson, "Governor Bill Richardson Signs Repeal of the Death Penalty," March 18, 2009. Available at www.governor.state.nm.us/press/2009/march/031809_02.pdf (accessed May 13, 2009).

Document 5.13
Nebraska Supreme Court Declares Electric Chair Cruel and Unusual Punishment, February 8, 2008

By 2008 Nebraska remained the only state that still employed the electric chair as the sole method of putting the condemned to death. In February of that year, the Supreme Court of Nebraska in Nebraska v. Mata *affirmed the conviction and death sentence of Raymond Mata Jr.; at the same time, it declared use of the electric chair unconstitutional cruel and unusual punishment under the state constitution. In effect, state officials were prohibited from continuing to use that method of execution. Nebraska's legislature responded by adopting a new death penalty law providing for lethal injection.*

OPINION BY: CONNOLLY
    CONSTITUTIONALITY OF ELECTROCUTION

Mata contends that the district court erred in failing to find that death by electrocution unconstitutionally imposes cruel and unusual punishment. The State, however, contends that Mata has failed to carry his burden of proof that electrocution is cruel and unusual punishment. It further contends no precedent exists to support Mata's position because neither this court nor the U.S. Supreme Court has ever held that a method of inflicting death is unconstitutional.

We pause to clarify what this case is not about. Mata does not argue that the death penalty in any form violates the U.S. and Nebraska Constitutions, nor could he. "[T]he death penalty, when properly imposed by a state, does not violate either the eighth or [the] fourteenth amendment [to] the United States Constitution or the Nebraska constitution." So the issue before us is not whether Mata will be executed, but only whether the current statutory method of execution is constitutional.

We have affirmed Mata's conviction and death sentence; we have affirmed the jury's finding that his crime was exceptionally depraved; and we have determined that the imposition of the death sentence in this case is proportional to that in the same or similar circumstances. But this court's finding that Mata's crime was heinous does not negate our duty to safeguard our state Constitution.

Obviously, all capital offenses involve heinous crimes. The people of Nebraska, through the Legislature, have determined that in some circumstances, the State may impose the death penalty. And we may not interfere unless the State's procedures in executing the prisoner violate constitutional requirements.

We limit our analysis to whether the State may constitutionally execute a sentence of death by electrocution. We must decide whether electrocution is prohibited by the Nebraska Constitution's proscription against inflicting cruel and unusual punishment. That determination, however, does not affect Mata's sentence of death.

(a) Nebraska Constitution Governs the Issue

It is correct that we have held that electrocution does not constitute cruel and unusual punishment within the meaning of the U.S. or Nebraska Constitution. But we have not previously had the opportunity to review a factual record showing electrocution's physiological effects on a prisoner, nor have we relied on any case in which such evidence was reviewed. Instead, we have relied on U.S. Supreme Court decisions. As explained below, those cases contain factual assumptions that some of the Court's more recent cases have called into question.

At the trial level, Mata moved for a declaration that electrocution is cruel and unusual punishment under both the federal and state Constitutions. The issue was developed and tried as a challenge under both Constitutions. Although in his brief, Mata assigned that electrocution violates the U.S. Constitution, he did not specifically cite to the Nebraska Constitution's prohibition against cruel and unusual punishment. Under our court rules, this oversight could preclude us from considering the state constitutional issue. However, because of the death penalty's severity and irrevocability, we have not strictly enforced briefing rules on capital defendants.

Moreover, we conclude that the Nebraska Constitution governs this issue. We have already decided that we have a constitutional responsibility to determine whether electrocution is lawful. We stayed the execution of Carey Dean Moore, another death row inmate, pending the outcome of that determination. Also, three other cases on our docket have raised the constitutionality of electrocution under the Nebraska Constitution. We conclude that it is imperative for this court to resolve this issue. In fulfilling our responsibility and in the interest of judicial economy, we excuse the technical omission in Mata's brief.

The Nebraska Constitution . . . mirrors the U.S. Constitution's Eighth Amendment: "Excessive bail shall not be required, nor excessive fines imposed, nor cruel and unusual punishment inflicted." Obviously, we cannot, under the U.S. Constitution, declare that electrocution violates its cruel and unusual punishment provision because the U.S. Supreme Court has held otherwise. And we have stated that the Nebraska Constitution's cruel and unusual punishment provision "does not require more than does the [Eighth Amendment to the] U.S. Constitution." But as we will explain, we now believe this issue should be resolved by this court.

Like this court, the U.S. Supreme Court has never reviewed objective evidence regarding electrocution's constitutionality. The Supreme Court based its holdings on state courts' factual assumptions, which, in turn, relied on untested science from 1890. Because we conclude that we can no longer rely on those factual assumptions and because no other state imposes electrocution as its sole method of execution, we will decide the issue under the Nebraska Constitution.

(i) Early U.S. Supreme Court Decisions on Electrocution

In 1890, in *In re Kemmler,* the U.S. Supreme Court decided the State of New York could proceed with the first execution by electrocution. . . . William Kemmler, the first prisoner scheduled to die by electrocution, challenged the method as cruel and unusual punishment. He alleged electrocution violated his right to due process under both the state and federal Constitutions.

On appeal, the U.S. Supreme Court said that cruel and unusual punishment could not be defined with precision. It stated, however, that certain types of punishment clearly fell within the Eighth Amendment's prohibition: "Punishments are cruel when they involve torture or a lingering death; but the punishment of death is not cruel, within the meaning of that word as used in the Constitution. It implies there [is] something inhuman and barbarous, something more than the mere extinguishment of life."

Over the last 118 years, the *In re Kemmler* standard has remained the baseline criterion under the Eighth Amendment for evaluating a method of execution. The Court did not, however, apply this standard in *In re Kemmler* to New York's newly enacted method, nor did it independently review the evidence regarding electrocution. Instead, it held that the 8th Amendment's protections were not applicable to state actions through the 14th Amendment: "The decision of the state courts sustaining the validity of [electrocution] under the state constitution is not re[e]xaminable here. . . ." The Court limited the 14th Amendment's protections to the prohibition of "arbitrary deprivation of life, liberty, or property," and "equal protection to all under like circumstances." Under that standard, it concluded the state's new execution method did not violate the prisoner's federal due process rights.

Therefore, the Court did not decide the case under the Eighth Amendment, and there was scant evidence about electrocution in 1890. Yet, lower courts, including this court, have traveled the well-worn path of summarily rejecting claims that electrocution is cruel and unusual punishment. Courts have "typically [relied] on the strength of th[e] Court's opinion in *In re Kemmler.*"

In *Francis v. Resweber,* a 1946 case challenging electrocution, eight justices assumed without deciding that a violation of the 8th Amendment would violate a prisoner's due process rights under the 14th Amendment. The issue was whether Louisiana could conduct a second electrocution after the prisoner's first electrocution failed to result in death—not whether electrocution was inherently cruel or unusual.

Our review of these early cases illustrates that the U.S. Supreme Court's case law on electrocution relies on unexamined factual assumptions about an electric current's physiological effects on a human. This obvious omission in the Court's jurisprudence results from three factors: (1) the Court's limited knowledge about an electrocution's effect on the human body, (2) the states' desire to find a more humane method of execution than hanging, and (3) the Court's view, when electrocution was first introduced, that the Eighth Amendment was not intended as a restraint on state legislatures' determinations of punishment. But that view has changed. The Supreme Court has specifically held that the Eighth Amendment is a restraint on legislative power to impose punishment. And it has held the 8th Amendment applies to the states through the 14th Amendment.

Yet since deciding *Resweber* in 1946, the U.S. Supreme Court has not addressed the constitutionality of any method of execution, and only indirectly in that case. We agree with Justice Souter that in light of modern knowledge about electrocution, the Court's decisions do not constitute a dispositive response to the issue.

(i) Substantial Risk That Prisoner Will Suffer Unnecessary and Wanton Pain

The baseline criterion in a challenge to a punishment is whether it imposes torture or a lingering death that is unnecessary to the mere extinguishment of life. "The traditional humanity of modern Anglo-American law forbids the infliction of unnecessary pain in the execution of the death sentence" and cruelty inherent in the execution method itself. "[T]he execution shall be so instantaneous and substantially painless that the punishment shall be reduced, as nearly as possible, to no more than that of death itself." Capital punishment "must not involve the unnecessary and wanton infliction of pain."

A single accident, however, does not show that a method of execution is inherently cruel. But a pattern of prisoners suffering unnecessary pain presents a different circumstance. A method of execution violates the prohibition against cruel and unusual punishment if there is a substantial foreseeable risk, inherent in the method, that a prisoner will suffer unnecessary pain.

The prohibition against cruel and unusual punishment is not a static concept and "must draw its meaning from the evolving standards of decency that mark the progress of a maturing society." A court must evaluate claims that punishment is cruel and unusual "in the light of contemporary human knowledge."

We decline to hold that under the Nebraska Constitution, evolving standards of decency apply only to claims of disproportional punishment. We conclude that evolving standards of decency must apply to claims that the State's intended method of execution inflicts unnecessary and wanton pain. To hold otherwise would not comport with the U.S. Supreme Court's consistent holdings since *Furman* that the death penalty is different, both in its severity and irrevocability. The constitutional prohibition against cruel and unusual punishment would be meaningless if the punishment would have to be rejected by every state before it could be cruel and unusual.

Responding to horror stories of "botched" electrocutions in Florida, some states selected lethal injection. It has been stated that courts have switched to lethal injection "because it is universally recognized as the most humane method of execution, least apt to cause unnecessary pain."

Faced with changing societal values, we cannot ignore Nebraska's status as the last state to retain electrocution as its sole method of execution. But this is not our only consideration. We must also consider whether electrocution comports with the "Eighth Amendment's protection of 'the dignity of man.'"

Scientific knowledge about electricity and its effects on the human body has vastly expanded since 1913, when the Nebraska Legislature first selected electrocution over hanging. "Time works changes, brings into existence new conditions and purposes." We presume that the Legislature intended to select an execution method within constitutional bounds. But we conclude that whether the Legislature intended to cause pain in selecting a punishment is irrelevant to a constitutional challenge that a statutorily imposed method of punishment violates the prohibition against cruel and unusual punishment.

In sum, we conclude that the relevant legal standards in deciding whether electrocution is cruel and unusual punishment are whether the State's chosen method of execution (1) presents a substantial risk that a prisoner will suffer unnecessary and wanton pain in an execution, (2) violates the evolving standards of decency that mark a mature society, and (3) minimizes physical violence and mutilation of the prisoner's body.

Whether a method of inflicting the death penalty inherently imposes a significant risk of causing pain in an execution is a question of fact. The ultimate issue, whether electrocution violates the constitutional prohibition against cruel and unusual punishment, presents a question of law.

(d) Parties' Contentions

Mata contends that his challenge to electrocution is not limited to the current protocol, which the Department of Correctional Services adopted in 2004. He argues that electrocution is cruel because it burns and mutilates the body and presents an unnecessary risk of pain. He also argues that electrocution no longer comports with evolving standards of decency because every state that authorizes the death penalty, except Nebraska, has rejected electrocution.

The State, of course, views the matter differently. The State contends that the district court concluded Mata failed to carry his burden of proof under the appropriate constitutional standard. That argument, however, relies upon a constitutional standard that we have rejected—a requirement that the prisoner show a legislative intent to cause pain and suffering. The State also argues that even if the prisoner remains conscious for 15 to 30 seconds, no basis exists for concluding that electrocution involves unnecessary pain. Finally, the State argues that it is "undisputed that electrocution can and does cause the instantaneous death of a condemned prisoner."

Although Mata contends that his challenge is directed at electrocution and not at the current protocol, an understanding of the current protocol is important because of its similarity to earlier electrocution procedures. We begin by explaining why the protocol was changed in 2004.

In 2000, the district court determined, in part, that [under] the State's 1994 electrocution protocol the current was not continuous. This order was part of the record ... that "[t]he mode of inflicting the punishment of death, in all cases, shall be by causing to pass through the body of the convicted person a current of electricity of sufficient intensity to cause death; and the application of such current shall be continued until such convicted person is dead." The 1994 protocol required prison officials to apply two 30-second sequences of electric current for a 155-pound person, with a 20-second pause in between shocks. In each sequence, the protocol called for officials to apply 2,450 volts for 8 seconds, followed by 480 volts for 22 seconds. In the 1990's, prison officials applied four sequences of current to electrocute three prisoners.

In response to the district court's order, prison officials changed the protocol in 2004. The new protocol is also standardized to a 155-pound person. But the new protocol requires prison officials to apply 2,450 volts of electric current in one 15-second continuous application.

The exact strength of the current is unknown. The protocol does not specify the amperage, which is the measure of electrical energy in a current. A retired prison administrator who developed the original protocol in the 1980's testified that he had an ammeter installed. He explained that he did this because the risk of fire from the sponges drying out increases if 8 to 10 amperes are applied for too long. He stated that the State uses 6 to 8 amperes and no more than 10. But the executing official for the 1990 electrocutions believed the ammeter simply showed the system was working within the correct range. He did not recall the amperage used or watch the voltage meter during the 1990 electrocutions. During electrocutions, prison officials do not record the amperage or voltage or use a regulator to ensure that the voltage does not drop below the required amount.

The strength of an electric current flowing through a conductor can be calculated if the voltage and a conductor's resistance to a current are known. But as the district court noted, experts do not agree on the human body's resistance as a conductor. Ronald K. Wright, M.D., the certified pathologist who recommended the State's 2004 protocol, testified that it would be unethical for physicians to make these determinations and that states do not measure the voltage exiting a prisoner's body during an electrocution. Because he had to rely on medical journals from the 1890's, he did not know whether a prisoner's size or height would affect the body's resistance. Because there has never been monitoring, the strength of the current flowing through a prisoner's body in Nebraska electrocutions is unknown. This evidence supports the district court's finding that the effect of electric current in a prisoner's body cannot be predicted. . . .

(f) Preparations for Electrocution

Before the execution, the prisoner's head and left leg are shaved where the electrodes will be placed. Both the State and defense experts agree that a high voltage electric current causes the body to violently react with muscle contractions. Shock victims have been known to suffer broken bones and dislocated joints from the force of these contractions. Consequently, officials must tightly strap the prisoner's torso, hips, arms, legs, ankles, and wrists to the electric chair. Witnesses observed prisoners slamming against these straps during an electrocution. Also, officials fasten the prisoner's head to the chair with a wide leather strap across the face, with a cutout for the nose.

After the prisoner is strapped in tightly, officials place a 3 1/4-inch circular electrode plate on the crown of the prisoner's head and a similar grounding electrode on the prisoner's left calf to create a circuit path through the body. They place larger natural sponges, which have been soaked in a saline solution, under each electrode next to the prisoner's skin. The saline ions form a bridge between the prisoner's body and the electrodes and are intended to keep the electricity from flowing outside the body. Electricity follows ions and will seek the path of least resistance. Wright testified that the sponge must be damp or the sponge and the prisoner may catch on fire.

(g) The Prisoner's Body is Burned

Burning of the prisoner's body is an inherent part of an electrocution. Wright testified that under the protocol he recommended, there would be burning and the possibility of severe skin burns in the last seconds of the 15-second application. He stated that the prisoner's skin could reach a temperature of 200 degrees. The protocol shows that the State expects burning and keeps a fire extinguisher close by.

During an electrocution, the executing official watches for smoke coming from the prisoner's head or leg. But the executing official for the three electrocutions performed in the 1990's testified that only smoke from the head would require interruption of the current, not smoke from the leg. Further, the protocol requires officials to interrupt the current only for extensive smoke; officials anticipate smoke equivalent to a burning cigar. If flames appear, the protocol requires officials to stop the current to check the sponges and tighten the electrodes.

Under the 1994 protocol used during the three 1990 electrocutions, witnesses testified that they saw smoke coming from the prisoner's leg and could smell burning flesh in the viewing room. A media witness of the 1997 electrocution reported seeing smoke coming from the prisoner's head also. A prison official testified that he had smelled a lingering odor of burning flesh in the death chamber after all three electrocutions. The coroner's reports showed that there were severe ring burns on the prisoners' heads where officials had attached the electrode plate. A witness also testified to viewing a prisoner's body after an electrocution. She reported sagging skin on the sides of the prisoner's head from the temple areas and cheeks to above and behind the ears.

The State concedes that burning is an inherent part of an electrocution but contends that it is localized. The district court, however, found that current density is highest at the electrodes and especially in the left leg. The left leg is where all of the current must pass to exit to the ground electrode. Third-degree burns and charring often appear at the head and left leg electrodes. Defense experts reviewing post mortem photographs of the prisoners concluded the electric current was causing severe burning and charring of the prisoners' left legs from the knee to the foot. In addition, the current vaporizes water in the skin causing severe steam burns and blistering, and leaving the skin in some areas separated and sagging following an electrocution. We disagree with the State's characterization of the burning as localized. The evidence shows that severe burning is also likely to be present under the 2004 protocol.

(h) 2004 Protocol Will Not Eliminate Risk of Prisoner Burning or Catching Fire

In 1994, prison officials changed the protocol to remove medical personnel from execution activities. Also, the 2004 protocol does not require a physician to be present. Under the 2004 protocol, after officials stop the current, they must wait 15 minutes before calling a coroner. The protocol, however, does not specify what officials should do if the coroner finds that a prisoner is still alive. But the warden testified that if a prisoner were alive after 18 minutes, an official would repeat the sequence. The executing official for the 1990 electrocutions also testified that if a prisoner were still alive, an official, after checking the equipment, would repeat the sequence.

Wright admitted that under the 2004 protocol, the sponge could be dry by the time a coroner arrives. He stated that the drying out of the sponge is one reason the current cannot be applied much longer than 15 seconds. He explained that the possibility of a fire is why officials must have a fire extinguisher close. So, by the time a coroner is called, 15 minutes after the current is stopped, if the prisoner is still alive, prison officials will need to replace the sponges before reapplying the current to avoid a fire from a dry sponge. But even if they do this, the risk remains that the prisoner's leg will burn at the exit point because the tissue will have already been deeply burned.

Nebraska used imported executioners to perform electrocutions from 1920 to 1959, and they employed different methods. For example, in 1959, the executioner applied 2,200 volts to the prisoner five separate times. In 1929, however, the State applied 2,300 volts for 19 seconds, which is a similar application to that of the 2004 protocol. Because physicians determined that the prisoner was still alive, officials applied the current again. Heavy brown smoke from the prisoner's burning leg filled the room. This shows the current protocol will continue the mutilation of prisoners' bodies. It also supports the district court's conclusion that some prisoners will be tortured during electrocutions.

(vi) Evidence Supports Court's Finding That Some Prisoners Will Experience Unnecessary Pain, Suffering, and Torture

This evidence substantially supports the district court's conclusion that electrocution "will result in unnecessary pain, suffering, and torture" for some condemned prisoners. Contrary to the State's argument, there is abundant evidence that prisoners sometimes will retain enough brain functioning to consciously suffer the torture high voltage electric current inflicts on a human body. The evidence also supports the district court's statement that the evidence shows one application of current will not always kill a prisoner. And sometimes, a prisoner will die more slowly from oxygen deprivation and damage to the body's vital organs. The State's expert admitted that a prisoner who can breathe could survive and regain more brain function, even assuming that the prisoner lost total consciousness during the application of the current. No one knows how long a prisoner could languish in agony, attempting to breathe, while the State passively waits to see if he or she dies.

We reject the State's argument that electrocution would not be cruel and unusual punishment if a prisoner remained conscious for 15 to 30 seconds. Fifteen to thirty seconds is not a blink in time when a human being is electrically on fire. We reject the State's argument that this is a permissible length of time to inflict gruesome pain. It is akin to arguing that burning a prisoner at the stake would be acceptable if we could be assured that smoke inhalation would render him unconscious within 15 to 30 seconds.

Given the evidence and the district court's finding thereon, we conclude that electrocution will unquestionably inflict intolerable pain unnecessary to cause death in enough executions so as to present a substantial risk that any prisoner will suffer unnecessary and wanton pain in a judicial execution by electrocution.

(j) Conclusion: Electrocution Is Cruel and Unusual Punishment

Besides presenting a substantial risk of unnecessary pain, we conclude that electrocution is unnecessarily cruel in its purposeless infliction of physical violence and mutilation of the prisoner's body. Electrocution's proven history of burning and charring bodies is inconsistent with both the concepts of evolving standards of decency and the dignity of man. Other states have recognized that early assumptions about an instantaneous and painless death were simply incorrect and that there are more humane methods of carrying out the death penalty. Examined under modern scientific knowledge, "[electrocution] has proven itself to be a dinosaur more befitting the laboratory of Baron Frankenstein than the death chamber" of state prisons. We conclude that death by electrocution violates the prohibition against cruel and unusual punishment in the Nebraska constitution.

(k) Resolution

Having concluded that electrocution is cruel and unusual punishment, we face the question of how to dispose of this appeal. The fact remains that although the Nebraska statutes currently provide no constitutionally acceptable means of executing Mata, he was properly convicted of first degree murder and sentenced to death in accord with Nebraska law. We have already affirmed his conviction. His sentence of death, although it cannot be implemented under current law, also remains valid.

Source: Nebraska v. Mata, 275 Neb. 1 (2008); 745 N.W.2d 229 (2008), at 3–108.

NOTES

1. *Gregg v. Georgia,* 428 U.S. 153 (1976).
2. For these statistics see www.deathpenaltyinfo.org/executions-year.
3. *Furman v. Georgia,* 408 U.S. 238 (1972).
4. Pub. L. No. 104–132, 110 Stat. 1214 (1996) (codified in scattered sections of 28 U.S.C.).
5. *Felker v. Turpin,* 518 U.S. 651 (1996).
6. *Atkins v. Virginia,* 536 U.S. 304 (2002), at 352–353. See also *Penry v. Lynaugh,* 492 U.S. 302 (1989).
7. *Blystone v. Pennsylvania,* 494 U.S. 299 (1990).
8. *Woodson v. North Carolina,* 428 U.S. 280 (1976); and *Sumner v. Shuman,* 483 U.S. 66 (1987).
9. *Blystone v. Pennsylvania,* at 300–309.
10. Ibid., at 319–323.
11. *Clemons v. Mississippi,* 494 U.S. 738 (1990).
12. *Brown v. Sanders,* 546 U.S. 212 (2006).
13. Ibid., at 231.
14. *McKoy v. North Carolina,* 494 U.S. 433 (1990).
15. *Simmons v. South Carolina,* 512 U.S. 154 (1994).
16. Ibid., at 185.
17. *Payne v. Tennessee,* 501 U.S. 808 (1991); and *Herrera v. Collins,* 506 U.S. 390 (1993).
18. *Booth v. Maryland,* 482 U.S. 496 (1987); and *South Carolina v. Gathers,* 490 U.S. 805 (1989).
19. *Payne v. Tennessee,* at 857–859. In December 2008, Justices Stevens, Souter, and Breyer urged the Court to hear two cases in order to reconsider *Payne* and victim-impact statements in capital sentencing. See *Kelly v. California* and *Zamudio v. California,* 555 U.S. ____ (2008).
20. See *Townsend v. Sain,* 372 U.S. 293 (1963).
21. *Herrera v. Collins,* at 427–428.
22. Ibid., at 417–418.
23. Ibid., at 432–433, 446.
24. Ibid., at 427.

25. *Johnson v. Texas*, 509 U.S. 350 (1993).

26. Ibid., at 375.

27. *Penry v. Johnson*, 532 U.S. 782 (2001), at 797.

28. *Atkins v. Virginia*, 536 U.S. 304 (2002), at 338.

29. See "An End to a Legal Saga—Deal Keeps Penry Imprisoned for Life," *Houston Chronicle*, February 16, 2008, B1; and "Avoiding Overkill—DA is Right to Let Penry Die in Prison," *Dallas Morning News*, February 20, 2008, 12A.

30. *Tennard v. Dretke*, 542 U.S. 274 (2004); and *Smith v. Texas*, 543 U.S. 37 (2004).

31. *Tennard v. Dretke*, at 281–284.

32. *Wiggins v. Smith*, 539 U.S. 510 (2003). See also *Strickland v. Washington*, 466 U.S. 668 (1984).

33. *Rompilla v. Beard*, 545 U.S. 374 (2005).

34. See *Thompson v. Oklahoma*, 487 U.S. 815 (1988).

35. *Stanford v. Kentucky*, 492 U.S. 361 (1989).

36. *Roper v. Simmons*, 543 U.S. 551 (2005), at 566–570, 576–578.

37. Ibid., at 622–628, 630.

38. "Gov. Ryan Empties Death Row," *Chicago Sun-Times*, January 12, 2003, 1.

39. *Brown v. Sanders*, at 221–225.

40. *Oregon v. Guzek*, 546 U.S. 517 (2006).

41. *Kansas v. Marsh*, 548 U.S. 163 (2006).

42. *Uttecht v. Brown*, 551 U.S. 1 (2007).

43. *Panetti v. Quarterman*, 551 U.S. 930 (2007). See also *Ford v. Wainwright*, 477 U.S. 399 (1986).

44. In *Wilkerson v. Utah*, 99 U.S. 130 (1878), the Court rejected an Eighth Amendment challenge to the territory's use of death by firing squad; twelve years later it turned down a Fourteenth Amendment claim against New York's first execution by electrocution in *In re Kemmler*, 136 U.S. 436 (1890).

45. "Texas Judge Draws Outcry For Allowing an Execution," *New York Times*, October 25, 2007, A18, C5. Lawyers for the condemned man, Michael Richard, failed to file their final state appeal with the Texas Court of Criminal Appeals before the court's 5 p.m. closing. The presiding judge, Sharon Keller, who turned them down, claimed she did not know the lawyers had experienced computer problems when they requested a twenty-minute extension to deliver their papers prior to the scheduled execution on September 25, 2007. Other judges on the court, however, said they were in the courthouse or available by phone and would have stayed late to hear an appeal if they had known about it.

46. Transcript of oral argument in *Baze v. Rees*, No. 07–5439, January 7, 2008, 4–5.

47. Ibid., at 6.

48. Ibid., at 7–8.

49. Ibid., at 14, 17, 21–22. Scalia vehemently rejected the idea that the Eighth Amendment mandated "the least painful" method of execution. "Where does that come from, that you must find the method of execution that causes the least pain? We have approved electrocution; we have approved death by firing squad. I expect both of those have more possibilities of painful death than the [Kentucky] protocol here." The Constitution, he concluded, prohibited only torture, which he defined as "unnecessary and wanton infliction of pain."

50. Ibid., at 33–34, 44.

51. Ibid., at 48.

52. *Baze v. Rees*, 553 U.S. ___ (2008), at 14–23.

53. Ibid., at 17.
54. Ibid., at 1–15.
55. Ibid., at 11.
56. "Death by Cocktail," *Xenia* (Ohio) *Daily Gazette,* June 16, 2008.
57. "Challenges Remain for Lethal Injection," *New York Times,* April 17, 2008.
58. *Kennedy v. Louisiana,* 554 U.S. _____ (2008).
59. *Coker v. Georgia,* 433 U.S. 584 (1977).
60. *Kennedy v. Louisiana,* at 8–10, 11–15.
61. Ibid., 1–21.
62. "Justices Bar Death Penalty for the Rape of a Child," *New York Times,* June 26, 2008, A1.
63. California Commission on the Fair Administration of Justice, "Reports and Recommendations on the Administration of the Death Penalty in California," June 30, 2008. Available at www.ccfaj.org/reports.html (accessed May 16, 2009). Spurred by growing evidence supplied by post-conviction DNA testing that innocent people were being convicted and even executed, the California State Senate established the California Commission on the Fair Administration of Justice in August 2004 to address issues of fairness in the state's administration of criminal justice and recommend safeguards to its effective application.
64. This brief summary of the tangled Nichols case is based on the following: Jeffrey Toobin, "Death in Georgia," *The New Yorker,* February 4, 2008, 32–37; "Public Defender System Out of Control," *Atlanta Journal-Constitution,* June 12, 2008; "Nichols' Lawyers Seek to Ban Audio of Fatal Shots," *Atlanta Journal-Constitution,* June 4, 2008; and "Nichols Accuses DA of Covering Up Ex-Prosecutor's Misconduct," *Atlanta Journal-Constitution,* June 25, 2008.
65. "The Brian Nichols Case: No Death Penalty Deadlocked Jury Will Mean Life for Killer," *Atlanta Journal-Constitution,* December 13, 2008, A1.
66. "In Georgia, Push to End Unanimity for Execution," *New York Times,* December 17, 2008, 18.
67. "Death Penalty Abolished in New Jersey," *New York Times,* December 17, 2007, A1.
68. "Electric Chair Likened to Torture," [Lincoln, Nebraska] *Journal Star,* February 9, 2008, 1–2.
69. "Other Views: Capital Punishment Can Be Costly," [Biloxi] *Sun Herald,* February 25, 2008, 2.
70. "Do Away With the Death Penalty," Connecticut *Courant,* April 7, 2009, 12.

Selected Bibliography

Acker, James R., Robert M. Bohn, and Charles S. Lanier, eds. *America's Experiment with Capital Punishment.* 2nd ed. Durham: Carolina Academic Press, 2003.

Amsterdam, Anthony G. "Race and the Death Penalty before and after *McCleskey.*" *Columbia Human Rights Law Review* 39 (2007): 34.

Banner, Stuart. *The Death Penalty: An American History.* Cambridge, Mass.: Harvard University Press, 2002.

Bedau, Hugo, ed. *The Death Penalty in America: Current Controversies.* New York, Oxford University Press, 1997.

Bedau, Hugo, and Paul G. Cassell. *Debating the Death Penalty: Should America Have Capital Punishment?* New York: Oxford University Press, 2004.

Berger, Raoul. "Incorporation of the Bill of Rights in the Fourteenth Amendment: A Nine Lived Cat." *Ohio Law Journal* 42 (1981): 435.

Caminker, Evan, and Erwin Chemerinsky. "The Lawless Execution of Robert Alton Harris." *Yale Law Journal* 102 (1992): 225.

Capozzola, Christopher. *Uncle Sam Wants You: World War I and the Making of the Modern American Citizen.* New York: Oxford University Press, 2008.

Carter, Dan. *Scottsboro: A Tragedy of the American South.* Baton Rouge: Louisiana State University Press, 1979.

Chessman, Caryl. *Cell 2455, Death Row.* Englewood Cliffs, N.J.: Prentice-Hall, 1960.

———. *Trial by Ordeal.* Englewood Cliffs, N.J.: Prentice-Hall, 1955.

Cortner, Richard C. *A Mob Intent on Death: The NAACP and the Arkansas Race Cases.* Middletown, Conn.: Wesleyan University Press, 1988.

Cox, Hank H. *Lincoln and the Sioux Uprising of 1862.* Nashville, Tenn.: Cumberland House, 2005.

Curtis, Michael K. "The Bill of Rights as a Limitation on State Authority: A Reply to Professor Berger." *Wake Forest Law Review* 16 (1980): 45.

———. "Further Adventures of the Nine Lived Cat: A Response to Mr. Berger on Incorporation of the Bill of Rights." *Ohio State Law Journal* 43 (1982): 89.

Dinnerstein, Leonard. *The Leo Frank Case.* Athens: University of Georgia Press, 1987.

Essig, Mark. *Edison and the Electric Chair: A Story of Light and Death.* New York: Walker and Co., 2003.

Fairman, Charles. "Does the Fourteenth Amendment Incorporate the Bill of Rights?" *Stanford Law Review* 2 (1949): 5.

Galliher, John F., David Patrick Keyes, Larry W. Koch, and Teresa J. Guess, eds. *America without the Death Penalty: States Leading the Way.* Boston: Northeastern University Press, 2002.

Gillespie, Kay. *Inside the Death Chamber: Exploring Executions.* Upper Saddle River, N.J.: Allyn and Bacon, 2002.

Goldberg, Faye. "Toward Expansion of *Witherspoon*: Capital Scruples, Jury Bias, and the Use of Psychological Data to Raise Presumptions in the Law." *Harvard Civil Rights–Civil Liberties Review* 5 (1970): 53.

Goodman, James. *Stories of Scottboro.* New York: Oxford University Press, 1995.

Gorecki, Jan. *Capital Punishment: Criminal Law and Social Evolution.* New York: Columbia University Press, 1983.

Green, James. *Death in the Haymarket: A Story of Chicago, the First Labor Movement and the Bombing that Divided America.* New York: Anchor Books, 2007.

Greenberg, Jack. "Capital Punishment as a System." *Yale Law Journal* 90 (1982): 912.

Haines, Herbert. *Against Capital Punishment: The Anti-Death Penalty Movement in America, 1972–1994.* New York: Oxford University Press, 1996.

Hamm, Theodore. *Rebel and a Cause: Caryl Chessman and the Politics of Death in Postwar California.* Berkeley: University of California Press, 2001.

Haney, Craig. "Juries and the Death Penalty." *Crime and Delinquency* 26 (1980): 512.

Harrison, Maureen, and Steve Gilbert, eds. *Death Penalty Decisions of the United States Supreme Court.* Carlsbad, Calif.: Excellent Books, 2003.

Haynes, Robert. *A Night of Violence: The Houston Riot of 1917.* Baton Rouge: Louisiana State University Press, 1976.

Higginbotham, A. Leon, Jr. *In the Matter of Color: Race and the American Legal Process—the Colonial Period.* New York: Oxford University Press, 1980.

Kennedy, Randall. *Race, Crime, and the Law.* New York: Random House, 1998.

Klarman, Michael. Brown v. Board *of Education and the Civil Rights Movement.* New York: Oxford University Press, 2007.

Latzer, Barry. *Death Penalty Cases: Leading United States Supreme Court Cases on Capital Punishment.* 2nd ed. New York: Butterworth Heinemann, 2002.

Liebman, James S. "Slow Dancing with Death: The Supreme Court and Capital Punishment, 1963–2006." *Columbia Law Review* 107 (2007): 1.

Lindemann, Albert. *The Jew Accused: Three Anti-Semitic Affairs (Dreyfus, Beilis, Frank), 1894–1915.* Cambridge: Cambridge University Press, 1992.

MacLean, Nancy. *Behind the Mask of Chivalry: The Making of the Second Ku Klux Klan.* New York: Oxford University Press, 1995.

Madow, Michael. "Forbidden Spectacle: Executions, the Public and the Press in Nineteenth-Century New York." *Buffalo Law Review* 43 (1995): 461.

Mailer, Norman. *The Executioner's Song.* New York: Little, Brown, 1979. Reprinted. New York: Vintage Books, 1994.

Martschukat, Jurgen. "The Art of Killing by Electricity: The Sublime and the Electric Chair." *Journal of American History* 89 (2002): 918.

Masur, Louis P. *Rites of Execution: Capital Punishment and the Transformation of American Culture, 1776–1865.* New York: Oxford University Press, 1991.

Michaelson, Howard C. "Post-Conviction Due Process Regarding Insanity Claims Prior to Execution." *Journal of Criminal Law and Criminology* 41 (1951): 639.

Miller, Arthur S., and Jeffrey H. Bowman. *Death by Installments: The Ordeal of Willie Francis.* Westport, Conn.: Greenwood Press, 1988.

Neff, James. *The Wrong Man: The Final Verdict on the Dr. Sam Sheppard Murder Case.* New York: Random House, 2001.

Newsome, Kevin Christopher. "Setting Incorporation Straight: A Reinterpretation of the Slaughter-House Cases." *Yale Law Journal* 109 (2000): 643.

Noonan, John. "Horses of the Night: *Harris v. Vasquez.*" *Stanford Law Review* 45 (1993): 1011.

Palmer, Louis J. *The Death Penalty: An American Citizen's Guide to Understanding Federal and State Laws.* Jefferson, N.C.: McFarland and Co., 1998.

Parker, Frank. *Caryl Chessman: The Red Light Bandit.* Chicago: Burnham, 1975.

Parrish, Michael E. "Cold War Justice: The Supreme Court and the Rosenbergs." *American Historical Review* 82 (1977): 808.

Patterson, Haywood, and Earl Conrad. *Scottsboro Boy.* London: Victor Gollanez, 1950.

Pollack, Jack Harrison. *Dr. Sam: An American Tragedy.* Chicago: Henry Regnery Co., 1972.

Polsby, Daniel D. "The Death of Capital Punishment? *Furman v. Georgia.*" *Supreme Court Review* 1 (1973): 1.

Rivkind, Nina, and Steven F. Shatz. *Cases and Materials on the Death Penalty.* Eagan, Minn.: West Group, 2005.

Rosen, Jeffrey. *The Most Democratic Branch: How the Courts Serve America.* New York: Oxford University Press, 2006.

Shapiro, Herbert. *White Violence and Black Response: From Reconstruction to Montgomery.* Amherst: University of Massachusetts Press, 1988.

Sheppard, Samuel H. *Endure and Conquer.* Cleveland: World Publishing, 1966.

Sigler, Mary. "Contradiction, Coherence, and Guided Discretion in the Supreme Court's Capital Sentencing Jurisprudence." *American Criminal Law Review* 40 (2003): 1151.

Slaughter, Thomas. *The Whiskey Rebellion: Frontier Epilogue to the American Revolution.* New York: Oxford University Press, 1986.

Stampp, Kenneth. *The Peculiar Institution: Slavery in the Ante-Bellum South.* New York: Random House, 1956.

Stevenson, Bryan A. "The Politics of Fear and Death: Successive Problems in Capital Federal Habeas Corpus Cases." *New York University Law Review* 77 (2002): 699.

Stockley, Grif, Jr. *Blood in Their Eyes: The Elaine Race Massacre of 1919.* Fayetteville: University of Arkansas Press, 2001.

T. L. M. "Rule 11 of the Federal Rules of Criminal Procedure: The Case for Strict Compliance after *United States v. Dayton.*" *Virginia Law Review* 66 (1980): 1169.

Turow, Scott. *Ultimate Punishment: A Lawyer's Reflections on Dealing with the Death Penalty.* New York: Farrar, Straus and Giroux, 2003.

U.S. Department of Justice, Bureau of Prisons. National Prisoner Statistics. Bulletin No. 45. *Capital Punishment, 1930–1968.* Washington, D.C.: Government Printing Office, 2005.

Wellerstein, Peter. "Race, Marriage and the Law of Freedom: Alabama and Virginia, 1860s–1960s." *Chicago-Kent Law Review* 70 (1994): 371.

Whitaker, John. *On the Laps of the Gods: The Red Summer of 1919 and the Struggle for Justice That Remade America.* New York: Crown Publishers, 2008.

Wiecek, William. "Felix Frankfurter, Incorporation and the Willie Francis Case." *Journal of Supreme Court History* 26 (2002): 53.

Wiener, Frederick Bernays. "The Seamy Side of the World War I Court Martial Controversy." *Military Law Review* 123 (1989): 109.

Yenne, Bill. *Indian Wars: The Campaign for the American West.* Yardley, Pa.: Westholme, 2008.

Zimring, Franklin E. "Inheriting the Wind: The Supreme Court and Capital Punishment in the 1990s." *Florida State Law Review* 20 (1992): 7.

Index